D1391284

A COMPANION TO SOCIAL ARCHAEOLOGY

For Nan Rothschild
LMM

For Gordon Willey
RWP

A Companion to
Social Archaeology

Edited by

Lynn Meskell and Robert W. Preucel

Blackwell
Publishing

© 2004 by Blackwell Publishing Ltd

350 Main Street, Malden, MA 02148-5020, USA
108 Cowley Road, Oxford OX4 1JF, UK
550 Swanston Street, Carlton, Victoria 3053, Australia

First published 2004 by Blackwell Publishing Ltd

Library of Congress Cataloging-in-Publication Data

Meskell, Lynn.
A companion to social archaeology / Lynn Meskell and Robert W. Preucel.
p. cm. – (Social archaeology)
Includes bibliographical references (p.) and index.
ISBN 0-631-22578-1 (alk. paper)
1. Social archaeology. I. Preucel, Robert W. II. Title. III. Series.

CC72.4.M47 2004
930.1–dc22

2003021516
A catalogue record for this title is available from the British Library.
Set in 10.5/12.5pt Garamond
by Kolam Information Services Pvt. Ltd, Pondicherry, India
Printed and bound in the United Kingdom
by TJ International, Padstow, Cornwall

For further information on
Blackwell Publishing, visit our website:
http://www.blackwellpublishing.com

Contents

Figures

Contributors

Wendy Ashmore is Professor of Anthropology at the University of California, Riverside. She has conducted field research in Guatemala (Quiriguá), Honduras (Gualjoquito and Copán), and most recently, Belize (Xunantunich). Recent publications include *Archaeologies of Landscape: Contemporary Perspectives* (co-edited with A. Bernard Knapp, Blackwell, 1999), "'Decisions and Dispositions': Socializing Spatial Archaeology" (*American Anthropologist*, 2002), "Spatial Order in Maya Civic Plans" (with Jeremy A. Sabloff, *Latin American Antiquity*, 2002), and "Classic Maya Landscapes and Settlement" (*Mesoamerican Archaeology*, edited by Julia A. Hendon and Rosemary A. Joyce, Blackwell, 2003).

Reinhard Bernbeck is Associate Professor of Anthropology at Binghamton University. He is currently co-director of the excavations at Toll-e Bashi, Iran and has previously done fieldwork in southeastern Turkey, Jordan, and Syria. Previous publications include *Die Auflösung der häuslichen Produktionsweise: das Beispiel Mesopotamiens* (1994) and *Theorien in der Archäologie* (1997).

Emma Blake is currently Visiting Assistant Professor in the Department of Classical Studies at the University of Michigan. She wrote her contribution to this book while a Humanities Teaching Fellow at Stanford University. Since completing her Ph.D. in Archaeology from Cambridge University, she has written a number of articles on spatial theory in archaeology. Her primary research area is the western Mediterranean in prehistory, and she is involved in an ongoing field project in western Sicily.

Victor Buchli is Reader in Material Culture at the Department of Anthropology, University College London. He has been co-editor of the *Journal of Material Culture* and is currently co-editor of *HomeCultures*. His previous publications include *The Material Culture Reader* (ed., 2002), *Archaeologies of the Contemporary Past* (with Gavin Lucas, 2001), and *An Archaeology of Socialism* (1999).

Clive Gamble is Director of the Centre for the Archaeology of Human Origins at the University of Southampton, UK. He has conducted research into all periods of the Paleolithic and has been involved in projects in all six continents. His recent publications include *The Palaeolithic Societies of Europe* (1999) and *Archaeology: The Basics* (2001). He is currently working on *Origins and Revolutions* a study of modern humans, wild and domestic.

Roberta Gilchrist is Professor of Archaeology at the University of Reading, and Archaeologist to Norwich Cathedral. She has written extensively on both gender and medieval archaeology. Her books include *Gender and Archaeology: Contesting the Past* (1999) and *Gender and Material Culture: the Archaeology of Religious Women* (1994).

Erica Gittins is a postgraduate at the Centre for the Archaeology of Human Origins at the University of Southampton. She is currently conducting research into the Late Glacial campsites in the Paris Basin. Her other research interests include the role of origins theory in archaeological interpretation, and the intellectual inheritance of the discipline from the Enlightenment. She most recently co-directed excavations in Guernsey.

Chris Gosden is a lecturer/curator in the Pitt Rivers Museum and School of Archaeology, University of Oxford. He has conducted excavations in Papua New Guinea, Turkmenistan, and Britain. His previous publications include *Social Being and Time* (Blackwell, 1994), *Collecting Colonialism* (with C. Knowles, 2001), and *Prehistory. A Very Short Introduction* (2003).

Julia A. Hendon is Associate Professor of Anthropology at Gettysburg College. She is a Maya archaeologist with field experience since 1980 in Belize, Guatemala, and Honduras, and is the former editor of *Anthropological Literature: An Index to Periodical Articles and Essays* (1988–96).

Ian Hodder is the Dunlevie Family Professor in the Department of Cultural and Social Anthropology at Stanford University. He is also a Fellow of the British Academy and of the McDonald Institute in Cambridge University. He directs the excavations of the prehistoric site of Catalhoyuk in Turkey. His main books are *Reading the Past* (1986), *The Domestication of Europe* (Blackwell, 1990), and *The Archaeological Process* (Blackwell, 1999).

Rosemary A. Joyce is Professor of Anthropology at the University of California, Berkeley. She has been engaged in archaeological fieldwork in Honduras since 1977. Her most recent publications include *Gender and Power in Prehispanic Mesoamerica* (2001), *The Languages of Archaeology* (2002), and *Embodied Lives: Egypt and the Ancient Maya* (with Lynn Meskell, 2003).

Ian Lilley is Reader in Aboriginal and Torres Strait Islander Studies at the University of Queensland. His research currently focuses on Torres Strait and New Caledonia. He is Secretary of the World Archaeology Congress, Secretary and past President of the Australian Archaeological Association, and an Executive Committee member of the Indo-Pacific Prehistory Association. Previous publications include *Histories of Old Ages. Essays in Honour of Rhys Jones* (with Atholl Anderson and Sue O'Connor, 2001), *Native Title and the Transformation of Archaeology in the Postcolonial World* (2000), and *Le Pacifique de 5000 à 2000 BP* (with Jean-Christophe Galipaud, 1999).

Randall H. McGuire received his Ph.D. from the University of Arizona in 1982. He is currently a Professor of Anthropology at Binghamton University in Binghamton,

New York. His interests and research include social theory in archaeology, reburial and repatriation, historical archaeology, and indigenous peoples of the American Southwest and northwest Mexico. His significant publications include (with Michael Shanks) "The craft of archaeology," *American Antiquity* 61 (1996); *A Marxist Archaeology* (1992); and "Archaeology and the First Americans," *American Anthropologist* (1992).

Lynn Meskell is Associate Professor of Anthropology at-Columbia University. She is founding editor of the *Journal of Social Archaeology* and her previous books include *Archaeology under Fire: Nationalism, Politics and Heritage in the Eastern Mediterranean and Middle East* (1998, ed.), *Archaeologies of Social Life: Age, Sex, Class etc. in Ancient Egypt* (Blackwell, 1999), *Private Life in New Kingdom Egypt* (2002), *Embodied Lives: Figuring Ancient Maya and Egyptian Experience*, (2003, with Rosemary Joyce) and most recently, *Object Worlds from Ancient Egypt: Material Biographies Past and Present* (2004).

Koji Mizoguchi is Associate Professor of Archaeology at the Graduate School of Social and Cultural Studies, Kyushu University, Japan. His current research interests are in modernity and archaeological discursive formation, and social stratification and the transformation of self-identity. His previous publications include *An Archaeological History of Japan, 30,000 B.C. to A.D. 700* (2002).

Paul R. Mullins is an Associate Professor of Anthropology at Indiana University-Purdue University, Indianapolis, where his research focuses on historical archaeology, popular culture, and race and consumption in the urban American Midwest. He is the author of *Race and Affluence: An Archaeology of African America and Consumer Culture* (1999).

Thomas C. Patterson is Distinguished Professor and Chair of Anthropology at the University of California, Riverside. His previous publications include *A Social History of Anthropology in the United States* (2001), *Marx's Ghost: Conversations with Archaeologists* (2003), and *Cultural Diversity in the United States: A Critical Reader*, edited with Ida Susser (Blackwell, 1999).

José Antonio Pérez Gollán (Ph.D., National University of Córdoba, Argentina) is a researcher at the National Science and Technology Council (Argentina). From 1977 to 1982 he was Researcher at the Department of Prehistory, INAH-Mexico, and from 1982 to 1987 Professor and Secretary of Research at the National School of Anthropology and History, INAH-Mexico. He is Director of the Ambato Archaeological Research Project and, since 1987, Director of the Ethnographic Museum, University of Buenos Aires. He has curated many archaeological exhibitions and has published over sixty articles and nine books.

Gustavo Politis is a researcher at CONICET (Consejo Nacional de Investigaciones Cientificas y Técnicas de Argentina) and Professor at the Universities of Centro de la Pcia. de Buenos Aires and La Plata. His main fields of research are the archaeology of the Pampean Region of Argentina, the early peopling of the Americas, the ethno-archaeology of tropical hunter-gatherers and the history and theory of Latin American archaeology. His publications include *Nukak* (1996); *Latin American Archaeology: An Inside View* (edited with Benjamin Alberti, 1999), and "The Theoretical Landscape and the Methodological Development of Archaeology in Latin America," *American Antiquity* (2003).

Susan Pollock is Professor of Anthropology at Binghamton University. She is co-director of excavations at Toll-e Bashi, Iran and has also worked in Turkey and Iraq. Her recent publications include *Ancient Mesopotamia: The Eden that Never Was* (1999) and the forthcoming *Archaeologies of the Middle East* (Blackwell), of which she is co-editor.

Robert W. Preucel is Associate Professor of Anthropology and Associate Curator of North American Archaeology at the University of Pennsylvania. He is editor of *Processual and Postprocessual Archaeologies: Multiple Ways of Knowing the Past* (1991), co-editor with Ian Hodder of *Contemporary Archaeology in Theory* (Blackwell, 1996), and most recently editor of *Archaeologies of the Pueblo Revolt: Identity, Meaning, and Renewal in the Pueblo World* (2002).

Bruce G. Trigger is James McGill Professor in the Department of Anthropology at McGill University. Educated at the University of Toronto (BA 1959) and Yale University (Ph.D.1964), he has specialized over the years in settlement archaeology, the development of archaeological theory, and the comparative study of early civilizations. His recent publications include *Sociocultural Evolution* (1998), *Artifacts and Ideas: Essays in Archaeology* (2003), and *Understanding Early Civilizations* (2003). He is currently working on a revised edition of *A History of Archaeological Thought*, originally published in 1989.

PART I

Knowledges

Robert W. Preucel and Lynn Meskell

Archaeology has been defined as the discipline that uniquely provides a world history extending humanity back into prerecorded time. It gives primary evidence for the three "rites of passage" in the human career, namely the emergence of anatomically modern humans, the origins of agriculture/first settled villages, and the rise of civilizations. The resulting narrative is a linear and processual story of technological progress and cultural evolution. Archaeology has also been described as the discipline that reveals the details of past human existence, including how people made their living, how they organized themselves into social groups, how they worshiped their gods, how they mourned their dead. In this case, the resulting account is a description of an individual's, family's or group's lived experience at a particular point in time. There is, therefore, for archaeology, even more so than for history, a natural tension between the individual and society, agency and structure, event and process that must be mediated by social theory as it articulates with the special characteristics of the archaeological record.

And yet there is another aspect of archaeology which we might call "social archaeology" that has always been present alongside the investigation of evolutionary questions and the study of past lives. Social archaeology refers to the ways in which we express ourselves through the things that we make and use, collect and discard, value or take for granted, and seek to be remembered by (Hall 2001). It is linked to how we conceptualize the relationships between ourselves and others, society and history in both past and present contexts. It involves an appreciation of the multiple entailments of our very being-in-the-world. This perspective is implicit in the organizations and institutions we have created to preserve the past, institutions such as English Heritage, UNESCO, Cultural Resource Management, the Louvre, and World Heritage monuments. It is implicated in nationalism and globalization because every form of political economy requires its own history and past narrative. The broadening influence of archaeology today across the humanities, social sciences, and beyond reveals a growing appreciation of archaeology in this "social" sense.

A social archaeology conceptualized as an archaeology of social being can be located at the intersections of temporality, spatiality, and materiality. To take these concepts as a focus of research is to explore the situated experiences of material life, the constitution of the object world and its shaping of human experience (Gosden 1994; Meskell 2004). This is related to, but not necessarily the same as, studying time, space, and material culture, categories that have often been identified as the dimensions of archaeology (Chang 1967; Spaulding 1960). Just as humans produce notions of time and space to mediate their existence in the world, so too do they produce notions of materiality and, indeed, these concepts are fundamentally interdependent because material culture practices serve to concretize and reproduce particular modes of space-time. There is now a large literature on social conceptions of time and historicity in the humanities and social sciences (Baert 1992; Fabian 1983; White 1973) and there is a developing literature on spatiality (Gregory 1994; Soja 1989). Without denying the significance of these contributions, what is missing from the majority of these formulations is a principled consideration of the materiality of human existence. This, we feel, is one of the areas where archaeology can make significant contributions to contemporary social theory.

The Social in Archaeology

Before discussing what we see as key constituents of a social archaeology, it is appropriate to review some of the different characterizations of the social in archaeology. Archaeology has always included a concept of the social, even if it has been understood in diverse ways and from a variety of perspectives (see Hodder, chapter 1, and Patterson, chapter 3). Without providing a comprehensive history, we wish to distinguish three broad engagements with the social in Anglo-American archaeology that might be termed "the social and the cultural," "the social and social theory," and "the social and contemporary society." At any one point in time, the discipline can be seen as a variegated field largely constituted by competing interpretations of these different relationships.

The social in archaeology can perhaps be said to begin with V. Gordon Childe (although see Chippindale 1989). As early as 1935, Childe argued that the study of past societies should be the goal of archaeology. For him, human consciousness could not be conceived of as being separate from society. Like the social anthropologists of his day, he distinguished society as a network of organic, self-perpetuating social relations from cultural traits as specific components of society that were transferable across societies through diffusion. Society was structure and culture was its content. Trigger (1980:144) has termed Childe's commitment to the social as "societal archaeology" and observed that it increased over his lifetime. There is little doubt that Childe's engagement with Marxism caused him, more than his contemporaries, to appreciate the close interrelationships between archaeology and modern society. He was particularly interested in creating an archaeology conceived of as a "science of progress" that would help elucidate major social issues and help establish a future (Childe 1946, 1947).

Grahame Clark regarded society as the central focus of archaeology. In his influential book *Archaeology and Society* (1939, 3rd edition 1957), he noted that the study of the production and use of artifacts is coextensive with the life of society. This meant that archaeologists needed to be conversant with the work of social and economic historians as well as the findings of social anthropology. For him, the emergence of a class society was not merely a consequence, but also a cause of social evolution. Clark also appreciated the social context of the practice of archaeology. He saw its main purpose as providing "sentiments needful to the stability and indeed to the very existence of society," since it "multiplies and strengthens the links which bind us to the past." This social use of archaeology was not to be confused with totalitarianism. In a sharp critique of Soviet archaeology, he argued for a "scientific humanism" committed to the study of universal world history that would appeal to both the underprivileged and the educated classes. For him, prehistory achieved its highest social purpose in promoting human solidarity and creating the conditions for freedom.

For K. C. Chang, the social was essential in the construction of archaeological interpretations. This is made clear in his statement that archaeology should "identify and characterize the social groups of archaeological cultures [and] ... look at archaeological sites as local social groups instead of as cultures or phases" (1958:324). Chang drew attention to the community (a camp, a village, or a town) as the elementary social group and considered it universally manifest in the archaeological record in terms of settlement (1967:15). This had implications for archaeological typologies, and he suggested that the standard archaeological practice of using "cultural" instead of "social" relationships was the result of privileging artifacts over settlements. Chang, like Clark, also recognized that the goals of archaeology were linked to contemporary social interests. He wrote: "[t]he greatest power of archaeological knowledge is at the mercy of its users, and it is the archaeologist's social responsibility to see that its use is appropriate to his own social consciousness and conscience" (1967:154).

With the emergence of processual archaeology in the 1960s, the social was defined as a subsystem within the broader cultural system. Lewis Binford (1962, 1965) defined the cultural system as the human organism's extrasomatic means of adaptation, and culture process as the dynamic articulation of environmental and sociocultural subsystems. This focus on culture process was legitimized by neoevolutionary theory borrowed from cultural anthropology, particularly Leslie White (1959) and Julian Steward (1955). One of the first applications of systems theory was Flannery's (1968) study of subsistence change in Mesoamerican societies. In an influential case study, he argued that hunter-gatherers altered their subsistence regimes to take advantage of genetic changes in maize and beans and this process set in motion a cycle of intensive agriculture that permitted the development of social hierarchies.

During this period, the study of complex societies reemerged as a key interest. Especially influential was the band–tribe–chiefdom–state typology introduced by Elman Service (1962). Considerable research focused on identifying and characterizing chiefdoms as the transitional type dividing simple and complex societies. According to Service, chiefdoms are kinship societies where authority is vested in a priest-chief. Archaeologists were quick to operationalize the chiefdom concept by focusing on food production and storage facilities. Renfrew (1973a), for example, provided a list of twenty characteristics of chiefdoms in his analysis of Neolithic Wessex society in southern England. However, problems soon began to emerge. Earle (1978), for example, called into question the trait-list approach to chiefdoms by showing that redistribution, a trait previously considered to be an essential requirement, did not exist within the Hawaiian context. Feinman and Neitzel (1984) conducted a cross-cultural survey of ethnographically known chiefdoms and documented considerable variability.

Their survey demonstrated that variation was continuous rather than discrete and implied that there were no readily apparent societal modes or subtypes. This result prompted a rethinking of neoevolutionary theory (e.g., Yoffee 1993).

Almost from the beginning, there were critiques of the technological determinism of the early processual archaeology. In his inaugural lecture at Southampton University, Renfrew (1973b) challenged the field to explore the emergence of symbolic systems and art styles. He attributed the reluctance to consider the social to the tendency to artificially separate mind and matter. It was widely believed that the material in the form of technology and subsistence was somehow more accessible than the spiritual as indicated by religious practices. Renfrew then argued that this view was erroneous and the religious and ceremonial observances of societies are not epiphenomenal, but rather crucial to their functioning. For him, social archaeology refers to the reconstruction of social organization of past societies, and "the way they themselves looked upon the world" (1973b:7). Similarly, Redman et al. (1978:1) expressed a frustration with the treatment of the social in contemporary archaeology. They observed that the debates over archaeological epistemology tended to yield two results. On the one hand were "theoretically bold" statements that often went beyond the sophistication of archaeological methods and, on the other, there were "theoretically timid" views often qualified as speculative and tentative. They advocated a social archaeology that integrated increasing methodological expertise and meaningful interpretations.

Among processual archaeologists, Renfrew (1984a) has provided perhaps the most explicit characterization of social archaeology. He is careful to distinguish it from social anthropology, noting that the concerns of the archaeologist overlap with, but are not identical to, those of the social anthropologist. The archaeologist is concerned with the social unit, its political organization, and its relationships with its neighbors. And most significantly, the archaeologist is concerned with material culture – the artifacts, buildings, and other human products that constitute the archaeological record. This has led archaeologists to conduct ethnoarchaeological research among contemporary societies with the goal of understanding regularities in the manufacture and use of material culture. Although Renfrew acknowledged that it was too early to write a manual of social archaeology, he specified five basic topics that it should tackle: societies and space and how landscapes of power are created; networks and flows (trade and interaction); structures of authority concerning monuments and the structure of pre-urban societies; the dynamics of continuous growth as approached through systems thinking; and issues of discontinuity and long-term change (Renfrew 1984b:10).

For most processual archaeologists, social relevance was assumed rather than explicitly discussed. In those cases where it was addressed, it was usually discussed in the context of the application of behavioral generalizations to the management of modern society. Fritz (1973), for example, suggested that since major contemporary problems result from undirected and poorly assimilated technological growth, greater understanding of these processes through archaeological research would be of considerable social benefit. Martin and Plog (1973) went so far as to argue that the analytic objectivity and archaeological derived statements about human behavior might help expose social prejudices and lead to more effective ways of designing social programs and public education. In a more critical vein, Ford (1973) noted that archaeology had yet to demonstrate its relevance and that its serviceability to humanity would be determined by expanding its research interests. Perhaps the most sophisticated considerations of relevance have been offered by those processual archaeologists influenced by Marxism. Paynter (1983) has observed that the increasing specialization of archaeological work most clearly seen in contract archaeology can be related to corporate interests in controlling a deskilled labor force. Patterson (1986, 1995) has extended this insight by developing an analysis of the class structure of American archaeology.

In 1980, Ian Hodder organized a series of graduate seminars at Cambridge University that, in retrospect, can be seen as the first explicit moves toward a postprocessual archaeology. In his introduction to the volume published from the seminar papers Hodder (1982) offered a sustained critique of processual archaeology and sketched the outlines of a new contextual approach. Hodder's critique singled out the artificial dichotomies between culture and function, individual and society, statics and dynamics, history and process, and the limits of positivism. He argued against Binford's view of culture as man's extrasomatic means of adaptation in favor of the perspective that it is meaningfully constituted. His contextual archaeology, later to be named postprocessual archaeology, was based in part upon Anthony Giddens's (1979) theory of structuration to mediate the excesses of both functionalism (the focus on ecology and economics) and "high" structuralism (the focus on rules and codes). The key element of this approach is the insight that material culture is not simply reflective of social practice but, rather, constitutive of it. He writes: "[t]he effects of symbols, intended and unintended, must be associated with their repeated use and with the 'structuration' of society" (Hodder 1982:10).

Shanks and Tilley (1987b) extended Hodder's critique in their view of social archaeology. Inspired by Laclau and Mouffe (1985), they argue against a social archaeology that is reductionist and essentialist, based upon a priori categories. They questioned the hierarchy of determination whereby the "economic" was privileged in social interpretation as opposed to other institutions such as the "political" and the "religious." Related to this is a skepticism toward universal social units, such as band, tribe, lineage, and mode of production. For them, the social is not a subsystem within the cultural system, but rather the practice of the construction of the social order. Finally, they argue that archaeology itself is a discursive practice and in the mediation of the past and present neither can be reduced to the other. They affirm the importance of rhetoric and the polemic since it is only in the context of the political that reason presents itself as a total system of representing reality. Some have interpreted this as espousing relativism (e.g., Watson 1990). But this seems too harsh, since while Shanks and Tilley (1987a:245) argue for a "radical pluralism" which recognizes multiple pasts produced in congruence with various ethnic, cultural, social, and political views, they explicitly say that all pasts are not equal. Their thesis is that archaeology as a social practice embedded in contemporary power relations should itself be subjected to ideology critique.

There have been several attempts at establishing a dialogue between processual and postprocessual approaches, often with a view toward constructing a unified approach (Preucel 1991; Schiffer 2000a; VanPool and VanPool 1999). Michael Schiffer, for example, has argued that the differences between various approaches are artificial since

all archaeological theory is social theory. He writes: "virtually all theories that archaeologists use to explain behavioral and/or social variability and change, including theories of Darwinian evolution and behavioral ecology, qualify as social" (2000b:1). In one
sense, of course, he is correct since all human practices, including archaeology, are
social. But it is not the case that all theories take the social as the object of inquiry. It
seems overly generous to claim that an approach like selectionism (O'Brien 1996), that
considers human agency only in the context of producing variation, can be considered
to be social. Bruce Trigger (Chapter 2, this volume) suggests that processual and
postprocessual approaches are not so much contradictory as complimentary.

There are, of course, significant non-Anglo-American approaches to the social that
have had and continue to have an effect on world archaeology. Here one can identify
European, Soviet, Chinese, and Latin American traditions (Hodder 1991; Malina and
Vasícek 1990; Patterson 1994; Trigger 1989). The social is often constituted as part of,
or alternatively, in reaction to, Marxist perspectives about social welfare in the nation-
state. One can also identify indigenous approaches that are beginning to emerge as part
of a broader postcolonial discourse (Layton 1989a, 1989b; Watkins 2000). In this case,
the social is often located in community health and well-being and not necessarily
associated with notions of the individual and free will. The relationships between
ideologies expressed by Western and non-Western archaeologies were showcased at
the World Archaeological Congress in 1986 where academic freedom and apartheid
came into sharp conflict (Ucko 1987). This event, perhaps more than any other,
demonstrated the indelibly political nature of archaeology. We now turn to a discussion
of social archaeology conceived of as an archaeology of social being and address the
concepts of temporality, spatiality, and materiality.

Temporality

It is no exaggeration to say that time is the central obsession of archaeology. The profession is devoted to understanding, in Childe's (1942) words, "what happened in history."
What counts as the past spans the gamut from "deep time," the domain of Paleolithic
archaeology, to the modern world, the domain of historical archaeology. However,
archaeology is itself a product of Time. It exists as a particular kind of disciplinary
practice with a historically situated character. Indeed, these two temporal issues are
intimately bound together since the birth of archaeology as a discipline is intertwined
with the question of the origins of humanity. Archaeology is both about and of Time.

The history of time in archaeology is one of the transition from religious to secular
chronologies and increasing technical control in measurement. In 1658 Archbishop
Ussher held that "from the evening ushering in the first day of the world, to that
midnight which began the first day of the Christian era, there were 4003 years, seventy
days, and six temporarie howers" and from this deduced that man was created on
Friday, October 28 (quoted in Daniel 1981:34). This view was extremely influential and
lasted until the second quarter of the nineteenth century. Two developments finally
laid it to rest. These were the doctrine of uniformitarianism developed in geology by
Charles Lyell and the recognition of the co-occurrence of stone tools and extinct
animals by prominent antiquarians such as Boucher de Perthes. In 1859 Charles

Darwin published his major work *On the Origin of Species*. Although it had little to say about the origins of man, later of his publications and those by Thomas Huxley presented the principles of human evolution. This new view of the antiquity of man and evolution of life was controversial among the devout, since it was seen as contradicting the book of Genesis and thus potentially dangerous to the Christian faith. Even today the tensions between religious fundamentalism and science are most concretely expressed with respect to evolution.

The necessary step in the control of time was the introduction of absolute dating as a means of marking universal Time. Prior to absolute dating, scholars such as Oscar Montelius and V. Gordon Childe relied upon relative dating based upon stylistic similarity to correlate archaeological sequences across broad geographical regions. The prevailing assumption was that basic technologies, such as metallurgy or megalithic architecture, emerged in "civilized" areas of the ancient Near East and diffused to the "barbarous" areas of Europe. In the late 1940s, radiocarbon dating revolutionized archaeology by permitting comparisons of archaeological sequences anywhere in the world. Later dendrochronological calibrations led to the discovery that monuments of Europe were older than those that had been posited to be their progenitors (Renfrew 1973c). Numerous other absolute dating methods have now been used in or developed for archaeology including potassium-argon, thermoluminescence, archaeomagnetism, obsidian hydration, etc. (Aitken 1990). The theory underlying these techniques varies, but the principle is the same. Time's arrow runs in one direction only and the passage of time can be measured by means of standardized units.

Coupled with the refinement of methods of indicating absolute time is a growing appreciation of different scales and rhythms of time. Especially influential has been the *Annales* school of social and economic history and the work of Fernand Braudel (1973). This approach is best known for its emphasis upon multiple temporal scales defined by short-term events or sociopolitical time, medium-term cycles or socioeconomic time, and long-term trajectories or environmental time. Hodder (1987), for example, has been inspired by this conception of time even as he has criticized it in favor of a structure and agency perspective. Similarly, Bradley (1991) uses Braudel's typology as a starting point, but argues that there are elements of social time, such as art styles, monuments, and depositions, that are better understood from the perspective of the long term. Knapp (1992) has observed that while most scholars find Braudel's structural-ecological determinism to be seriously flawed, they are attracted to its flexibility and capacity to grow with the demands of new developments in method and theory.

But time and temporality are not the same thing. Temporality can be glossed as the temporal imaginary. It is an inseparable part of our very being-in-the-world. Temporality is ultimately grounded in how people articulate with both the linear and recursive elements of their lived experience – initiations, marriages, divorces, the birth of children, the death of friends and relatives. According to Martin Heidegger (1962), humans possess no pre-given essence, rather we are what we become through our experiences in the life course. Our existence is "ahead of itself" in that our dealings with specific situations serve as models for future courses of action and each of our actions plays a role in shaping our lives. Edmund Husserl (1970, 1977) holds that we are aware of perceptual objects by virtue of being aware of our bodies and how they interact with objects. Stated another way, all awareness is mediated by our bodies. For Maurice Merleau-Ponty, the Self only exists as an embodied temporalization. He writes: "I am installed on a pyramid of time which has been me. I take up a field and invent myself (but not without my temporal equipment), just as I move about in the world (but not without the unknown mass of my body)" (1964:14–15). Taken together, these perspectives reveal the phenomenological nature of time as an embodied temporality.

In what is perhaps the first explicit archaeological engagement with temporality, Mark Leone (1978) has suggested that time can be seen as an ideology of capitalism and we, as archaeologists and as people, must understand how we use it to conceptualize the past. As he puts it, "the content of a segment of time as well as the segmentation of time itself is a creation stemming from a cultural assumption about what time is" (1978:35). This insight has been crucial to all subsequent treatments of temporality, even those from radically different theoretical frameworks (e.g., Ramenofsky 1998). Shanks and Tilley (1987a, 1987b), for example, have adopted this view and made it central to their vision of postprocessual archaeology. Their thesis is that time is not simply a neutral concept associated with a radiocarbon chronology or a book publication date. Rather it is a political judgment made in the present about a particular lived past. They are especially critical of cultural evolutionary theory which, they argue, promotes a homogeneous and abstract notion of time in order to permit cross-cultural comparisons. For them, in order to preserve the time of the past we must accept the past's coexistence with the present.

The notion of temporality has most recently been addressed by archaeologists inspired by the writings of Heidegger. Gosden (1994), for example, argues that time is not simply a mental ordering device but rather an aspect of bodily engagement with the world. It is a style of existence, a human dimension that unfolds in action. He observes that "human beings have a peculiar temporal relation to the world, and this temporality must be the starting point for all exploration" (1994:9). Similarly, Thomas (1996) has proposed that history is a lived process in which the relationships between humans and their world are continually transformed. He notes that it is "impossible to investigate time scientifically [as an external reality] without first having the kind of experiential temporality which distinguishes human beings" (1996:236). Karlsson (2001:55–56) has suggested that there is no gap between the past and present that can be bridged. Rather the temporality of the interpreter is such that "the character of having been" is intimately interwoven with both "the present" and "the future as approaching." Because our temporality is known only through our use of time, the traditional view of time is anchored in temporality.

In Chapter 5, Clive Gamble and Erica Gittins draw attention to the temporality of social archaeology through a consideration of Paleolithic archaeology. Their central thesis is that a social archaeology must acknowledge its origin myths, and preeminent among these is the idea of the Paleolithic. Origins research has considerable purchase because it is so deeply rooted in Western thought (Conkey with Williams 1991; Moser 1998). Indeed, the significance of the Paleolithic as a time period and type of archaeology is derived from its relationship to the origins of humanity. Inspired by Derrida's notion of logocentrism, Gamble and Gittins critique standard origins research as constraining and even misleading in its entanglement with "top-down" theories of social evolution. They advocate "bottom-up" theories of how individuals are constituted through their bodies, culture, self, and personhood because these issues relate to the creation of society through interaction. They conclude that a new Paleolithic archaeology constituted in these terms would significantly alter not only the Paleolithic's relationship with the rest of archaeology, but also the relationship that the West has with its own identity and past.

Spatiality

Archaeology is similarly about and located in space. It is about peoples, societies, and cultures that once inhabited, or indeed still inhabit, particular localities in the landscape. It addresses the movement of peoples and population diasporas, the trade and exchange of goods and commodities, and the circulation of ideologies and beliefs. Simultaneously, it is also a social practice largely based in Anglo-American institutions and largely dominated by the English language (Olsen 1991). Indeed, its spread throughout the world can be associated with the processes of colonialism (Trigger 1989) and, significantly, the emergence of postcolonial discourses is intimately tied to this process (Gosden, chapter 7 and 2001; Schmidt and Patterson 1995).

The history of archaeology's engagement with space can be characterized by a trend toward increased precision with which space is rendered. As Clarke (1977:2) has noted, while there was a strong interest in spatial information among all contemporary schools of archaeology, from the Russian to the Australasian, there has been a marked difference in emphasis. For example, the Austro-German school of anthropogeographers (1880–1900) developed the formal mapping of attributes and artifacts to explain the distribution of past cultures conceived of in ethnic terms. This was taken up most notably by Gustaf Kossinna (1912) in an attempt to support German nationalism. By the turn of the nineteenth century, archaeological distribution maps were a standard, if intuitive, approach in European archaeology. In many ways, British archaeology parallels the German model. There was a long tradition of relating archaeological sites to their environmental setting in the landscape. Both Crawford (1912) and Fleure (1921) were trained as geographers and their mapping helped establish a standard for future archaeological work.

By contrast, in America, the emphasis was largely upon ecological setting, social organization, and settlement pattern. Steward's (1938) pioneering work in Great Basin ethnography, in particular, stimulated the mapping of sites on a regional scale with the purpose of relating them to their environments. It directly stimulated Willey's (1953) settlement study of the Viru valley in Peru which established "settlement pattern archaeology." Willey (1953:1) defined his approach as the study of

> the way in which man disposed himself over the landscape on which he lived. It refers to dwellings, to their arrangement, and to the nature and disposition of other buildings pertaining to community life. These settlements reflect the natural environment, the level of technology on which the builders operated, and various institutions of social interaction and control which the culture maintained. Because settlement patterns are, to a large extent, directly shaped by widely held cultural needs, they offer a strategic starting point for the functional interpretation of archaeological cultures.

This approach involved the mapping of sites according to their functional and hierarchical places within the settlement system and became broadly influential throughout the world.

In the late 1970s, both British and American archaeologies converged upon a geographical paradigm consistent with the growing influence of positivism in the social sciences. They imported a series of sophisticated spatial techniques in order to enhance explanatory rigor (Flannery 1976; Hodder and Orton 1976). Among the techniques adopted were nearest neighbor analysis, network analysis, and activity area analysis, each of which were applied at different scales. These approaches permitted the comparison of empirical patterns to expectations under a random model. Although maps continued to be used, especially in the context of diffusion and trend surface simulations, graphic representations of site data fitted to probability distributions became an influential form of analysis. This approach to spatial representation, however, can be seen as mechanistic and asocial and a number of archaeologists, like many human geographers, began to have doubts about its ultimate value in understanding the past.

Unquestionably the most sophisticated spatial technique used in archaeology today is Geographical Information Systems (GIS) (Aldenderfer and Maschner 1996; Allen, Green, and Zubrow 1990; Lock and Stancic 1995). This approach was introduced in the early 1980s and has now come to dominate spatial analysis in both academic and cultural resource management contexts (Westcott and Brandon 2000; Wheatley and Gillings 2002). Basically, GIS approaches are spatially referenced databases that permit the collection, manipulation, and visualization of data through time and across space. They typically consist of two parts, a relational database which allows searching and a graphing database which permits visual representation. GIS has now been effectively applied to a range of problems such as predictive modeling, landscape analysis, and human ecology (Aldenderfer and Maschner 1996). Some have argued that GIS is a pure method, that is to say, "theory-free," and there is no necessary correlation between a particular data type or category and the use of GIS to solve a problem (Aldenderfer 1996:17). This view, however, cannot be maintained since the categories deemed relevant are in fact linked to, if not isomorphic with, the kinds of GIS techniques that are used in analysis.

Spatiality refers to the "objective" conceptions of space that are necessarily created through material practices and processes in the reproduction of social life. It has developed as a key issue in critical postmodern geography. One of the most important moves toward a consideration of spatiality is Gregory's (1978:120) observation that the analysis of spatial structure is not derivative and secondary to the analysis of social structure. As an example, he notes that class relations are not merely expressed within a spatial structure, they are in fact constituted through that same structure. Spatial structures and social structures have a recursive relationship: the one cannot be theorized without considering the other. Soja (1989) has provided a historical account of the devaluing of space brought about by the emergence of modernization. He notes that modernization can be linked to objective processes of structural change associated with the ability of capitalism to develop and survive. It is thus a continuous process of societal restructuring that is periodically accelerated owing to geographical and historical dynamics of modes of production. In a influential critique, Harvey (1989) has argued that capitalism is characterized by time–space compression where innovations in transportation annihilate space through time. There is a speeding up of the pace of life such that the world always seems just about to collapse on us. The despatialization of life is part of what he calls the "postmodern condition."

Spatiality has also been explored in anthropology through the creation of identities within local and global societies. Moore (1986), for example, has emphasized how spatial categories and orientations are linked to the ordering of social experience in her ethnographic research among the Endo. She notes that the importance of village life lies in its "architectonic" integration of the social, symbolic, and economic experiences. The houses, storage units, house compounds, and divisions of the fields all contribute to a sense of social being. Appadurai (1996) has emphasized the fragmentation of modern subjectivities and deterritorialization due to electronic media and mass migration. The product of this is the creation of ethnoscapes inhabited by people with hybrid identities and allegiances to multiple places. These new transnational and diasporic identities are gaining political power and he suggests that they pose a challenge to the dominance of the nation-state.

The study of spatiality is beginning to emerge as a significant focus in social archaeology. Much of this literature has been influenced by phenomenology. Tilley (1994), for example, has proposed that Neolithic British society can be understood from a consideration of the experience of the landscape. He notes that cairn and barrow, cursus and causeway enclosures signify a will to make manifest in the land ancestral powers, and that this is in turn linked to the control of knowledge of the ancestral past. These monuments objectified ancestral powers as resources to be manipulated according to the interests of particular individuals or social groups. Robin (2002) has proposed a concept of "lived space" that merges the material and the symbolic, and is socially constructed and socially experienced. She argues that the ways in which people organize living spaces defines and is defined by all aspects of their lives – social, political, economic, and ritual. In her study of the Maya community of Chan Noohol she shows that the ordered construction of place came into being as people lived out the spatial rhythms of their daily lives. She writes: "[j]ust as the places and meanings people construct influence subsequent actions in the world, people's ongoing actions continue to construct and reconstruct spatial meanings" (2002:262).

Materiality

Material culture is the traditional domain of archaeology and, in many ways, its very reason for being. It is seemingly an unproblematic category referring to the physical traces of past human activities, classically referring to artifacts, but also encompassing buildings, graves, caches, hoards, monuments, and the like. It is an indicator of humanity's intrusion into the natural world and our way of demarcating the natural and cultural with the knowledge that they inhabit permeable categories (Glassie 1999:1). And yet, material culture is not a natural category; it has its own genealogy. Material culture, as we understand it today, could be seen a product of the Victorian collecting traditions of the nineteenth century and intimately implicated in Enlightenment notions of universality, colonial expansion, industrialism, and the birth of consumer culture

(Buchli 2002:12). Archaeology has more recently moved from analyses of material culture as a corpus of objects and things, to understanding the more dynamic relationships forged under the rubric of materiality. Meskell (2004) argues that materiality "takes as its remit the exploration of the situated experiences of material life, the constitution of the object world and concomitantly its shaping of human experience."

There is a growing body of scholarship on materiality in anthropology and sociology (Appadurai 1986; Attfield 2000; Bourdieu 1977; Miller 1987; Strathern 1988; Toren 1999). It is now possible to identify a series of topics or research areas ranging from the philosophical to the practical including objectification, the social life of things, and consumption. Objectification is usually defined as the process by which people constitute themselves through things. This means more than simply objects signifying a particular kind of social distinction. Rather it implies that the meanings we give to things are intimately bound up in how we give meaning to our lives. Gell (1992, 1998) has even argued that artifacts have agency. His point is that although artifacts are inanimate they can be seen as agents because they produce real-world effects. The implication here is that the traditional subject–object divide can no longer be maintained and what is needed are studies of people–thing relationships. A sophisticated example from a semiotic perspective is Munn's (1986) study of the material practices of bodily spacetime among the Gawa in Papua New Guinea.

The social-life-of-things is a research focus on the circulation of objects though and across different commodity states. Appadurai (1996) positions commodities as things with precise forms of social potential and which are thus distinguishable from products, objects, goods, and artifacts. Specifically, he is concerned with the classic issue of exchange, circulation, and value as culturally embedded, and traverses the familiar ground of *kula* and *keda*, cargo cults, and commodity fetishism. Kopytoff (1986) provides a historical dimension to this view by considering things as having mutual or overlapping biographies. No object is isolated, unconnected from other objects or a dense network of relationships. Yet Kopytoff refers to inherently alienable commodities and networks of exchange. Perhaps his most evocative statement is that society constrains the world of people and the world of things, and in constructing objects society also constructs people. As Meskell (2004) suggests, archaeologists influenced by Kopytoff have tended to focus upon the afterlife of artifacts, the shifting contexts of things in and out of their original archaeological contexts (Hamilakis 1999; Seip 1999). Often these reflect the politics of museum display or colonial collection and disembedding, the renegotiation of meaning through the life-history of the object (Gosden and Marshall 1999: 170).

Yet another direction for approaching materiality is through the notion of consumption (Carrier 1995; Miller 1987, 1995, 1998b). The standard view of material culture drawn in part from Marxist perspectives on labor value has emphasized production and exchange. Indeed, Marx paid very little attention to consumption. This has had the unacknowledged consequence of treating consumption as a nonproblematic practice. There is a growing awareness of consumption as a social process and not as a simple economic transaction (Miller 1987, 1995). Indeed, consumption is part of how people define themselves and their identities from the clothes they wear to the furnishings in their homes. Social practices of consumption serve as ways of conforming to social norms and beliefs as well as a means of challenging power and authority. Recent research is focusing on seemingly mundane activities such as shopping, reconstructed as a social process mediated by values of love and sacrifice (Miller 1998a; Miller et al. 1998).

Archaeology is addressing materiality from several different directions, including social technology, material-culture-as-text, and embodiment. Elements of the social technology approach are seen in Lechtman's (1977) early work on "technological style" and her observation that technologies are not simply a means of adaptation, but "particular sorts of cultural phenomena that reflect cultural preoccupations and express them in the very style of the technology itself" (Lechtman and Steinberg 1979:139). This approach has been more fully developed through a consideration of the interrelations of technology and social agency. Dobres (2000) regards technology as embodied social practice that is a part of performance unfolding in, but not dictated by, the material world. For her, technology is best conceptualized as a verb, not a noun, and, as such, an unfinished process. Following a relatively independent French intellectual tradition, Leroi-Gourhan (1993) and, more recently, Lemonnier (1992, 1993), have pursued the material aspects of technology, interrogating the cultural logics that underlie choice and ultimately transform society.

The material-culture-as-text approach was an early move in the poststructural engagement with materiality. In his book *Reading the Past*, Hodder (1986) proposed the idea of material culture as a text to be read. His perspective is thoroughly structural and he argues that objective meanings need to be built up through a contextual consideration of similarities and differences. By 1988 Hodder (1989) adopted a poststructural interpretation of text. He regarded material culture to be implicated in practices designed to accomplish social goals. He outlined a series of comparisons between linguistic and material meanings, emphasizing the non-arbitrary nature of material meanings, their non-discursive and often subconscious quality, their inherent polysemy, and their durability. He concluded that the study of material culture raised, even more so than the study of language, the relationship between structure and context. This approach was initially influential among some postprocessualists (Tilley 1991), but has now been subjected to critique. Tilley (1999), for example, has proposed the concept of metaphor as a way of linking thought, action, and material culture.

Embodiment is emerging as a key approach to understanding materiality, specifically addressing the locus of the body as a material grounding for subjective experience. This is yet another significant domain where the once rigid taxonomies of subjects and objects are gradually being rethought through nuanced contextual analyses. According to Joyce (chapter 4), embodiment can be understood as the shaping of a person's experience of subjectivity that is simultaneously the outcome of material and discursive actions. Joyce (1998, 2000a, 2000b, 2000c, 2002) has carried out a series of analyses of material culture from pre-Columbian Maya and Aztec societies using insights drawn from the work of Judith Butler. These include ceramic and stone vessels, figurines, and ear ornaments, as well as burial practices. She identifies recursive relationships between the treatment of living and dead bodies that are mediated by artifacts in the objectification of moral values and bodily ideals. Meskell (1996, 1999, 2002; Meskell and Joyce 2003) has linked embodiment to bodily experience, focusing on the materiality of the body, the social context of the body, the operation of sex and/or gender on the body, and the singularity of living through our body. In her studies of ancient Egypt, she emphasizes the textual and material culture dimensions of Egyptian individuals whose very embodiment transcended death.

The challenge posed by the study of materiality entails deconstructing our own notions of objects and subjects as discrete and essential entities that inhabit particular, impermeable worlds. Recent writing on the specific contours of agentic objects or fetishes, as interlocutors between persons, things, and worlds, undermines the fixity of our imposed boundaries. Meskell (2004) cautions that we should acknowledge that humans create their object worlds, no matter how many different trajectories are possible and how subject-like objects become. Materiality manifests a presence of power in realizing the world, crafting thing from non-thing, subject from non-subject. This affecting presence is shaped through enactment with the physical world, project-ing or imprinting ourselves into the world (Armstrong 1981:19). Studies of materiality cannot simply focus upon the characteristics of objects but must engage in the dialectic of people and things.

Conclusions

Archaeology is popularly regarded as the purveyor of knowledge about human evolu-tionary processes and past lives. It provides an appreciation of where we are by revealing where we came from and, in this, gives us guidance for where we might be going. This is clearly an important social use of archaeology and one closely associated with its Enlightenment origins. It is part of the ethic of universal humanism espoused by science. In different ways, it is adopted by all types of nationalist archaeologies from Israel, to Iraq, to China, to the United States. Archaeology is also being used in a developing counter-hegemonic discourse by indigenous peoples throughout the world as they seek to control the representation of their pasts as a means of reclaiming their presents. This can best be seen in the debates over the antiquities trade (Brodie, Doole, and Renfrew 2001; Renfrew 2000) and repatriation (Fforde, Hubert, and Turnbull 2002; Fine-Dare 2002; Mihesuah 2000). This too is an appropriate social use of archae-ology, given the historical legacy of colonialism and the new homogenizing tendencies of globalization. The moving articulations of these different discourses will contribute to the shaping of future political forms and social interests.

While recognizing the centrality of these perspectives, we wish to offer a different, but related, view of archaeology, one that acknowledges the social construction of time, space, and material culture as constituent of social being. We have called this social archaeology. This approach is somewhat different from the study of the relation-ships of the social to culture, or the social to social organization, or the social and contemporary society. Rather it engages with how different peoples inscribe meaning in time–space, spacetime, and embodied time and, through this process of inscription, construct themselves. As Soja (1996:46) writes: "all social relations become real and concrete, a part of our lived social existence, only when they are spatially 'inscribed' – that is, *concretely represented* – in the social production of social space." Material culture is fundamentally implicated in the process of this concrete representation. Archaeology is particularly well positioned to address the material configurations of social time and social space. In this way, it can contribute to the broader project of developing social theory for the twenty-first century.

REFERENCES

Aitken, M. J. 1990. *Science-Based Dating in Archaeology*. London: Longman.

Aldenderfer, M. 1996. Introduction. In M. Aldenderfer and H. D. G. Maschner (eds.), *Anthropology, Space, and Geographic Information Systems*. Oxford: Oxford University Press, pp. 3–18.

——, and H. D. G. Maschner (eds.) 1996. *Anthropology, Space, and Geographic Information Systems*. Oxford: Oxford University Press.

Allen, K. M. S., S. W. Green, and E. B. W. Zubrow (eds.) 1990. *Interpreting Space: GIS and Archaeology*. London: Taylor & Francis.

Appadurai, A. 1986. Introduction: Commodities and the politics of value. In A. Appadurai (ed.), *The Social Life of Things: Commodities in Cultural Perspective*. Cambridge: Cambridge University Press.

——1996. *Modernity at Large: Cultural Dimensions of Globalization*. Minneapolis. University of Minnesota Press.

Armstrong R. P. 1981. *The Powers of Presence: Consciousness, Myth and Affecting Presence*. Philadelphia: University of Pennsylvania Press.

Attfield, J. 2000. *Wild Things: The Material Culture of Everyday Life*. Oxford: Berg.

Baert, P. 1992. *Time, Self, and Social Being: Temporality within a Sociological Context*. Brookfield, VT: Avebury.

Binford, L. R. 1962. Archaeology as anthropology. *American Antiquity* 28: 217–225.

——1965. Archaeological systematics and the study of culture process. *American Antiquity* 31: 203–210.

Bourdieu, P. 1977. *Outline of a Theory of Practice*. Cambridge: Cambridge University Press.

Bradley, R. 1991. Ritual, time and history. *World Archaeology* 23: 209–219.

Braudel, F. 1973. *The Mediterranean and the Mediterranean World in the Age of Philip II*. London: Collins.

Brodie, N., J. Doole, and C. Renfrew (eds.) 2001. *Trade in Illicit Antiquities: The Destruction of the World's Archaeological Heritage*. Cambridge: McDonald Institute for Archaeological Research.

Buchli, V. 2002. Introduction. In V. Buchli (ed.), *The Material Culture Reader*. Oxford: Berg, pp. 1–22.

Carrier, J. 1995. *Gifts and Commodities*. London: Routledge.

Chang, K. C. 1958. Study of the Neolithic social groupings: Examples from the New World. *American Anthropologist* 60: 298–334.

——1967. *Rethinking Archaeology*. New York: Random House.

Childe, V. G. 1942. *What Happened in History*. Harmondsworth: Penguin.

——1946. Anthropology and archaeology. *Southwestern Journal of Anthropology* 2: 243–252.

——1947. Archaeology as a social science. *University of London, Institute of Archaeology, Third Annual Report*, 4–11.

Chippindale, C. 1989. "Social archaeology" in the nineteenth century: Is it right to look for modern ideas in old places? In A. Christenson (ed.), *Tracing Archaeology's Past: The Historiography of Archaeology*. Carbondale: Southern Illinois University Press, pp. 21–33.

Clark, G. 1957 [1939]. *Archaeology and Society*. London: Methuen.

Clarke, D. L. (ed.) 1977. *Spatial Archaeology*. New York: Academic Press.

Conkey, M. W., with S. H. Williams. 1991. The political economy of gender in archaeology. In M. di Leonardo (ed.), *Gender at the Crossroads of Knowledge: Feminist Anthropology in a Postmodern Era*. Berkeley: University of California Press, pp. 102–139.

Crawford, O. G. S. 1912. The distribution of Early Bronze Age settlements in Britain. *Geographical Journal* August/September: 184–217.

Daniel, G. 1981. *A Short History of Archaeology*. London: Thames & Hudson.

Dobres, M-A. 2000. *Technology and Social Agency*. Oxford: Blackwell.

Earle, T. K. 1978. Economic and social organization of a complex chiefdom: The Halelea District Kaua'l, Hawaii. Ann Arbor: University of Michigan, Museum of Anthropology, Anthropological Papers 63.

Fabian, J. 1983. *Time and the Other: How Anthropology Makes its Object*. New York: Columbia University Press.

Feinman, G., and J. Neitzel 1984. Too many types: An overview of sedentary prestate societies in the Americas. *Advances in Archaeological Method and Theory* 7: 39–102.

Fforde, C., J. Hubert, and P. Turnbull 2002. *The Dead and their Possessions: Repatriation in Principle, Policy and Practice*. London: Unwin Hyman.

Fine-Dare, K. S. 2002. *Grave Injustice: The American Indian Repatriation Movement and NAGPRA*. Lincoln: University of Nebraska Press.

Flannery, K. V. 1968. Archaeological systems theory and early Mesoamerica. In B. J. Meggers (ed.), *Anthropological Archaeology in the Americas*. Washington, DC: Anthropological Society of Washington, pp. 67–87.

——(ed.) 1976. *The Early Mesoamerican Village*. New York: Academic Press.

Fleure, H. J. 1921. *Geographical Factors in History*. London: Macmillan.

Ford, R. I. 1973. Archaeology serving humanity. In C. L. Redman (ed.), *Research and Theory in Current Archaeology*. New York: John Wiley, pp. 83–93.

Fritz, J. 1973. Relevance, archaeology, and subsistence theory. In C. L. Redman (ed.), *Research and Theory in Current Archaeology*. New York: John Wiley, pp. 59–82.

Gell, A. 1992. The enchantment of technology and the technology of enchantment. In J. Coote and A. Shelton (eds.), *Anthropology, Art and Aesthetics*. Oxford: Oxford University Press, pp. 40–63.

——. 1998. *Art and Agency*. Oxford: Clarendon Press.

Giddens, A. 1979. *Central Problems in Social Theory*. London: Macmillan.

Glassie, H. 1999. *Material Culture*. Bloomington: Indiana University Press.

Gosden, C. 1994. *Social Being and Time*. Oxford: Blackwell.

——2001. Postcolonial archaeology: Issues of culture, identity, and knowledge. In I. Hodder (ed.), *Archaeological Theory Today*. Cambridge, Polity Press, pp. 241–261.

——, and Y. Marshall. 1999. The cultural biography of objects. *World Archaeology: The Cultural Biography of Objects* 31: 169–178.

Gregory, D. 1978. *Ideology, Science and Human Geography*. London: Hutchinson.

——1994. *Geographical Imaginations*. Oxford: Blackwell.

Hall, M. 2001. Social archaeology and the theatres of memory. *Journal of Social Archaeology* 1: 50–61.

Hamilakis, Y. 1999. Stories from exile: Fragments from the cultural biography of the Parthenon (or "Elgin") marbles. *World Archaeology: The Cultural Biography of Objects* 31: 303–320.

Harvey, D. 1989. *The Urban Experience*. Oxford: Basil Blackwell.

Heidegger, M. 1962. *Being and Time*. Oxford: Blackwell.

Hodder, I. 1982. Theoretical archaeology: A reactionary view. In I. Hodder (ed.), *Symbolic and Structural Archaeology*. Cambridge: Cambridge University Press, pp. 1–16.

——1986. *Reading the Past*. Cambridge: Cambridge University Press.

—— 1987. The contribution of the long term. In I. Hodder (ed.), *Archaeology as Long-term History*. Cambridge: Cambridge University Press, pp. 1–8.

—— 1989. Post-modernism, post-structuralism, and post-processual archaeology. In I. Hodder (ed.), *The Meaning of Things*. London: Unwin Hyman, pp. 64–78.

—— (ed.) 1991. *Archaeological Theory in Europe*. London: Routledge.

——, and C. Orton. 1976. *Spatial Analysis in Archaeology*. Cambridge: Cambridge University Press.

Husserl, E. 1970. *The Crisis of European Sciences*. Evanston, IL: Northwestern University Press.

—— 1977. *Cartesian Meditations*. The Hague: Martinus Nijhoff.

Joyce, R. A. 1998. Performing the body in Prehispanic Central America. *Res: Anthropology and Aesthetics* 33: 147–165.

——. 2000a. Heirlooms and houses: Materiality and social memory. In R. A. Joyce and S. Gillespie (eds.), *Beyond Kinship: Social and Material Reproduction in House Societies*. Philadelphia: University of Pennsylvania Press, pp. 189–212.

——. 2000b. A Precolumbian gaze: Male sexuality among the ancient Maya. In R. Schmidt and B. Voss (eds.), *Archaeologies of Sexuality*. London: Routledge, pp. 263–283.

—— 2000c. *Gender and Power in Prehispanic Mesoamerica*. Austin, University of Texas Press.

—— 2002. Beauty, sexuality, body ornamentation and gender in Ancient Mesoamerica. In S. Nelson and M. Rosen-Ayalon (eds.), *In Pursuit of Gender*. Walnut Creek, CA: AltaMira Press, pp. 81–92.

Karlsson, H. (ed.) 2001. *It's About Time: The Concept of Time in Archaeology*. Gothenburg: Bricoleur Press.

Knapp, A. B. (ed.) 1992. *Archaeology, Annales, and Ethnohistory*. Cambridge: Cambridge University Press.

Kopytoff, I. 1986. The cultural biography of things: Commoditization as process. In A. Appadurai (ed.), *The Social Life of Things: Commodities in Cultural Perspective*. Cambridge: Cambridge University Press, pp. 64–91.

Kossinna, G. 1912. *Die Deutsche Vorgeschichte: Eine hervorragend nationale Wissenschaft*. Mannus-Bibliothek 9.

Laclau, E., and C. Mouffe. 1985. *Hegemony and Socialist Strategy*. London: Verso.

Layton, R. (ed.) 1989a. *Conflict in the Archaeology of Living Traditions*. London: Unwin Hyman.

—— (ed.) 1989b. *Who Needs the Past? Indigenous Values and Archaeology*. London: Unwin Hyman.

Lechtman, H. 1977. Style in technology-some early thoughts. In H. Lechtman and R. S. Merrill (eds.), *Material Culture: Styles, Organization, and Dynamics of Technology*. St. Paul, MN: West Publishing Co., pp. 3–20.

——, and A. Steinberg. 1979. The history of technology: An anthropological perspective. In G. Bugliarello and D. B. Doner (eds.), *History and Philosophy of Technology*. Urbana: University of Illinois Press, pp. 135–160.

Lemonnier, P. 1992. *Elements for an Anthropology of Technology*. Ann Arbor: University of Michigan, Museum of Anthropology.

—— 1993. Introduction. In P. Lemmonier (ed.), *Technological Choices: Transformations in Material Cultures since the Neolithic*. London: Routledge, pp. 1–35.

Leone, M. P. 1978. Time in American archaeology. In C. L. Redman, M. J. Berman, E. V. Curtin, W. T. Langhorne, Jr., N. M. Versaggi, and J. C. Wanser (eds.), *Social Archaeology: Beyond Subsistence and Dating*. New York: Academic Press, pp. 25–36.

Leroi-Gourhan, A. 1993. *Gesture and Speech*. Trans. A. Bostock Berger. Cambridge, MA: MIT Press.

Lock, G., and Z. Stancic (eds.) 1995. *Archaeology and Geographical Information Systems: A European Perspective*. London: Taylor & Francis.

Malina, J., and Z. Vasicek. 1990. *Archaeology Yesterday and Today*. Cambridge: Cambridge University Press.

Martin, P. S., and F. Plog. 1973. *The Archaeology of Arizona: A Study of the Southwest Region*. Garden City, NY: Doubleday/Natural History Press.

Merleau-Ponty, M. 1964. *Signs*. Evanston, IL: Northwestern University Press.

Meskell, L. M. 1996. The somatisation of archaeology: Discourses, institutions, corporeality. *Norwegian Archaeological Review* 29: 1–16.

—— 1999. *Archaeologies of Social Life: Age, Sex, Class et cetera in Ancient Egypt*. Oxford: Blackwell.

—— 2002. *Private Life in New Kingdom Egypt*, Princeton, NJ: Princeton University Press.

—— 2004. *Object Worlds in Ancient Egypt: Material Biographies Past and Present*. Oxford: Berg.

——, and R. A. Joyce. 2003. *Embodied Lives: Figuring Ancient Maya and Egyptian Experience*. Routledge: Oxford.

Mihesuah, D. (ed.) 2000. *Repatriation Reader: Who Owns American Indian Remains?* Lincoln: University of Nebraska Press.

Miller, D. 1987. *Material Culture and Mass Consumption*. Oxford: Blackwell.

—— (ed.) 1995. *Acknowledging Consumption*. London: Routledge.

—— 1998a. *A Theory of Shopping*. Cambridge: Polity Press.

—— (ed.) 1998b. *Material Cultures: Why Some Things Matter*. Chicago: University of Chicago Press.

——, P. Jackson, N. Thrift, B. Holbrook, and M. Rowlands (eds.) 1998. *Shopping, Place and Identity*. London: Routledge.

Moore, H. 1986. *Space, Text and Gender: An Anthropological Study of the Marakwet of Kenya*. Cambridge: Cambridge University Press.

Moser, S. 1998. *Ancestral Images: The Iconography of Human Origins*. Stroud: Alan Sutton.

Munn, N. D. 1986. *The Fame of Gawa. A Symbolic Study of Value Transformations in a Massim (Papua New Guinea) Society*. Cambridge: Cambridge University Press.

O'Brien, M. J. (ed.) 1996. *Evolutionary Archaeology: Theory and Application*. Salt Lake City: University of Utah Press.

Olsen, B. J. 1991. Metropolises and satellites in archaeology: On power and asymmetry in global archaeological discourse. In R. W. Preucel (ed.), *Processual and Postprocessual Archaeologies: Multiple Ways of Knowing the Past*. Carbondale, IL: Center for Archaeological Investigations, pp. 211–224.

Patterson, T. C. 1986. The last sixty years: Toward a social history of Americanist archaeology in the United States. *American Anthropologist* 88: 7–26.

—— 1994. Social archeology in Latin America: An appreciation. *American Antiquity* 59: 531–537.

—— 1995. *Towards a Social History of Archaeology in the United States*. Orlando: Harcourt Brace.

Paynter, R. 1983. Field or factory? Concerning the degradation of archaeological labor. In J. M. Gero, D. M. Lacey, and M. L. Blakey (eds.), *The Socio-Politics of Archaeology*. Amherst: University of Massachusetts, pp. 17–29.

Preucel, R. W. (ed.) 1991. *Processual and Postprocessual Archaeologies: Multiple Ways of Knowing the Past*. Carbondale, IL: Center for Archaeological Investigations.

Ramenofsky, A. F. 1998. The illusion of time. In A. F. Ramenofsky and A. Steffen (eds.), *Unit Issues in Archaeology: Measuring Time, Space, and Material*. Salt Lake City: University of Utah Press, pp. 74–84.

Redman, C. L., M. J. Berman, E. V. Curtin, W. T. Langhorne, Jr., N. M. Versaggi, and J. C. Wanser (eds.) 1978. *Social Archaeology: Beyond Subsistence and Dating*. New York: Academic Press.

Renfrew, C. 1973a. Monuments, mobilization and social organization in Neolithic Wessex. In C. Renfrew (ed.), *The Explanation of Culture Change: Models in Prehistory*. London: Duckworth, pp. 539–558.

—— 1973b. *Social Archaeology*. Southampton: Camelot Press, University of Southampton.

—— 1973c. *Before Civilization: The Radiocarbon Revolution and Prehistoric Europe*. New York: Knopf.

—— 1984a. *Approaches to Social Archaeology*. Cambridge: Harvard University Press.

—— 1984b. Social archaeology, societal change and generalisation. In *Approaches to Social Archaeology*. Cambridge, MA: Harvard University Press, pp. 3–21.

—— 2000. *Loot, Legitimacy and Ownership*. London: Duckworth.

Robin, C. 2002. Outside of houses: The practices of everyday life at Chan Noohol, Belize. *Journal of Social Archaeology* 2: 245–267.

Schiffer, M. B. (ed.) 2000a. *Social Theory in Archaeology*. Salt Lake City: University of Utah Press.

—— 2000b. Social Theory in archaeology: Building bridges. In M. B. Schiffer (ed.), *Social Theory in Archaeology*. Salt Lake City: University of Utah Press, pp. 1–13.

Schmidt, P. R., and T. C. Patterson (eds.) 1995. *Making Alternative Histories: The Practice of Archaeology and History in Non-Western Settings*. Santa Fe: School of American Research Press.

Seip, L. P. 1999. Transformations of meaning: The life history of a Nuxalk mask. *World Archaeology: The Cultural Biography of Objects* 31: 272–287.

Service, E. 1962. *Primitive Social Organization*. New York: Random House.

Shanks, M., and C. Tilley. 1987a. *Reconstructing Archaeology*. Cambridge: Cambridge University Press.

—— 1987b. *Social Theory and Archaeology*. Cambridge: Polity Press.

Soja, E. W. 1989. *Postmodern Geographies: The Reassertion of Space in Critical Social Theory*. London: Verso.

—— 1996. *Thirdspace: Journeys to Los Angeles and Other Real and Imagined Places*. Oxford: Blackwell.

Spaulding, A. C. 1960. The dimensions of archaeology. In G. E. Doyle and R. L. Carneiro (eds.), *Essays in the Science of Culture in Honor of Leslie A. White*. New York: Thomas Crowell, n.p.

Steward, J. 1938. *Basin-plateau Aboriginal Sociopolitical Groups*. Washington, DC: US Government Printing Office, Smithsonian Institution, Bureau of American Ethnology Bulletin 120.

—— 1955. *Theory of Cultural Change*. Urbana: University of Illinois Press.

Strathern, M. 1988. *The Gender of the Gift: Problems with Women and Problems with Society in Melanesia*. Berkeley: University of California Press.

Thomas, J. 1996. *Time, Culture and Identity: An Interpretive Archaeology*. London: Routledge.

Tilley, C. 1991. *Material Culture and Text: The Art of Ambiguity*. London: Routledge.

—— 1994. *A Phenomenology of Landscape: Places, Paths, Monuments*. London: Berg.

—— 1999. *Metaphor and Material Culture*. Oxford: Blackwell.

Toren, C. 1999. *Mind, Materiality, and History: Explorations in Fijian Ethnography*. London: Routledge.

Trigger, B. G. 1980. *Gordon Childe: Revolutions in Archaeology*. London: Thames & Hudson.

—— 1989. *A History of Archaeological Thought*. Cambridge: Cambridge University Press.

Ucko, P. 1987. *Academic Freedom and Apartheid: The Story of the World Archaeological Congress*. London: Duckworth.

VanPool, C. S., and VanPool, T. L. 1999. The scientific nature of postprocessualism. *American Antiquity* 64: 35–53.

Watkins, J. 2000. *Indigenous Archaeology: American Indian Values and Scientific Practice*. Walnut Creek, CA: Alta Mira Press.

Watson, R. 1990. Ozymandias, king of kings: Postprocessual radical archaeology as critique. *American Antiquity* 55: 673–689.

Westcott, K. L., and R. J. Brandon (eds.) 2000. *Practical Applications of GIS for Archaeologists*. London: Taylor & Francis.

Wheatley, D. and M. Gillings. 2002. *Spatial Technology and Archaeology: The Archaeological Applications of GIS*. New York: Taylor & Francis.

White, H. 1973. *Metahistory: The Historical Imagination in Nineteenth Century Europe*. Baltimore: Johns Hopkins University Press.

White, L. A. 1959. *The Evolution of Culture*. New York: McGraw-Hill.

Willey, G. R. 1953. *Prehistoric Settlement Patterns in the Virú Valley, Peru*. Washington, DC: Bureau of American Ethnology, Bulletin 155.

Yoffee, N. 1993. Too many chiefs? (or, safe texts for the '90s). In N. Yoffee and A. Sherratt (eds.), *Archaeological Theory: Who Sets the Agenda*. Cambridge: Cambridge University Press, pp. 60–78.

1

The "Social" in Archaeological Theory: An Historical and Contemporary Perspective

Ian Hodder

The central importance of the social in archaeological theory has emerged over recent decades. Through the twentieth century as a whole one can identify an overall shift from the "cultural" to the "social" in theoretical discussions within archaeology. This is a grand claim and there are many exceptions and vicissitudes, but I hope in this chapter to demonstrate the shift and to explain its importance.

An Historical Perspective

It has long been recognized that the archaeology of the late nineteenth and early twentieth centuries in Europe and North America was primarily concerned with documenting culture-historical sequences and influences. In the United States these interests were intimately tied to the way in which cultural anthropology as a whole developed through the Boasian school and the codification of the four-field approach. In Britain and Europe, the concern with cultural definition grew out of the closer links between archaeology and history and the Classical world. Later changes in the definition of culture and society within archaeology also followed or responded to changes within anthropology and related disciplines. But my concern here is to focus on the effect of these changes within archaeology.

The culture concept, insofar as it was theorized by Childe and others, concerned shared traits. Stereotypically these shared traits were pot styles and fibulae types, but for many authors they included social features. Thus the social was seen as part of the cultural. For Walter Taylor (1948:103) the subject matter of archaeology was "cultural," and in his theorizing, the social aspects of culture are those involving shared traits. But there is little specific attention to the social itself; the focus is on culture.

A partitive notion of culture, in which the social is a subset of the cultural whole, is perhaps most clearly indicated in Hawkes's (1954) response to Taylor. Hawkes, in presenting his famous "ladder of inference," argued that in achieving understanding of past cultures it was relatively easy to infer from archaeological phenomena the techniques that produced them. On the next rung of the ladder it was possible to infer subsistence economies. Harder was inference about the social and political institutions of the group, and hardest of all, at the top of the ladder, was inference about religious institutions and spiritual life. For Hawkes, the social rung dealt with settlement patterns and it involved analyses in order to see if special, larger, chiefly huts could be identified. It dealt with burial data to see if ranking could be observed (1954:161–162).

For Grahame Clark too, the social was a subset of culture as a whole. As a prehistorian he valued information from social anthropology in assisting the interpretation of early cultures. In his book *Archaeology and Society* (1939 [1957]) he saw culture as made up of component parts such as transport, technology, trade, and religion, but also social organization (1939 [1957]:175). Social units are "the main groups through and by which culture is shared and transmitted from one generation to another" (ibid.:169). Clark certainly gives social organization a central role in the cultural system because of its place in the transmission of culture. He also discusses demography, trade, specialization of production, and social differentiation as key parts of the archaeological account of the social. Language, writing, art, science, and law are also seen as inextricably social. Although for Clark the social remains a component of the cultural, his links at Cambridge with social anthropologists possibly led him to a greater emphasis on the social than is found amongst American colleagues influenced by the opposing tradition of cultural anthropology.

Childe is often identified as one of the major theorists regarding the notion of culture in archaeology (e.g., 1925). But his Marxist interests also led him to describe (1960) the evolution of societies in stages defined by social theorists and ethnographers (as the savagery, barbarism, civilization scheme of Morgan). These same Marxist leanings also led Childe to discussions of the internal workings of societies that involved sophisticated accounts of social relations. In his 1939 book *Man Makes Himself* he looked at how cultural development in the Near East is very much concerned ultimately with adaptation to the environment. But he also recognized that it is social mechanisms that allow adaptation. He showed how information about survival is passed down through social traditions. He saw language as a social product, with its meanings created through the agreement of people. He saw discoveries and inventions in technologies as being social, linked to the emergence of specialized production and concentrations of wealth. Social and ideological mechanisms can also come to retard progress in his model, and in other work (e.g., 1952) he argued that cultural development became stagnated in the Ancient Near East in comparison with Europe, because of social differences between despotic and superstitious elites in the East and more entrepreneurial, independent specialists and elites in Europe. But in the end, even for Childe, the social was just a subsystem within a wider cultural whole. It was thus dependent on other aspects of life, especially the economy and environment. Thus, for example, "on the large alluvial plains and riverside flatlands the need for extensive public works to drain and irrigate the land and to protect the settlement would tend to consolidate social organization and to centralize the economic system" (1939:159).

There was another sense, too, in which archaeology had a social dimension during these culture-historical, diffusionist, and evolutionary periods. For many, archaeology had a social role. Many archaeologists in the nineteenth and early twentieth centuries felt a social responsibility to provide museums for wider publics, even if the message advocated in those museums was paternalistic, nationalist, and imperialist. Some theorized at great length about social responsibility. At the end of his *Methods and Aims in Archaeology* published in 1904, Flinders Petrie argued that the study of the past and archaeology led to social union and "the responsibility of man for man" (1904:193). Grahame Clark discussed in 1934 the political links between archaeology and the state, and Childe (1949) discussed the social construction of archaeological knowledge.

The notion that the social is a part of the cultural remained in the New Archaeology, and in processual archaeology. The social was now often identified as a subsystem within an overall system. The frequent use of the term "sociocultural system" to describe the system as a whole perhaps identifies an increased emphasis on the social in processual archaeology. Indeed, much emphasis was expended using social terms such as band, tribe, chiefdom or state to describe archaeological assemblages. Today a parallel practice is found amongst processual archaeologists who categorize societies in terms of social complexity (Johnson and Earle 1987). But in practice in much processual archaeology it remained the case that the social subsystem remained subordinate to the environment and to economic and technological subsystems. The intellectual debt owed by processual archaeology to ecological and materialist approaches assured that social relations were seen as deriving from or based upon other areas of life.

The continued partitive view of culture and the social is seen in Binford's (1962) distinction between technomic, sociotechnic, and ideotechnic artifacts. Some artifacts were part of the social subsystem but others were not. For David Clarke, too, the social was a subset of the overall "sociocultural system." The "social subsystem" is "the hierarchical network of inferred personal relationships, including kinship and rank status" (1968:102). His own work on the Iron Age Glastonbury site attempted to infer kinship organization from settlement data and material culture distributions (1972). In the United States, a parallel move sought postmarital residence behavior from ceramic distributions within sites (e.g., Longacre 1970). Although these early attempts to "play the ethnographer" in the past and infer prehistoric kinship were ultimately unsuccessful, they were part of a wider and successful effort by processual archaeologists to use settlement and burial data to make inferences about social group size and ranking.

A good example of a processual archaeologist with a strong commitment to the social is Colin Renfrew. He argued for the ability for archaeologists to reconstruct past social subsystems in his inaugural lecture at Southampton University (Renfrew 1973). Later, in his book *Approaches to Social Archaeology*, he said that he was concerned to make "inferences of a social nature from the archaeological data" (1984:4). Like Clark before him, he wanted to make alliances with social anthropology, and he defined social archaeology as the reconstruction of past social systems and relations. Most of his work at this stage involved trying to identify the degree of social ranking in society and the systems of exchange between elites and social groups. He was also interested in issues of past identity and ethnicity. In a later inaugural lecture, at Cambridge University (Renfrew 1982), he argued for a further shift from the social to the cognitive. In defining a cognitive-processual archaeology (see also Renfrew and Zubrow 1994), it can be argued that Renfrew saw the cognitive as somehow separable from the social – one can separate cognitive processes in the mind from their social contexts. This is a claim denied by much social theory and by postprocessual archaeology, as we shall see. The definition of a cognitive-processual archaeology again shows that for Renfrew the social is just a subsystem that can be separated from other realms of life, including the cognitive.

The Centrality of the Social in Postprocessual Archaeology

In recent decades, not only the mind, but even the economy and the environment have come to be seen as social. The body and sex, too, have been pried from biology and placed firmly within the social realm. The overall goal of interpretation in archaeology has come to be to understand the past in social terms (e.g., Tilley 1993). It is important to make a distinction here between society and the social. Shanks and Tilley (1987b:57) argued that "society, in the sense of the social totality of a logic of necessity, doesn't exist" and, because of this, it is impossible "to specify society as the object of archaeology." Their argument here was directed against the notion of society as a totality. They argued that it would be unhelpful to shift from cultural "wholes" to the societal "whole." Rather, the focus was to be placed on the active negotiation of social roles and processes as part of a continual process. All aspects of daily life could be seen as part of this social process.

This shift to the view that, crudely, "everything is social" has a number of causes. One is the shift within Marxist approaches inside and outside archaeology from the 1960s onwards toward the centrality of the social relations of production. Writers such as Friedman and Rowlands (1978) had much impact on European archaeology when they espoused a structural Marxism in which the search for prestige goods could be a prime mover in the evolution of social complexity. This move perhaps opened the way for postprocessual archaeologists to embrace social theorists from social anthropology (e.g., Bourdieu 1977) and sociology (Giddens 1979) who were interested in examining the micro-processes of daily life rather than the macro-economic constraints and interactions. These small-scale practices were seen as fundamentally linked to power. They were thus seen as social rather than as simply the product of "cultural" differences between societies. They were not just another cultural trait, but were the building blocks of society as a whole. Everything, from the body and its daily practices in the home, to the technology, economy, and landscape, came to be seen as social. There was no separate social subsystem or social rung on the inferential ladder as all aspects of life were seen as integrated and dispersed along chains of social meaning (Tilley 1993:20).

Thomas (1993:76) looks back from a postprocessual point of view and suggests that "generally, ever since we have had something which could be called a *social archaeology*, we have tended to set our sights on what might be seen as somewhat grandiose targets: social organization, ranking, stratification, empires." In a postprocessual perspective, the aims are perhaps yet more grandiose, as everything becomes social. But on the other hand, Thomas is right that in practice the focus becomes less grand as every mundane aspect of daily life is explored for social meaning. The aims become more particular and specific; more holistic and less partitive.

Another important factor that encouraged an emphasis on the social in all aspects of life was the critique of positivism. Most processual archaeologists had espoused some version of the idea that theories could be tested in archaeology. From whatever source hypotheses derived, there could be an independence and an objectivity in the testing process. Theory could be confronted with data. In particular, much play was given to the idea of "middle-range" theories that could mediate between high-level theory and data (Kosso 1991; Tschauner 1996). But the critiques of these positivist views had emerged early and continued through the last decades of the twentieth century. Wylie (1989) pointed out that it was ironic that processual archaeology should adopt a framework – positivism – just as it was undergoing radical critique within philosophy and in the social sciences. Gradually, this critique spilled over into archaeology and it is one of the main reasons behind the emergence of postprocessual archaeology.

But there were also more down-to-earth reasons for the critique of positivism. It became clear that many of the communities served by archaeology saw the idea of neutral testing of theories as itself a socially biased claim. Many indigenous groups found themselves in conflict with archaeological scientists over the idea that science was socially neutral. On behalf of the Tasmanian Aboriginal Community, Langford (1983) argued that objective science does not have a natural right to study her culture. Mamani Condori (1989) talked on behalf of the Aymara in Bolivia and maintained the value of traditional knowledge in opposition to the positivist scientific attitude. In the United States, the conflict over the reburial of human remains of Native Americans has resulted in much disillusion over the sustainability of a neutral science perspective. "Scientific knowledge does not constitute a privileged view of the past that in and of itself makes it better than oral traditions. It is simply another way of knowing the past" (Anyon et al. 1996:15). A critique of neutral science also emerged from a feminist critique – a wide range of studies have shown both flagrant and subtle gender bias in supposedly neutral archaeological science (e.g., Gero 1996).

In more general terms, I have argued (Hodder 1999) that the increased concern with alternative perspectives, multivocality, and identity issues in archaeology is linked to globalism, post-industrial societies, the information age, and so on. Writers such as Castells (1996) have looked at broad globalizing trends in economic systems, and Arjun Appadurai (1996), working from an anthropological perspective, has discussed the cultural components of this process, describing a new fluidity whereby the emphasis is on transnationalism and diaspora. Archaeology developed as a discipline in relation to nationalism and colonialism. Its embrace of the natural science model was a necessary part of its role as guardian of the nation's past. It can be argued today that the nation-state is being undermined by international companies, by the dispersal of production, consumption, and exchange, by large-scale environmental changes, by the internet, and so on. There has been much discussion of global and local processes that play off each other and together undermine the nation-state. This is still a highly unequal process that favors the already developed centers of economic wealth, but it has new characteristics in which fluidity and diversity are important components, and in which a wide range of alternative voices have made themselves heard.

So what is the alternative to a positivist, hypothesis-testing archaeology? Many positivist archaeologists have stuck to some form of watered-down version of the hypothesis-testing idea because they fear that the only alternative is a form of relativism in which "anything goes." In other words, they fear that if there is no possibility of objective testing, then anyone's statement about the past, including fascist manipulations of the past, is equally as good as anyone else's. I know of no archaeologist who would take this line. There are various forms of relativism (Lampeter Archaeology Workshop 1997; Wylie 1994), and most archaeologists would accept that archaeological interpretation is and should be answerable to data. The question is really just a matter of "how."

Most postprocessual archaeologists, and in my view most processual archaeologists in practice, use some form of hermeneutic relationship with their data. Even if processual archaeologists claim to be doing a positivist science, in my view (Hodder 1999) this is often false consciousness, and a desire to ape the natural sciences. In practice, archaeology is not for the most part an experimental science. Rather, it is an historical science that works not by testing theories against data but by fitting lots of different types of data together as best it can in order to make a coherent story. This emphasis on fitting rather than testing is at the heart of the hermeneutic approach. Hermeneutics deals with the theory of interpretation as opposed to explanation (Ricoeur 1971; Thomas 2001; Tilley 1991). Within the positivist, processual approach it was claimed that events in the past could be explained by showing that they were examples of general covering statements. Theories of interpretation place more emphasis on making sense of the event in relation to what is going on around it, whilst acknowledging that generalizations have to be used. In the hermeneutic approach it is recognized that the researcher comes to the data with much prior knowledge and prejudgments. The data are perceived within these prejudgments. The researcher then works by fitting all the data together so that the parts make up a coherent whole. The interpretation that works best both fits our general theories and prejudgments and it makes most sense of more data than other interpretations. The process is not circular – that is, one does not just impose one's prejudgments on the data. The objects of study can cause us to change our ideas about the whole. But never in a way divorced from society and from perspective. There is thus a dialectical (dialogical) relationship between past and present and between object and subject. There is never a socially neutral moment in the scientific process, but equally, socially biased accounts can be transformed by interaction with objects of study.

For all these reasons, then, postprocessual archaeologists came to place more emphasis on the social than in earlier approaches in archaeology. In early postprocessual archaeology, two good examples of this tendency are the ideas that material culture is meaningfully constituted and that it is active. One source of such ideas was ethnoarchaeological research carried out in the 1970s and 1980s by myself (Hodder 1982) and a group of students based at Cambridge (e.g., Braithwaite 1982; Donley 1982, 1987; Lane 1987; Mawson 1989; Moore 1982, 1987; Welbourn 1984). These studies, and the early development of postprocessual archaeology, were very much influenced by semiotic and structuralist approaches in anthropology (e.g., Barthes 1973; Douglas 1970; Leach 1976; Lévi-Strauss 1968, 1970; Tambiah 1969; Turner 1969). But parallel developments were underway in the United States within historical archaeology (Deetz 1977; Glassie 1975) and in feminist-inspired prehistoric studies (Conkey 1989). These semiotic and structuralist ideas led to the notion that material culture has a meaning which goes beyond the physical properties of an object, and derives from the network of social entanglements and strategies within which the object is embroiled. This idea was explored in relation to historical archaeology in the United States (e.g., Leone 1982), in relation to ethnoarchaeological studies of modern material culture (e.g.,

Parker Pearson 1982), and in relation to feminist understandings of, for example, space and ceramic variation (e.g., Moore 1986).

The second, and overlapping, idea is that material culture is not just a tool that is passively used by humans as they follow strategies dictated by environment, adaptation, or societal rules. Rather, material culture is used actively to have an effect in the social world. It is used by agents intentionally pursuing strategies and monitoring outcomes – even if the intentions are often not consciously understood. Thus it is difficult to predict how material culture will be used – an interpretation of particular strategies is needed. This second idea partly derives from the ethnoarchaeological work already described. For example, in my work in the Lake Baringo area in Kenya, I found that despite frequent interaction between three regional groups ("tribes"), their material culture exhibited a number of distinct stylistic differences (Hodder 1982). Rather than attributing such patterning to "cultural" norms, I argued instead that material culture styles were used strategically to maintain notions of difference between the three groups, and that in this sense material culture could be said to play an active role in the creation and re-creation of identities. The notion that material culture is actively involved in social processes rather than being merely a passive reflection of human behavior was subsequently elaborated upon by others (e.g., Shanks and Tilley 1987a). The development of this perspective was heavily influenced by the "practice" or "action" theories of social forms as developed by Bourdieu (1977) and Giddens (1979). The emphasis on material culture being actively manipulated in order to legitimate or transform society was also found in Marxist-inspired archaeological studies in prehistoric Europe (e.g., especially Kristiansen 1984) and in historical archaeology in the United States (Leone 1982).

These two ideas reinforce the pervasiveness of the social and they lie behind many of the later developments in the various approaches termed postprocessual archaeology. The underlying context for this shift toward a fuller recognition of radical cultural difference (differences in social meaning of material culture), and for the view that material culture is active, rather than passive, together with the shift from positivism, was the various economic, social, and cultural changes described by the term globalism (see above). The two ideas also led to two key areas of research in recent archaeology. The first concerns material culture as text, and the second theories of agency.

The Text Metaphor, Reading the Past, and Poststructuralism

If material culture is always meaningfully constituted, then perhaps it can be seen as a text that is read (Hodder 1986). This idea has several attractive aspects. It puts the emphasis on the reader – on the notion that meaning does not reside in the object itself, but in the way that the reader makes sense of that object. The "reader" here is both the past social actor and the present archaeologist. The reading metaphor foregrounds the fact that different people will read the same data differently, a tendency for which there is much historical evidence. The reading metaphor refers to interpretation and thus links us to hermeneutics as discussed above. It recognizes that interpretations are fluid and will change through time. The material object has to be read in terms of prejudgments but also in terms of contextual clues. The text metaphor encourages us to focus on context – "with text." Rather than studying pottery and animal bones separate from each other and from their find context, the emphasis is placed on looking at pottery, animal bones, and find circumstances in relation to each other. In each context there may be distinct or subtle changes of meaning, but there may also be overall codes or rules used in the "language" of the material objects. The text metaphor thus invites us to make use of the world of semiotics – the study of signs and the systems in which they are embedded.

There has in fact been widespread use of semiotics and structuralism in archaeology over recent decades (Bekaert 1998; Helskog 1995; Parker Pearson 1999; Yentsch 1991), and there has been a recent revival of interest as a result of a shift from Saussurean to Peircean perspectives (Preucel and Bauer 2001). There are clearly advantages to be gained from considering material objects as organized by codes and rules that give them meaning. Knowledge about symbols, signs, indices, icons, and so on can usefully be applied in archaeology. The layout of settlements or of decoration on pottery, the discard of animal bones, and the arrangement of artifacts in graves have all been subject to semiotic and structuralist analysis. But there are also difficulties with the text metaphor when applied to material culture. In some important ways, material culture is not like a written text. Perhaps most significantly, the relationship between a word and its signifier is normally arbitrary; but this is seldom the case with material culture. In most, if not all, material culture usage, there is some non-arbitrary link between material culture and its meaning – as when gold is used to indicate high status because it is rare and enduring. Also, material objects, such as those in a living room, are not arranged in a simple sequence as is the case with words in a sentence – there are often fewer clues about the sequence in which one is supposed to read objects on entering a room. In addition, many of the meanings of objects are sensual and non-discursive – they are less open to conscious definition. The very fact that one cannot often be sure of the meanings of objects, their sensual nature, and non-arbitrary relations, suggests that material objects are important mechanisms for manipulating social situations. Although the Peircean approach deals with many of these criticisms of the text model, it remains the case that semiotic approaches often deal inadequately with the social.

This same notion, that meaning cannot be adequately studied by reference to abstract "linguistic" codes, lies behind many of the poststructuralist approaches that have influenced archaeology (Bapty and Yates 1990; Derrida 1976; Tilley 1990). In Derridean poststructuralism, the critique focuses on the structuralist notion that signifiers have meaning through their difference from other signifiers. But these other signifiers themselves only have meaning by being opposed to yet other signifiers in an endless chain of signification. Also, the meaning of a signifier varies depending on the context in which it is found. It is thus always possible to deconstruct any analysis which claims a totality, a whole or an original meaning, a truth, because these "origins" of meaning must always depend on other signifiers. These forms of critique have been effective in undermining many of the a priori assumptions made by archaeologists. In other forms of poststructuralism influenced by Foucault (1979), the focus is on the forms of power that sustain particular forms of knowledge and regimes of truth. Foucault radically decenters the subject actor who is seen as caught within webs of power/knowledge. The meaning of texts or material culture is situated within discourse. By discourse I mean particular forms of knowledge that are historically generated within specific relations of power. Thus knowledge and meaning are always situated and always social. Meaning is not just meaning. It is always *of* something and *for* someone.

The poststructuralist critiques take us a long way from the interpretation of meaning divorced from society. They have led to large numbers of studies that explore the relationships between material culture, meaning, and power (e.g., see the volumes of collected papers edited by Hodder et al. 1995, Thomas 2001, and Tilley 1993). They have also led to attempts to explore new ways of writing that open up the meaning of the past to alternative readings by different groups, and which undermine the notion that there is only one valid interpretation. These experimental studies, often influenced by a parallel debate within feminist archaeology, involve the production of new textual strategies, ranging from self-reflexivity and dialogue, to hypertext and the inclusion of semi-fictional vignettes (Edmonds 1999; Joyce 1994; Moran and Hides 1990; Tringham 1991, 1994).

We thus see the importance of the social for any attempt to interpret meaning. But does all this critique of the text metaphor mean that we can no longer talk of "reading the past"? If material meanings are closely linked to power and to material context, if material culture is related to unconscious motivations and sensual experience, if its meanings are nonlinear and ambiguous, perhaps the very idea of reading the past is unhelpful. In my view, taking these various criticisms into account, it remains important to retain "reading" and interpretation as components of archaeological procedure. This is because we do not only read texts. As social actors we are involved in daily acts of making sense of, "reading," what is going on around us. This wider sense of reading refers to the larger process of interpretation – including making sense of textures, sounds, smells, power dynamics, and so on. Reading is a wider process than interpreting words on a page. It involves being thoroughly engaged in a social context and interpreting that context through a variety of senses.

Agency

One of the limitations of the structuralist and poststructuralist approaches is that, as we have seen, they often downplay the role of social agents. As already noted, the view that material culture is active, that it is wielded by agents to achieve social ends, was an important strut of early postprocessual archaeology. But what is meant by agency theory, and how can material objects be seen as active?

The emphasis on agency began as a reaction to the processual emphasis on behavioral responses to environmental and other forms of change. Is there really nothing to societies and their long-term development than the passive stimulus–response that seems implied by much processual and behavioral archaeology? In his recent description of a behavioral theory of material culture, Schiffer states:

> readers may be nonplussed at the absence in the new theory of much vocabulary ... such as meaning, sign, symbol, intention, motivation, purpose, goal, attitude, value, belief, norm, function, mind, and culture. Despite herculean efforts in the social sciences to define these often ethnocentric or metaphysical notions, they remain behaviorally problematic and so are superfluous in the present project. (1999:9)

The discussion of agency is a reaction against types of social theory in which intentionality is seen as irrelevant to the understanding of human behavior.

But beyond this starting point, how much can we say about past agency? Certainly, there has recently been increased archaeological interest in discussions of agency (e.g., Dobres and Robb 2000). In my view, the first step in making sense of these discussions is to recognize that agency is itself a complex process that needs to be broken down into its component parts. Different authors in archaeology refer to different aspects of agency. For example, Barrett (1994) mainly discusses the context for action – the fact that the actor has to be situated in relation to power/knowledge in order to have knowledge and resources to act. He discusses the mobilization of space and resources in prehistoric monuments in Britain in these terms.

A rather different approach argues that there is an intentionality to agency and that this intentionality cannot be reduced to the context for action. Of course, some intentions may be non-discursive in the sense that actors may not be fully consciously aware of their motivations. Intentions need, therefore, to be interpreted. Archaeologists routinely make these interpretations. When claiming that a ditch is defensive or that a large wall around a settlement was built to provide prestige, intentions are imputed. The defensive nature of the ditch may be determined from its shape, size, and position, and from evidence of warfare, and so on. The prestigious nature of the wall may derive from its non-defensive nature (in terms of construction material, location or effectiveness) and from a larger context of competitive symbolic behavior. Another form of intentional social action that has recently attracted the interest of archaeologists is resistance to dominant groups. The older Marxist view that subordinate groups are duped by dominant ideologies has suffered from theoretical and empirical inadequacies in the social sciences (Giddens 1979), and many archaeologists have sought to demonstrate that subordinate groups use material culture to counteract dominant forms of discourse. For example, Shackel (2000) detected hundreds of hidden beer bottles in his excavations of a nineteenth-century brewery in West Virginia. Shackel concluded that the workers were intentionally and covertly consuming the products of their labor, thus drinking the owner's profits (see also Beaudry, Cook, and Mrozowski 1991). As another example, Joyce (2000) argues that at the regional heart of Rio Viejo, on the Pacific coast of Oaxaca, Mexico, non-elites inhabited the monumental platforms of the site's civic-ceremonial center after the collapse of centralized institutions at the end of the Classic period. According to Joyce (2000), these commoners rejected the dominant ideology of the previous era by dismantling and denigrating the architecture and carved stones. Likewise, Brumfiel (1996) suggests that powerful Aztec ideologies of male dominance expressed in official carvings at the capital city are contested in the countryside by popular images that assert the high status of women in reproductive roles.

There are problems in these accounts of intentional resistance. As Joyce (2000) notes, is it not inadequate to reduce intentionality to a response to dominant groups – surely in most cases there are many more dimensions to agency? Also, resistance is often discussed as if groups acted as wholes, when in fact most societies have many cross-cutting divisions. This point has been made effectively by feminist archaeologists who have recently resisted the notion that "women" or "men" form one category. In fact, there may be many differences amongst women (or men) on the basis of age, class, sexual orientation, and so on. Meskell (2002b) in particular has attempted to break down social groups and study the varying actions of individuals within them. This raises the issue of whether groups can have intentions. In my view the existence of a group is part of the resources used for individual agency. To get at the intentionality of agency properly involves understanding the construction of self and private individual lives. While some examples are provided by Meskell (see also Hodder 1999), for most archaeological contexts the aim of accessing individual intentionality is an ideal. But it remains important to consider variability in intentionality within groups and to study the processes used within groups to negotiate and coordinate group behavior and consensus. It is also important to recognize that the atomized individual is itself a Western concept and that the very idea of "individual" agency is itself a social product. Conceptions of individuals and body boundaries vary through time and space. Indeed, these conceptions are part of the resources available to agency.

Any act can have intended and unintended consequences. Indeed, another approach to agency takes the focus away from intentionality and focuses more closely on the impact of action on others and on the material world. These consequences can be short-, medium- or long-term. They can be local or "global." Perhaps the main way that this impact-view of agency has been used in archaeology is in terms of "power over" (Miller and Tilley 1984). Dominant groups are described constructing a monument, controlling exchange, or holding a ritual that persuades others or manipulates them ideologically. Or elites may control the labor of others through the use of force. In these cases, there is almost no attempt to infer the intention of the actors: it is assumed that the intention is irrelevant to the outcome – domination. Since the specific intention or meaning behind the action is of little concern, analysis focuses narrowly on the effects of actions (see Barrett 1994:1).

To say that material culture is active is thus to argue that material objects are given meaning within agency. Material objects are part of the stocks of knowledge that provide the context for action. They are manipulated as part of intentional strategies (to hide, mask, legitimate, disrupt, and so on). And they endure, often resulting in unintended consequences long after individual actions – they spread agency over time. But consideration of the agency of material objects also leads to another nuance. Gell (1998) has provided many anthropological examples of objects that are apotropaic – that is, they protect people from illness or evil spirits. Boric (2003) provides archaeological examples from the prehistoric sites of the Danube Gorges. In some cases, apotropaic objects appear to act as people, to be agents themselves. In such cases the objects (appear to) have intentionality because they bring to mind associations that are meaningful to the person affected by the object. Indeed, much intentional action only has effects because it is perceived to be agentful. Thus we "give" powers to others and to objects such that they can act on us. Much ideology works in this way. So in exploring agency as intentional action we need to recognize two phases — the intentionality of an actor before or within an act, and the ascription of intentionality to an act by participants or observers.

Agency is likely to remain a fruitful area of discussion in archaeology. On the one hand, archaeologists deal with huge expanses of time in which change often seems slow and incremental. There seems little room for intentional action outside the structures within which agency is embedded. On the other hand, archaeologists deal with intimate moments – the loss of a bone awl (Spector 1993) or the burial of a relative.

To what extent are these small events determined by larger structures? To what extent is agency involved in transforming structures of power? To ask such questions is not to search for "free will." Such a notion implies that will and intention can somehow be external to society. The individual, will, and intentionality are themselves social. Rather, the aim is to understand the relationships between structure and agency when viewed over the long term.

Bodily Practices

It can be argued that these discussions of agency deal too much with power and with rather abstract agents. We get little sense in many discussions of agency of embodied individuals. Theorizing the body has become a central theme in many areas of research, including philosophy, literature, cultural studies, queer theory, and anthropology. In archaeology, the route toward a problematization of the body derives from two main strands – practice theory and feminist theory.

From early in the development of postprocessual archaeology, the writing of Pierre Bourdieu had a special place. His outline of a theory of practice (1977) was attractive to archaeology because it foregrounded the mundane aspects of daily life which archaeologists spend most of their time excavating – the pots and pans view of the world. Bourdieu showed how the daily practices of movement around domestic space, the discard of refuse, the construction of an oven, all had social weight. Alarm bells went off for archaeologists when Bourdieu said that it was possible to instill "a whole cosmology, an ethic, a metaphysic, a political philosophy, through injunctions as insignificant as 'stand up straight' or 'don't hold your knife in your left hand'" (1977:94). In his own ethnographic work, Bourdieu described how children learned social rules as they moved around the house, moving from "male" to "female" areas, from "light" to "dark." Boys may be encouraged to stand up straight, like spears, and girls to look down and be deferential. In this practical way, people gain an understanding of the world that is both practical and socially meaningful. Often they cannot articulate the understandings in conscious speech very well – they remain a set of dispositions or orientations – a habitus that is practical rather than conscious and verbal.

In fact, similar arguments had been made by a long line of sociologists from Goffman to Giddens, and anthropologists, from Mauss to Leroi-Gourhan. But it was Bourdieu and Giddens who had most direct impact in archaeology. Bourdieu in particular dealt with material very close to archaeology, and it was easy to see the application of his work. Also, he attempted to bridge between structuralism and Marxism while at the same time to give an adequate account of agency. Bourdieu recognizes that the habitus is not the only way in which practice is produced. The regularity that we observe in behavior is also produced by norms, symbols, rituals, and objective material considerations, such as the location of actors in socioeconomic hierarchies. But he was able to foreground the habitus in ways attractive to archaeologists. In doing so, he also pushed archaeologists toward a discussion of the body. He was concerned with bodily stance and with bodily movements about houses and other spaces. These were the prime mechanisms of social enculturation.

A similar move toward a consideration of the body derived from debates within various strands of feminist archaeology. One of the main aims of much feminist archaeology has been to put people back into the past, and to put faces on the "faceless blobs" that stalked the multi-hyphenated systems of processual archaeology (e.g., Tringham 1994). Beyond this general aim, in much early feminist archaeology a distinction was made between sex and gender, the first referring to the biological sex of the body, and the second to the cultural and social way in which that body was adorned or given meaning. This distinction was seen as being important methodologically, since skeletons in graves could first be identified by biological anthropologists, and then, on this reliable basis, patterns of artifact associations could be studied. More recently, archaeologies of sexuality have responded to a wide range of historical, literary, and anthropological work (e.g., Laqueur, Foucault, Haraway, Butler) which argues that simple dichotomies between sex and gender are difficult to maintain (Joyce 1998; Meskell 1999; Schmidt and Voss 2000; Yates 1993). Sex is not in fact a "given." Rather, descriptions of bodies and sexes change through time. There is no natural, stable sex, but rather a set of discursive practices that help define what is natural and biological.

Some examples of archaeological studies that use the idea that bodies are socially constructed include Treherne's (1995) account of the appearance of toilet articles at a particular horizon in the European Bronze Age. He argues for a changing aesthetic of the body and of personhood as a part of wider social changes. Joyce (1998) discusses human images from Prehispanic Central America and shows how they actively constituted theories of the body. Only certain postures were selected from the range of daily bodily movements to be represented in durable material such as fired clay and stone. This discourse, which materialized some representations of the body but not others, reinforced and naturalized a particular social philosophy.

At least in relation to practice theories, it can be argued that insufficient account is given of ways in which agents can transform structures. We are still left with rather faceless agents determined by larger forces. How can we get closer to what it feels like to "be," or to be inside someone's body? In an attempt to achieve a fuller account of embodiment, many archaeologists have been influenced by the phenomenology of Heidegger (e.g., Thomas 1996). Some of the most important aspects of the discussion of Heidegger in archaeology have been the critiques of binary oppositions between culture and nature, and between mind and body. What this means in archaeological applications is that attention is again focused on the ways in which bodies move around sites and landscapes. Rather than looking at the plan of a monument, attention is paid to the ways in which people moved around and experienced the monument.

In many of these archaeological accounts, the emphasis is placed on the way that relations of power are served in the layout of monuments and landscapes (Barrett 1994; Thomas 1996; Tilley 1994). In these accounts it is suggested that social actors are forced to perceive the world and to interact with each other in certain ways because their movements are constrained by the built environment. This focus on power again threatens to take the discussion away from lived experience and toward the structures of power that are seen as binding bodies and their movements. Often the accounts seem to assume a universal body. But two bodies moving around the same landscape or monuments may not see it in the same way. Much depends on the social meanings and values that are given to sites in the landscape, and much depends on the specific social positioning of actors.

It is inadequate to describe the movements of bodies and sensual experience without embedding bodily experience within social meaning. The studies discussed in this section have made great strides in that they have moved away from the body as a natural substance onto which the social is mapped, and they have rejected the idea that space is an abstract entity, a container for human existence. Rather they see space as part of the structuring of social existence, part of the process by which social actors experience and respond to the social world (Tilley 1993:10). But phenomenological approaches have their own problems. In particular, they need to be sensitive to radical cultural and social difference in basic ways of seeing the world, and they need to be reflexively critical about the different ways that different bodies can experience the same monuments and landscapes.

Conclusions

I hope it has become clear in this account how in contemporary social theory in archaeology "everything is social." We have seen how concepts that might seem neutral, natural or biological, like space, bodies, sex, the environment, have all come to be seen as social. The same could also be said for other terms not discussed here such as time (Lucas 2001). Certainly good arguments have been made that technology cannot be separated from the social (Dobres 2000; Lemonnier 1993). Even materiality itself is now seen as social, and Latour (1988) argues that objects are like people, in that both have agency or can act in the world. The notion that the meaning of a thing is not stable but depends on context and social entanglement has been made by Nicholas Thomas (1991). But we can go a step further and argue that our very selves develop in relationship with the object world, and that the boundaries between self and object vary historically and socially (Merleau-Ponty 1945).

The reasons for this shift from the dominance of culture to the centrality of the social have been discussed above, but they are part of a wider move against universalist and essentialist assumptions. Even truth is now seen as an effect of the social (Foucault 1979). In critiquing "culture" and "society" as essentialist or Western, the aim is to focus on the particular and the variable. No attempt is made to argue for a universal definition of the "social" and its workings. Rather, the term refers to the diversity of human experience. Of course, in other quarters of the social sciences there are counter-moves toward the real, the universal, and the evolutionary. Certainly one of the main challenges in social archaeology over coming decades will be reconciling the tensions between new advances in biological and biomolecular archaeology (Jones 2001) and social theoretical approaches.

I have not discussed at any length other "social" approaches in archaeology. This is because they do not attempt to engage with social theory in the social sciences and humanities as a whole. For example, Schiffer (2000) has edited a book entitled *Social Theory in Archaeology*, and in this and other work he has developed a behavioral theory of material culture. But I noted above that in developing his theory he rejects everything that most anthropologists, sociologists, and historians would regard as central components of the social. He focuses on material interactions and performance as if they could be isolated outside the social. Even in his edited volume, the tensions involved in trying to build a social theory without the social become clear. In that volume, Feinman describes an interesting categorization of societies into network and corporate. But he accepts (2000:49) that the important *why* questions remain. Unless one is allowed to explore the daily manipulation and reproduction of social micro-practices, knowledge, and power, it is difficult to see how a fuller account can be achieved. As another example, Nelson criticizes behavioral approaches to the choices involved in artifact deposition, saying "the social context of the choices could be more fully explored" (2000:61). She recognizes the need to introduce agency-based approaches to abandonment studies, but her account does not benefit from the full range of available social theory.

A similar indication of the need to embrace a fuller social theory is seen in Darwin-ian evolutionary archaeology. For example, O'Brien and Lyman (2000) try to build bridges to social theory by discussing the role of history in their theoretical perspective. Their own account of history focuses on the selective environment that led to the appearance of cultural traits and then on pursuing the historical lineages of the traits that ensue. A full account of the selective environments and performance characteristics that lead to some cultural variants being selected would need to consider social power, agency, meaning, and so on – i.e., all the rich social world (environment) in which cultural traits are embedded, are selected, and transmitted. Once all that has been done one is back with the full world of social theory, and with history as social, cultural, constructed, and created as well as being materially based. In order to provide an adequate account of an evolutionary process, a full social theory would need to be incorporated.

Much the same point can be made about cognitive processual archaeology (e.g., Renfrew and Zubrow 1994). Here an attempt is made to argue that one can talk in universal, non-social ways, about the mind and its cognitive processes. The focus is on the early evolution of the mind, the strategies used in knapping flint, the systems of weights and measures used by complex societies, and so on. The difficulty is again that this approach is underlain by the assumption that mind can be separated from society. For Bourdieu and Merleau-Ponty, the mind is born of the social world of objects. But Renfrew and his colleagues wish to maintain an objectivist position untrammeled by the meanings, desires, and intentions of the social world. Lakoff and Johnson in their book *Philosophy in the Flesh* (1999), however, argue that even color has no independent reality. "The qualities of things as we can experience and comprehend them depend crucially on our neural makeup, our bodily interactions with them and our purposes and interests" (1999:26). Cognition is not outside the social, and cognitive processual archaeology needs to become fully postprocessual if it is to be successful in understanding past minds.

On the other hand, to argue that everything is social is not to argue that it is only social. Clearly there are aesthetic, emotional, and material aspects of life which, while being thoroughly social, cannot be reduced to the social. Rather, the more important aim in foregrounding the social is to recognize the indivisibility of human experience – its non-partitive character. Most of the approaches discussed here try to be non-dichotomous – in terms of culture/nature, mind/body, agent/structure, self/society.

The central point is that everything is infused with the social, so that attempts to ignore the social are bound to be limited and partial. Future developments in the discipline, however biologically and naturally science they might be in initial motivation, will need to engage with the full range of social theory.

It might be argued that recognition of the social nature of material culture and of the way the past is constructed derives its influence from anthropology, history, and related disciplines. But there is also a sense in which recognition of the centrality of the social acts as a springboard for archaeologists to contribute to other disciplines. Certainly, there has been a widespread increase in the use of the archaeology metaphor in the social and humanistic disciplines. This metaphorical use of archaeology goes back to Freud, Husserl, Benjamin, and more recently to Foucault and Derrida. But there are more specific recent links that suggest a social archaeology can contribute more widely. Certainly, there is a widespread interest in many disciplines in materiality, in the ways that the social is constructed in the material, and in the ways in which materiality is active and constitutive. The success of the *Journal of Material Culture* is one indication of the extent of these interests and the archaeological contribution here is clear. Archaeology and heritage come together in accounts of monuments, identity, and memory (Meskell 2002a; Rowlands 1993) that are part of wider discussions in the social sciences (e.g., Connerton 1989). The archaeological and the material also allow windows into the non-discursive aspects of social life, especially when viewed over the long and very long term. The social present can be seen as the long-term product of slow moves in daily, non-discursive practices (e.g., Hamann 2002). In these various ways, the focus on the social in archaeology allows a port of entry for archaeology, heritage, materiality, and the long term to contribute to debates in a wide range of related disciplines.

ACKNOWLEDGMENTS

I would like to think Danielle Steen for her help in the literature search used for this paper, and Scott Hutson for discussions regarding theoretical points raised here.

REFERENCES

Anyon, R., T. J. Ferguson, L. Jackson, and L. Lane. 1996. Native American oral traditions and archaeology. *Society for American Archaeology Bulletin* 14(2): 14–16.

Appadurai, A. 1996. *Modernity at Large.* Minneapolis: University of Minnesota Press.

Bapty, I., and T. Yates. 1990. *Archaeology after Structuralism.* London: Routledge.

Barrett, J. 1994. *Fragments from Antiquity: An Archaeology of Social Life in Britain, 2900–1200 B.C.* Oxford: Blackwell.

Barthes, R. 1973. *Mythologies.* London: Paladin.

Beaudry, M., L. J. Cook, and S. A. Mrozowski. 1991. Artifacts and active voices: Material culture as social discourse. In R. H. McGuire and R. Paynter (eds.), *The Archaeology of Inequality.* Oxford: Blackwell, pp. 150–91.

Bekaert, S. 1998. Multiple levels of meaning and the tension of consciousness. *Archaeological Dialogues* 5: 7–29.

Binford, L. R. 1962. Archaeology as anthropology. *American Antiquity* 28: 217–225.

Boric, D. 2003. "Deep time" metaphor: Mnemonic and apotropaic practices at Lepenski Vir. *Journal of Social Archaeology* 3(1).

Bourdieu, P. 1977. *Outline of a Theory of Practice.* Cambridge: Cambridge University Press.

Braithwaite, M. 1982. Decoration as ritual symbol: A theoretical proposal and an ethnographic study in southern Sudan. In I. Hodder (ed.), *Symbolic and Structural Archaeology.* Cambridge: Cambridge University Press, pp. 80–88.

Brumfiel, E. 1996. Figurines and the Aztec state: Testing the effectiveness of ideological domination. In: R. P. Wright (ed.), *Gender and Archaeology.* Philadelphia: University of Pennsylvania Press.

Castells, M. 1996. *The Rise of the Network Society.* Oxford: Blackwell.

Childe, V. G. 1925. *The Dawn of European Civilization.* London: Kegan Paul.

—— 1939. *Man Makes Himself.* New York: Oxford University Press.

—— 1949. *Social Worlds of Knowledge.* London: Oxford University Press.

—— 1952. *New Light on the Most Ancient East.* London: Routledge & Kegan Paul.

—— 1960. *What Happened in History.* London: Max Parrish.

Clark, G. 1934. Archaeology and the state. *Antiquity* 8: 414–428.

—— 1957 [1939]. *Archaeology and Society.* 3rd edn. London: Methuen.

Clarke, D. 1968. *Analytical Archaeology.* London: Methuen.

—— 1972. A provisional model of an Iron Age society and its settlement system. In D. Clarke (ed.), *Models in Archaeology.* London: Methuen.

Condori, C. M. 1989. History and pre-history in Bolivia: What about the Indians? In R. Layton (ed.), *Conflicts in the Archaeology of Living Traditions.* London: Unwin Hyman, pp. 46–59.

Conkey, M. 1989. The structural analysis of Paleolithic art. In C. C. Lamberg-Karlovsky (ed.), *Archaeological Thought in the Americas.* Cambridge: Cambridge University Press, pp. 135–154.

Connerton, P. 1989. *How Societies Remember.* Cambridge: Cambridge University Press.

Deetz, J. 1977. *In Small Things Forgotten.* New York: Anchor Books.

Derrida, J. 1976. *Of Grammatology.* Baltimore, MD: Johns Hopkins University Press.

Dobres, M-A. 2000. *Technology and Social Agency.* Oxford: Blackwell.

——, and J. Robb (eds.) 2000. *Agency in Archaeology.* London: Routledge.

Donley, L. W. 1982. House power: Swahili space and symbolic markers. In I. Hodder (ed.), *Symbolic and Structural Archaeology.* Cambridge: Cambridge University Press, pp. 63–73.

—— 1987. Life in the Swahili town house reveals the symbolic meaning of spaces and artefact assemblages. *African Archaeological Review* 5: 181–192.

Douglas, M. 1970. *Natural Symbols.* New York: Vintage.

Edmonds, M. 1999. *Ancestral Geographies of the Neolithic: Landscapes, Monuments and Memories.* London: Routledge.

Feinman, G. 2000. New perspectives on models of political action and the Puebloan Southwest. In M. B. Schiffer (ed.), *Social Theory in Archaeology.* Salt Lake City: University of Utah Press, pp. 31–51.

Foucault, M. 1979. *Discipline and Punish: The Birth of the Prison.* London: Penguin.

Friedman, J., and M. Rowlands (eds.) 1978. *The Evolution of Social Systems.* London: Duckworth.

Gell, A. 1998. *Art and Agency.* Oxford: Clarendon Press.

Gero, J. 1996. Archaeological practice and gendered encounters with field data. In R. Wright (ed.), *Gender and Archaeology.* Philadelphia: University of Pennsylvania Press, pp. 251–280.

Giddens, A. 1979. *Central Problems in Social Theory.* London: Macmillan.

Glassie, J. 1975. *Folk Housing of Middle Virginia.* Knoxville: University of Tennessee Press.

Hamann, B. 2002. The social life of pre-sunrise things: Indigenous Mesoamerican archaeology. *Current Anthropology* 43.

Hawkes, C. F. C. 1954. Archaeological theory and method: Some suggestions from the Old World. *American Anthropologist* 56: 155–168.

Helskog, K. 1995. Maleness and femaleness in the sky and the underworld – and in between. In K. Helskog and B. Olsen (eds.), *Perceiving Rock Art: Social and Political Perspectives*. Oslo: Institute for Comparative Research in Human Culture, pp. 247–262.

Hodder, I. 1982. *Symbols in Action*. Cambridge: Cambridge University Press.

——. 1986. *Reading the Past*. Cambridge: Cambridge University Press.

——1999. *The Archaeological Process. An Introduction*. Oxford: Blackwell.

——, M. Shanks, A. Alexandri, V. Buchli, J. Carman, J. Last, and G. Lucas (eds.) 1995. *Interpreting Archaeology*. London: Routledge.

Johnson, A., and T. Earle. 1987. *The Evolution of Human Societies*. Stanford, CA: Stanford University Press.

Jones, M. 2001. *The Molecule Hunt: Archaeology and the Search for Ancient DNA*. London: Allen Lane.

Joyce, R. A. 1994. Dorothy Hughes Popenoe: Eve in an archaeological garden. In C. Claassen (ed.), *Women in Archaeology*. Philadelphia: University of Pennsylvania Press, pp. 51–66.

——1998. Performing the body in prehispanic Central America. *Res: Anthropology and Aesthetics* 33: 147–165.

——2000. *Gender and Power in Prehispanic Mesoamerica*. Austin: University of Texas Press.

Kosso, P. 1991. Method in archaeology: Middle range theory as hermeneutics. *American Antiquity* 56: 621–627.

Kristiansen, K. 1984. Ideology and material culture: An archaeological perspective. In M. Spriggs (ed.), *Marxist Perspectives in Archaeology*. Cambridge: Cambridge University Press, pp. 72–100.

Lakoff, G., and M. Johnson. 1999. *Philosophy in the Flesh: The Embodied Mind and its Challenge to Western Thought*. New York: Basic Books.

Lampeter Archaeology Workshop 1997. Relativism, objectivity and the politics of the past. *Archaeological Dialogues* 4: 166–175.

Lane, P. J. 1987. Reordering residues of the past. In I. Hodder (ed.), *Archaeology as Long-Term History*. Cambridge: Cambridge University Press, pp. 54–62.

Langford, R. F. 1983. Our heritage – your playground. *Australian Archaeology* 16: 1–6.

Latour, B. 1988. Mixing humans and nonhumans together: The sociology of a door closer. *Social Problems* 35: 298–310.

Leach, E. 1976. *Culture and Communication*. Cambridge: Cambridge University Press.

Lemonnier, P. 1993. *Technological Choices*. London: Routledge.

Leone, M. 1982. Some opinions about recovering mind. *American Antiquity* 47: 742–760.

Lévi-Strauss, C. 1968. *Structural Anthropology*. London: Allen Lane.

——1970. *The Raw and the Cooked*. London: Cape.

Longacre, W. 1970. *Archaeology as Anthropology*. Tucson: Anthropological Papers of the University of Arizona 17.

Lucas, G. 2001. *Critical Approaches to Fieldwork*. London: Routledge.

Mawson, A. N. M. 1989. The Triumph of Life: Political Dispute and Religious Ceremonial among the Agar Dinka of Southern Sudan. Unpublished Ph.D. dissertation, University of Cambridge.

Merleau-Ponty, M. 1945. *Phénoménologie de la perception*. Paris: Gallimard.

Meskell, L. 1999. *Archaeologies of Social Life*. Oxford: Blackwell.

——2002a. The intersections of identity and politics in archaeology. *Annual Review of Anthropology* 31: 279–301.

——2002b. *Private Life in New Kingdom Egypt*. Princeton, NJ: Princeton University Press.

Miller, D., and C. Tilley (eds.) 1984. *Ideology, Power and Prehistory*. Cambridge: Cambridge University Press.

Moore, H. L. 1982. The interpretation of spatial patterning in settlement residues. In I. Hodder (ed.), *Symbolic and Structural Archaeology*. Cambridge: Cambridge University Press, pp. 74–79.

—— 1986. *Space, Text and Gender*. Cambridge: Cambridge University Press.

—— 1987. Problems in the analysis of social change: An example from the Marakwet. In I. Hodder (ed.), *Archaeology as Long-Term History*. Cambridge: Cambridge University Press, pp. 85–104.

Moran, P., and D. S. Hides. 1990. Writing, authority and the determination of a subject. In I. Bapty and T. Yates (eds.), *Archaeology after Structuralism*. London: Routledge, pp. 205–221.

Nelson, M. C. 2000. Abandonment: Conceptualization, representation, and social change. In M. B. Schiffer (ed.), *Social Theory in Archaeology*. Salt Lake City: University of Utah Press, pp. 52–62.

O'Brien, M. J., and R. L. Lyman. 2000. Evolutionary archaeology: Reconstructing and explaining historical lineages. In M. B. Schiffer (ed.), *Social Theory in Archaeology*. Salt Lake City: University of Utah Press, pp. 126–142.

Parker Pearson, M. 1982. Mortuary practices, society and ideology: An ethnoarchaeological study. In I. Hodder (ed.), *Symbolic and Structural Archaeology*. Cambridge: Cambridge University Press, pp. 99–114.

—— 1999. Food, sex and death: Cosmologies in the British Iron Age with particular reference to East Yorkshire. *Cambridge Archaeological Journal* 9: 43–69.

Petrie, W. M. F. 1904. *Methods and Aims in Archaeology*. London: Macmillan.

Preucel, R. W., and A. Bauer. 2001. Archaeological pragmatics. *Norwegian Archaeological Review* 34(2): 85–96.

Renfrew, C. 1973. *Social Archaeology*. Southampton: University of Southampton.

—— 1982. *Towards an Archaeology of Mind*. Cambridge: Cambridge University Press.

—— 1984. *Approaches to Social Archaeology*. Edinburgh: Edinburgh University Press.

——, and E. Zubrow (eds.) 1994. *The Ancient Mind: Elements of Cognitive Archaeology*. Cambridge: Cambridge University Press.

Ricoeur, P. 1971. The model of the text: Meaningful action considered as a text. *Social Research* 38: 529–562.

Rowlands, M. 1993. The role of memory in the transmission of culture. *World Archaeology* 25: 141–151.

Schiffer, M. B. 1999. *The Material Life of Human Beings*. London and New York: Routledge.

—— (ed.) 2000. *Social Theory in Archaeology*. Salt Lake City: University of Utah Press.

Schmidt, R. A., and B. L. Voss (eds.) 2000. *Archaeologies of Sexuality*. London: Routledge.

Shackel, P. 2000. Craft to wage labor: Agency and resistance in American historical archaeology. In M-A. Dobres and J. Robb (eds.), *Agency in Archaeology*. London: Routledge, pp. 232–246.

Shanks, M., and C. Tilley. 1987a. *Re-constructing Archaeology*. Cambridge: Cambridge University Press.

—— 1987b. *Social Theory and Archaeology*. Oxford: Polity Press.

Spector, J. 1993. *What This Awl Means*. St. Paul: Minnesota Historical Society.

Tambiah, S. J. 1969. Animals are good to think and good to prohibit. *Ethnology* 8: 423–459.

Taylor, W. 1948. *A Study of Archaeology*. Carbondale: Southern Illinois University Press.

—— 1996. *Time, Culture and Identity*. London: Routledge.

Thomas, J. 1993. The hermeneutics of megalithic space. In C. Tilley (ed.), *Interpretative Archaeology*. Providence, RI: Berg, pp. 73–97.

—— (ed.) 2001. *Interpretive Archaeology: A Reader*. Leicester: Leicester University Press.

Thomas, N. 1991. *Entangled Objects*. Cambridge, MA: Harvard University Press.

Tilley, C. (ed.) 1990. *Reading Material Culture*. Oxford: Blackwell.

—— 1991. *The Art of Ambiguity: Material Culture and Text*. London: Routledge.

—— (ed.) 1993. *Interpretative Archaeology*. London: Berg.

—— 1994. *The Phenomenology of Landscape*. London: Berg.

Treherne, P. 1995. The warrior's beauty: The masculine body and self-identity in Bronze Age Europe. *Journal of European Archaeology* 3: 105–144.

Tringham, R. 1991. Men and women in prehistoric architecture. *Traditional Dwellings and Settlements Review* 3(1): 9–28.

—— 1994. Engendered places in prehistory. *Gender, Place, and Culture* 1(2): 169–204.

Tschauner, H. 1996. Middle-range theory, behavioural archaeology, and post-empiricist philosophy of science in archaeology. *Journal of Archaeological Method and Theory* 3: 1–30.

Turner, V. 1969. *The Ritual Process: Structure and Anti-Structure*. London: Routledge & Kegan Paul.

Welbourn, A. 1984. Endo ceramics and power strategies. In D. Miller and C. Tilley (eds.), *Ideology, Power and Prehistory*. Cambridge: Cambridge University Press, pp. 17–24.

Wylie, A. 1989. Archaeological cables and tacking: The implications of practice for Bernstein's "options beyond objectivism and relativism." *Philosophy of the Social Sciences* 19: 1–18.

—— 1994. On "capturing facts alive in the past" (or present): Response to Fotiadis and to Little. *American Antiquity* 59: 556–560.

Yates, T. 1993. Frameworks for an archaeology of the body. In C. Tilley (ed.), *Interpretative Archaeology*. Providence, RI: Berg, pp. 31–72.

Yentsch, A. 1991. The symbolic dimensions of pottery: Sex-related attributes of English and Anglo-American household pots. In R. McGuire and R. Paynter (eds.), *The Archaeology of Inequality*. Oxford: Blackwell, pp. 192–230.

2

Cross-Cultural Comparison and Archaeological Theory

Bruce G. Trigger

In the 1950s and 1960s, cross-cultural studies flourished in sociocultural anthropology alongside the neoevolutionary search for regularities in human behavior that could be "scientifically" explained (Ford 1967; Moore 1961). In archaeology, cross-cultural studies are generally associated with New Archaeology. Lewis Binford (1962, 2001) has maintained that comparative studies are essential, both for establishing middle-range regularities that provide a rigorous basis for the behavioural interpretation of archaeological data and for explaining such behavior. Yet neoevolutionary archaeologists never developed links with cross-cultural studies that were as close as those that existed between comparative ethnology and the Human Relations Area Files in the 1960s (Harris 1968: 612–615). This is reflected in the relatively informal use of cross-cultural comparison by archaeologists and its frequent employment to support rather than to test hypotheses (early exceptions include Binford 1971, 1980). In processual archaeology, the ethnoarchaeological collection of data, intended to be used to create middle-range generalizations (Binford 1977, 1978, 1981), was accorded more attention than was cross-cultural comparison. Nevertheless, neoevolutionary theorizing in archaeology was based on assumptions about cultural regularities, or the lack of such regularities, among societies at the same level of development. This chapter examines how cross-cultural studies have been used and abused in the study of early civilizations. It also demonstrates how cross-cultural data concerning seven early civilizations can be employed to test the validity and usefulness of competing theories that attempt to explain human behavior and the archaeological record (Trigger 1993; 2003).

The Comparative Study of Early Civilizations

Nineteenth-century evolutionists studied the development of culture in general rather than that of individual cultures. They assumed that general patterns of cultural development could be explained in terms of "psychic unity," or all people naturally tending to behave in the same manner, and a uniform, calculative human reason inevitably devising similar ways to deal more effectively with the natural world. Social and political systems, as well as knowledge, were assumed to develop everywhere along similar lines. Differences among societies at the same stage of development were attributed to environmental or racial factors. Herbert Spencer (1873–1934) collected vast amounts of data about individual societies around the world and Hobhouse, Wheeler, and Ginsberg (1915) sought to determine the extent to which forms of food production were correlated with other aspects of culture, such as political and judicial organization, family structure, warfare, social stratification, and property in a sample of 640 societies. Archaeological interest in studies of this sort declined as a culture-historical approach replaced an evolutionary one in the late nineteenth century.

Childe, even when he described himself as an evolutionist, focused almost exclusively on studying Europe and the Middle East. In his investigations of ancient Egypt and Mesopotamia, he concluded that for historical and environmental reasons these early civilizations had shared a similar technology and subsistence economy. Yet he observed that Mesopotamia had evolved as a series of city-states, while from very early times ancient Egypt was unified by a divine monarchy (Childe 1934). Childe, who was both a materialist and a possibilist, explained these differences as contingent divergences in the ways the ruling classes of these two early civilizations had devised to extract food surpluses from farmers. When he later learned that the Maya had created a civilization without knowledge of metallurgy, his definition of civilization became still more generalized and functional (Childe 1950: 9–16). Frankfort (1956), who was a humanist and idealist, attributed the differences between Egyptian and Mesopotamian civilizations to contrasting key ideas and beliefs that had existed prior to their development. Baines and Yoffee (1998) have recently re-examined with great insight the differing belief patterns of these two civilizations.

Wittfogel (1938, 1957) was a technological determinist who attributed the rise of early civilizations in various parts of the world to the development of irrigation systems. He maintained that increasing populations in arid environments that had abundant river water encouraged the development of ever-larger irrigation systems and that the authoritarian patterns that he believed were required to manage these irrigation systems were inevitably extended to control all aspects of life. Wittfogel also argued that these hydraulic societies provided a model for the development of states in areas where, because rainfall made agriculture possible, large polities would not have evolved on their own. These states were, however, less centralized and despotic than were those of hydraulic societies.

The ecological anthropologist Julian Steward (1949), although an advocate of multilinear evolution, accepted Wittfogel's idea that early civilizations arose only in arid or semi-arid regions where large-scale irrigation was possible. He maintained that, as populations grew, interstate competition increased and the theocratic control which characterized the initial development of early civilizations gave way to military leadership. Steward compared the development of early civilizations in five regions of the world: Egypt, Mesopotamia, North China, highland Mexico, and Peru, seeking to demonstrate that all five regions had followed the same trajectory. Yet demonstrating this uniformity required considerable selection and distortion of the evidence that was available in the 1940s. As a matter of policy, Steward confined his survey to investigating cross-cultural similarities and refused to assign any developmental significance to idiosyncratic differences.

Comparative studies of early civilizations became more common after the development of a world view of prehistory, which was made possible by the use of radiocarbon dating beginning in the late 1940s (Clark 1961). Radiocarbon dating permitted for the first time the construction of a worldwide cultural chronology and provided information about rates of cultural change in prehistoric times. The realization that cultures generally had changed more slowly since the end of the Ice Age than archaeologists had hitherto believed encouraged growing acceptance of the possibility that such alterations had occurred as a result of evolutionary processes rather than diffusion and migration.

Similarities among societies in different parts of the world once again were attributed to parallel evolution. In the 1960s, neoevolutionary anthropologists viewed early civilizations as a stage in the evolution of all more complex societies (Fried 1967; Sahlins 1968; Service 1971, 1975). Early civilizations were interpreted as complex ecological adaptations linked to circumscribed natural environments that were characterized by great potential for the development of more intensive food production, massive population increases requiring higher levels of agricultural productivity, spiralling warfare over land and resources, and an increasing need for state authority to protect privately and institutionally owned property. Interpretations emphasized either violence or the creation of consensus as factors leading to the development of early civilizations (Haas 1982). Service (1975) and Godelier (1986: 159–166) viewed early civilizations as theocracies, while Fried (1967) and Carneiro (1970) stressed the role of warfare and intimidation in creating and holding them together. In general, neoevolutionists followed Steward in viewing all early civilizations as being essentially similar.

Robert McC. Adams, whose settlement pattern research in Iraq had demonstrated that more complex irrigation systems were a consequence rather than a cause of the development of states (1965), undertook a detailed comparison of early civilizations in Mesopotamia and the Valley of Mexico (1966). He found these civilizations, which had both developed as a series of city-states, to be structurally very similar. Not being an ecological determinist, he attributed these similarities to functional limitations on what was possible in social and political organization. He also differed from Steward in regarding the differences as well as the similarities between these two civilizations as worthy of explanation.

Since that time, despite the contrasts that Childe and Frankfort had already delineated between Egyptian and Mesopotamian civilization, many archaeologists have tended to view city-states as the normal form of early civilization and territorial states, such as ancient Egypt, as rare aberrations. This view was adopted by many contributors to Nichols and Charlton's *The Archaeology of City-States* (1997, especially Norman Yoffee 1997: 262). Mann (1986) has rationalized this view by claiming that early rulers rarely possessed the resources needed to unify a larger area. Claessen and Skalník (1978), Renfrew (1997), Marcus (1998), and Feinman (1998) have argued that different types of early civilization represented successive stages in a unilinear process of development. They disagree, however, about how these stages are to be defined and the order in which they developed. Comparative historical evidence does not support any of these schemes (Trigger, in preparation). On the other hand, as early as 1983, Flannery and Marcus were arguing that not only environmental differences, but also different cultural traditions and different cultural encounters, had produced divergent cultural evolution among the early civilizations of highland Mexico.

By the 1980s, cross-cultural investigations were waning in anthropology, as the discipline once again focused on cultural studies and evolutionism, grand narratives, and cross-cultural uniformity became highly suspect (Clifford 1988; Diamond 1974; Geertz 1973; Patterson 1997; Turner 1967, 1975). Postprocessual archaeologists affirmed that ideas guided human behavior and that every culture was a unique mani-festation of the human spirit that must be understood on its own terms. Comparison was viewed as imposing arbitrary and misleading uniformity on concepts that could be understood only in relation to the cultural wholes of which they were a part. Hence cross-cultural comparison was declared to be impossible. On the other hand, many postprocessualists have utilized universal generalizations about how people think de-rived from structuralism (Hodder 1990) and more recently from the study of meta-phors (Lakoff 1987; Lakoff and Johnson 1980; Tilley 1999). This approach has its roots in the ideas of the late eighteenth-century German philosopher Johann Herder, who also influenced Franz Boas.

Theoretical Debates in Archaeology

When scientific debates continue for a long time with no signs of closure, it is worth enquiring whether the wrong questions are being asked. Since the 1980s, archaeology has been theoretically divided between so-called processual and postprocessual ap-proaches. Processual archaeology, the senior contender, stresses the study of human behavior; postprocessual archaeology, the rival newcomer, emphasizes the study of culture. Processual archaeology focuses on subsistence patterns and economic and political organization; postprocessual archaeology on values and religious beliefs. Pro-cessual archaeology investigates cross-cultural regularities; postprocessual archaeology cultural idiosyncrasies. Processual archaeology explains human behavior as rational accommodations to external forces; postprocessual archaeology treats behavior as de-termined by culturally defined goals and individual volition (Hodder 1986; Johnson 1999; Preucel 1991). Often this struggle is portrayed as a simple confrontation between irreconcilable opposites incarnated in Lewis Binford and Ian Hodder.

Yet things are not that simple. Postprocessual archaeology is a volatile mixture of trends derived from the new cultural anthropology, French Marxist anthropology, structuralism, poststructuralism, critical theory, Heiddegerian existentialism, and various liberation movements (Karlsson 1998; Patterson 1989). Processual archaeology, al-though it once prided itself on its methodological and theoretical unity, today offers a kaleidoscope of ecological explanations in which practical reason and culture are com-bined in various ways. While many archaeologists remain interested in ecology, an ever-decreasing number believe that environmental adaptation determines human behavior. As environmental determinism gives way to environmental possibilism, the external world is once again being seen as imposing limits on human behavior rather than determining it. Processual archaeology is also being challenged for control of the materialist end of the explanatory spectrum by evolutionary archaeology, which offers a Darwinian explanation of the archaeological record (Barton and Clark 1997; Dunnell 1980; Maschner 1996; O'Brien 1996; O'Brien and Lyman 2000; Teltser 1995), and by traditional Marxism, which proposes economic explanations of human behavior that make it the most humanistic and least deterministic variety of materialism (McGuire 1992; Spriggs 1984). The most significant dichotomy is thus no longer between processual and postprocessual archaeology, but between the materialist and idealist ends of a theoretical spectrum.

Yet processual and postprocessual archaeologists, however vigorously each side claims to be the sole possessor of the true explanation of the archaeological record, jointly believe that there are no undiscovered alternatives to the issues they debate. In doing so, they trap themselves in a dichotomy between Enlightenment rationalism and counter-Enlightenment romanticism that has dominated Western social thought since the eighteenth century (Trigger 1998). These trends are represented at the present time by a fading modernism and a pervasive postmodernism. Processualists seek to explain cross-cultural regularities, while postprocessualists strive to document cross-cultural diversity.

Explanations of early civilizations currently embrace the full spectrum from materialist to idealist. Ecological explanations stress environmental, technological, and demographic factors, or at a more abstract level energy efficiency, as determining factors bringing about behavioral and cultural change. Evolutionary or Darwinian archaeologists emphasize the "replicative fitness," of specific kinds of material culture. Marxists stress the organization of labor and distribution of goods, as well as the importance of property relations, as key factors shaping other spheres of behavior. Other, societally grounded, explanations stress functional constraints, often in the form of information theory. Idealist explanations assume the importance of cultural traditions, although there is much debate about the extent to which these traditions superorganically determine human behavior or are individually mediated. The ecologists Boyd and Richerson (1985) have argued in favor of the greater selective fitness of culturally transmitted knowledge over individual innovations. Those who focus on culture rather than behavior tend to emphasize particularities rather than cross-cultural uniformities.

Other archaeologists favor a more eclectic theoretical approach. The Annales school has attempted to associate different factors with processes that play themselves out over varying periods of time (Bintliff 1991), but, in my opinion, without much success. Marxism, Gidden's (1984) concept of structuration, and Bourdieu's (1977) idea of habitus seek to relate culture and behavior interactively in various ways. Curiously, little use has been made of cross-cultural comparison to test the validity of these specific explanations or of the broader processual and postprocessual approaches with which they are associated.

Cross-Cultural Methodology

To evaluate the usefulness of these approaches, I decided in the late 1980s to carry out a detailed cross-cultural study of seven early civilizations that had developed in various regions of the world. I rejected the proposition that the primary focus of cross-cultural studies was the investigation of cross-cultural similarities in human behavior. My objective was to examine both similarities and differences and define the sociocultural contexts in which each occurred.

Because hunter-gatherer cultures had spread round the globe, it is difficult to tell to what extent their cross-cultural similarities are a common heritage from the remote past or products of convergent evolution. There is strong archaeological evidence of the largely independent development of early civilizations in different regions. The common features that such early civilizations did not share with simpler societies can therefore be assumed mainly to be products of convergent development. To a considerable degree, the archaeological record permits us to distinguish features of early civilizations that resulted from parallel or convergent development from those that were the result of historical contacts. This makes early civilizations highly appropriate for a controlled study of sociocultural similarities and differences.

Archaeology has not yet reached the point where its practitioners can establish with any degree of certainty the social and political institutions, or beliefs, of those early civilizations for which written records are not available (Coe 1992; Cowgill 1997). I therefore decided to compare only the earliest civilization in each area for which significant written, as well as archaeological, documentation, either indigenous or European, was available. The early civilizations I selected were Old and Middle Kingdom Egypt, Early Dynastic to Old Babylonian Mesopotamia, Shang China, the Valley of Mexico in the fifteenth and early sixteenth centuries AD, the Classic Maya, the Inka of Peru in the early sixteenth century AD, and the Yoruba of West Africa in the eighteenth and nineteenth centuries AD. I systematically collected and compared information concerning their technologies and subsistence practices, their economic, family, social, and political organizations, their religious beliefs and practices, their geographical and cosmological knowledge, and their social values. This work required over a decade to complete.

I was aware that undertaking such a cross-cultural study would invite criticism from many quarters. In the 1950s, social anthropologists vehemently denounced George Peter Murdock for comparing data out of context (Köbben 1952, 1973). Having been his student, I knew that Murdock fundamentally agreed with this point. He maintained that the comparison of specific attributes using data abstracted from large numbers of societies was only a crude technique for discovering robust correlations among different forms of human behavior. He believed that understanding such behavior required the detailed, contextual analysis of specific, carefully chosen case studies (Murdock 1959). By analyzing only seven early civilizations, I sought to acquire a detailed understanding of how each of these societies had functioned before I started to compare specific features (Trigger 1993).

A more recent and fundamental criticism by new cultural anthropologists, such as Clifford Geertz (1973), affirms that cross-cultural comparisons are in fact impossible. Geertz has argued, as Johann Herder did two centuries ago and humanists have done ever since, that every culture is a unique expression of the human spirit. Such cultures may be understood and appreciated on their own terms, but they cannot legitimately be compared with one another. Geertz (1965) has also argued that what are often mistaken for cross-cultural regularities are classificatory fakes, produced by anthropologists imposing their ethnocentric prejudices on inadequately understood data.

I took these criticisms very seriously and tried to comprehend each early civilization on its own terms before applying any general analytical framework to all seven. From this research, it became obvious that the Aztec term for king, *tlatoani*, did not mean precisely the same as did the Egyptian *nswt*, the Shang Chinese *wang*, the Maya *kul ahaw*, or the Mesopotamian *lugal*. There may have been enough semantic overlap to justify glossing all these words as king for certain purposes, but each term had its own history and cultural meanings, which had to be taken into account in a cross-cultural study. Although unable to master the nine or more languages associated with these seven early civilizations, I glossed hundreds of technical terms in this manner.

It was also clear to me that, except for ancient Egypt, which I had studied intensively for a long time, I could not hope to become an expert on all seven early civilizations. I therefore based my research both on general and technical studies written by experts on each early civilization, mostly since 1960. By studying a large number of reports concerning each early civilization, I was able to compare the views of experts and determine to what extent they agreed or disagreed. I also noted their theoretical biases and assessed their work in relation both to the data and to these biases. In that way, I sought to evaluate as well as to understand my sources.

Finally, I had to accept that early civilization is an evolutionary stage and that, by adopting this concept as the generic criterion for what I was studying, I would draw the fire of postprocessualists, most of whom regard evolutionism as a tainted and bankrupt concept. I do not deny that one may define a concept so specifically as to make it self-fulfilling. I was, however, open to examining any large-scale society that occurred relatively early in the history of complex societies and was not caught up in the intricate webs of interacting large-scale societies that characterized later preindustrial Eurasian civilizations. I was also open to the possibility of considerable variation among early civilizations. In addition, in the course of my research, I subjected the concept of sociocultural evolution to a detailed analysis (Trigger 1998).

If the societies I examined had displayed no cross-cultural uniformities, the concept of early civilization would have been meaningless and claims by postprocessual archaeologists concerning the idiosyncracy and incomparability of societies would have been vindicated. This, it was evident from the beginning, was not the case. On the other hand, because my sample of early civilizations eventually turned out to exhibit two significant subtypes, I had to consider arguments by unilinear evolutionists that these variations represented two successive stages in the evolution of early civilizations. This issue was resolved using historical evidence, which did not confirm either an evolutionary or an ecological explanation of this variation.

As my research progressed, I learned something very interesting about the practice, as distinguished from the programmatic statements, of processual and postprocessual archaeology and their anthropological equivalents. When it came to studying the technology, economy, and political organization of early civilizations, the literature of the 1960s was abundant and very useful. The same was not true for understanding religion or what life appeared like from an indigenous perspective. Such insights were usually obtained from works published in the 1980s and 1990s. Initially, I despaired of learning anything about Inka religious concepts that was not hopelessly ethnocentric. Only in the publications of the past decade has such information become abundant (Salomon 1991). From work of the 1960s, some written by Yoruba scholars, it was possible to learn much about Yoruba land tenure, political organization, and economic activities. Yet only recent works, such as those by Andrew Apter (1992) and Karen Barber (1991), made it possible to perceive Yoruba culture from a Yoruba cultural perspective.

In other words, the products of processual and postprocessual orientations are not contradictory; they are complementary in the most productive and enriching manner.

The breadth of insight I gained into early civilizations would not have been possible had modernism not given way to postmodernism and processualism to postprocessualism. The reason that many archaeologists had for abandoning processual archaeology was not so much disbelief in its epistemology or utility, but disillusionment about its commitment, or ability, to address problems that were regarded as important for understanding the past, or the archaeological record, in a holistic manner.

Since 1970, I have taught a course on early civilizations at McGill University in which undergraduates are invited to write a paper on any related topic they choose. These papers have gradually shifted from an overwhelming preoccupation with economic, social, and political issues to an overwhelming concern with religion and culture. The holistic survey of early civilizations offered in the course has not changed. This shift in choices therefore suggests that the rise of postmodernism and the abandonment of positivism have pervasive social ramifications. The rejection of processualism represents growing discontent with the behaviorist approach's failure to address cultural and psychological issues. Yet to resolve a vast number of problems, it is essential that both sorts of research are pursued simultaneously.

I next consider some of the more interesting and counterintuitive findings of my research and their theoretical implications, beginning with subsistence patterns. This records an Alice in Wonderland adventure in which stubborn facts called cherished theories into question and opened unexpected and challenging theoretical perspectives.

Findings

Influenced by Wittfogel (1957), neoevolutionists and ecological anthropologists, beginning with Julian Steward (1949), argued that all early civilizations arose in arid environments where the need to construct complex irrigation systems inevitably led to the formation of the first states. All other early civilizations were assumed to be secondary ones that would not have evolved had irrigation civilizations not already existed. Yet, archaeological evidence demonstrates that early civilizations developed in many different environments: the temperate rainfall zone of North China, the tropical rain forests and savannahs of lowland Mesoamerica and Nigeria, and the highland valleys of Peru and central Mexico, as well as in the large river valleys of Egypt and Iraq that traditionally have been associated with early civilizations. Moreover, the very different configurations of the Nile and Tigris–Euphrates valleys required the hydraulic regimes that developed in these two regions to operate on very different principles (Adams 1981; Butzer 1976).

All early civilizations supported dense, sedentary populations using relatively simple agricultural technologies. Each civilization relied mainly on domesticated plants and animals and on various techniques of agriculture that had evolved regionally long prior to the rise of civilization. The Inka, Egyptians, and Mesopotamians combined growing crops with specialized herding; the Yoruba and Chinese practiced mixed farming. In Mesoamerica people mainly cultivated plants. Jared Diamond (1997) may be correct that the regional availability of cultigens influenced the chronological order in which early civilizations developed; but this factor did not determine the productivity of subsistence economies. Population densities varied from only about 60 people per square kilometre among the Yoruba, who practiced swidden agriculture (Bascom 1969: 2), to over 500 people per square kilometre of arable land in the southern part of the Valley of Mexico (Sanders, Parsons, and Santley 1979: 219, 378–380). The Maya lived in tropical forests and savannah as did the Yoruba; yet they had the second highest population density in my sample rather than one of the two lowest. The societies with the highest population densities were not the Egyptians and Mesopotamians, with their animal-drawn plows and grain fields, but the Mesoamericans, who had no large domestic animals and relied mainly on hand-cultivated vegetable produce.

Farmers in all early civilizations demonstrated the ability to increase food production as population densities rose. Sometimes the state intervened, such as with the building of massive dykes to reduce salinity in the shallow southern lakes in the Valley of Mexico. Yet it was farmers applying local traditions of intensive wetland farming who turned these lakes into centers of highly productive raised-field (*chinampa*) agriculture (Sanders, Parsons, and Santley 1979: 273–281).

My survey of agriculture shows subsistence patterns to have been highly variable and flexible, both geographically and temporally. Regional patterns inherited from the remote past were adapted in highly specific ways to the changing needs of the present. Contrary to what Julian Steward and other neoevolutionists expected, the evolution of agricultural regimes does not provide a simple, unilinear explanation of the development of early civilizations. Diversity is, moreover, precisely what ecological theory predicts: subsistence patterns are contingent, interactive adaptations to local environments and changing social conditions. Cultural ecology is useful for understanding the specific subsistence patterns of early civilizations, but it cannot be expected to provide a universal explanation for the development of specific complex cultures, any more than the synthetic theory of biological evolution can predict the evolution of any particular species of plant or animal. In the terminology of Sahlins and Service (1960), we are dealing with specific, rather than general, evolution. That is what ecological anthropologists studying early civilizations always should have expected.

The economies of early civilizations also displayed greater variation than unilinear evolutionists had anticipated. Crafts were produced by various combinations of household production, part-time specialists, full-time specialists serving a broad clientele, and elite craft workers creating luxury goods exclusively for the upper classes, by whom they may or may not have been employed. Long-distance trade was either in the hands of free agents or strictly controlled by the government. Markets played a crucial role in the total economy or were restricted to the circulation of goods among the lower classes (Trigger 1993: 71–74).

I found, however, that these differences were closely linked to social and political organization and in particular to whether early civilizations took the form of territorial states or city-state systems. Egypt, the Inka kingdom, and the Shang state of north China provide examples of territorial states, while Mesopotamia, the Yoruba, the Valley of Mexico, and the Classic Maya constituted examples of city-state systems. City-state systems consisted of clusters of small states, each composed of an urban center and its surrounding agricultural land. These urban centers were inhabited by a substantial percentage of the population, since farmers, as well as non-farmers, tended to live inside them for greater protection against interstate warfare. In Early Dynastic Mesopotamia, over 80 percent of the total population appear to have lived in urban centers, the majority of them farmers who tilled the surrounding countryside (Adams 1981). Full-time craft workers produced goods that were sold to the whole population through local markets, thereby giving farmers access to high-quality goods. Long-distance trade tended to be carried on by merchants who operated independently of the state, an arrangement that made it possible to obtain needed goods even during periods of intercity warfare. The Classic Maya may have been the one network of city-states where trade was controlled by the upper classes. In all city-state systems, the rulers of powerful city-states enriched themselves by levying tribute on defeated neighboring polities.

Territorial states were much larger polities governed by a hierarchy of officials acting at the national, provincial, and local levels. In some of these states, power to regulate most aspects of life was delegated to lower-level officials in return for the delivery of taxes and answering calls for military support from the central government. In others the central government sought to exert greater control over lower-level officials through a bureaucratic division of powers. Early civilizations often applied delegational and bureaucratic forms of control to different levels of government, or switched from one form of control to another, often quite rapidly and opportunistically.

Urban centers in territorial states were occupied by a much smaller percentage of the total population than was the case in city-states. They were inhabited only by the upper classes, government officials, soldiers, retainers, and craft workers employed by the government. Farmers, being relatively protected from foreign attack, lived in villages near the land they cultivated. They also manufactured the goods they required from locally available materials during slack periods in the agricultural cycle. They were thus part-time specialists. These goods, which were of modest quality, were exchanged at local markets. The government controlled the acquisition of exotic raw materials by monopolizing mining and foreign trade. These materials were transformed by elite craft workers attached to state institutions into high-quality luxury goods, which the king distributed among the upper classes. The control of the production and distribution of luxury goods by the central government played a major role in holding territorial states together (Trigger 1993: 8–14).

In general, the contrast was strongest between territorial states and those city-states in which upper-class status was not exclusively defined on a hereditary basis: in Mesopotamia and among the Yoruba (Stone 1997). In these city-states, political power tended to be shared heterarchically by various competing groups. City-states with hereditary upper classes, such as those in the Valley of Mexico, displayed more centralization. Yet such city states cannot be mistaken for territorial states because of clearly dissimilar settlement patterns and economic organization. Territorial states are not simply larger than city-states; they display an array of distinctive social and political features, many of which are archaeologically visible.

It is evident that in early civilizations the economy was powerfully influenced by social and political organization, as various theorists, including British social anthropologists, Marxist archaeologists, and Robert McC. Adams have long maintained. The evidence does not, however, support Polanyi's ideas that in early civilizations the economy was totally embedded in sociopolitical organization and that no profit motive existed (Polanyi, Arensberg, and Pearson 1957). Marxist and social anthropological theories remain useful for understanding the social, political, and economic organization of early civilizations.

The far-reaching dichotomy between city-states and territorial states also suggests that functionalism, though frequently repudiated by postprocessual archaeologists and poststructural anthropologists, has a significant role to play in understanding the archaeological record. Only certain features accord with each other sufficiently well to form a coherent system (Trigger 1982). Archaeologists must overcome the idea that functionalism necessarily idealizes homeostasis and hence has nothing to contribute to the study of systemic change. The social anthropologist Edward Evans-Pritchard (1949, 1962) refuted that view when he argued that studying social change was the best way to discover how the different components of a sociopolitical system were articulated. In the 1970s, archaeologists made important progress in furthering a functional approach when they began to employ information theory to understand the ways in which political structures at varying levels of complexity could be organized (Flannery 1972; Johnson 1973, 1981; Rathje 1975). This type of research deserves greater attention than it has received since the 1980s.

Some relativists believe that social inequality and states are optional, rather than inevitable, consequences of increasing social scale, leaving open the possibility that these are only accidental features of modern industrial societies (Kenoyer 1997; Maisels 1999: 186–259; Possehl 1998). Yet so little is known about the archaeological cultures that are cited as possible examples of stateless early civilizations that these conclusions are no more objective than are interpretations of ink blots. All early civilizations in my sample, and all other reasonably well-known early civilizations were hierarchical societies divided into largely endogamous classes on the basis of cross-culturally similar criteria. At the top was a small upper class headed by a king, who in his person symbolized the unity of the state and its various institutions and who possessed varying degrees of effective political power. Leading members of the upper class, which in total probably never amounted to more than a few percent of the population, made the high-level decisions about how society was to be managed. Commoners had no right to question the orders of the upper classes; doing so was regarded as tantamount to rebellion.

Below the upper class were various groups of commoners. At the top were various specialists. They were more numerous than the upper classes, but probably made up less than fifteen percent of the total population. Specialists were classified according to how much they engaged in manual labor. At the top were administrators who saw that the policies of the upper classes were carried out. Next came professional soldiers, who enforced the decisions of the upper classes. Full-time retainers and craft workers, with varying degrees of expertise and various economic relations to the upper classes, made up the lowest level of dependent specialists. Like farmers, craft workers worked with their hands.

The vast majority of people who lived in early civilizations, constituting 80 to 90 percent of the total population, were farmers. They were ranked according to whether they owned land, usually collectively, rented or sharecropped it, or worked land owned by others in return for pay, usually in the form of enough food to support themselves and their families. At the bottom of the social hierarchy were slaves. They were normally prisoners of war, debtors, purchased foreigners, or the descendants of slaves. Slaves tended to be few in number and were absorbed easily into the lower classes. They did no type of work that free individuals did not do (Trigger 1993: 55–61).

While a hierarchy of political authority may have been functionally necessary to manage complex states, the creation of class societies in which higher status always correlated with exemption from manual labor and the degree to which manual labor was specialized adds a cross-culturally uniform symbolic dimension to class structure. The upper classes not only possessed a monopoly of political power but also appropriated most of a society's surplus wealth by owning land, controlling labor, and being able to collect taxes. The management of society-wide information systems and intimidating and controlling the lower classes required wealth to pay officials and professional soldiers.

Yet why did the upper classes also develop their own distinctive and luxurious lifestyles and indulge in conspicuous consumption on a large scale, as invariably happened in early civilizations? Why, moreover, did the lower classes regard such behavior as a natural concomitant of status and power, even when they resented paying taxes? The cross-cultural uniformity of such behavior, which must have evolved separately as early civilizations came into existence in different parts of the world, suggests, as does the structure of the class system, that we are not dealing with behavior that was determined purely culturally.

Such practices may have developed because the general lack of substantial non-human energy sources in early civilizations, as well as in hunter-gatherer and early agricultural societies, meant that everyone intuitively appreciated the importance of the principle of getting the highest caloric returns for the least effort (Zipf 1949) as a desirable strategy for coping with subsistence. In class societies, the ability to violate the principle of least effort by engaging in conspicuous consumption may, as a result of this understanding, invariably have been admired as indicative of power and success (Trigger 1990a). Another possibility, also relevant to the development of hierarchical structures, may be that our nearest primate relatives, as well as our primate ancestors, were not only highly sociable but also intensely competitive (Conroy 1990). Hierarchical behavior was effectively suppressed in small-scale hunter-gatherer societies by gossip, ridicule, and witchcraft (Lee 1990; Trigger 1990b). Did the creation of larger societies permit a more direct expression of human nature? That makes it possible that early civilizations were shaped by psychological factors that are different from either the adaptively rational behavior that is of interest to processual archaeologists or the cultural factors studied by postprocessual archaeologists (Cowgill 1993).

Every early civilization evolved a distinctive style of art and architecture that was patronized by its upper classes. While the art and architecture that the lower classes produced for their own use is harder to distinguish, that produced for the upper classes of each early civilization was sufficiently coherent and idiosyncratic that today even a non-specialist can quickly learn to distinguish objects and buildings produced by different early civilizations. City-state systems shared a common elite style, but many city-states produced local variants of that style which expressed their own separate identity.

"Art" in early civilizations was not produced for art's sake, but consisted of religious objects, political propaganda, jewelry, fancy clothing, and richly ornamented weapons. Monumental architecture took the form of temples, palaces, upper-class tombs, and fortifications. Elite art was produced by skilled craft workers who sold most of their products to the upper classes or labored exclusively in government workshops. Especially in territorial states, even goods manufactured by different groups of craft workers from different raw materials shared the same style. This style was imposed on craft workers by their upper-class patrons. In some city-states, where craft workers were less controlled by upper-class patrons, either different materials were worked in different styles or goods produced for different purposes or clients were manufactured in different styles (Trigger 1993: 81–84).

Elite art styles tended to emerge quickly in the early stages of the development of a civilization. Hereafter, while these styles slowly changed, their basic pattern remained intact for long periods (Kemp 1989: 19–63; Townsend 1979). While each civilization had a distinct art style, there is no way to predict its specific features. All that can be done is to trace the style's historical origins and development. One of the main social purposes of elite styles of art and architecture was to signal the existence of the upper class as a dominant group in society. By imposing this style on public buildings, the upper classes symbolized their control of society as a whole. This required a distinctive style of art and architecture that could not be confused with that of any other known society or class, and that was homogenous enough that it expressed the collective identity and solidarity of the upper classes.

Evolutionary archaeologists would maintain that elite art and architectural styles were selectively neutral (Dunnell 1978). The alternative possibilities were sufficiently numerous that no two styles ever accidentally duplicated one another. Yet the social function of such art and architecture was so important that no early civilization failed to develop its own elite style. Art is clearly a ubiquitous, species-specific feature of human behavior that evolved at least as early as the Upper Palaeolithic period, and which in some manner is related to the human ability to symbolize (Mithen 1996). Elite art therefore has stylistic features that are quintessentially cultural and idiosyncratic, but also social and psychological aspects that must be understood cross-culturally.

The most behaviorally consequential idiosyncratic features of early civilizations were beliefs about the nature of a good life. These beliefs were pre-eminently associated with upper-class males, but influenced how everyone in these societies evaluated human conduct. Such views, like styles of elite art and monumental architecture, developed at an early stage in the evolution of civilizations and persisted for long periods. They made every early civilization a unique cultural experience in the Geertzian sense.

In ancient Egypt the ideal man was a bureaucrat: an administrator who sought at least overtly to please his superiors and never crossed them. Such men strove to appear modest, unacquisitive, calm in the face of extreme provocation, and good team players. In this way, they climbed the administrative ladder, leaving defeated rivals behind (Morenz 1973: 117–123). The Mesopotamian ideal, like that of their gods, was to acquire land and other forms of property and derive income from them. Men who were successful at doing this did not have to work with their hands but could serve on community councils, judge legal cases, and perform other community services (Van De Mieroop 1999: 212–213). The ideal in the Valley of Mexico was to be a successful warrior, which meant capturing enemy soldiers for sacrifice. No hereditary noble could qualify for public office without performing such feats, nor could a commoner who had not done so be granted noble status (Soustelle 1961: 217–224).

The Yoruba valued individual competitiveness, but this competitiveness took two different forms. The warrior-politician might start as a trader who invested his profits in recruiting armed retainers. These retainers enabled him to acquire more slaves in battle, who could be set to work producing food to support more retainers. Having an armed band to intimidate rivals and commoners helped an ambitious man to pursue a successful political career. The alternative option was to become a *babalawo*, or sage-priest of the Ifa cult. These priests were noted for their learning and ability to resolve disputes. Both warrior politicians and sages competed among themselves for influence and public recognition (Thompson 1976). The Shang nobility perceived military prowess, and closely related hunting skills, as the main factors defining nobility. Such activities also provided the wild game and human victims that were needed to empower the spirits of noblemen's ancestors and ensure their supernatural support (Lewis 1990).

Each of these ideals was elaborated until it became a design for living that substantially influenced the lives of everyone in a particular early civilization. Those who lived in the Valley of Mexico equated women who died in childbirth with men who died in battle, thereby symbolically identifying childbirth with military combat (Soustelle 1961: 190). In the Valley of Mexico, the preoccupation with warfare also created a cosmovision in which armed conflict was represented as an altruistic form of human behavior that sustained the universe. Honor, social mobility, and public office all depended on a man's ability to serve the gods as a warrior (Carrasco 1999). The Mesopotamian preoccupation with property led to an unparalleled elaboration of accounting, payment, and credit techniques in that civilization (Nissen, Damerow, and England 1993).

These ideals also imposed limitations on cultures. The Aztec desire to capture prisoners for sacrifice did not equip them to combat Spanish soldiers intent on military conquest. The Egyptian bureaucratic ideal may have created good quartermasters, but it did not make for outstanding military commanders, who, even at the height of Egyptian imperialism in the New Kingdom, were portrayed in their tombs as civilian officials or scribes. The Egyptian bureaucratic ideal developed at a time when the relatively isolated Egyptian state had no rivals. Yet this ideal did not disappear when Egypt eventually had to contend with aggressive rival powers in the Sudan, Southwest Asia, and Europe. Despite Egypt's wealth and substantial population, it became subject to a succession of foreign rulers. We thus find an important aspect of Egyptian culture that, despite its negative selective implications, persisted – arguably to the present. It is clear that values and ideals sometimes have the power to shape human behavior, even if that power is negative in the sense that it sustains, but does not transform, behavior.

There is no obvious reason why the distinctive personal values held in the Valley of Mexico, among the Yoruba, and in Mesopotamia should have been specific to those cultures, all of which evolved in the context of rivalrous city-states. Nevertheless, each of these city-state systems would have been significantly different had it embraced social values different from the ones it adopted. The development of social values seems to have been influenced by historical particularities, or perhaps even historical accidents, at an early stage in the development of each civilization. They may also have been, at least in part, a heritage from still earlier stages of development. Yet values are not like art styles, because they influence societies in ways that are not selectively neutral, as evolutionary archaeologists understand this concept. We must therefore conclude that aspects of ideational culture that affect societies at a particular level of development in functionally significant ways can display idiosyncratic cross-cultural variation and that even features that significantly reduce the competitive ability of specific early civilizations can persist for long periods (Hall 1986: 27–110; Hallpike 1986: 288–371). This calls for a rethinking of the range of strategies that may be effective in cultural, ethnic, and political competition.

Religious beliefs are phenomena that most ecological and postmodern archaeologists would agree ought, in the absence of historical connections, to display idiosyncratic variation. When it comes to specific deities and myths that is the case. Had I found seven early civilizations worshiping a sun god named Re, I would have concluded that Grafton Elliott Smith (1933) or Graham Hancock (and Faiia 1998) had something important to say.

One does, however, find general religious concepts that occur cross-culturally in these societies. One of these is the failure to distinguish the natural and supernatural realms. Gods are identified either with nature or as forces that animate the cosmos. Another shared belief is that human beings are animated by multiple souls, very often including a life force and a source of consciousness. These ideas both appear to have been inherited from earlier, less complex societies (Frankfort *et al.* 1949; Jacobsen 1976; Trigger 1993: 94–95, 105–107). The equation of the natural and the supernatural can be interpreted as the expression of a ubiquitous human tendency to anthropomorphize, first attested in Upper Palaeolithic art and interpreted as a significant feature of human thought thereafter. Anthropomorphization in turn, may be a specific expression of the important role played by metaphors in governing human thought and creating, reproducing, and transforming culture. Such concepts currently appear to be replacing or supplementing a rather moribund structuralism as a way to account for the patterning that paradigmatically relates symbols and makes them culturally meaningful (Lakoff 1987; Lakoff and Johnson 1980; Tilley 1999).

One of my least expected discoveries was that, underlying the seven early civilizations I was studying, lay a common pattern of religious belief. Finding this pattern was so contrary to my expectations that I spent much time trying unsuccessfully to disconfirm it. All the early civilizations believed that human life was created and sustained by the gods. This belief accorded with the close identification of the supernatural with the forces of nature in all early civilizations. Yet all early civilizations also believed that the gods, or supernatural powers, depended on humans for support and without that support would weaken or die, causing either the terrestrial realm or the entire cosmos to lapse into chaos.

This support took the form of sacrifices, usually consisting of food and drink or the lives of animals and human beings, which could be offered to major cosmic deities only by the king and possibly also by members of the high nobility. In Mesoamerica, the gods were believed to sacrifice their lives to produce corn to nourish humans, while humans in turn sacrificed their flesh and blood to feed the gods. The Mesopotamians described their gods, some of whom also died each year at harvest time, as growing faint with hunger when humans failed to offer sacrifices to them (Trigger 1993: 94–105).

What could account for such parallels, which are not associated with simpler societies, where the supernatural appears to have been approached either as benevolent parents or as powerful ancestors who had to be placated (Bird-David 1990; Ingold 1996)? Marshall Sahlins (1976: 211–212) has suggested that, when societies grew too complex for kinship to supply the metaphors used to understand all social relations, new metaphors were drawn first from the religious sphere. In early civilizations, farmers supported an upper class, who in turn maintained a political order that permitted dense populations to enjoy enough security that they might modestly prosper. This arrangement appears to have been projected into the supernatural realm: human farmers provided, and in some cases were, the food that the upper classes channeled into the supernatural realm to nourish the gods, who in turn maintained the cosmic order which allowed humans to grow food. In this analysis, farmers played as important a role as did the gods in maintaining the cosmic order, while the upper classes claimed a pivotal role in regulating the energy flows that permitted all things to exist.

What we appear to have here, couched in religious concepts appropriate for early civilizations, is a political constitution that defined both the obligations and the rights of the upper and lower classes within the framework of a cosmic order. An upper class which oppressed ordinary people to the point where the economy collapsed threatened not only its own future but also that of the gods. The lower classes, and local leaders, did not have the right to question how kings treated them, but they could question whether the gods, whose behavior affected the wellbeing of their district, were being properly served. Kings who wished to continue serving the gods had to uphold a social order in which the exploitation of the lower classes was maintained within conventional and acceptable limits and did not undermine the economic basis of society. In such ideas we see the beginning of what in Imperial China became the doctrine of the Mandate of Heaven. Thus, in the realm of religion, we find a striking example of cross-cultural uniformity which appears to result from practical reason being directed to the rational organization of political relations rather than to a narrowly ecological goal. The repeated success of such endeavors in curbing the rapacity of the upper classes may be seen in the long-term political stability of early civilizations by comparison with many later ones, where class conflict was less controlled and there was greater reliance on military force to maintain order.

Conclusions

Long ago, Gordon Childe (1949: 6–8) observed that all human behavior is culturally mediated. Humans do not adapt to the world as it is, but to the world as they imagine it to be. Childe was being profoundly postprocessual. Yet he also observed that human beings have bodily needs and to provide for these needs they must adapt to the real world. Thus, without contradiction, he was also being processual. Childe (1956: 58–60) further noted that the fact that most sociocultural systems manage to cope with changing conditions indicates that humans generally have a fairly objective understanding of the real world. This understanding is not necessarily framed in the same terms as are those of modern Western societies. A Cree hunter may know nothing about calories; yet what he believes about animal spirits may encode knowledge that more nourishing food usually can be obtained by hunting caribou than from hunting foxes (Tanner 1979).

There is clearly a lasting role for rationalist ecological and economic approaches in any study that considers how human beings have coped with scarce resources. Such studies are not, however, the opposite of the study of cultural traditions, as many processual and postprocessual archaeologists claim. The human ecologists Robert Boyd and Peter Richerson (1985) have demonstrated that cultural traditions are the major source of what every human being knows about what Sahlins (1976) has called practical as well as cultural reason. Cultural traditions supply knowledge that often has guided human behavior over long periods and hence has been tested for its social utility. It is also knowledge from which, on the basis of long experience, many flaws have been removed. Hence such knowledge is usually superior to *ad hoc* innovations by individuals, which tend to be self-interested, based on limited knowledge, and subjected to less informed judgment. The knowledge shared by members of a single culture also provides, not a set of simplistic prescriptions for human behavior, but multiple solutions for large numbers of problems (Salzman 2000). Hence cultural traditions constitute a rich guide for human behavior which both resists and assists innovation. This is what Karl Marx meant when he observed in 1852 that "human beings make their own history... not under conditions chosen by themselves, but ones directly encountered, given, and transmitted from the past" (Marx and Engels 1962, 1: 247).

Some aspects of cultural traditions are not selected by adaptive factors. These include art styles. Yet, to be aesthetically and socially meaningful, art styles need to be patterned, and to achieve this end they are selected to maintain their internal coherence. Value systems have competitive selective value but sometimes resist changing conditions to a much greater degree than rationalist theories would suggest. Finally, cross-culturally uniform beliefs can develop as a result of societies at similar levels of development managing similar social problems in analogous symbolic or religious ways.

From these observations, it becomes evident that the behavioral concerns of processual archaeology and the cultural concerns of postprocessual archaeology, when combined, do not provide a comprehensive basis for understanding human behavior past or present. They leave out what Victorian anthropologists labelled "psychic unity," but left largely unanalyzed. To understand how cultures change, we need to examine not only ecology and culture but also how the human mind works, as revealed by evolutionary psychology and neuroscience (Butterworth 1999; Gazzaniga 1992, 1998; Low 2000). Archaeologists, such as Steven Mithen (1996) are only now beginning to utilize these important fields. It must, however, be kept in mind that both evolutionary psychology and neuroscience are in their formative stages and may, at present, have more to learn from the social sciences than the social sciences have to learn from them.

Processual archaeology and psychological approaches are both capable of producing cross-cultural generalizations: processual archaeology about human behavior and psychology and neuroscience about general patterns of human thought. Together they may eventually provide a sound basis for what Colin Renfrew (1982; Renfrew and Bahn 2000; Renfrew and Zubrow 1994) calls a cognitive-processual approach to archaeology. At present the theoretical basis for such an approach is almost nonexistent. To know in any detail what people thought in the past requires texts that record the spoken word. Projecting culturally-specific ideas into the past by means of the direct historical approach (Trigger 1995) or inferring them contextually, as Ian Hodder (1987) advocates, is a highly speculative, and largely unverifiable, operation. In the hands of Heideggerian interpretative archaeologists, prehistory often becomes wholly speculative (Bender 1993; Gosden 1994; Karlsson 1998; Thomas 1996; Tilley 1984, 1993, 1994). Postprocessual archaeology clearly supplies an important cognitive dimension to historical archaeology, while prehistoric archaeology may remain largely restricted to processual and psychological approaches.

The expansion of the scope of archaeologists' current interests to embrace the findings of psychology and neuroscience, combined with a willingness to recognize that not all societies can be studied from every angle, provides a basis for drawing the current ecological and cultural approaches into a more elaborate and potentially far more fruitful theoretical synthesis. The future of archaeology, today as in the past, lies in exploiting innovations made in other disciplines while expanding archaeology's own theoretical perspectives. Contrary to those who fear that archaeology is falling apart as a result of intradisciplinary controversy, I believe that the scope of the debate must be substantially broadened, not narrowed, if we are to explain the archaeological record. Archaeologists have nothing to fear except their own narrowmindedness, lack of creative imagination, and complacency about their sectarian squabbles.

REFERENCES

Adams, R. McC. 1965. *Land Behind Baghdad: A History of Settlement on the Diyala Plains*. Chicago: University of Chicago Press.

—— 1966. *The Evolution of Urban Society: Early Mesopotamia and Prehispanic Mexico*. Chicago: Aldine.

—— 1981. *Heartland of Cities: Surveys of Ancient Settlement and Land Use on the Central Floodplain of the Euphrates*. Chicago: University of Chicago Press.

Apter, A. 1992. *Black Critics and Kings: The Hermeneutics of Power in Yoruba Society*. Chicago: University of Chicago Press.

Baines, J., and N. Yoffee. 1998. Order, legitimacy, and wealth in ancient Egypt and Mesopotamia. In G. M. Feinman and J. Marcus (eds.), *Archaic States*. Santa Fe, NM: School of American Research Press, pp. 199–260.

Barber, K. 1991. *I Could Speak Until Tomorrow: Orike, Women, and the Past in a Yoruba Town*. Washington, DC: Smithsonian Institution Press.

Barton, C. M., and G. A. Clark (eds.) 1997. *Rediscovering Darwin: Evolutionary Theory and Archeological Explanation*. Washington, DC: Archeological Papers of the American Anthropological Association 7.

Bascom, W. 1969. *The Yoruba of Southwestern Nigeria*. New York: Holt, Rinehart & Winston.

Bender, B. (ed.) 1993. *Landscape: Politics and Perspectives*. Oxford: Berg.

Binford, L. R. 1962. Archaeology as anthropology. *American Antiquity* 28: 217–225.

—— 1971. Mortuary practices: their study and their potential. In J. A. Brown (ed.), *Approaches to the Social Dimensions of Mortuary Practices*. Washington, DC: Memoirs of the Society for American Archaeology 25, pp. 6–29.

—— (ed.) 1977. *For Theory Building in Archaeology*. New York: Academic Press.

—— 1978. *Nunamiut Ethnoarchaeology*. New York: Academic Press.

—— 1980. "Willow smoke and dogs' tails": Hunter-gatherer settlement systems and archaeological site formation. *American Antiquity* 45: 4–20.

—— 1981. *Bones: Ancient Men and Modern Myths*. New York: Academic Press.

—— 2001. *Constructing Frames of Reference: An Analytical Method for Archaeological Theory Building Using Hunter-Gatherer and Environmental Data Sets*. Berkeley: University of California Press.

Bintliff, J. (ed.) 1991. *The Annales School and Archaeology*. Leicester: Leicester University Press.

Bird-David, N. 1990. The giving environment: another perspective on the economic system of gatherer-hunters. *Current Anthropology* 31: 189–196.

Bourdieu, P. 1977. *Outline of a Theory of Practice*. Cambridge: Cambridge University Press.

Boyd, R., and P. J. Richerson. 1985. *Culture and the Evolutionary Process*. Chicago: University of Chicago Press.

Butterworth, B. 1999. *What Counts: How Every Brain is Hardwired for Math*. New York: The Free Press.

Butzer, K. W. 1976. *Early Hydraulic Civilization in Egypt: A Study in Cultural Ecology*. Chicago: University of Chicago Press.

Carneiro, R. L. 1970. A theory of the origin of the state. *Science* 169: 733–738.

Carrasco, D. 1999. *City of Sacrifice: The Aztec Empire and the Role of Violence in Civilization*. Boston: Beacon Press.

Childe, V. G. 1934. *New Light on the Most Ancient East: The Oriental Prelude to European Prehistory*. London: Kegan Paul.

—— 1949. *Social Worlds of Knowledge*. London: Oxford University Press.

—— 1950. The urban revolution. *Town Planning Review* 21: 3–17.

—— 1956. *Society and Knowledge: The Growth of Human Traditions*. New York: Harper.

Claessen, H. J. M., and P. Skalník (eds.) 1978. *The Early State*. The Hague: Mouton.

Clark, J. G. D. 1961. *World Prehistory: An Outline*. Cambridge: Cambridge University Press.

Clifford, J. 1988. *The Predicament of Culture: Twentieth-Century Ethnography, Literature, and Art*. Cambridge, MA: Harvard University Press.

Coe, M. D. 1992. *Breaking the Maya Code*. London: Thames & Hudson.

Conroy, G. C. 1990. *Primate Evolution*. New York: Norton.

Cowgill, G. L. 1993. Beyond criticizing New Archaeology. *American Anthropologist* 95: 551–573.

—— 1997. State and society at Teotihuacan, Mexico. *Annual Review of Anthropology* 26: 129–161.

Diamond, J. M. 1997. *Guns, Germs, and Steel: The Fates of Human Societies*. New York: Norton.

Diamond, S. 1974. *In Search of the Primitive: A Critique of Civilization*. New Brunswick, NJ: Transaction Books.

Dunnell, R. C. 1978. Style and function: A fundamental dichotomy. *American Antiquity* 43: 192–202.

—— 1980. Evolutionary theory and archaeology. In M. B. Schiffer (ed.), *Advances in Archaeological Method and Theory*. Vol. 3. New York: Academic Press, pp. 35–99.

Evans-Pritchard, E. E. 1949. *The Sanusi of Cyrenaica*. Oxford: Oxford University Press.

—— 1962. Anthropology and history. In *Essays in Social Anthropology, by E. E. Evans-Pritchard*. London: Faber, pp. 46–65.

Feinman, G. M. 1998. Scale and social organization: perspectives on the archaic state. In G. M. Feinman and J. Marcus (eds.), *Archaic States*. Santa Fe, NM: School of American Research Press, pp. 95–133.

Flannery, K. V. 1972. The cultural evolution of civilizations. *Annual Review of Ecology and Systematics* 3: 399–426.

——, and J. Marcus (eds.) 1983. *The Cloud People: Divergent Evolution of the Zapotec and Mixtec Civilizations*. New York: Academic Press.

Ford, C. S. (ed.) 1967. *Cross-Cultural Approaches: Readings in Comparative Research*. New Haven, CT: HRAF Press.

Frankfort, H. 1956. *The Birth of Civilization in the Near East*. New York: Doubleday.

Frankfort, H. A., J. A. Wilson, and T. Jacobsen. 1949. *Before Philosophy: The Intellectual Adventure of Ancient Man*. Harmondsworth: Penguin.

Fried, H. M. 1967. *The Evolution of Political Society: An Essay in Political Anthropology*. New York: Random House.

Gazzaniga, M. S. 1992. *Nature's Mind: The Biological Roots of Thinking, Emotions, Sexuality, Language, and Intelligence*. New York: Basic Books.

——1998. *The Mind's Past*. Berkeley: University of California Press.

Geertz, C. 1965. The impact of the concept of culture on the concept of man. In J. R. Platt (ed.), *New Views of the Nature of Man*. Chicago: University of Chicago Press, pp. 93–118.

——1973. *The Interpretation of Cultures: Selected Essays*. New York: Basic Books.

Giddens, A. 1984. *The Constitution of Society: Outline of the Theory of Structuration*. Berkeley: University of California Press.

Godelier, M. 1986. *The Mental and the Material: Thought, Economy and Society*. London: Verso.

Gosden, C. 1994. *Social Time and Being*. Oxford: Blackwell.

Haas, J. 1982. *The Evolution of the Prehistoric State*. New York: Columbia University Press.

Hall, J. 1986. *Powers and Liberties: The Causes and Consequences of the Rise of the West*. Harmondsworth: Penguin.

Hallpike, C. R. 1986. *The Principles of Social Evolution*. Oxford: Oxford University Press.

Hancock, G., and S. Faiia. 1998. *Heaven's Mirror: Quest for the Lost Civilization*. London: Michael Joseph.

Harris, M. 1968. *The Rise of Anthropological Theory: A History of Theories of Culture*. New York: Crowell.

Hobhouse, L. T., G. C. Wheeler, and M. Ginsberg. 1915. *The Material Culture and Social Institutions of the Simpler Peoples: An Essay in Correlation*. London: Chapman & Hill.

Hodder, I. 1986. *Reading the Past: Current Approaches to Interpretation in Archaeology*. Cambridge: Cambridge University Press.

——(ed.) 1987. *The Archaeology of Contextual Meanings*. Cambridge: Cambridge University Press.

——1990. *The Domestication of Europe: Structure and Contingency in Neolithic Studies*. Oxford: Blackwell.

Ingold, T. 1996. Hunting and gathering as ways of perceiving the environment. In R. Ellen and K. Fukui (eds.), *Redefining Nature: Ecology, Culture and Domestication*. Oxford: Berg, pp. 117–155.

Jacobsen, T. 1976. *The Treasures of Darkness: A History of Mesopotamian Religion*. New Haven, CT: Yale University Press.

Johnson, G. A. 1973. *Local Exchange and Early State Development in Southwestern Iran*. Ann Arbor: University of Michigan, Museum of Anthropology, Anthropological Papers 51.

——1981. Monitoring complex system integration and boundary phenomena with settlement size data. In S. E. van der Leeuw (ed.), *Archaeological Approaches to the Study of Complexity*. Amsterdam: Van Giffen Institute, pp. 143–188.

Johnson, M. 1999. *Archaeological Theory: An Introduction*. Oxford: Blackwell.

Karlsson, H. 1998. *Re-Thinking Archaeology*. Gotarc Series, B,8. Gothenburg: Novum Grafiska.

Kemp, B. J. 1989. *Ancient Egypt: Anatomy of a Civilization*. London: Routledge.

Kenoyer, J. M. 1997. Early city-states in South Asia: Comparing the Harappan Phase and Early Historic Period. In D. L. Nichols and T. H. Charlton (eds.), *The Archaeology of City-States: Cross-Cultural Approaches*. Washington, DC: Smithsonian Institution Press, pp. 51–70.

Köbben, A. J. F. 1952. New ways of presenting an old idea: The statistical method in social anthropology. *Journal of the Royal Anthropological Institute* 82: 129–146.

——1973. Comparativists and non-comparativists in anthropology. In R. Naroll and R. Cohen (eds.), *A Handbook of Method in Cultural Anthropology*. New York: Columbia University Press, pp. 581–596.

Lakoff, G. 1987. *Women, Fire, and Dangerous Things: What Categories Reveal About the Mind*. Chicago: University of Chicago Press.

——, and M. Johnson. 1980. *Metaphors We Live By*. Chicago: University of Chicago Press.

Lee, R. B. 1990. Primitive communism and the origin of social inequality. In S. Upham (ed.), *The Evolution of Political Systems: Sociopolitics in Small-Scale Sedentary Societies*. Cambridge: Cambridge University Press, pp. 225–246.

Lewis, M. E. 1990. *Sanctioned Violence in Early China*. Albany: State University of New York Press.

Low, B. S. 2000. *Why Sex Matters: A Darwinian Look at Human Behavior*. Princeton, NJ: Princeton University Press.

Maisels, C. K. 1999. *Early Civilizations of the Old World: The Formative Histories of Egypt, the Levant, Mesopotamia, India, and China*. London: Routledge.

Mann, M. 1986. *The Sources of Social Power, Vol. I, A History of Power from the Beginning to A. D. 1760*. Cambridge: Cambridge University Press.

Marcus, J. 1998. The peaks and valleys of ancient states: An extension of the dynamic model. In G. M. Feinman and J. Marcus (eds.), *Archaic States*. Santa Fe, NM: School of American Research Press, pp. 59–94.

Marx, K., and F. Engels. 1962. *Selected Works in Two Volumes*. Moscow: Foreign Languages Publishing House.

Maschner, H. D. (ed.) 1996. *Darwinian Archaeologies*. New York: Plenum.

McGuire, R. H. 1992. *A Marxist Archaeology*. San Diego, CA: Academic Press.

Mithen, S. J. 1996. *The Prehistory of the Mind: A Search for the Origins of Art, Religion and Science*. London: Thames & Hudson.

Moore, F. W. (ed.) 1961. *Readings in Cross-Cultural Methodology*. New Haven, CT: HRAF Press.

Morenz, S. 1973. *Egyptian Religion*. Ithaca, NY: Cornell University Press.

Murdock, G. P. 1959. Evolution in social organization. In B. J. Meggers (ed.), *Evolution and Anthropology: A Centennial Appraisal*. Washington, DC: Anthropological Society of Washington, pp. 126–143.

Nichols, D. L., and T. H. Charlton (eds.) 1997. *The Archaeology of City-States: Cross-Cultural Approaches*. Washington, DC: Smithsonian Institution Press.

Nissen, H. J., P. Damerow, and R. K. Englund. 1993. *Archaic Bookkeeping: Early Writing and Techniques of Economic Administration in the Ancient Near East*. Chicago: University of Chicago Press.

O'Brien, M. J. (ed.) 1996. *Evolutionary Archaeology: Theory and Application*. Salt Lake City: University of Utah Press.

——, and R. L. Lyman. 2000. *Applying Evolutionary Archaeology: A Systematic Approach*. New York: Plenum.

Patterson, T. C. 1989. History and post-processual archaeologies. *Man* 24: 555–566.

—— 1997. *Inventing Western Civilization*. New York: Monthly Review Press.

Polanyi, K., C. M. Arensberg, and H. W. Pearson. 1957. *Trade and Market in the Early Empires*. Glencoe: The Free Press.

Possehl, G. L. 1998. Sociocultural complexity without the state: the Indus civilization. In G. M. Feinman and J. Marcus (eds.), *Archaic States*. Santa Fe, NM: School of American Research Press, pp. 261–291.

Preucel, R. W. (ed.) 1991. *Processual and Postprocessual Archaeologies: Multiple Ways of Knowing the Past*. Carbondale: Southern Illinois University at Carbondale, Center for Archaeological Investigations, Occasional Paper 10.

Rathje, W. L. 1975. The last tango in Mayapan: A tentative trajectory of production–distribution systems. In J. A. Sabloff and C. C. Lamberg-Karlovsky (eds.), *Ancient Civilization and Trade*. Albuquerque: University of New Mexico Press, pp. 409–448.

Renfrew, C. 1982. *Towards an Archaeology of Mind*. Cambridge: Cambridge University Press.

—— 1997. Review of *Early Civilizations*, by B. G. Trigger. *American Journal of Archaeology* 101: 164.

——, and P. Bahn. 2000. *Archaeology: Theories, Methods, and Practice*. 3rd edn. New York: Thames & Hudson.

——, and E. B. W. Zubrow (eds.) 1994. *The Ancient Mind: Elements of Cognitive Archaeology*. Cambridge: Cambridge University Press.

Sahlins, M. D. 1968. *Tribesmen*. Englewood Cliffs: Prentice-Hall.

——1976. *Culture and Practical Reason*. Chicago: University of Chicago Press.

——, and E. R. Service (eds.) 1960. *Evolution and Culture*. Ann Arbor: University of Michigan Press.

Salomon, F. (ed.) 1991. *The Huarochirí Manuscript: A Testament of Ancient and Colonial Andean Religion*. Austin: University of Texas Press.

Salzman, P. C. 2000. *Black Tents of Baluchistan*. Washington, DC: Smithsonian Institution Press.

Sanders, W. T., J. R. Parsons, and R. S. Santley. 1979. *The Basin of Mexico: Ecological Processes in the Evolution of a Civilization*. New York: Academic Press.

Service, E. R. 1971. *Primitive Social Organization: An Evolutionary Perspective*. 2nd edn. New York: Random House.

——1975. *Origins of the State and Civilization: The Process of Cultural Evolution*. New York: Norton.

Smith, G. E. 1933. *The Diffusion of Culture*. London: Watts.

Soustelle, J. 1961. *The Daily Life of the Aztecs on the Eve of the Spanish Conquest*. London: Weidenfeld & Nicolson.

Spencer, H. 1873–1934. *Descriptive Sociology; or, Groups of Sociological Facts, Classified and Arranged by Herbert Spencer*. 15 vols. London: Williams & Norgate.

Spriggs, M. (ed.) 1984. *Marxist Perspectives in Archaeology*. Cambridge: Cambridge University Press.

Steward, J. H. 1949. Cultural causality and law: A trial formulation of the development of early civilizations. *American Anthropologist* 51: 1–27.

Stone, E. C. 1997. City-states and their centers: The Mesopotamian example. In D. L. Nichols and T. H. Charlton (eds.), *The Archaeology of City-States: Cross-Cultural Approaches*. Washington, DC: Smithsonian Institution Press, pp. 15–26.

Tanner, A. 1979. *Bringing Home Animals: Religious Ideology and Mode of Production of the Mistassini Cree Hunters*. St. John's: Memorial University of Newfoundland, Institute of Social and Economic Research, Social and Economic Studies, 23.

Teltser, P. A. (ed.) 1995. *Evolutionary Archaeology: Methodological Issues*. Tucson: University of Arizona Press.

Thomas, J. 1996. *Time, Culture and Identity: An Interpretative Archaeology*. London: Routledge.

Thompson, R. F. 1976. *Black Gods and Kings: Yoruba Art at UCLA*. Bloomington: University of Indiana Press.

Tilley, C. Y. 1984. Ideology and the legitimation of power in the Middle Neolithic of southern Sweden. In D. Miller and C. Tilley (eds.), *Ideology, Power and Prehistory*. Cambridge: Cambridge University Press, pp. 111–146.

——(ed.) 1993. *Interpretative Archaeology*. Oxford: Berg.

——1994. *A Phenomenology of Landscape: Places, Paths, and Monuments*. Oxford: Berg.

——1999. *Metaphor and Material Culture*. Oxford: Blackwell.

Townsend, R. F. 1979. *State and Cosmos in the Art of Tenochtitlan*. Washington, DC: Dumbarton Oaks.

Trigger, B. G. 1982. Archaeological analysis and concepts of causality. *Culture* 2(2): 31–42.

——1990a. Monumental architecture: A thermodynamic explanation of symbolic behaviour. *World Architecture* 22: 119–132.

——1990b. Maintaining economic equality in opposition to complexity: An Iroquoian case study. In S. Upham (ed.), *The Evolution of Political Systems: Sociopolitics in Small-Scale Sedentary Societies*. Cambridge: Cambridge University Press, pp. 119–145.

—— 1993. *Early Civilizations: Ancient Egypt in Context*. Cairo: American University in Cairo Press.

—— 1995. Expanding middle-range theory. *Antiquity* 69: 449–458.

—— 1998. *Sociocultural Evolution: Calculation and Contingency*. Oxford: Blackwell.

—— 2003. *Understanding Early Civilizations: A Comparative Study*. Cambridge: Cambridge University Press.

Turner, V. 1967. *The Forest of Symbols: Aspects of Ndembu Ritual*. Ithaca, NY: Cornell University Press.

—— 1975. *Revelation and Divination in Ndembu Ritual*. Ithaca, NY: Cornell University Press.

Van De Mieroop, M. 1999. *The Ancient Mesopotamian City*. 2nd edn. Oxford: Oxford University Press.

Wittfogel, K. A. 1938. Die Theorie der orientalischen Gesellschaft. *Zeitschrift für Sozialforschung* 7: 90–122.

—— 1957. *Oriental Despotism: A Comparative Study of Total Power*. New Haven, CT: Yale University Press.

Yoffee, N. 1997. The obvious and the chimerical: city-states in archaeological perspective. In D. L. Nichols and T. H. Charlton (eds.), *The Archaeology of City States: Cross-Cultural Approaches*. Washington, DC: Smithsonian Institution Press, pp. 255–263.

Zipf, G. K. 1949. *Human Behavior and the Principle of Least Effort*. Cambridge, MA: Addison-Wesley.

3

Social Archaeology and Marxist Social Thought

Thomas C. Patterson

Archaeologists have used the label "social archaeology" to acknowledge the relation-ship between how we theorize society and history, on the one hand, and what we write about particular societies, including our own, that are known from archaeological, historical, and ethnographic evidence, on the other. In anglophone countries, for example, the initial impetus for social archaeology came in the late 1930s. In England, V. Gordon Childe (1935, 1983 [1936], 1946, 1947) and Grahame Clark (1957[1939]) urged their colleagues to begin thinking about the social relations and organization of the peoples who made the artifacts recovered in excavations and surveys. In the United States, William D. Strong (1936), Julian Steward, and Frank Setzler (1938), Clyde Kluckhohn (1939, 1940), and Walter Taylor (1948) in different ways prodded archae-ologists to think more clearly about their conceptual and social theoretical frameworks and to attempt to go beyond artifacts and associations when they wrote about past societies.

Reactions to such exhortations appeared in the mid-1950s. Christopher Hawkes (1954:161–162) claimed that, while it was "relatively easy" to infer the techniques of production from archaeological phenomena and "fairly easy" to infer subsistence eco-nomics, it was "considerably harder" to infer social–political institutions; the "hardest inference of all" concerned religious institutions and spiritual life. M. A. Smith was even more pessimistic. She insisted that efforts to re-create, reconstruct, or recover past societies from the surviving evidence was not really possible, because archaeo-logical remains support only a limited range of conclusions about human activity. In light of this limitation, she continued, it was important to recognize that "attempts to establish prehistoric societies... must rest on conjecture, not on argument" (1955:8). Archaeologists, she concluded, should recover what they can, look for observable regularities they can validly establish, and avoid claims about prehistoric cultures and societies they "can never *know*" (ibid., emphasis in original).

Responses taking cognizance of the views of both the boosters of functional social analyses and the pessimists appeared from the late 1950s onward. Joseph Caldwell (1959), for instance, pointed out that settlement pattern, ecological, and evolutionary studies in the 1950s promoted analyses of archaeological cultures as functionally integrated systems rather than as aggregates of discrete traits. John Rowe (1959, 1962) and Lewis Binford (1962, 1965) suggested in different ways that archaeologists should unpack and examine the implications of the methods and concepts they used.

Partly because of the real danger of political persecution,[1] what anglophone archaeologists did not consider overtly in the 1950s and 1960s was how different bodies of foundational social theory – such as liberal-positivist or Marxist – might affect the concepts and methods they used as well as the assumptions they were willing to make about culture, society, and history; the comparisons that were made were usually couched in terms of the differences between Childe's neolithic and urban revolutions and Steward's notion of increasing cultural complexity and emergence of successively greater levels of sociocultural integration (Adams 1960a, 1960b). This was less true for archaeologists residing in countries – like Italy, Mexico, or Peru, for instance – with longstanding traditions of intense analysis and discussion of various social theories and their political implications. Since archaeologists occasionally participated in the debates, their discussions of past societies tended to be more varied and theoretically textured than those in the anglophone countries (e.g. Bate 1977, 1978; d'Agostino 1991; Guidi 1988; Patterson 1994a).

By the 1970s, there were renewed calls in anglophone countries for the development of social archaeology. For Charles Redman and his associates, this was a plea to move beyond the study of subsistence activities and archaeological dating. Social archaeology in their view was a loosely defined direction that entailed using explicit models, adopting single and multicausal models, using broader databases, examining both individual and normative factors in society, and applying quantitative methods (Redman et al. 1978:14). For Colin Renfrew (1984:3–4), social archaeology marked a fundamental change in the methods, objectives, and aspirations of archaeologists as they sought to reconstruct past social systems; it was made possible by adopting the "body of explicit interpretive theory" developed in the 1960s and 1970s by the new archaeologists. From 1970 onward, the social archaeologists in Latin America – Luis Lumbreras (1974), Mario Sanoja and Iraida Vargas Arenas (1978; Vargas Arenas 1990), O. Hugo Benevides (2001) and others – viewed archaeology as a social science and used Marxism rather than liberal positivism as their foundational social theory.

The emergence of an explicitly social archaeology in the 1970s coincided with the appearance of critiques of the new (processual) archaeology both in anglophone countries and in Latin America. For example, Philip Kohl (1976) and Antonio Gilman (1976) were critical of the way in which Renfrew removed trade from its socioeconomic context, separated exchange from the economic relations in which the objects exchanged were produced and used, and treated trade as the determinant motor in sociocultural development. Manuel Gándara (1980, 1981) and Alison Wylie (1982) undertook extensive critiques of the epistemological and ontological foundations of the new archaeology, while Philip Kohl (1981) and Thomas C. Patterson (1981), among others, explored the advantages of Marxist historical materialism over the ecological, demographic, and technological materialisms underpinning processual archaeology. Ian Hodder and his associates at Cambridge criticized the positivist foundations of processual archaeology as well as its lack of attention to the social construction of meaning and to power relations (Hodder 1982; Miller and Tilley 1984; Spriggs 1984). In the wake of their critique, they deployed a number of alternative foundational theories, including several inspired by Marxist social thought, for the postprocessual archaeology they sought to develop.

By 1980, Luis Bate (1977) and Julio Montané (1980) had linked the words "Marxism" and "archaeology" in the titles of books, and, a decade later, Randall McGuire's (1992) *A Marxist Archaeology* and Bruce Trigger's (1993) survey of "Marxism in contemporary Western archaeology" appeared. At the same time, Ian Hodder (1991:15–16)) noted the rapidly increasing popularity and the diversity of Marxist theoretical positions adopted by European archaeologists during the 1970s and 1980s.

Marxism in Archaeology

In the Americas, the indigenous Marxist traditions were enriched in the late 1930s by refugees from Central Europe and by exiled veterans of the Spanish Civil War. A number of the exiles who went to Mexico City – Pedro Armillas, Angel Palerm, and Pedro Carrasco, to name only three – became anthropologists and brought with them textured appreciations of Marxist social thought. In the late 1940s and early 1950s, they collaborated with refugee and US scholars – notably Eric Wolf and René Millon – who brought their own understandings of Marxism to these international partnerships.[2]

Comparisons of their writings with those of contemporaries reveal their Marxist underpinnings. For example, in describing cultural development in Mesoamerica, Armillas (1948, 1951) spoke about the development of the productive forces, asked how the labor required to build the great pyramids was organized, and alluded to the extortion by the ruling classes preceding the destruction of Teotihuacán. Millon's (1954:178) early work at Teotihuacán was concerned with whether the valley was "large enough in and of itself to make possible the development of a class society based on production by means of irrigation." Wolf's (1959) *Sons of the Shaking Earth* was an extended analysis of the dialectics of class and state formation in Mesoamerica, first of the autochthonous processes and then of the processes that came into play as the region's peoples became enmeshed in colonial and capitalist social relations after 1500. Their publications were read widely and struck resonant chords for a number of North American scholars – including Robert Adams (1960a, 1960b, 1965, 1966) and Bruce Trigger (1967), whose own works in the 1960s were already exhibiting significant engagements with Marxist theory and methods.

The engagement of archaeologists with Marxist social thought took diverse turns in the 1970s and 1980s. In Latin America, it took place in the context of a wider debate among Marxist-Leninists who were concerned with the development of the productive forces and viewed the proletariat as the revolutionary class in contemporary society, Maoists who viewed poor peasants as the leading revolutionary class, and structural Marxists who were simultaneously rejecting the economic determination of history and developing the idea of an overdetermined, decentered totality. The Latin American social archaeologists rejected the mechanical forms of cultural evolutionism, reductionist methodologies, and claims that change was a consequence of exogenous factors impinging on social totalities. They argued instead that the world was structured by unobservable but nevertheless real processes and relations, that the processes of social development were historically constituted, and that there was no conceptual break between studying ancient and modern societies. They employed and refined analytical categories in their examinations of archaeological assemblages: mode of production, socioeconomic formation, mode of life, and culture (McGuire 1992:64–68; Patterson 1994a). By the mid-1970s, they had already raised the question of "archaeology for whom?" and were attempting to give voice to the sentiments of marginalized and disenfranchised classes and peoples. Since the 1980s, the Latin American social archae-ologists have had a continuing impact on the development of theoretical archaeology in Spain, where some view it as possibly "the most important Marxist tradition in the archaeology of the western world" (Vázquez Varela and Risch 1991:36).

From the mid-1960s onward, archaeologists working in the Near East had to take account of the writings of Igor M. Diakonov and the other members of the Soviet school of economic historians of the ancient Orient (Diakonoff 1969). As Philip Kohl (1991:xii) observed, this challenged dominant, grossly inaccurate Western images that portrayed Soviet scholarship as "a monolithic, dogmatic, highly entrenched orthodoxy to which everyone submits either through brainwashing or coercion." They were forced to take account of the disagreements among Soviet scholars over fundamental issues of interpretation that were debated openly in their literature. As Kohl (1991:xv) observed, "not all Soviet historians are Marxists" and "not all Marxists, including Soviet historians, interpret Marx and his successors in the same fashion." What unites Diakonoff and his colleagues is (1) their emphasis on the class structures of ancient societies and the status of direct producers which refract the social divisions of labor and property relations that exist in those societies; (2) their recognition of multiple paths of development in different societies in the ancient Orient; and (3) their efforts to reconstruct systems of though the use of texts concerned with mythology, world-view, and ethical-philosophical issues (Kohl 1991:xvi–xx). Their work influenced scholars of the ancient Near East in Scandinavia, Italy, and the United States (e.g., Larsen 1979; Liverani 1991; Tosi 1977; Zagarell 1986).

In England from the mid-1970s onward, archaeologists engaged with Marxist social thought in diverse ways. Some adopted the structural Marxism or Marxist structuralism of the French anthropologists – Maurice Godelier, Claude Meillassoux, Emmanuel Terray, and Pierre-Philippe Rey, who occupied different places in the French political spectrum. They simultaneously borrowed selectively and critiqued the work of the French Marxist anthropologists, Claude Lévi-Strauss and Louis Althusser. The archae-ologists variously asserted the primacy of social relations of production over the pro-ductive forces (Bender 1978); claimed erroneously that an "essential premise of Marxism" was a universal human nature in which all human beings are motivated by self-interest and the desire to accumulate power (Parker Pearson 1984:61); or insisted that structural transformations were more important motors of change than history or class struggle (Friedman 1975). Others were critical both of structural Marxism and of their colleagues' critiques of it (Gledhill 1981; Saunders 1990). Still others reasserted the importance of class structures, struggle, and the economic determination of history. Finally, a number turned to world systems theory or to the examination of core-periphery relations resulting from unequal exchange.

Barbara Bender, for example, examined trajectories of social development in north-west France and midcontinent North America. She argued that the underlying similar-ity in the social structures of foragers and peasant food-producers was often obscured

by an overemphasis on the mode of subsistence, and that neither was in fact completely autonomous or self-sufficient. The transition from foraging to food production
was brought about, in her view, by an intensification of intergroup alliances and
exchange relations. Alliance and exchange relations were ultimately concerned with
social reproduction of the participant communities (Bender 1978, 1981). Further examination of materials from different regions in midcontinent North America led her to
conclude that different conditions and structural constraints would lead to different
historical trajectories (Bender 1984, 1985).

Jonathan Friedman and Michael Rowlands (1977) examined the evolution of early
civilizations. What distinguished their work from evolutionist accounts was the idea of
the Asiatic state, which developed when the social relations of production which
organized horizontal flows of surplus through marriage exchange and feasting were
replaced by tributary relations that underwrote the emergence of an economy based on
the flow of wives and prestige goods from local communities to the chiefly estate
and the upper class. The epigenetic model they produced was concerned specifically
with the effects of dominant structures that were realized only with the passage of
time. In their view, areas outside those where primary civilizations emerged would
exhibit different trajectories of social development (Gledhill 1981:16–27).

John Gledhill's (1984) analysis of the social formation of late Prehispanic
Mesoamerica began with extended discussions of the Asiatic mode of production
and class structures in precapitalist societies. From there, he moved to examining the
characteristics of Aztec society – the dominant political power in central Mexico at
the time of the Spanish invasion in 1519. He began with a discussion of lands whose
produce was designated for the support of the temples, the army, and the secular
administration of the state, and of the duties and rights of the free members of peasant
communities who worked these lands. After pointing out that surplus was pumped out
of free peasants in a variety of ways, he proceeded to consider other categories of
landholding within the peasant communities themselves as well as lands that were
held/owned by the nobility. After exploring the relationships between landholding
and markets, Gledhill considered the constraints on and possibilities of structural
transformations in Aztec society, given the contradictions that existed within the
dominant classes. In this regard, he stressed the mediating role of politics.

By the mid-1980s, Friedman, Rowlands, and their colleagues in England and
Denmark had grafted the idea of world systems to their earlier concern with structural
transformation (Ekholm and Friedman 1979; Frankenstein and Rowlands 1978;
Friedman 1982; Hedeager 1987; Kristiansen 1982; Rowlands 1987). They adopted
Immanuel Wallerstein's (1974) argument that the expansion of trade and the market
created an international division of labor and laid the foundations for exploitation
to occur. Wallerstein's critics have pointed out that world-systems theory placed
the motor for development in the industrializing countries of Europe and that it did
not adequately deal with class struggles internal to the social units on the periphery.
Rowlands (1987:3) has correctly pointed out that Wallerstein was not particularly concerned with precapitalist societies – which were the focus of the archaeologists. Unlike
Wallerstein, Ekholm and Friedman (1979) emphasized the "long-term continuity which
exists between precapitalist and capitalist world economies" and noted that "the transition to the modern era was itself the product of a previously unified medieval Euro-

pean/Mediterranean world economy" (Rowlands 1987:3). Rowlands (1987:3) proceeded to point out that the archaeologists were using world systems theory to rethink the "significance of large-scale spatial/temporal shifts in geopolitical centers;...the correlation of expanding peripheral formations with political decentralization in faraway core areas and...the theorisation of irreversible change."

The archaeologists in anglophone North America confronted different conditions from their colleagues in Europe. First, they lived and worked in countries that had originally been settler colonies whose indigenous populations had, in many instances, been dispossessed from their means of production.[3] Second, from the 1970s onward, they had to confront issues raised by politically well-organized First Nation descendant communities and African-American diasporic communities; these included the repatriation and reburial of Native American human remains from museum and university collections as well as the excavation and interpretation of sites such as the African Burial Ground in New York City (Epperson 1999; McGuire 1997).

This has several consequences. One is that the question of "archaeology for whom" has had a profound impact on the US and Canadian archaeologists whose writings make use of Marxist social thought. A second is that many of them are historical archaeologists concerned with the archaeology of capitalism and the spread of Europeans into non-European parts of the world after 1500. As a result, questions about "colonialism, imperialism, racism, the spread and mechanisms of capitalism, [and] the creation of categories based on gender and ethnicity" are important ones (Orser 1996:2).

Inspired initially by Louis Althusser's (1984[1970]) essay "Ideology and ideological state apparatuses" and later by the writings of Georg Lukács (1971[1922]) and Jürgen Habermas (1979), Mark Leone and his associates have focused on issues of ideology. On the one hand, they have sought to show how present-day ideologies influence the views both archaeologists and the public hold about past societies (Leone 1994; Leone, Potter, and Shackel 1987). On the other hand, they have sought to show how the dominant ideologies of past societies have shaped the archaeological record from the plan and construction of the garden of an upper-class household in Annapolis to the conceptualization, spatial arrangement, and construction of entire cities and how subordinated classes resisted these impositions at different scales (Leone 1995; Leone and Hurry 1998).

A number of anglophone North Americans have used Marxist concepts of class, class formation, and class structure as points of entry to study historically specific socioeconomic formations and their transformation. For example, Robert Paynter (1985:409; 1988) has stressed the ways in which surplus was extracted from direct producers and pointed to the need for class analyses to understand the formation and working of the capitalist mode of production in North America. In a series of publications, Charles Orser (1990, 1991, 1999) traced processes of class formation and social transformation in the American South from the time of the Antebellum slave plantations to the post-Reconstruction tenant farms that were located on the old plantations.

However, efforts at class analysis have not been limited entirely to class-stratified societies with bookkeeping and writing systems. For instance, Randall McGuire and Dean Saitta (1996) built on Stephen Resnick and Richard Wolff's (1987:117–131) discussion of subsumed classes to analyze how the contradiction between communal life and social hierarchy was a major motor of change in the Prehispanic western pueblos of the American Southwest. Jon Muller (1997) countered arguments based on core-periphery models and on discussions of power with an argument built around the "mode of production" concept and examinations of processes of social change focusing on tendencies toward class formation and resistance to those tendencies to analyze the Mississippian political economy of midcontinent North America. Thomas Patterson (1991) deployed the analytical concepts of mode of production and class struggle to examine processes of class and state formation and resistance in the central Andes, both before and after the arrival of the Spaniards in the 1530s; in his view, the socio-economic transformation marked by the transition from prehistory to history – i.e., the consolidation of the capitalist mode of production – was complex and not gradual.

North American archaeologists have deployed several strands of Marxist thought to discuss the origins of inequality and resistance to the processes involved. Bruce Trigger (1990:120) pointed out that the French Marxist anthropologists had argued that the differences of age, gender, and personal standing found among the members of primitive communities gave rise to conflicts and that these conflicts, like class struggle in capitalist societies, were the motor of social change. He countered these claims, arguing that primitive communal societies were radically different from those class-stratified polities. A number of archaeologists, Marxist and otherwise, adopted this perspective. Trigger explored Pierre Clastres's (1977:6) claim that coercion and subordination of one group by another are not universal features of human society, and asserted that many primitive communal societies "possess well-integrated mechanisms to defend equality that must be eliminated if hierarchical organizations are to develop" (Trigger 1990:145).

Christine Gailey and Thomas Patterson (1988) deployed the concepts of mode of production and articulation to examine the relationships between centers and peripheries in the process of state formation. They indicated that not all states were the same and that emergence of state-based societies has immediate effects on the production relations and stratification of nearby societies, including those organized on the basis of the primitive communal mode of production. Kinship and production relations, they argued, were distorted as primitive communal societies were simultaneously en-snared in the exploitative relations of tributary states and sought to retain control over their members and the goods they produced.

Anglophone North American archaeologists also turned their attention to the ways in which the categories of gender, ethnicity, and race (in capitalist societies) intersected with class position and, indeed, were constitutive of those positions in the social division of labor. They considered how the analytical categories of ethnicity and race were forged in the context of class-stratified societies, both historic and prehistoric (Delle, Mrozowski, and Paynter 2000; Patterson 2001).

Elizabeth Brumfiel's applications of Marxist class analysis were the most textured of the 1980s and 1990s. Using data from the Aztec social formation in central Mexico, she pointed out that considerations of the dialectical interplay of ecology, existing social structures, and political dynamics would significantly enhance our understanding of class and state formation (Brumfiel 1983). Her studies of the relationships between agricultural development and class stratification in the southern Valley of Mexico (1991a) were followed by analyses of craft specialization and the identity of craft specialists (1987, 1998), of the gendered division of labor in Aztec society (1991b), of factional competition within the Aztec ruling class (1994a), of tribute, commerce, and non-compliance in Central Mexico (1991c, 1993), of resistance and class warfare in Aztec ethnohistory (1994b), and of the effectiveness of ideological domination (1996).

While Brumfiel's writings provided a model of what an archaeology informed by Marxist social looks like, Patterson's *Theory and Practice of Archaeology: A Workbook* (1994b) explored how social theoretical frameworks shape the questions archaeologists ask; his perspective is explicitly Marxist as he engages the "middle range theory and practice" that exists between the accumulation of data, on the one hand, and the interpretation of its significance, on the other. William Marquardt (1992) examined the implications of dialectical analysis in archaeology, paying particular attention to the analytical categories of agency, contradiction, structures, power relations, and scale. Marquardt, Carole Crumley, and their associates undertook dialectical analyses of Burgundian landscapes – i.e., the changing relations between humans and their environments from the Iron Age through the Middle Ages (Crumley and Marquardt 1987).

There have been several explicitly Marxist commentaries on the practice of archaeology in anglophone North America. For instance, Bruce Trigger (1984) has examined dominant perceptions of American Indians in his portraits of US archaeology during its colonialist and imperialist phases of development; this led him to raise the issue of power relations and the question of who owns the past (Trigger 1985). Patterson (1986, 1995) has periodized the historical development of archaeology in the United States and related its development to wider political-economic and social currents in the society. He subsequently explored the political economy of archaeology in the United States at the end of the century, pointing to significant changes in the labor market from the 1970s onward, to the potential unionization of field technicians and graduate students, and to the emerging dynamics between archaeologists and politically mobilized descendant and diasporic communities (Patterson 1999).

Toward a Critical Social Archaeology

Both Marxists and non-Marxists have participated in the development of social archaeology. The largest impediments to the development of a critical social archaeology exist in states where ethico-philosophical standards that are actually local knowledge claims are held to be natural or universal and where such standards constitute part of everyday social discourse; this was particularly true of the United States during the repressive years of the Cold War. Philosophical standards that are held to be natural or universal are actually more inhibiting than overt, covert, and institutionalized forms of discrimination. Since these claims are hegemonic and assumed to be correct, it is difficult to conceive of alternative explanations simply because alternatives are either not discussed nor taken seriously when they are posed. This is not the same as saying that the circumstances which sustain these standards are immutable.

It seems clear to me that perspectives critical of hegemonic standards most frequently come from groups – descendant or diasporic communities – that feel the injustice of such claims every day of their lives. Secondly, they have been able to convey the depth and content of their feelings to the disaffected members of classes that would normally adhere to these standards; this potentially allows alliances to be forged and nurtured. One moment when such alliances occurred in the United States was in the 1960s and early 1970s with the convergence of the civil rights, labor, women's, peace, student, and counter-culture movements; for too brief a moment, they overlapped and crosscut one another. Another moment occurred in Eastern Europe in the early 1990s when, in country after country, twenty to thirty political parties – representing every possible position on the political spectrum and every conceivable alliance – vied for office. A third, specifically archaeological moment occurred in the mid-1980s around the organization of the World Archaeological Congress. A critical social archaeology is most likely to develop when real political and intellectual debate occurs, especially when archaeologists participate meaningfully in those wider politicized discussions and are not fickle consumers of new ideas.

Marxists, as Terry Eagleton (1996:118) observed, are often accused of being universalists. He proceeded to point out that universality does not exist in any positive sense, and that Marxists have historically been critical of the kind of false universality which claims that everyone will enjoy freedom and justice once the values of Western Man are extended to the rest of the globe. "The political goal of socialism is not a resting in difference, which is then the flipside of a spurious universalism, but the emanicipation of difference at the level of human mutuality or reciprocity" (Eagleton 1966:120).

In sum, a Marxist-informed social archaeology is now fixed on the intellectual landscape of archaeology in ways that it was not fifty years ago or even two decades ago. The obvious question at this juncture is where does it go from here? Given current trends, I see it developing along four strands that intertwine, separate, and come back together. The first entails critical examinations of the diverse strands of Marxist social thought itself, of the real and potential dialogues they have or could have with other theoretical perspectives, and of the utility they might have for developing social archaeology. The second involves the elaboration of theoretically informed, comparative core-periphery, world-systems, or articulation of modes of production arguments about the diverse kinds of relationships that have existed between state and non-state societies. The third builds on those studies that have been concerned with the intersection of class, race/ethnicity, and gender relations both in past societies as well as in a profession that is shaped partly by the ideology of nation-states and partly by topically based discourses such as the rise of civilization or the origins of states. The fourth calls for continued and more thoughtful political engagement with the members of non-ruling classes and descendant communities at home and abroad as means of charting alternatives to the development strategies promoted by states, international agencies, and ruling classes that too often overlook the welfare and well-being of working people everywhere.

ACKNOWLEDGMENTS

This paper has profited from the advice, comments, and observations of Wendy Ashmore, Sandra Harding, Lynn Meskell, Robert Paynter, Robert Preucel, and Bruce Trigger.

NOTES

1   Political persecution and repression of the Left has been a continuous, persistent feature of US society for more than a century. The Congress of Industrial Organizations unions were purged of their progressive leadership after World War II; university professors who refused to sign loyalty oaths or who became enmeshed in the webs of legislative bodies, such as the House Un-American Activities Committee (HUAC), lost their jobs (Schrecker 1986). Marxists, independent and otherwise, were simultaneously portrayed as dupes, Soviet agents, and hence as internal enemies of the state during the Cold War. Legions of young men and women who expressed curiosity about Marxist social thought while they were graduate students from the 1950s onward were "blackballed" by unsympathetic teachers and were not able to secure academic positions once they graduated. This was especially true when their social theory informed their political praxis and they engaged in activities – such as the civil rights, peace or labor movements – that attracted the attention of various state agencies. Activism rather than theory was the key. Merely talking about Marxism annoyed people; organizing or participating in demonstrations opposed to the actions of the government captured its attention and often incurred the wrath of its agents.

William Peace (1992) described the political activities of V. Gordon Childe and the persecution he experienced in Australia, England, and the United States. Eleanor Leacock (1982:255), who had a lifelong identification with the Left, wrote that, during the 1950s, "Marxist formulations were often blurred" and that on one occasion she chose to cite a chance statement by an establishment anthropologist when she should have cited Karl Marx.

2   Spanish translations of many of Childe's books were published in the two decades following World War II, beginning with *Man Makes Himself*, which appeared in 1936. In Mexico, José Luis Lorenzo studied with Childe at the Institute of Archaeology in 1953–4, and Julio Olivé Negrete (1958) wrote a master's thesis using Childe's approach to organize archaeological information from Mesoamerica (Olivé Negrete 1987).

3   The European immigrants to colonial-settler states – the United States, Australia, South Africa, and Israel, for example – were imbued with a chauvinism that saw "any territory as 'empty' and available if its indigenous population had not yet achieved national independence and recognized statehood" (Buch 1973:12). Trigger (1984:360–363) has described the dominant features of the archaeologies that developed in these circumstances.

REFERENCES

Adams, R. McC. 1960a. Early civilizations, subsistence, and environment. In C. H. Kraeling and R. M. Adams (eds.), *City Invincible: A Symposium on Urbanization and Cultural Development in the Ancient Near East*. Chicago: University of Chicago Press, pp. 269–295.

—— 1960b. The evolutionary process in early civilization. In S. Tax (ed.), *Evolution After Darwin: The University of Chicago Centennial, Vol. II, The Evolution of Man*. Chicago: University of Chicago Press, pp. 153–168.

—— 1965. *Land Behind Baghdad: A History of Settlement on the Diyala Plain*. Chicago: University of Chicago Press.

—— 1966. *The Evolution of Urban Society: Early Mesopotamia and Prehispanic Mexico*. Chicago: Aldine.

Althusser, L. 1984 [1970]. Ideology and ideological state apparatuses. In *Essays on Ideology*. London: Verso, pp. 1–60.

Armillas, P. 1948. A sequence of cultural development in Meso-America. In *A Reappraisal of Peruvian Archaeology*, assembled by Wendell C. Bennett. Salt Lake City: Memoirs of the Society for American Archaeology 4, pp. 105–112.

——1951. Tecnología, formaciones socio-económicas y religión en Mesoamérica. In S. Tax (ed.), *Selected Papers of the XXIX Congress of Americanists, Vol. 1, The Civilizations of Ancient America*. Chicago: University of Chicago Press, pp. 19–30.

Bate, L. F. 1977. *Arqueología y materialismo histórico*. México, DF: Ediciones de Cultura Popular.

——1978. *Sociedad, formación económico social y cultura*. México, DF: Ediciones de Cultura Popular.

Bender, B. 1978. Gatherer-hunter to farmer: A social perspective. *World Archaeology* 10(2): 204–222.

——1981. Gatherer-hunter intensification. In A. Sheridan and G. Bailey (eds.), *Economic Archaeology*. Oxford: British Archaeological Reports, International Series 95, pp. 149–157.

——1984. Emergent tribal formations in the American midcontinent. *American Antiquity* 50(1): 52–62.

——1985. Prehistoric developments in the American midcontinent and Brittany, northwest France. In T. D. Price and J. A. Brown (eds.), *Prehistoric Hunter-Gatherers: The Emergence of Cultural Complexity*. Orlando, FL: Academic Press, pp. 21–57.

Benevides, O. H. 2001. Returning to the source: Social archaeology as Latin American philosophy. *Latin American Antiquity* 12(4): 355–370.

Binford, Lewis R. 1962. Archaeology as anthropology. *American Antiquity* 28(2): 217–225.

——1965. Archaeological systematics and the study of culture process. *American Antiquity* 31(2): 267–275.

Brumfiel, E. M. 1983. Aztec state making: Ecology, structure, and the origin of the state. *American Anthropologist* 85(2): 261–284.

——1987. Elite and utilitarian crafts in the Aztec state. In E. M. Brumfiel and T. K. Earle (eds.), *Specialization, Exchange, and Complex Societies*. Cambridge: Cambridge University Press, pp. 102–118.

——1991a. Agricultural development and class stratification in the southern Valley of Mexico. In H. R. Harvey (ed.), *Land and Politics in the Valley of Mexico*. Albuquerque: University of New Mexico Press, pp. 43–62.

——1991b. Weaving and cooking: Women's production in Aztec Mexico. In J. M. Gero and M. W. Conkey (eds.), *Engendering Archaeology: Women and Prehistory*. Oxford: Basil Blackwell, pp. 224–251.

——1991c. Tribute and commerce in imperial cities: The Case of Xaltocan, Mexico. In H. J. M. Claessen and P. van de Velde (eds.), *Early State Economics*. New Brunswick, NJ: Transaction Books, Political and Legal Anthropology, vol. 8, pp. 177–198.

——1993. Tribute and Noncompliance in Cloth Production in Central Mexico. Paper presented at the annual meeting of the American Anthropological Association, San Francisco, CA.

——1994a. Factional competition and political development in the New World: An introduction. In E. M. Brumfiel and J. W. Fox (eds.), *Factional Competition and Political Development in the New World*. Cambridge: Cambridge University Press, pp. 1–13.

——1994b. Three Incidents of Resistance and Class Warfare in Aztec Ethnohistory. Paper presented at the annual meeting of the American Anthropological Association, Atlanta, GA.

——1996. Figurines and the Aztec state: Testing the effectiveness of ideological domination. In R. P. Wright (ed.), *Gender and Archaeology: Research in Gender and Practice*. Philadelphia: University of Pennsylvania Press, pp. 143–166.

——1998. The multiple identities of Aztec craft specialists. In C. L. Costin and R. P. Wright (eds.), *Craft and Social Identity*. Arlington, VA: Archeological Papers of the American Anthropological Association 8, pp. 145–152.

Buch, P. 1973. Introduction. In M. Rodinson, *Israel: A Colonial–Settler State*. New York: Monad Press, pp. 9–26.

Caldwell, J. 1959. The New American Archaeology. *Science* 129(3345): 303–307.

Childe, V. G. 1935. Changing methods and aims in prehistory. Presidential Address for 1935, *Proceedings of the Prehistoric Society* I(1): 1–15.

—— 1983 [1936]. *Man Makes Himself*. New York: New American Library.

—— 1946. Archaeology and anthropology. *Southwestern Journal of Anthropology* 2(1): 243–251.

—— 1947. *Archaeology as a Social Science*. London: University of London Institute of Archaeology, Third Annual Report, pp. 49–60.

Clark, G. 1957 [1939]. *Archaeology and Society: Reconstructing the Prehistoric Past*, 3rd edn. New York: Barnes & Noble.

Clastres, P. 1977. *Society against the State*. New York: Urizen Books.

Crumley, C. L., and W. H. Marquardt (eds.) 1987. *Regional Dynamics: Burgunidan Landscapes in Historical Perspective*. San Diego, CA: Academic Press.

d'Agostino, B. 1991. The Italian perspective on theoretical archaeology. In I. Hodder (ed.), *Archaeological Theory in Europe: The Last Three Decades*. London: Routledge, pp. 52–64.

Delle, J. A., S. A. Mrozowski, and R. Paynter (eds.) 2000. *Lines That Divide: Historical Archaeologies of Race, Class, and Gender*. Knoxville: University of Tennessee Press.

Diakonoff, I. M. (ed.). 1969. *Ancient Mesopotamia: A Socio-Economic History*. Moscow: "Nauka" Publishing House.

Eagleton, T. 1996. *The Illusions of Postmodernism*. Oxford: Blackwell.

Ekholm, K., and J. Friedman. 1979. "Capital," imperialism and exploitation in ancient world systems. In M. Trolle Larsen (ed.), *Power and Propaganda: A Symposium on Early Empires*. Mesopotamia: Copenhagen Studies in Assyriology 7. Copenhagen: Akademisk Forlag, pp. 41–58.

Epperson, T. W. 1999. The contested commons: Archaeologies of race, repression, and resistance in New York City. In M. P. Leone and P. B. Potter, Jr., *Historical Archaeologies of Capitalism*. New York: Kluwer/Plenum, pp. 81–110.

Frankenstein, S., and M. Rowlands. 1978. The internal structure and regional context of early Iron Age society in southwest Germany. *Bulletin of the Institute of Archaeology of London* 15: 73–112.

Friedman, J. 1975. Tribes, states, and transformations. In M. Bloch (ed.), *Marxist Analyses and Social Anthropology*. London: Malaby Press, pp. 161–202.

—— 1982. Catastrophe and continuity in social evolution. In C. Renfrew, M. J. Rowlands, and B. A. Segraves (eds.), *Theory and Explanation in Archaeology*. New York: Academic Press, pp. 175–196.

——, and M. J. Rowlands. 1977. Notes toward an epigenetic model of the evolution of "civilisation." In J. Friedman and M. J. Rowlands (eds.), *The Evolution of Social Systems*. London: Duckworth, pp. 201–276.

Gailey, C. W., and T. C. Patterson. 1988. State formation and uneven development. In J. Gledhill, B. Bender, and M. Trolle Larsen, *State and Society: The Emergence and Development of Social Hierarchy and Political Concentration*. London: Unwin Hyman, pp. 77–90.

Gándara, M. 1980. La vieja "nueva arqueología," primera parte. *Boletín de Antropología Americana* 2: 59–97.

—— 1981. La vieja "nueva arqueología," segunda parte. *Boletín de Antropología Americana* 3: 99–159.

Gilman, A. 1976. Bronze Age dynamics in southeast Spain. *Dialectical Anthropology* 1(4): 307–319.

Gledhill, J. 1981. Time's arrow: Anthropology, history, social evolution and Marxist theory. *Critique of Anthropology* 16: 3–30.

——1984. The transformations of Asiatic formations: The case of late Prehispanic Mesoamerica. In M. Spriggs (ed.), *Marxist Perspectives in Archaeology*. Cambridge: Cambridge University Press, pp. 135–148.

Guidi, A. 1988. *Storia della palentologia*. Rome: Laterza & Figli.

Habermas, J. 1979. *Communication and the Evolution of Society*. Boston, MA: Beacon Press.

Hawkes, C. 1954. Archeological theory and method: Some suggestions from the Old World. *American Anthropologist* 56(2): 155–168.

Hedeager, L. 1987. Empire, frontier and barbarian hinterland: Rome and Northern Europe, A D 1–400. In M. Rowlands, M. Larsen, and K. Kristiansen (eds.), *Centre and Periphery in the Ancient World*. Cambridge: Cambridge University Press, pp. 125–140.

Hodder, I. (ed.) 1982. *Symbolic and Structural Archaeology*. Cambridge: Cambridge University Press.

——1991. Archaeological theory in contemporary European societies: The emergence of competing traditions. In I. Hodder (ed.), *Archaeological Theory in Europe: The Last Three Decades*. London: Routledge, pp. 1–24.

Kluckhohn, C. 1939. The place of theory in anthropological studies. *Philosophy of Science* 6(3): 328–344.

——1940. The conceptual structure in Middle American studies. In C. L. Hay, R. L. Linton, S. K. Lothrop, H. L. Shapiro, and G. C. Vaillant (eds.), *The Maya and Their Neighbors*. New York: Appleton-Century, pp. 41–51.

Kohl, P. 1976. The balance of trade in Southwestern Asia in the mid-third millennium B.C. *Current Anthropology* 19(3): 463–492.

——1981. Materialist approaches in prehistory. *Annual Review of Anthropology* 10: 89–118.

——1991. Foreword. In I. M. Diakonoff (ed.), *Early Antiquity*. Chicago: University of Chicago Press, pp. vii–xxiii.

Kristiansen, K. 1982. The formation of tribal systems in later European prehistory: Northern Europe 4000–500 B.C. In C. Renfrew, M. J. Rowlands, and B. A. Segraves (eds.), *Theory and Explanation in Archaeology*. New York: Academic Press, pp. 241–280.

Larsen, M. T. 1979. The tradition of empire in Mesopotamia. In M. T. Larsen (ed.), *Power and Propaganda: A Symposium on Early Empires*. Mesopotamia: Copenhagen Studies in Assyriology 7. Copenhagen: Akademisk Forlag, pp. 75–105.

Leacock, E. B. 1982. Marxism and anthropology. In B. Ollman and E. Vernoff (eds.), *The Academy Left: Marxist Scholarship on American Campuses. New York: McGraw-Hill, pp. 242–276.*

Leone, M. P. 1994. The archaeology of ideology: Archaeological work at Annapolis since 1981. In P. A. Shackel and B. J. Little (eds.), *Historical Archaeology of the* Chesapeake. Washington, DC: Smithsonian Institution Press, pp. 215–229.

——1995. A historical archaeology of capitalism. *American Anthropologist* 97(2): 251–268.

——, and S. D. Hurry. 1998. Seeing: The power of town planning in the Chesapeake. *Historical Archaeology* 32(4): 34–62.

Leone, M. P., P. B. Potter, Jr., and P. A. Shackel. 1987. Toward a critical archaeology. *Current Anthropology* 28(3): 283–302.

Liverani, M. 1991. *Antico oriente: Storia, società, economia*. Rome: Laterza & Figli.

Lukács, G. 1971 [1922]. Reification and the consciousness of the proletariat. In *History and Class Consciousness: Studies in Marxist Dialectics*. Cambridge, MA: MIT Press, pp. 83–222.

Lumbreras, L. 1974. *La arqueología como ciencia social*. Lima: Ediciones Histar.

Marquardt, W. H. 1992. Dialectical archaeology. In M. B. Schiffer (ed.), *Archaeological Method and Theory*, Vol. 4. Tucson: University of Arizona Press, pp. 101–140.

McGuire, R. H. 1992. *A Marxist Archaeology*. San Diego, CA: Academic Press.

——1997. Why have archaeologists thought the real Indians were dead and what can we do about it? In T. Biolsi and L. J. Zimmerman (eds.), *Indians and Anthropologists: Vine Deloria Jr. and the Critique of Anthropology*. Tucson: University of Arizona Press, pp. 63–91.

——, and D. J. Saitta. 1996. Although they have petty captains, they obey them badly: The dialectics of Prehispanic Western Pueblo social organization. *American Antiquity* 61(2): 197–216.

Miller, D., and C. Tilley (eds.) 1984. *Ideology, Power and Prehistory*. Cambridge: Cambridge University Press.

Millon, R. 1954. Irrigation at Teotihuacan. *American Antiquity* XX(2): 177–180.

Montané, J. 1980. *Marxismo y arqueología*. México, DF: Ediciones de Cultura Popular.

Muller, J. 1997. *Mississippian Political Economy*. New York: Plenum.

Olivé Negrete, J. C. 1958. Estructura y dinámica de Mesoamérica. *Acta Antropológica*, época 2, 1(3), 00–00.

——1987. The presence of Vere Gordon Childe in Mexican archaeology. In L. Manzanilla (ed.), *Studies in the Neolithic and Urban Revolutions: The V. Gordon Childe Colloquium, Mexico, 1986*. Oxford: BAR International Series 349, pp. 9–17.

Orser, C. E., Jr. 1990. Archaeological approaches to New World plantation slavery. In M. B. Schiffer (ed.), *Archaeological Method and Theory*, Vol. 2. Tucson: University of Arizona Press, pp. 111–154.

——1991. The continued pattern of dominance: Landlord and tenant on the postbellum cotton plantation. In R. H. McGuire and R. Paynter (eds.), *The Archaeology of Inequality*. Oxford: Basil Blackwell, pp. 40–54.

——1996. Historical archaeology for the world. *World Archaeology Bulletin* 7: 2–5.

——1999. Archaeology and the challenges of capitalist farm tenancy in America. In M. P. Leone and P. B. Potter, Jr. (eds.), *The Historical Archaeologies of Capitalism*. New York: Kluwer/ Plenum, pp. 143–168.

Parker Pearson, M. 1984. Social change, ideology and the archaeological record. In M. Spriggs (ed.), *Marxist Perspectives in Archaeology*. Cambridge: Cambridge University Press, pp. 59–71.

Patterson, T. C. 1981. *Archaeology: The Evolution of Ancient Societies*. Englewood Cliffs, NJ: Prentice-Hall.

——1986. The last sixty years: Toward a social history of Americanist archaeology in the United States. *American Anthropologist* 88(1): 1–26.

——1991. *The Inca Empire: The Formation and Disintegration of a Pre-Capitalist State*. Oxford: Berg.

——1994a. Social archaeology in Latin America: An appreciation. *American Antiquity* 59(3): 531–537.

——1994b. *The Theory and Practice of Archaeology: A Workbook*. Rev. 2nd edn. Englewood Cliffs, NJ: Prentice-Hall.

——1995. *Toward a Social History of Archaeology in the United States*. Fort Worth, TX: Harcourt, Brace.

——1999. The political economy of archaeology in the United States. *Annual Review of Anthropology* 28: 155–174.

——2001. Diversity and archaeology. In I. Susser and T. C. Patterson (eds.), *Cultural Diversity in the United States: A Critical Reader*. Oxford: Blackwell, pp. 140–154.

Paynter, R. 1985. Surplus flow between frontiers and homelands. In S. W. Green and S. M. Perlman (eds.), *The Archeology of Frontiers and Boundaries*. Orlando, FL: Academic Press, pp. 163–211.

——1988. Steps to an archaeology of capitalism: Material change and class analysis. In M. P. Leone and P. B. Potter, Jr., *The Recovery of Meaning: Historical Archaeology in the Eastern United States*. Washington, DC: Smithsonian Institution Press, pp. 407–433.

Peace, W. J. 1992. The Enigmatic Career of Vere Gordon Childe: A Peculiar and Individual Manifestation of the Human Spirit. Ph.D. Dissertation in Anthropology, Columbia University. Ann Arbor, MI: University Microfilm International 94221386.

Redman, C. L., E. V. Curtin, N. M. Versaggi, and J. C. Wanser. 1978. Social archaeology: The future of the past. In C. L. Redman, M. J. Berman, E. V. Curtin, W. T. Langhorne, Jr., N. M. Versaggi, and J. C. Wanser (eds.), *Social Archaeology: Beyond Subsistence and Dating*. New York: Academic Press, pp. 1–18.

Renfrew, C. 1984. Social archaeology, societal change and generalisation. In *Approaches to Social Archaeology*. Edinburgh: Edinburgh University Press, pp. 3–21.

Resnick, S. A., and R. D. Wolff. 1987. *Knowledge and Class: A Marxian Critique of Political Economy*. Chicago: University of Chicago Press.

Rowe, J. H. 1959. Archaeological dating and cultural process. *Southwestern Journal of Anthropology* 15(4): 317–324.

——1962. Stages and periods in archaeological interpretation. *Southwestern Journal of Anthropology* 18(1): 40–54.

Rowlands, M. 1987. Centre and periphery: A review of concepts. In M. Rowlands, M. Larsen, and K. Kristiansen (eds.), *Centre and Periphery in the Ancient World*. Cambridge: Cambridge University Press, pp. 1–11.

Sanoja, M., and I. Vargas Arenas. 1978. *Antiguas formaciones y modos de producción venezolanos*. 2nd edn. Caracas: Monte Avila.

Saunders, T. 1990. Prestige and exchange: Althusser and structuralist–Marxist archaeology. In F. Baker and J. Thomas (eds.), *Writing the Past in the Present*. Lampeter: St. David's University College, pp. 69–77.

Schrecker, E. W. 1986. *No Ivory Tower: McCarthyism and the Universities*. New York: Oxford University Press.

Smith, M. A. 1955. The limitations of inference in archaeology. *Archaeology News Letter* 6(1): 3–7.

Spriggs, M. (ed.) 1984. *Marxist Perspectives in Archaeology*. Cambridge: Cambridge University Press.

Steward, J. H., and F. M. Setzler. 1938. Function and configuration in archaeology. *American Antiquity* IV(1): 4–10.

Strong, W. D. 1936. Anthropological theory and archaeological fact. In R. H. Lowie (ed.), *Essays in Anthropology in Honor of Alfred Louis Kroeber*. Berkeley: University of California Press, pp. 359–370.

Taylor, W. W. 1948. *A Study of Archeology*. Menasha, WI: Memoirs of the American Anthropological Association 69.

Tosi, M. 1977. The archaeological evidence for protostate structures in eastern Iran and central Asia at the end of the 3rd millennium B.C. In J. Deschayes (ed.), *Le Plateau Iranien et l'Asie Centrale des origines à la conquête islamique*. Paris: Colloques Internationaux du Centre National de la Recherche Scientifique 567, pp. 45–66.

Trigger, B. G. 1967. Engels on the part played by labour in the transition from ape to man: An anticipation of contemporary anthropological theory. *Canadian Review of Sociology and Anthropology* 4(2): 165–176.

——1984. Alternative archaeologies: Nationalist, colonialist, imperialist. *Man* 19(3): 355–370.

——1985. The past as power: Anthropology and the North American Indian. In I. McBryde (ed.), *Who Owns the Past?* Oxford: Oxford University Press, pp. 49–74.

——1990. Maintaining economic equality in opposition to complexity: An Iroquoian case study. In S. Upham (ed.), *The Evolution of Political Systems: Sociopolitics in Small-Scale Sedentary Societies*. Cambridge: Cambridge University Press, pp. 119–145.

——1993. Marxism in contemporary Western archaeology. In M. B. Schiffer (ed.), *Archaeological Method and Theory*, Vol. 5. Tucson: University of Arizona Press, pp. 159–200.

Vargas Arenas, I. 1990. *Arqueología, ciencia y sociedad: Ensayo sobre teoría y la formación económico social tribal en Venezuela*. Caracas: Editorial Abre Brecha.

Vázquez Varela, J. M., and Risch, R. 1991. Theory in Spanish archaeology since 1960. In I. Hodder (ed.), *Archaeological Theory in Europe: The Last Three Decades*. London: Routledge, pp. 25–51.

Wallerstein, I. 1974. *The Modern World-System: Capitalist Agriculture and the Origins of the European World-Economy in the Sixteenth Century*, Vol. 1. New York: Academic Press.

Wolf, E. 1959. *Sons of the Shaking Earth*. Chicago: University of Chicago Press.

Wylie, A. 1982. Positivism and the New Archaeology. Ph.D. dissertation in philosophy, State University of New York at Binghamton. Ann Arbor, MI: University Microfilms International no. 8201043.

Zagarell, A. 1986. Structural discontinuity – A critical factor in the emergence of primary and secondary states. *Dialectical Anthropology* 10(3–4): 155–179.

4

Embodied Subjectivity: Gender, Femininity, Masculinity, Sexuality

Rosemary A. Joyce

Central to what we might think of as the "socialization" of archaeology since the early 1980s have been concerns with the exploration of ancient subjectivities. These concerns cannot simply be equated with earlier debates about the place of the individual in archaeology (e.g., Hill and Gunn 1978). As Ian Hodder (1992: 98–99) perceptively noted in 1982, this earlier concern with the place of the individual was limited by functionalism that allowed "little emphasis to individual creativity and intentionality. Individual human beings become little more than the means to achieve the needs of society.... Adequate explanations of social systems and social change must involve the individual's assessments and aims. This is not a question of identifying individuals...but of introducing the individual into social theory" (see also Hodder 2000). Whether or not archaeologists can identify specific, individual historical persons, as they can where rich textual records can be related to archaeological remains (e.g., Meskell 1998a, 2002), their models either explicitly posit specifically situated subjects or they risk implicitly assuming an undifferentiated subject who tends to approximate the self-contained, rational, implicitly masculine individual of modern social thought.

Construed as social subjects, actors in the past must be theorized as specifically situated: as men and women, children and elders, celibate and sexually active, and above all constantly in a state of transformation. Archaeologists interested in theorizing agency have realized that, in the absence of specificity about the subjectivity of the agent, it is likely that they will reproduce an emphasis on a few "hyperactive" agents like those that have been the subject of critiques of methodological individualism (Clark 2000). Archaeological attention to subjectivity thus raises important questions about the status of the person and of individuality in the past. It also should bring into focus consideration of the embodied subject in archaeology, particularly given the key role archaeology can play in contemporary interests in historicizing embodiment (Meskell and Joyce 2003).

Studies of embodiment are a central part of contemporary explorations of subjectivity in the social sciences. A long Western tradition privileged the mind as a non-material site of identity, opposed to the body, seen as an object of cognition, separable from the thinking subject's mind (Grosz 1994: 3–10; Turner 1984: 30–59; cf. Knapp and Meskell 1997: 183–187). The body had needs or desires that stood in the way of the realization of full subjectivity and that had to be subordinated to the ends of society (Turner 1984: 10–22; see also Turner 1991; Frank 1991). Against this tradition, phenomenological approaches offer a vision of the body as "both an object for others and a subject for myself" (Merleau-Ponty 1962: 167). For Merleau-Ponty, the body is "the instrument by which all information and knowledge is received and meaning is generated. It is through the body that the world of objects appears to me; it is in virtue of having/being a body that there are objects for me" (Grosz 1994: 87; see pp. 86–111 for a critique from a feminist perspective of the universalism of Merleau-Ponty's phenomenological project). Anthropologist Thomas Csordas (1994: 7–10) considers further implications of taking embodiment as the ground of subjectivity, linking this perspective to Charles Taylor's (1985, 1989) critiques of subjectivity as the projection of internal, monological, self-representation, and to anthropologist Michael Jackson's (1989) "radical empiricism." Csordas (1994: 10–11) suggests that these approaches to embodiment converge in an emphasis on "lived experience" or "being-in-the-world" that requires a hermeneutic interpretive perspective in place of a semiotic one, and a shift from analysis of an objectified "body" to active "embodiment." At the present time, little archaeological work fully takes these currents of social theory into account.

In archaeology, related concerns have a history that can be traced most readily to roots in the archaeology of gender, as discussed in greater detail below. Similar issues also arise in household archaeology (Hendon, chapter 12, this volume), social theory of materiality, and analyses of temporality. In its attention to the materiality and historicization of embodied subjectivity, archaeology is in a position to contribute substantively to wider social theory, beyond its present use as a source of exotic examples to support positions in contemporary debates. To realize that potential, archaeologists will need to consistently emphasize the distinctive aspects of our analyses while making use of the most contemporary social theory.

Where We Are Today

With the almost simultaneous publication of collections of papers devoted to sexuality (Schmidt and Voss 2000) and queer theory (*World Archaeology* vol. 32, 2000), and of sustained studies of specific ancient societies and historical traditions that treat questions of embodiment as open to archaeological examination (e.g., Joyce 2001a; Meskell 1999), it would seem that sexually embodied subjects at last are an acknowledged focus of archaeological analyses. Of course, any such inference would need to be moderated by observing that mainstream archaeological writing has hardly accepted gender as a central dimension of social difference, and has not embraced the experience of embodiment as an archaeological subject. Discussion of some topics – sexuality perhaps most obviously – continues to be treated for the most part as ungrounded speculation going far beyond what we can know archaeologically.

The substantive contributions made by archaeological investigations of embodiment refute such characterizations, and demonstrate the importance of reflexive, theoretically grounded, sustained analyses. For example, a number of archaeologists have invoked the work of Judith Butler (1990, 1993) in studies of embodiment in settings ranging from the ancient Mediterranean (Alberti 2001) to the Prehispanic Southwest United States (Perry and Joyce 2001: 66–72). At a minimum, archaeologists draw on Butler to support the argument that "there is no atemporal, fixed 'core' to a person's identity... outside the acts and gestures that constitute it" (Alberti 2001: 190). Rather than constituting unfettered performance of idiosyncratic gender identities, the centrality of performative *citation* of precedents for embodiment has been critical to the integration of Butler's work in archaeology, providing grounds to explore both individual subjectivity and sociality. Thus, Alberti (2001: 194) argues that the reproduction of categorical relations of similarity among figurines produced in Knossos can best be understood as the result of citation of prior practices, rather than as the representation of predetermined universals of sex. He suggests that on these figurines, "breasts are an integral part of the costume of the figurines" that helps to produce a legible gender representation through citation of embodied sexed subjectivities (Alberti 2001: 200).

Citationality has been critical in linking Butler's work to archaeological investigations. Butler argued that an unwarranted presumption of the natural priority of the body undercut the claim that genders were culturally distinct ways of interpreting a given, prediscursively sexed body (Butler 1990: 24–25). Instead, she argued that gender performance produced, as one of its effects, an impression of the priority of sex (Butler 1990: 7). The illusion that the body is a natural given is thus a byproduct of discourse about bodily materiality within society (Butler 1993: 1–16). This does not represent an evasion of the materiality of bodies, but rather a critical realization that we always experience our body through the mediation of cultural concepts. Materiality is critical to the production and reproduction of sex, and other aspects of subjectivity, and is fundamental to Butler's (1993: 12–16, 101–119) concept of performance. For Butler, performance is not a theatrical free play unconstrained by social or material factors. Instead, performance is discussed as a repeated citation of a disciplinary norm, a largely or normally nondiscursive (not prediscursive) enactment of a mode of being shaped by culturally situated precedents, that in turn shapes new cultural performances.

Rosemary Joyce (1998, 2000a, 2000b, 2001a, 2001b, 2002a, 2002b) has carried out a series of analyses of Central American materials that demonstrate how Butler's theoretical perspectives transform a wide range of archaeological remains into potential evidence for embodiment. Joyce takes embodiment as the shaping of the physical person as the site of the experience of subjectivity, a shaping that is simultaneously the product of material and discursive actions. She traces connections between the manufacture of objects (such as ceramic and stone vessels and figurines) representing isolated body parts (notably the head, but also legs, feet, and hands) and of other objects used in practices of body ornamentation that marked the same sites on the body (such as ear ornaments), and identifies traces of post-mortem body-processing in burials in which the same body parts (e.g., crania) were singled out for continued attention (Joyce 1998). The recursive relationships Joyce identifies between the treatment of living bodies, bodies of the deceased, and manufactured objects foregrounds the critical role of material objects, including but not limited to human representations, as precedents for repeated performances aimed at approximating, or in Butler's terms, citing, bodily ideals.

Joyce (2000a) extended this theoretical perspective to an analysis of actions through which children were transformed into adults with specific subject positions within late prehispanic Aztec society, identifying ear ornaments as particularly significant material media for the materialization of adult embodiment. Joyce (2000b, 2002a, 2002b) further pursues the implication that human bodies represented in artworks served as idealized precedents toward which successive generations of youths aspired in a series of articles concerned with the predominance of youthful bodies, primarily those of young men, as objects of the gaze of spectators within and outside artworks and performances in Precolumbian Maya and Aztec societies. By pursuing links between human representations, objects used to adorn bodies, and the physical alteration of bodies to approximate ideals, Joyce demonstrates that embodiment and aspects of subjectivity such as desire, central to sexuality, can be open to archaeological investigation.

Despite the relatively recent history of explicit attention to sexuality, archaeological explorations of sexual sites, practices, and desires have already been attempted for a wide range of societies. The inclusion of sexual attraction as one of the factors shaping material culture has transformed understanding of images previously analyzed primarily in terms of fertility, and has expanded the consideration of sexuality to encompass masculinity and same-sex desires and practices. Zainab Bahrani (1996) argues that nudity and explicit depiction of the body of Mesopotamian female figures referenced female sexual pleasure (Marcus, 1993, 1996). Meskell (1999: 94–103, 2000, 2002) shows that sexuality was integrated throughout New Kingdom Egyptian life, not segregated in a separate sphere, and demonstrates that male sexual pleasure and male–male sexuality were subject to representation without apparent stigma. Joyce (2000b) explores similar evidence for homoerotics in Classic Maya society that she demonstrates is not based on an opposition of heterosexuality and homosexuality, since the same representations of youthful male bodies are the subject of both female and male gaze (Joyce 2002a; cf. Stone 1988). Gilchrist (1994, 1997, 2000) has broadened consideration of sexual subjectivity to explicitly encompass celibate subjects usually entirely absent from archaeological interpretations, despite historical indications that celibacy was significant in a number of cultural traditions and historical moments. Multiple historical archaeological studies directly address the identification of sites of sexual practices that would have been stigmatized, such as prostitution (Costello 2000; Siefert, O'Brien, and Balicki 2000) and magical practices related to sexuality (Wilkie 2000).

An archaeology of the embodied subject is a necessary requirement for the pursuit of any of the currently valued perspectives in archaeology drawing on broader social theories of practice, structuration, and agency. There can be no such thing as a generalized agent or actor. Each agent or actor is specifically situated within society and history in such a way that what that agent sees as possible and valuable to attempt is related to the agent's own subjectivity. Similarly, phenomenological approaches in archaeology demand attention to the experience of embodied subjects, and these again must be specifically situated.

The relatively small group of articles published to date that deal with masculinity demonstrate the close connection between theoretical perspectives grappling with agency and experience and the requirement for an explicit concern with embodied subjectivities. One of the earliest explicit attempts to pursue an archaeology of masculinity was developed by Timothy Yates (1993; see also Nordbladh and Yates 1990) in order to address the interpretation of human figural representations in Norwegian rock art. His survey of these images defines explicit sexual characteristics identified as evidence of male sexual identity, but also includes delineation of prominent calf muscles as a possible marker of a particular kind of male body (Yates 1993:35–36; cf. Parkington 2002:106–113). Yates (1993:41–48) thus identifies representational schema depicting distinct masculinities, contrasting in their degree of phallicism and aggression. His analysis of these images led him to consider theories of subjective formation of the self and its relation to embodiment in order to better specify the conditions required for theorizing an active social agent (Yates 1993:60). Yates (1993:62–64) juxtaposed his analysis of representations of embodied difference to an analysis of difference (or the lack thereof) in contemporary burials. While his treatment of the body as a surface open to apparently unconstrained signification exemplifies a weakness shared with a number of other studies of embodiment, Yates has rightly been singled out for praise for his serious and pathbreaking exploration of embodiment as the ground for masculinity (Meskell 1996: 7). Few other studies at the time even treated the male body, leading Meskell (1996:4–5) to caution that "the body" in archaeology was unselfconsciously being constituted as inherently feminine.

Practice theory in particular should encourage archaeologists to examine the objects and settings that disciplined past bodies over time, contributing to creating shared, largely uninterrogated ways of acting and the reflexive self-monitoring through which social structures are reproduced. Sophisticated research on embodiment replaces the identification and description of objects that signal gender status (gender attribution) with exploration of how the experience of being gendered (and sexed, and aged) was induced through the habitual use of specific modes of dress, of working with specific tools, and of inhabiting specific spaces (see Perry and Joyce 2001). This alternative way of examining artifacts in search of sexually embodied subjects is as likely to create avenues to examine masculinity as it is to bring to light unexamined femininities. In another early study of masculinity, Treherne (1995) argued that a material culture devoted to body modification that developed in Bronze Age Europe was evidence of an ideal of the beautiful body of the male warrior. His arguments can be criticized for their broad temporal and regional sweep. More recent analysis of the material culture of a college fraternity, one of the historically recorded institutions through which upper-class masculinity was reproduced in American universities at the turn of the twentieth century (Wilkie 1998), exemplifies the great potential of such analyses when temporal and spatial control are stronger.

Theories of practice (in the broad sense) suggest that subjectivity is complex and interactive, continually in a process of being shaped and reshaped. This process of shaping, partly a project of the self and partly the regulation of the self by other social actors, has become a focus of contemporary archaeologies of embodied subjectivity, often explicitly grounded in phenomenological thought, partly displacing earlier conceptualizations of the subject in terms of static categories (e.g., Meskell and Joyce 2003). Categorical conceptualizations of identity, although thoroughly critiqued throughout their history of investigation, persist as objects of study for many archaeologists who explicitly identify with an archaeology of gender but decline to consider embodiment and sexuality as part of their explorations. To understand both why these earlier concerns persist untouched by critique and unmoved by the positive attractions of more complex approaches to embodied subjectivity, we need to take a brief look at

the history of the development of the archaeology of gender and the growth of archaeologies of sexuality and embodiment from those roots.

How We Got Here

Many studies of the eruption of gender as an archaeological topic have stressed the
diversity of research projects that were pursued by the large number of writers, the
majority women, who explicitly identified gender as an object of their archaeological
analyses in the 1980s. Perhaps most useful for understanding the implications of the
development of gender as a topic by a diverse group of scholars simultaneously pursuing
multiple different agendas is Alison Wylie's (1991:31–32, 38–41) classic discrimination
between three projects pursued under the common rubric of archaeology of gender: a
critique of androcentrism; a "remedial" recovery of women; and a re-examination of
naturalized assumptions in which "gender relations and gender must be treated as
contextually and historically specific constructs" (p. 40) and "localized strategies by
which social categories and structures are constructed" (p. 41) become central objects of
analysis. As Wylie notes, these projects cannot simply be considered stages in a temporal
sequence. But pursuit of the third project, re-examining naturalized assumptions, does
seem to lag behind critiques of androcentrism and remedial research on women, which
take place in parallel and are based on shared assumptions. The first two projects can, to
a great extent, assume a female subject as a focus; the third project by definition has
to critically examine the stability of the category "woman" itself. The first two projects
can fit comfortably within a positivist framework while the last challenges it and
demands hermeneutic approaches, consistent with Csordas's (1994:11) linking of phenomenological approaches to embodiment and hermeneutic strategies of interpretation.

Because the first two projects developed rapidly and at the same time, gender
archaeology as it initially developed was made coherent by an emphasis on women as
an improperly understudied category of actors in the past. The essentialism involved in
identifying women as an object of analysis transhistorically was not foregrounded,
particularly because, whatever the weaknesses of specific studies, many richly detailed
and highly original archaeological analyses were produced by archaeologists pursuing
these two projects. In its task of identifying a second, understudied group that contrasted with the implicitly male subject of mainstream archaeology, the gender archaeology of the 1980s and early 1990s often employed an implicit or explicit structural
analysis. Women's tools, spaces, and images could be identified whenever a contrast
could be drawn with tools, spaces, and images understood as those of an equally
unitary male subject. Questions of embodied subjects and their experiences of sexuality
and gender were subordinated to the identification of structural classes most easily
perceived in terms of fixed positions in divisions of labor, social organization, and
political hierarchies. But even initial structural studies raised issues of embodiment and
sexuality, as when the stereotyping of weaving and spinning as "typical" female labor
among the Aztecs was shown to be related to metaphors of public dancing and sexual
intercourse (McCafferty and McCafferty 1991:23–25).

Embodiment, personhood, and individuality routinely cropped up as issues in
figurine studies and burial analyses pursued as part of the initial projects of gender

archaeology. Burials appeared to promise a specially privileged site for exploration of gender, understood variably but always in relation to sexed being. Starting in the 1960s, mortuary studies operated with an explicit theory of individual identity in which a person's categorical roles during life, including sex, were reflected in burial. Multiple critiques of the model of personhood that supported mortuary analysis were produced throughout the 1980s and 1990s, leading to an understanding of mortuary contexts as charged sites where personhood and social relations were formulated and transformed (see Gillespie 2001). Under the programmatic assumptions of mortuary studies, sex, taken as the ground of gender, could theoretically be independently assessed using culture-free biological criteria. In the continuing development of this generalizing project, skeletal remains identified as male or female are viewed as recording traces of habitual action by the individual person, which can be compared categorically as indications of gendered behavior (Cohen and Bennett 1993). But even when such traces of individual experience are abstracted as attributes of a categorical kind, they simultaneously constitute evidence of unique and irreducible biographies of specific bodies, specific persons.

Early on, the tendency of burial populations to exhibit features that resisted dichotomous classification, or to have noncoincident patterns of biological sex and other dichotomous traits, served as a spur for analyses that began to examine a broader range of aspects of difference, including age and social rank. Some key studies of sexuality, particularly work on the potential to recognize third or additional genders, also built on nondichotomous variability in burial populations.

Sandra Hollimon (1997, 2000) explicitly aimed at evaluating whether archaeological mortuary assemblages would allow identification of persons of third-gender status historically attested in numerous Native American societies (compare Schmidt 2000 for a parallel inquiry for the European Mesolithic). Hollimon documented considerable experiential diversity based on descriptions of the lives and actions of historical individuals who occupied such third-gender statuses among the California Indian groups she studied. Nonetheless, she was tentatively able to identify burials of individuals who possibly occupied such statuses (Hollimon 1997:186–188). The proportion of possible third-gender individuals identified in Hollimon's Chumash population was comparable to ethnographically reported frequencies. The criteria she found useful included both artifact patterns (although no simple binary sexual patterns of artifact use were established overall) and osteological evidence of habitual actions.

Perhaps most intriguing was Hollimon's observation that in the California groups she studied, the third gender was effectively an "undertaking gender" (ibid.: 182–183), defined by a set of practices that have no recognizable link to reproductive sexuality but were closely related in native thought to the spiritually powerful sexual status of a third-gender person. In a later study amplifying her engagement with the question of third-gender individuals in Chumash society, Hollimon (2000) pursued the links between nonprocreative sexuality and the special status required for undertaking. As Hollimon's work exemplifies, burial studies, as a methodological subset of work on gender in archaeology, required a re-engagement with gender as sexed experience, enacted through a body. Burial studies forcefully posed questions of the experiences of the person and of individuality that more categorical gender studies in archaeology did not bring into focus.

The challenges posed to an explicit archaeology of gender by figurine studies similarly led to renewed attention to the conjunction of embodiment, sexuality, and personhood. Like burial analyses, figurine studies have enjoyed a long history of explicit engagement with a practice of sexing, and of theorization, however impoverished, about relations between material traces and the actual life experiences of categories of people and of individuals. Until very recently, hand-modeled figurines from Paleolithic and Neolithic Europe, and Archaic and Formative societies of the Americas, were commonly viewed even within archaeology as evidence of "fertility cults" centered on women's bodies (e.g., Roosevelt 1988). Debate about the implications of Upper Palaeolithic images popularly labeled "Venus" figurines for understanding embodiment and sexuality charts changing approaches and continuing controversies in archaeology.

At the beginning of the 1980s, it was possible to argue that Upper Palaeolithic European figurines were regarded by most archaeologists as related to fertility (Rice 1982). Classifying a sample of these figurines in terms of the apparent depiction of bodily features correlated with changes over the life course of reproductive females, Rice (1982:409–412) suggested that the answer to the question of why these images were created would most likely come from the specific "cultural life" of the group, rather than from a universal concern with fertility and reproduction. Rice raised the issue of the significance of theorizing the standpoint of figurine makers and users, noting the potential for differences in attitudes of women toward self-representation and men toward representation of others that could only be understood by positing the sex of figurine makers.

By the mid-1990s, the terms of engagement had changed, and debate about the rationale for production of the figurines moved to the intentions of artists. Those who argued for male figurine makers, based on the assumption that the figurines sexualized female bodies as objects for male viewers, were roundly criticized for assuming a stable, modern, heterosexist erotics (see Dobres 1992a:10–18, 1992b). New arguments were proposed for female figurine makers, based on the assertion that the figurines realistically depict limitations of self-observation and portrayal of the artist's own body (e.g., McCoid and McDermott 1996; McDermott 1996). The argument that the makers were females observing their own bodies by looking down at them from a standing position assumed that the subjective consciousness of women figurine makers was most significantly shaped by experiences of pregnancy, ironically keeping intact an assumed transhistorical meaning of the female body.

Nonetheless, this analysis raised the issues of reflexivity, of the effects of making images on self-perception, and of self-perception on representation, that haunts all attempts to use representations as evidence for ancient personhood. McDermott (1996:247) argued that these figurines were "self-portraits centered on individual reproductive events," by and of specific pregnant women recording their self-consciousness about their changing bodies. As Whitney Davis (1996) cautioned, even if a particular visual perspective is convincingly demonstrated, such an analysis cannot imagine unmediated observation and representation, since objects like Upper Palaeolithic figurines require both a process of transcription of observed reality and of fabrication through which distance between self-consciousness and representation is introduced: "to 'represent' the 'self' is to treat it as an object. What has its origin in . . . egocentricity, modulates into the experience of the alienated social person or 'subject'" (p. 252). James Elkins (1996:255) was pressed by the same analysis to urge engagement with the work of Merleau-Ponty, arguing that his "phenomenology of the body stresses the unproportional, unoptical possibilities that follow on a more somatic, less visual aware-ness of the body: for example, a foot or a hand might be depicted overly large because it is experienced that way."

Other approaches to figurines as individualistic representations took these prob-lems of representation more seriously (e.g., Bailey 1994; Knapp and Meskell 1997; Kokkinidou 1997). Combining these approaches to personhood with categorical ana-lyses of gender, not only identifications of gendered forms of embodiment but also of cross-cutting dimensions of bodily experience, could be identified as subjects of self-conscious reflection by the persons who created these images in the past. Embodiment itself could be seen as a topic of past concern, toward which an extraordinary array of body practices were directed, whose traces archaeologists encounter in other parts of archaeological assemblages. Everything from the provision of food, to the practice of sports, and the use of specific ornaments that engaged people in the past in the modification of their bodies, came into focus as evidence for studies of embodiment and its experience in the past (e.g., Alberti 2001; Hamilakis 1999; Hamilakis, Pluciennik, and Tarlow 2002; Joyce 2002b; Loren 2001; Meskell and Joyce 2003).

Some of the earliest forays into exploration of sexuality using archaeological mate-rials emerged from art history, both in the ancient world (Kampen 1996; Brown 1997) and in the Americas (Miller 1988). While much of this literature involved analysis of representations, some authors made connections between representation and experi-ence, and interpreted the use of archaeologically recovered artifacts in terms of femi-ninities, masculinities, and sexualities (e.g., Stone 1988; Winter 1989, 1996). Although there are exceptions, most of this literature assumed a binary sex/gender model. In addition, as Meskell (1996) noted in an influential paper, archaeological writing tended to equate the body with women, or women with the body (see also Meskell 1998b). Contributions to an emerging archaeology of masculinity in the 1990s (e.g., Knapp 1998; Nordbladh and Yates 1990; Treherne 1995; Yates 1993) necessarily contested this conflation (see also Knapp and Meskell 1997).

Where Do We Go from Here?

Given this brief sketch of the trajectory of archaeological attention to embodiment, it is surprising that there still are very few studies that take up fully and forthrightly issues of embodied experience, except those experiences that can be taken as specific to women and therefore, as feminist social theorists have long noted, most easily treated as "natural" (see Meskell 1996). The number of articles treating male subjectivity and sexuality can still be individually enumerated and discussed in a short article, long after the production of work on female experience has outstripped even the most dedicated attempts at bibliographic tracking.

Some progress in broadening consideration of embodied subjectivity in archaeology has been made by analysts concerned explicitly with variation in age within what traditionally have been treated as unitary male and female categories. Thus, for example, Cyphers Guillén (1993) identified representations of distinct stages in the female life course in a sample of figurines from Formative period Central Mexico. Richard Lesure's studies of figurines from Formative period Pacific coastal Mexico explored cross-cutting dimensions of sex and age, identifying the assemblage as composed of representations of male and female elders and of young women (Lesure 1997). Both analysts argue that what is represented is an outcome of the way that these societies differentially valued different bodies, particularly as they underwent changes over individual lives (see also Gilchrist, Chapter 6).

These and other contributions to archaeological research on aging and the life course seem unlikely to lead to a sealed-off "archaeology of children," a fate that seems to have befallen work on archaeology of gender, which has been accepted in "normative" archaeology as an added topic of special interest to some people – primarily women – but not of general significance. Childhood, as a topic, demands consideration as part of a process, because no one thinks of the child status as one that is permanent. As a consequence, archaeological work on childhood and aging may be one way of continuing the project of examining the formation, structuration, and resignification of embodied subjectivity as a dynamic experience.

Another promising avenue for maintaining momentum in the archaeological analysis of embodiment is the current broadening of perspectives drawn from wider social theory. The unproductive tendency to divide archaeology into two camps, one materialist and the other idealist, is no longer convincing or tenable. Archaeology that might once have been seen as processualist has, with the integration of perspectives from theories of agency, structuration, and practice, introduced necessary attention to human action, motivations, and dispositions, differing between differently positioned subjects (Pauketat 2001). Archaeology explicitly grounded in the tradition labeled postprocessual has turned from the use of discourse as a metaphor for all experience to examination of materiality and experience as points of intersection of past structuration and present interpretation (e.g., Meskell 1999). But while the breaking down of this unproductive divide has revitalized archaeology rooted in each of the major contemporary traditions, it has not necessarily provided theoretical resources best suited for pursuing archaeologies of embodiment in the most thoroughgoing fashion.

Among the strands of social theory for a materially based exploration of past experiences of embodiment, phenomenological and feminist theories of subjectivity would seem to be particularly promising (Meskell and Joyce 2003). A phenomenological perspective directs our attention to the body as the grounding of the self and the subject of perception, and to the recursive experience of discovery of the world and the self through the body (Merleau-Ponty 1962). Butler's (1990, 1993) insistence on the reproduction of embodiment as a process of citation, repetition aimed at recapitulating precedents internalized as ideals that one always falls short of reproducing, has already proved useful for a number of archaeologists (Perry and Joyce 2001; see Alberti 2001; Joyce 1998, 2000a, 2001b). Comparative analyses of the historical development of theories of embodiment (Laqueur 1990) already inform contemporary archaeology, and could be more influential in directing archaeologists to explore how experience, representation, and ideas about embodiment might have been intertwined. Feminist analyses of embodiment and the formation of subjectivity (e.g., Grosz 1994) could be applied more broadly to sustain interpretation of past subjectivities.

The goal of continued archaeological exploration of embodied personhood should be something more than the description of previously ignored categories of persons. Instead, we might hope to finally disassemble some of the received systems of classification that so consistently persist in archaeological analysis. Rather than seek ever more extreme examples of alternative genders or queer sexualities, we might use an archaeology of embodied personhood to consistently ask questions about how human beings in the past may have experienced their world through the body, and experienced their bodies through their specific cultural positions. Through an emphasis on the body as instrument for knowledge, an archaeology of the body might engage both with discursive forms of embodied knowledge (Johnson 1987; Lakoff and Johnson 1999) and the non-discursive experiences (Kus 1992) that we know were significant in past societies.

REFERENCES

Alberti, B. 2001. Faience goddesses and ivory bull-leapers: The aesthetics of sexual difference at late Bronze Age Knossos. *World Archaeology* 33: 189–205.

Bahrani, Z. 1996. The Hellenization of Ishtar: Nudity, fetishism, and the production of cultural differentiation in ancient art, *Oxford Art Journal* 19: 3–16.

Bailey, D. W. 1994. Reading prehistoric figurines as individuals. *World Archaeology* 25: 321–331.

Brown, S. 1997. "Ways of seeing" women in antiquity: An introduction to feminism in classical archaeology and ancient art history. In A. O. Koloski-Ostrow and C. L. Lyons (eds.), *Naked Truths: Women, Sexuality, and Gender in Classical Art and Archaeology*, London: Routledge, pp. 12–42.

Butler, J. 1990. *Gender Trouble: Feminism and the Subversion of Identity*. New York, Routledge.

—— 1993. *Bodies That Matter: On the Discursive Limits of "Sex."* New York: Routledge.

Clark, J. E. 2000. Towards a better explanation of hereditary inequality: A critical assessment of natural and historic human agents. In M-A. Dobres and J. Robb (eds.), *Agency in Archaeology*. London: Routledge, pp. 92–112.

Cohen, M. N., and S. Bennett. 1993. Skeletal evidence for sex roles and gender hierarchies in prehistory. In B. Miller (ed.), *Sex Roles and Gender Hierarchies*. Cambridge: Cambridge University Press, pp. 273–296.

Costello, J. G. 2000. *Red light voices*: An archaeological drama of late nineteenth-century prostitution. In R. Schmidt and B. Voss (eds.), *Archaeologies of Sexuality*. London: Routledge, pp. 160–175.

Csordas, T. J. 1994. Introduction: The body as representation and being-in-the-world. In T. J. Csordas (ed.), *Embodiment and Experience: The Existential Ground of Culture and Self*. Cambridge: Cambridge University Press, pp. 1–24.

Davis, W. 1996. Comment on "Self-representation in Upper Paleolithic female figurines" by L. McDermott. *Current Anthropology* 37: 251–252.

Dobres, M-A. 1992a. Re-presentations of Palaeolithic visual imagery: Simulacra and their alternatives. *Kroeber Anthropological Society Papers* 73–4: 1–25.

—— 1992b. Reconsidering Venus figurines: A feminist inspired re-analysis. In A. S. Goldsmith, S. Garvie, D. Selin, and J. Smith (eds.), *Ancient Images, Ancient Thought: The Archaeology of Ideology*. Calgary, AL: Archaeological Association of the University of Calgary, pp. 245–262.

Elkins, J. 1996. Comment on "Self-representation in Upper Paleolithic female figurines" by L. McDermott. *Current Anthropology* 37: 255–258.

Frank, A. W. 1991. For a sociology of the body: An analytical review. In M. Featherstone, M. Hepworth, and B. S. Turner (eds.), *The Body: Social Process and Cultural Theory*. London, Sage, pp. 36–102.

Gilchrist, R. 1994. *Gender and Material Culture: The Archaeology of Religious Women.* London: Routledge.

——1997. Ambivalent bodies: gender and medieval archaeology. In J. Moore and E. Scott (eds.), *Invisible People and Processes: Writing Gender and Childhood into European* Archaeology. London: Leicester University Press, pp. 88–112.

——2000. Unsexing the body: The interior sexuality of medieval religious women. In R. Schmidt and B. Voss (eds.), *Archaeologies of Sexuality.* London: Routledge, pp. 89–103.

Gillespie, S. D. 2001. Personhood, agency, and mortuary ritual: A case study from the Ancient Maya. *Journal of Anthropological Archaeology* 20: 73–112.

Grosz, E. 1994. *Volatile Bodies: Toward a Corporeal Feminism.* Bloomington: Indiana University Press.

Guillén, A. 1993. Women, rituals, and social dynamics at ancient Chalcatzingo. *Latin American Antiquity* 4: 209–224.

Hamilakis, Y. 1999. Food technologies/technologies of the body: The social context of wine and oil production and consumption in Bronze Age Crete. *World Archaeology* 31: 38–54.

——, M. Pluciennik, and S. Tarlow (eds.) *Thinking Through the Body: Archaeologies of Corporeality.* New York: Kluwer/Plenum.

Hill, J. D., and J. Gunn (eds.) 1978. *The Individual in Prehistory.* New York: Academic Press.

Hodder, I. 1992. *Theory and Practice in Archaeology.* London: Routledge.

——2000. Agency and individuals in long-term processes. In M-A. Dobres and J. E. Robb (eds.), *Agency in Archaeology.* London: Routledge, pp. 21–33.

Hollimon, S. E. 1997. The third gender in native California: Two-spirit undertakers among the Chumash and their neighbors. In C. Claassen and R. A. Joyce (eds.), *Women in Prehistory: North America and Mesoamerica.* Philadelphia: University of Pennsylvania Press, pp. 173–188.

——2000. Archaeology of the 'aqi: Gender and sexuality in prehistoric Chumash society. In R. Schmidt and B. Voss (eds.), *Archaeologies of Sexuality.* London: Routledge, pp. 179–196.

Jackson, M. 1989. *Paths Toward a Clearing: Radical Empiricism and Ethnographic Inquiry.* Bloomington: Indiana University Press.

Johnson, M. 1987. *The Body in the Mind: The Bodily Basis of Meaning, Imagination, and Reason.* Chicago: University of Chicago Press.

Joyce, R. A. 1998. Performing the body in Prehispanic Central America. *Res: Anthropology and Aesthetics* 33: 147–165.

——2000a. Girling the girl and boying the boy: The production of adulthood in ancient Mesoamerica. *World Archaeology* 31: 473–483.

——2000b. A Precolumbian gaze: Male sexuality among the Ancient Maya. In R. Schmidt and B. Voss (eds.), *Archaeologies of Sexuality.* London: Routledge, pp. 263–283.

——2001a. *Gender and Power in Prehispanic Mesoamerica.* Austin, University of Texas Press.

——2001b. Negotiating sex and gender in Classic Maya society. In C. F. Klein (ed.), *Gender in Pre-Hispanic America.* Washington, DC: Dumbarton Oaks, pp. 109–141.

——2002a. Desiring women: Classic Maya sexualities. In L. Gustafson and A. Trevelyan (eds.), *Ancient Maya Gender Identity and Relations.* Westport, CT: Greenwood, pp. 329–344.

——2002b. Beauty, sexuality, body ornamentation and gender in Ancient Mesoamerica. In S. Nelson and M. Rosen-Ayalon (eds.), *In Pursuit of Gender.* Walnut Creek, CA: AltaMira Press, pp. 81–92.

Kampen, N. (ed.) 1996. *Sexuality in Ancient Art: Near East, Egypt, Greece and Italy.* Cambridge: Cambridge University Press.

Knapp, A. B. 1998. Who's come a long way, baby? *Archaeological Dialogues* 2: 91–106.

——, and L. M. Meskell. 1997. Bodies of evidence on prehistoric Cyprus. *Cambridge Archaeological Journal* 7: 183–204.

Kokkinidou, D. 1997. Body imagery in the Aegean Neolithic: Ideological implications of anthropomorphic figurines. In J. Moore and E. Scott (eds.), *Invisible People and Processes: Writing*

Gender and Childhood into European Archaeology. London: Leicester University Press, pp. 88–112.

Kus, S. T. 1992. Toward an archaeology of body and soul. In J-C. Gardin and C. Peebles (eds.), *Representations in Archaeology*. Bloomington: Indiana University Press, pp. 168–177.

Lakoff, G., and M. Johnson. 1999. *Philosophy in the Flesh: The Embodied Mind and its Challenge to Western Thought*. New York: Basic Books.

Laqueur, T. 1990. *Making Sex: Body and Gender from the Greeks to Freud*. Cambridge, MA: Harvard University Press.

Lesure, R. G. 1997. Figurines and social identities in early sedentary societies of coastal Chiapas, Mexico, 1550–800 B.C. In C. Claassen and R. A. Joyce (eds.), *Women in Prehistory: North America and Mesoamerica*. Philadelphia: University of Pennsylvania Press, pp. 227–248.

Loren, D. 2001. Social skins: Orthodoxies and practices of dressing in the early colonial lower Mississippi Valley. *Journal of Social Archaeology* 1: 172–189.

Marcus, M. I. 1993. Incorporating the body: Adornment, gender, and social identity in ancient Iran. *Cambridge Archaeological Journal* 3: 157–178.

——1996. Sex and the politics of female adornment in pre-Achaemenid Iran (1000–800 BCE). In N. Kampen (ed.), *Sexuality in Ancient Art: Near East, Egypt, Greece and Italy*. Cambridge, Cambridge University Press, pp. 41–54.

McCafferty, S. D., and G. G. McCafferty. 1991. Spinning and weaving as female gender identity in post-Classic Mexico. In J. C. Berlo, M. Schevill, and E. B. Dwyer (eds.), *Textile Traditions of Mesoamerica and the Andes: An Anthology*. New York: Garland, pp. 19–44.

McCoid, C. H., and L. D. McDermott. 1996. Toward decolonizing gender: female vision in the Upper Palaeolithic. *American Anthropologist* 98: 319–326.

McDermott, L. 1996. Self-representation in Upper Paleolithic female figurines. *Current Anthropology* 37: 227–275.

Merleau-Ponty, M. 1962. *The Phenomenology of Perception*. Trans. C. Smith. London: Routledge & Kegan Paul.

Meskell, L. M. 1996. The somatisation of archaeology: Discourses, institutions, corporeality. *Norwegian Archaeological Review* 29: 1–16.

——1998a. Intimate archaeologies: The case of Kha and Merit. *World Archaeology* 29: 363–379.

——1998b. The irresistible body and the seduction of archaeology. In D. Montserrat (ed.), *Changing Bodies, Changing Meanings: Studies on the Human Body in Antiquity*. London: Routledge, pp. 139–161.

——1999. *Archaeologies of Social Life: Age, Sex, and Class in Ancient Egypt*. Oxford: Blackwell.

——2000. Re-em(bed)ding sex: Domesticity, sexuality, and ritual in New Kingdom Egypt. In R. Schmidt and B. Voss (eds.), *Archaeologies of Sexuality*. London: Routledge, pp. 253–262.

——2002. *Private Life in New Kingdom Egypt*. Princeton, NJ: Princeton University Press.

——, and R. A. Joyce. 2003. *Embodied Lives: Figuring Ancient Maya and Egyptian Experience*. London: Routledge.

Miller, V. (ed.) 1988. *The Role of Gender in Precolumbian Art and Architecture*. Lanham, MD: University Press of America.

Nordbladh, J., and T. Yates. 1990. This perfect body, this virgin text: Between sex and gender in archaeology. In I. Bapty and T. Yates (eds.), *Archaeology After Structuralism*. London: Routledge, pp. 222–237.

Parkington, J. 2002. Men, women and eland: Hunting and gender among the San of southern Africa. In S. Nelson and M. Rosen-Ayalon (eds.), *In Pursuit of Gender*. Walnut Creek, CA: AltaMira Press, pp. 93–117.

Pauketat, T. R. 2001. Practice and history in archaeology: An emerging paradigm. *Anthropological Theory* 1: 73–98.

Perry, E. M. and R. A. Joyce. 2001. Providing a past for *Bodies that Matter*: Judith Butler's impact on the archaeology of gender. *International Journal of Sexuality and Gender Studies* 6: 63–76.

Rice, P. C. 1982. Prehistoric Venuses: Symbols of motherhood or womanhood? *Journal of Anthropological Research* 37: 402–414.

Roosevelt, A. C. 1988. Interpreting certain female images in prehistoric art. In V. Miller (ed.), *The Role of Gender in Precolumbian Art and Architecture*. Lanham, MD: University Press of America, pp. 1–34.

Schmidt, R. 2000. Shamans and northern cosmology: the direct historical approach to Mesolithic sexuality. In R. Schmidt and B. Voss (eds.), *Archaeologies of Sexuality*. London: Routledge, pp. 220–235.

Schmidt, R. A., and B. L. Voss (eds.) 2000. *Archaeologies of Sexuality*. London: Routledge.

Siefert, D., E. B. O'Brien, and J. Balicki. 2000. Mary Ann Hall's first-class house: The archaeology of a capital brothel. In R. Schmidt and B. Voss (eds.), *Archaeologies of Sexuality*. London: Routledge, pp. 117–128.

Stone, A. J. 1988. Sacrifice and sexuality: Some structural relationships in Classic Maya art. In V. Miller (ed.), *The Role of Gender in Precolumbian Art and Architecture*. Lanham, MD: University Press of America, pp. 75–103.

Taylor, C. 1985. The person. In M. Carrithers, S. Collins, and S. Lukes (eds.), *The Category of Person: Anthropology, Philosophy, History*. Cambridge: Cambridge University Press, pp. 257–281.

—— 1989. *Sources of the Self: The Making of the Modern Identity*. Cambridge: Cambridge University Press.

Treherne, P. 1995. The warrior's beauty: The masculine body and self-identity in Bronze-Age Europe. *Journal of European Archaeology* 3: 105–144.

Turner, B. S. 1984. *The Body and Society*. Oxford: Basil Blackwell.

—— 1991. Recent developments in the theory of the body. In M. Featherstone, M. Hepworth, and B. S. Turner (eds.), *The Body: Social Process and Cultural Theory*. London: Sage, pp. 1–35.

Wilkie, L. A. 1998. The other gender: The archaeology of an early 20th-century fraternity. *Proceedings of the Society for California Archaeology* 11: 7–11.

—— 2000. Magical passions: Sexuality and African-American archaeology. In R. Schmidt and B. Voss (eds.), *Archaeologies of Sexuality*. London: Routledge, pp. 129–142.

Winter, I. 1989. The body of the able ruler: Toward an understanding of the statues of Gudea. In H. Behrens, D. Loding, and M. T. Roth (eds.), *Dumu-E-Dub-Ba-A: Studies in Honor of Åke W. Sjöberg*. Philadelphia: Samuel Noah Kramer Fund, pp. 573–583.

—— 1996. Sex, rhetoric and the public monument: The alluring body of Naram-Sin of Agade. In N. Kampen (ed.), *Sexuality in Ancient Art*. Cambridge: Cambridge University Press, pp. 11–26.

Wylie, A. 1991. Gender theory and the archaeological record: Why is there no archaeology of gender? In J. Gero and M. W. Conkey (eds.), *Engendering Archaeology: Women and Prehistory*. Oxford: Blackwell, pp. 31–54.

Yates, T. 1993. Frameworks for an archaeology of the body. In C. Tilley (ed.), *Interpretive Archaeology*. Oxford: Berg, pp. 31–72.

5

Social Archaeology and Origins Research: A Paleolithic Perspective

Clive Gamble and Erica Gittins

Introduction

A social archaeology is at once both an obvious and permeable concept. It hardly seems necessary to qualify the study of the human past as a social enterprise, and yet what archaeologists mean by social is, as illustrated so well by this *Companion*, always polyphonous and often conceptually fluid. Social archaeology is part of an archaeologist's *habitus*, that landscape of habit (Gosden 1999), where much activity takes place because of routine, rather than because it is discussed. But when the latter does occur it is usually to reflect on either the perceived practices or institutions that allow people to associate and which occur when people interact.

In this chapter we take a single archaeological period, the Paleolithic, to examine the obvious and the permeable in social archaeology. Selection is necessary because every time we consider an aspect of social archaeology a specific, contextually derived understanding is required on the part of the archaeologist. It is for this reason that the term acts as a locus through which archaeologists express a wide variety of often competing ideas. For example, a social archaeology of the Paleolithic frequently involves making a distinction between the capacity for social *practice* with that of either economic or technological *behavior*.

Therefore, while we readily recognize "social archaeology," the distinction between capacities which this concept relies upon produces a definition which is too general to be of immediate use. Hence in this chapter we will take a different tack and define social archaeology in the Paleolithic as the practice of questioning the fundamental premises of archaeology in order to provide an analysis of the way the permeable parts of the discipline fit together to form a coherent and obvious structure. We will argue that social archaeology, taken broadly, must be recognized as a practice that questions the motives and construction of the discipline for the reason that archaeology is itself a social practice. It is from this self-reflexive position that Paleolithic archaeologists can formulate questions and offer interpretations of the past in response to bodies of ancient data.

Our Deep-Time Social Background

The Paleolithic period, from the first stone tools to the widespread appearance of agriculture (see table 5.1), has served a particular purpose within the broadly-based theoretical enterprise known as anthropological archaeology (Gamble 2001). In particular, the period has provided a point of origin for different approaches to the interpretation and reconstruction of social life from the material remains of later prehistory and the historic, text-aided, periods. These interpretive projects, which we refer to collectively as social archaeology, began with Childe (1951) and continued under various methodological and theoretical guises for the next half-century. The weakness of such approaches from the Paleolithic point of view is, however, revealed by the fact that while they need a Paleolithic they have, paradoxically, produced little by way of what a Paleolithic social archaeology might be. Margaret Conkey has observed that "It is increasingly recognized that the study of social phenomena in hunter-gatherer life has been relatively underdeveloped. Concomitant with this has been an over-emphasis on ecological determinants ... The lifeways of the prehistoric hunter gatherer ... have been homogenized and cast in utopian imagery" (1984:254).

Here we will argue that irrespective of theoretical approach – culture-history, processual, postprocessual or Marxist archaeology – all that these social archaeologies require is a standard account of the Paleolithic. Therefore, we contend that there can be no such thing as social archaeology without the underpinning provided by the Paleolithic, but this structure means the Paleolithic is rarely allowed any social content. By examining this asymmetrical relationship we will ask: what future is there for social archaeology if this disciplinary indifference to Paleolithic society, as pointed out by Conkey, is maintained? The assumption remains, whether discussed or not, that both our biological beginnings and the inception of cultural complexity were attained during our early prehistory. Our approach to this question is to review current approaches and briefly consider the perspective offered by Derrida in his notion of logocentrism. Our intention in adopting his perspective is to throw into sharp relief the way that the position of the Paleolithic within the disciplinary structure of archaeology sets what are regarded as its legitimate questions. Furthermore, these questions are in turn derived from the traditions of Western thought that archaeologists have inherited. It is from this embedded position that the Paleolithic derives its importance as a disciplinary enquiry, but which also forms its greatest restriction.

We will discuss these issues through an examination of two origins questions which a social approach to the Paleolithic has pursued (table 5.1).

The first question is the origins of group identity and where social boundaries which are the building blocks of all subsequent archaeological periods from the Neolithic to the recent, more familiar, past. Anthropological analogy, in particular the global sample of fisher-gatherer-hunters (Binford 2001; Lee and DeVore 1968; Service 1962), underpins approaches to this question in the Paleolithic. The second question, derived from the insights of social studies of primates, casts the process differently. Here it is how social relations were extended in time and space, which is at issue. Both questions illustrate the importance of interdisciplinary approaches for a social archaeology of the Paleolithic. The results, as might be expected with such permeable relations, are often

Table 5.1   *The investigation of Paleolithic society*

Years before Present		Terms Used Here	Evolutionary Trajectory	Origin Question	Basis for Analogy
	Mesolithic	Late Paleolithic			
10,000					
	Upper Paleolithic		Complicated society, complexity of material culture	Group closure (Band Society)	Hunter/gatherer ethnography
60,000					
	Middle Paleolithic	Early Paleolithic		Release from proximity	
300,000					
	Lower Paleolithic		Complex society, uniformity of material culture		Primate social life
2.7 million					

Note: Terms such as Paleolithic and Mesolithic only have currency in Europe and are used here as a form of shorthand.

quite different. In this brief contribution our examples are mostly drawn from the Old World, although the prehistoric hunters and gatherers of Australia and the Americas would furnish abundant data for question one.

Social Archaeology and the Paleolithic: The Origins of Group Closure

Anthropological archaeology replaced the Childe of the 1950s with a child of the 1960s. This replacement involved a reworking of Gordon Childe's (e.g., 1956) method of identifying the revolutions in human history. This involved establishing criteria to determine the break-points in a stadial model of our progress toward civilization. For example, the appearance of urbanization and civilization was identified with a ten-point checklist (Gamble 1986a). However, in Childe's influential trinitarian approach to social evolution, adopted from Morgan (1877), the Paleolithic lay in the primordial stage of Savagery, crushed by the succeeding weight of Barbarism and Civilization to which such checklists really applied.

Anthropological archaeology, in its processual guise, adopted a similar approach by determining the correlates of social types, most famously bands, tribes, chiefs, and states in the neo-evolutionist framework of Service (1962) and Sahlins (1963). The central proposition was that material remains directly reflected both the positions people held within these societies and the institutions that defined them. Evidence from graves and settlements concerning status, rank, subsistence, and exchange was particularly important. The approach produced remarkable results for many prehistoric and early state societies and opened up a comparative approach on a worldwide scale.

However, in the euphoria of uncovering early states and chiefdoms from Wessex to Waikiki (Redman et al. 1978; Renfrew 1973), it went largely unremarked that, apart from labeling the Paleolithic as examples of band society, no further social comment was possible. Childe's assessment that "The archaeological record is found to be regrettably but not surprisingly deficient in indications of the social organisation or lack of it in Lower Paleolithic hordes. *From the scraps available no generalisations are permissible*" (1951:85, our emphasis) was uncontested. Consequently, the Early Paleolithic has never been part of social archaeology as described above (for discussion see Gamble 1999). Any social content for this period usually rests solely in the implicit assumption, shared by many culture historians, that Paleolithic artifacts, irrespective of period, express group identity founded on ethnic, racial, or psychological variation (e.g., Bordes 1968; Bordes and de Sonneville-Bordes 1970). This assumption during a lively debate was singed, rather than burnt, at the stake of functionalism (Binford 1973).

A social archaeology which depended on correlates to reflect social structure and reveal social positions fared better in the Late Paleolithic (table 5.1), with its more differentiated material record (Conkey 1978; Conkey 1980; King 1978; Lourandos 1997; Price and Brown 1985). But even so, Late Paleolithic stone tools, shell jewelry, campsites and the occasional skeleton yielded slim pickings for the social archaeologist more accustomed to elite cemeteries, urban landscapes, wall paintings, and lapis lazuli.

The result was to abandon the Late Paleolithic to the broader interests of neo-evolutionary typologies. The key concern for the period became the origins of group closure (Gilman 1984). Closure was regarded as an important issue since it was assumed to correlate with the deliberate use of material culture to signal a more complex social geography (compare Conkey 1978 with 1984). The implicit assumptions of the culture historians were now being made explicit by equating social differences with variable information flows (Gamble 1982).

Johnson and Earle (1987) provide a neo-evolutionist analysis which shows how little is required of Paleolithic data. They follow a cultural materialist perspective by proposing that population growth is the primary determinant of all social development. The "natural unit" of human social and economic organization is the family, for the reason that it has been around for a very long time in human evolution, its analytical legitimacy rooted in biological capacities and tendencies (1987: 63). Within families they identify individuals as active agents; but active only in the sense that they seek to meet their basic biological needs and those of their families (1987: 3). These individuals are also helped and constrained by the natural and cultural environment. Johnson and Earle illustrate their family-level groups with the San peoples of southern Africa, and archaeologically by the Early Paleolithic of Olduvai Gorge and the Middle Paleolithic of the Dordogne. They compare the next level in their evolutionary typology, the local group, to the Alaskan Nunamiut and the Upper Paleolithic of Europe. The close parallels with Sollas's (1911) long discredited scheme of equating ancient hunters with their modern representatives should be noted.

Fortunately, not all approaches to the origins of group closure have been so unproductive. The main gain lay in the demonstration that the Paleolithic could be interpreted at a regional scale (Gamble 1986b), and to achieve this a conceptual shift about

Table 5.2   *The postulates of Band Society* (Williams 1974)

---

1 A species divided into social groups which are autonomous with respect to food supply or vital resources will exhibit territoriality.

2 Given that food is shared within the family and that a sexual division of labor, with respect to hunting-gatherering activities, exists, then territorial groups will tend to be patrilocally based.

3 Social units in hunting-gathering societies are kinship units.

4 In hunting-gathering society, the kinship unit having maximal autonomy with respect to resources is the lineage band.

5 The lineage band is exogamic.

6 Optimal band size is the minimal size in which marriage alliances can be maintained with all surrounding bands indefinitely.

---

settlement, mobility, and interaction, as originally advocated by the Binfords (1966), had to be made.

However, the problems with this origins-driven approach to group closure are well illustrated by Williams's (1974) study of the generic concept of Band Society. Six postulates (table 5.2) are put forward, but they deal only with the residential and territorial aspects of social organization.

The most influential application of these postulates appeared in the locational and stylistic analyses of Wobst (1974a, 1974b, 1976, 1977). While Wobst's model revolutionized the study of regional behavior in the Paleolithic, at its heart lay Williams's equation of society with connubia, or marriage networks (see also Gilman 1984). While this was a necessary step in approaching the study of Paleolithic materials in a systematic and rigorous manner, it left a void where a Paleolithic social life should be.

A similar missing center can be found in the ethnographically based approaches to the European Late Paleolithic by Newell and Constandse-Westermann (1986; Houtsma et al. 1996). When they refer to "Paleolithic society" what they are describing is a traditionally defined archaeological culture as identified through the distribution of traits in time and space. What they are then seeking is an analogy based upon the spatial dimensions of their archaeological units with the ethnographic record of North America. Their analysis of this record isolated two demographic levels, band and tribal (Constandse-Westermann and Newell 1991), and where population density is identified as a crucial variable.

An equally thorough analysis of the ethnography of hunters and gatherers has recently been conducted by Binford (2001). Its application to archaeology is presented as a regional framework for the analysis of the transition from hunting to farming (2001: Chapter 12). As with Newell and Constandse-Westermann, the environment provides Binford with a strong warrant for the framework of analogy he advocates. Central to Binford's analysis is his definition of packing as "the patterned reduction in subsistence range arising from a regional increase in population" (2001:442). Moreover, packing at critical thresholds (table 5.3) is regarded as important in the transformation of the adaptive system, the society.

However, what exactly is being "packed" at the larger scale? The "packed" are identified as "increasing numbers of social units within a region" (2001:438), a form of complex social geography. Such units are analogous to Wobst's connubia and Newell

Table 5.3   *Two packing thresholds and their systemic responses* (Binford 2001:434). *An example of a top-down, group approach to studying the social in the Paleolithic*

>1.6 people per $100\,\mathrm{km}^2$

- Expanded niche using aquatic resources
- Extensified niche using land animals
- Mobility the key tactic to adapt to variation in resources

>9.1 people per $100\,\mathrm{km}^2$

- No longer a primary dependence on land animals
- Mobility is no longer the key tactic
- The use of aquatic resources indicates that intensification is underway

and Constande-Westermann's band and tribal level of organization. Indeed, the latter take the goal of Paleolithic social archaeology as producing a satisfactory answer to the question of why closed, rather than open, marriage networks exist (Newell and Constandse-Westermann 1986:245; see also Binford 1968; Gilman 1984; Wobst 1974a:vi). Furthermore, and independently of Binford, they settle on a threshold figure of 9.9 people per $100\,\mathrm{km}^2$ (Newell and Constandse-Westermann 1986: Table 9) for the regular appearance of group closure, where at least 80 percent of marriages are endogamous. They conclude that in Europe it was only in the Late Mesolithic that such population densities were exceeded, allowing closed connubia. In their terms this means that the Early and Middle Mesolithic are band-level, open societies while Late Mesolithic societies are tribal level, closed groups (1986: 293). However. as Conkey noted more generally, "Structural and materialist emphasis turned out to be at the expense of the social geographic or more contextual perspectives. The definition of bounded Upper Paleolithic groups, or what amounts to a complex social geography, remains to be defined" (1984:265).

These analogy-based studies have produced interesting structural patterns. However, although Binford reminds us that packing is an achieved rather than environmentally ascribed condition (2001: Proposition 12.04) we are never told about the character and composition of those doing the achieving. The system achieves packing because of the number of social units which need to be packed. The system transforms because the region remains constant within the life span of such units. Social archaeology and social evolution, it seems, are the preserve of evolutionary processes best understood through the products of groups and the organization of systems. There is very little room for any conception of "society" or "people" in the broader sense.

The Primate Alternative and the "Release from Proximity"

Ethnographic analogy has not been the only route to a social archaeology directed at the "scraps" of evidence from the Early Paleolithic. With primates providing the warrant for analogy (table 5.1) the issue for human evolution now revolves around the release from proximity, rather than the closure of the group, in the construction of social life.

Ever since Washburn's interdisciplinary exploration, *Social Life of Early Man* (1961), investigations of the societies of hominids and primates have proceeded at a different pace. In marked contrast to Paleolithic studies of hominids with brains often three times larger than their closest animal cousins, primatologists have devised ways to examine the varied societies of monkeys and great apes (de Waal 1982; 1991; Dunbar 1988; Goodall 1986; Maryanski and Ishii-Kuntz 1991; Parish 1996; Quiatt and Reynolds 1993). They have achieved this without recourse to notions that artifacts reflect status, rank, and the structure of social relations.

Primatologists have stressed a number of key points, few of which have a place in standard accounts of Paleolithic society:

- the importance of the individual;
- the importance of attention and intention during social interaction;
- the importance of networking, achieved through grooming, and its expression in alliances;
- the power of performance to achieve social goals;
- the social skills of the body;
- the presence of social memory;

But primatologists are not united in their approach. Many adopt a top-down rather than a bottom-up approach to the study of social origins using primates as a comparative framework. (Aiello and Dunbar 1993; Dunbar 1993; Foley and Lee 1996; Foley 1989; Maryanski 1993, 1996; Maryanski and Turner 1992; Steele and Shennan 1996). For example, Rodseth et al. (1991) present a model for hominid society that is built from comparisons with living primates (table 5.4).

The unit of analysis they propose is the community where bonds are strengthened and relationships maintained to produce variable outcomes. Moreover, they identify the goal of such studies as understanding how hominids achieved a "release from proximity" (1991: 240), by which they mean the capacity to sustain relationships *in absentia*. Their preferred solution is a fission–fusion model of hominid society where collective

Table 5.4 *A framework for understanding variation in early hominid society* (Rodseth et al. 1991: 237)

Strengthening bonds,
1 between males and females
2 or, between related males
3 or, a combination of 1 and 2.

Maintaining relationships,
1 either with dispersing offspring
2 or, by forming alliances with affines in other groups.

rituals, performed in co-presence, act to create a stable, but temporary, face-to-face society. In their view the tensions of social life, that extended periods of absence would exacerbate, are increasingly mediated by culture and language.

Such models are very much in the tradition started by Washburn and DeVore (1961) when they compared primates and human societies. But many of these primate-based studies are in contrast to a methodology first articulated by Hinde (1976). Here he compared primate and human society and stressed the equal importance of bottom-up and top-down approaches.

In Hinde's model primate and human social life is founded on interaction, while relationships and social structure are seen as emergent rather than pre-established properties. This emphasis on a bottom-up approach to primate sociality stands in marked contrast to the Paleolithic view described above which is very much top-down: the adaptive system, or connubium, or the band comes first and only then the individual.

The social insights that come with Hinde's approach are clearly expressed by Strum and Latour (1987) in their discussion of the performative question and social life. Rather than a pre-existing, top-down framework they argue that primate society emerges from the interaction of individuals. They characterize these performers as "competent members." These are social actors who have some difficulty in negotiating one factor at a time, particularly so because they are constantly being distracted by others with exactly the same problem (1987: 41). In Strum and Latour's opinion this leads to *complex* society based on the performance of bonds which create social life. Among these fingertip societies, society is literally groomed into existence (see Dunbar 1996). Human societies are different, they argue, because they are *complicated* rather than complex (table 5.1). Complication describes a succession of simple operations. Rather than competent members we now have "skilled practitioners" who are able to bring more to social interaction than just their bodies and immediately negotiated social skills. Instead they also have symbols and material culture to channel those interactions. What emerges is a complicated society based on the complexity of material culture.

The Standard View of the Paleolithic

The implications of an origins-based approach to the social archaeology of the Paleolithic can now be summarized. The contrast in the standard view draws distinctions between an Early and a Late Paleolithic (table 5.5).

Two important differences immediately stand out. In the first place there are differences in hominid anatomy (1) suggesting to many a biological basis for social and cultural difference. When combined with the second difference, a uniformity of material culture when compared to its complexity in the Late Paleolithic (2–9), it matters little if the origins question is either group closure or release from proximity. The result is the same with the origin point for such issues fixed firmly in the material complexity of the Late Paleolithic. The Early Paleolithic then becomes the analytical outgroup which, by default, has open-access systems and only limited release. Equal competence in basic provisioning (10) merely serves to emphasize the cultural gulf.

Table 5.5 *A ten-point checklist presenting the standard view of the evidence for social differences between the Early and Late Paleolithic* (see Gamble 1993; Stringer and Gamble 1993)

		Early Paleolithic	Late Paleolithic
1	Anatomy and phrenology of *Homo sapiens sapiens*		X
2	Architecture for dwelling in		X
3	Art for reflexive discourse		X
4	Expressions of self through items of personal identity	?	X
5	Hearths for talking around		X
6	Long-distance exchange facilitating social storage		X
7	Overwater colonization indicating extended absence	?	X
8	Ownership of local territory marked by open-air cemeteries with grave goods		X
9	The complex social geography of regional space–time culture groups	?	X
10	Top dog in the trophic pyramid by virtue of hunting prime-age animals	X	X

However, the opposition of simple and complex social systems is also widespread in Late Paleolithic studies as well as among the ethnographic analyses of contemporary hunters and gatherers. Price and Brown (1985) identify the first appearance of complexity in social life during the Late Paleolithic. The complex centres stand out from the surrounding simple hunting and gathering societies on the following criteria:

- population density
- maximum settlement size
- permanent shelter
- permanent ceremonial grounds
- art styles
- differences in burials due to grave wealth, location, and the energy investment in grave preparation (Brown and Price 1985:437).

A similar approach can be found in Keeley's (1988) dichotomy of simple and complex hunters as well as Woodburn's (1980) immediate and delayed systems of return (for further discussion see Gamble 1999:14–26)

The dichotomy continues when the Late Paleolithic, and by extension the Early Paleolithic, is then compared to the Neolithic and the agriculturally based complex societies which followed. Judged at this scale, the whole of the Paleolithic now forms an analytical outgroup for the discussion of later social agendas. The standard view of the Paleolithic from this perspective can be summarized as emphasizing absence:

- Not enough chronological control (too much time, therefore everything is fuzzy because the missing time somehow needs to be filled).
- Not enough social contexts (where are the cemeteries, tombs, villages, tells, mounds, cities, temples, ball-courts and general purpose ceremonial monuments?).
- Not enough variety in material culture (where are the basketry, textile, wooden, paper, metal, and ceramic technologies?).
- Not enough differentiation (one Paleolithic technocomplex, either Early or Late, looks to the uninitiated very much like another, unlike the polities of the ancient Near East, Mesoamerica or China).
- Not enough changes (one set of stone tools follows another. The dramatic material changes between the Tasmanians and the British or the Iron Age and the Romans is never found. By contrast, modern humans in Europe replaced Neanderthals stone for stone, and a few beads (Graves 1991).

All of these unfavorable comparisons contribute to the standard view of Early Paleolithic society summed up in Childe's phrase "the scraps available." And when it comes to another Neolithic archaeologist looking back to the Late Paleolithic we find an equally familiar, albeit utopian, judgment: "I believe that if the nature of late Mesolithic society in southern Scandinavia could adequately be described by a modern political term, 'primitive communism' might still be very apposite. I am politically old-fashioned enough even to want to describe it as a kind of Garden of Eden before the fall" (Tilley 1996:68).

Origins and Logocentrism

So far we have argued that the standard "Childean" heritage of the Paleolithic has left a void where a concept of society should be. This displacement stems from the privileging of biology over culture and a reliance on notions of human development from simplicity to complexity. In turn these developments chart the rise of what we would recognize as modern institutions, a point made previously by Conkey (1984:254) in her discussion of presentist perspectives on the Upper Paleolithic.

However, the failing does not lie with each new theoretical position that archaeology adopts. Neither is it simply the case that culture historians and processualists have always refused to consider Paleolithic society (see David 1973; Mueller-Wille and Dickson 1991). Instead, this condition stems from the inherited intellectual framework of Western thought that predates the existence of archaeology but within which archaeology operates. So far, this discourse has received limited examination.

Derrida has sought to uncover the principles or "desires" that drive Western intellectual traditions. His work has been used in some postprocessual texts to support notions of material culture and archaeological writing as a variable field of meanings and signifiers (e.g., Hodder 1991; Johnson 1999). For our purposes in this chapter, this particular interpretation of Derrida is somewhat limited. The principal desire that we are interested in here is *logocentrism* (from the Greek *Logos*, meaning logic, reason, the word, God), the metaphysical desire for foundation. Metaphysics and Western thought are, in Derrida's terms, the same phenomena, and logocentrism is concerned with all

"discourse that relies on foundational metaphysical ideas such as truth, presence, identity, or origin to centre itself" (Hugdahl 1999:740). The great questions of Western
thought carry a motivation to center themselves on a fundamental truth or principle.
This truth is considered a pure, undivided point of "self-presence" – where truth is
assured and known to itself.

In his early work on the philosophy of language, Derrida (1976 [1967]) initially
illustrated that Saussure's privileging of speech over writing relied on a particular mode
of logocentrism, which he called *phonocentrism*. The opposition he identified between
the spoken and written word was subsequently extrapolated to the entire Western
tradition of language so that "it is along the axis of the opposition between phoneme
(unit of speech) and grapheme (written letters) that Derrida unfolds his deconstruction
of western metaphysics" (Hugdahl 1999:740). This extrapolation led him to a belief
that *all* signification (whether literally linguistic or not) was radically indeterminate,
and consequently that meaning could not be frozen or made stable. As this is the
condition of all signification it applies equally to meaning, metaphysics, and therefore
archaeology.

Archaeology is therefore logocentric, in that it is a metaphysical construct that
cannot exist outside of language or signification. Furthermore, the Paleolithic implies a
search for an unproblematic center – a point of origin which allows unequivocal
meaning to be possible.

This logos can appear in a number of guises. Central ideas acting as logoi can be
identified within texts which allow the structure of an argument around them. This
center has the effect of making the structure appear natural,

> and this by a process of giving it a centre or referring it to a point of presence, a fixed
> origin. The function of this centre was not only to orient, balance, and organize the
> structure – one cannot in fact conceive of an unorganized structure – but above all to
> make sure that the organizing principle of the structure might limit what we might call the
> play of the structure. (Derrida 1997 [1967]:278)

This center, as logos, is considered whole and indivisible and provides coherence for
the structure of the argument. However, because this center is considered indivisible, it
escapes structure. It cannot be part of a structure or argument that relies on binary
oppositions or tension between concepts because it must be a pure concept in itself;
"Thus it has always been thought that the centre, which by definition is unique,
constituted that very thing within a structure which while governing the structure,
escapes structurality" (ibid.:279). Therefore the center is an impossible core, a nonexistent point of truth.

However, argument and debate will continue as if this center exists, because the
desire for fundamental ground is a discipline's desire for the security of authority.
Therefore we can expose the Paleolithic's real motivation for the notion of common
origins as a need for security. In opposition to a questioning of our normative academic practice, we have a system of metaphors which support pre-existing sets of
values and truths about human nature and Western identity. The history of the idea of
this center must be thought of "as a series of substitutions of centre for centre, as a

linked chain of determinations of the centre…in a regulated fashion, the centre receives different forms and names" (ibid.). In all its different reincarnations, each is a permutation of self-present being.

The idea of origin has immense power because it is so deeply rooted in the basis of Western thought. The Paleolithic derives its significance and historically its very existence from the notion of the origin. Looking for origins is essentially an attempt to define the moment we became human (Alexandri 1995). The Paleolithic was literally *essential* for the invention of archaeology. Furthermore, it is this beginning which provides earliest human prehistory with its apparent relevance. Finding the "first" or the beginning of a phenomenon is both the structure and the center for Paleolithic practice. The aim or desire for the logos in the Paleolithic – identification of a common origin – provides both the question and justification for the existence of the Paleolithic. It is very difficult for the Paleolithic to be anything other than a provider of origins, stranded as it is in the metaphysical logos as much as a perceived, literal one.

The desire for foundation and truth forces archaeologists to repeat the same statements over and over. The statements we make appear sound and reasonable, because logoi provide "coherence" for arguments, but in fact our arguments are "neutralized" around the center or logos of an argument. This prevents radical departure from what is generally accepted. There is a tangible notion of "proper" or formal archaeology – the standard Paleolithic is an example (see above) – which allows us to entertain many notions, but which would normally exclude serious consideration of, say, extra-terrestrials painting the caves of the Dordogne. But our reaction to such "obvious nonsense" exposes the real motivation behind the notion of origin; a need for security. In direct opposition to a questioning academic practice, we have instead a system of metaphors which support a pre-existing set of values and truths. This is the mechanism by which we produce logical and coherent stories about familiar institutions (Conkey and Williams 1991). It is also ethnocentric, and as Derrida (1974) would describe it, a "white mythology." It is our own story of our own beginning which we create for ourselves by studying other cultures. This story has always privileged the biological or technological realms. In a classic binary scheme, nature is opposed to culture, and nature acts as the location of our origin, our logos. The beginning is seen as so close to nature that social activity and cultural variation are neither academically nor politically expedient.

Conkey and Williams (1991) make the observation that this kind of research leads to essentialism, reductionism, and the authorization of dominant masculine agendas. But not all researchers agree that the quest for origins is necessarily flawed. Others see origins research as essentially practical, claiming that, after all, the "ultimate meaning of a thing is its essence" (Alexandri 1995:59). For Alexandri, the questions we ask do not predetermine the answers we give. Futhermore, she argues, a total rejection of the origins of meaning loses sight of the durability and general public appeal of this question and its role in shaping our identity as humans (1995: 60).

We do not take issue with the notion that we have a link to our past, nor that the past has a role to play in the construction of identity. However, we do contest the idea that origins research is somehow neutral, or that it provides a set of discourses which even at a superficial level can be controlled or rendered harmless. The idea of the first, the beginning, the undivided pure center of institution, is a powerful metaphysic that requires examination if archaeology as a whole, and the Paleolithic archaeology, are to successfully grasp its own exapted structure. The relationship appears natural, hence obvious and neutral. But we must recognize that we are engaging with a historically specific discourse.

The search for the *Logos* keeps the same research questions in motion that not only constrict the relevance of society in early prehistory, but which also act to maintain our own perceptions of the role and place of the West in the world, together with social and political aspects in our own society. It is no coincidence that the loss of Europe as the primary cultural reference through colonialism resulted in the birth of ethnology and, of course, the Paleolithic (Derrida 1997 [1967]; Young 1990). The titles of the founding texts of Paleolithic archaeology demonstrate this point:

Sir John Lubbock (1865) *Pre-Historic Times, as illustrated by Ancient Remains and the Manners and Customs of Modern Savages*

W. J. Sollas (1911) *Ancient Hunters and Their Modern Representatives.*

A Role for the Individual in the Paleolithic

The *Logos* conditions and constrains. As a result it is difficult to find much discussion of Paleolithic society beyond such issues as cooperative hunting (Klein 1989), central place foraging (Isaac 1976) and origins questions concerning the first Americans (Adovasio and Page 2002), intensification (Lourandos 1997), symbolism (Knight 1991a, 1991b), language (Aiello 1996; Noble and Davidson 1996; White 1985), meaning (Alexandri 1995), and modern cognition (Mithen 1996). Moreover, such studies are invariably top-down and group-based (e.g., Mithen 1994), to the extent that some, understandably perhaps, want to be told another story (Latour and Strum 1986).

For this reason the recent interest in the individual is welcome. As a unit of analysis the individual has been championed in the context of decision making (Mithen 1990, 1993) and the transmission of cultural information (Shennan 1989), although still within a group-based approach to the study of the period. But the individual is also an unpopular concept, regarded by Clark (1992:107) as beyond the resolution of Paleolithic evidence where only the activities of groups are preserved. Clark's assessment, which is widely shared, is a further example of the standard view and can be traced back directly to Childe's "available scraps."

As long as a top-down approach is applied to the study of the Paleolithic there will be no social archaeology and no room for the individual. Moreover, merely turning the analysis upside down is not enough to rectify the situation (Gamble 1998b). But, while a bottom-up approach does not solve all the problems at a single stroke it does present social life as a creative process, enacted by individuals as they go about their daily lives. The task of social archaeology therefore moves away from defining institutions, for example, Band Society, and their relative condition as measured by the degree of complexity they exhibit. Instead we want to know more about how individuals are constituted through their bodies, culture, self, and personhood, because these issues relate to the creation of society through interaction. In other words, we require a consideration of people.

One consequence affects the search for social origins. There is no origin point for the self or embodiment. Rather there is a continual, creative social process which archaeological evidence indicates has been running for at least 2.7 million years. Accordingly, social life in the Paleolithic, or any archaeological period, can be described as:

- embodied, as much as en-minded (Ingold 2000);
- routinized, because much of what we do is "unthinking"; muscle memories, techniques of the body (Mauss 1979), the durable dispositions of the *habitus* (Bourdieu 1977), and the landscape of habit (Gosden 1994, 1999);
- material and mutual, because interacting agents and artifacts are both responsible for the creation and constant becoming of social life;
- hybrid, composed of persons and things (Strathern 1996) and where the traditional analytical distinctions between thing : person, animal : human, nature : culture are no longer supported because of the social relationship contained in the notion of hybrid.

This change in emphasis has been examined by Gamble (1996, 1998a, 1998b, 1999). He sets out an interactional model based on the individual as the primary focus. The analytical device he uses are the networks which individuals construct and through which they live their social lives. His warrant stems from the observation of how people grow their networks in contemporary societies of very different scale. In particular, emotional, material, and symbolic resources are used differentially to define a person's overlapping social networks described as intimate, effective, and extended (table 5.6).

The intimate network, which happens to be of Western family size, but not necessarily made up of family members (Milardo 1992), is very much part of our complex primate heritage. But, just as is the case with the great apes, there is nothing natural about it (Wilson 1988). Rather, these small-scale networks are created through negotiation and interaction.They embody social skills as much as biology. The effective and extended networks have contributed to our complicated social lives (as discussed above and in table 5.1). They involve material culture as much as people. Ancestors, animals, and artifacts are all interwoven in a personal network (table 5.6) whose analytical force lies in the notion that social life is hybrid.

Gamble also addresses the issue of the release from proximity, but not as a point of origin. The question instead provides an opportunity to see how individuals constructed their varied social lives through material culture and how, in turn, they were constituted by it. Certainly the Paleolithic record of all periods has opportunities to study the performance of social life as people encountered each other at locales (Gamble 1999:153–172, 251–264, 387–414), attended to one another in their taskscapes (Ingold 1993), made tracks across landscapes, and constituted their self and

Table 5.6 *A network approach to social life based on the individual* (based on Gamble 1999: Table 2.8)

Ego-Centred Networks	Principal Resource for Network Negotiation	Status of Network Partners	Form of Exchange	Number of People in Each Network
Personal				
Intimate	Emotional	Significant others	Generalized	3–7
Effective	Material	Colleagues and friends	Generalized	10–23
Extended	Symbolic	Friends of friends	Balanced	100–400
Global		Strangers	Negative	Unbounded

personhood through rhythms and gestures applied to making, doing, and living (Leroi-Gourhan 1993).

Such a social approach based on active, individual agents is exhaustively explored by Dobres (2000; Dobres and Hoffman 1994). The concept of agency, closely associated with the work of Giddens (1984) and Bourdieu (1977), empowers the individual, turning them from cipher to actor in the sense noted earlier by Strum and Latour. The key, as Dobres emphasizes, is a reformulation of our understanding of technology. Rather then seeing technology as a response to adaptive solutions, and hence under selection, it is instead a set of practices that both define and are defined by social life: "Technology can be thought of as a web that both metaphorically and literally weaves together people and their products" (Dobres 2000:130).

Through such a definition technology becomes hybrid, and is best described as a social technology (Gamble 1999:80–87). It is, moreover, an example of a network, itself a hybrid construct.

It is here that agency, a multifaceted concept at the best of times (Dobres and Robb 2000), achieves definition and fills that void at the center of what most people understand by social life in the Paleolithic. An example is provided by Wobst (2000:42) in his move away from the position that artifacts merely either afford action, or that action takes place and artifacts, in his phrase, "rain down." Instead he refers to artifacts as "material interferences" linked to people's intentions. Rather than bemoaning Childe's scraps, "The Paleolithic appeals to me because it is a particularly rich constellation of contexts to think about artifacts as material interventions in society"; (2000:43) "in its variability and variation in time and space, the Paleolithic record is the richest reservoir of agency in the archaeological record" (2000: 48).

However, what is currently lacking is a methodology to elucidate social practice and material interventions. Dobres (2000), for example, sets great store by the *chaîne opératoire* applied to bone and stone tool manufacture (Karlin and Julien 1994; Leroi-Gourhan 1993; Schlanger 1994). As utilized by Geneste (1988a, 1988b, 1989) in his study of technology and the acquisition of raw materials in Middle Paleolithic France, the *chaîne opératoire* promises much in uniting embodied social practice with material product (table 5.7).

Table 5.7 *A framework for studying the different scales and activities of Paleolithic society* (after Gamble 1999: Table 3.1)

LOCALES	*RHYTHMS*	*REGIONS*
Encounters	*Chaîne opératoire*	Landscape of habit
Gatherings		
	Taskscape	
Social occasions		
Place	*Paths and tracks*	Social landscape
INDIVIDUALS	<---------->	NETWORKS

What kind of individual?

But there is still some way to go with such approaches before a social archaeology can be said to exist for the Paleolithic. For example, the notion of the person usually remains normative, occasionally filled with essences (Bender 1978) to produce someone gendered, active, and knowledgeable, but hardly social.

Furthermore, there is a debate which needs to be entered concerning the concept of the individual. There are currently two polarized views. On the one hand is the familiar Western concept of the individual, someone who literally stops at the skin. As far as the Paleolithic individual has been investigated this would be the current understanding of the term: someone who first recognizes social categories and then uses resources to achieve them.

The alternative stems from Strathern's work in Melanesia (1988; Bird-David 1999), where she discussed the dividual, a person constituted by relationships. Rather than recognizing categories as the Western concept prefers, Strathern's relational model does away with the opposition between individuals and society. Due to the relationships through which a person is constituted, people can be said to be partible. And because those relationships are hybrid, involving people and things, persons can be distributed through networks. Of course, the reality is less dichotomized, as forcefully argued by Gosden (1999) and, as noted by LiPuma (1998:56). All cultures have both individual and dividual modalities of personhood. What is important, as Ingold (1999:81) points out, is that currently it is Western rather than relational ways of characterizing the individual which have most authority.

Chapman (2001) has investigated the material signatures of these social modalities by examining the intentional breaking of artifacts in the past. This results in parts of objects, such as ceramic potsherds, standing in relation to whole items and persons. His observations are particularly pertinent for the Paleolithic: "Dividing the flakes from a single flint core between two or more persons is one of the simplest forms of fragmentation that can be imagined. The personal stamp of the knapper on the tool ensured that s/he would travel wherever the tool journeyed" (2001: 40).

Chapman provides a means to examine the social practice of enchainment by which the person is constituted through the act of partition and distribution. The other social practice he identifies relates to accumulation, where distributed elements are brought together to form sets, for example deer canines, harvested through networks from a social landscape (table 5.7) to make a necklace (D'Errico and Vanhaeren 2002). As Wobst noted above, a change of perspective regarding the way that social life is conceived in the Paleolithic reveals that its potential for such analysis is vast. Moreover, as Dobres noted previously, here is a methodology to trace how technology wove people and their products, and to potentially produce a new understanding of a social archaeology of the Paleolithic.

Conclusions: The Future Social Paleolithic

The Paleolithic is used to define the direction of human development and add original authority to the institutions of later societies, including our own. Ever since the progressive evolution of Morgan (1877) and Engels (1884 [1902]) the Paleolithic has played this role on the broadest of political stages.

In this chapter we have argued that the formal framework by which the Paleolithic is studied affects archaeology as a whole. Moreover, the theoretical constraints are complex rather than simply being a straightforward matter of choice. Any research that stresses alternative interpretations to the one offered here of the material evidence, and role, of the Paleolithic would present later archaeological periods with a fundamental challenge to their uncontested existence. It would seem like an act of betrayal from that safe family member who has always been there, sitting quietly in the corner, but now wants to be heard.

But safety has nothing to do with it. Instead we are dealing with powerful notions that maintain a naturalized order. Their presence may go unnoticed but they are nevertheless our most restrictive sources of authority. They pay no attention to broad changes in theoretical discourse such as those which archaeology has recently undergone (Gamble 2001).

Derrida was the first to recognize that this metaphysical construction could not be easily sidestepped: "We can pronounce not a single destructive proposition which has not already had to slip into the form, the logic, and the implicit postulations of precisely what it seeks to contest" (Derrida 1997 [1967]:280–281).

The Paleolithic lacks the language to break the chains of such constructions. This is not because an appropriate language is readily available elsewhere, but rather because we are bound to use the same terms and logic that we are contesting (Derrida 1997 [1967]).

This would seem to put us all in a position of servitude to the present until we remember that "If no-one can escape this necessity, and if no-one is therefore responsible for giving in to it, however little he may do so, this does not mean that all the ways of giving in to it are of equal pertinence" (Derrida 1997 [1967]:282).

The alternative approaches discussed above indicate that it is possible to view differently many of the interpretive processes traditionally used in the Paleolithic and which we started out by characterizing as both obvious and permeable. The obvious, that social life had no origin but must be part of all archaeology, including the Paleolithic, may make it difficult to avoid a normative interpretation. But by acknowledging this circumstance we can begin to limit some of the constraints that a Paleolithic social archaeology currently finds itself in. One of the biggest constraints is the widespread indifference amongst archaeologists to a Paleolithic social archaeology. This indifference can be blamed on the lack of data, the monotony of what we have, and the length of time waiting for something, anything, to happen. Overcoming this status quo is only possible by recognizing the permeable character of social archaeology as we defined it earlier. The period since the 1980s has seen the introduction of many discourses, practices, and theories into archaeology. Interdisciplinarity permeates the entire process of responding to bodies of data which concern the past. Many of these currents have been explicitly social although it has to be said that the flow has been rather one-way. Archaeology has yet to be taken seriously by social theorists. The Paleolithic, because of its bedrock position in the structure of social origins, might be the place to reverse the flow by providing a critique of this very Western enterprise. Such a critique would significantly alter not only the Paleolithic's relationship with the rest of archaeology, but also the relationship that the West has with its own identity and past. To paraphrase Engels, "the Paleolithic has nothing to lose but its *chaînes* in this revolution. It has a social world to win!" Social archaeology therefore begins here.

ACKNOWLEDGMENTS

We would like to thank our editors for their patience and all those at the Centre for the Archaeology of Human Origins at Southampton for stimulating discussions on these issues. Yvonne Marshall and Matt Leivers deserve a special mention for their continual support. The chapter was written while Clive Gamble held a British Academy Research Readership.

REFERENCES

Adovasio, J. M., and J. Page. 2002. *The First Americans: In Pursuit of Archaeology's Greatest Mystery*. New York: Random House.

Aiello, L., and R. Dunbar. 1993. Neocortex size, group size and the evolution of language. *Current Anthropology* 34: 184–193.

Aiello, L. C. 1996. Terrestriality, bipedalism and the origin of language. In W. G. Runciman, J. Maynard-Smith, and R. I. M. Dunbar (eds.), *Evolution of Social Behaviour Patterns in Primates and Man*. Oxford: Oxford University Press, pp. 269–289.

Alexandri, A. 1995. The origins of meaning. In I. Hodder, M. Shanks, A. Alexandri, V. Buchli, J. Carman, J. Last, and G. Lucas (eds.), *Interpreting Archaeology; Finding Meaning in the Past*. London: Routledge, pp. 57–67.

Bender, B. 1978. Gatherer-hunter to farmer: A social perspective. *World Archaeology* 10: 204–222.

Binford, L. R. 1973. Interassemblage Variability – the Mousterian and the "Functional" argument. In C. Renfrew (ed.), *The Explanation of Culture Change*. London: Duckworth, pp. 227–254.

—— 2001. *Constructing Frames of Reference: An Analytical Method for Archaeological Theory Building Using Ethnographic and Environmental Datasets*. Berkeley: University of California Press.

——, and S. R. Binford. 1966. A preliminary analysis of functional variability in the Mousterian of Levallois facies. *American Anthropologist* 68: 238–295.

Binford, S. R. 1968. Early Upper Palaeolithic adaptations in the Levant. *American Anthropologist* LXX: 707–717.

Bird-David, N. 1999. "Animism" revisited: Personhood, environment, and relational epistemology. *Current Anthropology* 40: 67–91.

Bordes, F. 1968. *The Old Stone Age*. London: Weidenfeld & Nicolson.

——, and D. de Sonneville-Bordes. 1970. The significance of variability tn palaeolithic assemblages. *World Archaeology* 2: 61–73.

Bourdieu, P. 1977. *Outline of a Theory of Practice*. Cambridge: Cambridge University Press.

Brown, J. A., and T. D. Price. 1985. Complex hunter-gatherers: Retrospect and prospect. In T. D. Price and J. A. Brown (eds.), *Prehistoric Hunter-Gatherers: The Emergence of Cultural Complexity*. Orlando, FL: Academic Press, pp. 435–442.

Chapman, J. 2001. *Fragmentation in Archaeology: People, Places and Broken Objects in the Prehistory of South-Eastern Europe*. London: Routledge.

Childe, V. G. 1951. *Social Evolution*. London: Watts.

——1956. *Piecing Together the Past: The Interpretation of Archaeological Data*. Harmondsworth: Penguin.

Clark, G. A. 1992. A comment on Mithen's ecological interpretation of Palaeolithic art. *Proceedings of the Prehistoric Society* 58: 107–109.

Conkey, M. 1984. To find ourselves: Art and social geography of prehistoric hunter gatherers. In C. Schrire (ed.), *Past and Present in Hunter Gatherer Studies*. New York: Academic Press, pp. 253–276.

Conkey, M. W. 1978. Style and information in cultural evolution: Toward a predictive model for the Palaeolithic. In C. L. Redman, M. J. Berman, E. V. Curtin, W. T. Langhorne, N. M. Versaggi, and J. C. Wanser (eds.), *Social Archaeology*. New York: Academic Press, pp. 61–85.

——. 1980. The identification of prehistoric hunter-gatherer aggregation sites: The case of Altamira. *Current Anthropology* 21: 609–630.

——, and S. H. Williams. 1991. The political economy of gender in archaeology. In M. di Leonardo (ed.), *Gender at the Crossroads of Knowledge: Feminist Anthropology in a Postmodern Era*. 1st edn. Berkeley: University of California Press, pp. 102–139.

Constandse-Westermann, T. S., and R. R. Newell. 1991. Social and biological aspects of the western European mesolithic population structure: A comparison with the demography of North American Indians. In C. Bonsall (ed.), *The Mesolithic in Europe*. Edinburgh: Edinburgh University Press, pp. 106–115.

David, N. 1973. On Upper Palaeolithic society, ecology, and technological change: The Noaillian case. In C. Renfrew (ed.), *The Explanation of Culture Change: Models in Prehistory*. London: Duckworth, pp. 277–303.

D'Errico, F., and M. Vanhaeren. 2002. Criteria for identifying red deer (*Cervus elaphus*) age and sex from their canines. Application to the study of Upper Palaeolithic and Mesolithic ornaments. *Journal of Archaeological Science* 29: 211–232.

Derrida, J. 1976 [1967]. *Of Grammatology*. Baltimore, MD: Johns Hopkins University Press.

——1997 [1967]. *Writing and Difference*. London: Routledge.

——1974. The white mythology: Metaphor in the text of philosophy. *New Literary History* 6: 7–74.

de Waal, F. 1982. *Chimpanzee Politics*. London: Johnathan Cape.

——1991. *Peacemaking among Primates*. London: Penguin.

Dobres, M-A. 2000. *Technology and Social Agency*. Oxford: Blackwell.

——, and C. R. Hoffman. 1994. Social agency and the dynamics of prehistoric technology. *Journal of Archaeological Method and Theory* 1: 211–258.

Dobres, M-A., and J. Robb. 2000. Agency in archaeology: paradigm or platitude? In M-A. Dobres and J. Robb (eds.), *Agency in Archaeology*. London: Routledge, pp. 3–17.

Dunbar, R. I. M. 1988. *Primate Social Systems*. London: Croom Helm.

—— 1993. Coevolution of neocortical size, group size and language in humans. *Behavioural and Brain Sciences* 16: 681–735.

—— 1996. *Grooming, Gossip and the Evolution of Language*. London: Faber & Faber.

Engels, F. 1884 [1902]. *The Origin of the Family*. Chicago: Charles H. Kerr.

Foley, R., and P. C. Lee. 1996. Finite social space and the evolution of human social behaviour. In J. Steele and S. Shennan (eds.), *The Archaeology of Human Ancestry: Power, Sex and Tradition*. London: Routledge, pp. 47–66.

Foley, R. A. 1989. The evolution of hominid social behaviour. In V. Standen and R. A. Foley (eds.), *Comparative Socioecology*. Oxford: Blackwell Scientific, pp. 473–494.

Gamble, C. S. 1982. Interaction and alliance in Palaeolithic society. *Man* 17: 92–107.

—— 1986a. Hunter-gatherers and the origin of states. In J. A. Hall (ed.), *States in History*. Oxford: Basil Blackwell, pp. 22–47.

—— 1986b. *The Palaeolithic Settlement of Europe*. Cambridge: Cambridge University Press.

—— 1993. *Timewalkers: The Prehistory of Global Colonization*. Cambridge, MA: Harvard University Press.

—— 1996. Hominid behaviour in the Middle Pleistocene; an English perspective. In C. S. Gamble and A. J. Lawson (eds.), *The English Palaeolithic Reviewed*. Salisbury: Trust for Wessex Archaeology, pp. 63–71.

—— 1998a. Handaxes and Palaeolithic individuals. In N. Ashton, F. Healy, and P. Pettitt (eds.), *Stone Age Archaeology: Essays in Honour of John Wymer*. Oxford: Oxbow Monograph 102, pp. 105–109.

—— 1998b. Palaeolithic society and the release from proximity: A network approach to intimate relations. *World Archaeology* 29: 426–449.

—— 1999. *The Palaeolithic Societies of Europe*. Cambridge: Cambridge University Press.

—— 2001. *Archaeology: The Basics*. London: Routledge.

Geneste, J-M. 1988a. Les industries de la Grotte Vaufrey: Technologie du débitage, économie et circulation de la matière première lithique. In J-P. Rigaud (ed.), *La Grotte Vaufrey à Cenac et Saint-Julien (Dordogne), Paleoenvironments, chronologie et activités humaines*, Vol. 19, *Mémoires de la Société Préhistorique Française*, pp. 441–518.

—— 1988b. Systèmes d'approvisionnement en matières premières au paléolithique moyen et au paléolithique supérieur en Aquitaine. *L'Homme de Néandertal* 8: 61–70.

—— 1989. Economie des resources lithiques dans le mousterien du sud-ouest de la France. In M. Otte (ed.), *La Subsistance, Vol. 6, L'Homme de Néandertal*. Liège: ERAUL, pp. 75–97.

Giddens, A. 1984. *The Constitution of Society*. Berkeley: University of California Press.

Gilman, A. 1984. Explaining the Upper Palaeolithic revolution. In M. Spriggs (ed.), *Marxist Perspectives in Archaeology*. Cambridge: Cambridge University Press, pp. 115–126.

Goodall, J. 1986. *The Chimpanzees of Gombe: Patterns of Behaviour*. Cambridge MA: Belknap Press.

Gosden, C. 1994. *Social Being and Time*. Oxford: Blackwell.

—— 1999. *Anthropology and Archaeology: A Changing Relationship*. London: Routledge.

Graves, P. M. 1991. New models and metaphors for the Neanderthal debate. *Current Anthropology* 32: 513–41.

Hinde, R. A. 1976. Interactions, relationships and social structure. *Man* 11: 1–17.

Hodder, I. 1991. *Reading the Past*. 2nd edn. Cambridge: Cambridge University Press.

Houtsma, P., E. Kramer, R. R. Newell, and J. L. Smit. 1996. *The Late Palaeolithic Habitation of Haule V: From Excavation Report to the Reconstruction of Federmesser Settlement Patterns and Land Use*. Assen: Van Gorcum.

Hugdahl, F. P. 1999. Poststructuralism: Derrida and Foucault. In R. H. Popkin (ed.), *The Pimlico History of Western Philosophy*. London: Pimlico, pp. 737–744.

Ingold, T. 1993. The temporality of the landscape. *World Archaeology* 25: 152–173.

——1999. Comment on Bird-David. *Current Anthropology* 40: 82–3.

——2000. *The Perception of the Environment: Essays in Livelihood, Dwelling and Skill*. London: Routledge.

Isaac, G. 1976. The activities of early African hominids: A review of archaeological evidence from the time span two and a half to one million years ago. In G. Isaac and E. McCown (eds.), *Human Origins: Louis Leakey and the East African Evidence*. Menlo Park, CA: Benjamin, pp. 483–514.

Johnson, A. W., and T. Earle. 1987. *The Evolution of Human Societies*. Stanford, CA: Stanford University Press.

Johnson, M. 1999. *Archaeological Theory: An Introduction*. Oxford: Blackwell.

Karlin, C., and M. Julien. 1994. Prehistoric technology: A cognitive science. In C. Renfrew and E. Zubrow (eds.), *The Ancient Mind: Elements of Cognitive Archaeology*. Cambridge: Cambridge University Press, pp. 152–164.

Keeley, L. H. 1988. Hunter-gatherer economic complexity and "population pressure": A cross-cultural analysis. *Journal of Anthropological Archaeology* 7: 373–411.

King, T. F. 1978. Don't that beat the band? Nonegalitarian political organisation in prehistoric central California. In C. L. Redman, M. J. Berman, E. V. Curtin, W. T. Langhorne, N. M. Versaggi, and J. C. Wanser (eds.), *Social Archaeology*. New York: Academic Press, pp. 225–248.

Klein, R. G. 1989. *The Human Career*. Chicago: University of Chicago Press.

Knight, C. 1991a. *Blood Relations: Menstruation and the Origins of Culture*. New Haven, CT: Yale University Press.

——1991b. *The Origins of Human Society*. 4th edn. London: Radical Anthropology Group.

Latour, B., and S. C. Strum. 1986. Human social origins: Oh please, tell us another story. *Journal of Social Biological Structure* 9: 169–187.

Lee, R. B., and I. DeVore (eds.) 1968. *Man the Hunter*. Chicago: Aldine.

Leroi-Gourhan, A. 1993. *Gesture and Speech*. Cambridge, MA: MIT Press.

LiPuma, E. 1998. Modernity and forms of personhood in Melanesia. In M. Lambek and A. Strathern (eds.), *Bodies and Persons: Comparative Perspectives from Africa and Melanesia*. Cambridge: Cambridge University Press., pp. 53–79.

Lourandos, H. 1997. *Continent of Hunter-Gatherers: New Perspectives in Australian Prehistory*. Cambridge: Cambridge University Press.

Maryanski, A., and M. Ishii-Kuntz. 1991. A cross-species application of Bott's hypothesis on role segregation and social networks. *Sociological Perspectives* 34: 403–425.

Maryanski, A., and J. H. Turner. 1992. *The Social Cage: Human Nature and the Evolution of Society*. Stanford, CA: Stanford University Press.

Maryanski, A. R. 1993. The elementary forms of the first protohuman society: An ecological/social network approach. *Advances in Human Ecology* 2: 215–241.

——1996. African ape social networks: A blueprint for reconstructing early hominid social structure. In S. J. Shennan and J. Steele (eds.), *The Archaeology of Human Ancestry; Power, Sex and Tradition*. London: Routledge, pp. 67–90.

Mauss, M. 1979. Body techniques. In *Sociology and Psychology: Essays*. Trans. Ben Brewster. London: Routledge & Kegan Paul, pp. 97–123.

Milardo, R. M. 1992. Comparative methods for delineating social networks. *Journal of Social and Personal Relationships* 9: 447–461.

Mithen, S. 1990. *Thoughtful Foragers*. Cambridge: Cambridge University Press.

—— 1993. Individuals, groups and the Palaeolithic record: A reply to Clark. *Proceedings of the Prehistoric Society* 59: 393–398.

—— 1994. Technology and society during the middle pleistocene: Hominid group size, social learning and industrial variability. *Cambridge Archaeological Journal* 4: 3–32.

—— 1996. *The Prehistory of the Mind*. London: Thames & Hudson.

Morgan, L. H. 1877. *Ancient Society*. New York: World Publishing.

Mueller-Wille, S., and D. B. Dickson. 1991. An examination of some models of late pleistocene society in southwestern Europe. In G. Clark (ed.), *Perspectives of the Past: Theoretical Biases on Mediterranean Hunter Gatherer Research*. Philadelphia: University of Pennsylvania Press, pp. 25–55.

Newell, R. R., and T. S. Constandse-Westermann. 1986. Testing an ethnographic analogue of mesolithic social structure and the archaeological resolution of mesolithic ethnic groups and breeding populations. *Proceedings of the Koninklijke Nederlandse Akademie van Wetenschappen* 89: 243–310.

Noble, W., and I. Davidson. 1996. *Human Evolution, Language and Mind*. Cambridge: Cambridge University Press.

Parish, A. R. 1996. Female relationships in Bonobos (*Pan paniscus*): Evidence for bonding, cooperation, and female dominance in a Male-Philopatric species. *Human Nature* 7: 61–96.

Price, T. D., and J. A. Brown (eds.) 1985. *Prehistoric Hunters and Gatherers: The Emergence of Cultural Complexity*. New York: Academic Press.

Quiatt, D., and V. Reynolds. 1993. *Primate Behaviour: Information, Social Knowledge, and the Evolution of Culture*. Cambridge: Cambridge University Press.

Redman, C., M. J. Berman, E. V. Curtin, W. T. Langhorne, N. M. Versaggi, and J. C. Wanser (eds.) 1978. *Social Archaeology*. New York: Academic Press.

Renfrew, C. (ed.) 1973. *The Explanation of Culture Change*. London: Duckworth.

Rodseth, L., R. W. Wrangham, A. Harrigan, and B. B. Smuts. 1991. The human community as a primate society. *Current Anthropology* 32: 221–254.

Sahlins, M. 1963. Poor man, rich man, big man, chief: Political types in Melanesia and Polynesia. *Comparative Studies in Society and History* 5: 285–303.

Schlanger, N. 1994. Mindful technology: unleashing the *chaîne opératoire* for an archaeology of mind. In C. Renfrew and E. Zubrow (eds.), *The Ancient Mind: Elements of Cognitive Archaeology*. Cambridge: Cambridge University Press, pp. 143–151.

Service, E. R. 1962. *Primitive Social Organization: An Evolutionary Perspective*. 2nd edn. New York: Random House.

Shennan, S. 1989. Introduction: Archaeological approaches to cultural identity. In S. J. Shennan (ed.), *Archaeological Approaches to Cultural Identity*. London: Unwin Hyman, pp. 1–32.

Sollas, W. J. 1911. *Ancient Hunters and their Modern Representatives*. London: Macmillan.

Steele, J., and S. Shennan (eds.) 1996. *The Archaeology of Human Ancestry; Power, Sex and Tradition. Theoretical Archaeology Group (TAG)*. London: Routledge.

Strathern, M. 1988. *The Gender of the Gift: Problems with Women and Problems with Society in Melanesia*. Berkeley: University of California Press.

—— 1996. Cutting the network. *Journal of the Royal Anthropological Institute* 2: 517–535.

Stringer, C., and C. Gamble. 1993. *In Search of the Neanderthals: Solving the Puzzle of Human Origins*. London: Thames & Hudson.

Strum, S. S., and B. Latour. 1987. Redefining the social link: From baboons to humans. *Social Science Information* 26: 783–802.

Tilley, C. 1996. *An ethnography of the Neolithic*. Cambridge: Cambridge University Press.

Washburn, S. L. (ed.) 1961. *Social Life of Early Man*. New York: Wenner-Gren.

——, and I. DeVore. 1961. Social behaviour of baboons and early man. In S. L. Washburn, *Social Life of Early Man*, pp. 91–105. New York: Wenner-Gren.

White, R. 1985. Thoughts on social relationships and language in hominid evolution. *Journal of Social and Personal Relationships* 2: 95–115.

Williams, B. J. 1974. A model of Band Society. *Memoirs of the Society for American Archaeology* 29.

Wilson, P. 1988. *The Domestication of the Human Species*. New Haven, CT: Yale University Press.

Wobst, H. M. 1974a. The archaeology of Band Society: Some unanswered questions. *Memoirs of the Society for American Archaeology* 29: v–xiii.

——1974b. Boundary conditions for palaeolithic social systems: A simulation approach. *American Antiquity* 39: 147–78.

——1976. Locational relationships in Palaeolithic society. *Journal of Human Evolution* 5: 49–58.

——1977. Stylistic behavior and information exchange. In *Papers for the Director: Research Essays in Honor of James B. Griffin, Vol. 61, Anthropological Papers*, ed. C. E. Cleland. Ann Arbor: Museum of Anthropology, University of Michigan, pp. 317–342.

——2000. Agency in (spite of) material culture. In M-A. Dobres and J. Robb (eds.), *Agency in Archaeology*. London: Routledge, pp. 40–50.

Woodburn, J. 1980. Hunters and gatherers today and reconstruction of the past. In E. Gellner (ed.), *Soviet and Western Anthropology*. London: Duckworth, pp. 95–117.

Young, R. 1990. *White Mythologies: Writing, History and the West*. London: Routledge.

Part II

Identities

Lynn Meskell and Robert W. Preucel

Archaeology, like the social sciences in general, has begun to reorient itself around the notion of identity. Theorizing identity forms a critical nexus in contemporary academic discourse, bringing together sociologists, anthropologists, political scientists, psychologists, geographers, historians, and philosophers (Gosden 1999; Hall 1996; Jenkins 1996; Yaeger 1996). However, it is only since the 1980s that archaeology engaged with, and contributed to, identity discourse. In the 1980s the debate focused upon single-issue social categories such as gender or ethnicity which were often viewed as radical taxonomies that resided on the fringe of archaeological possibility. Within a decade, from the mid-1990s onwards, archaeological interpretations have become more nuanced, complex, and altogether more relevant to the lived experiences of people, past and present. This is one of the most exciting aspects of a burgeoning social archaeology and one that encompasses not only Euro-American archaeologies, but those from Australia, Latin America, Africa, South Asia, and so on.

In framing identity today, archaeologists and other scholars who concern themselves with the social world investigate how individuals and collectivities are distinguished in their social relations with other individuals and collectivities (Jenkins 1996:4). In the "social and cultural sciences, what was once called 'identity' in the sense of social, shared sameness is today often discussed with reference to difference. Difference points to the contrastive aspect of identities and thereby emphasizes the implicit condition of plurality" (Sökefeld 1999:417–18). Self-definition today coalesces around genealogy, citizenship, shared histories, and religious unity and sameness, but underlying that reside troubling contemporary concerns about disenfranchisement, dislocation, and difference. The constitutive outside, premised on exclusion and alterity, forms the corona of difference through which identities are enunciated (Meskell 2002a). Identity as a discursive category extends back to the Greeks, yet as an analytical concept it achieved its saliency in the 1960s, primarily in the social sciences, through the influential works of Erikson, Merton, Goffman, and Berger. Identity has proven to be simultaneously a productive and challenging concept since it crosses multiple theoretical frames and embodies contradictory and heterogeneous definitions. The 1980s saw the rise and sedimentation of the trinity of race, class, and gender. It was only in the 1990s that archaeology considered this convergence of identities as both a possible and fruitful mode of analysis. Identity may be constituted by categories of practice, but we must recognize that individuals associate and live within multiple categories in the course of their life trajectory and further connect to others by various practices of identification. This lack of ultimate fixity has led many scholars to bemoan the slippery fluidity of identity and challenge its political stability and thus, utility. Others have celebrated this lack of boundedness and essential categorization as more akin to lived experience and personal politics, arguing that a more contingent politics of location should be embraced. These debates are currently at the forefront of research on identity, whether conducted by feminists, sociologists, anthropologists or archaeologists.

The debate can be characterized as oscillating between hard or soft constructionism, between those who would argue for fixed categories reliant on foundational differences and those who advocate a more mutable, fluid set of identifications that are open to re-evaluation and reflexivity. Identity remains an elusive term embodying contradictory and heterogeneous definitions. Its theoretical purview encompasses two extreme poles of thought and many diverse positions in between. Identity is thus a topos, a challenging terrain that has not only academic interest but serious real-time effects for living people, descendant communities and relations among diverse interest groups. As Brubaker and Cooper encapsulate the dilemma:

> Clearly the term identity is made to do a great deal of work. It is used to highlight non-instrumental modes of action; to focus on self-understanding rather than self-interest; to designate sameness across persons or sameness over time; to capture allegedly core, foundational aspects of selfhood; to deny that such core, foundational aspects exist; to highlight the processual, interactive development of solidarity and collective self-understanding; and to stress the fragmented quality of the contemporary experience of "self," a self unstably patched together through shards of discourse and contingently "activated" in differing contexts. (2000:8)

Identity as a processual phenomenon, rather than a set of taxonomic specificities, may be one way to ameliorate the polarities and bring the debate to a closer understanding of how our individual identities congeal or solidify over our lifetime as a dynamic practice of marking difference. Subjectivity and human agency are clearly central to reformulating our discursive identity practices (Foucault 1978:xiv). Bauman astutely notes (1996:19) that identity has come to operate as a verb, rather than a noun and occupies the ontological status of both a project and a postulate. These are inherently political practices, grounded in spatio-temporal contexts – what has come to be described as the *politics of location* (see below). Language and the terminologies we chose to deploy are similarly key to those political incursions and it is to that terrain that we now turn.

Taxonomies

Western conventions of taxonomizing, especially in terms of identity, be it race, class, gender, or sexual preference, has been effectively inculcated in our own scholarship even when examining past lives. These conventions necessitate that all individuals be neatly pigeonholed and categorized according to a set of predetermined labels. So too in our archaeological investigations we have concentrated on single-issue questions of identity, focusing singularly on gender or ethnicity, and have attempted to locate people from antiquity into a priori Western taxonomies: heterosexual/homosexual, male/ female, elite/non-elite, etc. Archaeologists have tended to concentrate on specific sets of issues that coalesce around topics like gender, age or status, without interpolating other axes of identity, be they class, ethnicity or sexual orientation, for example, because it has been seen as too vast or complex a project. As previously argued (Meskell 2001), we need to break the boundaries of identity categories themselves, blurring the crucial domains of identity formation, be they based on gender, sexuality, kin, politics, religion or social systems. Only through deconstruction of the domains we see as "natural" or prediscursive can we contextualize archaeologies of difference. One can even go further and interrogate the traditional classifications of people and things. In chapter 7 of this volume Gosden, drawing on the work of Latour, also seeks to challenge the epistemic force of conventional taxonomies: the world is thus composed of a series of hybrids, of quasi-objects. These quasi-objects are human products refracting past human actions and intentions, but they are also human beings who have a series of physical characteristics as well as social intentions (see also Buchli, chapter 8, this volume). At a meta-level, all social worlds are made up of dense networks of quasi-objects (people and things) that are effective in creating states of affairs by virtue both of their physical efficacy and embodied sets of intentions. Gosden also directs us toward a more relational view of persons and their networked relations, extending out from Strathern's influential work on individuals and dividuals.

Moving beyond a list of salient identity markers, archaeologists might profitably interrogate the very foundations of our imposed categories and try to understand social domains in their cultural context. Focusing on the social domains that are crucial for the formation of people's identity – family, sexuality, race, nation, religion – we cannot assume a priori that what *we* consider as natural, no matter how institutionalized, is fundamental. Whether in ethnographic or archaeological settings,

> [t]he verities on which identity – whether gender, sexual orientation, nationality, ethnicity, or religion – have traditionally been based no longer provide the answers, in part because of the contact and conflict between peoples and in part because the explanatory schemes upon which identity was based have been shown to rest not on the bedrock of fact but suspended in narratives of origin. (Yanagisako and Delaney 1995b: 1)

In archaeology, the foundational premises of sex and gender have only recently been challenged (Gilchrist 1999; Meskell 1996, 1999b; Wylie 1991). Archaeologists have found it difficult to extricate themselves from "naturalized power" in the discourses of identity that are fundamental to our own culture. Thus we have construed gender in the past, for instance, as simplistically mirroring specific contemporary terms and agendas, or connoted sexuality as existing primarily in a modern European guise. What we see as natural exists largely within our own temporal and cultural borders, yet we take this as fixed and "natural" and thus transferable to ancient contexts. The erasure of difference results in a familiar and normative picture of the past that may bear little relation to ancient experience. Alternatively, anthropologists, feminists, and social scientists might draw upon archaeology's provision of a deep temporal sequence in terms of cultural difference, often as it is mediated through the discursive production of material culture. These rich strata of evidence can only enhance, and contribute to, the complex picture already emerging of identity as having both contextual and embedded entanglements.

Only culture makes the boundaries of domains seem natural, gives ideologies power, and makes hegemonies appear seamless. Even the seemingly implacable dichotomy of subjects and objects, things and people, has now been interrogated, suggesting that these taxonomies may prove inadequate in our understandings of others (Gell 1998; Meskell 2004; Myers 2001; Pinney and Thomas 2001). In ancient contexts we can rarely be clear where one cultural domain ends and another begins. It might prove more interesting to inquire how meanings migrate across domain boundaries and how specific actions are multiply constituted. We also have to interrogate what we have constructed as the facts of life, calling into question the constructions of motherhood (Wilkie 2003), the domain of kinship (Joyce and Gillespie 2000; Strathern 1992), and the spheres of sexuality and religiosity (Meskell 2000), for example. Anthropologists, and by extension archaeologists, have read seamlessly across other people's cultural domains. We cannot assume that in other societies cultural domains are structured like ours and expect the same analytic constellations. Social or contextual archaeology is premised on the recognition of local patterns of meanings-in-practice (Meskell 2001: 203).

Identity provides a salient case for both moderns and ancients – as one of the most compelling issues of our day it is appropriate that we focus on the social experiences of ancient people, yet what makes these questions so intriguing is how specific societies evoked such different responses prompted by categorical differences in their understandings and constructions of social domains. It is inseparable from the experience of everyday life where individuals are positioned or made aware of certain aspects of themselves whether it is their age, sex, race, religion or social status. Some vectors of identity are internalized, others are discursive, yet it is their particular intensities, experienced in certain settings and certain times, that crystallizes into structures or is rendered political. There is also a significant difference between self-identification and the ways in which others identify and taxonomize people, what one might see as the relational versus the categorical (Brubaker and Cooper 2000). One need only recall that the census and other state apparatuses were also operative in various ways in antiquity as devices of governmentality. Identification might also be seen as a process, a *sens practique* that defies the fixity of categorization. But before archaeologists began to explore the possibilities of identity broadly construed or as reconfigured in specific space–time contexts, single-issue studies held sway. It is to this periodization that we now turn.

Issues of Power, Class, and Status

Within a social archaeology single-issue studies have been of great interest over the past few decades. Most scholars acknowledge that we all have a number of social identities which entail constant negotiation and organize our relationships to other individuals and groups within our social world (Craib 1998:4–9), yet we often forget the subjective, inner world of the individual. There has been an outward focus on uncovering the top-down implementations of power that have effects on people or the "technologies of the self" that infer a disembodied force. Here the writings of Giddens, Foucault, and Bourdieu on power and social reproduction have been influential (Barrett 1994; Barrett 2000; Gardner 2002; Shanks and Tilley 1987a, 1987b; Thomas 1996; Tilley 1990, 1994). Understanding society often requires a metanarrative, just as awareness of individual selves requires that identity and life experience be inserted into that equation (Craib 1998:28). In fact, there are two levels of operation: one is the broader social level in which identities have certain formal associations or mores; the other is the individual or personal level where a person experiences many aspects of identity within a single subjectivity, fluid over the trajectories of life. The latter is more contingent, immediate, and operates at a greater frequency, whereas society's categories and constraints may take longer to reformulate.

The first studies of social identity tended to focus upon rank and status as a means of examining the origins of social complexity. In Britain this was largely stimulated by the work of Childe, Clarke, Renfrew, and the Cambridge postprocessual school. Following the work of Elman Service and Morton Fried, archaeologists in the United States pursued evolutionary models derived from anthropology. Of special interest were those societies lying between bands and states that came to be called chiefdoms or ranked societies. Earle (1997, 2002), for example, argued that the standard defin-itions of chiefdoms that identified reciprocity were flawed. Many archaeologists were aiming to identify institutionalized status inequality, i.e., any hierarchy of statuses that form part of social structure and extend beyond age, sex, individual characteristics, and intrafamilial roles (Wason 1994:19). Whilst this is one important layer in the social stratum, so is the substratum Wason attempts to avoid – the individual dimension. Both are interdependent categories that must be addressed in order to offer a represen-tative and accurate picture of social life, as experienced by individuals and not categor-ies. Lewis Binford once talked about the social persona as a composite of the social identities maintained in life (Chapman and Randsborg 1981:7; O'Shea 1984:4). However, he was more interested in generalizing strategies rather than contextual ones and in accessing the larger social system at the expense of individuals in all their variability.

Throughout the 1980s and 1990s archaeologists focused firmly on the materializa-tion of power strategies and the negotiation of rank, status, and prestige display (Earle, Renfrew and Shennan 1982). Concomitantly, individuals were reduced to passive social actors fulfilling prescribed roles (Meskell 1996, 1999b). Prior mortuary analyses focused on the expression and negotiation of social relationships. From this perspec-tive, deceased individuals were manipulated for the purposes of status aggrandizement for the living (Parker Pearson 1982:112): people were largely motivated by self-interest and the desire to accumulate power. Since the burial context is manipulable and not necessarily reflective of social reality, archaeologists recognized that the negotiation of symbolic meanings was constitutive of social relationships (see also Parker Pearson 2001). Yet the centrality of power overshadowed the realization that death could, in specific contexts, be a deeply moving, personal experience (Tarlow 1999). In this critique others suggested that death and burial are not always necessarily driven by social aspirations (Meskell 1996; Nordström 1996): an archaeology of burial is not tantamount to an archaeology of death (e.g., Barrett 1988). Subsequently, more multi-dimensional analyses have focused upon the experience and creation of memory, identity, agency, and embodied being in contextually rich settings (Bradley 2000; Chesson 2001; Gilchrist 1999; Jones 2001; Joyce 2000a, 2001; Meskell 1999b, 2003; Meskell and Joyce 2003).

A significant move in the archaeology of social inequality was Brumfiel's (1992) consideration of status, class, faction, and gender. Here she argued against the system-based (or ecosystem) approach in favor of an agent-centered one that acknowledged the play of gendered, ethnic, and class interaction. She suggested that elites were not the only prime movers of change and that subordinate groups could affect the structure of hierarchy. Whether culture-historical, processual or social archaeologies, the study of relationships between elite and non-elite has been central (e.g., Bailey 2000; Kristiansen and Rowlands 1998; Miller, Rowlands, and Tilley 1989; Miller and Tilley 1984; Yoffee 1998, 2000). Yet the degree to which this has coalesced around social identity rather than simply examining exchange, bureaucracy, and power is debatable.

In fields such as historical archaeology (Hall 1992, 1994, 2000, 2001) or archaeologies of the recent past (Buchli 2000; Buchli and Lucas 2001), our findings have socio-political inflections and many researchers feel impelled to engage with living communities. Writing on identity and consumption in chapter 9 of this volume, Mullins draws our attention to the myriad ways in which African heritage may be material-ized and argues that this subjectivity is itself actively fashioned by consumers in specific social, political, and material circumstances. For archaeologists, he argues, the aim should be to examine how African, black, white, middle class, and similar identity taxonomies have been constructed by various social groups over time, the ways in which apparently distinct categories are entangled in each other, and how archaeology itself can identify the historical discontinuities in such identities. This reiterates the importance of classification and taxonomy as constructed, albeit with tremendous residual and lasting power. He argues that while the presence of traditional African objects is a powerful and important testament to African-American agency, it is equally salient that these individuals became producers, marketers, shoppers, and consumers in a society in which all public rights were denied to people of color. For Mullins, any research that examines consumption as uncomplicated patterning of well-established identities risks attenuating individual agency, reducing the distinct factors shaping any given consumption context, and ignoring the complexities of power altogether. Many theories have sought to present communities as cohesive and undifferentiated, making groups different on a comparative scale yet undermining the social variability internal to the group. Concepts such as culture and ethnicity still have interpretive power, and that power has repercussions in contemporary society. That being said, a focus on wealth, status, and consumption should problematize the presumed fixity of identities and their construction.

Another development within the archaeology of social difference stemmed from Marxist notions (see Patterson 2003) of class struggle and oppression that have found their fullest expression in historical archaeology (Paynter and McGuire 1991; Saitta 1994; Spriggs 1984). As Mullins outlines, the concept of ideology has been crucial in these debates particularly in the 1980s (see Miller, Rowlands, and Tilley 1989; Miller and Tilley 1984), and has been most articulately championed by Mark Leone (1984); drawing upon the work of Althusser. From this perspective, ideology is lived relations that give human subjects coherence, though that coherence is an illusion produced by structures that exist outside our everyday practical consciousness. Leone's formulation of ideology adopts Althusser's concept of ideological state apparatuses and combines it with the Habermasian notion of ideology as intentionally distorted communication. For Leone, ideology is a dominant class-interested discourse that finds its way into various everyday behaviors and beliefs that the masses internalize without critical self-reflection. From the 1980s onward, many archaeologists have been inspired by Giddensian structuration theory: the notion that modes of economic relationships are translated into noneconomic social structures (Giddens 1981:105, 1984, 1991). Some, like Hodder (1982), viewed it as a means of bridging the opposition of functionalism and structuralism. Similarly, Bourdieu has been embraced by archaeologists for his attempts to dissolve the structure–agency dualism and for allowing agents some contribution to their construction in the world (Bourdieu 1977, 1980, 1998; Bourdieu and Eagleton 1994; see also Hodder, this volume). Other social theorists are now being integrated within an archaeology of identity, including Butler, Hacking, Habermas, and Hall.

Race and Ethnicity

The broader question of identifying ethnicity materially and symbolically extends back to early writers such as Montelius and Childe, through to Hawkes, Piggott, the ethnoarchaeological work of Hodder (1982), processual approaches (Auger et al. 1987; Emberling 1997), and contextual ones (Aldenderfer 1993; Wells 1998; Yoffee and Emberling 1999). Yet isolating ethnic specificities has proven to be illusive and potentially teleological in archaeological writing. From this perspective, racial and ethnic studies share a common ontological terrain. As Upton (1996:3) demonstrates, while archaeologists view "slave culture" as a product of racial experience, and a response to the social, economic, legal, and interpersonal conditions of the institution, we have come to expect a particular material resistance. Their artifacts are supposed to be distinctive and we are suspicious when they are indistinguishable from those of their masters. Studies often focus on the articulation of difference in reductive terms, by examining ceramics, textiles, architecture, food, burials, etc. Looking for ethnicity mirrors the strategies of gender archaeology, which simply looked for women as discrete and familiar entities. And, like gender, theories of ethnicity have moved from a focus on the biological to the social, and from the category to the boundary. The axial ideational, social, and subjective dimensions are lived and potentially porous or changeable, yet often materially invisible. Assuming a specific ethnic identification "must depend on ascription and self-ascription: only in so far as individuals embrace it, are constrained by it, act on it, and experience it will ethnicity make organizational difference" (Barth 1994:12). Hall (1997:4) reminds us that "identities are constructed within, not outside, discourse" and are "produced in specific historical and institutional sites within specific discursive formations and practices, by specific enunciative strategies." The fluidity and permeability of those identities produces real problems for archaeologists in contexts lacking historical documentation, and even text-aided settings can be complex (Meskell 1999a, 1999b).

There has been a longstanding archaeological interest in ethnicity and ethnogenesis, while the related trajectories of politics and nationalism are relatively more recent. There has never been any consensus in terminology and "ethnicity" has been used to denote the individual versus the group, the contents of an ethnic identity versus its instrumental expression, personal feelings versus the instrumental expression of identity, etc. (Banks 1996:47). Ethnic identity is only one social determinate that is intersected by status, occupation, gender, and so on. But it involves the social negotiation of difference and sameness, and it often entails larger tensions between individuals, the group, and the state. Ethnic identity is not fundamentally hierarchical like class and status in either a Marxist or Weberian sense (Emberling 1997:305). It is a concept aligned to the construct of kinship, albeit larger than the group, clan, or lineage. Archaeologists have shown that ethnicity is not always synonymous with a single language, race, location, or material culture. Some markers are more telling than others for archaeologists, such as styles of food or household arrangements, rather than language or pottery (Baines 1996; Baldwin 1987; Cheek and Friedlander 1990; Emberling 1997; Hall 1997; Jones 1996; McGuire 1982; Odner 1985; Spence 1992; Staski 1990; Stine 1990; Wall 1999). In chapter 8 of this volume, Buchli specifically addresses both the material and immaterial dimensions that shaped the socialist and post-socialist experience in Russia and Kazakhstan. He outlines how two competing materialities created and reworked new realms of material culture and radically different social visions. One form of architecture was iconoclastic and preoccupied with the fabrication of utopian order (European Modernism). The alternative form intended to refashion that order in diverse ways and scales (Stalinist Classicism). Architectural styles configured the material world in very distinct and antagonistic fashions in relation to shifting fields of power. In Kazakhstan, Buchli documents the construction of the new Capitol of Kazakhstan in Astana, where competing materialities are similarly in contentious and fluid engagement with post-socialist and independent Kazakhstani identity. Ironically, this has entailed the construction of a postmodern capital city with a new nationalist architecture, while what one might consider an authentic national tradition is subsequently being destroyed. Buchli highlights the complexity of identity construction, even in contemporary and well-documented contexts. This underscores that archaeologists must negotiate an in-between terrain at the unstable interface between the material and immaterial.

Following Bourdieu's concept of habitus, Jones's (1996) synthetic work on ethnicity provides a detailed account of the discipline's engagement and its problematics. Teasing out ethnic difference from the complex fabric of identity is fraught, if not impossible, in many archaeological contexts. If, indeed, ethnicity is grounded in the shared subliminal dispositions of social agents and shaped by practice, how might we approach this materially? Historically, theorizing ethnicity seems to have either correlated pots with people or written material culture out of the record almost entirely. Other studies took tangential routes to cultural identity in an attempt to move beyond these isomorphic and deterministic studies (Shennan 1994). Some argue that not all archaeologists can study ethnicity or that social structures may not indeed correspond to our current classifications, which impels us to revisit anthropological and sociological literatures (Hegmon 1998:274). The discipline's most evocative studies of ethnicity emanate from historical (Rothschild 2003; Staski 1990; Wall 1999; Woodhouse-Beyer 1999) or ethnohistorical contexts (David et al. 1991; Dietler and Herbich 1998; Torrence and Clark 2000), where diverse sources are inflected with the nuanced valences that represent social complexity. Newer research has moved from ethnicity to coalesce around issues of community, as a more localized perspective on identity formation (Blake 1999; Canuto and Yaeger 2000). Research into the specificities of ethnic identity and the longevity of community lies at the intersection of identity politics. On the one hand, investigating ethnicity answers questions about social difference in past societies while on the other, in extreme circumstances, it forms a locus for extrapolation to contemporary political questions about origins, legitimacy, ownership and, ultimately, rights. That entanglement has singled "ethnicity" out as the dangerous vector of difference, as opposed to gender or age taxonomies (see Part IV: Politics).

Plantation archaeology is a salient example, situated within the larger framework of African-American archaeology – the latter developing out of social, political, and intellectual movements such as black activism, historic preservation legislation, academic interest in ethnicity, and the role of public archaeology (Singleton 1995:122, 1999). The focus of study has moved from the identification of slave quarters to more nuanced discussions of power and identity and the complex machinations between plantation owners and their slaves. The archaeology of racism is prefigured in all such discussions, and while there might seem an obvious connection to ethnicity theory, the two should not be conflated (Babson 1990; Orser 1999:666). As Orser warns, whiteness must also be denaturalized. Moreover, archaeologists should consider the material dimensions of using whiteness as a source of racial domination, which is inexorably linked to capitalism (Leone 1995). Historical archaeologists are, however, faced with a complex mosaic of racial, ethnic, and class reflections in material culture, which has proven difficult to disentangle. More recently, single-issue theories have been displaced by multifaceted explanations involving race, class, gender, religion, lineage, and representation (Delle, Mrozowski, and Paynter 2000; Mullins 1999; Rotman and Nassaney 1997; Russel 1997; Stine 1990; Wall 1999; Wilkie 2003; Wilkie and Bartoy 2000) and the recognition of contemporary sociopolitical relevance.

Gender and Feminism

The salience of gender as an identifiable marker arrived relatively late on the theoretical scene (Conkey and Spector 1984); first through the lens of first-wave feminist theory (Claassen 1992a; Engelstad 1991; Gilchrist 1991) and followed by a number of substantive case studies outlining women's place in the past (Gero and Conkey 1991; Gibbs 1987; Gilchrist 1994). It went hand in hand with contemporary concerns over the position of women as practitioners and academics within the discipline (Claassen 1994; Claassen and Joyce 1997; Diaz-Andreu and Sørensen 1998; Dommasnes 1992; Nelson, Nelson, and Wylie 1994). Gender studies in archaeology suffered from being considered the domain of women, rather than the more dialogic or holistic study of gendered relations that considered men as gendered beings with a concomitant construction of sexed identity (Knapp 1998; Knapp and Meskell 1997; Meskell 1996).

Some earlier studies took more radical paths to sexed identity (Yates and Nordbladh 1990), yet were not seen as representing engendered studies, due to their lack of explicit focus upon women as a category. A more inclusive third-wave feminist perspective positioned gender as relational to a host of other identity markers such as age, class, ethnicity, sexuality, and so on (Meskell 1999b; 2002). Its positionality must also be contextualized through other modalities of power such as kinship or social status (Brumfiel 1992; Joyce and Gillespie 2000; Meskell & Joyce 2003; Sweely 1999). Identity, in its various manifestations, operates under erasure in the interstices of reversal and emergence (Hall 1996:2), which entails interrogating the old taxonomies and categories that we have reified as doxic and impermeable.

Part of this reformulation has been undertaken within the locus of gender archaeology. Gender has now been instantiated within the wider social context of the life cycle (Gilchrist 2000; Meskell 2002b) or linked to age (Moore and Scott 1997), expanding the social milieu, rather than restricting it to single-issue polemics. In chapter 6 of this volume, Gilchrist evinces this more holistic approach, advocating a constructionist position on age, and consideration of the life-course model that has become central within the social sciences. Rather than focusing on successive stages of the life cycle in isolation, such as childhood, adolescence, old age, and so on, the life-course perspective attempts to understand the experience of human life as a continuum. Archaeologists have shown how material culture was used to articulate the transition from child to adulthood and how it was mobilized by children to learn adult skills and modes of interacting. In archaeology, as in many social disciplines, the theme of the body has been interwoven with studies of the life cycle through emerging anthropologies of personhood. As Gilchrist demonstrates, this has been adopted through the lens of embodied approaches within feminist archaeology, but also in subfields such as evolutionary biology.

Axiomatically, our identities are constantly under negotiation as we experience life, and open to manipulation if we have the opportunity. People do not always perform as "men" or "women" and identities are not coherent or prior to the interactions through which they are constituted. Individuals are gendered through discursive daily practices: "gender is thus a process of becoming rather than a state of being" (Harvey and Gow 1994:8). The concept of identity politics does not necessarily entail objective needs or political implications, but challenges the connections between identity and politics and positions identity as a factor in any political analysis. Thus, we can say that though gender is not natural, biological, universal, or essential, we can still claim that it is relevant because of its political ramifications.

Other dimensions of identity that are burgeoning are those of age, the body, intimate relations, and sexuality (Gamble 1998; Hamilakis, Pluciennik, and Tarlow 2002; Joyce 2000b; Lyons 1998; Meskell 1998a; Rautman 2000). Refiguring the body has recently provided an important nexus for reconciling issues such as biological imperatives, cultural markers, personal embodiment and experience, diachronic diversity, and social difference. There have been numerous case studies from prehistoric contexts (Knapp and Meskell 1997; Marcus 1993; Shanks 1995; Shanks and Tilley 1982; Thomas and Tilley 1993; Yates 1993; Yates and Nordbladh 1990) to historically embedded examples (Gilchrist 1997, 1999; Joyce 1993, 1998, 2001; Meskell 1998b, 1998c, 1999b; Meskell & Joyce 2003; Montserrat 1998; Osborne 1998a, 1998b). These studies suggest that archaeology has much to offer other social sciences in being able to discuss the cultural specificities of corporeality, as well as a long temporal trajectory. Many of the initial studies drew heavily from Foucauldian notions of bodily inscription, namely the literal marking of society upon the body of the individual. Social constructionism, largely influenced by poststructuralist theorizing, conceives bodies and identities as being constructed through various disciplines and discourses. These studies were followed in the 1990s by more contextual readings of embodiment on both cultural and individual levels, influenced by feminist and corporeal philosophies. Identity and experience are now perceived as being deeply implicated and grounded in the materiality of the body (Meskell & Joyce 2003). Yet this emphasis on materiality conjoins with the immaterial dimensions of subjectivity, selfhood, agency, emotionality, and memory (Blake 1999; Dobres 2000; Dobres and Robb 2000; Meskell 2003; Tarlow 2000; van Dyke and Alcock 2003; Williams 2003).

Studies of the body in all its sexed specificity have prompted new discussions of sexuality in archaeology (Hollimon 1998; Joyce 2000b; Koloski-Ostrow and Lyons 1997; McCafferty and McCafferty 1999; Meskell 2000; Robins 1996; Winter 1996). Sexuality is embedded within deeply situated historical contexts that bring together a host of different biological and psychical possibilities, such as gender identity, bodily differences, reproductive capacities, needs, desires, and fantasies. These need not be linked together and in other cultures have not been (Weeks 1997:15). It is variety, not uniformity, that is the norm. Like the other strands of identity discussed, "sexuality may be thought about, experienced and acted on differently according to age, class, ethnicity, physical ability, sexual orientation and preference, religion, and region" (Vance 1984:17). Archaeologists have begun investigating how sexuality might be shaped and iterated by economic, social, and political structures, and what the relationship is between sex and power specifically in terms of class and race divisions. Throughout much gendered archaeology heterosexuality was taken to be a normative category that remained unquestioned, although the rise of queer theory, and the enormous popularity of Judith Butler's writings, exposed this position as untenable (Claassen 1992b; Dowson 2000; Joyce 1996; Meskell 1996; Meskell & Joyce 2003). As Gilchrist underscores, Butler has been influential in archaeology since the late 1990s in part because of her explicit linkage between the body and the material world, a connection that links in important ways to a social archaeology.

The Politics of Location

Any discussion of locatedness necessitates evaluating the historicity of our conceptual frameworks and challenging their seemingly "natural" or foundational constitution. Identity construction and maintenance may have always been salient in the past, yet categories such as "ethnicity", "gender", or "sexuality," for example, may not have always existed as the discrete categories we find so familiar (Meskell 1999b, 2001). Indeed, many of these domains are now being refigured in contemporary society (Strathern 1999; Weston 2003; Yanagisako and Delaney 1995a). These contexts should be carefully examined before their insights are applied to archaeological or historical contexts. If we fail to push these questions further we risk an elision of difference, conflating ancient and modern experience in the process. What makes questions of identity so compelling is the ways in which specific societies evoked such different responses, prompted by categorical differences in their understandings and construc-tions of social domains. Much of this positioning works on at least two levels: first is the commitment of the researcher and their own politics, second is their situated understandings of those that they study and their particular identity configurations. These two sets of ontologies are inseparable and mutually constitutive, especially when one is constructing a narrative of the ancient past.

This has recently come to the fore within circles of feminist theory and devolves to whether feminists want to operate within spheres of inclusion or exclusion. This has prompted disciplinary concerns, ostensibly whether feminists should privilege gender above all else, or to expand the debates to encompass other subject positions and research agendas. It stands as an important example, relevant to other constituent domains within identity studies. Certainly in archaeology there has been somewhat of a reticence to embrace a broader view of feminism that would extend our scholarship into the wider sphere of identity. Historically, too, the study of gender has been synonymous with the study of women in the past and has largely resisted the epistemic insights of masculinist theory (Harrison 2002; Joyce 2000b; Knapp 1998; Meskell 1996), sexuality (Meskell and Joyce 2003; Schmidt and Voss 2000; Steele and Shennan 1995), and so on. While many major theoreticians have failed to speculate on the recent developments in both feminism and gender studies, and their real-world political implications, younger archaeologists are doing exactly that in practice (e.g. Franklin 2001; Lazzari 2003; Loren 2001): they are writing identity, more broadly construed. Yet even the notion of location has its own inertial fixity that several feminists find troub-ling and in need of deconstruction. Sylvia Walby imputes that "the politics of differ-ence, or of location, assumes that it is possible to separately identify holistic communities each with their own distinctive values, but this is a dubious proposition ... divisions run through most communities; for instance, gender, generation and class cross-cut most ethnic 'communities', creating both differences and inequalities" (Walby 2000:195). Many scholars have drawn on Braidotti's (1989, 1994) metaphor of the nomad and nomadic theory to understand the postmodern position of the feminist whose subject position and theory migrates across domains.

Returning to a central question for feminists (and, indeed, all those interested in identity politics), if we expand our horizons do we again risk minimizing the position of women for the constitution of a subject of difference more broadly construed? Certainly, some of the primacy of gender will have to be relinquished in attempts to address the complications of race, class, religion, sexuality, and so on that are similarly embedded and not easily disentangled from individuals' lives. If we take identity as a series of situated practices and embodied relations then gender relations can only be explicated by looking at *relations*. This is true also with reference to the other axes of difference: whom and what do they separate, and interconnect, by what kinds of relationality, that cannot be comprehended by looking solely at one category: women. What would we lose with a relational model? Axeli Knapp (2000:219) has usefully identified the following pragmatic concerns that stand for all vectors of identity and their ultimate coalescence:

- the dilemma of equality: equal treatment of unequals leads to the continuation of inequality
- the dilemma of difference: differential treatment of what is different is likely to perpetuate the reasons for discrimination
- the dilemma of identity: presupposing substantial group identities leads to an inherent exclusion of the non-identical
- the dilemma of deconstruction: attacking the conceptual conditions of possibility for statements about individual identities tends to undermine their political mobilization.

Perhaps the way around these dilemmas of positioning is to accept the embedded and embodied nature in which our identities are bound with other various constitutive communities – that gender, for example, is only one of numerous framing devices that situate us as individuals. Hekman (2000:304) has recently offered a solution to the identity politics debate, suggesting that "we move from identity politics to a politics of identification." She advocates a

> politics in which political actors identify with particular political causes and mobilize to achieve particular political goals. The identifications that political actors choose are rooted in aspects of their identities; the reasons for those identifications vary, but embracing an identification does not entail fixing the whole of the individuals' identity in a particular location. The politics of the women's movement is illustrative. In a strict sense, the women's movement is about identification, not identity. Many who possess the identity "woman" have not identified with the women's movement. Those who have, embrace it as an identification that reflects a particular aspect of their identity.

Conclusions

In constituting identity and its social location, Brubaker and Cooper (2000:6–8) have outlined the most common ways in which identity is conceived. Identity is thought to revolve around a set of particularistic categorical attributes in a universally conceived social structure. These are often formulated as a tension between the assumed structures of sameness and difference. Identity at the level of the self or selfhood is thought to be deeper and more foundational, according to psychologists, as compared to the fleeting and superficial aspects of contingent identities. Identity is also presented as the product of social and political action, instantiated through practice and iteration with others. It is both a product of action and a basis of action, as outlined by Hekman above. Lastly, identity is demarcated through multiple and competing discourses that are unstable, fragmented, and situational. This contextualist understanding of the term is inflected with postmodernist and poststructuralist thought, in keeping with more recent trends evidenced in social archaeology as well.

As the foregoing illustrates, many scholars are now endeavoring to situate identity relationally and complexly, whereas, as others are still locked into the premise of examining identity as a separate list of factors: the historicity of this trend is well evidenced. Moreover, we must address the task of reconfiguring identity in antiquity and that entails challenging our original taxonomies.

Social archaeology since the 1980s has seen a flourishing activity in the arena of identity. Made possible through the plurality of a postprocessual archaeology, our debates have been most ardently influenced by the recent outgrowth of gender and feminist archaeologies, but also underpinned by longstanding commitments to the study of race, class, and ethnicity in the discipline. In this arena archaeology as a discipline has something to contribute to other social sciences. Identity issues in the past, be they studies of class inequality, gender bias, sexual specificity, or even more fundamental topics like selfhood, embodiment, and being, have the capacity to connect our field with other disciplines in academia, but equally importantly with the wider community at large.

REFERENCES

Aldenderfer, M. S. (ed.) 1993. *Domestic Architecture, Ethnicity and Complementarity in the South-Central Andes.* Iowa City: University of Iowa Press.

Auger, R., M. F. Glass, S. MacEachern, and P. H. McCartney (eds.) 1987. *Ethnicity and Culture.* Calgary, AL: Archaeological Association at the University of Calgary.

Babson, D. W. 1990. Archaeology of racism and ethnicity on southern plantations. *Historical Archaeology* 24: 20–28.

Bailey, D. 2000. *Balkan Prehistory: Exclusion, Incorporation and Identity.* London: Routledge.

Baines, J. 1996. Contextualizing Egyptian representations of society and ethnicity. In J. S. Cooper and G. M. Schwartz (eds.), *The Study of the Ancient Near East in the 21st Century.* Eisenbrauns, IN: Winona Lake, pp. 339–384.

Baldwin, S. J. 1987. Roomsize patterns: A quantitative method for approaching ethnic identification in architecture. In R. Auger, M. F. Glass, S. MacEachern, and P. H. McCartney (eds.), *Ethnicity and Culture.* Calgary, AL: Archaeological Association at the University of Calgary, pp. 163–174.

Banks, M. 1996. *Ethnicity: Anthropological Constructions.* London: Routledge.

Barrett, J. C. 1988. The living, the dead and the ancestors: Neolithic and Early Bronze Age mortuary practices. In J. C. Barrett and I. A. Kinnes (eds.), *The Archaeology of Context in the Neolithic and Bronze Age: Recent Trends.* Sheffield: University of Sheffield Department of Archaeology and Prehistory, pp. 30–41.

——1994. *Fragments from Antiquity: An Archaeology of Social Life in Britain, 2900–1200 BC.* Oxford: Blackwell.

——2000. A thesis on agency. In M-A. Dobres and J. Robb (eds.), *Agency in Archaeology.* London: Routledge, pp. 61–68.

Barth, F. 1994. Enduring and emerging issues in the analysis of ethnicity. In H. Vermeulen and C. Grovers (eds.), *The Anthropology of Ethnicity.* Amsterdam: Het Spinhuis, pp. 11–32.

Bauman, Z. 1996. From pilgrim to tourist – or a short history of identity. In S. Hall and P. du Gay (eds.), *Questions of Identity.* London: Sage, pp. 18–34.

Blake, E. C. 1999. Identity mapping in the Sardinian Bronze Age. *European Journal of Archaeology* 2: 55–75.

Bourdieu, P. 1977. *Outline of a Theory of Practice.* Cambridge: Cambridge University Press.

——1980. *The Logic of Practice.* Stanford, CA: Stanford University Press.

——1998. *Practical Reason: On the Theory of Action.* Cambridge: Polity Press.

——, and T. Eagleton. 1994. Doxa and common life: An interview. In S. Zizek (ed.), *Mapping Ideology*. London: Verso, pp. 265–277.

Bradley, R. 2000. *An Archaeology of Natural Places*. London: Routledge.

Braidotti, R. 1989. The politics of ontological difference. In T. Brennan (ed.), *Between Feminism and Psychoanalysis*. London: Routledge, pp. 89–105.

—— 1994. *Nomadic Subjects: Embodiment and Sexual Difference in Contemporary Feminist Theory*. New York: Columbia University Press.

Brubaker, R., and F. Cooper. 2000. Beyond "identity." *Theory and Society* 29: 1–47.

Brumfiel, E. M. 1992. Distinguished lecture in archaeology: Breaking and entering the ecosystem – gender, class, and faction steal the show. *American Anthropologist* 94: 551–567.

Buchli, V. (2000). *An Archaeology of Socialism*. Oxford: Berg.

——, and G. Lucas (eds.) (2001). *Archaeologies of the Contemporary Past*. London: Routledge.

Canuto, M. A., and J. Yaeger (eds.) 2000. *The Archaeology of Communities: A New World Perspective*. London: Routledge.

Chapman, R., and K. Randsborg. 1981. Approaches to the archaeology of death. In R. Chapman, I. Kinnes, and K. Randsborg (eds.), *The Archaeology of Death*. Cambridge: Cambridge University Press, pp. 1–24.

Cheek, C. D., and A. Friedlander. 1990. Pottery and pigs' feet: Space, ethnicity, and neighborhood in Washington, D.C., 1880–1940. *Historical Archaeology* 24: 34–60.

Chesson, M. (ed.) 2001. *Social Memory, Identity and Death: Ethnographic and Archaeological Perspectives on Mortuary Rituals*. Washington, DC: American Anthropological Association.

Claassen, C. (ed.) 1992a. *Exploring Gender Through Archaeology: Selected Papers from the 1991 Boone Conference*. Madison, WI: Prehistory Press.

—— 1992b. Questioning gender: An introduction. In C. Claassen (ed.), *Exploring Gender Through Archaeology: Selected Papers from the 1991 Boone Conference*. Madison, WI: Prehistory Press, pp. 1–9.

—— (ed.) 1994. *Women in Archaeology*. Philadelphia: University of Pennsylvania Press.

——, and R. A. Joyce (eds.). 1997. *Women in Prehistory: North America and Mesoamerica*. Philadelphia: University of Pennsylvania Press.

Conkey, M. W., and J. D. Spector. 1984. Archaeology and the study of gender. *Advances in Archaeological Method and Theory* 7: 1–38.

Craib, I. 1998. *Experiencing Identity*. London: Sage.

David, N., K. Gavua, A. S. MacEachern, and J. Sterner. 1991. Ethnicity and material culture in north Cameroon. *Canadian Journal of Archaeology* 15: 171–177.

Delle, J., S. A. Mrozowski, and R. Paynter (eds.) 2000. *Lines that Divide: Historical Archaeologies of Race, Class, and Gender*. Knoxville: University of Tennessee Press.

Diaz-Andreu, M., and M. L. S. Sørensen (eds.) 1998. *Excavating Women: A History of Women in European Archaeology*. London: Routledge.

Dietler, M., and I. Herbich. 1998. Habitus, techniques, style: An integrated approach to the social understanding of material culture and boundaries. In M. T. Stark (ed.), *The Archaeology of Social Boundaries*. Washington, DC. Smithsonian Institution Press, pp. 232–263.

Dobres, M-A. 2000. *Technology and Social Agency*, Oxford: Blackwell.

——, and J. Robb (eds.) 2000. *Agency in Archaeology*. London: Routledge.

Dommasnes, L. H. 1992. Two decades of women in prehistory and in archaeology in Norway. A review. *Norwegian Archaeological Review* 25: 1–14.

Dowson, T. A. (ed.) 2000. *World Archaeology: Queer Archaeologies* 32(2).

Earle, T. (ed.) 1991. *Chiefdoms: Power, Economy and Ideology*. Cambridge: Cambridge University Press.

—— 1997. *How Chiefs Come to Power: The Political Economy in Prehistory*. Palo Alto, CA: Stanford University Press.

——2002. *Bronze Age Economics: The First Political Economies*. Boulder, CO: Westview Press.

Emberling, G. 1997. Ethnicity in complex societies: archaeological perspectives. *Journal of Archaeological Research* 5: 295–344.

Engelstad, E. 1991. Images of power and contradiction: feminist theory and post-processual archaeology. *Antiquity* 65: 502–514.

Foucault, M. 1978. *The History of Sexuality*. London: Routledge.

Franklin, M. 2001. A Black feminist-inspired archaeology. *Journal of Social Archaeology* 1: 108–125.

Gamble, C. 1998. Palaeolithic society and the release from proximity: A network approach to intimate relations. *World Archaeology* 29: 426–449.

Gardner, A. 2002. Social identity and the duality of structure in late Roman-period Britain. *Journal of Social Archaeology* 2: 323–351.

Gell, A. 1998. *Art and Agency: An Anthropological Theory*. Oxford: Oxford University Press.

Gero, J. M., and M. W. Conkey (eds.) 1991. *Engendering Archaeology: Women and Prehistory*. Oxford: Blackwell.

Gibbs, L. 1987. Identifying gender in the archaeological record: A contextual study. In I. Hodder (ed.), *The Archaeology of Contextual Meanings*. Cambridge: Cambridge University Press, pp. 79–89.

Giddens, A. 1981. *The Class Structure of the Advanced Societies*. London: Hutchinson.

——1984. *The Constitution of Society: Outline of a Theory of Structuration*. Cambridge: Polity Press.

——1991. *Modernity and Self-Identity: Self and Society in the Late Modern Age*. Cambridge: Polity Press.

Gilchrist, R. 1991. Women's archaeology? Political feminism, gender theory and historical revision. *Antiquity* 65: 495–501.

——1994. *Gender and Material Culture: The Archaeology of Religious Women*. London: Routledge.

——1997. Ambivalent bodies: Gender and medieval archaeology. In J. Moore and E. Scott (eds.), *Invisible People and Processes: Writing Gender and Childhood into European Archaeology*. London: Leicester University Press, pp. 42–58.

——(ed.) 2000. *World Archaeology: Lifecycles*, 31(3).

Gilchrist, R. L. 1999. *Gender and Archaeology: Contesting the Past*. London: Routledge.

Gosden, C. 1999. *Anthropology and Archaeology: A Changing Relationship*. London: Routledge.

Hall, J. M. 1997. *Ethnic Identity in Greek Antiquity*. Cambridge: Cambridge University Press.

Hall, M. 1992. Small things and the mobile, conflictual fusion of power, fear, and desire. In A. Yentsch and M. Beaudry (eds.), *The Art and Mystery of Historical Archaeology*. Boca Raton, CA: CRC Press, pp. 373–399.

——1994. The secret lives of houses: Women and gables in the eighteenth-century Cape. *Social Dynamics* 20: 1–48.

——2000. *Archaeology and the Modern World: Colonical Transcripts in South Africa and the Chesapeake*. London: Routledge.

——2001. Social archaeology and the theaters of memory. *Journal of Social Archaeology* 1: 50–61.

Hall, S. 1996. Introduction: Who needs "identity"? In S. Hall and P. du Gay (eds.), *Questions of Identity*. London: Sage, pp. 1–7.

Hamilakis, Y., M. Pluciennik, and S. Tarlow (eds.) 2002. *Thinking Through the Body: Archaeologies of Corporeality*. New York: Kluwer.

Harrison, R. 2002. Archaeology and the colonial encounter: Kimberley spearpoints, cultural identity and masculinity in the north of Australia. *Journal of Social Archaeology* 2: 352–377.

Harvey, P., and P. Gow. 1994. Introduction. In P. Harvey and P. Gow (eds.), *Sex and Violence: Issues in Representation and Experience*. London: Routledge, pp. 1–17.

Hegmon, M. 1998. Technology, style, and social practices: Archaeological approaches. In M. T. Stark (ed.), *The Archaeology of Social Boundaries*. Washington, DC and London: Smithsonian University Press, pp. 264–279.

Hekman, S. 2000. Beyond identity: Feminism, identity and identity politics. *Feminist Theory* 1: 289–308.

Hodder, I. 1982. *Symbols in Action*. Cambridge: Cambridge University Press.

Hollimon, S. E. 1998. Gender and sexuality in prehistoric Chumash society. In R. Schmidt and B. Voss (eds.), *The Archaeologies of Sexuality*. London: Routledge, pp. 179–196.

Jenkins, R. 1996. *Social Identity*. London: Routledge.

Jones, A. 2001. "Drawn from memory": The archaeology of aesthetics and the aesthetics of archaeology in Earlier Bronze Age Britain and the present. *World Archaeology: Archaeology and Aesthetics* 33: 334–356.

Jones, S. 1996. *The Archaeology of Ethnicity: Constructing Identities in the Past and Present*. London: Routledge.

Joyce, R. A. 1993. *Embodying Personhood in Prehispanic Costa Rica*. Wellesley, MA: Davis Museum and Cultural Center, Wellesley College.

——1996. The construction of gender in Classic Maya monuments. In R. P. Wright (ed.), *Gender and Archaeology*. Philadelphia: University of Pennsylvania Press, pp. 167–195.

——1998. Performing the body in Prehispanic Central America. *Res: Anthropology and Aesthetics* 33: 147–166.

——2000a. Heirlooms and houses: Materiality and social memory. In R. A. Joyce and S. Gillespie (eds.), *Beyond Kinship: Social and Material Reproduction in House Societies*. Philadelphia: University of Pennsylvania Press, pp. 189–212.

——2000b. A Precolumbian gaze: Male sexuality among the ancient Maya. In R. Schmidt and B. Voss (eds.), *Archaeologies of Sexuality*. London: Routledge, pp. 263–283.

——2001. *Gender and Power in Prehispanic Mesoamerica*. Austin: University of Texas Press.

——, and S. D. Gillespie (eds.) 2000. *Beyond Kinship: Social and Material Reproduction in House Societies*. Philadelphia: University of Pennsylvania Press.

Knapp, A. 2000. More power to argument. *Feminist Theory* 1: 207–223.

Knapp, A. B. 1998. Who's come a long way, baby? Masculinist approaches to a gendered archaeology. *Archaeological Dialogues* 5: 91–106.

——, and L. M. Meskell. 1997. Bodies of evidence in prehistoric Cyprus. *Cambridge Archaeological Journal* 7: 183–204.

Koloski-Ostrow, A. O., and C. L. Lyons (eds.) 1997. *Naked Truths: Women, Sexuality, and Gender in Classical Art and Archaeology*. London: Routledge.

Kristiansen, K., and M. Rowlands. 1998. *Social Transformations in Archaeology: Global and Local Perspectives*. London: Routledge.

Lazzari, M. 2003. Archaeological visions: Gender, landscape and optic knowledge. *Journal of Social Archaeology* 3: 194–222.

Leone, M. 1984. Interpreting ideology in historical archaeology: Using rules of perspective in the William Paca garden in Annapolis, Maryland. In D. Miller and C. Tilley (eds.), *Ideology, Power and Prehistory*. Cambridge: Cambridge University Press, pp. 25–28.

Leone, M. P. 1995. A historical archaeology of capitalism. *American Anthropologist* 97: 251–268.

Loren, D. 2001. Social skins: Orthodoxies and practices of dressing in the early colonial lower Mississippi Valley. *Journal of Social Archaeology* 1: 172–189.

Lyons, D. 1998. Witchcraft, gender, power and intimate relations in Mura compounds in Déla, northern Cameroon. *World Archaeology* 95: 344–362.

Marcus, M. I. 1993. Incorporating the body: Adornment, gender, and social indentity in ancient Iran. *Cambridge Archaeological Journal* 3: 157–178.

McCafferty, G. G., and S. D. McCafferty. 1999. The metamorphosis of Xochiquetzal. In T. Sweely (ed.), *Manifesting Power: Gender and the Interpretation of Power in Archaeology*. London: Routledge, pp. 103–125.

McGuire, R. H. 1982. The study of ethnicity in historical archaeology. *Journal of Anthropological Archaeology* 1: 159–178.

Meskell, L. M. 1996. The somatisation of archaeology: Institutions, discourses, corporeality. *Norwegian Archaeological Review* 29: 1–16.

——1998a. Intimate archaeologies: The case of Kha and Merit. *World Archaeology* 29: 363–379.

——1998b. The irresistible body and the seduction of archaeology. In D. Montserrat (ed.), *Changing Bodies, Changing Meanings: Studies on the Human Body in Antiquity*. London: Routledge, pp. 139–161.

——1998c. Size matters: Sex, gender, and status in Egyptian iconography. In M. Casey, D. Donlon, J. Hope, and S. Welfare (eds.), *Redefining Archaeology: Feminist Perspectives*. Canberra: Australian National University, pp. 175–181.

——1999a. Archaeologies of life and death. *American Journal of Archaeology* 103: 181–199.

——1999b. *Archaeologies of Social Life: Age, Sex, Class in Ancient Egypt*. Oxford: Blackwell.

——2000. Re-embedding sex: Domesticity, sexuality and ritual in New Kingdom Egypt. In R. Schmidt and B. Voss (eds.), *Archaeologies of Sexuality*. London: Routledge, pp. 253–262.

——2001. Archaeologies of identity. In I. Hodder (ed.), *Archaeological Theory: Breaking the Boundaries*. Cambridge: Polity Press, pp. 187–213.

——2002a. The intersection of identity and politics in archaeology. *Annual Review of Anthropology* 31: 279–301.

——2002b. *Private Life in New Kingdom Egypt*. Princeton, NJ: Princeton University Press.

——2003. Memory's materiality: Ancestral presence, commemorative practice and disjunctive locales. In R. van Dyke and S. E. Alcock (eds.), *Archaeologies of Memory*. Oxford: Blackwell, pp. 34–55.

——2004. *Object Worlds in Ancient Egypt: Material Biographies Past and Present*. Oxford: Berg.

——, and R. A. Joyce. 2003. *Embodied Lives: Figuring Ancient Maya and Egyptian Experience*. London: Routledge.

Miller, D., M. Rowlands, and C. Tilley (eds.) 1989. *Domination and Resistance*. London: Allen & Unwin.

Miller, D., and C. Tilley (eds.) 1984. *Ideology, Power and Prehistory*. Cambridge: Cambridge University Press.

Montserrat, D. (ed.) 1998. *Changing Bodies, Changing Meanings: Studies on the Human Body in Antiquity*. London: Routledge.

Moore, J., and E. Scott (eds.) 1997. *Invisible People and Processes: Writing Gender and Childhood into European Archaeology*. London: Leicester University Press.

Mullins, P. R. 1999. *Race and Affluence: An Archaeology of African America and Consumer Culture*. New York: Kluwer/Plenum.

Myers, F. (ed.) 2001. *The Empire of Things*. Santa Fe, NM: School of American Research.

Nelson, M., S. M. Nelson, and A. Wylie (eds.) 1994. *Equity Issues for Women in Archaeology*. Washington, DC: Archaeological Papers of the American Anthropological Association 5.

Nordström, H-A. 1996. The Nubian A-Group: Ranking funerary remains. *Norwegian Archaeological Review* 26: 17–39.

Odner, K. 1985. Saamis (Lapps), Finns and Scandinavians in history and prehistory. Ethnic origins and ethnic process in Fenno-Scandinavia (and comments). *Norwegian Archaeological Review* 18: 135.

Orser, C. E. J. 1999. The challenge of race to American historical archaeology. *American Anthropologist* 100: 661–668.

Osborne, R. 1998a. Men without clothes: Heroic nakedness and Greek art. *Gender and History: Gender and Body in the Ancient Mediterranean* 9: 80–104.

——1998b. Sculpted men of Athens: Masculinity and power in the field of vision. In L. Foxhall and J. Salmon (eds.), *Thinking Men: Masculinity and its Self-Representation in the Classical Tradition.* London: Routledge, pp. 23–42.

O'Shea, J. M. 1984. *Mortuary Variability: An Archaeological Investigation.* Orlando, FL: Academic Press.

Parker Pearson, M. 1982. Mortuary practices, society and ideology: An ethnoarchaeological study. In I. Hodder (ed.), *Symbolic and Structural Archaeology.* Cambridge: Cambridge University Press, pp. 99–114.

Parker Pearson, M. 2001. *The Archaeology of Death and Burial.* Stroud: Sutton.

Patterson, T. C. 2003. *Marx's Ghost: Conversations with Archaeologists,* Oxford: Berg.

Paynter, R., and R. H. McGuire. 1991. The archaeology of inequality: Material culture, domination, and resistance. In R. H. McGuire and R. Paynter (eds.), *The Archaeology of Inequality.* Oxford: Blackwell, pp. 1–27.

Pinney, C., and N. Thomas (eds.) 2001. *Beyond Aesthetics: Art and the Technologies of Enchantment.* Oxford: Berg.

Rautman, A. (ed.) 2000. *Reading the Body.* Philadelphia: University of Pennslyvania Press.

Renfrew, C. and S. Shennan (eds.) 1982. *Ranking, Resource and Exchange.* Cambridge: Cambridge University Press.

Robins, G. 1996. Dress, undress, and the representation of fertility and potency in New Kingdom Egyptian Art. In N. Boymel Kampen (ed.), *Sexuality in Ancient Art.* Cambridge: Cambridge University Press, pp. 27–40.

Rothschild, N. 2003. *Colonial Encounters in a Native American Landscape: The Dutch and Spanish in the New World.* Washington, DC: Smithsonian Institution Press.

Rotman, D. L., and M. S. Nassaney. 1997. Class, gender, and the built environment: Deriving social relations from cultural landscapes in southwest Michigan. *Historical Archaeology* 31: 42–62.

Russel, A. E. 1997. Material culture and African-American spirituality at the Hermitage. *Historical Archaeology* 31: 63–80.

Saitta, D. 1994. Agency, class and archaeological interpretation. *Journal of Anthropological Archaeology* 13: 201–227.

Schmidt, R., and B. Voss (eds.) 2000. *Archaeologies of Sexuality.* London: Routledge.

Shanks, M. 1995. Art and archaeology of embodiment: Some aspects of Archaic Greece. *Cambridge Archaeological Journal* 5: 207–244.

——, and C. Tilley. 1982. Ideology, symbolic power and ritual communication: A reinterpretation of Neolithic mortuary practices. In I. Hodder (ed.), *The Archaeology of Contextual Meanings.* Cambridge: Cambridge University Press, pp. 129–154.

——1987a. *Social Theory and Archaeology.* Cambridge: Polity Press.

——1987b. *Re-Constructing Archaeology: Theory and Practice.* London: Routledge.

Shennan, S. (ed.) 1994. *Archaeological Approaches to Cultural Identity.* London: Routledge.

Singleton, T. A. 1995. The archaeology of slavery in North America. *Annual Review of Anthropology* 24: 119–140.

——1999. *"I, too, am America": Archaeological Studies of African-American Life.* Charlottesville: University Press of Virginia.

Sökefeld, M. 1999. Debating self, identity, and culture in anthropology. *Current Anthropology* 40: 417–447.

Spence, M. W. 1992. Tlailotlacan, a Zapotec enclave in Teotihuacan. In J. C. Berlo (ed.), *Art, Ideology, and the City of Teotihuacan.* Washington, DC: Dumbarton Oaks, pp. 59–88.

Spriggs, M. (ed.) 1984. *Marxist Perspectives in Archaeology*. Cambridge: Cambridge University Press.

Staski, E. 1990. Studies of ethnicity in North American historical archaeology. *North American Archaeologist* 11: 121–145.

Steele, J., and S. Shennan (eds.) 1995. *The Archaeology of Human Ancestry: Power, Sex and Tradition*. London: Routledge.

Stine, L. F. 1990. Social Inequality and turn-of-the-century farmsteads: Issues of class, status, ethnicity, and race. *Historical Archaeology* 24: 37–49.

Strathern, M. 1992. *After Nature: English Kinship in the Late Twentieth Century*. Cambridge: Cambridge University Press.

—— 1999. *Property, Substance and Effect: Anthropological Essays on Persons and Things*. London: Athlone.

Sweely, T. (ed.) 1999. *Manifesting Power: Gender and the Interpretation of Power in Archaeology*. London: Routledge.

Tarlow, S. A. 2000. Emotion in archaeology. *Current Anthropology* 41: 713–746.

—— 1999. *Bereavement and Commemoration: An Archaeology of Mortality*. Oxford: Blackwell.

Thomas, J. 1996. *Time, Culture and Identity*. London: Routledge.

——, and C. Tilley. 1993. The axe and the torso: Symbolic structures. In C. Tilley (ed.), *Interpretive Archaeology*. Oxford: Berg, pp. 225–324.

Tilley, C. 1990. Foucault: Towards an archaeology of archaeology. In C. Tilley (ed.), *Reading Material Culture*. London: Basil Blackwell, pp. 281–347.

—— 1994. *A Phenomenology of Landscape: Places, Paths and Monuments*. Oxford: Berg.

Torrence, R., and A. Clark (eds.) 2000. *Archaeology of Difference: Negotiating Cross-Cultural Engagements in Oceania*. London: Routledge.

Upton, D. 1996. Ethnicity, authenticity, and invented traditions. *Historical Archaeology* 30: 1–7.

Vance, C. S. (ed.) 1984. *Pleasure and Danger: Exploring Female Sexuality*. Boston, MA: Routledge & Kegan Paul.

van Dyke, R., and S. E. Alcock (eds.) 2003. *Archaeologies of Memory*. Oxford: Blackwell.

Walby, S. 2000. Beyond the politics of location. *Feminist Theory* 1: 189–206.

Wall, D. 1999. Examining gender, class and ethnicity in nineteenth-century New York City. *Historical Archaeology* 33: 102–117.

Wason, P. K. 1994. *The Archaeology of Rank*. Cambridge: Cambridge University Press.

Weeks, J. 1997. *Sexuality*. London: Routledge.

Wells, P. S. 1998. Identity and material culture in the later prehistory of Central Europe. *Journal of Archaeological Research* 6: 239–298.

Weston, K. 2003. *Gender in Real Time: Power and Transience in a Visual Age*. London: Routledge.

Wilkie, L. A. 2003. *An Archaeology of Mothering*. London: Routledge.

——, and K. M. Bartoy. 2000. A critical archaeology revisited. *Current Anthropology* 41: 747–777.

Williams, H. (ed.) 2003. *Archaeologies of Remembrance: Death and Memory in Past Societies*. New York: Kluwer/Plenum.

Winter, I. J. 1996. Sex, rhetoric, and the public monument: The alluring body of Naram-Sîn of Agade. In N. B. Kampen (ed.), *Sexuality in Ancient Art: Near East, Egypt, Greece and Italy*. Cambridge: Cambridge University Press, pp. 11–26.

Woodhouse-Beyer, K. 1999. Artels and identities: Gender, power, and Russian America. In T. Sweely (ed.), *Manifesting Power: Gender and the Interpretation of Power in Archaeology*. London: Routledge, pp. 129–154.

Wylie, A. 1991. Gender theory and the archaeological record: Why is there no archaeology of gender? In J. M. Gero and M. W. Conkey (eds.), *Engendering Archaeology: Women and Prehistory*. Oxford: Blackwell, pp. 31–54.

Yaeger, P. (ed.) 1996. *The Geography of Identity*. Ann Arbor: University of Michigan Press.

Yanagisako, S., and C. Delaney (eds.) 1995a. *Naturalizing Power: Essays in Feminist Cultural Analysis*. New York: Routledge.

——1995b. Naturalizing power. In S. Yanagisako and C. Delaney (eds.), *Naturalizing Power: Essays in Feminist Cultural Analysis*. New York: Routledge, pp. 1–22.

Yates, T. 1993. Frameworks for an archaeology of the body. In C. Tilley (ed.), *Interpretive Archaeology*. Oxford: Berg, pp. 31–72.

——, and J. Nordbladh. 1990. This perfect body, this virgin text: Between sex and gender in archaeology. In I. Bapty and T. Yates (eds.), *Archaeology after Structuralism*. London: Routledge, pp. 222–237.

Yoffee, N. 1998. The economics of ritual at Late Old Babylonian Kish. *Journal of the Economic and Social History of the Orient* 41: 310–343.

——2000. Law courts and the mediation of social dispute in ancient Mesopotamia. In J. E. Richards and M. Van Buren (eds.), *Order, Legitimacy, and Wealth in Ancient States*. Cambridge: Cambridge University Press, pp. 46–63.

——, and G. Emberling. 1999. Thinking about ethnicity in Mesopotamian archaeology and history. In H. Kuehne, K. Bartl, and R. Bernbeck (eds.), *Fluchtpunkt Uruk: Archaeologische Einheit aus Methodologischer Vielfalt: Schriften fuer Hans J. Nissen*. Rahden: Marie Leidorf Verlag, pp. 272–281.

6

Archaeology and the Life Course: A Time and Age for Gender

Roberta Gilchrist

Introduction: The Invisibility of Age

This chapter examines the increasing emphasis placed on aspects of age within arch-aeological perspectives on gender and the body, and explores the wider intellectual influences and interpretative potential of this approach. To date, the most prominent element of aging to be studied archaeologically has been the archaeology of children, or childhood (Derevenski 2000; Moore and Scott 1997). Broader interpretations have sought to integrate age in the analysis of social identity, through explorations of the relationship of age in combination with gender, social status, ethnicity, and sexuality, through the concept of the life course (Derevenski 1997; Gilchrist 1999, 2000; Meskell 1999). These latter approaches are strongly grounded in recent developments in femi-nist theory, anthropologies of the body, and new developments in sociology that, during the 1990s, were inaugurated as "age studies." The principle linking gender and age is the constructionist premise that these are not solely biological factors, but also cultural constructions, that combine to produce different life experiences for men and women (either individually, or as social groups).

It is therefore not surprising that the case for a specific archaeological interrogation of aging bears striking similarity to discussions in the 1980s of the need for a gendered archaeology. A crucial difference between the themes of gender and age is that while both have contemporary political movements allied with them, only gender has enjoyed political advocacy from within archaeology. The feminist critique proposed that archae-ologists were perpetuating a "gender mythology," by failing to consider gender rela-tions explicitly (Conkey and Spector 1984). It was argued that archaeologists instead drew implicitly on contemporary gender stereotypes to interpret social relations in the past, implying a longstanding continuity of gender roles (Bertelsen, Lillehammer, and Naess 1987). Feminist archaeology called for a constructionist position on gender, which would move beyond biological definitions of sex, to consider historical vari-ations and cultural diversities in the cultural construction of gender. We might argue today that this simplistic opposition between biological sex and cultural gender in itself lacks an appreciation of how the body is historically created and contextually perceived

(Laqueur 1990; Parker 1998). Nevertheless, paralleling age with the development of gender studies makes a persuasive case.

The biological characteristics of age are culturally created and historically contingent, to the same degree as those of sex. Contemporary age and gender stereotypes are equally constructed, and equally inappropriate for universal application to the past. A more reflexive approach to age is critical, which questions our own cultural attitudes toward aging and particular phases in the life cycle. Contemporary prejudices and presumptions regarding age – including, for example, the notion of a dependent child-hood, a rebellious adolescence, a "prime of life," a "mid-life crisis," and a neglected, reviled old age – are no more appropriate for projection on to the prehistoric past than stereotypes of the nuclear-age housewife and her family.

The role of age in constructing social relations and identities has been under-theorized in archaeology. Although the long tradition of burial archaeology has in-volved a study of the physical anthropology of human skeletons (Chapman, Kinnes, and Randsborg 1981), until recently these analyses have assigned sex and age determin-ations with little consideration of their associated cultural meanings. In addition, the methods employed in bioarchaeology have an inbuilt bias in their tendency to focus on adult categories. While the sex of an adult skeleton can be assigned with up to 95 percent confidence where the pelvis is present, and 85–95 percent where the skull is complete (Brown 1998), aging skeletal remains are far more problematic. The result is that the two extremes of age are regularly underrepresented. The very old are rendered invisible through the consistent underestimation of ages at death, leading to the overrepresentation of young and middle adult categories. The very young, infants and young children, are particularly underrepresented in archaeological samples. Their bones are more vulnerable to destruction through taphonomic processes and archaeo-logical excavation, and may be overlooked, especially where children's remains have been disposed of through different mortuary practices than those that were employed for adults (Chamberlain 2000: 210; Gowling 2001). Osteological approaches are begin-ning to address the differential impact of biological and cultural aging on the male and female body; for example, through sex-related differences in iron-deficiency anaemia, responses to episodes of nutritional stress, and bone loss in old age (Grauer and Stuart-Macadam 1998).

More explicit considerations of the gendered body within archaeology have equally failed to engage with the cultural issue of age. This omission is apparent, for example, in Paul Treherne's study of the European "warrior" grave. The male weapon burial de-veloped in Bronze Age Europe, and continued in some regions throughout the Iron Age. Treherne proposes that prestige goods were used in graves to signal a potent male symbolism, through the use of artifacts representing warfare, drinking, horse-riding and bodily ornamentation. He argues that material culture was used to create a cultural aesthetic of the male body, which became naturalized over time as a "specific form of masculine beauty unique to the warrior" (Treherne 1995: 106). Treherne presents a static picture of the masculine body, with the idealized image of the warrior at the height of his prowess. At what ages did the male gain and relinquish his warrior identity, and how was material culture used to mark such transitions? How did the warrior interrelate with other males of different ages, social roles, and ethnicities? Treherne stresses the signifi-cance of long hair and grooming in warrior symbolism, yet fails to address the cultural perception of crucial physical changes to the male body, such as the onset of facial hair at puberty, and loss of hair color and abundance in later years.

A more holistic approach to gender archaeology requires a constructionist position on age, and consideration of the model of the life course that is used increasingly in other social disciplines. The particular terminology and definition of the life course developed in the branch of sociology concerned with social policy, is aimed at analyzing and improving the quality of different stages of contemporary life. Rather than focusing on successive stages of the life cycle in isolation, such as childhood, adolescence, old age, and so on, the life-course perspective attempts to understand the experience of human life as a continuum. This particular concept developed rapidly in the 1980s, as sociologists and gerontologists confronted the burgeoning elderly population in the West. Life-course approaches are frequently termed "longitudinal" in their attempt to examine both trajectory and transition in human lives: "how society gives social and personal meanings to the passing of biographical time" (Hagestad 1990: 151). Applied to archaeological contexts, the life-course approach has the potential to identify age thresholds that may not correspond with modern Western constructs of age and gender identity (Gowland 2001: 162).

Within the disciplines of history and ancient history, an interest in the life course has developed from demographic studies, and in particular the analysis of funerary monuments and their inscriptions (e.g., Harlow and Laurence 2002). In relation to Ancient Rome, for example, it has been demonstrated that there was a great deal of variation in the naming and representation of age across the Empire (Parkin 1992). There is now widespread acknowledgement that age is one of four dimensions that construct individual and social experience in the past, together with gender, ethnicity, and class (Laslett 1995: 4). Historical disciplines have engaged with more sociological perspectives on the life course, in contrast with archaeology's greater attraction to anthropological perspectives. The life-course framework assists sociologists in analyzing the life experience of different groups and individuals, and connects the discrete human life with varying time scales, emphasizing "the interaction between the passage of individual time, family time and historical time" (Arber and Evandrou 1993: 11). The nascent concept of the life course has the potential to link gender with current concerns in other branches of social archaeology, including phenomenological approaches to time and place, social memory, and embodiment.

Rites of Passage: The Birth of New Disciplines

Since the early twentieth century, anthropologists have remarked on the diversity of cultural practices surrounding age. Much early work was concerned with the dramatic public ceremonies and bodily modifications connected with "rites of passage." These cultural rites mark the transitions between stages in the life cycle, and are said to involve three classic phases: separation, marginality, and reincorporation (Turner 1969; Van Gennep 1960 [1908]). From this model, archaeologists have inferred that particular spaces may have played an important role in prehistoric rites of initiation, particularly in connection with the transmission of "esoteric knowledge" to young men. A poignant example is that of the caves of Upper Palaeolithic Europe, natural places that have been impressed with small human footprints and handprints that survive in cave-paintings (Owens and Hayden 1997). While early anthropological studies emphasized the more flamboyant rituals associated with male adolescence, contemporary anthropologists have examined more private female rites, and a wider range of "life-cycle rites" (Roscoe 1995), including birth, naming, puberty, initiation, marriage, widowhood, and death. Significantly, it has been recognized that the classic model of the "rites of passage" is itself culturally loaded, and should not be applied universally: an understanding of age structures is required beyond their public and ceremonial face. Since the 1980s, anthropologists have aimed to identify the experience of aging in specific cultural and social contexts, and to understand the mechanisms that influence individuals' experiences of aging (Keith 1980, 1990: 91).

During this same period, the impact of feminism resonated throughout the social sciences. "Second-wave" feminists[1] of the 1960s and 1970s were concerned with issues of equality in the public and private sphere, and were united by the theory of patriarchy: power relations that structure the subordination of women through institutions such as the family, education, religion, and government. Feminist anthropologists were concerned with the origins, cultural classifications, and symbolism through which universal female subordination had been perpetuated (Rosaldo and Lamphere 1974). Universals were proposed also in relation to gender and aging, such as the theory that women's status improved with increasing age. Women's lot is supposedly improved once menopause has released them from reproductive roles, and they achieve a senior place within the family, through institutionalized roles of grandmothers and mothers-in-law (Brown 1982; Kerns and Brown 1992).

Within archaeology, second-wave feminism stimulated an interest in women's work, their cultural connection with the household and domestic reproduction, and their agency in bringing about cultural change (Gero and Conkey 1991). Many of these studies approached women as a single group or an essential cultural category, undifferentiated by age, class or, to some extent, historical and cultural position. Perspectives on the female life cycle were a by-product of documenting women's work; for example, the impact of aging on female foraging and mobility patterns, and the apprenticeship of women's tasks between female generations of the same family (Spector 1983; Brumbach and Jarvenpa 1997).

A major shift in scholarship resulted from two related, but distinct, movements: "third-wave" feminism, and interest in the body. With the advent of the third wave, feminists transferred their attention from issues of inequality to issues of difference (Meskell 1996). The notion of an essential experience shared by all women (or all men) was rejected in favor of examining the differences between men and women, or among men and women of contrasting sexualities, ethnicities, or social classes (Harding 1991). Third-wave feminism offered the insights of Black Feminism and Queer Theory (e.g., Amos and Parmar 1984; Lauretis 1991), arguing respectively for the specificity of gendered experience created through ethnicity and sexuality, perspectives now being explored in archaeology (Franklin 2001; Dowson 2000; Schmidt and Voss 2000). The relative lack of archaeological attention given to age suggests that this element of identity is regarded as more biologically determined than those of gender, ethnicity, and sexuality.

A contemporary but very different approach to human "life history" had its lineage in evolutionary biology (Morbeck, Galloway, and Zihlman 1997). "Life-history theory" developed to counter the view of social scientists that "all evolutionary views of human behavior are the same, unified by their inherent genetic determinism and insensitivity to historical contingencies – especially those affecting inequalities due to race, class and gender" (Chisholm 1993: 1). The "life-history" model analyzes human life events from an evolutionary perspective, in order to highlight reproductive and survival strategies from infancy to adulthood. This approach characterizes humans in contrast with other primates and mammals, and has identified the development of certain life-cycle stages as defining aspects of human evolution. For example, the "grandmother hypothesis" argues that the prolonged human life span developed to allow the survival of post-menopausal women, in order that they could assist with the provisioning of grand-children (Hawkes, O'Connell, and Blurton 1997).

The Body's Legacy

Third-wave feminists engaged closely with the explosion of interest in the body. This work was stimulated in part by the works of Michel Foucault, and his premise that each human subject draws meaning and experience from competing, multiple dis-courses, and that this complex constitution of the subject continues to develop through the span of the human life (1981). Earlier studies had emphasized taboos and restrictions on the body, and proposed that its metaphors mirrored and structured cultural views (Douglas 1966). These approaches had failed to take full account of the extent to which the body is historically created, and experienced individually. Foucault "reintroduced history to an anthropology of the body" (Lock 1993: 137–40), but already Pierre Bourdieu had profoundly influenced the discipline's ideas about bodily practices (1977), and challenged the view that the body was merely a template upon which culture was imprinted.

Bourdieu's theory of *habitus* – the practical logic and sense of order that is learned through the enactment of everyday life – has been widely influential in archaeology (e.g., Gilchrist 1994). Application of Foucauldian principles has been more problematic (Meskell 1996), but has been attempted by Lin Foxhall in exploring contrasting gen-dered discourses of time, aging and monumentality in Classical Greece. Women married earlier and lived longer than men, with differing periods of social influence. A woman's influence grew with age, since her power over kin and the household increased until she dominated three generations of the family. Men, in contrast, achieved greater public power and a larger-scale past, but held this authority for a shorter period, with influence decreasing with age and the cessation of military activity. Men adopted larger-scale notions of past and future, and cultivated a concern with monumentality, for example, through rhetoric about fame, glory, reputation, and memory, and material culture ranging from grave stelae to monumental architecture. These artifacts of a "hegemonic masculinity" marked "their relatively short period of full, powerful adulthood" (Foxhall 1994: 137).

By the 1990s, anthropologists were theorizing the body explicitly, and grappling with challenges to the truth claims of medical science (Fausto-Sterling 1985) and the trad-itional dichotomies of mind/body and nature/culture (Jordanova 1989). Historical scrutiny of the body revealed that apparently "natural" categories of sex had been forged culturally. Thomas Laqueur argued cogently that sexual difference between men and women was not voiced clearly until the end of the eighteenth century, when such distinctions became critical to political debates over the participation of women in education and public life (Laqueur 1990). He showed that in the classical and medieval worlds a "one-sex model" was prominent, in which men and women were perceived physically as more or less the same sex, with degrees of maleness and femaleness determined by the balance of bodily fluids and temperatures ("humours"). Sex was considered unstable and changeable, and under certain circumstances, the female could actually change her sex by extruding the sexual organs outwards. Importantly, Laqueur demonstrated that categories of biological sex have not always been regarded as fixed and binary. This scholarship combined to render the body "elusive, fluid and uncontrollable" (Lock 1993:134). Moreover, it had banished the second wave's dualistic and static notion of biological sex versus cultural gender: definitions of both sex and gender are culturally contingent. But how are they connected with age?

Critically, the theme of the body was linked to the life cycle through emerging anthropologies of "personhood," particularly in Melanesia and Africa. These studies moved away from concentration on the body, self, or individual, to consider the whole living person, and how they were constituted through their relationships with other people and entities, including cosmologies and material culture (Strathern 1988: 268–274). The development of the body and personhood seems frequently to be linked to gendered substances. In her study of the American Navajo, for example, Maureen Schwarz shows how:

> Personhood is developed gradually in the Navajo world by controlling the influence of various substances and events on the body and parts of the body such as umbilical cords, voice, hair, and menstrual blood. The complex manipulations of the body … are framed around the critical events in the lifecycle of a Navajo, from conception through puberty. (Schwarz 1997: xix)

Gilbert Herdt has shown how control of gendered substances among the Sambia is used to create six stages of initiation leading to masculinization (Herdt 1987). In order to achieve and maintain maleness, Sambian men must orally ingest male substance (semen), which is believed to stimulate the development of secondary sexual characteristics, and expel female substance (blood).

Herdt's study of the Sambia was the direct inspiration for Tim Yates's archaeological analysis of the Bronze Age rock carvings of the west coast of Sweden (Yates 1993). Yates classifies the human figures in the rock carvings according to the presence or absence of weapons or horned helmets, and by four physical characteristics: an erect phallus, exaggerated calf muscles, exaggerated hands and/or fingers, and long hair (ibid.: 35–36) (figure 6.1). He draws particular attention to the contrast between phallic and non-phallic figures, proposing that a distinction existed between male, and not-yet male. He argues that the weapons and exaggerated physical features were intended to assist with the process of acquiring masculinity: "Masculine identity must be guaranteed by signs applied to the surface of the body, and these signs are detachable – they do not inhere in the body, but can be separated from it" (ibid.: 66).

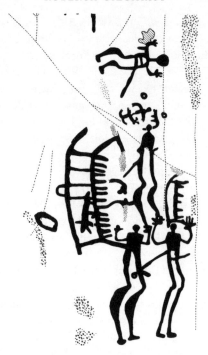

Figure 6.1 *An example of Swedish rock art from Torsbo Kville, showing human figures with exaggerated phalluses, calf muscles, and hands* (Gilchrist 1999: 74)

Gender archaeology's increasing emphasis on the body has dealt predominantly with representations in ancient art of particular social categories or groups, including men, women, and children (Kampen 1996; Koloski-Ostrow and Lyons 1997; Moore and Scott 1997; Rautman 2000). For example, Mesoamerican representations of women have been analyzed according to stages in the female life cycle, connecting them with broader cosmologies, female roles in production, and with female ceremonies and social networks (e.g., Guillén 1993). The cultural interpretation of specific phases in the life cycle has been addressed more rarely, for example in relation to classical Athenian iconography, where male and female adolescence was marked differently (Beaumont 2000).

More theoretically expansive studies have linked anthropological approaches to the body with third-wave feminist perspectives. In particular, the work of the feminist philosopher Judith Butler has been influential in social archaeology since the late 1990s (e.g., Schmidt and Voss 2000), in part for its linkage of the body with the material world. Butler's concept of "performance" proposes that gender and sexual identity are merely an effect created by repetitions that present the appearance of a coherent personal identity, performed as the repeated citation of a gendered norm (Butler 1993). Rosemary Joyce has used Butler's theory of performance to analyze the practices through which life-cycle transitions were marked on the bodies of Aztec children (Joyce 2000). She observes that ethnohistorical texts emphasize the strict disciplining of Aztec children's bodies in order to produce "a properly decorous adult": children were likened to raw materials, such as precious stones and feathers, that were shaped into body ornaments. The Aztec experience of embodiment was socially produced, through the repeated performance of particular ways of being that are represented as *citational precedents*; in other words, a sense of tradition, or a desire to equal the acts of ancestors or elders. Life-cycle rituals reinforced the careful repetition of actions, and bonded groups of individuals together through membership of age grades. Through habitual action, costume, and ornaments, by their early teens Aztec children had been shaped to fit one of three genders (potentially reproductive male, potentially reproductive female, and celibate) (ibid.: 474). In its concern with disciplining the body, Joyce's study owes equal intellectual debts to Butler and Foucault (Foucault 1981).

In commenting on Foucauldian approaches in archaeology, Lynn Meskell (1996) has argued that particularly in British prehistory, these have amounted to an artefactual approach to the body. The individual body is subsumed by "the social body," and described in relationship to landscapes or monuments, without reference to corporeal experience or individual identity. She links the queer theory of Judith Butler with more phenemenological approaches (after Merleau-Ponty 1962 [1945]), in advocating a more experiential approach to the body that probes the embodied experience of individuals. She has explored the potential for examining the multiple constitution of the individual in the historical context of Egyptian culture (1999), and in prehistoric Cyprus (Knapp and Meskell 1997). Meskell's call for an archaeological enquiry into individual embodiment has not been welcomed universally: some prehistorians consider the approach inappropriate for nonliterate societies (Sørensen 2000: 55–56). Understanding the processes affecting the individual agent is crucial, however, in connecting gender and age with embodiment, personhood, and social constructions of time.

Time, Memory, and Metaphors

Despite archaeology's intrinsic concerns with measuring the sequence and chronology of the past, until recently there has been little consideration given to the social meaning of time (e.g., Murray 1999). Time has been neglected somewhat by the discipline of anthropology also, exacerbated by its inherent invisibility, and by the temptation for ethnographers to take time for granted, projecting the values and measures of their own society (Adam 1994: 503). Anthropologists formerly contrasted "modern" constructions of time with those of "traditional" societies, arguing that "linear" perceptions of time characterized the former, and "cyclical" measures of time prevailed in the latter. Such assumptions were overturned by anthropologists who demanded more contextual understandings of time, and more reflexive considerations of the values of time in other societies (Fabian 1983; Adam 1990). Barbara Adam has demonstrated that cyclicity and irreversible linearity are not dichotomies of traditional and modern societies, but rather that both principles are integral to all rhythmically structured phenomena (Adam 1990: 70–76; 87–90). In other words, the seasons do not run backwards, and living, organic entities do not get younger. She stresses that all societies measure time in some fashion, but that industrial time has become reified by its dependence on "artefactual time"; the measurement of equal, spatialized units, losing sight of natural rhythms.

Philosophers have proposed that our human "sense of time" develops from an awareness of duration, and that resulting ideas of time are intellectual constructions, arising from personal experience and action (Whitrow 1988: 5–6). Within archaeology, a simplistic and false opposition is often maintained between "science time" and "social time" (Murray 1999: 3): or; in other words, the measurement of archaeological contexts and phenomena, versus the interpretation of perceptions of lived time in the past. Alfred Gell, borrowing from the philosopher McTaggart (1934), distinguished these contrasting measures as A-series time, concerned with perceptions of past, present, and future, and B-series time, events which exist "before" or "after" a particular moment (Gell 1992). The former comprises the "social time" experienced subjectively by individuals, while the latter represents the "science time" that provides a common measure for comparing temporal phenomena between cultures.

Phenomenological approaches to archaeology have linked the concepts of time and embodiment through their consideration of the structures of the everyday world and the life cycles of individual actors (Thomas 1996; Gosden 1994). The sociologist Bryan Turner has observed that phenomenological approaches have the potential to connect long-term, generational time with the individual's experience of aging, through the concept of "social memory" (Turner 1995: 251). Richard Bradley has further elaborated the place of material culture in imprinting social memory. He suggests that two key processes actively perpetuate a connection with the collective past: *performance*, bodily practice through rituals and ceremonies, and *inscription*, the creation of durable material culture and monuments (Bradley 2002: 12). The former process links the individual life course to generational time, while the latter connects individual actors to a collective past, present, and future.

Material culture is sometimes used as a metaphor for the human life course, drawing together the life cycles of people and things. This approach follows Igor Kopytoff's influential study of "the cultural biographies of things." He directs particular questions to objects, including: "What are the recognized 'ages' or periods in the thing's 'life', and what are the cultural markers for them? How does the thing's use change with its age, and what happens to it when it reaches the end of its usefulness?" (Kopytoff 1986: 66–67). Maureen MacKenzie has used this biographical approach in her anthropological study of string bags and gender among the Telefol people of Central New Guinea (MacKenzie 1991). She shows that the *bilum*, the ubiquitous looped string bag, possessed complex and overlapping meanings, as a metaphor for gender relations, a symbol for passage through the life cycle, and a connection with past generations and ancestors.

From Small Beginnings: An Archaeology of Children

From an early point in its development, feminist archaeology showed a strong interest in developing a subdiscipline around the archaeology of children (Lillehammer 1989). One might be tempted to link this to feminism's overtly political concerns with aging. Since Simone de Beauvoir's *The Coming of Age* (1972), there have been attempts to integrate age into feminist theory and practice: "Feminist age studies provide a basis for theory and resistance by firmly re-placing old age – and other ages – within the continuum of particular life courses" (Gullette 2000: 13). The origins of the archaeology of children were rooted within second-wave feminism, but they were not connected to broader theoretical considerations of aging. Retrospective justification by Grete Lillehammer suggested an affinity with studies of women's work, and in particular their roles as mothers: "perhaps we ought to lighten mother's load by seeing children as worthy subjects of study in relation to material culture" (Lillehammer 2000: 18). In a refreshing riposte, Laurie Wilkie argued that studies of women and children should not be too closely linked, because the association relies "too much on biological rather than cultural associations it also conjures the distressing image of a sinking ship" (Wilkie 2000: 111).

The first studies in this movement focused on infants and children, highlighting their visibility in archaeological contexts, and attempting to draw cross-cultural generalizations concerning their engagement with material culture (Lillehammer 1989). Previous archaeological interpretations had neglected children entirely: this very omission demonstrates the need for a better developed theory of age in archaeology. Perhaps because contemporary Western society regards children as socially passive, economically non-productive, and culturally peripheral, children were largely disregarded in archaeological interpretations. It was assumed that people in the past shared our own society's attitudes toward children and childhood, until the feminist critique drew attention to this blatantly "presentist" bias. Archaeologists began to consider the ways in which childhood might be culturally constructed and historically specific, benefiting from parallel developments in social history (Ariès 1965).

In the modern West, childhood is characterized as a prolonged and cosseted period of dependency on adults; further, it is sentimentalized as a period of asexual innocence (Derevenski 2000: 4–5). Archaeological studies have shown that such assumptions cannot be projected universally onto the past (Derevenski 2000; Moore and Scott 1997). Children fulfilled active economic roles in past societies, assisting with food gathering or production, and serving as apprentices in craft or tool production; and ancient art sometimes represents children, even infants, with pronounced sexual characteristics (Meskell 1999: 101).

Recent studies of children have contributed to the emergence of a life-course perspective. Archaeologists have shown how material culture was used to mark the threshold and transition from child to adulthood, evidenced by grave goods (Crawford 2000; Gowland 2001), and how specialist material culture was used by children to learn adult skills and ways of interacting (Park 1998). Joanna Sofaer Derevenski has noted that the category of "child" has been used in archaeology to explore the construction of "adult," but that the more experiential aspects of childhood have been neglected. She calls for new archaeologies of children that explore the identity, experience, and agency of children (Derevenski 2000: 8). These aims are addressed in a case study by Laurie Wilkie, who examines the treatment of toys by particular children in known historical contexts of the eighteenth to twentieth centuries. Wilkie (2000) interprets the "children's intentions and experiences" on the basis of their interaction with the toys, and suggests that material culture used by children can comment on their "sense of identity, world-view, priorities and social networks". Wilkie approaches children through biographies of artifacts associated with them, but few archaeologists will have recourse to such richly documented contexts.

The Life Course: Linking Age, Gender, Time, and Space

Considerable progress has been achieved in exploring the contextual nature of child-hood and how it may be expressed materially. However, there have been few attempts to address other stages of life archaeologically, such as adolescence and old age. In-stead, the influence of third-wave feminist and somatic perspectives has led to more holistic approaches that study age within the continuum of the life course. Two examples are recounted briefly here.

Lynn Meskell's work on "Age, Sex, Class, *et cetera* in Ancient Egypt" (1999) pays homage to Judith Butler's assertion that we should examine the relationships *between* the proverbial commas that separate these elements (Butler 1993: 168). The *"et cetera"* addresses the relationships between these aspects, and how they work together to create the social identity of individuals (Meskell 1999: 105). Meskell focuses on excavated evidence from the New Kingdom village of Deir el Medina, home to the workers who built the royal tombs in the adjacent Valley of the Kings. The cemeteries associated with this village were based around two hills, the eastern and western necropolises. Meskell demonstrates how age was the major factor in determining the method and location of burial, with marital status being the next most incisive deter-minant (ibid.: 169). During the eighteenth dynasty, the prestigious tombs were con-structed only in the western necropolis, perhaps because the west was associated with the sacred domain of the dead. The western necropolis was reserved for individ-uals and couples, while the eastern necropolis was used for the burials of children, adolescents, and single people, often women, who may have been divorced wives (ibid.: 146).

The mode of burial was determined by age, with infant burials interred in jars, baskets, boxes or coffins, regardless of the wealth of the family (ibid.: 171). Positions of graves within the eastern necropolis were zoned according to age, with the lowest part of the slope reserved for infants, neonates, and foetuses, adolescents assigned to the middle section of the hill, and adults located on the upper portion (figure 6.2; ibid.: 163). Commenting on measures of aging, Meskell remarks that the concept of the life cycle is more appropriate to Egypt than the model of "rites of passage." She observes that life stages were more marked for men, while women were socialized and sexual-ized at an early age, with less variation with the progression of age than men (Meskell 2000: 425).

In medieval Europe, the life course is demonstrated most vividly by the archaeology of the parish church (Gilchrist 1999: 83–87). By the twelfth century, the fully de-veloped ground plan of the church represented the body of the crucified Christ, and the siting of particular rites, features, and images connected physical movement through the spaces of the church with the passage of a Christian life (figure 6.3). In contrast with the Egyptian example, the most revered space was in the east, toward the holy city of Jerusalem. Fonts for infant baptism were placed at the western end of the nave, to denote both entry to the Church and initiation to the life course, and infant burial was also concentrated to the west of the church. Popular iconography for the font included representations of the seasons and the labors of the months, combining images of the agricultural cycle with the human life cycle.

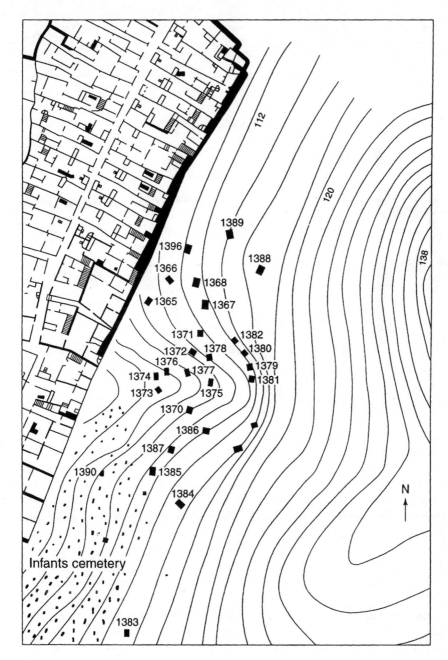

Figure 6.2 *Plan of the Eastern Necropolis, Deir el Medina, Egypt. Numbered tombs with adult burials are marked with a circle, adolescents with a triangle, and children with a square. The lower portion of the cemetery was for infants and neonates* (Meskell 2000:430)

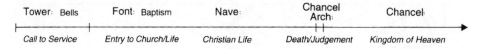

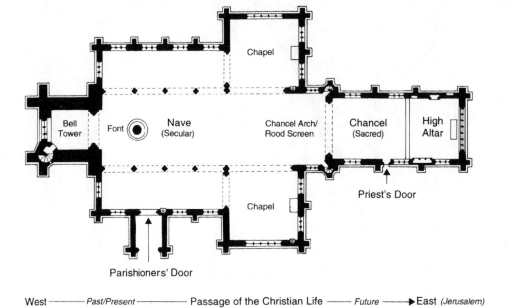

Figure 6.3 *Plan of a late medieval English parish church, illustrating the conjunction of the passage of a Christian life with physical movement from west to east through the spaces of the church* (Gilchrist 1999:86)

The most arresting imagery was reserved for the space over the chancel arch, above the crucifixion on the rood screen. Here, visions of doom and the judgment day depicted the weighing of good and bad souls, and the passage to heaven or hell (figure 6.4). Its placement underlined the transitions of the Christian life: entry through baptism at the western extreme of the nave; moving eastward through life toward judgment at the rood screen; and the promise of heavenly afterlife in the mystified, eastern area of the chancel. These spaces were experienced differently according to social status, sex, and age: proximity to the high altar during services was influenced by sex and status, and position of burial was affected especially by age. The spaces and visual imagery of the parish church gave meaning to the personal experience of aging, while its burials and tombs linked past and present generations. Its monumentality provided a sense of temporal and spatial order that united cosmological and human time scales with public and private memory.

Conclusions: "The Coming of Age"

This chapter has argued that the historically contingent and culturally constructed qualities of age demand critical consideration in archaeology. It has shown that age is

Figure 6.4 *A medieval panel painting depicting the Judgment, from above the chancel arch at Wenhaston parish church, Suffolk, England* (author's photograph)

viewed increasingly as a vital element of social identity, integrated with gender and other factors. The diverse intellectual strands behind these themes have been drawn together, revealing the significance of feminist third-wave and age studies, together with anthropological approaches to the body. In contrast with the disciplines of history and ancient history, archaeology has engaged less directly with sociological literature on the life course, and has resisted creating a subdiscipline devoted to gerontology. The largest corpus of archaeological work to address age concerns children, but the theme has influenced studies of gender and the body. The framework of the life course has been advocated; a "longitudinal" approach which examines trajectory and transition across the continuum of the human life, and which situates the human life span within social measures of time. The *life-course* model should be distinguished from the *life cycle*, which carries overtly biological and cross-cultural overtones. The contrast between life course and life cycle is greater than mere terminology. In the formative stages of theorizing age, this distinction may be as significant as that which contrasted the terms "gender" and "sex" in the fledgling discipline of gender archaeology.

The life course promises a more embodied and experiential perspective to gender archaeology, one that interacts with archaeologies of time and memory. The most developed studies to date have been within the sphere of historical archaeology, allowing nuanced interpretations of individuals and their intentions (e.g., Meskell 1999; Wilkie 2000). Even without the association of textual sources, the evidence of burial archaeology and ancient art have the potential for a life-course analysis of age and gender categories, such as Derevenski's study of Copper Age burials from Tiszapolgár-Basatanya (1997), and Gowland's analysis of age thresholds in the burials of Romano-British children (2001). Finally, the study of aging bridges social and biological concerns, and perhaps offers the opportunity to mediate traditional tensions between constructionist and evolutionary approaches to human social life (Chisholm 1993).

In common with earlier feminist archaeology, the perspective of the gendered life course demands new scales of archaeological analysis. Alison Wylie (1992) concluded that feminist scholarship in archaeology in the 1980s and 1990s had prompted an innovative concern for local, micro-scale, empirical detail. In drawing connections between age and gender, attention is now shifting to temporal measures of analysis. This new scale of gender archaeology remains grounded in contextualism, but reaches for a feminist meta-narrative: or; one that conceptualizes the gendered body and life experience in relation to time, space, and memory.

ACKNOWLEDGMENTS

I am grateful to my colleague Ray Laurence for our discussions on shared interests in the life course and historical archaeology.

NOTE

1   Feminist thought is understood to have developed in three waves, although there is some disagreement amongst feminists as to the precise dates and accomplishments of these three

movements. "First wave" refers to the suffrage movements of between roughly 1880 and 1920, devoted to the public emancipation of women. "Second wave" is used here to refer to the feminism which emerged in the late 1960s, which concentrated more on personal issues of equality, and was linked with a concern for identifying the root causes of women's oppression. Second-wave feminism is connected with the theory of patriarchy, which provided a universal, explanatory framework for women's experience. "Third-wave" feminism has been influenced by postmodernism, and rejects the idea of an "essential" experience for women or men. It incorporates a greater pluralism of approaches to investigate gender difference (Gilchrist 1999: 2–3).

REFERENCES

Adam, B. 1990. *Time and Social Theory*. Cambridge: Polity Press.

—— 1994. Perceptions of time. In T. Ingold (ed.), *Companion Encyclopedia of Anthropology. Human Culture and Social Life*. London: Routledge, pp. 503–526.

Amos, V., and P. Parmar. 1984. Challenging imperial feminism. *Feminist Review* 17: 3–21.

Arber, S., and M. Evandrou. 1993. Mapping the territory. Ageing, independence and the life course. In S. Arber and M. Evandrou (eds.), *Ageing, Independence and the Life Course*. London: Jessica Kingsley, pp. 9–26.

Ariès, P. 1965. *Centuries of Childhood*. New York: Jonathan Cape.

Beaumont, L. 2000. The social status and artistic presentation of "adolescence" in fifth-century Athens. In J. S. Derevenski (ed.), *Children and Material Culture*. London: Routledge, pp. 39–50.

Beauvoir, S. de. 1972. *The Coming of Age*. Trans. P. O'Brian. New York: Norton.

Bertelsen, R. A. Lillehammer, and J. Naess (eds.) 1987. *Were They all Men? An Examination of Sex Roles in Prehistoric Society*. Norway: Stavanger.

Bourdieu, P. 1977. *Outline of a Theory of Practice*. Cambridge: Cambridge University Press.

Bradley, R. 2002. *The Past in Prehistoric Societies*. London: Routledge.

Brown, J. 1982. Cross-cultural perspectives on middle-aged women. *Current Anthropology* 23:2: 143–156.

Brown, K. A. 1998. Gender and sex: distinguishing the difference with ancient DNA. In R. D. Whitehouse (ed.), *Gender & Italian Archaeology. Challenging the Stereotypes*. London: Accordia, pp. 35–44.

Brumbach, H. J., and R. Jarvenpa. 1997. Woman the hunter: Ethnoarchaeological lessons from Chipewyan life-cycle dynamics. In C. Claassen and R. Joyce (eds.), *Women in Prehistory*. Philadelphia: University of Pennsylvania Press, pp. 17–32.

Butler, J. 1993. *Bodies that Matter: On the Discursive Limits of "Sex."* London: Routledge.

Chamberlain, A. 2000. Minor concerns: A demographic perspective on children in past societies. In J. S. Derevenski (ed.), *Children and Material Culture*. London: Routledge, pp. 206–212.

Chapman, R. W, I. Kinnes, and K. Randsborg (eds.) 1981. *The Archaeology of Death*. Cambridge: Cambridge University Press.

Chisholm, J. S. 1993. Death, hope and sex. Life-history theory and the development of reproductive strategies. *Current Anthropology* 34(1): 1–24.

Conkey, M. W., and J. Spector. 1984. Archaeology and the study of gender. In M. W. Conkey and J. Spector, *Archaeological Method and Theory* 7. New York: Academic Press, pp. 1–38.

Crawford, S. 2000. Children, grave goods and social status in early Anglo-Saxon England. In J. S. Derevenski (ed.), *Children and Material Culture*. London: Routledge, pp. 169–179.

Derevenski, J. S. 1997. Age and gender at the site of Tiszapolgár-Basatanya, Hungary. *Antiquity* 71: 875–889.

——2000. Material culture shock: Confronting expectations in the material culture of children. In J. S. Derevenski (ed.), *Children and Material Culture*. London: Routledge, pp. 1–16.

Douglas, M. 1966. *Purity and Danger: An Analysis of Concepts of Pollution and Taboo*. London: Routledge.

Dowson, T. (ed.) 2000. Queer archaeologies. *World Archaeology* 32(2).

Fabian, J. 1983. *Time and the Other*. New York: Columbia University Press.

Fausto-Sterling, A. 1985. *Myths about Gender: Biological Theories about Women and Men*. New York: Basic Books.

Foucault, M. 1981. *The History of Sexuality: An Introduction. Volume 1*. Harmondsworth: Penguin.

Foxhall, L. 1994. Pandora unbound: A feminist critique of Foucault's *History of Sexuality*. In A. Cornwall and N. Lindisfarne (eds.), *Dislocating Masculinity*. London: Routledge, pp. 133–146.

Franklin, M. A. 2001. A Black feminist-inspired archaeology? *Journal of Social Archaeology* 1(1): 108–125.

Gell, A. 1992. *The Anthropology of Time*. Oxford: Berg.

Gero, J. M., and M. W. Conkey (eds.) 1991. *Engendering Archaeology: Women and Prehistory*. Oxford: Blackwell.

Gilchrist, R. 1994. *Gender and Material Culture. The Archaeology of Religious Women*. London: Routledge.

——1999. *Gender and Archaeology: Contesting the Past*. London: Routledge.

——ed. 2000. Human lifecycles. *World Archaeology* 31(3): 325–328.

Gosden, C. 1994. *Social Being and Time*. Oxford, Blackwell.

Gowland, R. 2001. Playing dead: Implications of mortuary evidence for the social construction of childhood in Roman Britain. In G. Davies, A. Gardner, and K. Lockyer (eds.), *TRAC 2000. Proceedings of the Tenth Annual Theoretical Roman Archaeology Conference*. Oxford: Oxbow, pp. 152–168.

Grauer, A. L., and Stuart-Macadam, P. (eds.) 1998. *Sex and Gender in Paleopathological Perspective*. Cambridge: Cambridge University Press.

Guillén, A. C. 1993. Women, rituals, and social dynamics at Ancient Chalcatzingo. *Latin American Antiquity* 4(3): 209–224.

Gullette, M. M. 2000. Age studies and gender. In L. Code (ed.), *Encyclopedia of Feminist Theories*. London: Routledge, pp. 12–14.

Hagestad, G. O. 1990. Social perspectives on the life course. In R. H. Binstock and L. K. George (eds.), *Handbook of Ageing and the Social Sciences*. 3rd edn. San Diego, CA: Academic Press, pp. 151–168.

Harding, S. 1991. *Whose Science? Whose Knowledge? Thinking from Women's Lives*. Milton Keynes: Open University Press.

Harlow, M., and R. Laurence. 2002. *Growing Up and Growing Old in Ancient Rome: A Life Course Approach*. London: Routledge.

Hawkes, K., J. F. O'Connell, and N. G. Blurton. 1997. Hadza women's time allocation, offspring provisioning, and the evolution of long postmenopausal life spans. *Current Anthropology* 38(4): 551–577.

Herdt, G. 1987. *The Sambia: Ritual and Gender in New Guinea*. New York, Holt, Rinehart & Winston.

Jordanova, L. 1989. *Sexual Visions*. London: Harvester Wheatsheaf.

Joyce, R. A. 2000. Girling the girl and boying the boy: The production of adulthood in ancient Mesoamerica. *World Archaeology* 31(3): 473–484.

Kampen, N. B. (ed.) 1996. *Sexuality in Ancient Art. Near East, Egypt, Greece and Italy*. Cambridge, Cambridge University Press.

Keith, J. 1980. "The best is yet to be": Toward an anthropology of age. In B. J. Siegal (ed.), *Annual Review of Anthropology*. Palo Alto, CA: Annual Reviews, pp. 339–364.

——1990. Age in social and cultural context: Anthropological perspectives. In R. H. Binstock and L. K. George (eds.), *Handbook of Ageing and the Social Sciences*. 3rd edn. San Diego, CA: Academic Press, pp. 91–111.

Kerns, V., and J. K. Brown. 1992. *In Her Prime*. Urbana, University of Illinois Press.

Knapp, B., and L. Meskell. 1997. Bodies of evidence in Cypriot prehistory. *Cambridge Archaeological Journal* 7(2): 183–204.

Koloski-Ostrow, A., and C. L. Lyons (eds.) 1997. *Naked Truths. Women, Sexuality and Gender in Classical Art and Archaeology*. London: Routledge.

Kopytoff, I. 1986. The cultural biography of things: Commodification as process. In A. Appadurai (ed.), *The Social Life of Things. Commodities in Cultural Perspective*. Cambridge: Cambridge University Press, pp. 64–91.

Laqueur, T. W. 1990. *Making Sex: Body and Gender from the Greeks to Freud*. Cambridge, MA: Harvard University Press.

Laslett, P. 1995. Necessary knowledge: Age and aging in the societies of the past. In D. I. Kertzer and P. Laslett (eds.), *Ageing in the Past: Demography, Society and Old Age*. Berkeley: University of California Press, pp. 3–77.

Lauretis, T. de (ed.) 1991. Queer Theory. *Differences* 3, Special Issue.

Lillehammer, G. 1989. A child is born. The child's world in an archaeological perspective. *Norwegian Archaeological Review* 22: 89–105.

——2000. The world of children. In J. S. Derevenski (ed.), *Children and Material Culture*. London: Routledge, pp. 17–26.

Lock, M. 1993. Cultivating the body: Anthropology and epistemologies of bodily practice and knowledge. *Annual Review of Anthropology* 22: 133–155.

MacKenzie, M. A. 1991. *Androgynous Objects. String Bags and Gender in Central New Guinea*. Amsterdam: Harwood Academic.

McTaggart, J. M. E. 1934. *Philosophical Studies*. London: Edward Arnold.

Merleau-Ponty, M. 1962 [1945]. *The Phenomenology of Perception*. London: Routledge.

Meskell, L. 1996. The somatisation of archaeology: Discourses, institutions, corporeality. *Norwegian Archaeological Review* 29(1): 1–16.

——1999. *Archaeologies of Social Life, Age, Sex, Class et cetera. in Ancient Egypt*. Oxford, Blackwell.

——2000. Cycles of life and death: Narrative homology and archaeological realities. *World Archaeology* 31(3): 423–441.

Moore, J., and E. Scott (eds.) 1997. *Invisible People and Processes: Writing Gender and Childhood into European Archaeology*. London: Leicester University Press.

Morbeck, M. E., A. Galloway, and A. L. Zihlman (eds.) 1997. *The Evolving Female: A Life-History Perspective*. Princeton, NJ: Princeton University Press.

Murray, T. 1999. Introduction. In T. Murray (ed.), *Time and Archaeology*. London: Routledge, pp. 1–7.

Owens, D., and B. Hayden. 1997. Prehistoric rites of passage: A comparative study of transegalitarian hunter-gatherers. *Journal of Anthropological Archaeology* 16: 121–161.

Park, R. W. 1998. Size counts: The miniature archaeology of childhood in Inuit societies. *Antiquity* 72: 269–281.

Parker, H. N. 1998. The Tetratogenic grid. In J. P. Hallett and M. B. Skinner (eds.), *Roman Sexualities*. Princeton, NJ: Princeton University Press, n.p..

Parkin, T. 1992. *Demography and Roman Society*. Baltimore, MD: Johns Hopkins University Press.

Rautman, A. E. (ed.) 2000. *Reading the Body. Representations and Remains in the Archaeological Record*. Philadelphia, University of Pennsylvania Press.

Rosaldo, M. Z., and L. Lamphere (eds.) 1974. *Woman, Culture and Society*. Stanford, CT: Stanford University Press.

Roscoe, P. B. 1995. Initiation in cross-cultural perspective. In N. C. Lutkehaus and P. B. Roscoe (eds.), *Gender Rituals*. London: Routledge, pp. 219–238.

Schmidt, R. A., and B. L. Voss (eds.) 2000. *Archaeologies of Sexuality*. London: Routledge.

Schwarz, M. T. 1997. *Moulded in the Image of Changing Woman. Navajo Views on the Human Body and Personhood*. Tucson, University of Arizona Press.

Sørensen, M. L. S. 2000. *Gender Archaeology*. Cambridge, Polity Press.

Spector, J. 1983. Male/female task differentiation among the Hidatsa: Toward the development of an archaeological approach to the study of gender. In P. Albers and B. Medicine (eds.), *The Hidden Half*. Washington, DC: University Press of America, pp. 77–99.

Strathern, M. 1988. *The Gender of the Gift. Problems with Women and Problems with Society in Melanesia*. Berkeley: University of California Press.

Thomas, J. 1996. *Time, Culture and Identity: An Interpretive Archaeology*. London: Routledge.

Treherne, P. 1995. The warrior's beauty: The masculine body and self-identity in Bronze-Age Europe. *Journal of European Archaeology* 3(1): 105–144.

Turner, B. 1995. Aging and identity: Some reflections on the somatization of the self. In M. Featherstone and A. Wernick (eds.), *Images of Aging. Cultural Representations of Later Life*. London: Routledge, pp. 245–260.

Turner, V. 1969. *The Ritual Process: Structure and Anti-Structure*. Ithaca, NY: Cornell University Press.

Van Gennep, A. 1960 [1908]. *The Rites of Passage*. Trans M. B. Vizedom and G. L. Caffee. Chicago: University of Chicago Press.

Whitrow, G. J. 1988. *Time in History. Views of Time from Prehistory to the Present Day*. Oxford: Oxford University Press.

Wilkie, L. 2000. Not merely child's play: Creating a historical archaeology of children and childhood. In J. S. Derevenski (ed.), *Children and Material Culture*. London: Routledge, pp. 100–113.

Wylie, A. 1992. Feminist theories of social power: Some implications for a processual archaeology. *Norwegian Archaeological Review* 25.1: 51–68.

Yates, T. 1993. Frameworks for an archaeology of the body. In C. Tilley (ed.), *Interpretative Archaeology*. Oxford: Berg, pp. 31–72.

7

The Past and Foreign Countries: Colonial and Post-Colonial Archaeology and Anthropology

Chris Gosden

Understanding a past that is unlike the present is a complex process. This was the challenge facing those constructing the first systematic prehistories in the nineteenth and twentieth centuries. Creating a different past requires some, or all, of the following things: a desire to know the past and the thought that an understanding of the past allows different views of the present and future; some images of societies different from one's own; a defined sense of self and the society one lives in; a theory or theories that make it possible to construct self and other from general principles; a theory or theories of change. Anthropology and archaeology have, since the 1850s, created theories and images of self, other, and change that have opened up the possibility of prehistory, first in Europe and North America and later in other parts of the world. This was a process not of discovering self and other, but of creating them, and it draws on a longer history of cross-cultural encounters. We can gloss this longer history as colonialism. Colonialism gave Europeans a sense of themselves through an understanding of all the peoples that they were not, which crystallized in the late nineteenth and early twentieth centuries. A European past emerged out of the gap between self and other. Since the 1960s the discrete and oppositional nature of self and other have been breaking down, as images of savagery and primitivism are used less freely, which has fundamentally altered the way prehistory is constructed or discovered.

Westerners have changed their views of others, but slightly less obviously, they have changed their views of themselves. What individuals consist of, how societies are constituted, can be questioned, as can the relationship between the Western researcher and groups of non-Western origin. Anthropologists are now self-conscious about using the term "informant," which implies someone who supplies raw empirical detail about their own culture on which the anthropologist can carry out the sophisticated work of analysis and theory-building to translate this empirical detail into real knowledge. Anthropologists work with people, not through them, acknowledging that theoretically informed analysis can be carried out by anyone, even though the theory may derive from non-Western traditions. A similar process has happened in archaeology, although it is less discussed and recognized. Many archaeologists still write about the prehistory of North America, West Africa or Australia in a manner in tune with their own interests and training, but increasing numbers don't. A growing proportion of the profession realize that cooperation with local indigenous communities is not just a matter of social courtesy or legal necessity, but is a theoretically informed process through which the ideas that an archaeologist initially brings to an investigation will be modified or even thrown out through discussions with local people. This is now seen as a sign of intellectual strength and not weakness: learning about the past is learning about ways of life not our own, and it is a process which requires a Western investigator to give up some of the values they hold dear. Constructive self-criticism is crucial to the understanding of difference.

Given the longevity and pervasiveness of colonial influences, it is no simple matter to become postcolonial. The end of formal colonial and imperial structures does not immediately bring about a total shift in forms of thought and feeling. In order to explore what it might mean to be postcolonial, we need to look at the range and depth of colonial influences, their continuing influence, and how we might unlearn these influences. In this chapter I shall concentrate on the postcolonial context of the present and argue that there is an emerging body of theory within anthropology which can help us rethink the nature of personhood, the constitution of groups, and human relations with the material world, which is useful to current archaeological purposes. The study of colonialism of the recent and ancient pasts is a useful testing ground for this theory, showing as it does the fluidity of colonial cultures and helping us to further distance ourselves from overly rigid ideas of groups, cultures, and otherness.

Creating the Other

Archaeology and anthropology are often seen as the academic outcome of a process of discovering alterity: just how different people are around the globe with all their various ways of life, customs, forms of speech, and thought. I see this process not as one of discovering Otherness, but of creating it. The joined history of archaeology and anthropology is linked by this central thread, which becomes apparent in modern guise through nineteenth-century discussions about race, systems of marriage and religion, or the social systems lying behind the prehistoric evidence from Europe and North America.

Archaeology and anthropology have enjoyed a fluctuating relationship. They were close, indeed inseparable, in the evolutionary anthropology of the late nineteenth century, where an evolutionary model of bands, tribes, chiefdoms, and states was used to contain and order a mass of detail brought together without any notion of structure. Structures and their analysis came to dominate anthropology in the earlier twentieth century, just as the critique of structure came to dominate its end. Archaeology developed an enthusiasm for structure (and structuralism) at the point where the notion was coming under attack in anthropology, which confused things a little as archaeology became poststructuralist without ever having fully embraced structuralism. Crucially, the exploration of poststructuralist thought in archaeology from the 1980s onward set the conditions for closeness between both archaeology and anthropology in Britain, not found in quite the same manner elsewhere. Poststructuralism was allied to postcolonialism in its urge to deconstruct Western certainties and superiorities. Key areas like material culture, landscape, cultural property, identity, and representation have been usefully explored in tandem by both archaeologists and anthropologists in Britain, leading to some cross-fertilization between the disciplines, which has been rather slower to happen in North America or in the southern hemisphere. To understand the nature of the debates since the 1980s we need to look at the longer history of anthropology and how it has influenced archaeology.

Anthropology of the early twentieth century, through the figures of Malinowski and Radcliffe-Brown, sought to distinguish itself from the earlier evolutionary ethnology of Tylor and Pitt Rivers. Instead of change, the new social anthropologists focused on the complexity of ways of life at any one moment in time: how a society worked and functioned in the "ethnographic present." Social structure was the key to understanding primitive societies, and the innovation which led to the systematic investigation of social structure was Rivers's development of the so-called "genealogical method." The stress on social relations, as continued in the work of Malinowski and Radcliffe-Brown, became the key feature of British social anthropology, remaining so until the 1980s. Radcliffe-Brown (1952) was not just interested in structure, but also function. How did forms of thought and action function to make a viable and sustainable form of life? Although he was interested in particular cases, he also wanted to use these in order to create broader generalizations. "The Australian idea of what is here called 'opposition' is a particular feature of that association by contrariety that is a universal feature of human thinking, so that we think by pairs of contraries, upwards and downwards, strong and weak, black and white" (Radcliffe-Brown 1958:118). In statements such as these Radcliffe-Brown was moving from structural analysis to structuralist forms, and may have predisposed British anthropology to this new French theory which it would start to embrace in the post-war period. Lévi-Strauss is the key originating figure.

The search for deep structures giving rise to diversity is a theme of all aspects of Lévi-Strauss's work. Of both his writings on kinship and that on mythology which followed, he asked: "in the presence of a chaos of social practices or religious representations, will we continue to seek partial explanations, different for each case? Or will we try to discover an underlying order, a deep structure whose effect will permit us to account for this apparent diversity and, in a word, to overcome this incoherence?" (Lévi-Strauss and Eribon 1991:141). From Boas, Lévi-Strauss took the idea that cultures have their own sets of logic and in some ways are sufficient unto themselves. He obviously differed from the older man in seeing order underlying variety, whereas for Boas local variety was all (Stocking 1996). Boas set up the culture-historical approach in the United States, which was also a reaction against an earlier evolutionary anthropology practiced by the Bureau of American Ethnology. Lévi-Strauss's intellectual means of grasping underlying structure was through the influence of structural linguistics of Saussure and which Lévi-Strauss first encountered through a meeting with the prominent linguist Roman Jakobson.

Structuralist linguistics made it possible to probe the workings of individual languages, but made a comparative project difficult unless one posited some more universal structure. Like Chomsky in linguistics, Lévi-Strauss overcame this relativism through finding a commonality in the structure of the human mind. A direct indication of the workings of the mind was contained in myth, the sets of stories, metaphors, and images through which a group tried to make sense of the world.

For Lévi-Strauss cultural schemes of thought and representation were codes to be unscrambled, providing the key to social relations and connections with the phenomenal and spirit worlds. A myth is only superficially about the story it purports to tell. It can be made to reveal a set of underlying analogies and resemblances at the heart of the culture in question: this is the *real* story. Kuper (1996:161) says that Lévi-Strauss's ideas hit Britain from 1960 onward with the force of revelation, and that the leaders of the new British structuralism, such as Leach, Needham, and Mary Douglas, introduced these ideas in a proselytizing spirit.

A further complex reciprocal influence was with cultural anthropology in the United States. Here structuralism was partly confronted by a new evolutionary anthropology based on the work of Leslie White. However, there were elements of American anthropology more sympathetic to structuralism. Kroeber and Kluckhohn wrote a review of the concept of culture in which they listed 164 definitions of the word, before settling on their own view of culture as an ensemble of "patterns, explicit and implicit, of and for behavior acquired and transmitted by symbols" (1952:181). Such a view had striking resonances with that of Lévi-Strauss, without invoking the same set of complex intellectual influences. Clifford Geertz, a student of Kluckhohn's, was to develop this view of culture "as a system of symbols by which man confers significance on his own experience" (1993 [1973]:250).

An emphasis on structuralism and symbolism came late to archaeology, after much of the heat had gone out of the arguments over these topics in anthropology and the light generated by symbolic and structural approaches had started to dim. Historical archaeology saw the first and possibly the best application of structuralism in Deetz's little gem *In Small Things Forgotten* (1977). Deetz analyzed the framework of thought and feeling created by the Georgian order found in seventeenth-century Virginia. Colonial housing, material culture, and sensibility were structured around an order of thought and symbolism imported from Britain, which gave a rational shape and direction to the social world. The influence of Deetz's work continues today as a point of debate (Leone 1988). More polemical and less convincing empirically was Hodder's edited volume *Symbolic and Structural Archaeology* (1982), which could not quite bring itself to use the word structuralism in the title through an awareness that this might look passé. The poststructuralist move in archaeology focused on meaning and its generation through local context, which took archaeology back to the concerns of Boas and the early work of Childe. Boas carried out fieldwork amongst Inuit groups on Baffin Island in 1883–4 and came to realize the importance of the peoples' cultural perceptions of the world in which they lived and the history of the cultures that framed those perceptions. These are ideas that he carried with him to subsequent work on the art and representation of the Canadian northwest coast, and meant that he had no place for a theory of evolution in which everyone in the world was supposed to move through the same set of stages. Hodder's contextual archaeology shared many of the same elements (Hodder 1986). Archaeology gradually moved away from structure into a concern for meaning and how this is generated.

Both Marxists and symbolic anthropologists share an interest in discursive and practical consciousness. However, the former tend to stress the practical as the place to start in generating understanding, whereas the latter emphasize that the world must be conceived of symbolically before it can be acted upon practically. Many have noted the parallels between Marx's thought and that of Lévi-Strauss, and much French Marxist anthropology has borrowed the notion of structure. Althusser (Althusser and Balibar 1970) and others have combined structuralist ideas, common in French intellectual life, with Marxism to show that there may be different speeds in the development of the forces and relations of production, plus more than one mode of production present in any one social formation (Hindness and Hirst 1975).

Ideas emphasizing structure allowed archaeology and anthropology to codify different forms of otherness in exactly the terms Lévi-Strauss used – to seek deep structures underlying superficial similarity. The idea of structure was good for many purposes, forming the crucial term in structural-functionalism, structuralism, and structural Marxism. Recent thought has been termed "poststructuralism," but might be better thought of as an attack on structure in all its forms, a poststructurism. The attack on structure has helped bring about new conceptions of otherness.

Deconstructing the Other and Attacking Structure

From the mid-1960s onward the idea of structure started to come under attack, first in France through the work of Foucault, Derrida, and Lacan, and later in all parts of the globe and all the social sciences. Structuralism was seen by many as the last grand theory that tried to explain all human life through the universal structuring powers of the human mind, which divided the world into opposites and reveled in the tension this created. The criticisms of structuralism saw a return to smaller and more detailed accounts of human life, stressing the local and the particular, looking at how individuals dealt with their lives and the emotions this engendered, as well as the forms of thought. The stress on detail might have returned anthropology to the styles of the late nineteenth century. Who can now read Tylor, Fraser or Haddon without being overwhelmed and bewildered by the piles of details and endless examples? The main difference between the works of the end of the nineteenth century and the next was that the later work was centrally concerned with the link between power and knowledge. Who is telling a particular story, why, and how all became central questions both to ask of the work of other people and oneself. The notion of voice opened up the possibility that excluded voices ought to speak, so that black, feminist, and other subaltern writers critiqued hitherto dominant traditions. Structuralism was also criticized for ignoring history, the material dimension of life, and change, but the issue of power links poststructuralism to another great current affecting archaeology and anthropology today: postcolonialism.

Postcolonial theory derives from the decline of formal colonial structures and the forms of thought that went along with them after World War II. Postcolonial theory was developed by thinkers and activists in former colonies, together with theorists from former colonial powers dealing with the unpalatable consequences of racism or other forms of Western triumphalism. The key postcolonial text is Edward Said's

Orientalism (1978) in which Said criticizes the clichéd view that Europe holds of the East as being static, exotic, theocratic, and backward, exactly the views held by Marx, Weber, and other key European theorists.

At the heart of most postcolonial thought is the need for local histories, not global theory (Thomas 1994: ix). A central paradox for many postcolonial theorists is that, while using the terms colonial or postcolonial in a general fashion, they demand recognition of local differences and nuances in power relations which can be used to critique broader models. Local differences arise due to the agency of local people, who resist colonials with a variety of instruments, from armed resistance to subtle cultural subversions. Difference also derives from the contradictory nature of colonial powers. In the British Empire at its height there was a vast range of attitudes of "native" populations, from gentle exoticism to vicious racism, so that the Empire varied over space and time in the manner in which colonies were administered and represented back "home." Attitudes of all parties were historically rooted, with fixed racial categories only arising after the eighteenth century, so that encounters between the Pilgrim Fathers and the "Indians" in the seventeenth century were very different from those in the interior of Africa in the later nineteenth. The main distrust of grand narratives is due to Foucault's link between knowledge and power. Foucault felt that knowledge was not produced due to disinterested study of the world, but through structures of power and of government. People come to know themselves as subjects, or others as objects, through the interests of government, with the modern world of the last two centuries seeing the rise of new codifications of people as variously solid citizens, criminals, the insane or the native (Foucault 1979). In this he was following Gramsci's desire to understand how the consent of subjects was solicited through cultural practice and education, as well as through force and domination. If knowledge and power are linked, then all forms of study should be subject to deconstruction, and we should understand what the imperatives are behind the need to know the world in a particular manner. A big story, like that created by the evolutionary theorists, is seen as a projection of a European obsession with politics and economics onto the world screen and an attempt to decide who was the dominant world force at any one time. Wole Soyinka, for instance, sees Marxism as an attempt to impose Western humanistic attitudes as universals.

Much of the effort of postcolonial thinkers has been to uncover the roots, the effects, and the outward appearances of colonial forms of discourse and representation (Bhabha 1994; Said 1978, 1993; Spivak 1987 – see also discussions in Gosden 1999, 2001). This has led to the criticism by some that postcolonial theory is more about Western discourse than Third World problems – like a tar-baby, Western forms of thought have trapped even those who struggle against them. Another common criticism is the complexity and opacity of the prose of many postcolonial thinkers, surprising in those so concerned with discourse and representation. So-called "subaltern studies" (Guha 1988) have attempted to develop views less dominated by forms of discourse and more focused on the conditions of peoples' lives. Both elements of approach, deconstruction and a concentration on the "weapons of the weak," are vital in helping us to excavate vestiges of colonial forms of thought.

Where does archaeology stand within these discussions on colonialism? Archaeology, in its earlier history, often told versions of the "rise of the West" story. Childe echoed

Marx and Weber, the former consciously, the later less so, in seeing Eurasian prehistory as the triumph of Europe through the Industrial Revolution, despite the fact that the two previous Neolithic and Urban revolutions had occurred in the Middle East. "Among the Early Bronze Age peoples of the Aegean, the Danube valley, Scandinavia and Britain, we can recognise already those very qualities of energy, independence and inventiveness which distinguish the Western world from Egypt, India and China" (Childe 1925: xiii–xiv). The ultimate triumph of Europe, following this view, only occurred since the fifteenth century when European ways of life spread across the globe, not least to Childe's native Australia. The branch of archaeology which has concerned itself with this spread is historical archaeology started by Deetz and others, using excavated evidence of settlements, pots, and animal bones which can be combined with written accounts of peoples' lives. Historical archaeology only dates back to the 1960s, having started in North America as the study of settler societies there from the beginning of the seventeenth century onwards.

> The theoretical basis for this perspective is the idea that the world became a different place when colonizing Europeans began to travel across the globe, meeting and interacting with diverse peoples as they went. The hybrid cultures that were subsequently created in the Americas, Asia, Africa and the South Seas, and even in Europe are the outcomes of these dramatic cultural exchanges. (Orser 1996: 11)

Although uncertain about its status as handmaiden to history, this strand of historical archaeology has rightly stressed the ability archaeology has to throw light on the lives of the poor, slaves, or ethnic minorities whose lives are not documented in written records. But this concentration on the world system post-1500 is exactly what some historical archaeologists are uneasy with. Johnson (1999: 28) is worried about inherited master narratives, and particularly the concentration on the shift from feudalism to modernity/capitalism that has dominated much of recent historical archaeology, which has often concentrated on the rise of the "Georgian order" on both sides of the Atlantic between the sixteenth and the eighteenth centuries. Increasingly, historical archaeologists want the subdiscipline to be broadly comparative, ranging across all the cases over the last five thousand years where written records and archaeological evidence can be combined (see discussions in Funari, Hall, and Jones 1999). Colonial forms and sentiments circulate in both space and time. The British Empire was constructed partly through conscious references to earlier empires, especially Rome, which in turn sought precedents for its tropes of power and forms of conquest. To ignore the past history of colonial forms makes no more sense than to ignore the movement of material and cultural forms across the colonial world in all directions. Colonial forms are created as hybrids across time and space.

Approaches to power and legitimacy in archaeology have overlapped with a consideration of colonialism, without highlighting the term explicitly. The explorations in *Domination and Resistance* (Miller, Rowlands, and Tilley 1989), as the title implies, look at how authority may be both claimed and challenged, drawing on the work of a range of theorists from Marx to Althusser. A framework set up around domination and resistance prejudices the terms of encounter and is only strictly relevant to some sets of human power structures, many of which have arisen since the 1500s. Few have looked at colonialism in a comparative light, a notable exception being Rowlands (1998), who feels that colonialism has been ignored as a specific topic of study within archaeology. Rowlands feels that the use of the past to legitimize modern colonialism has made people wary of drawing specific parallels between past and present forms, which has not led to conceptual clarity when thinking about both variety of forms of colonialism and their similarities (Rowlands 1998:327). We need to be aware of both the particular features of modern colonialism, such as the creation of fixed orders of racial and cultural difference which were not found in the same manner amongst the Romans or the Greeks, for instance, and of the variety of earlier forms of colonial power, which may have operated through different forms of power, means of conceiving of cultural variability, and forms of materiality. I believe it is possible to carry out an exercise of comparison, but also to disrupt the old grand narratives that have underpinned earlier archaeological attempts to understand long-term continuity and change within regimes of power and their material forms (Gosden in preparation).

The Current Situation

The broad trends I have briefly sketched out here played themselves out differently in various parts of the world. In the United States an evolutionary archaeology has continued to dominate into the twenty-first century, leaving little space for structuralism, poststructuralism or Marxism, which only really thrive within historical archaeology, by far the most theoretically aware and politically sensitive area of archaeology. Debate in historical archaeology tends to be both lively and good-humoured, a rare combination – see, for instance, the Gramscian Marxism of Leone (1988, 1999), with its North American orientation, debating with those who advocate a more obviously global approach (Orser 1996, 1999). Such trends (both the humor and the theory) are writ very small in considerations of earlier periods. Political concerns and the theoretical discussions they tend to spark cannot be avoided in the post-NAGPRA (Native American Graves Protection and Repatriation Act (1990) era, but even in areas concerning native American histories and their rights of cultural determination the numbers entering into the discussion are few (Anyon et al. 1996; Biolsi and Zimmerman 1997; Bray and Killion 1994; Deloria 1970; Preucel 2002; Zimmerman 1997). Archaeology in the United States has an unusual degree of distance from much of anthropology at present; an occasionally uncomfortable fact for those archaeologists and anthropologists in anthropology departments. Postcolonial theory is becoming more influential in North American archaeology than links with anthropology as such.

In Britain evolutionary archaeology is alive and well, but is just one of the many healthy elements of the discipline. Poststructuralist influence on archaeology has been profound, which helps unite the discipline with anthropology, where the same has been true. Social anthropology in Britain is moving away from the sole emphasis on social structures and kinship central to its first few decades (1920–60) and has incorporated the material world in the form of material culture and landscape. Theories of practice and practical action, stemming from Bourdieu (1990), have offered a theoretical basis for those studying the material world. Approaches which study practice look at how life is learned and lived, through concentrating on embodied skills inculcated through the process of socialization. Life is not learnt or enacted all of a piece, and different elements of social action are created in and create varying locales of action and efficacy. The same roster of interests apply to archaeology and anthropology in Britain today: questions of identity, gender, sexuality, consumption, and the nature of history vie with those of representation, politics, and disciplinary history in creating a politically informed and generally critical approach to the subject matter and forms of study of the discipline (fieldwork, writing, and exhibitions). Postcolonialism is a concern for British archaeologists, but its consequences are seen mainly to affect others with internal forms of colonialism and are something to be studied rather than lived. Much of archaeology in Britain is, of course, driven by local concerns and takes a culture-historical approach.

In Australia and New Zealand there is something of a generational split between an older group of processualists and a succeeding group influenced by poststructuralist and certainly postcolonialist concerns (Lilley 2000; Torrence and Clarke 2000). Whether these interests will bring archaeology and anthropology closer together remains to be seen, as they exhibit considerable distance at present.

The global situation is one of complex regional differences overwritten by archaeology fragmenting into a series of subfields inspired by varying aspects of social theory. Feminist thought focuses on sex, gender, and representation, and overlaps with, but differs from, identity theorists, and both hold things in common with indigenous groups arguing for a control over their own past. It is not just that different voices are speaking, but also that they have their own sets of theoretical languages.

Reconstructing Other and Self

The initial attack on structure was a destructive, deconstructive one. More recently this has been replaced by a more constructive turn, which emphasizes relations. Entities and structures are both seen as problematical in current forms of thought: structures are a figment of the analyst's mind concerned to seek out order at all costs; entities, such as the individual, the group, and the society, are thought not to have inherent characteristics of their own, but rather to derive from relationships between people and things which give the terms they link special characteristics and forms of appearance. A stress on relationships makes it impossible to focus on essential characteristics of individuals, groups, or objects, but still allows us to think about how such terms might be built up and created. Surprisingly, recent emphasis on the individual as the most sensitive locus of analysis have often not been very concerned with definitions of the individual, or whether personhood always takes the form of individuals cross-culturally.

At the heart of the alternative framework I shall sketch briefly here is the idea that entities (persons and things) do not have their own properties, but take on varying characteristics depending on how they are linked to other entities. People and things gain values through their relations rather than starting with these values. Relations rather than entities become important, so that we should replace "I think, therefore I am" with "You are, therefore I am." Relations to others, although formative, are not necessarily benign – the I in question could be formed as a slave through relations to others, for instance.

My initial inspiration comes from the work of Marilyn Strathern (1988, 1998), who has developed a relational view, in which persons do not have invariant qualities which they carry around with them but rather take on qualities from the network of relations with others in which they are enmeshed. Male and female characteristics belong less to persons than to the social matrix as a whole, and can be attached to people in different manners under varying circumstances. In Melanesia, at least, people are not always individuals, but rather dividuals: flexible parts of a social network taking on the characteristics of the network. In an extension of Strathern's ideas, LiPuma (1998) has argued that all societies create forms of personhood ranging in a spectrum between the dividual and the individual, and the point of analysis is to discover under what sorts of circumstances people appear as individuals and when they are created as dividuals. This erodes the radical separation Strathern has made between Melanesia and the West, but gives these ideas broader forms of applicability. A further idea deriving from Strathern is that people's agency is not limited to the current location of their body, but is distributed. Distributed personhood takes place through the circulation of objects a person has previously made and used, which in a situation of gift exchange, have unbreakable connections to past makers and transactors. Someone's effects can range far beyond their physical body and last long after they have died. Strathern's thought about the individual and group is part of a long tradition within anthropology going back to Mauss, Benedict, Mead, and Dumont, to name just some (rather similar ideas, but deriving from a different intellectual tradition are found in the work of Milton Singer, 1984), but is useful because it contains not just critique of the views of others, but a theory for generating new views on personhood.

Here Strathern's work has been partly influenced by Gell (1998) who, in his analysis of art objects, concentrates on how social relations are created and shaped through things. Gell shifted the analysis of art from an understanding of meaning to an appreciation of effect, concentrating on how objects have effects on human relations. Real appreciation of effects can only come about through an analysis of the formal properties of objects, so that in many ways his ideas could be applied to any form of material culture, and not just ideas that might be designated as art.

I would like to take elements of all of the above forms of thought, which take seriously the mutual effects of people and material culture, but which also put in question fixed categories of people and of objects. However, in both Strathern and Gell there is the feeling that social relations are primary, with objects included in their analyses to the extent that they support social relations. If material culture can be seen as the objectification of people's capacities, then people are subjectifications of things' potentialities. People are socialized in and through a material world, which makes sense to people at a visceral level. Material culture exists not as a series of external and opposing objects, but as a set of things whose potentials can be revealed by people in tune with their possibilities. There are no social relations, but only material – social relations, as one cannot exist without the other. This is close to cyborg view (Haraway 1991) in which people and objects mingle and modify the other. Distributed personhood usefully reminds us that people's efficacy is not limited to the confines of the body and a social persona may consist of things as well as a body. Under certain circumstances people can present themselves as individuals and be accepted as such, at the expense of broader connections to others. Individuals need objects to possess, that they alone can claim and control, and to this extent the possessive individual is still a valid concept, but is now only seen as one relatively limited form of personhood. Distributed personhood operates through assemblages of objects, that do not so much have properties in their own right, but through sets of physical and aesthetic links to other objects. Mention of aesthetics reminds us that people's sensory responses to objects are vital in attaching values to social–material relations, so aesthetic appreciation arises from all aspects of sensory experience and is not just or mainly to do with beauty and refinement.

Such views help reconfigure the debates about structure and agency (Dobres and Robb 2000). A longstanding question is: how far do broader structures of life determine individual people's behavior, or are individuals able to alter structures? The scheme I have sketched here does not start with the nature of individuals, but tries to constitute them in varying ways out of relations. It also refuses to accept the idea of structures. The question then becomes: how do different forms of power create individuals and groups at various times, and what forms of material culture help create and sustain these forms of power? Agency and power exist at all social levels, which interact in complex and contradictory ways. Whether the individual is dominated by structures or able to change them through novel action becomes a non-issue.

I am not trying to set up a dichotomy here between social forms where individuals dominate versus those where dividuals or distributed personhood is the norm, but rather to say that all social forms provide conditions under which individuation and distributed personhood are possibilities (table 7.1).

The study of colonialism shows that colonial cultures were fluid and changeable, so the historical forms which gave those in the nineteenth century essentialized views can be studied anew to destabilize key terms. Older views of colonial forms saw three possibilities for colonized cultures: they could succumb to the superior force of the colonizing culture and die out; they could succumb to the superior force of

Table 7.1 The relationships between persons, things, and knowledge

People	Things	Knowledge
Distributed	*Assemblages*	*Intimate*
People are composed of relationships, rather than having relationships. No fixed boundaries between people and things.	Material culture composed of a dense, interrelated field, where qualities of single things are given by links to the mass of material culture. Assemblages accumulate relationships.	Knowledge is intimate and strongly felt, most important aspects of which concern the mutually creative properties of people and things. Evaluated in terms of efficacy.
Individuals	*Objects*	*Knowledge*
Individuals have relations with people and things, rather than being composed of relations. More fixed boundaries between people and things.	Exist external to people and have their own characteristics. They are possessed by individuals.	Knowledge becomes information, being depersonalized and general. Knowledge becomes an object, through writing and machines and is evaluated in terms of its truth.

the colonizing culture and acculturate (seen positively by the colonizers as development); or they could stay the same. Many have recently pointed out that another option is not just possible but common: new hybrid cultural forms were created through the creative engagement of the colonized with the colonizing culture. A stress on hybridity acknowledges the agency of the colonized in a broader manner than that contained within a simple model of domination and resistance. Colonial relations are transformative in all directions, profoundly altering all those involved. The center did not dominate the periphery, as active components were to be found throughout the network of colonial relations. To give more substance to these views let us look briefly at two quite contrasting colonial instances, one modern (the fur trade in north America) and one ancient (activities on the edges of the Roman Empire).

Self, Other, and Colonial Cultures

A key statement of the fluidity of colonial relations is presented by the historian Richard White, who investigated the fur trade in the Great Lakes region of present-day Canada and the United States between the seventeenth and nineteenth centuries. White (1991: ix) points out that the interaction between Europeans and "natives" could create new cultural forms, influenced by both sets of cultural logics but not identical to either. From the 1650s onward Algonquians and the French constructed an alliance out of mutual dependency and need, which was cemented by the exchange of gifts and both allowed the French to live in a new social and physical landscape and the Algonquians to come to terms with the novel set of strangers in their land. The alliance created a middle ground in which many people lived for a number of centuries, helping to create new sets of meanings and forms of interaction. The middle ground only broke up in the nineteenth century, when Indians were constructed as Other and could no longer force American society into forms of mediation and alliance. The egalitarian American republic forced Indians to do what the French and British empires could not: to become true colonial subjects.

Anthropological study of the Indians was a part and an outcome of the greater distance between American society and Native American culture and the distance that made the study of Native American society possible and necessary was the final form of colonial form of usurpation, leading to cultural decline, although not destruction. White (1991: xv) feels that we have seen all earlier historical periods through a nineteenth-century lens, imputing forms of distance and views of Otherness to periods where they did not exist in the same manner.

The alliance between the French and the Algonquians, based around the exchange of European trade goods against furs, was driven by aesthetics and values. Hamell (1983, 1987; Miller and Hamell 1986) has attempted to define basic religious beliefs of the Algonquian, Iroquian, and Siouan-speakers in the seventeenth century. Marine shells, native copper and silver, rock crystals, and coloured stones, all of which came from beneath the earth or water, were connected with supernatural beings, such as the horned serpent, the panther or the dragon, who were the spirit patrons of medicine societies. Hamell's interpretations remain controversial in detail but help explain the occurrence of marine shell, native copper, and rock crystals in Eastern

Woodlands burials from the late Archaic (6000 BP) until after European contact. Indians equated European copper, brass, and tin with native copper and silver and glass beads with rocks and crystals. This helps explain the Native interest in glass and metal and why brass and copper kettles were cut into tiny fragments and exchanged widely in the sixteenth century, and also why most European goods are found in burials and not habitation sites.

By definition, the middle ground of the Great Lakes was one of mediation. The middle ground was composed of a series of links between people, French and Native American, who could act as representatives of their group. No decisions or links were binding without gifts and gifts had to be culturally appropriate, appealing to the values of both sides. These novel forms of trade and connection allowed people to individuate themselves differently, offering possibilities to those who would not previously have enjoyed any and offering new scope to those already socially powerful, where this scope might often be restricted rather than extended. In a vital sense the middle ground was not a spatial or geographical phenomenon, but concerned values, such that the values attached to people and things could be played with and mutually understood, a pragmatic commensurability of value systems. The middle ground did not just join different groups, previously not in contact, but helped reorganize material, individual, and group relations. Such recent examples allow archaeologists to think in more subtle terms about earlier colonial contacts. The idea of the middle ground also resolves the question of agency. All parties influenced the operations of these social forms, but the outcome of any action was not easily predictable for any of the parties. Everyone exercised but no one was in control. A similar view has been developed by Chantal Knowles and myself when looking at Australian New Guinea (Gosden and Knowles 2001).

The late Iron Age in southern Britain (150 BC to AD 43) is somewhat parallel to the two cases just discussed. During the late Iron Age southern Britain made the transition from a hillfort-dominated landscape to one in which some form of urban centers existed and new structures of rule came into being through kingship and a possible warrior caste. Roman and Gallo-Roman traders were active across the English Channel, probably seeking metals, grain, and slaves, in exchange for gold, coins, fine metal, and pottery (Creighton 2000). In the two centuries before Britannia became a province of the Empire, Britons were exposed to Roman values and vice versa. The British elite used Roman pottery and metalwork and Roman-style coinage, and some of the new urban centers (such as Silchester) employed rectangular buildings arranged on an orthogonal grid, unlike earlier circular forms of architecture. By the Claudian invasion of AD 43 much of the Southeast had adopted a Romano-British lifestyle and did not need to be conquered by force of arms; fighting only started in the West Country and the Midlands. Artifacts and architecture altered forms of miraculation, giving them new sets of possibility and constraint.

We might easily see this as a process of "Romanization," with the native inhabitants willingly adopting a new, civilized lifestyle which looks rather more like our own than anything that went before, and the attractions of which thus appear obvious (Millett 1990). Romanization is problematical (Hingley 2000), partly because it was a two-way process which created a blend of local and adopted cultural forms, partly because Roman culture itself was created through the making of the Empire, and partly because "civilizing the natives" is an idea so weighed down with nineteenth-century colonial values that it is more likely to produce clichés than insights. Woolf sums up the problems of Romanization succinctly – "Gauls were not 'assimilated' to a pre-existing social order, but participated in the creation of a new one" (Woolf 1997: 347). This is middle grounding of a sophisticated order, creating a working accommodation between two different cultural forms. Such an accommodation did not just affect the edges of the Empire in Britain or Gaul, but reached to its heart, because the heart of the Empire lay not so much in Rome itself, but rather in a core set of values defining what it meant to be Roman. "A symbolic centre did exist in the Roman cultural system, but it was located not in any one place or region but rather in the set of manners, tastes, sensibilities and ideals that were the common property of an aristocracy that was increasingly dispersed across the empire" (Woolf 1998: 241). Cultural change amongst aristocrats at any one point in the Empire could effect those elsewhere, so that Roman culture was a system of circulation of ideas, values, and material culture and as new circuits were added, such as Gaul or Britain, the culture as a whole was subtly altered. It was not just the Britons that were Romanized through contacts and expansion of Empire, but all Romans, because being Roman was not a state but a process with differing dynamics as the Empire expanded.

Becoming Roman entailed complex reorganizations of groups, individuals, and forms of material culture, as new values and networks came into being. The late Iron Age probably saw the rise of degree of personal possession of land and objects forming the basis for forms of individualism. Groups were also more obviously defined through coins and the distribution of other artifacts. Change was both fundamental and subtle.

Given the entanglement of so many colonial relations, it is ironic that nineteenth-century thinkers used the relationships of colonialism to emphasize differences between Westerners and others. These differences have been given intellectual shape in such schemes as the evolutionary ladder of bands, tribes, chieftains, and states where those on different rungs on the ladder have little or nothing in common. The mass of links and changes that took place through White's middle ground or New Guinean colonial culture have been erased from cultural memory by the emphasis on difference and the integrity of groups and persons. Essentialism is now an issue for both archaeology and anthropology, with archaeologists realizing that much social action within and between groups puts people and those groups at risk on some occasions, whilst solidifying them on others. More subtle and malleable notions of the social world past and present should be crucial elements of any postcolonial archaeology, which in turn necessitates new views of the colonial period itself. Colonial forms show the subtlety of human actions and their effects and a concentration on the hybrid nature of people and groups is useful in allowing us to think about noncolonial situations, making the study of colonialism an area of key theory-building.

Looking to the Future

Prediction is dangerous and my thoughts here are more about how I would like archaeology to develop than how it necessarily will develop. Self-evidently I think closeness between archaeology and anthropology has been a good thing where it has occurred, although there have been costs. A major price that some archaeologists have paid is in wanting to be anthropologists. The lure of the fine detail of human life has been too great to resist, even for prehistoric archaeologists dealing with periods where most of that detail vanished long ago. Anthropologists can talk to and about real persons, each with their own views, fears, and hopes for the future. Only some archaeologists can talk about real people in some individualized sense, mainly those with textual records. Meskell (2002) can write about ancient Egyptian experience in a convincing and provocative manner and the problems with concepts such as "private life" when applied to New Kingdom Egypt. We do not know the nature of experience in Neolithic Britain or the mid-Holocene Pacific at the personal level, but we might be able to sketch the sorts of relations that form the basis for peoples' experience. Those archaeologists who are close to anthropology, of whom I am one, now need to think what differentiates the two disciplines, as well as what joins them; continued collaboration is vital but needs to happen in a manner which plays to the strengths of each.

Issues of ownership are important now and may become more important as time goes by in this period of hyper-capitalism. Our views of the past act as a guide to control and ownership of land, cultural property, and a sense of identity in the present. The aspirations of the present animate desires for control and ownership of the past. This complex interaction between past and present is as important in a place like Britain, where local, regional, and national identities are all at issue, as it is for indigenous groups using the past to create a more healthy present. Not everyone in the world is the same or lives by identical values, and how we deal with the discreteness of cultural forms versus cultural fluidity and change raises a set of questions concerning sexuality, race, individuals, and groups. Ontology is as important as representation. The manner in which the material world is shaped for cultural purposes and also shapes us culturally needs more consideration. In an increasingly virtual world the sensory impact of material things and the manner in which their qualities shape human relations need to be looked at more closely.

Archaeology is a hybrid discipline and continually takes on influences from others, while maybe contributing less influence than it might. What we think about the discipline is often a question of how we position archaeology within an array of cognate disciplines. Is archaeology a form of history, supplying information on the full temporal span that humans and the ancestors have lived and worked? Should it be seen as a form of ecology, charting the relationships of the human species within a network of relationships within ecosystems; or sociobiology looking for the genetic basis of social imperatives? Might it be a form of politics where the needs of the present shape our views of the past? Or philosophy, throwing questions of ethics, mind and body, and human social relations into long-term perspective. For me, archaeology should be an emancipatory science, one that allows us to think differently, using the unlikely nature of the past to think the future anew, but within a present context of political claims and aspirations. Links to anthropology are vital as they provide theory and images of forms of life other than our own; but history and a deconstructive philosophy are also important in providing temporal depth and deconstructive rigor. Archaeology was developed for and by a particular segment of global society, the white middle classes in the later nineteenth century. It is now outgrowing the sets of interests that focused on the rise of civilization, technology, and the West as the locus of real historical change. Archaeology is now being re-created by new global links, which bring new parties into the conversation, as well as being critical of those links. We now know that the past can be used to be critical of the present and we hope to use it to be constructive of the future.

GUIDE TO FURTHER READING

There is a small but emerging literature on colonialism and postcolonial issues in archaeology, with a slightly larger one on the links between archaeology and anthropology. The former area includes C. Gosden (ed.) (1977), "The archaeology of colonialism and culture contact," *World Archaeology* 28(3) and Rowlands (1988). There is a large literature on historical archaeology, some of which explicitly uses a colonial perspective and some of which does not. For one of the most explicit discussions of historical archaeology and colonialism see J. Delle, M. P. Leone, and P. R. Mullins, "Archaeology of the modern state: European colonialism," in G. Barker (ed.), *Companion Encyclopedia of Archaeology* (London: Routledge, 1999), pp. 1107–1159. Also Funari, Hall, and Jones (1999) contains excellent discussions of the nature of colonial archaeology. A high-quality single-author work combining both method and theory is M. Hall, *Archaeology and the Modern World* (London: Routledge, 2000). For the mutual influences between colonial histories and archaeology, see B. G. Trigger, *Natives and Newcomers. Canada's "Heroic Age" Reconsidered* (Kingston, ON: McGill-Queen's University Press, 1985).

Postcolonial approaches have been little addressed within archaeology. An exception is Gosden (2001). There is an interesting literature mainly from North America on relationships between archaeologists and indigenous groups and the implications that archaeological research has for land rights and more general political aspirations: Biolsi and Zimmerman (1997), Bray and Killion (1994), Deloria (1970), Lilley (2000), and Zimmerman (1997). Introductions to postcolonial theory in general include B. Moore-Gilbert, *Postcolonial Theory: Contexts, Practices, Politics* (London: Verso, 1997), Said (1978, 1993), and Bhabha (1994).

Anthropological approaches to colonialism are many. A few of the better known examples are: N. Thomas, *Entangled Objects: Exchange, Material Culture and Colonialism in the Pacific* (Cambridge, MA: Harvard University Press, 1991), J. Comaroff, *Body of Power, Spirit of Resistance: The Culture and History of a South African People* (Chicago: Chicago University Press, 1985), and Thomas (1994).

On the relationship between archaeology and anthropology, there are a number of works: Gosden (1999), Hodder (1982), and B. Orme, *Anthropology for Archaeologists: An Introduction* (London: Duckworth, 1981).

REFERENCES

Althusser, L., and E. Balibar. 1970. *Reading Capital*. Trans. B. Brewster. London: New Left Books.

Anyon, R., T. J. Ferguson, L. Jackson, and L. Lane. 1996. Native American oral traditions and archaeology. *Society for American Archaeology Bulletin* 14: 14–16.

Bhabha, H. 1994. *The Location of Culture*. London: Routledge.

Biolsi, T. L., and L. J. Zimmerman (eds.) 1997. *Indians and Anthropologists. Vine Deloria Jr. and the Critique of Anthropology*. Tucson: University of Arizona Press.

Bourdieu, P. 1990. *The Logic of Practice*. Cambridge: Polity Press.

Bray, T. L., and T. W. Killion (eds.) 1994. *Reckoning with the Dead, The Larsen Bay Repatriation and the Smithsonian Institution*. Washington, DC: Smithsonian Institution Press.

Childe, V. G. 1925. *The Dawn of European Civilization*. London: Kegan Paul.

Creighton, J. 2000. *Coins and Power in Late Iron Age Britain*. Cambridge: Cambridge University Press.

Deetz, J. F. 1977. *In Small Things Forgotten*. New York: Anchor Books.

Deloria, V. 1970. *Custer Died for your Sins: An Indian Manifesto*. New York: Avon.

Dobres, M-A., and J. Robb. 2000. *Agency and Archaeology*. London: Routledge.

Foucault, M. 1979. *Discipline and Punish: The Birth of the Prison*. Trans. A. Sheridan. Harmondsworth: Peregrine.

Funari, P. P., M. Hall, and S. Jones (eds.) 1999. *Historical Archaeology. Back from the Edge*. London: Routledge.

Geertz, C. 1993 [1973]. Deep play; notes on the Balinese cockfight. In *The Interpretation of Cultures*. London: Fontana, pp. 412–453.

Gell, A. 1998. *Art and Agency. Towards a New Anthropological Theory*. Oxford: Clarendon Press.

Gosden, C. 1999. *Archaeology and Anthropology. A Changing Relationship*. London: Routledge.

—— 2001. Post-colonial archaeology: Issues of culture, identity and knowledge. In I. Hodder (ed.), *Archaeological Theory Today*. Oxford: Polity Press, pp. 241–261.

—— in preparation. *Archaeology and Colonialism*. Cambridge: Cambridge University Press.

——, and C. Knowles. 2001. *Collecting Colonialism. Material Culture and Colonial Change*. Oxford: Berg.

Guha, R. (ed.). 1988. *Selected Subaltern Studies*. Oxford: Oxford University Press.

Hamell, G. R. 1983. Trading in metaphors: The magic of beads. Another perspective on Indian-European contact in northeastern North America. In C. F. Hayes III (ed.), *Proceedings of the 1982 Glass Bead Conference*. Rochester, NY: Rochester Museum, pp. 5–28.

—— 1987. Strawberries, floating islands and Rabbit Captains: Mythical realities and European contact in the Northeast during the sixteenth and seventeenth centuries. *Journal of Canadian Studies* 21: 72–94.

Haraway, D. 1991. *Simians, Cyborgs and Women: The Reinvention of Nature*. London: The Free Association.

Hindness, B., and P. Q. Hirst. 1975. *Pre-Capitalist Modes of Production*. London: Routledge & Kegan Paul.

Hingley, R. 2000. *Roman Officers and English Gentlemen. The Imperial Origins of Roman Archaeology*. London: Routledge.

Hodder, I. (ed.) 1982. *Symbolic and Structural Archaeology*. Cambridge: Cambridge University Press.

—— 1986. *Reading the Past*. Cambridge: Cambridge University Press.

Johnson, M. 1999. Rethinking historical archaeology In P. Funari, M. Hall, and S. Jones (eds.), *Historical Archaeology. Back from the Edge*. London: Routledge, pp. 23–36.

Kroeber, A. L., and C. Kluckhohn. 1952. *Culture: A Critical Review of Concepts and Definitions*. Cambridge: Papers of the Peabody Museum of American Archaeology and Ethnology XLVII.

Kuper, A. 1996. *Anthropology and Anthropologists*. 3rd edn. London: Routledge.

Leone, M. P. 1988. The Georgian order as the order of merchant capitalism in Annapolis, Maryland, America. In M. P. Leone and P. B. Potter (eds.), *The Recovery of Meaning. Historical Archaeology in the United States*. Washington, DC: Smithsonian Institution Press, pp. 235–261.

——1999. Setting some terms for historical archaeologies of capitalism. In M. P. Leone and P. B. Parker (eds.), *Historical Archaeologies of Capitalism*. New York: Kluwer/Plenum, pp. 3–20.

Lévi-Strauss, C., and D. Eribon. 1991. *Conversations with Lévi-Strauss*. Chicago: University of Chicago Press.

Lilley, I. (ed.) 2000. *Native Title and the Transformation of Archaeology in the Post-Colonial World*. Sydney: Oceania Monographs 50.

LiPuma, E. 1998. Modernity of forms of personhood in Melanesia. In M. Lambek and A. Strathern (eds.), *Bodies and Persons. Comparative Perspectives from Africa and Melanesia*. Cambridge: Cambridge University Press, pp. 53–79.

Meskell, L. 2002. *Private Life in New Kingdom Egypt*. Princeton, NJ: Princeton University Press.

Miller, C. L., and G. R. Hamell. 1986. A new perspective on Indian–White contact: Cultural symbols and colonial trade. *Journal of American History* 73: 311–328.

Miller, D., M. Rowlands, and C. Tilley (eds.) 1989. *Domination and Resistance*. London: Routledge.

Millett, M. 1990. *The Romanization of Britain*. Cambridge: Cambridge University Press.

Orser, C. E. 1996. *A Historical Archaeology of the Modern World*. New York: Plenum.

——1999. Negotiating our "familiar" pasts. In S. Tarlow and S. West (eds.), *The Familiar Past? Archaeologies of Later Historic Britain*. London: Routledge, pp. 273–285.

Preucel, R. (ed.) 2002. *Archaeologies of the Pueblo Revolt. Identity, Meaning and Renewal in the Pueblo World*. Albuquerque: University of New Mexico Press.

Radcliffe-Brown, A. R. 1952. *Structure and Function in Primitive Society*. London: Cohen & West.

——1958. The comparative method in social anthropology. In M. N. Srinivas (ed.), *Method in Social Anthropology: Selected Essays*. Bombay: Asia Publishing House, pp. 108–129.

Rowlands, M. 1998. The archaeology of colonialism. In K. Kristiansen and M. Rowlands, *Social Transformations in Archaeology: Global and Local Perspectives*. London: Routledge, pp. 327–333.

Said, E. W. 1978. *Orientalism*. New York: Vintage.

——1993. *Culture and Imperialism*. New York: Knopf.

Singer, M. 1984. *Man's Glassy Essence: Explorations in Semiotic Anthropology*. Bloomington: Indiana University Press.

Spivak, G. 1987. *In Other Worlds: Essays in Cultural Politics*. London: Routledge.

Stocking, G. W. 1996. *After Tylor: British Social Anthropology 1888–1951*. London: Athlone.

Strathern, M. 1988. *The Gender of the Gift: Problems with Women and Problems with Society in Melanesia*. Berkeley: University of California Press.

——1998. *Property, Substance and Effect: Anthropological Essays on Persons and Things*. London: Athlone.

Thomas, N. 1994. *Colonialism's Culture: Anthropology, Travel and Government*. Oxford: Polity Press.

Torrence, R., and A. Clarke (eds.) 2000. *The Archaeology of Difference: Negotiating Cross-Cultural Engagement in Oceania*. London: Routledge.

White, R. 1991. *The Middle Ground. Indians, Empires, and Republics in the Great Lakes Region, 1650–1815*. Cambridge: Cambridge University Press.

Woolf, G. 1997. Beyond Romans and natives. *World Archaeology* 28: 339–350.

——1998. *Becoming Roman. The Origins of Provincial Civilization in Gaul*. Cambridge: Cambridge University Press.

Zimmerman, L. 1997. Remythologising the relationship between Indians and archaeologists. In N. Swidler, K. E. Dongoske, R. Anyon, and A. S. Downer (eds.), *Native Americans and Archaeologists. Stepping Stones to Common Ground*. Walnut Creek, CA: AltaMira Press, pp. 4–56.

8

Material Culture:
Current Problems

Victor Buchli

Introduction

Archaeology has always been identified with the study of material culture and, probably more than any other discipline, it has problematized material culture with the highest degree of sophistication. Before it was a science of material culture it was preceded by an archaeological practice focused on the constitution and collection of objects. Palaeolithic assemblages, ancient Chinese and Roman antiquarians, and the cabinets of curiosities established by Europeans during the Renaissance all evince the archaeological preoccupation with artifacts (Schnapp 1996). In the Euro-American tradition this concern with the significance of the material world culminated with the establishment of the great museums of the Western tradition (the Louvre, the Hermitage, the Smithsonian, the British Museum) that formed the collections of artifacts constituting material culture and the focus of archaeological thought. In their nineteenth-century forms these museum collections were the culmination of collecting traditions (both archaeological and ethnographic) that emerged from liberal Enlightenment era notions of universality, the political and administrative expansion of European colonies, the florescence of industrial society, and the birth of what we now refer to as consumerism. Krystoff Pomian suggested (1990) that these European collections functioned at a higher conceptual level as a means to mediate between two realms of experience: the known (visible/Western/present) and the unknown (invisible/non-Western/past). He describes this process as inherently destructive and wasteful – rendering something once useful useless. Like the equally destructive archaeological act (see Shanks 1992, 1998) – the collection destroys all potential utilities, subjugating them to one sole purpose as a view onto another realm of experience (the Egyptian past, British prehistory, the folkways of Russian peasants or the Triobriand islanders) – in short, archaeology and material culture studies in general are productive of various and at times conflicting materialities within and through which we shape our understandings of social reality.

Materialities of Archaeology

Archaeology has worked with different understandings of materiality throughout its history and with different analytical and social effects. Within archaeology one could hazard describing several different understandings of materiality characterizing the study of material culture. The first one might describe arises within the late nineteenth-century tradition of evolutionary thought, as can be seen in the works of Ratzel, Morgan, and Pitt-Rivers, amongst others. As described famously by Karl Marx, material culture functions much like a fossil record of economic forms – and as such, one can chart by it the evolution and social progress of Man from prehistory to the present. The entailing evolutionary and cultural-historical approach saw an almost isomorphic association of material culture with people and social evolution: with the result that pots equalled people. The evolution, migration, and ethnogenesis of peoples could be "read" directly from material culture as direct signs of their presence, movement, and evolution. The formal attributes of artifacts were delineated, divorced from their cultural contexts and understood in terms of their place within larger evolutionary schema such as those described by Lewis Henry Morgan (1978). The early twentieth-century tradition of structural functionalism considerably diminished the significance of such materialities within material culture studies in general for anthropology, heralding its decline, despite its significance for the evolutionary and cultural-historical approaches in archaeology. Malinowski's work on Kula exchange focused on the material artifact in terms of its place within a social network of exchange rather than in terms of the artifact per se (MacKenzie 1991:251), as in earlier approaches where the materiality of the artifact was so exquisitely recorded and articulated in collections and detailed drawings (Lucas 2001; Thomas 1991).

With the advent of the New Archaeology of the mid-twentieth century the cultural-evolutionary approach was displaced, breaking the discipline's so-called theoretical slumber. Material culture and its materiality were understood in rather distinct ways – as Binford famously described – as an "extrasomatic means of adaptation" (1965: 205). Objects did not signify people or levels of social and technological evolution, rather the focus was on people making "rational" decisions – making and using things to adapt to the particular circumstances of their environment. The artifact itself was not so significant except as an adaptive device; its materiality, design variation, etc., were subservient to its role within environmental adaptation. Formal attributes that were so extensively documented in terms of color, design, form, etc., in earlier times were ignored in favor of function within adaptive systems – a radically different constitution of materiality predominated – favouring a spare adaptational functionality of forms and materials.

Roughly about the same time, structuralism and linguistic analogies began to emerge, sitting rather comfortably with the adaptive systems approaches of the New Archaeology for all of its inherent "systemness" (see Hodder 1986: 34–35). The work of information-exchange theorists (Wobst 1977) within the New Archaeology argued for the communicative function of material culture as a material means of communication within and between groups which shaped the materiality of the world. Thus the material artifact is reconstituted yet another way, eliminating or reducing in significance certain attributes at the expense of others (as a system of communication), in the pursuit of a particular vision of the social and material world – reshaped and retooled yet again as contingencies require.

Within this prevailing understanding, the work of linguists such as Noam Chomsky had a profound influence, particularly on key figures such as the folklorist and material culture expert Henry Glassie (1975) and archaeologists such as James Deetz (1977). Similarly, semioticians such as Barthes and Baudrillard also perceived material culture as a form of communication which could be analyzed like a text. Underlying structures organizing and generating material culture could be determined to provide an overall "generative grammar" for understanding material and social life – such as key oppositions that structure a given society materially and socially – or they could in fact mask them, as Lévi-Strauss has observed (1973, as cited in Shanks and Tilley 1987). Thus the materiality of the artifact is constituted in yet another and distinct way – but not unlike earlier work where certain formal principles prevailed – this time internal structural ones rather then external ones characterizing earlier typological approaches. The work of Bourdieu and his notion of habitus in this respect had a decisive impact (1977), as well as Hodder's earlier work and the semiotic approaches found in the works of anthropologists such as Forge (1973) and Munn (1973). However, the rather deterministic nature of some structuralist approaches meant it was rather difficult to understand human agency and social change if much of human interaction within the material and social world was seen to be already "pre-wired."

The poststructuralist response within archaeology, most notably at the hands of Michael Shanks and Christopher Tilley, sought to break up the perceived Procrustean hold of structuralism on the understanding of human agency and explored the possibility of understanding material culture according to a textual metaphor heavily influenced by the works of Derrida and others. This understanding was open-ended, indeterminate, and the product of social contingencies. Material culture no longer was seen as the fossilized sign representing a social group or economic formation, or the "extra-somatic" means of production or the result of a "generative grammar." Instead, it was seen as produced by and productive of existing relationships, meanings, and contingencies that are contested, open-ended, and socially negotiated.

In the 1980s a notable shift was evinced in anthropology with the revival of an interest in material culture studies. In the United States the works of Munn, Appadurai, Keene, and others entailed a re-evaluation of the works of Marcel Mauss and the insights brought on from the works of Pierre Bourdieu. Simultaneously in Britain, the postprocessualist preoccupation with ethnoarchaeology saw a re-evaluation of the role of the ethnography of material culture for its own sake, notably in the works of Daniel Miller, Christopher Tilley, Michael Rowlands, and Barbara Bender, forming the basis of what can be called the University College London school of material culture studies. Alongside these developments the anthropological study of art received an added impetus as an independent anthropological endeavor through the pioneering work of Alfred Gell, a student of Anthony Forge. On both sides of the Atlantic, material culture studies became increasingly an interstitial field of study drawing anthropologists, archaeologists, art historians, and students of consumerism together. Up until this moment, the dimension of time demarcated (at times rather arbitrarily, depending on the respective research traditions) the division of labor between archaeological and anthropological approaches to the study of material culture. The legacy of the New Archaeology and the significance it ascribed to ethnoarchaeology saw the development in the United States of a distinctly archaeological approach to modern material culture studies, notably William Rathje's garbology and Shiffer's ethnoarchaeology, amongst others, as well as the distinctly Marxist approaches found in the works of McGuire and Paynter. Similarly, the study of the present for its own sake emerged within Britain and later postprocessual approaches, notably Hodder's pet-food factory study (1987) and Shanks and Tilley's study of contemporary beer cans (Shanks and Tilley 1987). At the same time the 1980s also saw the revised interest in technology in the works of Appadurai (1986), Latour (2000), Lemonnier (1986), Miller (1987), and Pfaffenberger (1988), amongst others. These studies, particularly those within the French tradition (Lemonnier, Latour), are indebted to Marcel Mauss's "Les techniques du corps" (1935; see Mauss 1973), which focused on the total social context in which technologies emerged. Another key concept was that of the *chaîne opératoire* developed by the prehistorian Leroi Gourhan, which looked at the processes whereby raw materials became finished artifacts and their social context. Objects in this tradition are understood within a broader social context of "action upon matter" (Lemonnier 1992). This contextual approach has been expanded to see objects as functioning within widely different cultural, social, and temporal contexts through the "biographical" approaches championed by Appadurai and Kopytoff (see Kopytoff 1986). Here materiality is subservient to the various social contexts in which it is entailed and is as underdetermined in terms of its materiality as in the days of structural functionalism. However, the interest in technology expanded functionalist adaptational arguments and earlier formal arguments of technological evolution. The focus was instead on the social and cultural context in which technologies emerge and their attendant forms of social organization, and their shifting material/human interfaces as most recently discussed by Latour (1999). The materiality of the artifact becomes more the focus of study as an aspect of the social and technological forces that bring to bear a specific technology or corpus of material culture. This interest in technology has coincided with an interest in the body and phenomenological studies of material culture (MacKenzie 1991; Pinney 2002; Tilley 2002), and most notably on the materiality of things in relation to their corporeal and phenomenological dimensions.

More recently the legacy of ethnoarchaeology for the development of material culture studies between anthropology and archaeology has resulted in an increasingly specialized approach toward the archaeology of the present. This inheritance from the New Archaeology has opened up some interesting prospects for the increased interdisciplinary work of material culture studies (consumption, design history, architectural history, etc.) as well as for intradisciplinary work. Processual and postprocessual approaches seem to coexist much more happily when addressing the recent past. The epistemological concerns around the dimension of time, especially with regard to analogy, once factored out, creates a space for greater intradisciplinarity as well as interdisciplinarity as seen in texts such as Gould and Schiffer's *Modern Material Culture* and, more recently, Buchli and Lucas's *Archaeologies of the Contemporary Past* (2001) and Mayne and Murray's *The Archaeology of Urban Landscapes: Explorations in Slumland* (2001). Amongst these diverse works one can see a surprising congruence of approaches and interpretive sensibilities, despite the epistemological perspectives brought to bear.

Materiality and Dimension

As the issue of time suggests, throughout these discussions of material culture and the shifting terms of materiality lurks the passage of dimensionality: the shifting dimension-alities of earlier approaches and what is being suggested in terms of materiality in the present. Much of this work that follows both postprocessual and processual sens-ibilities is characterized by an abiding concern with the terms by which the material world is manifest; in short, the transformative processes that shape the material world. The inherently destructive and wasteful nature of archaeological and material culture studies (contrary to the "intuitive" logic of conservation practices and heritage manage-ment) suggests a certain emphasis on negation or diminishment in the varying forms of dimensionality constituted within our inquiries. More recently, the understanding of the feminine as "lack" – as that which is "predisposed," to use Marilyn Strathern's felicitous term to ensure a specific category such as maleness in the construction of gender – is instructive in terms of understanding the terms by which material signifiers are actually presenced, such as material culture itself. Only a few observers have noted the inherent masculinist bias in the manner in which materiality is unproblema-tized in material culture studies (Oldenziel 1996). More explicitly in the matter that concerns us here, is the realm of the unmaterialized and "predisposed" which ensures the stability of social categories, narratives, and origin myths through such things as the "wasted" artifacts hidden away in museum storage rooms or displayed as deathlike still lifes (*natures mortes*). Bataille offers useful insights here in terms of his discussions of sacrificial economies whose cultural logics are determined by elaborate rituals of waste (notably the Potlatch of the Pacific Northwest Coast [1991]). Such wastage ensures inalienability and the near-absolute signification of ideal worlds and states.

Most material culture either as ethnographic or archaeological artifact, museum display or textural representation transforms a mostly inarticulate realm of sensual experience felt over time and space and with many senses into something inevitably static. This is typically the near two-dimensional *nature morte* of the museum display or the emphatically two-dimensional representation of the ethnographic drawing (Thomas 1991) or photograph. Peculiarly, this translation of ostensibly ephemeral objects as performed through the archaeological act (retrodictively manufacturing a "discovery" as a consequence of the archaeological encounter [see Shanks 1998; Latour 1999]) unearthing that which has been forgotten and is unseen into the durable artifact of material culture diminishes the sensual physicality of the object from three rich sensual ones to the two dimensions we typically encounter. Such physical transformations are inherently manifest in the analytical metaphors constantly used within recent material culture studies – all suggestive of the fact that the study of material culture is itself an intervention involving a manipulation of the physicality of the material world along various continua of dimensionality through our analytical endeavors. Increased dimen-sionality is rendered through the building up of aggregates "thick description" (per Geertz), "cultural thickening" (per Löfgren 1997), or "aura" (another dimensionality further articulating three per Walter Benjamin [Shanks 1998]). Or alternatively, dimen-sionality is decreased through the breaking down of aggregates along other continua:

"deconstruction," or "micro-physics" (per Foucault). The archaeological artifact can be described as emerging from a virtually dimensionless reality of no mass, neither social or physical ("unseen," unearthed,' and undiscovered'), to the highly three-dimensional and social "massive" artifact of material culture and then moving further along and diminishing in dimension and social "mass" almost full circle to the yet again "buried" artifact of the archive and hidden museum collection.

Thus the materialization of material culture involves a certain modulation of physicality across dimensions, from the unearthed artifact to the "buried" item of a collection, unseen and mostly unused (except at the time of excavation, collection, analysis, and deposition; see Holtorf 2002). An intensively constituted and rich sensual reality is rendered increasingly dead, useless, dimensionless, and invisible. The "fetish" of conservative Marxist critiques is neutralized and suppressed – its enchanting and promiscuous effects are curtailed (Belk 2001; Editorial 1996). Various observers (Gell, and Thomas, Kuechler, Pinney, Tilley) have noted how the promiscuous effects of material culture – its phenomenological and sensual dimensions – are sacrificed to our preoccupation with textuality and the textual metaphors used to contain, explain, and represent the material culture we study. The promiscuous and dangerous effects of artifacts are more recently underscored with recent problems in conservation practices. Recently repatriated Native American artifacts have been found to be conserved with poisonous substances, rendering them physically dangerous to the communities and individuals to which they have been returned; permanently inalienable and incapable of any further material transformation or appropriation.

These various transformations of artifacts in varying degrees of promiscuity, alienability, and dimensionality along many dimensions suggest that alienability represents a certain fluidity. This is a loss of "cultural mass" as it moves from one highly fixed denotative context (the diagnostic artifact of material culture in a museum collection) along the axis of time to a more permeable, connotative, promiscuous, and increasingly immaterial state. The weight of tradition or consensus (cultural or scientific) is shed, allowing the physical artifact to be transformed in terms of socially produced durability into something less so. This is not unlike the process of durability Thompson describes in Rubbish Theory which is the result of extensive social interventions: "Those people near the top have the power to make things durable and to make things transient" (1994:271). Here I am adopting a more traditional understanding of "mass" as a degree of physical substantiability rather than, as Cooper notes, "a mutable and inexhaustible source from which worlds are continually being made through the repeated double movement of collection and dispersion (2001:16). However, I would argue that both understandings are not mutually exclusive but represent degrees of concrescence; a growing together of social and empirical circumstances (Whitehead 1978 [1929]; Latour 1999) that constitute empirical and social realities – the 'factishes" of Latour. Such concrescences that assume the durability of material culture are the result of extensive social interventions such as exchange values generated in the market or the cultural and scientifically mediated effects of museum curation. These social interventions produce an "artefactual effect" (Fletcher 1997), with varying consequences and utilities as the brief history of archaeology's various materialities suggests. What occurs here is a profound social alchemy (see Shanks's discussion of alchemy and archaeology [Shanks 1992]).

Gilles Lipovetsky (1994) has argued that the cultural mass that produces this artifactual effect is also undermined by the ephemerality of fashion and consumption. The ephemerality of fashion (see also Appadurai 1996) actively wears away at the gravity and mass of tradition. The crushing ephemerality of late capitalism, which Lipovetsky refers to as its "tragic lightness," conspires against the fixity or artifactual effects of material culture as we traditionally know it. Increasingly social agency is exerted less effectively through material means, contradicting the logic of Foucault, as we know through the significance of information technology over production, the mobility of capital (Slater and Tonkiss 2001), and the extraordinary rates of consumption and waste production (Rathje and Murphy 1992). The traditional nineteenth-century conceptual category of material culture seems increasingly unable as a cultural tool and concept to engage with the conditions that characterize the "tragic lightness" of late capitalist and post-socialist modernity. This is a point more recently made by Ingold in relation to the persistent insistence within archaeology and many material culture studies to view material culture as "the imposition of conceptual form on inert matter" (2000:52) – materiality and its effects is utterly unproblematized, despite its varied history.

More recent work in material culture has focused increasingly on the instability of artifacts, their materiality, and their "artefactual effects" (Fletcher 1997). Studies on waste (Rathje and Murphy 1992), destruction (Saunders 2000), recycling and divestment (Marcoux 2001), capital flows (Miller and Carrier 1998; Slater and Tonkiss 2001), and the socially mediated effects of artifactuality (Holtorf 2002; Jensen 2000; Latour 1999) all combine to stress the importance of the processes of materiality that are of equal if not of greater significance to the artifact itself. The artifact of material culture is just one peculiar moment and social effect of these processes. As Ingold has observed: "the forms of objects are not imposed from above but grow from the mutual involvement of people and materials in an environment. The surface of Nature is thus an illusion: we work from within the world, not upon it" (2000:68).

The politics of destruction and conservation are fraught and foreground the significance of the terms by which materiality is realized rather than any a priori understandings. Michael Rowlands (2002) has discussed the complexities of Hindu and Muslim iconoclasms and conservation as explicitly destructive yet the means according to which social viabilities are actually predicated. These materialities fly in the face of orthodox Western materialities that emphasize the integrity of material culture and its conservation. In these respects the Euro-American preoccupation with dense materiality and conservation is much more problematic and in need of reconsideration (as might be said for other Western liberal democratic ideals as well). Even within the Western tradition, Gilles Lipovetsky's emphasis on the ephemerality and inherently alienable and constantly fleeting and cast-off nature of fashion as the paradigm for capitalist and late capitalist understandings of materiality, stresses how this inherent instability forges the conditions whereby social viability and an enfranchised subjectivity are possible. The ephemerality of fashion described by Lipovetsky evinces in many ways the importance of this instability and open-endedness for Neopragmatist thinkers such as Rorty and Radical Democratic theorists such as Mouffe (see Mouffe 1993). Waste and production are two points along the same continuum of materialization forming our understandings of material culture. The emphasis is more on the latter than the former. It is, however, on that side of the spectrum where that which is "predisposed" (Strathern 2001) facilitates the terms of social life, shaping its inclusions and exclusions, while simultaneously reworking them and challenging them (see also Butler 1993). Both suggest that the terms of personal liberty are secured by the ephemerality of the material world and ideology. No one materiality or ideology is ever able to gain the upper hand and is rapidly wasted toward the realization of social reform as soon as their social utility wanes. It is here, in the territory of the abject beyond the constitutive realm of materiality, where critical work increasingly is being done and needs to be continued. Indeed, it is here that much of the dynamism of late capitalist societies is located as a consequence of its speedy and ever-increasing ephemerality (see Buchli and Lucas 2001). The "tragic lightness" of ephemerality described by Lipovetsky suggests that no one regime is ever able to prevail, rendering ontological security unstable and contingent at best. However, as Lipovetsky points out: "The consummate reign of fashion pacifies social conflict; it allows more individual freedom but it generates greater malaise of living ... which renders us increasingly problematic to ourselves and others" (1994:241). How people are able to negotiate this territory which is increasingly immaterial and alienable is one of the significant challenges which faces material culture studies.

However, this vigilant optimism is challenged by the legal scholar Jonathan Simon, who has noted in his studies of new actuarial practices that the Foucauldian preoccupation with the material and spatial aspects of social discipline forming subjectivities is rendered increasingly irrelevant by new actuarial practices in the redistribution of social risk in social policy and law. This marks a change from the way power is exerted over and constitutive of subjects from the highly intensive and extensive disciplinary regimes of Foucault – which require great material and economic inputs (prisons, town planning, hygiene, medical regimes, etc.) to discipline and form new subjectivities to a new actuarial regime where behavior is predicted and accommodated (Simon 1988:773). This is a shift from bodies to populations – a much less fixed and considerably more immaterial entity. The incorporeal, despatialized, and immaterial nature of these new social aggregates according to which society is increasingly more organized makes it extremely difficult for individuals to form common goals and purposes (Simon 1988:774). As Bauman notes, these new configurations form a new kind of mass in the many multiple senses of the word: "Mass is a gaseous substance, an aggregate of atoms with little mutual attraction. The atoms are similar – but similarity does not make a community" (Bauman 2001:105). This very "light" (Lipovetsky) and "gaseous" (Bauman) configuration is notoriously unstable, incorporeal, and immaterial, yet increasingly the medium within which social life is formed. The disciplines that produced new subjectivities of resistance to the exertion of state power are unable to concresce, to use Latour's apt phrase borrowed from Whitehead. Individual coherent, materialized, and spatialized identities are not the terms by which discipline is exerted – rather deterritorialized, incorporeal, and fragmented attributes that are aggregated become the terms by which social hierarchies and control are exerted.

In short, to echo E. P. Thomson and quote Simon: "Rather than making people up, actuarial practices unmake them" (1988:792) and, furthermore, "barricades are useless against a power that operates in the abstract space of statistical tables" (1988:798). The terms whereby subjectivities are dematerialized means that material culture studies has even more important work to do than it has in the past and requires an even more finely attuned understanding of materiality and its constitutive effects than ever before.

This requires ever more detailed analysis of the terms of materiality (the effects of our analytical metaphors, be it "cultural thickening" or "micro-physics" exerted on communities and individuals) and the nexus of concrescences that facilitate empirical reality and the inclusions and exclusions that are entailed. As Whitehead suggests (in a good neopragmatist manner that would please Rorty): "The simple notion of an endur-ing substance sustaining persistent qualities, either essentially or accidentally, expresses a useful abstract for many purposes of life. But whenever we try to use it as a fundamental statement of the nature of things, it proves itself mistaken" (1978 [1929]:79). Thus, according to Whitehead, "the question as to whether to call an enduring object a transition of matter or of a character is very much a verbal question as to where you draw the line between various properties (cf. the way in which the distinction between matter and radiant energy has now vanished)" (1978 [1929]:109). Holtorf's elegant essay on the naming and constitution of the "ancientness" of a potsherd is an excellent example of the process whereby such lines are drawn (2002; see also Ingold (2000) regarding the arbitrariness of boundaries between material cul-ture artifacts and mind and Jensen 2000). Archaeology and material culture studies are only now grappling with the consequences of these insights concerning the social contingencies of the materialities we constitute, most notably in the works of Ingold (2000), Shanks (1998), and Holtorf (2002).

By refocusing on the constitutive materialities of our endeavors we might be able to obviate the difficulties often encountered in recent material culture studies in terms of the competing primacies of "visuality," "textuality," "materiality" or "phenomenological experience." Thus these issues are just that – highly contingent "verbal questions," propositions within a particular social nexus, ultimately arbitrary but profoundly con-tingent and strategic. It is the necessities of such transitions between nexus, the move-ment between them, their historical necessity, and the social accommodations they aspire to which should be more the focus of our endeavors rather than an insistence of one over the other (phenomenological versus visual versus textual, etc.).

Archaeologies of Immateriality

The data that constitute material culture studies, of course, can be understood in terms of the varying socially contingent materialities that are constituted and experienced. I would like to discuss here some examples from my own work on the various materi-alities shaping the socialist and post-socialist experience in Russia and Kazakhstan.

In my recent research on the materiality of Soviet socialism in *An Archaeology of Socialism* (Buchli 1999), I outlined how two competing materialities – one denotative, and one contextual – created and reworked new realms of material culture and materi-ality and radically different social visions. One form of materiality was iconoclastic and preoccupied with the dematerialization of the material world in order to realize a utopian order of socialist life, characterized by the architectural and aesthetic principles of European Modernism. While in conflict with that view, an alternative form of materiality was envisioned which sought to refigure that order in diverse ways at once highly ephemeral (in terms of people's individual manipulations of domestic space) and massively material (in terms of the bombastic projects of Stalinist Classicism). Both approaches manipulated the dimensionality of material culture to achieve those social aims at various scales. These were often hybrid in terms of the different scales they addressed and the agents and agencies able to manipulate these dimensionalities. They nonetheless configured a material culture that functioned in very distinct and antagonistic fashions as contingencies and shifting fields of power required. The dimensionality and materiality of the artifact was never assumed but always deliberately reconfigured to achieve specific social aims.

My more recent research explores some of the contemporary consequences of these issues in relation to the construction of the new Capitol of Kazakhstan in Astana, where competing materialities are yet again in contentious and fluid engagement over the terms by which a post-socialist and independent Kazakhstani identity is shaped and the conflicts that arise in materializing this embattled identity. Here I am thinking of the construction of a "postmodern" capital to express a new nationalist architecture while what one might consider to be an authentic national tradition is being destroyed. In this case a particular traditional architectural element of material culture – the *shanrak* or circular birch-twig opening of the nomadic yurt that lets smoke out and air and light in – represents a particular problem (figure 8.1). At the level of urban architectural forms, particularly the forms of the new Capitol, the *shanrak* is a ubiquitous element figured in many different ways appearing as a somewhat empty signifier of Kazakhness and state sovereignty for a newly independent Kazakhstan. It has considerable purchase despite the highbrow words of detractors and critics: appearing

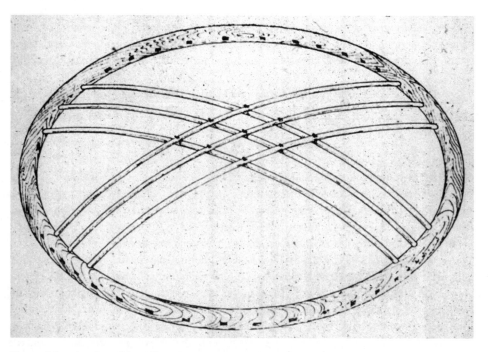

Figure 8.1   *A traditional* shanrak (author's photograph)

everywhere from banknotes, presidential palace schemes, ceiling rosettes, railings, and furniture store logos.

The apparent incongruity of this form within the built and visual environment of the new Capitol might be better understood in terms of the semiotic dimension of the *shanrak* and the implication of its indexicality for the materiality of the new Capitol. This might offer a more satisfactory means of explaining the built environment of Astana, rather than as a failure of distinction, signification, and the general malaise of corruption plaguing the construction of the new Capitol. What might appear as incongruity and failure is in fact the logical expression of a more general principle governing notions of continuity.

At this point conventional notions of physicality and signification are at stake. The issue of physicality and the ability of the material world to denote explicit meanings has been very problematic in this part of the world. Imperial Russian and Soviet ethnographers variously reported on the lack of a significant body of material culture: the absence of those physical signifiers by which Europeans gauged the advancement of peoples and societies. The Soviet period was a time when this "lack" was directly addressed and overcome. This was the time of massive urban growth and industrial development. When Russians speak of their legacy they speak of and point to the buildings they built and the industrial infrastructure, all of which, of course, are collapsing all around, particularly industries and dying regional urban centers.

There is, of course, a persistent sense on one hand that the material environment does not adequately signify things as they are or as they should be – a failure, in short, to realize modernity. Old Soviet-era architectural forms and industrial infrastructures are bankrupt, and new ones are suspect and corrupt in terms of kickbacks, backroom deals, and bribes and physically corrupt in terms of shoddy construction and workmanship and the use of cheap, untested materials. The city itself could disappear overnight as easily as it appeared – Astana's "five minutes of Las Vegas," as one Kazakhstani observed, could be over very quickly (figure 8.2).

While the materiality of these overt expressions of Kazakhness is unstable, ephemeral and corrupt, the more durable forms of the Kazakh built environment that, according to orthodox Western preservation standards, would be the most obvious candidates for an indigenous architectural tradition are being torn down left and right. This is an ancient mud-brick tradition which resembles the pueblo construction of the American Southwest (figure 8.3). Preservation law is powerless, and enforcement hopeless within the prevailing climate of corruption and kickbacks. What to Western eyes (and to a very small number of local ethnographers and architects) might represent an authentic national Kazakh building tradition is rejected in favor of new constructions that phantasmagorically evoke Santa Barbara, St. Petersburg, Las Vegas, and Stalinist Moscow as the more appropriate attempts with which to realize new Kazakhstani urban forms – these are the fantasies of the nouveau-riche "New Kazakhs" and the bureaucratic, court tastes surrounding the President.

It is here that I am reminded how incongruous it might seem when a young Kazakh mother might point to the prefabricated ceiling of her Soviet-era flat as a *shanrak* and scold her children, saying, "Whose *shanrak* is this?"[1] When they misbehave, the honor of their lineage is at stake (represented by the *shanrak*) – as a *shanrak* is inherited from youngest son to youngest son, it is only said to exist when a male child is born to the

Figure 8.2 *Astana's new skyline* (Khazakhstan), *2001* (author's photograph)

Figure 8.3 *A traditional northern Kazakh permanent dwelling, Astana, Kazakhstan, 2001* (author's photograph)

next generation in expectation of the continuity of the lineage. The indexical slippage that signifies the successful lineage between the *shanrak* of the yurt and the prefabricated concrete Soviet ceiling seems to gather together all these improbable and otherwise antagonistic material elements into a coherent narrative of successful and expectant continuity, irrespective of what conventional understandings of these appar-

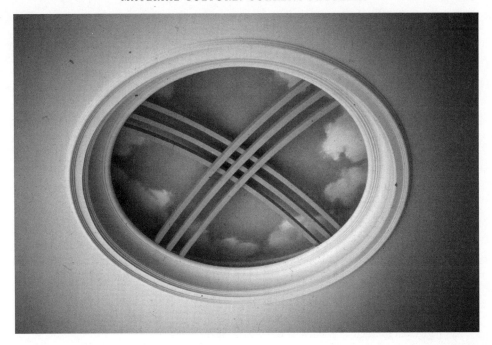

Figure 8.4 *Shanrak as trompe-l'oeil ceiling decoration in a recently constructed post-Soviet institutional building, Astana, Kazakhstan, 2001* (author's photograph)

ently incongruous material forms might suggest. The materiality of these built forms signifies in an unexpected fashion from the conventional notions of Western and Soviet materiality and meaning. I suggest that the contradictory, materially unstable and otherwise corrupt and corrupting material environment of the new Capitol might be understood according to the seemingly incongruous terms of the mother's admonishment of her child and might be adequately contained within the wide compass of the indexical qualities of the *shanrak*, designating a momentary consolidation and continuity: one that is fraught (when was it ever assured?), highly contested, and contradictory, but nonetheless invokes the admiration of local citizens, proud of the brash and shiny newness of the Capitol and the social and economic opportunities it affords, despite its shortcomings. Traditionally the *shanrak* frames one's vision onto the sacred sky-blue of the cosmos (figure 8.4). The *shanrak* is described as sky-blue not because of what it is materially (an old one is actually black), but because of what it frames and indexes, and this is what the built environment of Astana might be seen as doing as well in a highly contested but hopeful way in all its material incongruity. It is indexing this improbable yet momentary continuity and articulation of tradition very differently from orthodox Western and Soviet understandings of tradition and materiality. As such it indexes a view from one realm onto another as yet intangible, unfathomable, and unknowable, but expectant and hopeful. The *shanrak*'s dimensionality is at times highly attenuated, realized by merely pointing to a prefabricated concrete ceiling, dispersed iconically on banknotes and as government symbols, or given highly dimensional and massive expression in the form of presidential palace schemes – it is negotiating this futurity along varying axes of dimensionality.

The Kazakhstani example here suggests another way in which immateriality might seem to function, as well as the ambivalent political implications of such an understanding, and the issues surrounding individual complicity and potential agency entailed within these varying terms of materiality. These examples might suggest that there is some purchase in examining this terrain at the unstable interface between the material and immaterial to better understand the role of agency in social change and the diverse and contested terms of materiality itself, its varying states of dimensionality, and their implications socially, politically, and ontologically, within the various social nexus in which they function. Archaeology, with its methods and practices, is very well placed to examine these processes – after all, archaeology always deals with the "abject" and "constitutive outsides" of social life – the wasted and forgotten – and it is here, on the unstable terrain of the immaterial, where the problem of agency and change and the shifting terms of late capitalist materialities might be more fruitfully addressed and understood.

NOTE

1   I am very grateful to K. M. Kizamadieva-Kasenova for her observations from her research on traditional northern Kazakhstani material culture.

REFERENCES

Appadurai, A. (ed.) 1986. *The Social Life of Things: Commodities in Cultural Perspective*. Cambridge: Cambridge University Press.

——1996. *Modernity at Large: Cultural Dimensions of Globalization*. Minneapolis: University of Minnesota Press.

Bataille, G. 1991. *The Accursed Share*, Vol. 1. New York: Zone Books.

Bauman, Z. 2001. On mass, individuals and peg communities. In N. Lee and R. Munro (eds.), *The Consumption of Mass*. Oxford: Blackwell, pp. 102–113.

Belk, R. W. 2001. *Collecting in a Consumer Society*. London: Verso.

Binford, L. 1965. Archaeological systematics and the study of culture process. *American Antiquity* 31: 203–210.

Bourdieu, P. 1977. *Outline of a Theory of Practice*. Cambridge: Cambridge University Press.

Buchli, V. 1999. *An Archaeology of Socialism*. Oxford: Berg.

——, and G. Lucas. 2001. *Archaeologies of the Contemporary Past*. London: Routledge.

Butler, J. 1993. *Bodies that Matter*. London: Routledge.

Cooper, R. 2001. Interpreting mass: Collection/dispersion. In N. Lee and R. Munro (eds.), *The Consumption of Mass*. Oxford: Blackwell, pp. 16–43.

Deetz, J. 1977. *In Small Things Forgotten: The Archaeology of Early American Life*. Garden City, NJ: Anchor Press/Doubleday.

Editorial. 1996. *Journal of Material Culture* 1(1): 5–14.

Fletcher, G. 1997. Excavating the Social. Paper presented at *Rethinking the Social* Conference, Griffith University, Queensland, Australia.

Forge, A. (ed.) 1973. *Primitive Art and Society*. London and New York: Oxford University Press.

Glassie, H. 1975. *Folk Housing in Middle Virginia*. Knoxville: University of Tennessee Press.

Gould, R. A., and M. B. Schiffer (eds.) 1981. *Modern Material Culture: The Archaeology of US*. New York: Academic Press.

Hodder, I. 1986. *Reading the Past*. Cambridge: Cambridge University Press.

——1987. Bow ties and pet foods: Material culture and the negotiation of change in British industry. In I. Hodder (ed.), *The Archaeology of Contextual Meanings*. Cambridge: Cambridge University Press, pp. 11–19.

Holtorf, C. 2002. Notes on the life history of a potsherd. *Journal of Material Culture* 7(1): 49–71.

Ingold, T. 2000. Making culture and weaving the world. In P. Graves-Brown (ed.), *Matter, Materiality and Modern Culture*. London: Routledge, pp. 50–71.

Jensen, O. W. 2000. The many faces of stone artefacts: A case of the shift in the perception of thunderbolts in the late 17th and early 18th century. In O. W. Jensen and H. Karlsson (eds.), *Archaeological Conditions: Examples of Epistemology and Ontology*. Gothenburg: Department of Archaeology, University of Gothenburg.

Kopytoff, I. 1986. The cultural biography of things: Commoditisation as a process. In A. Appadurai (ed.), *The Social Life of Things: Commodities in Cultural Perspective*. Cambridge: Cambridge University Press, pp. 64–91.

Latour, B. 1999. *Pandora's Hope: Essays on the Reality of Science Studies*. Cambridge MA: Harvard University Press.

——. 2000. The Berlin Key or how to do words with things. In P. Graves-Brown, *Matter, Materiality and Modern Culture*. London: Routledge, pp. 10–22.

Lemonnier, P. 1986. The study of material culture today: Towards an anthropology of technical systems. *Journal of Anthropological Archaeology* 5(2): 147–186.

——1992. *Elements for an Anthropology of Technology*. Ann Arbor, MI: Museum of Anthropology, University of Michigan.

Lévi-Strauss, J-C. 1973. *Tristes Tropiques*. Harmondsworth: Penguin.

Lipovetsky, G. 1994. *The Empire of Fashion: Dressing Modern Democracy*. Princeton, NJ: Princeton University Press.

Löfgren, O. 1997. Scenes from a troubled marriage: Swedish ethnology and material culture studies. *Journal of Material Culture* 2(1): 95–113.

Lucas, G. 2001. *Critical Approaches to Fieldwork: Contemporary and Historical Archaeological Practice*. London: Routledge.

MacKenzie, M. 1991. *Androgynous Objects: String Bags and Gender in Central New Guinea*. Chur: Harwood Academic Press.

Marcoux, J. S. 2001. The "casser maison" ritual: Constructing self by emptying the Home. *Journal of Material Culture* 6(2): 213–235.

Mauss, M. 1973. *Sociology and Psychology*. London: Routledge.

Mayne, A., and T. Murray. 2001. *The Archaeology of Urban Landscapes: Explorations in Slumland*. Cambridge: Cambridge University Press.

Miller, D. 1987. *Material Culture and Mass Consumption*. Oxford: Basil Blackwell.

——, and J. Carrier (eds.) 1998. *Virtualism: A New Political Economy*. Oxford: Berg.

Morgan, L. H. 1978. *Ancient Society*. New York: Labor Press.

Mouffe, C. 1993. *The Return of the Political*. London: Verso.

Munn, N. 1973. The spatial presentation of cosmic order in Walibri iconography. In A. Forge (ed.), *Primitive Art and Society*. Oxford: Oxford University Press.

Oldenziel, R. 1996. Object/ions: Technology, culture and gender. In W. D. Kingery (ed.), *Learning From Things: Method and Theory in Material Culture Studies*. Washington, DC: Smithsonian Institution Press, pp. 55–69.

Pfaffenberger, B. 1988. Fetishised objects and humanised nature: Towards an anthropology of technology. *Man* 23(2): 236–52.

Pinney, C. 2002. Visual culture. In V. Buchli (ed.), *The Material Culture Reader*. Oxford: Berg, pp. 81–86.

Pomian, K 1990. *Collectors and Curiosities: Paris and Venice, 1500–1800*. Cambridge: Polity Press.

Rathje, W., and C. Murphy. 1992. *Rubbish! The Archaeology of Garbage*. New York: HarperCollins.

Rowlands, M. 2002. Insert title of this chapter at proof stage. In V. Buchli (ed.), *The Material Culture Reader*. Oxford: Berg.

Saunders. N. 2000. Bodies of metal, shells of memory: "Trench art" and the Great War recycled. *Journal of Material Culture* 5(1): 43–67.

Schnapp, A. 1996. *The Discovery of the Past: The Origins of Archaeology*. London: British Museum Press.

Shanks, M. 1992. *Experiencing the Past: On the Character of Archaeology*. London: Routledge.

——1998. The life of an artefact in an interpretive archaeology. *Fennoscandia Archaeologica* XV: 15–30.

——, and C. Tilley. 1987. The design of contemporary beer cans. In *De-Constructing Archaeology*. Cambridge: Cambridge University Press.

Simon, J. 1988. The ideological effects of actuarial practices. *Law and Society Review* 22: 771–800.

Slater, D., and F. Tonkiss. 2001. *Market Society: Markets and Modern Social Theory*. Cambridge: Polity Press.

Strathern, M. 2001. The aesthetics of substance. In N. Cummings and M. Lewandowka (eds.), *Capital*. London: Tate Publishing, pp. 45–63.

Thomas, N. 1991. *Entangled Objects: Exchange, Material Culture, and Colonialism in the Pacific*. Cambridge, MA: Harvard University Press.

Thompson, 1994. The filth in the way. In S. Pearce (ed.), *Interpreting Objects and Collections*. London: Routledge.

Tilley, C. 2002. Metaphor, materiality and interpretation. In V. Buchli (ed.), *The Material Culture Reader*. Oxford: Berg.

Whitehead, A. 1978 [1929]. *Process and Reality: An Essay in Cosmology*. New York: The Free Press.

Wobst, M. 1977. Stylistic behavior and information exchange. *Anthropological Papers of the University of Michigan* 61: 317–342.

9

Ideology, Power, and Capitalism: The Historical Archaeology of Consumption

Paul R. Mullins

Since the 1980s, many thinkers have tackled the complications of consumption and crafted a sophisticated interdisciplinary scholarship on the marketing, acquisition, and symbolism of material goods in capitalist societies (e.g., Agnew 1993; Appadurai 1986; Bourdieu 1984; Campbell 1987; Miller 1987, 1995a). It would seem appropriate for archaeologists to lead this charge: armed with the tangible evidence of everyday materialism in a vast range of social and historical contexts, archaeology is distinctively positioned to confront the multivalent meaning of goods, probe the ideological roots of material symbolism, and emphasize that even the most commonplace objects provide insight into meaningful social struggles. Yet archaeologists have been relatively slow to embrace consumption as an appropriate research focus.

Much of the archaeological reluctance to tackle consumption reflects longstanding disdain of mass materialism (cf. Horowitz 1985). By the mid-nineteenth century, for instance, Thoreau's (1854) assessment of American life characterized it as "unconscious despair" fueled by ever-increasing, dissatisfying labor. For Thoreau, such labor became necessary simply to secure seemingly essential goods that ultimately provided no genuine gratification. Perhaps the most intriguing and influential of these moralistic commentaries came from Thorstein Veblen (1899), whose distaste for vacuous materialism was the predominant scholarly view of consumption into the 1970s. Veblen argued that a newly rich Victorian "leisure class" manufactured an illusory sense of self-importance and distinction through their consumption of superficial material goods. Veblen acknowledged that materialism had a social purpose and was not simply an economic act, however, he argued that consumption's fundamental social purpose was hierarchical status competition in which goods publicly displayed status and identity.

In the subsequent century many of these sentiments remained remarkably resilient. Stuart Ewen's (1988) incisive assessment of contemporary consumer culture nearly a century after Veblen is no more optimistic. Ewen despairs that consumers invest powerful desires and values into goods, even though they are left perpetually unfulfilled by their pursuit of insubstantial things. In a similar vein, Juliet Schor (2000) laments that Americans "want so much more than they need": we are dissatisfied with our material lives, Schor argues, yet we are unable to transform this private discontent into

a public discourse critical of objective inequalities. These critics share with their predecessors an apprehension of consumption's defamiliarizing instability: for Veblen and
many Victorians, for instance, consumption was a demasculinizing assault on patriarchy
that risked eroding women's subordination, not simply an exercise in bourgeois emulation. Observers then and now often have been unnerved by the dynamic, potentially
transformative nature of material consumption, handicapped by their inability to
fathom the social meaning of consumption, and bogged down in distinguishing between genuine needs and inauthentic wants.

In the 1960s, scholars in newly emerging academic niches laid a substantial ground-
work to rethink scholarly visions of everyday life and, by extension, consumption.
Social histories from the "bottom up," such as E. P. Thompson's (1963) examination
of British working-class life, embraced the idea that everyday life took shape through
self-conscious will and might reveal something beyond mere subjugation. *Annales*
school historians such as Fernand Braudel (1973) championed a sweeping analysis of
everyday life that avoided focusing on major events and instead paid close attention to
long spans of time and prosaic material culture. Henry Glassie's (1975) research on
vernacular architecture and folk objects stressed long-term cultural continuities in the
face of radical social change. Such research stressed the importance of everyday material life as a mechanism to understand broad social collectives, and it was part of an
ambitious interdisciplinary scholarship to illuminate the genuine impact of a vast range
of relatively unknown individuals and social groups. Both of these impulses have had
significant effects in archaeology.

By the 1980s, a series of sophisticated studies appeared that attempted to offset the
predominant scholarly emphasis on producers, supply-side economics, and the elite.
Mary Douglas and Baron Isherwood's (1978) *The World of Goods* was the first sustained
anthropological study of consumption that examined the social meaning of materialism
outside economically based perspectives. Douglas and Isherwood pushed beyond
Veblen's influential assumption that consumption was simply instinctive and driven by
emulation, competitive display, and economic rationality. Douglas and Isherwood instead assumed that consumption was a social, contextually distinctive process in which
goods functioned as symbolic category systems linked to collective values rather than
atomized individual decisions. Pierre Bourdieu (1984) followed with an exhaustive
analysis of French consumer patterns. He retained an appreciation for the limits imposed by structures such as class and status, but he argued that such structures do not
determine human agency. Bourdieu argued that material "taste" is acquired by education and social influences and serves to legitimize social differences. He stressed that
even the most prosaic goods naturalized systems of difference, defining consumption
as a symbolic process that established social distinctions and did not simply reflect
existing economically determined differences.

In subsequent years, the literature has rapidly expanded, and consumer scholars hail
from numerous disciplinary niches with quite distinct ways of defining and assessing
consumption. However, most of these researchers share common interests in compen-
sating for longstanding scholarly disinterest in consumption and confronting the political impact of material consumption. The former effort to push beyond an economistic
production focus and represent consumers' agency seems settled: there are few, if any,
scholars who would argue that consumers were powerless in the face of widespread

material and social changes. The genuine social impact of everyday consumption, however, is a complicated issue, and various scholars have cast the "politics" of consumption in a vast range of forms. How various scholars see consumption's "politics" – if they accord it the status of politics at all – depends on their visions of ideology, resistance, power, desire, identity, and consumption itself.

This vast corpus of consumer scholarship has not yet had a significant influence on archaeology, and archaeology has had very little impact on interdisciplinary consumer scholarship. This seems unusual because archaeology is distinctively positioned to confront the multivalent meaning of goods, probe the ideological roots of material symbolism, and emphasize that even the most commonplace objects provide insight into meaningful social struggles. An archaeology of consumption should represent a complex range of politicized consumption patterns that variously reproduce, negotiate, and resist dominant ideology and structural inequalities. Ultimately this scholarship can destabilize stock archaeological research topics, document the historical contours of capitalist materialism, and illuminate the deep-seated contradictions of contemporary consumer culture.

Capitalism and Consumption

An archaeology of consumption could be conducted in any material context: consumption is a social practice through which people simultaneously construct understandings of themselves and are positioned within the world, and this process certainly applies to prehistoric and pre-capitalist contexts. Many complex societies clearly had mass manufacture and consumption, a vast range of societies can make a claim to using goods to fashion individual and social identity, and the identity formation issues stressed by consumption scholarship certainly are relevant to prehistorians. Most analyses of consumption, however, have examined the period since the early eighteenth century, highlighting commodity consumption and the global structural shifts associated with capitalism. Much of this scholarship has focused on the twentieth-century emergence of a mass consumer culture. In a "consumer culture," Jean-Christophe Agnew (1993) argues, social identity is shaped by commodity consumption rather than discourses such as religion or nationalism, and states themselves have become committed to safeguarding consumer privilege as a consequential citizen right. The archaeological interest in capitalism and consumption's material dimensions may have its most profound implications in historical archaeology, which examines the period since European colonization and is consciously focused on the roots of contemporary society. Historical archaeology is most clearly established in the United States, but it has a foothold throughout much of the world.

Since the 1990s some historical archaeologists have ventured that the discipline's appropriate focus should be capitalism (e.g., Delle 1998; Delle, Mrozowski, and Paynter 2000; Leone 1995; Orser 1996; Paynter 1988), and most have at least conceded that capitalism has some impact on the material record. Capitalism has been defined in a wide range of ways by consumption scholars, and various thinkers accord it divergent roles in material transformations. Chandra Mukerji (1983), for instance, traces modern mass consumption to fifteenth-century Europe, arguing that non-utilitarian consumption existed prior to capitalism's emergence and concluding that modern consumption

actually preceded capitalism. Colin Campbell (1987) instead looks to the eighteenth century for consumer society's origins and links it to sociocultural shifts rather than capitalist
economic processes. Like Campbell, Neil McKendrick (McKendrick, Brewer, and Plumb
1982) also looks to the eighteenth century; however, he attributes consumer society's
emergence to astute marketing and production reorganization by capitalists like Josiah
Wedgwood. Rather than focus on capitalism, Arjun Appadurai (1986) instead suggests
that consumer research's focus should be modernity and the relations between systemic
and local contexts. Appadurai shifts consumer research's emphasis to how a given object
can be commodified in various ways over time and from one context to the next.

Most researchers have developed a complex vision of consumption that routinely
melds capitalism, Westernization, and materialism into a more-or-less synonymous phenomenon implicated in the interests of various states and capitalists as well as distinct
local experiences and identities. Daniel Miller (1997:7) argues that modern consumer
research's focus is primarily on the shift of power from production to consumption, a
transformation that was not determined by capitalism or states. Capitalism may provide a
flexible framework for consumption research, but Miller (1997:16–17) argues that
scholars have paid too little attention to its myriad local variants and have instead fallen
back on a monolithic model of capitalism. Miller's (1997) own ethnography of consumption in contemporary Trinidad focuses on the everyday experience of consumers negotiating the production and marketing system that provides commodities. Miller pushes
beyond market acquisition alone to probe manufacturing, marketing, retailing, and shopping as coeval processes, and he stresses that consumers' everyday material patterns and
meanings often differ considerably from those of mass producers. Miller questions the
degree to which places like Trinidad are assumed to be peripheral to or structured by
worldwide capitalism, instead suggesting that "local" capitalism can take on a very distinct contextual form quite unlike the dominant economic model of capitalism.

Many archaeologists have likewise probed the complex relations between local and
systemic contexts, examining links between communities and global producers. Charles
Orser's (1996) archaeology of the modern world, for instance, assesses colonization
and capitalism by ranging across sociocultural contexts from Brazil to Ireland to the
United States. Neil Silberman (1989) emphasizes that Ottoman pipes reflect connections between the Ottoman world, Native Americans, and English colonizers, and Uzi
Baram (2000) likewise sees an "archaeology of entanglement" between European commodities and the Ottoman world where those goods were consumed and assumed
quite distinct meanings. Aron Crowell (1997) probes the development of worldwide
capitalism by archaeologically examining trade between colonizers and indigenous
peoples in Alaska. Matthew Johnson's (1996) analysis of agrarian capitalism in Britain
advocates a global archaeology of capitalism that reaches back to examine medieval
antecedents of capitalism, discarding simplistic divisions between capitalism and pre-
capitalist formations. Clearly, archaeologists define consumption so broadly that archaeologies of consumption weave together processes of production, exchange, and acquisition across a vast range of social systems and historical periods. When consumption
studies meld production and acquisition along with use and social symbolism, layering
that with subjectivity construction and power relations over vast spans of time, there is
relatively little left "outside" consumption, and many scholars wish to define consumption this ambitiously. Søren Askegaard and A. Fuat Firat (1997), for instance, offer the

solution of simply collapsing the dualism of production and consumption into a single seamless process. They argue for jettisoning the modernist dichotomy of production and consumption realms so scholars can study "consumption as production." This sentiment may reflect that in contemporary consumer culture goods are, as Orwell put it, "the air that we breathe," but this definition of an all-encompassing consumption is somewhat problematic to project onto even the recent past. If consumption does indeed monolithically blanket the social world and is essentially indistinguishable from production, then consumer scholarship's purpose risks being reduced to documenting myriad local contexts and continually defining ethnic, class, and social variables within largely unexamined structural conditions.

Historical archaeology usually illuminates capitalism and consumer identity from the standpoint of local, household-based commodity patterns, illustrating the quantity, variety, and range of goods acquired, used, and discarded by a particular group of consumers. Most archaeologists at least implicitly interpret these assemblages as reflections of a specific facet of identity, such as a household's cultural affiliations or social standing. This tendency to see objects simply as reflections of some "real" identity has been one of the central hurdles to a rigorous archaeology of consumption: i.e., objects are interpreted as expressions of an identity that preceded consumption and is merely "accented" by the process of acquiring and giving meaning to material things. This is significant, because when consumption is viewed as a "reflection" it becomes less an active and meaningful negotiation of personal and social subjectivity than a recurring patterned expression of an essential identity.

Various forms of culture history have had a significant influence on historical archaeologists' tendency to see culture as the steadfastly embedded core of identity and the discipline's appropriate focus. James Deetz's (1977) *In Small Things Forgotten* provides the most influential example of this perspective. Deetz examined colonial American material culture as patterned expressions of deep-seated cultural mindsets, a structuralist interpretation most articulately championed in material culture studies by Henry Glassie (1975). Anne Yentsch's (1994) study of colonial Chesapeake English slaveholders and enslaved Africans provides a similar analysis of material patterns reflecting distinct cultural identities. Yentsch focuses on local, contextually distinct expressions of cultural mindsets that are connected to broader systems but best understood from local perspectives.

Any archaeology focused on cultural tradition in its most inflexible sense risks posing culture as an appropriate mechanism to explain material patterns, rather than the subject that needs to be explained itself (cf. Barrett 2001:157). Archaeologists examining African heritage, for instance, have tended to at least implicitly look at material objects as expressions (conscious or unrecognized) of an African cultural identity. Most of this research has focused on aesthetic motifs and material goods known as "Africanisms"; objects that either have clear connections to African cultural practice or show significant commonalities among New World diaspora (e.g., Ferguson 1992). Warren Perry and Robert Paynter (1999) applaud such research but warn that it hazards assuming an unreasonably monolithic African culture and often lacks a sophisticated understanding of African cultural and material diversity. When Africanisms' studies do examine commodity consumption, they often stress unique cultural meanings that were invested in mass-produced goods. Laurie Wilkie's (2000) examination of enslaved Bahamians, for example, argues for an African "cultural sensibility" that incorporated mass-produced goods and used them in "uniquely African ways." Such analyses attempt to preserve cultural identity despite the appearance of commodity homogenization: these "authentic" identities appear as the inverse of the "inauthentic" meanings presented in commodities and consumption. Paul Gilroy (2000:107) believes that widespread efforts to recover such stable and authentic identities reflect a commonplace anxiety many people feel in the face of globalization. Yet archaeologists pursuing such enduring identities risk projecting onto the past their own deep-seated desires for identity stability, and this scholarship generally evades how those archaeologically validated identities subsequently function in contemporary ethnic and disciplinary politics.

Historical archaeologists may stress the persistence of cultural identities to temper the appearance of capitalist homogenization suggested by mass consumption. Commodity consumption is indeed bound to have some genuine homogenizing effect, but the form and meaning of that "homogenization" vary significantly from one place and time to another. Some thinkers certainly view such homogenization apprehensively. The "McDonaldization" thesis, for example, proposes that mass corporations have materially and socially reorganized almost all elements of contemporary production and consumption into what Weber called a rationalized society (Ritzer 1993). This critique resonates with anthropologists' longstanding misgivings about Westernization: producers like McDonald's pose significant economic and cultural threats to a vast range of local contexts. Daniel Miller (1995b:268), however, suggests that the social differentiation and diversity within capitalist societies ensures that various social groups will have heterogeneous experiences, even under quite comparable conditions. For instance, Andrew Heinze's (2000) account of Jewish immigrant consumption notes that women assumed the role of household consumer in America. Jewish women frequented the same stores and purchased most of the same goods as their neighbors, yet turn-of-the-century Jewish women assumed significant family importance based on their role as material arbiters securing high-quality, inexpensive, and stylish goods. Rather than see consumption as a homogenizing threat to traditional culture or women's agency, Jewish immigrants instead embraced it.

Archaeologists' tendency to view identity in rather self-contained, historically "authentic" packages certainly did not emerge from archaeology: many contemporary people are attracted to a pleasant positivism that demonstrates clear ethnic distinctions, deep-seated identities, and cultural resilience in the face of often-overwhelming inequality. In most contemporary theory, however, the notion of an "authentic" identity has either been significantly destabilized or rejected altogether. Don Slater (1997:83) argues that the contemporary world is a pluralized "post-traditional" society in which selfhood is neither assigned nor unambiguous. He suggests that contemporary social life is mediated by commercialization, media, and commerce that make possible a vast range of fluid identity options. Many theorists focus on how consumers actively "produce" meaning from goods and discourses circulating in contemporary space; this shifts the most significant social construction of material meanings from producers and ideologues to consumers. For instance, the subculture studies most closely associated with Birmingham's Centre for Contemporary Cultural Studies (e.g., Cohen 1993; Hebdige 1979) examine how subcultures manipulate dominant symbolism in consumer goods and discourses as a form of resistance that expresses the contradictions in the "parent" culture. Subcultural consumers constantly appropriate material and popular symbols and reconstruct their dominant meanings through bricolage, a process that constructs an oppositional identity negotiating structural contradictions such as class inequality. In a similar form, post-subculturalists (e.g., Bennett 1999; Redhead 1997) have focused on consumers' distinctive material tactics and social values. Post-subculturalists, however, reject the notion of a clearly defined mainstream culture or structural conditions against which consumption patterns are hegemonically positioned, instead focusing on quite dynamic individuality and subjective lived experiences. Jean Baudrillard (1988) champions perhaps the most radical vision of consumption and social reality in general, arguing that we consume signs that refer to realities that do not themselves exist. Fredric Jameson (1984) suggests that the unique autonomous self no longer exists, and, in fact, that bourgeois individual may never have existed.

In contemporary life, the boundaries that social factions draw between authentic and fake, or periphery and mainstream are ambiguous and utterly dynamic, and contrast radically with the inflexible identity categories social scientists routinely reproduce. Such thinking can productively destabilize inflexible identity frameworks, but it examines radical sociocultural hybridity that is not a particularly apt archaeological analog: identity formation in postwar consumer culture clearly is historically distinct and cannot be transferred wholesale to every context. Stuart Hall (1993) argues that in the contemporary world marginality has become celebrated and is now viewed as the representative experience. Hall cautions that even in the face of infinitely dispersed marginal identities groups still must sociopolitically articulate across lines of difference. Terry Eagleton (1991:38–39) concludes that by rejecting all but the most provisional forms of subjectivity, many theorists fail to distinguish between qualitatively different forms of social subjectivity and, by extension, their political claims. African heritage, for instance, may be materialized in a vast range of ways, but this subjectivity is itself actively fashioned by consumers – and archaeologists – in specific social, political, and material conditions. The archaeological objective should be to examine how African, Black, White, middle class, and similar identity taxonomies have been constructed by various social groups over time, the ways in which apparently distinct categories are entangled in each other, and how archaeology itself can identify the historical discontinuities in such identities. The presence of objects associated with African traditions is a powerful and important testament to African-American agency, but it is also significant that African Americans became producers, marketers, shoppers, and consumers in a society in which all public rights were denied to people of color. It might seem uplifting to paint a marginalized African subject vigilantly maintaining oppositional identity, but identifying African-American agency in White consumer space may well have a more radical effect on how archaeologists define and interpret difference across the color line: focusing on how African Americans negotiated White public spaces should nuance essentialized notions of cultural continuity by confronting the impression of anti-Black racial ideology and the continuities between White and Black materialism. Any archaeology that examines consumption as uncomplicated patterning of well-established identities or domination alone risks diminishing individual agency, minimizing the distinct factors shaping any given consumption context, and ignoring the complexities of power altogether. Concepts such as culture and ethnicity still have interpretive power, but a focus on consumption should problematize such identities and their construction; this is quite different from explaining consumption patterns based on their agreement with existing identity categories.

Ideology, Politics, and Consumption

Working classes and subordinated groups have often identified consumer privileges as one of Western society's most significant citizen "rights" (e.g., Edsforth 1987). T. H. Breen (1993:501), for instance, reaches the stunning conclusion that the American Revolution was defined "around participation in a newly established consumer marketplace," rather than the conventional notion that Americans thirsted for individual and national freedoms. Instead, Breen argues that American colonists saw themselves as participants in an expanding British trade empire, and when the Crown restricted Americans' consumer privileges colonists responded in ways that had profound political and social effects. After the Revolution, however, Americans continued to purchase English goods, underscoring that the Revolution may not have been a radical shift in Americans' cultural identity.

Shopping for, and possessing goods can be a significant privilege for many citizens; however, shopping and material desire demand some implication in wage labor and a cash economy, as well as at least provisional acceptance of a consumer discipline that accepts stunning inequalities. If Westerners have been participants in a consumer revolution, the degree of inequality in the contemporary world suggests it was decidedly conservative. In his examination of American society between the world wars, Warren Susman (1984) reached the conclusion that, in the 1920s, to be "American" was to be a consumer. For Susman, Americans' most deeply held values by the 1930s were no longer God, country, region, or similar monoliths; instead, what Americans shared was a society in which their individual materialism, the state's dedication to support and "protect" consumer privileges, and access to consumer space were our most deeply held "rights" (Agnew 1993). Susman concluded that this was a true consumer "culture" in which our commonly held social values and state interests revolved around material consumption.

Many consumers feel empowered by contemplating, acquiring, and possessing goods; consumers' ability to actually change structural conditions or eliminate inequalities, however, has historically been very limited, and such structural change is not normally considered a goal of material consumption. The significance of consumption in many peoples' lives reflects that it has a genuine impact on how people see themselves and their society and perhaps even how they articulate their politics. However, it is worth being critical of the empowering aspects of material consumption and probing precisely how goods meaningfully negotiate ideology and actually reproduce dominant structural conditions.

The notion of ideology appears in a vast range of consumption and archaeological studies alike: ideology is variously cast as a belief system, a seamless social medium, a body of socially interested misrepresentations, a discourse of power, or the uneasy marriage of reality and representation, among many other definitions. Some thinkers have lobbied for the dissolution of an idealistic sense of ideology; leery of ideology's deterministic capacity, Michel Foucault (1972) champions a broad definition of discourse embedded in diffuse power relations. In contrast, Louis Althusser (1971) embraces the problematic extreme that everything is ideological. Terry Eagleton (1991:8) concludes that it is not essential to settle on a definition of ideology that can be applied to any context; instead, the notion of ideology provides us with a powerful concept to assess socially consequential power struggles. Archaeologists' interest in the ideological dimension of commodities seems to revolve around how objects can display, mask, negotiate, or evade such power struggles.

In historical archaeology the concept of ideology has been most articulately championed by Mark Leone (1984), whose formulation of ideology borrows most from Althusser (1971). For Althusser, ideology is lived relations that give human subjects coherence, though that coherence is an illusion produced by structures that exist outside our everyday "practical" consciousness (Eagleton 1991:140–142). Leone's formulation of ideology adopts Althusser's concept of "ideological state apparatuses" and combines it with Jürgen Habermas's (1976) notion of ideology as intentionally distorted communication. For Leone, ideology is a dominant class-interested discourse that finds its way into various everyday behaviors and beliefs that the masses internalize without critical self-reflection. There are some genuine problems with defining precisely what constitutes such "internalization": e.g., does consumption of a fork, which is part of a well-defined disciplinary ideology, imply the consumption of those dominant ideas, or does it necessarily reflect a consistent elite discourse that underlies those objects? Rather than focus on the construction of dominant ideologies, as Leone does, many archaeologists are most interested in how they can identify meaningful ideological "breakdowns"; tensions with ideologies, and resistance to them. Leone's assessment of capitalist ideologies does not disavow resistance, but he tends to see such resistance being somehow reincorporated.

Analyses of consumption and ideology alike often wrestle with the notion of resistance. Michel de Certeau (1984), for instance, suggested that the sort of situational subversion typical in consumer space is a "tactics": i.e., it has no long-run strategic goals, or it does not articulate a particular political plan to move from evading experienced injustices to eradicating the conditions that permit and reproduce them. Consumer tactics can have concrete political effects through their repetition by numerous people, but de Certeau frames consumption as the commonplace, situational empowerment within everyday experience. It may be tempting to celebrate consumers who appropriate goods and symbolically turn them against the producer elite, but consumption commonly takes prosaic forms that negotiate lived inequalities and place consumers on a fluid terrain both within and outside ideologies. For example, Erica Carter (1984) argues that postwar West German women were both agents and objects in consumer space. She paints a complex picture of women's consumption that muddies the facile distinction between domination and resistance: on the one hand, material patterns were profoundly structured by consumer culture's economic structures and ideological conventions; but on the other hand, those structuring mechanisms never dictated women's everyday material consumption patterns, and women were made both subjects and citizens by consumer disciplines. John Fiske (1989) argues that shopping is empowering to women because it opens up public space, provides a legitimate public identity, and allows women to access what are otherwise considered exclusively masculine pleasures. However, Fiske recognizes that shopping does not upset patriarchal ideology that assumes such public privileges and pleasures should be more accessible to men.

In historical archaeology, the dispute over ideology has usually centered on its deterministic efficacy, or, more specifically, on the tension between human agency and structural dominance. Martin Hall (1992), for instance, levels the charge of determinism at Leone and favors instead dissecting power struggles as "discourses," a move championed by Foucault. Hall sees meaning and identity being formed in discourses that have patterned regularities but are still quite diffuse, shaped by complex power relations, and not always especially well controlled by the elite. John Barrett (2001) argues a similar case by advocating Anthony Giddens's (1984) notion of structuration, which argues that agency and structure are inseparable phenomena that conjointly form social space. For Barrett, power is materialized in a vast range of ways that express various struggles in a diverse range of ideological forms. Ian Hodder (1986:67–73) pins the shortcomings of ideology on Marxism and what he concludes is its assumption of class determinism. He prefers to pose ideology as simply one dimension of symbolic systems that is generated and experienced in contextually distinct forms.

Hall, Barrett, and Hodder alike argue much of this case articulately and persuasively. Yet some archaeologists seem eager to junk the concept of ideology altogether and substitute an utterly fluid, agent-centered vision of social life. Laurie Wilkie and Kevin Bartoy (2000), for instance, accuse Leone of ideological determinism in which people succumb to a "false consciousness." Even Althusser's quite deterministic notion of ideology does not argue that people have a "false" consciousness of reality: Althusser's conclusion is that a dominant ideological discourse provides a coherent vision of subjectivity in the first place, producing social subjects and enabling certain forms of agency, rather than simply repressively controlling subjects. Yet many of the archaeological critiques of ideology reduce it to its most deterministic and repressive caricature as elite falsehoods uniformly projected onto the masses, often mechanically invoking the "dominant ideology thesis" that suggests a unified ideology bonds society (Abercombie, Hill, and Turn 1980). In the place of ideology, Wilkie and Bartoy instead champion an experiential archaeology revolving around individual consciousness, ambiguous structures, and continual semiotic discontinuity. Dennis Pogue's study of emergent consumption in the Chesapeake (2001:50–51) sounds a similar lament that studying ideology "reduces all behaviors to issues of power" and inevitably ignores common folks' agency in favor of a focus on what he dubs the "capitalist conspiracy." Simplistic divisions between capitalist elite and the masses or the implication that ideology provides a universal signifying system generally are rhetorical maneuvers; critics use these caricatures to launch transparent attacks on whatever forms of determinism they choose to evade, which has often meant stressing individual decision-making and everyday resistance over ideology and structural domination. Historical archaeologists have often dismantled ideology and then lapsed into explaining consumption as a natural outgrowth of economic and production shifts: Pogue, for instance, attributes eighteenth-century materialism to population growth and the emergence of socially competitive gentry who used goods in status hierarchies like those Veblen modeled.

Most archaeologists are uneasy with the suggestion that a single coherent body of elite values and practices could actually repress the masses, who certainly retain some measure of autonomy in even the most repressive circumstances. Ross Jamieson's (2000) analysis of household consumption in colonial Ecuador notes that most accounts of Spanish colonial life assume that powerful Spanish colonizers simply imposed changes on indigenous peoples. However, Jamieson argues for a quite dynamic relationship between colonizers and colonized in Ecuador, which is reflected in diverse consumption patterns among urban and rural, elite and impoverished, that incorporated local and colonial objects alike.

Dominant ideological discourses clearly have vast ambiguity in any lived circumstance, and resistance and experience are themselves shaped by ideology, which is itself dynamic, uncoordinated, and unevenly articulated. Consequently, it is infeasible to argue that people simply "see through" ideological misrepresentation or alternatively are "taken in" by it. Most consumer ideology is contested in some fashion and with some genuine measure of personal efficacy, but personally empowering consumption does not necessarily work significant structural change. Desire and the hopes consumers invest in goods are key to consumption's genuine transformative potential; however, consumption usually expresses a quite personal "politics" that imagines individual and situationally distinct social possibilities, which may subsequently lead to structural change, reproduce existing conditions, or work wholly meaningful personal changes with ambiguous social and structural effects.

To assess something as dynamic and ambiguous as a consumer "politics," it is necessary to examine both desire and ideology and assess how and why certain consumers invest specific ambitions into consumption and particular objects. Historical archaeology's standard approach to desire has been to examine how consumers use material goods to display their hierarchical social position or pose the social identity to which they aspire. This idea was most clearly articulated by Veblen (1899), and in a similar form Weber (1958) argued for the presence of social status groups that distinguished themselves from others by unique consumption patterns. Bourdieu (1984) has argued for comparable class-distinguishing processes in contemporary material consumption.

Veblen's perspective has been most clearly embraced by Neil McKendrick, John Brewer, and J. H. Plumb (1982), who argue that the emulation of upper-class style by the masses was central to why English consumer society unleashed unprecedented materialism throughout the Empire. Emulation is infeasible in its most mechanical caricature as poor people instrumentally parroting the elite, but it is not without some genuine interpretive power. Paul Shackel's (1993:162) analysis of colonial Chesapeake consumption accepts that cross-class emulation was commonplace; however, he argues that such emulation masked a complex range of conflicts and class-specific interests. Many consumers at least provisionally reproduced ideals that were circulated in discourses such as etiquette books and advertising. Shackel focuses on the former, and Roland Marchand (1985) is among the many scholars who have examined the latter. There is clear evidence that many middling or impoverished consumers were swayed by consumer goods and consumption patterns they literally saw displayed in public space: African-American and European immigrant domestics, for example, often were introduced to particular goods through their labor in White genteel homes, and department store display windows were productive theaters for many working-class urbanites (cf. Abelson 1989). But this sort of emulation is a rather piecemeal and highly individualistic reproduction of ideals that were themselves ambiguous, dynamic, and dispersed. Such emulation does not "imitate" a coherent set of dictates (or an elite class) as much as it reproduces an equivocal ideal that did not exist in objective reality: i.e., consumers negotiated various threads of material discourses and particular experiences in public space that produced a quite diverse range of consumption patterns loosely linked back to dominant disciplinary ideals.

Historical archaeologists still tend to share Veblen's presumption that commodities' central meanings are dependent on what goods "communicate" to society through their display. Historical archaeologists usually have ended up reducing goods' "communicative" use value to their instrumental capacity to display "cost status": i.e., costly and stylish goods are consumed with the fundamental intention of publicly communicating (and perhaps improving or masking) the consumer's socioeconomic standing. Methodologically, most of this work in American historical archaeology has focused on ceramic pricing research conducted by George Miller (1991). Miller's assessments of Staffordshire price-fixing agreements provide a quantitative mechanism to evaluate the wholesale value of a ceramic assemblage. Usually these studies are directed toward some measure of status reflected in an assemblage's economic value, though "status" has been relatively poorly defined. Suzanne Spencer-Wood (1987), for example, provides one of the most systematic status analyses based on ceramic scaling, concluding that higher-status consumers demonstrated their social standing through tea and coffee vessel consumption; lower-status households, in contrast, tended to purchase cheaper wares in similar decorative types. A flood of studies have probed the diversity of consumption patterns and related them to other documentary measures of affluence and social status. However, the mechanisms spurring consumption pass largely unexamined, and they seem to assume economically rational consumers who instrumentally buy things to display their legitimate right to (or desire for) socioeconomic privilege.

This vision of materialism concedes consumers relatively little consequential impression over the meaning of material goods; it implies that middling consumers will generally purchase whatever the marketplace provides or dominant social tastes dictate; and it tends to pose consumption as a rather logical goal-oriented social activity. Reacting to such visions of economically rational consumers, Colin Campbell (1987) argues that modern consumption (i.e., since the first quarter of the eighteenth century) is instead rooted in individual desire that is focused less on displaying meaning to society than personally imagining how goods can reconceive the individual and society. For Campbell, the most critical moments in consumer experience fall between manufacture and acquisition; in the consumer musing over how acquiring and possessing a particular good will gratify them. Consumers imaginatively invest various sentiments into goods, but this imagination is tempered by discipline that suppresses or postpones some pleasures while it allows itself others. The apparent tension between a puritanical discipline and a romantic hedonism is not so much a contradiction for Campbell as it is a productive and inseparable amalgam. Stressing the broad implications of such desire, George Yudice (2001:229) emphasizes that there is a significant social dimension to consumer desire. Yudice concludes that consumers fantasize about material fulfillment of desires and project this onto social space as a mechanism to collectively negotiate what constitutes a "need" or "satisfaction," both of which are fluid and vary from one group to another.

Methodologically, it may seem somewhat daunting to divine such individualistic desires in commodities, but the key lies in examining how ideology, power, and social position encourage particular forms of desire in certain contexts. Paul Mullins (1999, 2001) has argued that objects that do not symbolically "fit" within an assemblage or a material system often offer the most possibilities for consumer imagination, because they provide equivocal aesthetic and material cues that a consumer can interpret in a variety of forms. Novel objects may feature exotic styles or ambiguous functions, but in some form they pose distinctions to other goods in the same assemblage or the goods available in a given time and place. Novel material style could have a wide range of meanings, and that meaning might well differ from one person to the next: a novel object could distinguish the consumer from others, homogenize them within the guise of individual symbolic manipulation, or provide the symbolic means to rethink and even critique their social conditions.

Paul Willis (1990) sounds a similar thesis, arguing that "commerce and consumerism have helped to release a profane explosion of everyday symbolic life and activity" because commodities are intended for exchange that attempts to address desires and needs; consequently, commodities generally are relevant to what he calls "socially necessary symbolic work." Willis suggests that this "work" in consumption and every facet of everyday life has contextually distinctive dynamics in which "symbols and practices are selected, reselected, highlighted and recomposed to resonate further appropriated and particularized meanings." Willis argues against seeing such symbolic potential strictly defined by either the thing's properties or dominant aesthetic meanings; instead, he argues that analysis should focus on everyday social relations. This is a process akin to what Daniel Miller (1987) calls "recontextualization." Miller (1987:174–176) frames recontextualization as the creative manipulation of the symbolism of mass-produced goods, a process in which consumers define the meaning of commodities in ways that are perceived to positively contribute to or reproduce personal and social identity. Miller argues that particular goods have distinct possibilities in certain consumers' hands. The challenge is moving from the realm of imaginative individuals to collectives whose agency has some impact on dominant structural relations: this need not be structurally revolutionary change as much as it should suggest ways that collectives rethought social contradiction, which may or may not lead to structural change.

A Social Archaeology of Consumption

Daniel Miller has gone so far as to argue that consumption is the "vanguard to history," a pronouncement he believes is warranted by consumption's global socio-economic transformations and the stampede of scholars who have examined consumption. Archaeology has always been focused on the material evidence of consumption, so it seems unusual that archaeologists are not in the midst of this interdisciplinary turn to consumption research. However, the distance that archaeologists need to traverse to do a social archaeology of consumption is not particularly great: archaeologists clearly have conducted an extensive amount of research on a vast range of consumption patterns, the ways in which material culture shapes and mirrors identity, and the historical continuities between contemporary and past consumer societies. It also would appear that archaeology has a great deal to offer consumption scholarship: consumption research often relies on impressionistic data analysis that falls well below archaeological expectations of methodological rigor; objects are routinely examined through mechanical typological frameworks; and consumption patterns usually are defined based on textual evidence rather than concrete assemblages. Consequently, despite the overwhelming turn to consumption, it seems that few scholars have wrestled with how systematic object analysis might provide fresh insight into how things structure and encourage various forms of desire and identity formation.

Archaeology's insular methodologies and narrative forms likely have discouraged interdisciplinary scholars from using archaeological data and insights. Historical archaeologists, for instance, have marshaled a stunning inventory of household consumption data, but most of this analysis has focused on prefabricated patterns rather than the complicated entanglements between social groups. In historical archaeology the reluctance to embrace consumption theory seems to revolve around the identity fluidity painted by most consumer theorists. Accepting that identity is dynamic, fluid, and situational, ensnaring it in a vast range of local capitalist experiences, and then confronting its tense relationship with ideology could potentially transform some of historical archaeology's most cherished assumptions about the stability of culture and identity. A social archaeology of consumption also will inevitably stress that the key characteristics of historical contexts – mass consumption, identity fluidity and factionalism, and the roots of material inequality – extend well into the prehistoric past, illuminating the continuities between past and present and productively eroding historical archaeology's own insularity.

An archaeology of capitalist consumption should be utterly dynamic and confront the tense confluence of ideology, power, and desire, and this shift likely will impact how we interpret all commonplace things. The historic and prehistoric past have not been inhabited by consumers just like ourselves, so even if we accept consumption's long-term identity fluidity and social complexity archaeologists still should resist peopling the past with self-empowered shoppers. Archaeology offers a critical mechanism to assess the politics of consumption across time and space, and it certainly reveals both significant similarities and profound differences between consumers in the past and present.

GUIDE TO FURTHER READING

The most wide-ranging interdisciplinary review of consumption scholarship is Daniel Miller's edited *Acknowledging Consumption: A Review of New Studies* (New York: Routledge, 1995). Campbell (1987) is a fascinating and imaginative examination of the roots of contemporary consumption. Agnew (1993) is a brilliant exposition of consumer culture historiography. Susman (1984) rethinks most of modern American society by placing consumption at the heart of the American Dream. Horowitz (1985) provides a thoughtful intellectual history of Americans' ambivalence toward goods. For a more sober vision of consumer culture, see Ewen (1988). Jean Baudrillard has had a significant impact on the most radical theories of consumption; see his essays in Baudrillard (1988). Bourdieu (1984) is a thorough study of French consumption patterns. Researchers examining subcultures have stressed the political potential of goods, such as

Dick Hebdige's succinct and insightful *Subculture: The Meaning of Style* (1979). Among the vast range of studies on ideology, Eagleton (1991) is especially thorough, critical, and clever. Orser (1996) outlines American historical archaeology's turn toward capitalism, colonization, and cultural complexity in the past decade. Leone (1995) summarizes his application of Frankfurt School critical theory to archaeological interpretation.

REFERENCES

Abelson, E. S. 1989. *When Ladies Go A-Thieving: Middle-Class Shoplifters in the Victorian Department Store*. New York: Oxford University Press.

Abercombie, N., S. Hill, and B. S. Turner. 1980. *The Dominant Ideology Thesis*. London: Allen & Unwin.

Agnew, J-C. 1993. Coming up for air: Consumer culture in historical perspective. In J. Brewer and R. Porter (eds.), *Consumption and the World of Goods*. New York: Routledge, pp. 19–39.

Althusser, L. 1971. *Lenin and Philosophy and Other Essays*. New York: Monthly Review Press.

Appadurai, A. 1986. *The Social Life of Things: Commodities in Cultural Perspective*. Cambridge: Cambridge University Press.

Askegaard, S., and A. F. Firat. 1997. Towards a critique of material culture, consumption and markets. In S. M. Pearce (ed.), *Experiencing Material Culture in the Western World*. London: Leicester University Press, pp. 114–139.

Baram, U. 2000. Entangled objects from the Palestinian past: Archaeological perspectives for the Ottoman period, 1500–1900. In U. Baram and L. Carroll (eds.), *A Historical Archaeology of the Ottoman Empire: Breaking New Ground*. New York: Kluwer/Plenum, pp. 137–159.

Barrett, J. C. 2001. Agency, the duality of structure, and the problem of the archaeological record. In I. Hodder (ed.), *Archaeological Theory Today*. Malden, MA: Blackwell, pp. 141–164.

Baudrillard, J. 1988. *Jean Baudrillard: Selected Writings*. Stanford, CA: Stanford University Press.

Bennett, A. 1999. Subcultures or neo-tribes? Rethinking the relationship between youth, style and musical taste. *Sociology* 33(3): 599–610.

Bourdieu, P. 1984. *Distinction: A Social Critique of the Judgement of Taste*. Cambridge, MA: Harvard University Press.

Braudel, F. 1973. *Capitalism and Material Life 1400–1800*. London: Weidenfeld & Nicolson.

Breen, T. H. 1993. Narrative of commercial life: Consumption, ideology, and community on the eve of the American Revolution. *William and Mary Quarterly* 50(3): 471–501.

Campbell, C. 1987. *The Romantic Ethic and the Spirit of Modern Consumerism*. Cambridge, MA: Blackwell.

Carter, E. 1984. Alice in the consumer wonderland: West German case studies in gender and consumer culture. In A. McRobbie and M. Nova (eds.), *Gender and Generation*. London: Macmillan, pp. 185–214.

Cohen, P. 1993. Subcultural conflict and working-class community. In A. Gray and J. McGuigan (eds.), *Studying Culture: An Introductory Reader*. New York: St. Martin's Press, pp. 95–103.

Crowell, A. 1997. *Archaeology and the Capitalist World System: A Study from Russia America*. New York: Plenum.

de Certeau, M. 1984. *The Practice of Everyday Life*. Berkeley: University of California Press.

Deetz, J. 1977. *In Small Things Forgotten: The Archaeology of Early American Life*. New York: Anchor/Doubleday.

Delle, J. A. 1998. *An Archaeology of Social Space: Analyzing Coffee Plantation in Jamaica's Blue Mountains*. New York: Kluwer/Plenum.

——, S. A. Mrozowski, and R. Paynter (eds.) 2000. *Lines that Divide: Historical Archaeologies of Race, Class, and Gender*. Knoxville: University of Tennessee Press.

Douglas, M., and B. Isherwood. 1978. *The World of Goods: Towards and Anthropology of Consumption*. New York: Routledge.

Eagleton, T. 1991. *Ideology: An Introduction*. New York: Verso.

Edsforth, R. 1987. *Class Conflict and Cultural Consensus: The Making of a Mass Consumer Society in Flint, Michigan*. New Brunswick, NJ: Rutgers University Press.

Ewen, S. 1988. *All Consuming Images: The Politics of Style in Contemporary Culture*. New York: Basic Books.

Ferguson, L. 1992. *Uncommon Ground: Archaeology and Early African America, 1650–1800*. Washington, DC: Smithsonian Institution Press.

Fiske, J. 1989. *Reading the Popular*. Boston: Unwin Hyman.

Foucault, M. 1972. *The Archaeology of Knowledge and the Discourse on Language*. New York: Pantheon.

Giddens, A. 1984. *The Constitution of Society*. Berkeley: University of California Press.

Gilroy, P. 2000. *Against Race: Imagining Political Culture Beyond the Color Line*. Boston: Harvard University Press.

Glassie, H. 1975. *Folk Housing in Middle Virginia: A Structural Analysis of Historic Artifacts*. Knoxville: University of Tennessee Press.

Habermas, J. 1976. *Legitimation Crisis*. Boston: Beacon.

Hall, M. 1992. Small things and the mobile, conflictual fusion of power, fear, and desire. In A. E. Yentsch and M. E. Beaudry (eds.), *The Art and Mystery of Historical Archaeology: Essays in Honor of James Deetz*. Boca Raton, FL: CRC Press, pp. 373–399.

Hall, S. 1993. Minimal selves. In A. Gray and J. McGuigan (eds.), *Studying Culture: An Introductory Reader*. New York: St. Martin's Press, pp. 134–138.

Hebdige, D. 1979. *Subculture: The Meaning of Style*. New York: Routledge.

Heinze, A. 2000. Jewish women and the making of an American home. In J. Scanlon (ed.), *The Gender and Consumer Culture Reader*. New York: New York University Press, pp. 19–29.

Hodder, I. 1986. *Reading the Past: Critical Approaches to Interpretation in Archaeology*. Cambridge: Cambridge University Press.

Horowitz, D. 1985. *The Morality of Spending: Attitudes Toward the Consumer Society in America, 1875–1940*. Baltimore, MD: Johns Hopkins University Press.

Jameson, F. 1984. Postmodernism, or the cultural logic of late capitalism. *New Left Review* 146: 53–93.

Jamieson, R. 2000. *Domestic Architecture and Power: The Historical Archaeology of Colonial Ecuador*. New York: Kluwer/Plenum.

Johnson, M. 1996. *An Archaeology of Capitalism*. Cambridge, MA: Blackwell.

Leone, M. P. 1984. Interpreting ideology in historical archaeology: The William Paca Garden in Annapolis, Maryland. In D. Miller and C. Tilley (eds.), *Ideology, Power, and Prehistory*. Cambridge: Cambridge University Press, pp. 25–35.

——1995. A historical archaeology of capitalism. *American Anthropologist* 97(2): 251–268.

Marchand, R. 1985. *Advertising the American Dream: Making Way for Modernity, 1920–1940*. Berkeley: University of California Press.

McKendrick, N., J. Brewer, and J. H. Plumb. 1982. *The Birth of a Consumer Society: The Commercialization of Eighteenth-Century England*. Bloomington: Indiana University Press.

Miller, D. 1987. *Material Culture and Mass Consumption*. New York: Blackwell.

——1995a. Consumption and commodities. *Annual Reviews of Anthropology* 24: 141–161.

——1995b. Consumption studies as the transformation of anthropology. In D. Miller (ed.), *Acknowledging Consumption: A Review of New Studies*. New York: Routledge, pp. 238–263.

——1997. *Capitalism: An Ethnographic Approach*. Oxford: Berg.

Miller, G. L. 1991. A revised set of CC Index values for classification and economic scaling of English ceramics from 1787 to 1880. *Historical Archaeology* 25(1): 1–25.

Mukerji, C. 1983. *From Graven Images: Patterns of Modern Materialism*. New York: Columbia University Press.

Mullins, P. R. 1999. *Race and Affluence: An Archaeology of African America and Consumer Culture*. New York: Kluwer/Plenum.

——2001. Racializing the parlor: Race and Victorian bric-à-brac consumption. In C. E. Orser, Jr. (ed.), *Race and the Archaeology of Identity*. Salt Lake City: University of Utah Press, pp. 158–176.

Orser, C. E., Jr. 1996. *A Historical Archaeology of the Modern World*. New York: Kluwer/Plenum.

Paynter, R. 1988. Steps to an archaeology of capitalism: Material change and class analysis. In M. P. Leone and P. B. Potter, Jr. (eds.), *The Recovery of Meaning: Historical Archaeology in the Eastern United States*. Washington, DC: Smithsonian Institution Press, pp. 407–433.

Perry, W., and R. Paynter 1999. Artifacts, ethnicity, and the archaeology of African Americans. In T. A. Singleton (ed.), *"I, Too, Am America": Archaeological Studies of African-American Life*. Charlottesville: University of Virginia Press, pp. 299–310.

Pogue, D. J. 2001. The transformation of America: Georgian sensibility, capitalist conspiracy, or consumer revolution? *Historical Archaeology* 35(2): 41–57.

Redhead, S. 1997. *Subcultures to Clubcultures: An Introduction to Popular Cultural Studies*. Malden, MA: Blackwell.

Ritzer, G. 1993. *The McDonaldization of Society: An Investigation into the Changing Character of Contemporary Social Life*. London: Pine Forge Press.

Schor, J. B. 2000. Towards a new politics of consumption. In J. B. Schor and D. B. Holt (eds.), *The Consumer Society Reader*. New York: The New Press, pp. 446–462.

Shackel, P. 1993. *Personal Discipline and Material Culture: An Archaeology of Annapolis, Maryland, 1695–1870*. Knoxville: University of Tennessee Press.

Silberman, N. A. 1989. *Between Past and Present: Archaeology, Ideology, and Nationalism in the Modern Middle East*, New York: Henry Holt.

Slater, D. R. 1987. *Consumer Culture and Modernity*, Cambridge: Polity Press.

Spencer-Wood, S. 1987. *Consumer Choice in Historical Archaeology*. New York: Plenum.

Susman, W. 1984. *Culture as History: The Transformation of American Society in the Twentieth Century*. New York: Harper & Row.

Thompson, E. P. 1963. *The Making of the English Working Class*. New York: Vintage.

Thoreau, H. D. 1854. *Walden*. Boston: Ticknor & Fields.

Veblen, T. 1899. *The Theory of the Leisure Class: An Economic Study of Institutions*. New York: Mentor.

Weber, M. 1958. *The Protestant Ethic and the Spirit of Capitalism*. New York: Charles Scribner's Sons.

Wilkie, L. A. 2000. Culture bought: Evidence of creolization in the consumer goods of an enslaved Bahamian family. *Historical Archaeology* 34(3): 10–26.

——, and Bartoy, K. M. 2000. A critical archaeology revisited. *Current Anthropology* 41(5): 747–777.

Willis, P. 1990. *Common Culture: Symbolic Work at Play in the Everyday Cultures of the Young*. London: Open University Press.

Yentsch, A. E. 1994. *A Chesapeake Family and their Slaves: A Study in Historical Archaeology*. New York: Cambridge University Press.

Yudice, G. 2001. Comparative cultural studies traditions: Latin American and the US. In T. Miller (ed.), *A Companion to Cultural Studies*. Malden, MA: Blackwell, pp. 217–231.

Part III

Places

Robert W. Preucel and Lynn Meskell

Place has come to be a key organizing concept in the social sciences. It has infused such diverse fields as philosophy, human geography, literature, sociology, anthropology, and cultural studies (Adams, Hoelscher, and Till 2001; Agnew and Duncan 1989; Dainotto 2000; Feld and Basso 1996; Gupta and Ferguson 1997; Hirsch and O'Hanlon 1995; Jackson 1994; Keith and Pile 1993; Low 1996; Malpas 1999; Massey 1994; McDowell 1999). One reason for its broad appeal is that the term retains a sense of its Cartesian origins as a physical quality and, at the same time, implies the affective and the phenomenological. Allied with this is a new appreciation of the multisitedness of culture, the fact that culture is always in motion and differentially expressed across space (Olwig and Hastrup 1997). Indeed, placemaking is widely regarded as a central process in identity formation and integral to the construction of social orders. Archaeology is well positioned to produce accounts of placemaking, since it is directly involved in constructions of identities and meanings over the long term and the subsequent histories of spatiality.

It is useful at the outset to differentiate space and place. Space is usually defined as a natural science concept, the physical setting within which everything occurs. It is modeled in mathematics and physics as Euclidean, topological, and infinite. This approach is generally attributed to Descartes, who regarded space as an absolute containing all senses and bodies (Lefebvre 1991). Places can be regarded as the outcome of the social process of valuing space. They are the products of the imaginary, of desire, and are the primary means by which we articulate with space and transform it into a humanized landscape. The crucial distinction here is that places require human agents and spaces do not. This characterization has been extremely productive in the human sciences. However, it is important to note that some have argued that place is the more general concept from which space is derived (Casey 1996). This view is based upon the idea that place is a premodern concept with deep historical roots, while space is a recent, modern notion. Still others regard both space and place as social constructs (Harvey 1996). In this context, the focus needs to shift from the distinctions between space and place to the interpretation of the ever-changing meanings of the production of spaces and places within the social order across the social process.

In many ways, space and place are "natural" concepts for archaeology. The mapping of peoples and cultures across space and time as evidenced by the distribution of artifacts, households, settlements, and monuments is one of the most basic forms of archaeological analysis. Since the 1990s it has led to new understandings of the colonizations of the Pacific Islands, the peopling of the Americas, the origins and spread of agriculture in the Near East and China, and the emergence of premodern world systems. The new interest in place can be seen as part of a broader reassertion of the individual in the human sciences and a recognition of the importance of phenomenology. There is a growing concern for the social nature of these processes and how they articulate with the cultural imaginary and lived experience. The result is a new appreciation of the politics of location and the social construction of space and place.

Spatial Science

The pre-eminent science of social space is, of course, human geography. In its formative years during the 1930s, it encompassed an uneasy marriage between environmental determinism and regionalism (Hartshorne 1939). The first of these approaches, environmental determinism, sought to identify causal linkages between the distributions of human activities and the natural environment. Almost always, the causal arrow went in one direction, from the natural to the human. The second was an emphasis upon the specific variables of different regions of the earth that produced their unique character. In the views of the followers of Paul Vidal de la Blache, each area was held to have its own personality (see Blake, chapter 10). Although in theory regionalism was a reaction to environmental determinism, in practice, both shared a common focus on the determinative features of the natural environment.

In the 1950s and 1960s a movement known as the "New Geography" emerged in the United States and then quickly spread to the United Kingdom. It was positivist in content and explicitly concerned with spatial forms and morphological laws (Chorley and Haggett 1967). As David Harvey (1969:191) put it, "the whole practice and philosophy of geography depends upon the development of a conceptual framework for handling the distribution of objects and events in space." The conceptual framework of geography was built up from a loose association of related theories, including Central Place theory, Land-Use theory, and Industrial Location theory, among others, and came to be known as economic geography. All of these theories treated distance as a cost to be overcome, either in maximizing the location of a market, in determining the proper mix of alternative agricultural strategies, or in minimizing production costs in the locations of factories. Coupled with this was an impressive battery of quantitative methods and techniques, many of which had to be devised specifically for spatial contexts because of confounding issues such as spatial autocorrelation (Cliff and Ord 1973).

By the late 1970s, four reactions to the New Geography developed. The first was the emergence of behavioral geography (Gold 1980). This approach was a response to the abstract, depersonalized spatial approach and an attempt to reintroduce the individual by emphasizing psychological and cognitive perspectives. The second response was humanist geography (Gregory 1981; Ley 1982; Ley and Samuels 1978). This perspective emphasized the centrality of human creativity and the significance of individual events. One of the most eloquent of the humanists was Yi-Fu Tuan (1974, 1977), who articulated a phenomenology of space and place. For him, the ultimate goal of such an approach is "to increase the burden of awareness" of the nature of our existence. The third approach was historical geography (Baker 1972). This approach addressed the historical dimension of geographical patterns. Finally, there was a newfound sense of social relevance. This was expressed in the growing concern for social justice in urban contexts (Harvey 1973) and in the spatial distribution of inequality and poverty (Peet 1977). In retrospect, it is possible to see these reactions as the constitutive elements of a new postmodern geography.

Today, the positivist emphasis upon spatial forms and morphological laws has lessened and new engagements have emerged (Dear 2001). Some parts of human geography have begun to articulate with cultural anthropology in their focus on problems of representation, the politics of postmodernity, feminist geography, and postcolonialism. Other parts have focused on quality of life issues such as nature and environment, place and health, and social justice. It is significant that geographers have been among the most eloquent commentators on postmodernism. David Harvey (1989, 1996), for example, has been one of its sharpest critics. For him, it is nothing more than capitalism speeded up and those studies that embrace it do so without acknowledging that they are complicit in reproducing capitalism. Edward Soja (1989, 1996), on the other hand, has written approvingly of postmodernism and its challenges. He sees it as a strategic reconstitution of conventional modernist epistemologies and his notion of "Thirdspace" is his attempt to reconsider how we might think about the interrelationships of space, history, and society.

The spatial science approach has been extremely influential in archaeology and the field has followed a parallel trajectory with human geography (see Earle and Preucel 1986; Hodder 1987; Wagstaff 1987). During the early development of European archaeology, the mapping of ethnic regions and population movements was central to understanding national origins and identities. One influential development was the German school of anthropogeography which linked ethnicity and the culture-area approach to the environment (Ratzel 1882–91). In the United States, however, ethnicity was suppressed due to its political overtones in favor of a focus upon culture. For example, William Henry Holmes (1914) published a map of sixteen "cultural characterization areas" based upon archaeological traits. In the 1950s, Gordon Willey (1953), inspired by the culture ecologist Julian Steward, introduced settlement-pattern archaeology. This approach used the size and distribution of sites and buildings to infer social function and hierarchies in the Prehispanic settlement of the Virú Valley of Peru.

In the early 1960s, the so-called "New Archaeology" emerged on both sides of the Atlantic. Like the New Geography, it adopted positivism and espoused general laws of human behavior (Binford 1962; Fritz and Plog 1970). According to Watson, LeBlanc, and Redman (1971:3), this new approach was defined by a "self-conscious concern with the formation and testing of hypothetical general laws." A central element of the New Archaeology was spatial modeling and pattern recognition which came to be called locational analysis (Clark 1977; Hodder and Orton 1976). Classic examples of this kind of research are Timothy Earle's (1976) nearest-neighbor analysis of Aztec cities in the Valley of Mexico and Ian Hodder's (1972) central-place study of market towns in Romano-Britain. With the growing significance of applied archaeology and Cultural Resource Management, this spatial science approach was turned toward predictive modeling (Kohler and Parker 1986).

In the early 1980s a sharp critique of the New Archaeology developed from the quarters of structuralism and Marxism and, to a lesser degree, feminism. Especially influential was a volume published by Hodder (1982a) based upon a Cambridge seminar on structuralism and archaeology. In his introduction, Hodder (1982b:5) wrote that "(m)y own involvement in spatial archaeology, a sphere where statistical prediction has been most successful, has shown most clearly that prediction has little to do with explanation." The volume included two influential studies of social space. Linda Donley (1982) conducted an ethnoarchaeological study of the gendered construction of the Swahili house that drew upon insights from Pierre Bourdieu. Henrietta Moore (1982) examined spatial patterning of refuse in settlement as a part of a structured symbolic order. At the same time in the United States, Mark Leone developed a critique of the assumptions of Historical Archaeology from a structural Marxist and critical theory perspective. In a classic study of William Paca's garden, he argued that the layout of the garden served to rationalize space and the contradictory nature of Georgian ideology (Leone 1984).

There is currently a new rapprochment between human geography, cultural anthropology, and social archaeology. This can be seen in the methodological shift in scale at both ends of the social space spectrum from settlement to landscape and from site-based to household archaeology. In their discussion of landscape as an ideology of settlement, how people inscribe land with meaning in a process of domestication, Snead and Preucel (1999) emphasize the close interrelationships between villages, shrines, trails, mountains, and lakes. In her chapter (chapter 12), Hendon argues that the household becomes a useful analytic category when we seek to connect social identity and economic production with a locale. A social archaeology of household production and social relations must therefore not only come to terms with the household but also with the house, recognizing that houses and the people who live in them are in a "mutually constituting" relationship. This rapprochement can also be seen in the growing interest in distinctive theories of landscape, borderlands, diaspora, and globalization.

Landscape

Landscape has recently reemerged as a compelling framework in the analysis of space and place in human geography (Cosgrove 1984; Cosgrove and Daniels 1988; Duncan 1990), anthropology (Hirsch and O'Hanlon 1995), and now archaeology (Anschuetz et al. 2001; Ashmore and Knapp 1999; Bender 1993; Tilley 1994). The word landscape is itself derived from the Dutch word *landschap* and was introduced into English during the sixteenth century as a technical term used by painters. According to Keith Thomas, "(t)he initial appeal of rural scenery was that it reminded the spectator of landscape pictures (and)... the scene was only called a 'landscape' because it was reminiscent of a painted 'landskip'; it was 'picturesque' because it looked like a picture" (1984:265). Here we see some of the complexities embedded in the term since representation, memory, and nature are all intertwined.

Early uses of the concept in the social sciences have tended to emphasize the landscape as the physical or ecological setting for social action. Brian Roberts summarizes a long tradition of work in geography and archaeology when he defines landscapes as "assemblages of real world features – natural, semi-natural and wholly artificial – (which) give character and diversity to the earth's surface, and form the physical framework within which human societies exist" (1987:79). The focus of these landscape studies was on settlement patterns, field systems, village forms, and building styles. With the development of the New Geography and the New Archaeology, a common group of formal models and quantitative methods were applied, such as site-catchment analysis for reconstructing subsistence economies, the rank-size rule for settlement hierarchies, and the gravity model for social interaction (Chisholm 1962; Hodder and Orton 1976; Vita-Finzi and Higgs 1970).

The crucial move was the shift from landscape-as-passive to landscape-as-active pioneered in both British geography and archaeology. For Denis Cosgrove (1984:13), landscape is not merely the world we see, but rather a way of seeing the world. It is an ideological concept that represents how specific classes of people have signified themselves and their world through their imagined relationships with nature. Christopher Gosden (1989) has argued that the ways in which social groups interact with landscapes are partly structured by how previous social groups interacted with the landscape. The social landscape is thus both context and content. A similar point is made by Christopher Tilley (1994:23) who argues, following Anthony Giddens, that landscape is both the medium for and the outcome of action and previous histories of action. He regards landscape as having ontological import since it is lived and replete with meanings and symbolism, not simply something just looked at or thought about. This means that, as Barbara Bender (1993, 1998) points out, there is never a single landscape but always many landscapes. Landscapes are an outcome of the practices of identity formation since "people create their sense of identity – whether self, or group, or nation state – through engaging and re-engaging, appropriating and contesting the sedimented pasts that make up the landscape."

Landscape is often aligned with memory (Schama 1995). Western concepts of memory are inflected with the Aristotelian principle that memory is a physical imprinting. According to this classic view, material substitutes are necessary to compensate for the fragility of the human memory. Alternatively, anthropologists and historians have imputed that collective memory does not necessarily dwell in ephemeral monuments. Following Paul Connerton (1989), they argue that embodied acts and rituals may be more successful in iterating memory than simply the creation of objects, war memorials being an oft-cited example. Physical memorials supposedly serving as perpetual reminders are typically overlooked and considered less effective iterative strategies than commemorative performances. Thus studies of remembering must necessarily oscillate between the physicality of monuments, things, and representations and the often immaterial practices that locate subjects within new timespace understandings: trajectories that fuse past, present, and future.

The recent examination of landscape in archaeology has often entailed the study of the relation of myth to memory. Paul Taçon (1999) has discussed the antiquity of landscape as a mythological charter and moral order in Aboriginal Australia, one that is reproduced in contemporary art. The landscape itself is defined by different levels of sacredness. As people acquire different knowledge-bases through initiation, they receive the rights to access more varied sacred sites and landscapes. Tim Pauketat and Susan Alt (2003) focus on "mound memory," how mound-construction knowledge was transmitted across generational and cultural divides in the mid-continental United States. They suggest that the persistence of four-side platform mound construction can be interpreted as the inscription of social memory in landscapes. They also suggest that local variability in mound construction reveals contested social fields. Archaeologists are thus poised to examine both material and immaterial registers of social memory, if we broaden our scope of analysis and unravel the complexities of remembering and forgetting in diverse cultural moments.

Borders

Borders can be conceptualized as barriers or bridges real or imagined and can be accordingly marked or unmarked, permeable or impermeable. They can be the sites of control, as with the Great Wall of China; sites of identity, such as American Indian reservations; or sites of transgression, as with the US–Mexico border. And, of course, they can be simultaneously all three. There is a growing interest across the humanities and social sciences in borders of all kinds and the lived experience of border peoples and communities that inhabit these places of ambiguity (Barkan and Shelton 1998; Michaelsen and Johnson 1997). The study of borders is directly associated with social subjectivities such as gender, class, and ethnicity (Lugo 1997). It encompasses the crafting of hybrid identities in charged loci, where various intersections of difference meet and are played out materially. Borders research traverses different understandings of spacetime, culture clash, symbolic landscapes, and social and economic manipulations. From this perspective, borders can be seen as an "interstitial zone of displacement and deterritorialization that shapes the identity of the hybridized subject" (Gupta and Ferguson 1992:19).

There are two related strains that are contributing to this interest, feminist critiques and Borderlands studies. Feminists have argued that because all knowledge is "situated" there is no possibility of the "God trick," a neutral, detached view of the world (Haraway 1988). Objectivity thus becomes not an absence of bias, but rather an acknowledgment of the necessarily local and partial nature of one's knowledge. As Meskell (1999:68–69) observes, this insight has implications for the feminist project; it implies that we need to be wary of the reification of gender and identify the variable construction of identity as a methodological and political goal. Similarly, Borderlands scholars have emphasized the power of the "view from the margin." A classic example is the work of Gloria Anzaldúa (1987) who extends the geographical to include cultural, physical, spiritual, sexual, and linguistic spaces where "two or more cultures edge each other, where people of different cultures occupy the same territory, where under, lower, middle, and upper classes touch, where the space between two individuals shrinks with intimacy." She writes that the space of the Borderlands creates a new form of consciousness, the consciousness of the *mestiza*. Soja (1996) has identified this perspective as critical to the rethinking of Thirdspace.

In geography and archaeology, borders have traditionally been treated as objective, disembodied forces consistent with the positivist view of cultural systems. Examples include wave-of-advance models (Ammerman and Cavalli-Sforza 1973) used in explaining the spread of agriculture in Europe and frontier-zone models used to explain the process of the colonization of the American West (Green and Perlman 1984). Among the most exciting studies are those that are approaching borders as socially constituting, multiethnic sites of identity formation. Mike Davis has drawn attention to Los Angeles as an edge city. He writes that its Spanish-speaking neighborhoods constitute "more than melting pots for eventual assimilation to some hyphenated ethnicity"; they create "a virtually parallel urban structure – a second city... with its own distinctive urbanity" (1990:77–78). Another example is Minette Church's (2002) analysis of the varied ethnic landscapes in southern Colorado. She identifies Anglo, Hispanic, and Native American conceptions of the land and suggests they played a central role in transforming land into homeland. Significantly, her archaeological work reveals considerable variability in land use that is not apparent from the historical record.

Diaspora

Since the 1990s, diaspora has been a central concept in the study of postmodern culture. James Clifford has discussed diasporas as "a history of dispersal, myth/memories of the homeland, alienation in the host country, desire for the eventual return, ongoing support for the homeland, and a collective identity importantly defined by this relationship" (1994:305). Diaspora is, in this sense, a culture without a country. It produces a postcolonial subjectivity, a position that is both the subject and object of the discourse on identity. However, as Lilley (Chapter 13) points out, there are other definitions of diaspora that simply implicate population movements such as colonization and migration.

The recent social articulation of diaspora is a direct offshoot from developments in historical archaeology. Paraphrasing Agorsah (1996:222), the examination of diasporic cultures brings together such compelling issues as family, gender, race, and minority communities, and is enmeshed with issues of cultural interaction and transformation, transfers, exchanges, race and power relations, and heritage development. This might be seen as a more theorized extension of anthropology's longstanding interest in migration (Cavalli-Sforza and Cavalli-Sforza 1995), albeit imbued with a more critical stance toward correlating assemblages and enclaves with specific groups. Archaeologists have used the language of diaspora to circumvent the heavily ascriptive associations of ethnicity, while still allowing a discussion of community and identity that cross-cuts spatial lines (Goldstein 2000:182). Others have linked archaeological discourse on places and landscapes to some central concerns within diaspora studies, such as migration, displacement, and dislocation (Bender 2001). This has obvious contemporary salience, as well as offering a resonant critique of phenomenological studies of placemaking in the past.

Diasporic studies in archaeology have, in themselves, been highly localized. In the Caribbean, a politicized archaeology is currently being forged through this analytic lens

(Haviser 1999; Sued Badillo 1995; Wilkie and Bartoy 2000). Prior to this emergence, few studies sought to document the nexus between archaeology, transnationalism, and political faction. There is little doubt that diasporic issues articulate with a broader engagement with social theory in the Caribbean countries, and in Cuba this was intimately connected to the 1959 revolution and the predominance of Marxism (Davis 1996). Diasporic sites in the Dominican Republic, Jamaica (Agorsah 1999), Brazil (Funari 1995, 2001, 2004), and the Americas (Weik 1997) have recently been published. However, the archaeology of the African diaspora still remains confined to studies of New World slavery, despite rich variability in African experience outside Africa, whether in Europe, South Asia, and so on. Suffice it to say, archaeologists have lagged behind historians and anthropologists, explained to some degree by a disciplinary reticence toward Islamic history and its role in the modern world (Orser 1996:63).

Utopia

Place can be a powerful social imaginary and the basis for constructing a new society. This is perhaps best seen in the definition of utopia, alternatively interpreted as a "good place" (*eu topos*) and "no place" (*ou topos*). Almost all examples of utopian societies presume that social engineering can be effected through spatial form. The phalansterian landscape of the utopian theorist Charles Fourier, for example, was to consist of a grand communal building set in a picturesque, varied location with distributed work areas that enhanced communal interaction (Hayden 1976). All utopian architecture and landscapes, because of their rigid design, can be both static and authoritarian, as is well described in Orwell's *1984*. The boundaries between utopia and distopia, thus, are not always clear and, depending upon one's political agenda, the one can be seen as the other.

Utopianism has recently been reintroduced into social theory as a means of responding to the disillusionment of postmodernism. Harvey (2000), for example, has argued that we need to recuperate a notion of utopianism that follows through on the Enlightenment project of building a better society. He suggests that we need to adopt a utopianism that is explicitly spatiotemporal, a dialectical utopianism. This is, at its core, a system of translations across and between qualitatively different but related areas of social and ecological life that link the individual, the collective, mediating institutions, and the built environment. Harvey writes: "(t)he chicken-and-egg problem of how to change ourselves through changing our world must be set slowly but persistently in motion... . I, as a political person, can change my politics by changing my positionality and shifting my spatiotemporal horizon (2000:238).

Sarah Tarlow has recently reviewed why archaeologists should study utopian communities. She argues that the study of such communities provides special opportunities for analyzing some of the complexities and contradictions of Western society. In particular, she suggests that it can cause us to question our assumptions of what constitutes a household, settlement or farm and the relationships of social and sexual reproduction. As she puts it, "the legacy of modernity is not wholly to be despised" (2002:319). There are, as yet, few archaeological studies of utopian communities that emphasize space and place. One example is Robert Preucel and Steven Pendery's (2003) study of the utopian landscapes of Brook Farm in West Roxbury, Massachusetts, in the mid nineteenth century. They suggest that the architectural features built during the Transcendentalist phase helped create certain habits of thought and action that actively resisted the complete transition to Fourierism.

The term heterotopia was introduced by Foucault in his book *The Order of Things* (Foucault 1971) and developed in a later lecture originally given in 1967 and published posthumously. For him, heterotopia refers to "a space of illusion that exposes every real space, all the sites inside of which human life is partitioned" (Foucault 1986). Edward Relph (1991:104–105) regards heterotopia as the geography of our times, one that is marked by centerless flows of information and deep social inequalities. As Soja notes, Foucault's heterotopologies are "frustratingly incomplete, inconsistent, incoherent (1996:162)". And yet, he concluded that "they are also marvelous incunabula of another fruitful journey into Thirdspace, into the spaces that difference makes, into the geohistories of otherness." For many postmodern theorists, then, heterotopias are the key loci for social change. Indeed Marc Augé's (1995) "non-places" characteristic of supermodernity can, in fact, be seen as heterotopias. The archaeology of heterotopias would seem to be an especially productive area of research since it must necessarily address places used for the production and representation of the past such as museums, monuments, parks, and archaeological sites.

Globalization

Globalization is one of the most compelling frames for the study of the growing interconnectedness of the contemporary world. Indeed, Featherstone, Lash, and Robertson have gone so far as to characterize it as "the successor to the debates on modernity and postmodernity" and "the central thematic for social theory" (1995:1). Most interpretations of globalization emphasize its economic character as a new transnational force associated with the growth of international trade and the rise of multinational corporations. It can be seen as an extension of World Systems theory whereby the world's variegated economic systems are subsumed into a single all-encompassing economic system (Wallerstein 1974, 1980). This system is itself a product of economic internationalization and the spread of capitalist market relations.

In popular discourse, globalization is sometimes discussed as "Coca-Colonization" and "McDonaldization," with the attendant implications of homogenization and standardization. Giddens has argued that "in a general way, the concept of globalisation is best understood as expressing fundamental aspects of time–space distanciation" (1991:21). Distanciation is defined as the stretching of social systems across time–space. Physical proximity is no longer the sole determinant of interaction as the rate, volume, and scale of communication and transportation increase functional interdependence between places. Globalization thus involves the "interlacing of social events and social relations 'at distance' with local contextualities" (Giddens 1991:22). It is an inherently dialectical phenomenon since events at one scale impact and potentially contradict events at another.

For Robertson (1992), globalization refers to a new consciousness of the growing interdependence between people and places. He regards the global field as consisting of four elements – the self, the national society, the world system of societies, and humankind. The relationships between these elements become highlighted through a process he terms "compression." Compression refers to the bringing together of previously unrelated societies and to the heightened awareness of their differences and similarities. These new perceptions, in turn, lead to relativizations of identity, citizenship, and nationality. He has coined the term "glocalization," borrowed from Japanese business, to refer to the local in the global (Robertson 1995). Homogenization and heterogenization tendencies are thus mutually implicative. Appadurai (1990) takes a more materialist view, emphasizing the global circulation of commodities and ideas. He identifies five dimensions of flow: "ethnoscapes," the interconnections of social affinity groups; "mediascapes," the distribution of the capacity to disseminate information and the mediated images of the world; "technoscapes," the global configuration and flow of technologies; "finanscapes," the shifting global disposition of capital; and "ideoscapes," the global dispersion of political–ideological constructs. These "scapes" are differentially inhabited by individuals, and this leads to parallel imagined worlds. Globalization is thus the reproduction of these different imagined worlds and the unnamed spaces that lie between them.

Archaeologists have engaged with the processes of globalization in two main ways. The first of these is a focus on the modern world system. Robert Schuyler (1970:87) observed that the global presence of Europeans provided a perfect context for the anthropological study of historical contact. The classic studies of globalization are the now numerous accounts of slavery and plantation life (Delle 1998; Delle, Mrozowski, and Paynter 2000). Few archaeologists, however, have sought to develop a theoretical response to a global approach. One exception is Charles Orser (1996), who has recast historical archaeology as the study of the modern, global world. For Orser, a global historical archaeology must confront four "haunts" – colonialism, Eurocentrism, capitalism, and modernity and, in the process, liberate the field. The second engagement is a focus on heritage. Ian Hodder (1999) has analyzed heritage from the perspective of the contradictory processes of homogenization and fragmentation. He regards the idea of universal heritage as exemplified by World Heritage sites as part of the global networked economy that depends upon a dispersed, deregulated, de-unionized process of labor. This lends itself to a "theme-parking" of history and the past. He sees the notion of national and local heritage as a reaction against homogenizing tendencies associated with the dispersal and concealment of power. It is associated with rights, sense of place, ownership, and origins. Hodder (1999:164) observes that in one way or another the globalization process wins out, since "either heritage serves the global economy by fragmenting into pastiche and individual nostalgia or the process of negotiating heritage rights homogenizes and makes same." And yet, the same processes of global networking and flow have the potential to empower individuals and groups.

Conclusions

Place, in its multiple manifestations of landscape, border, utopia, diaspora, and globalization, is serving to establish and extend a productive dialogue across the social sciences. There is a common rejection of the rigid and deterministic views of space that were so influential in positivist spatial science, and a growing appreciation of its dynamic and varigated character. This much is clear. What is less often understood is that these views are themselves products of specific forms of political economy and the outcomes of power relations. This implies that a focus on the processes of globalization and transnationalism is critical not only to understand the present and how we live, but also to understand the categories and imperatives we take for granted in constructing the past. In the end, all views of the global are local, produced from particular sites of power. As Flusty puts it, globalization is "nonsovereign" since it is "constituted by and it constitutes the human and nonhuman actors who stand in or move through concrete places while engaging in production and consumption, transporting, and meaning-making" (2001:144). He continues to say that an understanding of the global is necessarily insufficient until we approach it "from its most intimate basis in localized everyday existence." A social archaeology can contribute to a new understanding of place, one that is contoured by the lived experiences of past and present social actors as they mutually constitute one another through the processes of placemaking.

REFERENCES

Adams, P. C., S. Hoelscher, and K. E. Till (eds.) 2001. *Textures of Place: Exploring Humanist Geographies*. Minneapolis: University of Minnesota Press.

Agnew, J., and J. Duncan (eds.) 1989. *The Power of Place: Bringing Together Geographical and Sociological Imaginations*. London: Unwin Hyman.

Agorsah, E. K. 1996. The archaeology of the African diaspora. *African Archaeological Review* 13: 221–224.

———. 1999. Ethnoarchaeological consideration of social relationship and settlement patterning among Africans in the Caribbean diaspora. In J. B. Hauser (ed.), *African Sites Archaeology in the Caribbean*. Princeton, NJ: Mark Diener, pp. 38–64.

Ammerman, A. J., and L. L. Cavalli-Sforza. 1973. A population model for the diffusion of early farming in Europe. In C. Renfrew (ed.), *The Explanation of Culture Change: Models in Prehistory*. Pittsburgh: University of Pittsburgh Press, pp. 343–357.

Anschuetz, K. F., R. H. Wilshusen, and C. L. Scheick. 2001. An archaeology of landscapes: Perspectives and directions. *Journal of Archaeological Research* 9: 157–211.

Anzaldúa, G. 1987. *Borderlands/La Frontera: The New Mestiza*. San Francisco: Spinsters/Aunt Lute.

Appadurai, A. 1990. Disjunction and difference in the global cultural economy. *Public Culture* 2(2): 1–24.

Ashmore, W., and A. B. Knapp (eds.) 1999. *Archaeologies of Landscape: Contemporary Perspectives*. Oxford: Blackwell.

Augé, M. 1995. *Non-Places: Introduction to an Anthropology of Supermodernity*. London: Verso.

Baker, A. R. H. 1972. *Progress in Historical Geography*. Newton Abbot: David & Charles.

Barkan, E. and M-D. Shelton (eds.) 1998. *Borders, Exiles, Diasporas*. Stanford, CA: Stanford University Press.

Bender, B. (ed.) 1993. *Landscape, Politics and Perspective*. Oxford: Berg.

——— 1998. *Stonehenge: Making Space*. Oxford: Berg.

——— 2001. Landscapes-on-the-move. *Journal of Social Archaeology* 1: 75–89.

Binford, L. R. 1962. Archaeology as anthropology. *American Antiquity* 28: 217–225.

Casey, E. 1996. How to get from space to place in a fairly short stretch of time: A phenomeno-logical prolegomena. In S. Feld and K. Basso (eds.), *Senses of Place*. Santa Fe, NM: School of American Research Press, pp. 13–52.

Cavalli-Sforza, L. L., and F. Cavalli-Sforza. 1995. *The Great Human Diasporas: The History of Diversity and Evolution*. Reading, MA: Addison-Wesley.

Chisholm, M. 1962. *Rural Settlement and Land Use*. London: Hutchinson.

Chorley, R., and P. Haggett (eds.) 1967. *Models in Geography*. London: Methuen.

Church, M. 2002. The grant and the grid: Homestead landscapes in the late nineteenth-century borderlands of southern Colorado. *Journal of Social Archaeology* 2: 220–244.

Clark, D. L. 1977. *Spatial Archaeology*. London: Methuen.

Cliff, A. D., and J. K. Ord. 1973. *Spatial Autocorrelation*. London: Pion.

Clifford, J. 1994: Diasporas. *Cultural Anthropology* 9(3): 302–338.

Connerton, P. 1989. *How Societies Remember*. Cambridge: Cambridge University Press.

Cosgrove, D. 1984. *Social Formation and Symbolic Landscape*. London: Croom Helm.

——, and S. Daniels (eds.) 1988. *The Iconography of Landscape*. Cambridge: Cambridge University Press.

Dainotto, R. M. 2000. *Place in Literature: Regions, Cultures, Communities*. Ithaca, NY: Cornell University Press.

Davis, D. D. 1996. Revolutionary archaeology in Cuba. *Journal of Archaeological Method and Theory* 3: 159–188.

Davis, M. 1990. *City of Quartz: Excavating the Future in Los Angeles*. London: Verso.

Dear, M. 2001. The postmodern turn. In C. Minca (ed.), *Postmodern Geography: Theory and Praxis*. Oxford: Blackwell, pp. 1–34.

Delle, J. A. 1998. *An Archaeology of Social Space: Analyzing Coffee Plantations in Jamaica's Blue Mountains*. New York: Plenum.

——, S. A. Mrozowski, and R. Paynter (eds.) 2000. *Lines That Divide: Historical Archaeologies of Race, Class, and Gender*. Knoxville: University of Tennessee Press.

Donley, L. 1982. House power: Swahili space and symbolic markers. In I. Hodder (ed.), *Symbolic and Structural Archaeology*. Cambridge: Cambridge University Press, pp. 63–73.

Duncan, J. S. 1990. *The City as Text: The Politics of Landscape Interpretation in the Kandyan Kingdom*. Cambridge: Cambridge University Press.

Earle, T. K. 1976. A nearest-neighbor analysis of two formative settlement systems. In K. V. Flannery (ed.), *The Early Mesoamerican Village*. New York: Academic Press, pp. 196–222.

——, and R. W. Preucel, 1986. Processual archaeology and the radical critique. *Current Anthropology* 28: 501–538.

Featherstone, M., S. Lash, and R. Robertson (eds.) 1995. *Global Modernities*. London: Sage.

Feld, S. and K. Basso (eds.) 1996. *Senses of Place*. Santa Fe, NM: School of American Research Press.

Flusty, S. 2001. Adventures of a Barong: A worm's-eye view of global formation. In C. Minca (ed.), *Postmodern Geography: Theory and Praxis*. Oxford: Blackwell, pp. 129–146.

Foucault. M. 1971. *The Order of Things: An Archaeology of the Human Sciences*. New York: Pantheon Books.

——. 1986. Of other spaces. *Diacritics* 16: 22–27.

Fritz, J. M., and F. Plog. 1970. The nature of archaeological explanation. *American Antiquity* 35: 405–412.

Funari, P. P. A. 1995. Mixed features of archaeological theory in Brazil. In P. J. Ucko (ed.), *Theory in Archaeology: A World Perspective*. London: Routledge, pp. 236–250.

—— 2001. Archaeology and slave resistance and rebellion. *World Archaeology* 33: 61–72.

——— 2004. The archaeological study of the African diaspora in Brazil. In T. Falola and A. Ogundiran (eds.), *The Archaeology of Atlantic Africa and the African Diaspora*. Gainesville: University of Rochester Press, forthcoming.

Giddens, A. 1991. *Modernity and Self-Identity*. Oxford: Polity Press.

Gold, J. R. 1980. *An Introduction to Behavioural Geography*. Oxford: Oxford University Press.

Goldstein, P. S. 2000. Communities without borders: The vertical archipelago and diaspora in the southern Andes. In M. A. Canuto and J. Yaeger (eds.), *The Archaeology of Communities: A New World Perspective*. London: Routledge, pp. 182–209.

Gosden, C. 1989. Prehistoric social landscapes of the Arawe Islands, West New Britain Province, Papua New Guinea. *Archaeology in Oceania* 24: 45–58.

Green, S. W., and S. M. Perlman (eds.) 1984. *The Archaeology of Frontiers and Boundaries*. Orlando, FL: Academic Press.

Gregory, D. 1981. Human agency and human geography. *Transactions of the Institute of British Geographers* 6: 1–18.

Gupta, A. and J. Ferguson 1992. Space, Identity, and the Politics of Difference. *Cultural Anthropology* 7: 6–23.

Gupta, A., and J. Ferguson (eds.) 1997. *Culture, Power, Place: Explorations in Critical Anthropology*. Durham, NC: Duke University Press.

Haraway, D. 1988. Situated knowledges: The science question in feminism as a site of discourse in the privilege of partial perspective. *Feminist Studies* 14: 575–600.

Hartshorne, R. 1939. *The Nature of Geography: A Critical Study of Current Thought in Light of the Past*. Lancaster, PA: Association of American Geographers.

Harvey, D. 1969. *Explanation in Geography*. London: Edward Arnold.

——— 1973. *Social Justice and the City*. London: Edward Arnold.

——— 1989. *The Condition of Postmodernity: An Enquiry into the Origins of Cultural Change*. Oxford: Blackwell.

——— 1996. *Justice, Nature and the Geography of Difference*. Oxford: Blackwell.

——— 2000. *Spaces of Hope*. Berkeley: University of California Press.

Haviser, J. B. (ed.) 1999. *African Sites: Archaeology in the Caribbean*. Princeton, NJ: Markus Wiener.

Hayden, D. 1976. *Seven American Utopias: The Architecture of Communitarian Socialism, 1790–1975*. Cambridge, MA: MIT Press.

Hirsch, E., and M. O'Hanlon (eds.) 1995. *The Anthropology of Landscape: Perspectives on Place and Space*. Oxford: Clarendon Press.

Hodder, I. 1972. Locational models and the study of Romano-British settlement. In D. L. Clarke (ed.), *Models in Archaeology*. London: Methuen, pp. 887–909.

——— (ed.) 1982a. *Symbolic and Structural Archaeology*. Cambridge: Cambridge University Press.

——— 1982b. Theoretical archaeology: A reactionary view. In I. Hodder (ed.), *Symbolic and Structural Archaeology*. Cambridge: Cambridge University Press, pp. 1–16.

——— 1987. Converging traditions: The search for symbolic meanings in archaeology and geography. In J. M. Wagstaff (ed.), *Landscape and Culture: Geographical and Archaeological Perspectives*. Oxford: Blackwell, pp. 134–145.

——— 1999. *The Archaeological Process*. Oxford: Blackwell.

———, and C. Orton. 1976. *Spatial Analysis in Archaeology*. Cambridge: Cambridge University Press.

Holmes, W. H. 1914. Areas of American culture characterization tentatively outlined as an aid in the study of antiquities. *American Anthropologist* 16: 413–446.

Jackson, J. B. 1994: *A Sense of Place, A Sense of Time*. New Haven, CT: Yale University Press.

Keith, M., and S. Pile (eds.) 1993. *Place and the Politics of Identity*. London: Routledge.

Kohler, T. A., and S. C. Parker. 1986. Predictive models for archaeological resource location. *Advances in Archaeological Method and Theory* 9: 397–443.

Lefebvre, H. 1991. *The Production of Space*. Trans. D. Nicholson-Smith. Oxford: Blackwell.

Leone, M. P. 1984. Interpreting ideology in historical archaeology: The William Paca Garden in Annapolis, Maryland. In D. Miller and C. Tilley (eds.), *Ideology, Power and Prehistory*. Cambridge: Cambridge University Press, pp. 25–35.

Ley, D. 1982. Rediscovering man's place. *Transactions of the Institute of British Geographers* 7: 248–253.

——, and M. Samuels. 1978. *Humanistic Geography: Prospects and Problems*. London: Maaroufa Press.

Low, S. M. 1996. The social production and social construction of public space. *American Ethnologist* 23(4): 861–879.

Lugo, A. 1997. Reflections on border theory, culture, and the nation. In S. Michaelsen and D. E. Johnson (eds.), *Border Theory: The Limits of Cultural Politics*. Minneapolis: University of Minnesota Press, pp. 43–67.

Malpas J. E. 1999. *Place and Experience: A Philosophical Topography*. Cambridge: Cambridge University Press

Massey, D. 1994. *Space, Place, and Gender*. Minneapolis: University of Minnesota Press.

McDowell, L. 1999. *Gender, Place, and Identity: Understanding Feminist Geographies*. Minneapolis: University of Minnesota Press.

Meskell, L. M. 1999. *Archaeologies of Social Life: Age, Sex, Class et cetera in Ancient Egypt*. Oxford: Blackwell.

Michaelsen, S., and D. E. Johnson (eds.) 1997. *Border Theory: The Limits of Cultural Politics*. Minneapolis: University of Minnesota Press.

Moore, H. L. 1982. The interpretation of spatial patterning in settlement residues. In I. Hodder (ed.), *Symbolic and Structural Archaeology*. Cambridge: Cambridge University Press, pp. 74–79.

Olwig, F., and K. Hastrup, 1997. *Siting Culture: The Shifting Anthropological Object*. London: Routledge.

Orser, C. E., Jr., 1996. *A Historical Archaeology of the Modern World*. New York: Plenum.

Pauketat, T. R., and S. M. Alt. 2003. Mounds, memory, and contested Mississippian history. In R. M. Van Dyke and S. E. Alcock (eds.), *Archaeologies of Memory*. London: Routledge, pp. 151–179.

Peet, R. (ed.) 1977. *Radical Geography*. London: Maaroufa Press.

Preucel, R. W., and S. R. Pendery. 2003. Envisioning utopia: Transcendentalist and Fourierist landscapes at Brook Farm, West Roxbury, Massachusetts. *Historical Archaeology*, forthcoming.

Ratzel, F. 1882–91. *Anthropogeographie*. Stuttgart: Englehorn.

Relph, E. 1991. Post-modern geography. *Canadian Geographer* 35: 98–105.

Roberts, B. 1987. Landscape archaeology. In J. M. Wagstaff (ed.), *Landscape and Culture: Geographical and Archaeological Perspectives*. Oxford: Blackwell, pp. 77–95.

Robertson, R. 1992. *Globalization: Social Theory and Global Culture*. London: Sage.

——1995. Glocalization: Time–space and homogeneity–heterogeneity. In. M. Featherstone, S. Lash, and R. Robertson (eds.), *Global Modernities*. London: Sage, pp. 25–44.

Schama, S. 1995. *Landscape and Memory*. New York: Knopf.

Schuyler, R. L. 1970. Historical archaeology and historic sites archaeology as anthropology: Basic definitions and relationships. *Historical Archaeology* 4: 83–89.

Snead, J., and R. W. Preucel. 1999. The ideology of settlement: Ancestral Keres landscapes in the Northern Rio Grande. In W. Ashmore and A. B. Knapp, *Archaeologies of Landscape: Contemporary Perspectives*. Oxford: Blackwell, pp. 169–197.

Soja, E. W. 1989. *Postmodern Geographies: The Reassertion of Space in Critical Social Theory*. London: Verso.

——1996. *Thirdspace: Journeys to Los Angeles and Other Real-And-Imagined Places*. Oxford: Blackwell.

Sued Badillo, J. 1995. The theme of the Indigenous in the national projects of the Hispanic Caribbean. In P. R. Schmidt and T. C. Patterson (eds.), *Making Alternative Histories: The Practice of Archaeology and History in Non-Western Settings*. Santa Fe, NM: School of American Research Press.

Taçon, P. S. C. 1999. Identifying ancient sacred landscapes in Australia: From physical to social. In W. Ashmore and A. B. Knapp, *Archaeologies of Landscape: Contemporary Perspectives*. Oxford: Blackwell, pp. 33–57.

Tarlow, S. 2002. Excavating utopia: Why archaeologists should study "ideal" communities of the nineteenth century. *International Journal of Historical Archaeology* 6(4): 209–323.

Thomas, K. 1984: *Man and the Natural World: Changing Attitudes in England 1500–1800*. Harmondsworth: Penguin.

Tilley, C. 1994. *A Phenomenology of Landscape: Places, Paths and Monuments*. London: Berg.

Tuan, Y-F. 1974: *Topophilia*. Englewood Cliffs, NJ: Prentice-Hall.

——1977. *Space and Place: The Perspective of Experience*. Minneapolis: University of Minnesota Press.

Vita-Finzi, C., and E. S. Higgs, 1970. Prehistoric economy in the Mount Carmel area of Palestine: Site catchment analysis. *Proceedings of the Prehistoric Society* 36: 1–37.

Wagstaff, J. M. 1987. The new archaeology and geography. In J. M. Wagstaff (ed.), *Landscape and Culture: Geographical and Archaeological Perspectives*. Oxford: Blackwell, pp. 26–36.

Wallerstein, I. 1974: *The Modern World System*, I. New York: Academic Press.

——1980. *The Modern World System*, II. New York: Academic Press.

Watson, P. J., S. A. LeBlanc, and C. L. Redman 1971. *Explanation in Archaeology: An Explicitly Scientific Approach*. New York: Columbia University Press.

Weik, T. 1997. Archaeology of maroon societies in the Americas: Resistance, cultural continuity, and transformation in the African diaspora. *Historical Archaeology* 31: 81–92.

Wilkie, L. A., and K. M. Bartoy. 2000. A critical archaeology revisited. *Current Anthropology* 41: 747–777.

Willey, G. R. 1953. *Prehistoric Settlement Patterns in the Virú Valley, Peru*. Washington, DC: Bureau of American Ethnology, Bulletin 155.

10

Space, Spatiality, and Archaeology

Emma Blake

Space is no longer the sole purview of geography but is a thematic thread linking theoretical discourse across the humanities and social sciences. The growing currency of spatial terms is closely linked to the recognition of space's key role in the processes by which people construct their understandings of the world. This chapter presents an up-to-date account of theories of space in the social sciences, providing a brief introduction to the most topical concepts and recent literature on them, and weighing these themes' salience to archaeologists. In considering directions for further research, it offers a case study for moving beyond the isolated issue of spatiality to a conjoining of multiple themes, here charting the role of place in a diasporic community from the archaeological record.

Common Ground: Early Intersections between Archaeology and Geography

Geography and archaeology draw from a shared corpus of social theory and confront the same task of inferring the ideational from material evidence. The two disciplines have adopted similar theoretical projects: human geographers have highly evolved concepts of the links between spatial form and social process, and archaeologists have effectively theorized the long-term narratives of place through time. Indeed, archaeology is inherently a spatial discipline, its data based on the positioning of objects in space, whether in strata or the co-occurrence of objects at a site or sites in a region. These common interests have not engendered the type of mutually beneficial exchange of ideas that one might hope for, however. While archaeologists have benefited from both theoretical and methodological advances in geography, borrowing ideas and techniques, there has been little cross-pollination, as archaeological scholarship continues to attract limited attention from geographers.[1] This may in part be because geography has traditionally had far greater emancipatory ambitions and a more prescriptive discourse than archaeology, largely as a result of the enormous impact of Marxist political economy on the field of human geography since the early 1970s (see Harvey 1973). Indeed, archaeology on the whole has remained somewhat removed from issues of social injustice, with the subdisciplines of gender and Marxist archaeologies operating far more peripherally than their counterparts in geography. Now, however, a growing minority of archaeologists are arguing for a deeper political engagement (e.g., Gathercole and Lowenthal 1990; Meskell 1998). The first part of this chapter will consider how the most recent theoretical developments of both disciplines cohere. The early inter-sections between geography and archaeology have been documented extensively else-where (Ashmore 2002; Earle and Preucel 1987; Green, Haselgrove, and Spriggs 1978), so what follows is a brief overview only. Of particular interest here is that while the two disciplines have always shared both methodologies and theoretical frameworks, it is ironically with the advent of the "spatial turn" across the social sciences that we see the furthest distancing of archaeology from geography.

The earliest and most sustained links between archaeology and geography have been forged through the former discipline's dependence on physical data. It is standard for archaeological reports to open with a physical description of the land, climate, and geology (e.g., van Dommelen 1998). Data from geography and the earth sciences are drawn on to determine environmental conditions in the past in order to reconstruct past landscapes. There have long been scholars operating at the interstices of both disciplines: paleoeconomists, human ecologists, and the like. Human ecology is trad-itionally treated as a subdiscipline of geography, but this study has been present in the field of archaeology since the 1940s, following the anthropologist Julian Steward's "cultural ecology" (1937), in which the natural environment was seen as structuring human behavior (Coe and Flannery 1967). Even earlier, the French geographer Paul Vidal de la Blache similarly studied the impact of the environment on human land use (1926). For Steward and Vidal de la Blache, the environment was conceptualized as a constraint on human action, though both recognized that while the environment limits the possibilities of human behavior, it does not determine them. Now the discipline's causal questions have been inverted, focusing on the impact of humans on the envir-onment (e.g., Nicholson and O'Connor 2000). Paleoeconomists Eric Higgs and Derek Jarmann (1975) looked at the economic impact of the landscape on early peoples, tying subsistence practices to environmental conditions. The subdiscipline of environmental archaeology is closely tied to physical geography, as it takes into account such themes as topography, geology, climate, vegetation, and soils. Increasingly, specialized environ-mental archaeologists such as paleobotanists, geoarchaeologists, paleomicromorpholo-gists, and zooarchaeologists tackle this research themselves. These subdisciplines' ties with the earth sciences (and life sciences) are strong, but their approach to space has little to do with the emergent spatial theories of their colleagues in the same discipline. Indeed, in general, the fragmented nature of geography and archaeology means that scholars of physical geography or archaeological science have less in common with others in their disciplines working on theories of spatiality and the like than they do with other scientists across disciplines.

Apart from these associations in the scientific subdisciplines, geography and archae-ology have shared similar research agendas and methods. A fundamental step in arch-aeological research is the plotting of the geographic location of sites and finds in a region, a practice it shares with geography. The history of this approach in archaeology goes back to the early days of the so-called "settlement archaeology" in the 1950s, and specifically to Gordon Willey's work. Willey was the first to propagate the idea of moving beyond the isolated settlement as an object of study, to examine instead interconnected settlements across a landscape (Willey 1953). The resulting distribution maps were at first seen as an end in itself, charting demographic change through the shifting placement of sites through time, or serving simply to provide context for a particular site being excavated.

In the 1960s, archaeologists recognized that the spatial patterns observed on the distribution maps could be more than descriptive, serving as the basis for explaining behavior and thereby deriving predictive models. Unique instances were ignored in favor of statistically verifiable universals. This emphasis on explanation was an outgrowth of the earlier ecological and environmental approaches and postwar scientific advances, and a part of a general positivist outlook and a privileging of scientific and quantitative techniques that were evident throughout the social sciences. Lagging behind geography by about a decade, archaeology adopted the methods of spatial analysis of the former discipline in the early 1970s, in efforts to reconstruct past environments and also determine the human impact on the environment. This was the period of greatest apparent convergence of the two disciplines, though already a significant group of geographers had moved on, and were launching a radical critique of these same analytical methods. This slippage was noted even at the time, as was the miscommunication between the two disciplines (see Green and Haselgrove 1978: xiii). Archaeology borrowed much from geography's methodology, from a general emphasis on the analytical value of spatial patterning and the search for non-random distributions to specific techniques such as site-catchment analysis, central place theory, nearest neighbor analysis, spatial modeling, and statistical analysis (see Clarke 1977; Hodder and Orton 1976; Renfrew 1975). Though subjected to postpositivist critiques, and even critiques from other positivists who recognized the problems inherent in quantifying the spatial patterning of human activity without taking into account specific cultural factors (see Taaffe 1974), the abstract models generated by this positivist approach had considerable persuasive power and continue to be used in archaeological analyses. Kent Flannery's important study of the Oaxaca region is a more recent example of the application and refinement of quantitative spatial methods (1986), and the Fish and Kowalewski (1990) volume compiles a number of regional studies incorporating quantitative spatial methods. Interpreting non-random distribution patterns is challenging and has itself generated much scholarship (e.g., Kroll and Price 1991).

If spatial analysis is used with greater reservations nowadays, specific methodological overlaps with geography carry on: recent examples of geographic approaches finding use in archaeology include network analysis and biogeography. Network analysis has been undertaken by archaeologists since the 1960s, as a way of understanding social categories through their relations with other categories, individuals, and institutions, in short, by mapping their networks of interaction between proximal points (see Broodbank 2000; Wobst 1974). Likewise, the archaeologist Mark Patton (1996) has applied theories from biogeography to explain the cultural manifestations of islands in the Mediterranean, replacing the term biogeography with "sociogeography." Island biogeographers focus on the biological variability of insular environments, the classic study being MacArthur and Wilson (1967). Patton seeks to explain the cultural variability of islands, focusing specifically on the monumentality of certain Mediterranean islands as examples of the wayward development of isolated island communities. This approach is useful in explaining the initial human colonization of islands based on geographic factors of size, distance from other landforms, and range of available resources (see Cherry 1984). However, it is less helpful once insular populations are established and cultural factors come to the fore, as the environmental factors always underdetermine the specificities of the insular cultures.

As a tool for handling spatial data, Geographical Information Systems (GIS) technology has found adherents in both disciplines. At first glance GIS technology may seem merely a refinement in technique rather than a theoretical innovation. However, a growing body of scholarship proposes that GIS research offers more than mere descriptive information, but opens up a space for more developed theorizing of spatiality (e.g., Aldenderfer and Maschner 1996; Lock and Stancic 1995; Zubrow 1994). As proponents of the method write: "GIS is not, under such circumstances, to be considered as an objective observer of patterns implicit within spatial data; rather, it is a tool to create spatial relationships according to values we regard as important" (Gaffney, Stancic, and Watson 1995: 213). This ambitious agenda for GIS is similar to earlier claims for spatial analysis and distribution maps, and points to the recurring interest in translating static spatial data into social dynamics. However, though the methodology is transdisciplinary, publications going beyond the level of instructions to consider theoretical implications and impact of GIS tend to remain discipline-specific, whether the field is meteorology, geology, archaeology, or geography.

Postmodernism and the "Spatial Turn"

While geography and archaeology have reached a degree of consensus on quantitative and scientific approaches to space, in the extrapolation of social behavior from the spatial record (past and present) the links are limited to a particular set of themes. Some aspects of spatial theory in geography remain unexplored by archaeologists. This is surprising, given the impact of the "spatial turn" on both disciplines. This spatial turn is a feature of the advent of postmodernism in the academy, characterized by a general crisis of representation and a shift in focus to questions of the experiential, constructivism, and subjectivity. Geography's critique of positivism in its own field began in the 1970s, slightly earlier than in archaeology, and, as mentioned above, emerged just as archaeology itself was adopting geography's positivist analytical models (see Green and Haselgrove 1978). It was marked by the emergence of the subdiscipline of humanistic geography, which emphasized the impact of place on human experience, power, and knowledge (see Ley and Samuels 1978; Tuan 1976). When archaeologists began exploring postmodernist ideas in the early 1980s, the two disciplines separately drew from a common well of social theory when confronting these issues, rather than engaging in a direct dialogue. Thus, humanistic geographers discovered the phenomenology of Edmund Husserl, and adopted the concept of Heidegger's lifeworld, apparently independently of archaeology's own foray into studies of cosmology and phenomenology (cf. Seamon and Mugerauer 1985 and Thomas 1996).

Much like postprocessual archaeology, humanistic geography, following greater theoretical specialization and the maturation of social theory, has fragmented to the degree that few geographers would label themselves as "humanistic" now, styling themselves instead as cultural or social geographers (Adams, Hoelscher, and Till 2001: xvi). Nevertheless, humanistic geography and its heirs have been at the forefront of social theory's current privileging of the spatial dimension over the temporal, contributing significantly to discourses on globalism and localism, identity politics, and postcolonialism. The recognition of space as a generative force is at the heart of the movement that has come to be known as the "spatial turn," originating with the writing of Henri Lefebvre and Michel Foucault in the late 1960s and early 1970s (Foucault 1986; Lefebvre 1991 [1974]). If the movement has proved less radical than was originally intended, it has nevertheless had a significant influence, conditioning scholars to recognize the importance of space in shaping social processes, identities and actions. The present generation of social geographers has been theorizing this revitalized notion of space for several decades: see Agnew and Duncan (1989); Barnes and Gregory (1998); Blake (2002); Duncan and Ley (1993); Massey (1985); Pred (1986); Soja (1989, 2000). Michel Foucault (1980:149) wrote: "A whole history remains to be written of spaces – which would at the same time be the history of powers (both of these terms in the plural) – from the great strategies of geopolitics to the little tactics of the habitat." Here he would seem to be speaking to archaeologists as much as to historians and geographers. However, archaeology has hardly risen to the call: it has generally lagged behind somewhat in entering these debates, and has been extremely selective in its choice of spatial subjects. Archaeology's own "spatial turn" is evident in burgeoning studies on landscape, monumentality, the life histories of ancient places, and space and power. The remainder of this section considers archaeology's spatial turn, and then some of the themes as yet unexplored by archaeology.

Out of this "spatial turn" has come the realization that space, as much as portable artifacts, can feature in identity formation and expression. An entire issue of the *Journal of Social Archaeology* (2002) was devoted to the topic of spatial theory, demonstrating just how important space has become. Indeed, it may be the most powerful evidence we can obtain of social groupings and identities, as territory may be said to define people. However, the relationship between territory and identity is rarely straightforward, as is discussed further below. The manipulation of space is nevertheless a key strategy in self-definition, as archaeologists are increasingly recognizing. Lisa Kealhofer's (1999) work on seventeenth-century Virginia landscapes is an example of such a study, in which she considered how different facets of identity may be played out at nested spatial scales. She observed the way in which early immigrants from Britain sought to carve out new identities both at the individual and community levels, and the active role that landscapes played in this process. Kealhofer correlates scales of identity (individual, family, community, region) with scales of space (house, garden, field systems, region), highlighting the temporal dimension of each of these spatial scales. The differential rates of change of these spaces can lead to apparent disjunctures between them, dividing constructed from conceived landscapes. The settlers may have conceived of their landscape in a particular way, but it took time to alter it to fit that vision (1999: 58–60). Thus, a garden could be designed quickly, and serve as a more immediate expression of a changed mindset, whereas regional patterns will take far longer to emerge, and thus may be delayed manifestations of social transformations.

Other key concepts to have found crossdisciplinary currency are "place" and "locale." A strict definition of place may be given as "the spot in which something is located," while "'space' refers to the physical reality of where things are not located" (Orser 1996: 136). But the concept of place goes way beyond that, to encompass all social and physical surroundings, natural and constructed space. The use of the term opens up the possibility of focused work rather than abstract, decontextualized spatial analyses. A human element is implicit in the very idea of "place," of the conscious demarcation of space. World views emerge from, and are embedded in, the always-situated practices. This leads to a revalorization of space, not as an inert backdrop, but as an active component of human activities and lifeworlds. The sociologist Anthony Giddens's definition of the term "locale" as the "setting for social action...making it "essential to specifying [an action's] contextuality" highlights this shift in approach (1985: 271). Examples of work being done in this vein include the general study of the relationships between community, locality, and identity-making in the anthropologist Nadia Lovell's (1998) volume; or the historian Lisa Tolbert's *Constructing Townscapes* (1999), in which she examined the role of town layout and sense of place in shaping small-town ideology and social identities. The emotive qualities of place make it a dangerous concept as well. The characterization of a place may be negative, as when working-class urban neighborhoods have been labeled "slums" with their connotation of crime, filth, and unhappiness. This denigration of place affects the inhabitants of that place's self-identity, and may lead to conditions of resistance or resignation. Mayne and Murray's recent volume focuses on just this issue, as they attempt to move beyond the slum narrative of the past to present more accurate "ethnographies of place" for these economically marginal zones (Mayne and Murray 2001). The spatial component of power is a theme running through many of these studies, and has been addressed directly by some scholars. Historical archaeologists in particular have studied the links between power relations and space, and the ways in which ideology can be hidden or dissembled spatially, just as social relations can be obscured or reified spatially (Leone 1984; Orser 1996:131–58).

It is the study of landscape that has provided the two disciplines with their most significant recent point of contact. Archaeologists exploring new ways of conceptualizing landscape and problematizing environmental determinism and functionalist explanations looked to geographical writings. These new approaches to landscape emphasized its symbolic value, that is, its role as a signifying system. A landmark work in this regard has been Barrett, Bradley, and Green's 1991 volume, *Landscape, Monuments and Society: The Prehistory of Cranborne Chase*, in which the three authors conducted a regional study of the modifications made to the land in a particular part of southern England from the Neolithic through the Iron Age, demonstrating that these alterations were inextricable from corresponding social developments. John Barrett's subsequent work on the construction of the subject through the spaces in which they move explicitly spatializes the structured conditions posited by agency theorists (Barrett 1994). The steady spate of publications on landscape in archaeology demonstrate the continued salience of this topic (see Ashmore and Knapp 1999; Bender 1993).

The Annaliste perspective, a model developed by the historian Fernand Braudel (1972 [1949]), has been taken up in certain branches of archaeology, primarily in studies in the Mediterranean (Barker 1995; Bintliff 1991; Knapp 1992). The Annales approach offers an explanatory mechanism for integrating causative factors operating at different temporal scales, including the long-term ecological scale. The Annaliste perspective provides a more nuanced approach to the environment's impact, distinguishing between the conditions of the natural environment and human perception of those conditions. It has proved particularly useful in regional studies and in interpreting survey data, by providing greater temporal control of spatial variables.

Not all archaeological approaches to space operate at the scale of landscapes or regions. The microscale study of space, particularly built space, is central to the archaeological project. Theories of architecture and built space aid in understanding the social impact and function of monumentality and buildings in the past. As the purposeful characterization of a space, architecture shapes human practices and contributes to one's perceptions of self in relation to the world. Of course, the social impact of architecture is not a new discovery: architectural historians, folklore scholars, and anthropologists have long been attuned to its significance (see Glassie 1975; Rapoport 1969, 1982). More recently, Daphne Spain's *Gendered Spaces* combines the fields of sociology and planning to demonstrate how space configures gender relations (1992). In the late 1980s and early 1990s, archaeologists focused particular attention on interior space and society (see Kus and Raharijaona 1990; Lane 1994; Parker Pearson and Richards 1994; Sampson 1991; Wallace Hadrill 1988). Though in most cases archaeologists and architectural historians have worked in isolation, Susan Kent's 1990 edited volume, *Domestic Architecture and the Use of Space: An Interdisciplinary Cross-Cultural Study*, is a notable exception, containing contributions from archaeologists, ethnographers, and architects. In Kent's volume the contributors focus on the cultural significance of the built environment, examining such topics as the links between cosmology and house form, and the gendered division of activity areas.

In Europe, the experiential aspect of architecture has been of particular interest to prehistorians investigating the meanings of megalithic monuments. These studies blend theories of architecture and landscape much as the monuments themselves are both built spaces and features of the landscape. Phenomenological theory in archaeology, explored most fully in studies of the British and northern European Neolithic (Bradley 1996, 1998; Richards 1993; Thomas 1993, 1996; Tilley 1994, 1996), has brought archaeologists much further toward accepting the social impact of space, and in recognizing that routinized practices occurring in space are a form of cultural conditioning. In the absence of durable meaning attributable to these monuments, phenomenology constitutes a way of getting at how the monuments were "lived through." According to Julian Thomas, the routinized experience of living with the monuments would have enabled human beings to be constituted as subjects (1993). However, the danger of phenomenological approaches to space and monuments lies in their tendency to universalize the way humans experience, treating experience as a precultural process onto which contingently derived meanings are pasted. More carefully theorized treatments of monumentality in mortuary contexts are found in Silverman and Small's recent volume (2002).

Cities and Urban Space

Geography is not the only field to which archaeology is beholden for spatial theory: the burgeoning field of urban planning embodies a similar fusion of the spatial and the social. Some of the best and earliest work linking space and society was done in the field of urban studies or urban sociology. The field of urban studies looks at the processes by which the particular spatial configurations of a city came about, and the social repercussions of those spaces. Since the nineteenth century scholars have observed the benefits and ills of urban life, theorizing the condition of large, dense, nucleated populations. Ferdinand Toennies and Emile Durkheim contrasted the earlier preindustrial social networks, based on kinship that extended to shared space, with new industrial-era bonds based on shared occupations and economic status. These new industrial communities were always forged in an urban setting. Reformers deplored the degradations wrought by the industrial system, as played out in urban society. The Chicago School of Urban Sociology put urban studies on the map. Through their studies of Chicago itself, the scholars, adopting a reformist perspective, identified the causes of urban ills in spatial terms, noting such concrete factors as cramped and unsanitary housing and lack of public space (Thomas 1983). After dominating the field for many decades, the Chicago School came under critique for overlooking underlying causes for these conditions in the forms of the inequities of the capitalist system. Their perception of the city as an organic structure downplayed specific cultural factors, social interests, and negotiations (Bulmer 1984). There are ongoing debates over whether cities really do engender social distancing among their occupants, that is, whether or not city life inevitably entails a loss of community. Some scholars critique the whole debate, noting that these discussions apply only to Western industrial urban processes, with little bearing on the circumstances of the cities of developing nations, where community ties continue much as before (Abu-Lughod and Hay 1979). Indeed, few archaeologists have incorporated the concerns of the modern-day city into their understandings of premodern ones, presuming the same sorts of community ties evident today in the cities of developing nations.

If the nexus of early urban studies was Chicago, the focus has now shifted to Los Angeles as the quintessential postmodern metropolis. The latter half of the twentieth century saw the growth of vast amorphous metropolitan regions with no clear center. The corresponding rise of suburbs and exurbs is tied to the introduction of the automobile and, with it, the possibility of further distancing of residence from workplace. To confront these complex new arrangements, factor analysis became the predominant spatial tool, of geographers measuring multiple variables to analyze the spatial configuration of cities, beginning with Bell and Shevsky's influential work of the mid-1950s (Bell 1955). The new urban conditions generated not just a new set of methods but new theoretical frameworks as well. In the 1970s, a group of Marxist-inspired scholars, led by David Harvey and Manuel Castells, critiqued the organic system-based approach to urban structures, emphasizing instead the political and economic relations underlying the condition of urban areas. This political economy approach has helped to explain otherwise anomalous occurrences, emphasizing conflicts behind the urban structure, and advocating change in the economic systems that produce these spatial conditions. The result was a reconceptualization of the city as a locus for social movements and contestations. As Castells argued, "there is no theory of space that is not an integral part of a general social theory" (1977:115).

Of the variables shaping the urban structure, social rank, gender, and ethnicity recur as the three critical vectors of social and spatial difference. While class had been the primary variable, analysts came to recognize the importance of the latter two dimensions in shaping distributions of people. For example, in the distribution of populations across a city, racial segregation was often a stronger pattern than segregation by income bracket. Indeed, the real effects of the spatial configurations are particularly evident in the case of racial segregation, where the lack of interaction between racial groups serves to perpetuate social distancing. These studies may be inverted to a focus on the identity politics of the city. *Contra* initial claims that the city was the source of the decline of community, studies have shown that one cannot simply program in variables of size and population density to determine the propensity for community. As Janet Abu-Lughod argued, cultural values shape the effects of ecological variables on spatial and social structures (1961, 1969).

The experiential and poetic aspects of urban life have followed a different trajectory, as seen in Michel de Certeau's work on the city (1984). His identification of "pedestrian speech acts" in the manner in which one moves through urban space owes much to Baudelaire's *flâneur* and Walter Benjamin's writings (1983: 97). The dystopian vision of the city of films such as *Blade Runner* is conceived as prophetic in the popular imaginary, tapping into the feared alienation and facelessness of the city-dweller. The work of Jean Baudrillard (1994) likewise has been influential in understanding, or better, conceiving, the excesses of post-industrial space and society, drawing attention to imagined and virtual places. Simulacra, hyperreality, imagined places, and placelessness are generally explored in an urban context (Eco 1986). Because of the distinctly contemporary, even prescient character of these works, however, archaeologists have found little use for them in describing the premodern past.

Thus, in spite of this dynamism of urban studies, archaeology's contribution to, or adoption of, these topics has been limited, undoubtedly because today's city seems so radically different from those of the distant past. A further practical reason for this is that archaeology in cities is usually contract work rather than academic research, so the archaeologists do not have the luxury of theorizing (Mayne and Murray 2001: 2). The archaeological concern with urbanism has been one primarily of teleology and closely linked to tracing the path of social complexity: how, when, and why cities formed. The result has been an emphasis on the *functions* of cities, treating them as a coherent system akin to the Chicago School's early approaches. Newer approaches to urbanism have had relatively little impact. Indeed, some of the most innovative scholars of urbanism, notably Jane Jacobs (1969) and more recently Ed Soja (2000), have drawn on archaeology for precisely this sort of data, in order to trace the origins of the first cities. There is much room here for a re-evaluation of cities in the past. The architectural historian Diane Favro (1996) provides a refreshing exception to the dearth of theoretically informed literature on the ancient city. Historical archaeologists have been studying cityscapes for some time now, notably in New York City and Los Angeles (Cantwell and Wall 2001; Greenwood 1996; Rothschild 1990). However, there has been little attempt to engage with the theories of urban studies discussed above. The Cantwell and Wall volume is typical in its emphasis on the one-way impact of social factors on the structuring of urban space, and the authors go to great lengths to assert that urban sites are like any other archaeological sites, and that the research questions and methods are the same (2001:190). While this insistence that what they are doing is no different from the work of other archaeologists serves as a justifiable claim to disciplinary relevance, it closes off avenues for uniquely urban analyses, such as the transformation from industrial to post-industrial metropolis, the urban as a site of Appadurai's transnational flows, and so on. Dell Upton's work is an exception to this undertheorizing. Upton evaluates the notion of the city as a unitary "artifact," teasing out both the strengths and problems with this label. It has an obvious heuristic appeal and it confirms our common-sense notion of a city as an entity. However, drawing together the fragmented piecemeal elements that constitute a city into a single coherent whole might be an oversimplification. In the framework of a city, how does the archaeologist distinguish the causative influences of intentionality or accident? Are the built features the by-products of collective action or individual agency? At the smaller scale of portable objects or single-period sites, these questions are taken for granted, while the multivalent spaces of the city demand more theorizing, at the same time offering great opportunities for interpretation (Upton 1992).

Borderlands

Along with cities, national boundaries have become focal points for research in the social sciences, offering the possibility to study the interactions of nested identities in the form of local border communities that overlie larger political groupings. Border cultures would seem, at first glance, a product of the modern emergence of the nation-state. The historical specificity of nationalism, famously explored by Anderson (1983), entails a notion of cultures contained within unitary territories. The messiness of border zones undercuts the naturalism of nations, and can thus be a threat to their integrity. Border zones, as interstices, serve as laboratories for observing the conflicts between varying identities, and have been studied by anthropologists for that reason (Donnan and Wilson 1999: 33). More and more, scholars are coming around to the idea that borders, far from exceptional spaces, are representative of the ways in which identities are constructed as hybrid, in the absence of any true "core" territory or culture. Though these studies have burgeoned recently, they predate the spatial turn. The activities in border zones tend to undermine the traditional understandings of territorial behavior. Of course, there have been exceptions to the standard relationships of people to territory, a fact that was observed before there were theoretical models for explaining it. Thus the anthropologist Fredrik Barth, writing in 1961, observed Persian nomadic communities and described them as having no sense of territory or concept of boundaries (1961:5). Barth's later, evocative description of tribal grazing rights is worth quoting in its entirety:

> these grazing rights were conceptualized not as bounded territories, but as migration schedules, called *il-rah*, i.e., tribal roads. Each such "road" was composed of rights of pasture and of passage during particular time periods. I have compared these rights to a train schedule: a train does not have rights to railway lines and stations, but the "right" to be at certain points at certain times (2000: 19).

We need to be aware of these sorts of approaches to space that differ so much from our own culture's territorial possessiveness. More recently, in Casimir and Rao's (1991)

volume, the contributors offer a wide range of case studies that contradict the normative accounts of territorial behavior. Interestingly, all of the contributors are anthropologists rather than geographers.

Mary Louise Pratt's work on contact zones has expanded the concepts of border
beyond the linear boundary separating groups and the adjacent skirt of borderlands.
These contact zones, as arenas of encounter and collision, replace the linearity of
the border with the image of a liminal mosaic (1992). Indeed, the term "border" has
come to signify any literal or figurative contact zone between groups, and for some
this dilution of its original geopolitical sense is regrettable (Donnan and Wilson 1999:
33–40). The complexities inherent in border cultures have found poetic expression in
numerous works, perhaps most notably Gloria Anzaldúa's *Borderlands/La Frontera: The
New Mestiza* (1987). While borders resonate in current social theorizing, they remain
under-explored in archaeology.

Globalism, Localism, and Mobility

The discussions of border zones play out against a broader backdrop of globalism and
its ramifications. The call for an increased emphasis on the spatial, at borders and
elsewhere, comes just as the bounded, grounded given of the space of cultures is being
challenged. No longer is it possible to locate culture in terms of a single territory.
Cultures are not tidy, autonomous units: they are always relational, forged through
interaction. Mobility is the norm, and diaspora and displacement challenge our standard conceptions of ethnicity and cultural identity. Markets, social networks, cultural
frameworks, political structures, and people are increasingly spread across the planet,
disrupting the integrity of local spaces and societies in a trajectory of uneven development that results from the global capitalist economy. These social transformations are
inherently spatial. This movement of people and goods is, of course, nothing new, as
archaeologists can attest, but what has changed is its breadth and intensity. The structural inequalities characterizing this globalization mean that though it may offer opportunities to new groups, on the whole the experience is a challenge to our
conceptualizations of self and other, as boundaries and identities are rewritten on lines
other than territory and nationhood. But as geographers have also noted, this era of
globalism does not result in the loss of place, but rather in a revision of its role.

While this phenomenon is unique to the contemporary moment, those studying the
past can benefit from an awareness of the implications of these movements. One may
take as an example the ambivalence of migration, both in terms of its causes and its
effects. The particular features of modern-day migration may be without precedent, but
the phenomenon of the movement of peoples is not. Mobility is a feature of the
human condition. Indeed, rather than ask, why did people move, one may ask, why did
people stay put in some cases? Is this fixity self-imposed, or are we observing the
restriction of subaltern groups from the *freedom* of displacement? Sedentism may be
appreciated anew as a choice. James Clifford, in the prologue to his book *Routes*,
observes that not traveling "may be a form of resistance, not limitation, a particular
worldliness rather than a narrow localism" (Clifford 1997: 5). Likewise, the impact of
population movements cannot be simply characterized by the benign exchange

of knowledge and diffusion of new technologies on the one hand, or by violent invasions on the other, but involves more complex costs and benefits in terms of economic stability and identity politics. Cultural contact may not itself be the most significant outcome of movement: that is to say, the impact of moving between cultures or nations may be less great than a shift from rural to urban within a culture. More recently, the term "glocalization" has emerged to reconcile the global/local binary and account for the ways in which these scales are nested inextricably. As Soja writes:

> In rethinking localization, for example, it is recognized that we always act (and think) locally, but our actions and thoughts are also simultaneously urban, regional, national, and global in scope, affecting and being affected by, if often only in the smallest way, the entire hierarchy of spatial scales in which our lives are embedded. Similarly, rethinking globalization leads to the recognition that it is not a process that operates exclusively at a planetary scale, but is constantly being localized in various ways and with different intensities at every scale of human life, from the human body to the planet. (2000: 199–200)

Work on glocalization is not widespread, and is primarily done by political economists studying regionalist organizations, whether supranational associations with economic agendas such as the EU or subnational zones that have closer links to regions outside of their nations than to regions within, such as northern Italy. Homi Bhabha approaches globalism through culture, looking at what he sees as the unsettling "attenuation of 'local' space" of "cultural globality" (1994: 216). He recognizes the "anxiety of enjoining the global and local" (ibid.), a project that can only be accomplished in the interstices of culture. "It is, ironically, the disintegrative moment, even movement, of enunciation – that makes possible the rendering of culture's global reach" (ibid.: 217). The literature on globalization encourages a rethinking of archaeologists' core-periphery models and even a reconsideration of the spatialized practice of archaeology itself, marked as it is by the ongoing punctuated encounters with communities where we repeatedly conduct fieldwork for a season and then leave.

Consumption and Tourism

Today's rootless and agonistic perception of identity has propelled consumption and the spaces in which it occurs to a new level of social importance. Indeed, consumption has become a central topic in geographic studies, as it has elsewhere in the social sciences. Consumption was formerly treated solely by economists as a function of demand and income of the consumer, with little interest in motivations behind consumer choice. Daniel Miller's 1995 edited volume, *Acknowledging Consumption*, demonstrated chapter by chapter the impact of consumption on a broad selection of disciplines, including sociology, history, anthropology, psychology, and geography. The spaces of consumption have been of great scholarly interest in geography. Studies of shopping malls, amusement parks, even the gentrification of neighborhoods, abound, blending geography, cultural studies, and anthropology (e.g., Gibian 1997; Goss 1993; Zukin 1991). This blurring of disciplinary boundaries is evident in neighborhood studies. Seemingly the purview of urban studies, these are also a subject for consumer studies in which the residences are treated as objects of consumption (Jackson and Thrift 1995: 209). Likewise, the sites of performances and events such as world's fairs and expositions, as Walter Benjamin first observed (1983), fall under the rubric of sites of consumption, in the form of experience.

While many of these studies are positing a recent shift in sensibility that is part of the larger patterns associated with postmodernism, post-Fordism, late capitalism, or glocalization, and therefore perhaps of limited applicability to the spaces of consumption in the past, the approaches taken contribute to a more refined approach to the spatial analyses of artifacts and their life histories, and have immediate implications for studies of the design of identities. Studies of feasting in the past, for example, a burgeoning topic in archaeology (see Dietler and Hayden 2001), offer a possibility of retheorizing the sites of commensal activities, from the forecourts of megalithic monuments to medieval great halls, as spaces of consumption. While it is true that individuals in modern industrial societies have the ability to design an identity from consumption practices to a degree that is utterly unprecedented, this link between consumption and social relations, even of power, is hardly new and can certainly be teased out further.

Place and the practice of consumption fuse in tourism, which may be conceived as the consumption of explicitly spatialized experience. Urry has written on the pleasure afforded the tourist, the novelty of the objects under the tourist's gaze, in short, the objectification of those sites/sights for tourist consumption. Urry further spatializes the practice of tourism by emphasizing the importance of the journey itself in delimiting the tourist experience as something original (1990: 119). A goal of the tourist is the search for authenticity. But as soon as the residents of the destination recognize the tourists' agenda, they self-consciously maintain or even fabricate the previously unconscious authentic traditions (MacCannell 1976). This has had an impact on the practice of archaeology and the politics of heritage (Lowenthal 1996). Though the explosion of tourism is a distinct feature of modernity, it has been practiced since antiquity, and therefore is yet another theme to which archaeological inquiry may be profitably directed. A premodern variant on tourism may be pilgrimage, where the authenticity of the destination is critically important, and the journey itself is a central component of the experience, serving as *payment* for the consumption of the pilgrimage site itself. If the link between pilgrimage in the past and the modern-day tourist's quest for authenticity and the consumption of places seems tenuous, consider the fictional Pardoner's business of selling fake religious relics to pilgrims in Chaucer's *Canterbury Tales*, written in the fourteenth century AD. Nevertheless, archaeological approaches to pilgrimage have been reluctant to engage with this literature of tourism and the consumption of place (see Bauer and Stanish 2001; Coleman and Elsner 1995; Graham-Campbell 1994).

Community is another theme that is linked to the expanding discourse on space, that has been the subject of renewed focus in the humanities and social sciences. Traditionally in archaeology, "community" has meant a spatially bounded group, a mappable base unit of social organization, structured around proximate affiliations. In such a perspective, the space of community is taken for granted as a unifying backdrop, either by design or accident. To this definition of community one may add more recent conceptualizations of the term that stress feelings of belonging or common interests over territory. A growing literature has explored myriad communities that cannot be mapped onto a single space: diasporae, cyber communities, gay and lesbian groups, and so on. In this area anthropology has stepped to the fore: ethnographic studies of traditional, small-scale nucleated settlements have problematized many of our basic assumptions, showing, for example, that their boundaries are often porous, and that public places such as plazas or monuments may be seen in very different ways by factions within the community (see Cohen 1999; Just 2000; Low 2000). These places are subject to appropriation by interest groups and may breed internal fragmentation as much as cohesion. The meanings of communal places are negotiated, contested, ignored. There is nothing inevitable, then, about the associations between a people and their immediate locality. In archaeology these themes are being picked up just recently, inter-estingly often without direct reference to the growing literature on spatiality (see Lewis and Stout 1998; but see Canuto and Yaeger 2000 for more explicit theoretical discussion).

Recent work seeks to fuse these two intellectual trends, dissolving the seeming para-dox of this slippage between community and place on the one hand, and the heightened emphasis on space on the other. Diaspora studies have proven to be a fertile ground for thinking critically about the links between space and community (see Lilley, chapter 13, this volume). Safran defines diasporas as "expatriot [sic] minority communities" that are spread out in several places other than their original homeland but who maintain emo-tional ties to their origins, and define themselves through both their roots and their current location. He suggests that the homeland always holds the possibility of return (1991: 83–4). For the prehistoric archaeologist, Safran's definition poses some difficul-ties, because the emotive links with the homeland, the dream of return, cannot be directly confirmed materially. However, if one observes a lack of material integration into an adopted culture over a long period of time, it may be appropriate to surmise that the ties to the homeland remained strong (see Clifford 1997: 250).

These extended links mean that the concept "diaspora," by definition, cannot be understood through the normative perception of grounded identities. This is not a mere academic issue. The claims to authenticity of diasporic identities challenge more traditional indigenous and nation-based claims (ibid.: 249). Diaspora communities are forged through fusion and hybridity and have a very different relationship to space than local communities. It is not that diaspora communities are somehow extra-local, it is rather that their identities at once incorporate immediate surroundings and networks extending across space. What is particularly exciting is that this spatial fragmentation, the condition of transnationalism, may serve as a prism of critique, opposing the outdated rootedness of nation-states with their exclusivity and calls to tradition. Dias-pora communities have their own take on tradition: "Identifications not identities, acts of relationship rather than pregiven forms: this *tradition* is a network of partially con-nected histories, a persistently displaced and reinvented time/space of crossings" (ibid.: 268). Such communities are not simply products of modernity but can also be identi-fied in the past.

Case Study: Place and Community in a Phoenician Colony

So how does an archaeologist take on board these innovative approaches to space? In other words, how can contemporary notions of spatiality inform our understanding of past spaces? What follows is an example of how one may approach spatial evidence from a new angle, taking into account the complexities but also the rich potentialities of these alternate approaches. Picking up specifically on the links between place and community, this study of the Phoenician colony of Motya considers the multivalent roles of space(s), and the entanglement of locality and distance in this community.

The site of Motya, just off the coast of western Sicily, would seem at first glance to provide a textbook example of a spatially self-contained community. Occupying the entirety of a small island, Motya's immediate boundaries are clearly defined, and as a social group Motya's population of Phoenician traders shared a common origin and common purpose, the hallmarks of a stable community. Yet on closer examination it is evident that there is no consistent isomorphic relationship between community and locality at Motya. The founding community was forged not through this shared place, but through a common purpose and ties to the homeland. Subsequently, the community transformed itself into an imperial outpost. These changes are visible in the spatial transformations of the town over time, but rather than merely reflecting these broader political and social changes, the timing of the spatial changes points to the latter having an active role in the community transformations.

Motya was the largest and most important of the three primary Phoenician settlements on Sicily, reaching close to an estimated 16,000 inhabitants by the sixth century BC. With a foundation date toward the end of the eighth century BC, Motya constituted one node of Phoenicia's overseas commercial and shipping network, headed by the city of Tyre (Phoenicia itself corresponds roughly to modern-day Lebanon). At about the same time as the Greek colonization of the Mediterranean, Phoenicians established permanent outposts for trade and interaction in southern Iberia, North Africa, Sardinia, Malta, Cyprus, and Sicily, in a sustained project of displacement that constituted a diaspora. The Phoenicians are known to have traded in a wide variety of items, most notably, the famous purple-dyed textiles, metalworking, ivory, and faience (see Aubet 1997). The traditional account of the site's history maintains that over the course of the sixth century BC Motya progressively fell under the control of the largest Phoenician colony, Carthage, and was transformed from a node in the Phoenician diaspora to a part of the Carthaginian Empire, as a step in the absorption of all of western Sicily under Carthaginian control. In a seemingly neat manner, the spatial changes in the town in the sixth century are seen as reflections of these political shifts. However, this account of Motya's history has been called into question of late. Peter van Dommelen has weighed the evidence, both textual and archaeological, for this story of Carthaginian imperialism and convincingly argued that the Phoenician colonies in the west remained independent until as late as the end of fifth century in some areas. The evidence for this is particularly strong in Sicily. As independent support for this claim, at the indigenous sites of Monte Polizzo and Monte Adranone in western Sicily, which should have been saturated with Carthaginian goods by the sixth century, it is not until the fourth century that Carthaginian influence is visible in the material record (Holloway 1991: 156; Morris et al. 2003). This new chronology has important implications for understanding the spatial transformations at Motya.

Enough of Motya has been excavated over the last century to give us some picture of this cosmopolitan and mobile community during more than 300 years of continuous occupation. At the start, Motya's ties were with her homeland, Tyre, and this is evident spatially, in the insular siting of the town itself. The placement of Motya on a small coastal island is traditionally seen in functionalist terms, as a result of Phoenician strategy, one that was repeated in the Spanish sites of Gadir and Cerro del Villar (Aubet 1997: 200; Bondì 1988: 248). In light of evidence that the Phoenicians had frequented the western Mediterranean in the precolonial period (though see van Dommelen 1998: 71–3), we can surmise that they knew the area well and chose carefully before settling there. The standard explanation for Motya's insular location is that the Phoenicians wanted a quick getaway if trouble arose with the native peoples on the mainland. But with a limited food supply on the island, and given the short distance to shore, this explanation is unconvincing. Their precarious position would have made Motya's inhabitants *dependent* on good relations with the mainland. That the island was without defensive walls for the first hundred years is further evidence that attacks were not foremost on Motyans' minds. Therefore the choice of the insular setting cannot be explained in solely functionalist terms. More telling is that the home city of Tyre herself is also on a small island just offshore. Aubet acknowledges this similarity but implies that it is a bow to tradition and the above-mentioned function. However, the residents of Tyre had nothing to fear on their mainland (at least initially, before the Assyrians became a threat), so the purported defensive function is inconsistently applied in one case but not the other. Drawing on the new approaches to spatiality, we can reread this choice and perceive the setting in a more active light. Motya's location may be seen as an objectification of her Near Eastern links. Not only are Tyre and Motya both islands, but they are virtually the same size: Motya covers about 45 hectares (Tusa 1989a:7), close to Tyre's estimated size of 53 hectares (Aubet 1997:29). I suggest, then, that Motya's setting is a spatial reference to the home city of Tyre herself: the colonists' Near Eastern heritage was literally being inscribed on the land, an iteration of a distant place, a diasporic tactic to make the new place familiar and to reinforce links with the homeland.

Subsequently, Motya's ties to the other Phoenician colonies manifest themselves spatially, in the many similarities in urban layout. There are a number of characteristics that distinguish the colonies from their Near Eastern progenitors. The siting of the island's archaic period necropolis, containing eighth- and seventh-century graves, at some remove from the settlement area, was a trait of all Phoenician necropoli, west and east (Gras, Rouillard, and Teixidor 1989:62). However, Motya residents' overwhelming preference for cremations was in keeping with other Phoenician colonies but in contrast to the homeland, where inhumation prevailed. Even more significant is Motya's *tophet*, the sacred enclosure for child sacrifice. It is situated in the north of the town and at some distance from the residential area, also true of tophets at the Phoenician colonies of Nora and Tharros on Sardinia. Motya's tophet was in use from the beginning of the seventh century BC. It was expanded in the sixth century and a temple was built. There are several levels of depositions of urns containing the burnt remains of the sacrifices (Aubet 1997: 202, 207–213). The tophet is a common feature of a number of Phoenician colonies in the central Mediterranean but not elsewhere, suggesting a tighter network of interaction in that region. No tophets are known from the Phoenician homeland, where child sacrifice was not practiced to the extent it was in the colonies. That the tophet's sad depositions carry on throughout the site's history up to the fourth century BC, if not later, points to the community's sustained associations with other nodes in the diaspora: Sardinia, Iberia, the Balearics, and so on, and of course Carthage.

Motya also shared with its sister colonies an economic purpose that structured everyday life on the island, evident in the priority of space given to storehouses and industrial areas, dating from the sixth century. The same types of storerooms are found at other Phoenician colonies, such as Toscanos (Gras, Rouillard, and Teixidor 1989: 62). The "industrial zone" contained kilns used for producing storage vessels, brick-making, and a dye-manufacturing area. The *absence* of a plaza or public space at Motya is also a characteristic of Phoenician cities (1989:63). Perhaps the commercial and mercantile activities were collective to such a degree that the storehouses and industrial areas fulfilled the purpose of the public square. From these spatial similarities and from what we know of Phoenician commerce, it is evident that Motya retained close bonds with the other colonies, and that this collective enterprise underpinned these communities.

A surrounding wall is another standard feature of Phoenician colonies, usually built during the life of the site rather than at the moment of its foundation (1989:62). Motya is no exception, with walls appearing for the first time in the sixth century BC. Its fortifications more closely resemble other western Phoenician colonies in the Mediter-ranean than they do their Near Eastern counterparts. Indeed, the construction tech-niques are similar enough to suggest the swapping around of builders between the colonies rather than mere emulation (Isserlin and du Plat Taylor 1974: 87–89). In the sixth century, also, we see the expansion of the sacred zone known as the Cappidazzu, the construction of a second harbor, and a causeway to the mainland. All this building activity has typically been attributed to the Carthaginian control of the island.

The spatial evidence, however, speaks to progressive Greek influence, which one would not expect in a Carthaginian colony. Indeed, we know that the relations with the Greeks often turned violent. This violence eventually resulted in the sacking of the island in 397 BC at the hands of another Greek colony, Siracusa. This uneasy mixture of intimacy and antagonism that characterized Motya's relations with the Greek col-onies is evident spatially. This influence should not be overstated. Isserlin and du Plat Taylor postulate that the gates to the city may instead have been measured out in Phoenician long units and Egyptian cubits (1974:95). Nor did Motya adopt one of the crucial features of a Greek city, a uniform grid system: while there is a limited grid system in the center of the site, along the coast the buildings simply follow the shoreline. This mixed layout has Near Eastern antecedents (ibid.: 87). However, a degree of Greek influence is evident. A Greek-style temple with Doric capitals was built sometime in the sixth century outside the north wall of the town (Ciasca 1980; Spanò Giammellaro 1989: 23). Even more telling is the suggestion that certain public structures in Motya – a sanctuary, the town wall, and the channel of the inner harbor – seem to have been planned in Attic feet.

Portable artifacts show a similar incorporation of Greek elements. From the earliest period of settlement the island yielded Corinthian fine wares and amphorae along with the expected Phoenician pottery, and Greek imports continued to appear in funerary assemblages (Tusa 1989b). The famous fifth-century-BC marble statue known as the "Youth of Motya" is Greek in style, and possibly of Greek manufacture (Spanò Giammellaro 1990). By the early fifth century, Motya had begun minting coins that alternated Greek and Punic writing (Cutroni Tusa 1989). The small private altars found on Motya are also typical finds at Greek colonies in the west and have no Phoenician antecedents (Isserlin and du Plat Taylor 1974: 95). These finds demonstrate that the residents of Motya were subject to influences other than Carthage.

The Phoenicians on Sicily are seen by scholars as maintaining a marked cultural distance from the native peoples. This is superficially supported materially by the near-absence of indigenous goods at Motya and other Phoenician sites, and the correspondingly low numbers of Phoenician goods on native sites. However, there is growing spatial evidence that Motya's residents had increasingly close contacts with the native inhabitants of the region. The absence of early defenses on the island is an indication that Motya established peaceable relations with the native peoples from the beginning. Thucydides himself spoke of good relations between the Phoenicians and the native populations in the area (Thucydides 1972: VI.2.6), and textual accounts tell of two different times in the sixth century when the locals united with the Phoenicians to repulse attempts by the Greeks to settle nearby (van Dommelen 1998: 119). In support of the spatial evidence is the presence of indigenous cooking pots at Phoenician colonies in Sicily (Bisi 1967). That the ties between island and mainland were growing is evident in the mid-sixth century BC, when Motya's residents began burying their dead on the mainland. This is also the moment of the construction of the causeway linking the island and mainland. Clearly the physical boundaries of the island had become more porous. In this light, the defensive walls that appeared in the early sixth century are unlikely to signify a shift in relations with the mainland populations, but instead may have been intended to keep out the Greeks.

All of these changes in the sixth century fit neatly into the traditional picture of Motya's history that attributes its evolution from trading post to city to its economic success and political shifts. However, in light of the evidence that Motya was not under Carthaginian control until the end of the fifth century at the earliest, then all the spatial changes in fact *predate* the island's political transformations. This realization permits another way of looking at the changes in the space of Motya, interpreting them as indicative of a changed relationship between community and place. This approach puts space at the forefront of the story of Motya, recognizing the specifically *spatial* component of this story. Motya was a community derived first from a *network* of far-flung places, then increasingly structured according to its immediate locality. This changing relationship of community and place may be read in the urban features of the town.

Motya's initial diasporic community was forged through the act of displacement, rather than through a strong connection to its new locality. We see this in the spatial referencing of the homeland, while the absence of monumental, permanent structures points to an initial lack of emotional investment in the place. By the sixth century there is a growing rootedness, a community increasingly committed to a single locality. The fortifications, the expanded tophet, the new temple, the closer physical links with the mainland signaled by the causeway and the new necropolis: all these public works point to an articulated urban identity and a new sense of locality, rather than to a political change. Ironically, just when Motya seems most grounded in its island locale, it spills over to the mainland, demonstrating that the neat associations between a bounded space and a bounded community cannot be taken for granted. The growing independence and emergent urban identity at Motya may serve as harbingers of subsequent changes: a similar process at the other Phoenician colonies, and particularly at Carthage, may have resulted in the same territoriality. This pride of place, in the case of Carthage, may have been a source for its later platform of territorial aggression.

By studying communities such as Motya we are made aware of the surprising *impermanence* of locality and the inherent dynamism of community. If we focus just on the social as determining the spatial, we cannot explain the specificities of the site's history. If we position space at the forefront of our understanding of Motya, the transformation of the site over time makes more sense. At first, Motya's spatial links extended far beyond its coastline, as its residents were distinctly outward-looking. While the town's role as a node in a larger network carried on, the residents' own focus shifted inward, as a new appreciation of place developed. Archaeologists should take the lessons of geography and the new spatial studies to heart, then, and generate new understandings of past places and peoples.

ACKNOWLEDGMENTS

This chapter was written while I was working as a postdoctoral teaching fellow in Stanford University's IHUM program. I would like to extend my heartfelt thanks to Lynn Meskell and Robert Preucel for their guidance, patience, and excellent suggestions. I alone am responsible for all errors.

NOTE

1   I'm referring to the Anglo-American context here: in France, interestingly, it is archaeology that has the greater influence on historical geography (see Leveau 1984).

REFERENCES

Abu-Lughod, J. 1961. Migrant adjustment to city life: The Egyptian case. *American Journal of Sociology* 67: 22–2.
—— 1969. *The City is Dead-Long Live the City: Some Thoughts on Urbanity*. Berkeley, CA: Center for Planning and Development Research of the University of California Monograph 12.
——, and R. Hay, Jr. (eds.) 1979. *Third World Urbanization*. New York: Methuen.
Adams, P. C., S. Hoelscher, and K. E. Till. 2001. Place in context: Rethinking humanist geographies. In P. C. Adams, S. Hoelscher, and K. E. Till (eds.), *Textures of Place: Exploring Humanist Geographies*. Minneapolis: University of Minnesota Press, pp. xiii–xxxiii.
Agnew, J. A., and Duncan, J. S. (eds.) 1989. *The Power of Place: Bringing Together Geographical and Sociological Imaginations*. Boston: Unwin Hyman.
Aldenderfer, M., and H. Maschner (eds.) 1996. *Anthropology, Space, and Geographic Information Systems*. Oxford: Oxford University Press.
Anderson, B. 1983. *Imagined Communities: Reflections on the Origins and Spread of Nationalism*. London: Verso.
Anzaldúa, G. 1987. *Borderlands/La Frontera: The New Mestiza*. San Francisco: Aunt Lute.

Ashmore, W. 2002. "Decisions and dispositions": Socializing spatial archaeology. *American Anthropologist* 104(4): 1172–1183.

——, and A. B. Knapp (eds.) 1999. *Archaeologies of Landscape: Contemporary Approaches*. Oxford: Blackwell.

Aubet, M. E. 1997. *The Phoenicians and the West: Politics, Colonies and Trade*. Trans. M. Turton. Cambridge: Cambridge University Press.

Barker, G. 1995. *A Mediterranean Valley: Landscape Archaeology and Annales History in the Biferno Valley*. London: Leicester University Press.

Barnes, T., and D. Gregory (eds.) 1998. *Reading Human Geography: The Poetics and Politics of Inquiry*. London: Arnold.

Barrett, J. 1994. *Fragments From Antiquity: An Archaeology of Social Life in Britain, 2900–1200* B.C. Oxford: Blackwell.

——, R. Bradley, and M. Green. 1991. *Landscape, Monuments and Society: The Prehistory of Cranborne Chase*. Cambridge: Cambridge University Press.

Barth, F. 1961. *Nomads of South Persia*. Oslo: Oslo University Press.

——2000. Boundaries and connections. In A. P. Cohen (ed.), *Signifying Identities: Anthropological Perspectives on Boundaries and Contested Values*. London and New York: Routledge, pp. 17–36.

Baudrillard, J. 1994. *Simulacra and Simulation*. Trans. S. F. Glaser. Ann Arbor: University of Michigan Press.

Bauer, B. S., and C. Stanish. 2001. *Ritual and Pilgrimage in the Ancient Andes: The Islands of the Sun and the Moon*. Austin: University of Texas Press.

Bell, W. 1955. Economic, family and ethnic status: An empirical test. *American Sociological Review* 20: 45–52.

Bender, B. (ed.) 1993. *Landscape: Politics and Perspectives*. London: Berg.

Benjamin, W. 1983. *Charles Baudelaire: Lyric Poet in the Era of High Capitalism*. London: New Left Books.

Bhabha, H. K. 1994. *The Location of Culture*. London and New York: Routledge.

Bintliff, J. 1991. *The Annales School and Archaeology*. London: Leicester University Press.

Bisi, A. M. 1967. L'irradiazione semitica in Sicilia in base ai dati ceramici dei Centri Fenicio-Punici dell'Isola. *Kokalos* 13: 30–65.

Blake, E. 2002. Spatiality past and present: An interview with Edward Soja, Los Angeles, 12 April 2001. *Journal of Social Archaeology* 2(2): 139–158.

Bondì, S. F. 1988. L'urbanistica e l'architettura. In S. Moscati (ed.), *I Fenici*. Milan: Bompiani, pp. 248–283.

Bradley, R. (ed.) 1996. Sacred geography. *World Archaeology* 28(2).

——1998. *The Significance of Monuments: On the Shaping of Human Experience in Neolithic and Bronze Age Europe*. London and New York: Routledge.

Braudel, F. 1972 [1949]. *The Mediterranean and the Mediterranean World in the Age of Philip II*. London: Fontana.

Broodbank, C. 2000. *An Island Archaeology of the Early Cyclades*. Cambridge: Cambridge University Press.

Bulmer, M. 1984. *The Chicago School of Sociology: Institutionalization, Diversity, and the Rise of Sociological Research*. Chicago: University of Chicago Press.

Cantwell, A. M., and D. Wall. 2001. *Unearthing Gotham: The Archaeology of New York City*. New Haven, CT and London: Yale University Press.

Canuto, M. A., and J. Yaeger (eds.) 2000. *The Archaeology of Communities: A New World Perspective*. London and New York: Routledge.

Casimir, M. J., and A. Rao (eds.) 1991. *Mobility and Territoriality: Social and Spatial Boundaries among Foragers, Fishers, Pastoralists and Peripatetics*. New York and Oxford: Berg.

Castells, M. 1977. *The Urban Question: A Marxist Approach*. Trans. Alan Sheridan. London: Edward Arnold.

Cherry, J. F. 1984. The initial colonization of the West Mediterranean islands in the light of island biogeography and paleogeography. In W. H. Waldren, R. Chapman, J. Lewthwaite, and R-C. Kennard (eds.), *The Deya Conference of Prehistory: Early Settlement in the Western Mediterranean Islands and the Peripheral Areas*. Oxford: British Archaeological Reports, International Series 229, pp. 7–23.

Ciasca, A. 1980. Mozia: note sull'architettura religiosa. In M. J. Fontanna, M. T. Piraino, and F. P. Rizzo (eds.), *Miscellanea di studi classici in onore di Eugenio Manni*. Rome: Giorgio Bretschneider, pp. 501–513.

Clarke, D. L. (ed.) 1977. *Spatial Archaeology*. London: Academic Press.

Clifford, J. 1997. *Routes: Travel and Translation in the Late Twentieth Century*. Cambridge, MA: Harvard University Press.

Coe, M. D., and K. V. Flannery, 1967. *Early Cultures and Human Ecology in South Coastal Guatemala*. Washington, DC: Smithsonian Institution Press.

Cohen, J. H. 1999. *Cooperation and Community: Economy and Society in Oaxaca*. Austin: University of Texas Press.

Coleman, S., and J. Elsner. 1995: *Pilgrimage: Past and Present in the World Religions*. Cambridge, MA: Harvard University Press.

Cutroni Tusa, A. 1989. La monetazione. In A. Ciasca, A. Cutroni Tusa, M. L. Fama, A. Spanò Giammellaro, and V. Tusa (eds.), *Mozia*. Rome: Libreria dello Stato, pp. 93–95.

de Certeau, M. 1984. *The Practice of Everyday Life*. Berkeley: University of California Press.

Dietler, M., and B. Hayden (eds.) 2001. *Feasts: Archaeological and Ethnographic Perspectives on Food, Politics, and Power*. Washington, DC: Smithsonian Institution Press.

Donnan, H., and T. M. Wilson. 1999. *Borders: Frontiers of Identity, Nation and State*. Oxford and New York: Berg.

Duncan, J., and D. Ley (eds.) 1993. *Place/Culture/Representation*. London and New York: Routledge.

Earle, T. K., and R. W. Preucel. 1987. Processual archaeology and the radical critique. *Current Anthropology* 28(4): 501–538.

Eco, U. 1986. *Travels in Hyper Reality*. Trans. W. Weaver. San Diego: Harcourt Brace.

Favro, D. 1996. *The Urban Image of Augustan Rome*. Cambridge: Cambridge University Press.

Fish, S. K., and S. A. Kowalewski (eds.) 1990. *The Archaeology of Regions: A Case for Full Coverage Survey*. Washington, DC: Smithsonian Institution Press.

Flannery, K. V. (ed.) 1986. *Guila Naquitz: Archaic Foraging and Early Agriculture in Oaxaca, Mexico*. New York: Academic Press.

Foucault, M. 1980. Questions on geography. In C. Gordon (ed. and trans.), *Power/Knowledge: Selected Interviews and Other Writings 1972–1977*. Brighton: Harvester Press, pp. 63–77.

—— 1986. Of other spaces. Trans. J. Miskowiec. *Diacritics* 16: 22–27.

Gaffney, V., Z. Stancic, and H. Watson. 1995. The impact of GIS on archaeology: A personal perspective. In G. Lock and Z. Stancic (eds.), *Archaeology and Geographical Information Systems*. London: Taylor & Francis, pp. 319–334.

Gathercole, P., and D. Lowenthal (eds.) 1990. *The Politics of the Past*. London: Unwin Hyman.

Gibian, P. 1997. The art of being off-center: Shopping center spaces and the spectacles of consumer culture. In P. Gibian (ed.), *Mass Culture and Everyday Life*. London and New York: Routledge, pp. 238–291.

Giddens, A. 1985. Time, space and regionalisation. In D. Gregory and J. Urry (eds.), *Social Relations and Spatial Structures*. London: Macmillan, pp. 265–295.

Glassie, H. 1975. *Folk Housing in Middle Virginia: A Structural Analysis of Historic Artifacts*. Knoxville: University of Tennessee Press.

Goss, J. 1993. The "magic of the mall": An analysis of form, function and meaning in the contemporary retail built environment. *Annals of the Association of American Geographers* 83(1): 18–47.

Graham-Campbell, J. (ed.) 1994. The archaeology of pilgrimage. *World Archaeology* 26(1).

Gras, M., P. Rouillard, and J. Teixidor. 1989. *L'Univers phénicien*. Paris: Editions Arthaud.

Green, D., and C. Haselgrove. 1978. Some problems in cross-disciplinary communication as viewed from archaeology and geography. In D. Green, C. Haselgrove, and M. Spriggs (eds.), *Social Organisation and Settlement: Contributions from Anthropology, Archaeology and Geography*. Oxford: BAR International Series Supp. 47, pp. vii–xxxvi.

——, and M. Spriggs (eds.) 1978. *Social Organisation and Settlement: Contributions from Anthropology, Archaeology and Geography*. Oxford: BAR International Series Supp. 47.

Greenwood, R. S. 1996. *Down by the Station: Los Angeles Chinatown, 1880–1933*. Los Angeles: UCLA Institute of Archaeology, Monumenta Archaeologica 18.

Harvey, D. 1973. *Social Justice and the City*. London: Edward Arnold.

Higgs, E., and D. Jarmann. 1975. Palaeoeconomy. In E. Higgs (ed.), *Palaeoeconomy: Being the second volume of Papers in economic prehistory by members and associates of the British Academy Major Research Project in the Early History of Agriculture*. Cambridge: Cambridge University Press, pp. 1–7.

Hodder, I., and C. Orton. 1976. *Spatial Analysis in Archaeology*. Cambridge: Cambridge University Press.

Holloway, R. R. 1991. *The Archaeology of Ancient Sicily*. London and New York: Routledge.

Isserlin, B. S. J., and J. du Plat Taylor. 1974. *Motya: A Phoenician and Carthaginian City in Sicily. Vol. I: Fieldwork and Excavation*. Leiden: E. J. Brill.

Jackson, P., and N. Thrift. 1995. Geographies of consumption. In D. Miller (ed.), *Acknowledging Consumption: A Review of New Studies*. London and New York: Routledge, pp. 204–237.

Jacobs, J. 1969. *The Economy of Cities*. New York: Random House.

Journal of Social Archaeology 2(2), June 2002. Spatial Theory and Archaeological Ethnographies.

Just, R. 2000. *A Greek Island Cosmos*. Santa Fe, NM: School of American Research Press.

Kealhofer, L. 1999. Creating social identity in the landscape: Tidewater, Virginia, 1600–1750. In W. Ashmore and A. B. Knapp (eds.), *Archaeologies of Landscape: Contemporary Perspectives*. Oxford: Blackwell, pp. 58–82.

Kent, S. (ed.) 1990. *Domestic Architecture and the Use of Space: An Interdisciplinary Cross-Cultural Study*. Cambridge: Cambridge University Press.

Knapp, A. B. (ed.) 1992. *Archaeology, Annales, and Ethnohistory*. Cambridge: Cambridge University Press.

Kroll, E. M., and T. D. Price (eds.) 1991. *The Interpretation of Archaeological Spatial Patterning*. New York and London: Plenum.

Kus, S., and V. Raharijaona. 1990. Domestic space and the tenacity of traditions among the Betsileo of Madagascar. In S. Kent (ed.), *Domestic Architecture and the Use of Space: An Interdisciplinary Cross-Cultural Study*. Cambridge: Cambridge University Press, pp. 21–33.

Lane, P. 1994. The temporal structuring of settlement space among the Dogon of Mali: An ethnoarchaeological study. In M. Parker Pearson and C. Richards (eds.), *Architecture and Order: Approaches to Social Space*. London and New York: Routledge, pp. 196–216.

Lefebvre, H. 1991 [1974]. *The Production of Space*. Trans. D. Nicholson-Smith. Oxford: Blackwell.

Leone, M. P. 1984. Interpreting ideology in historical archaeology: Using the rules of perspective in the William Paca Garden, Annapolis, Maryland. In D. Miller and C. Tilley (eds.), *Ideology, Power, and Prehistory*. Cambridge: Cambridge University Press, pp. 25–35.

Leveau, P. 1984. La question du territoire et les sciences de l'antiquité: La géographie historique, son évolution de la topographie à l'analyse de l'espace. *Revue des Etudes Anciennes* 86: 85–115.

Lewis, R. B., and C. Stout (eds.) 1998. *Mississippian Towns and Sacred Spaces: Searching for an Architectural Grammar.* Tuscaloosa: University of Alabama Press.

Ley, D., and M. Samuels (eds.) 1978. *Humanistic Geography: Prospects and Problems.* Chicago: Maroufa Press.

Lock, G., and Z. Stancic (eds.) 1995. *Archaeology and Geographical Information Systems.* London: Taylor & Francis.

Lovell, N. (ed.) 1998. *Locality and Belonging.* London and New York: Routledge.

Low, S. M. 2000. *On the Plaza: the Politics of Public Space and Culture.* Austin: University of Texas Press.

Lowenthal, D. 1996. *The Heritage Crusade and the Spoils of History.* London: Viking.

MacArthur, R. J., and E. O. Wilson. 1967. *The Theory of Island Biogeography.* Princeton, NJ: Princeton University Press.

MacCannell, D. 1976. *The Tourist: A New Theory of the Leisure Class.* New York: Shocken Books.

Massey, D. 1985. New directions in space. In D. Gregory and J. Urry (eds.), *Social Relations and Spatial Structures.* London: Macmillan, pp. 9–19.

Mayne, A., and T. Murray. 2001. The archaeology of urban landscapes: Explorations in slumland. In A. Mayne and T. Murray (eds.), *The Archaeology of Urban Landscapes: Explorations in Slumland.* Cambridge: Cambridge University Press, pp. 1–7.

Meskell, L. (ed.) 1998. *Archaeology under Fire: Nationalism, Politics and Heritage in the Eastern Mediterranean and Middle East.* London and New York: Routledge.

Miller, D. 1995. Consumption studies as the transformation of anthropology. In D. Miller (ed.), *Acknowledging Consumption: A Review of New Studies.* London and New York: Routledge, pp. 264–295.

Morris, I., T. Jackman, E. Blake, and S. Tusa. 2003. Stanford University excavations at Monte Polizzo in Sicily, 2: Preliminary report on the 2001 season. *Memoirs of the American Academy in Rome 48.*

Nicholson, R. A., and T. P. O'Connor (eds.) 2000. *People as an Agent of Environmental Change.* Oxford: Oxbow Books.

Orser, C. E., Jr. 1996. *A Historical Archaeology of the Modern World.* New York and London: Plenum.

Parker Pearson, M., and C. Richards (eds.) 1994. *Architecture and Order: Approaches to Social Space.* London and New York: Routledge.

Patton, M. 1996. *Islands in Time: Island Sociogeography and Mediterranean Prehistory.* London and New York: Routledge.

Pratt, M. L. 1992. *Imperial Eyes: Travel Writing and Transculturation.* London and New York: Routledge.

Pred, A. 1986. *Place, Practice and Structure: Social and Spatial Transformation in Southern Sweden: 1750–1850.* Cambridge: Polity Press.

Rapoport, A. 1969. *House Form and Culture.* Englewood Cliffs, NJ: Prentice-Hall.

—— 1982. *The Meaning of the Built Environment: A Nonverbal Communication Approach.* Beverly Hills: Sage.

Renfrew, C. 1975. Trade as action at a distance: Questions of integration and communication. In J. A. Sabloff and C. C. Lamberg-Karlovsky (eds.), *Ancient Civilization and Trade.* Albuquerque: University of New Mexico Press, pp. 3–60.

Richards, C. 1993. Monumental choreography: Architecture and spatial representation in later Neolithic Orkney. In C. Tilley (ed.), *Interpretative Archaeology.* Oxford: Berg, pp. 143–81.

Rothschild, N. A. 1990. *New York City Neighborhoods, the Eighteenth Century*. Orlando, FL: Academic Press.

Safran, W. 1991. Diasporas in modern societies: Myths of homeland and return. *Diaspora* 1(1): 83–99.

Sampson, R. (ed.) 1991. *The Social Archaeology of Houses*. Edinburgh, Edinburgh University Press.

Seamon, D., and R. Mugerauer (eds.) 1985. *Dwelling, Place, and Environment: Towards a Phenomenology of Person and World*. New York: Columbia University Press.

Silverman, H., and D. B. Small (eds.) 2002. *The Space and Place of Death*. Arlington, VA: Archaeological Papers of the American Anthropological Association 11.

Soja, E. W. 1989. *Postmodern Geographies: The Reassertion of Space in Critical Social Theory*. London: Verso.

——2000. *Postmetropolis: Critical Studies of Cities and Regions*. Oxford: Blackwell.

Spain, D. 1992. *Gendered Spaces*. Chapel Hill and London: University of North Carolina Press.

Spanò Giammellaro, A. 1989. Strutture extramurarie e vie principali di comunicazione. In A. Ciasca, A. Cutroni Tusa, M. L. Fama, A. Spanò Giammellaro, and V. Tusa (eds.), *Mozia*. Rome: Libreria dello Stato, pp. 23–29.

——1990. La statua marmorea di Mozia: un aggiornamento della questione. *Sicilia Archeologica* 23(72): 19–37.

Steward, J. 1937. Ecological aspects of southwestern society. *Anthropos* 32: 87–104.

Taaffe, E. J. 1974. The spatial view in context. *Annals of the Association of American Geographers* 64(1): 1–16.

Thomas, J. 1983. The Chicago School: The tradition and the legacy. *Urban Life* 11 (January), special edition.

——1993. The hermeneutics of megalithic space. In C. Tilley (ed.), *Interpretative Archaeology*. Oxford: Berg, pp. 73–97.

——1996. *Time, Culture and Identity: An Interpretative Archaeology*. London and New York: Routledge.

Thucydides, 1972. *History of the Peloponnesian War*. Trans. Rex Warner. London: Penguin.

Tilley, C. 1994. *A Phenomenology of Landscape: Places, Paths and Monuments*. Oxford: Berg.

——1996. *An Ethnography of the Neolithic*. Cambridge: Cambridge University Press.

Tolbert, L. 1999. *Constructing Townscapes: Space and Society in Antebellum Tennessee*. Chapel Hill and London: University of North Carolina Press.

Tuan, Y-F. 1976. Humanistic geography. *Annals of the Association of American Geographers* 66: 266–276.

Tusa, V. 1989a. L'isola di S. Pantaleo nella storia. In A. Ciasca, A. Cutroni Tusa, M. L. Fama, A. Spanò Giammellaro, and V. Tusa (eds.), *Mozia*. Rome: Libreria dello Stato, pp. 7–13.

——1989b. Necropoli. In A. Ciasca, A. Cutroni Tusa, M. L. Fama, A. Spanò Giammellaro, and V. Tusa (eds.), *Mozia*. Rome: Libreria dello Stato, pp. 41–3.

Upton, D. 1992. The city as material culture. In A. Yentsch and M. Beaudry (eds.), *The Art and Mystery of Historical Archaeology: Essays in Honor of James Deetz*. Boca Raton, FL: CRC Press, pp. 51–74.

Urry, J. 1990. *The Tourist Gaze*. London: Sage.

van Dommelen, P. 1998. *On Colonial Grounds: A Comparative Study of Colonialism and Rural Settlement in First Millennium BC West Central Sardinia*. Leiden: Leiden University Archaeological Studies.

Vidal de la Blache, P. 1926. *Principles of Human Geography*. New York: Henry Holt.

Wallace Hadrill, A. 1988. The social structure of the Roman House. *Papers of the British School at Rome* 56: 43–97.

Willey, G. R. 1953. *Prehistoric Settlement Patterns in the Virú Valley, Peru.* Washington, DC: Bureau of American Ethnology Bulletin 155.

Wobst, M. 1974. Boundary conditions for Palaeolithic social systems: a simulation approach. *American Antiquity* 39: 147–178.

Zubrow, E. 1994. Knowledge representation and GIS: A cognitive example using GIS. In C. Renfrew and E. Zubrow (eds.), *The Ancient Mind: Elements of Cognitive Archaeology.* Cambridge: Cambridge University Press, pp. 107–119.

Zukin, S. 1991. *Landscapes of Power: From Detroit to Disney World.* Berkeley and Los Angeles: University of California Press.

11

Social Archaeologies of Landscape

Wendy Ashmore

[L]andscape archaeology is ... central to the archaeological programme as a whole because the history of human life is about ways of inhabiting the world. (Barrett 1999a:30)

What is clear is that landscape is a major industry of intellectual production. The very diversity of approaches is part of the success of landscape studies today. (Stoddart 2000:373)

Barrett's statement is exhortatory and programmatic; Stoddart's statement affirms that contemporary archaeologists agree with Barrett's words, if not necessarily with the same theoretical foundations from which he wrote. Landscape has been part of archaeologists' purview for well over a century. Each of the terms "landscape," "landscape approach," and "landscape archaeology" support multiple definitions. Although most of these acknowledge interaction between physical environment and human presence, they vary markedly in the roles and relative importance accorded to people and the land in production of landscape. The source of variation, of course, is the theoretical stance of the archaeologist.

There is a tendency to dichotomize current archaeological treatments of landscape, a stark contrast to the ecological and economic approaches of American processualist archaeology and the interpretative approaches of predominantly British postprocessualists. At the same time, some scholars decry the attendant polarization, along with the rhetoric that perpetuates it. Despite acknowledged theoretical differences, the mediators contend that more is to be gained from communication than from mutual disregard, and see landscape studies as a domain for bridging theoretical and practical divides (e.g., Anschuetz, Wilshusen, and Scheick 2001; Ashmore and Knapp 1999; Crumley and Marquardt 1990; Lekson 1996).

In this chapter, I review recent developments in archaeologies of landscape, emphasizing trends in the United Kingdom and the United States, and diversity within those trends. Sundry strands of social theory inform this diversity, and link archaeologies of landscape to like pursuits in geography, social anthropology, and other disciplines.

Explicitly *social archaeological* perspectives, described below, partake of distinct categories of theory, choices among which encourage – or discourage – particular lines of inquiry.

Landscapes Defined

Whereas some scholars equate *landscape* with physical environment irrespective of human presence, others hold the opposite view, that human involvement is what distinguishes landscape from environment (Ingold 1986; Knapp and Ashmore 1999; Schama 1995). Layton and Ucko (1999:2–3) link the two poles broadly with goals, respectively, for scientific explanation of human adaptation and for humanistic inter- pretation of meaningful action. These correspond broadly to positivist and postpositi- vist philosophies. Positivist scholars tend to seek a single, umbrella approach to landscape study (e.g., Feinman 1999; Rossignol 1992: 4–5). Not all do, however, and postpositivist writers are most likely to tolerate, and sometimes extol, greater diversity in approach. For example, recognizing the interplay of approaches, Gosden and Head (1994) famously label landscape a "usefully ambiguous" concept. Alternatively, even as Anschuetz, Wilshusen, and Scheick are unsurprised that "landscape concepts in geog- raphy and other sciences have a multiplicity of meanings that fall variously along the nature-culture continuum" (2001: 158), they do offer specific proposals for a unifying "landscape paradigm." For Stoddart and Zubrow (1999), the most important conclu- sion to draw from the current literature is that, while the diversity of inquiry is intellec- tually productive, it *precludes* subsuming or reducing landscapes to a single definition or approach. Social archaeologies of landscape, as we shall see, feature prominently in the assemblage.

Multiple authors outline contemporary *themes* in landscape research, inventorying archaeological approaches to landscapes as materializing – or as entries to understand- ing – particular kinds of human custom, social practice or belief in spatial terms (e.g., Anschuetz, Wilshusen, and Scheick 2001; Knapp and Ashmore 1999; Muir 2000; Stoddart 2000; Stoddart and Zubrow 1999). Prominent themes include landscape as ecology, palimpsest, meaning, memory, identity, social order, morality, and social trans- formation. In theory and in practice, the themes overlap, and multiple themes are evident in single bodies of work. Although many of the themes in this non-exhaustive array are evident in both US and UK contexts, the theory underlying their investigation commonly differs, often dramatically. As Bender (1999a) remarks, archaeologists on either side of the Atlantic seem to draw from distinct reading lists; Stoddart and Zubrow maintain that "different traditions of landscape on both sides of the Atlantic... show some cross-fertilization, but enduring differences and diversity" (1999: 686). The focus of this chapter is precisely those commonalities and distinctions, and their historical and theoretical bases.

This is not another review of topical themes, however. Like most classifications, such orderings vary with the classifier. Rather than adopt one or another approach to categorizing study topics, I isolate five clusters of issues for and implications from landscape archaeologies. The goal is to explore how theory shapes archaeologists' engagement with these issues and implications. The aforementioned topic themes are the interpretive settings in which the issues and implications emerge. Links to other scholarly fields inform the discussion, as does consideration of alternative views from beyond mainstream UK and US writers. The chapter closes with thoughts on emergent and future trends.

Histories and Contexts

Commonalities include shared ties to other disciplines, and overlapping, but far from identical intellectual histories. Following Hirsch, for example, Anschuetz and his colleagues (2001) consider variable Anglo-American landscape concepts to be legacies of late nineteenth-century debates between Ratzel and Durkheim in their organismic models of society. Writing specifically of Europe, however, Sherratt (1996) draws more general distinctions to consider swings between settlement patterns and landscape studies in how scholars have examined human space at a regional scale. Reviewing historical variation in traditions of thought since the Renaissance, he links the former with social contexts of economic prosperity, political security, and scientific positivism. Landscape studies, in contrast, prevail under conditions of markedly greater uncertainty, tolerance of ambiguity, and intellectual reflexivity. He glosses the associated metanarratives as *evolution* and *genealogy*, respectively (Sherratt 1996: 141), and argues (149) that both approaches are necessary to spatial studies of regions.

In the United States of the late nineteenth century, Euro-American observers had relatively shallow genealogical ties to the land. For them, landscape was not a social construct, but held strong implications of being nature "untainted by human presence" (Spirn 1996:111). Even openly modified places quickly became naturalized anew in popular thought, as illustrated dramatically in perceptions of Yosemite, Niagara Falls, Boston's Fens, and other US places that landscape architect Frederick Olmsted reshaped for human health and enjoyment. After World War I, Carl Sauer (1925) formally distinguished "cultural" landscapes from "natural" ones. Still, the notion of landscapes as pristine nature remains frequent in the United States, among scholars as well as the public, in part a continuing legacy of Enlightenment thought (Kirch 2000: 315). Among colonized parts of the world, however, casting landscape as primeval nature has been critiqued for naïve shallowness of land histories (e.g., Cronon 1996; Kirch 1999).

Archaeological landscape studies in the United States are linked most directly to currents of theory and method nearer mid-century, especially research conducted at a regional scale, and inquiry into the "human/environment dialectic" (Fisher and Thurston 1999: 630). Anschuetz and his colleagues (2001; Knapp 1997) provide a historical and theoretical review of landscape archaeology, with thoughtful insight into US traditions. Cultural ecological studies of Steward and Willey's settlement pattern research are commonly cited as primary sources inspiring these American traditions (e.g., Billman 1999; Sabloff and Ashmore 2001). Both were significant foundations for the positivist, processualist ideas dominating US-based archaeology in the second half of the twentieth century. Theoretical trends in this US "New Archaeology" broadly paralleled those in a "New Geography" at mid-century, and archaeologists cited widely from Chisholm, Chorley, Haggett, and (early) Harvey. The decades following World

War II were times of relative prosperity and growth, and of energy and optimism among scientists, including archaeologists, anthropologists, and geographers (e.g., Flannery 1976). From a research vantage, landscapes and other kinds of space were objects to be measured and compared, analyzed, and interpreted via powerful statistical models in which the land remained a neutral and passive object, used by people but otherwise relatively detached from them.

In Britain, by contrast, many recognize a deeper, longstanding interest in prehistoric and historical landscapes, associated with genealogical interest in local and regional traditions. And given an immense boost after World War I from availability of aerial photography and production of the Ordnance Survey maps. Several authors provide useful historical overviews of varying length and perspective (e.g., Johnson 1999; Knapp 1997; Muir 2000; Stoddart 2000; Tilley 1994). Amid the economic and ecological perspectives of the 1960s and 1970s, however, scientific approaches prevailed. Higgs, Jarman, Vita-Finzi, and their colleagues built from Clark's economic and environmental archaeology and led in examining landscapes with a functional view to reconstructing ancient land use. Clarke and Renfrew inferred social and economic dimensions of a range of spatial frames, including landscapes. All these approaches were broadly consistent with models dominating archaeological thinking on both sides of the Atlantic at that time, and like their counterparts in the United States, drew on contemporary positivist works of the geographers mentioned previously (e.g., Hodder and Orton 1976).

Already in the 1970s, however, in both the United States and the United Kingdom, positivist stances increasingly were challenged by postpositivist philosophies, humanist concerns, and calls for social relevance – and social justice – in uncertain times of economic flux and the Vietnam War. Space (including landscapes) and human action were recast as matched participants in perpetual dialectic of mutual constitution. The new stream in geographic thinking built from existentialism, feminism, idealism, phenomenology, and interactionism (Anschuetz, Wilshusen, and Scheick 2001: 165). Supporting and challenging voices from other disciplines, from Jackson and LeFebvre, to Giddens, Cosgrove, and McHarg, maintained vigorous, socially engaged dialogues on space and landscape into which archaeologists entered unevenly and for the most part, relatively recently (Groth and Bressi 1997; Lekson 1996).

Landscape Archaeologies Today

In the United States, positivist archaeology remains strong, with widening exploration of postpositivist stances. In landscape research, most invoke theory from economic geography, ecology, and anthropology, for examining social and economic dimensions of land use. Some focus more closely on the physical landscape in itself, with theory drawn at least as often from the physical and natural sciences as from the social. In all of the foregoing, location and distribution of material resources figure importantly, with growing attention to monuments and rock art or other symbolic markings, and to landscapes materializing ideology or meaning. Those who explore the latter draw more explicitly on social theory with a humanistic cast. Historical archaeologists in the United States likewise tend to be more inclined to humanistic stances, by writing landscapes primarily (but not exclusively) in terms of colonial gardens. Prehistorians examine landscapes more expansively in space and time, as long-term palimpsests of human interactions with the land. They treat landscapes whose locations collectively span the globe, for periods anytime from the Paleolithic forward. One can recognize social archaeologies of landscapes in several forms. Although reference remains relatively sparse for much of the social theory sparking social geography – existentialism, feminism, idealism, and phenomenology – growing attention emerges for practice theory, structuration, and Marxist thought.

In the United Kingdom, landscape research is generally more humanistic and postpositivist, as in British archaeology at large. In landscape study, archaeologists invoke social theory from a range of sources, especially structural Marxism, phenomenology, and various strands of practice theory. Feminist thought is also evident in some works. Most practitioners stress interpretive and phenomenological approaches, turning on the idea of landscape as socially constructed and emphasizing that the same piece of ground holds different attachments and contrasting meanings for different people and groups, at any one time and through time as well. Attachments and meanings may be attested materially, inscribed on the land through architecture, rock art or other media; additionally, or alternatively – and more challenging for archaeologists – the attachments and meanings may reside in memories, shared orally, if at all. Location and distribution of material markings figure importantly in most landscape writings, especially stone monuments, construction, and rock art, and material expressions commonly coupled with ritual. The majority of those studied were created in the Neolithic and Bronze Age. Many authors write of the markings' naturalization as primordial landscape elements; variable details are offered for social processes by which naturalization occurs. Attention to what appear to be materially *un*marked landscape elements emerges with intermittent strength in particular lines of inquiry. Whether expressed materially or not, however, the attachments and meanings are commonly considered fundamental for orienting individuals and societies, integral to social identities and often, to moral grounding. For the most part, economics and ecology have receded greatly in interpretive importance.

Issues and Implications

Multiple epistemic and theoretical matters challenge archaeologists in landscape study, raising issues they have engaged in different ways and to variable degrees. The following five broad, overlapping areas capture the most prominent issues: relating nature, culture, and society; time and history; social and spatial scale; meaning and its attachment; and roles of alternative voices.

Relating nature, culture, and society

Phrasing the situation in various ways, most archaeologists consider landscape a product of human interaction with the environment. It is in the nature of that interaction, and of its results, that scholars differ along theoretical lines. This is the crux for recognition of *social archaeologies* of landscape.

In the United States, the issue frequently centers on settlement ecology and land-use (e.g., Anschuetz, Wilshusen, and Scheick 2001). As Fish comments: "Despite new disciplinary trends...the ecological configuration of prehistoric societies is a line of inquiry that is far from exhausted" (1999: 206). Most such research is positivist, primarily economic and ecological in orientation, and seeks to understand landscapes in terms of land-use strategies and practices of adaptive risk-management. Some scholars conduct direct land-use experiments (e.g., Erickson 1993). Stone (e.g., 1996) draws from settlement pattern and systems approaches, highlighting writings by Boserup, Flannery, and Netting. To set peasant land-use strategies in explanatory contexts, Erickson takes a less fully positivist tack, turning to such "New Ecologists" as Botkin because of their explicit recognition "that environments are dynamic *and historically contingent*" (Erickson 1999: 635, my emphasis).

Broadly parallel in goal, if less social in standpoint, is the "place-use history" approach of Rossignol, Wandsnider, and their colleagues (Rossignol and Wandsnider 1992; Wandsnider 1998). With inspiration from Butzer's archaeological human ecology, their principal theory sources are geology, ecology, positivist geography, archaeological formation processes and, in addition, selectionist evolution. In assessing human presence on the landscape, they look to off-site and distributional approaches, rather than plotting of sites, which they view as arbitrary archaeological constructs. They outline a *landscape approach* for archaeology, but criticize others' *landscape archaeology* for emphasis on historical (i.e., social) matters at the expense of ecological and geological system variables.

Dramatically different are conceptions of landscapes as records of social history. While retaining interest in land-use strategies, for example, Bradley criticizes most land-use analysts' prevalent economic and functionalist bias. Following Ingold, Bradley contrasts *landscape* as pertaining primarily to natural elements (and the sites and paths that connect them) with *land* as a two-dimensional measure of area in agricultural societies. His studies of monuments and rock art (1993, 1997) thus are entries for understanding landscape as documenting social history. In consequence he draws on historians (e.g., Hobsbawm), anthropologists (e.g., Ingold, Morphy), and other theorists, in exploring how landscape features are socialized and how cultural features become naturalized. Crucial in the process is creation of memory, by repeated movement of the body through the landscape. He attends increasingly to ruins and other elements ambiguous in their cultural/natural identity, and to their prospective social roles (1993, 1998, 2000).

For Bender and Tilley, also, landscapes are primarily social constructs. Bender's structural Marxism, together with influence from Foucault and Williams, among others, sustains in landscape inquiry her longstanding attention to social inequality. For Bender, landscape is process, intensely political, a way of perceiving, experiencing, and remembering the world (1993a, 1993b, 1998). She challenges the gendering of landscape, the male and mercantilist gaze that permeates thinking about landscape (1999b). In her more recent research, Heidegger's phenomenology plays a greater role (Bender, 1998; Bender, Hamilton and Tilley 1997).

Similarly, both Heidegger and Merleau-Ponty prominently inform Tilley's views, in which dwelling and the body mediate between thought and the world (1993, 1994). Indeed, the experience is synesthetic, "an affair of the whole body moving and sensing" (Tilley, in Bender 1998: 81), both creating and engaging a narrative linking the body – individual and social group – with the land. Like Bender and Bradley, he stresses links between landscape and social memory, in an ongoing dialectic of mutual constitution.

Thomas, also, considers landscape a way of "being in the world." In his writings since the 1990s, reference to de Certeau's everyday practice (e.g., Thomas 1991) has been supplanted by increasingly explicit allusion to hermeneutics and Heidegger's phenomenology, to creation of memory narratives through actions of the body (e.g., Thomas 1993a, 1993b, 2001). Following Moore and others, he once considered monuments and their (landscape) settings as texts to be read (e.g., 1990). Departing from this stance, he now rejects distancing terms like "perception" and "view" in concepts of landscape, instead advocating recognition of more direct immersion of people in the world: landscape is *disclosed* through experience (2001). Along with others, Thomas decries objectification, gendering, and distancing of nature – and with it, landscape – in Cartesian, Enlightenment, and capitalist thought.

Time and history

Issues of conceptualizing *time* clarify and amplify the foregoing distinctions, and how various approaches articulate with social theory. Shorter and longer time frames contrast the immediacy of phenomenological landscape experience (e.g., Thomas 1993a; Tilley 1994) with the long-term, palimpsest accumulation of people–landscape interactions over the *longue durée* (e.g., Bradley 1987; Erickson 1999; Muir 2000; Wandsnider 1998). For many archaeologists, this leads further, to engagement with landscapes today, although the focus of engagement differs with theoretical foundations.

Combining adaptationist, ecological approaches and historical sensibilities with material evidence, Kirch (e.g., 1999, 2000) describes the archaeological record as documenting millennia of human decisions and their consequences on the varied landscapes of Oceania; he contends that this understanding enables archaeologists to contribute significantly to understanding global environmental change, and to affecting current decisions on that global scale.

With theoretical wellsprings in ecology, history, geography, and dialectical Marxism, Crumley and Marquardt's historical ecology yields a history of decision-making in the Burgundy landscape, from the Iron Age through medieval times (Crumley 1994; Crumley and Marquardt 1987, 1990). Implications of the social strategies and impacts of such cumulative decisions – alternately continuous and disjunctive in aim and content – support the same authors' involvement with landscape and ecological activism today (e.g., Crumley 1994; Crumley, van Deventer, and Fletcher 2001).

Similarly, Bender refuses to relegate social involvement with Stonehenge to antiquity, embracing instead fully five millennia of inscribing social presence and conflict in that landscape (Bender 1993b, 1998). She also attends to landscapes today, but more particularly as means for understanding social fragmentation in the current postimperial world (2001).

Complementary inquiry on time emerges from Bradley's focus on the "afterlife of monuments," presaged earlier in reference to how landscape features are socialized and how cultural features are naturalized. He joins others (e.g., Barrett, Bender, Shennan,

Schlanger) who highlight the persistence of monuments and places in the landscape. Whereas Schlanger (1992) foregrounds economic resources in persistence of place use, Bradley and others look more emphatically at persistence and flux in meaning. Monuments and landscapes are reinterpreted by each generation. In that vein, he writes of the diverse ways in which physical persistence in the landscape articulates with social relations. Going further, and following Bloch, Leach, Lévi-Strauss, Ingold, Hobsbawm, and others, Bradley (1987) distinguishes cyclical, historical/linear, and magical (mythical) time, their differential impact on social memory, and their quite varied utility for recognizing continuities and breaks in human involvement with monuments and landscapes. Historical time invites defining linear sequences of events and actors; cyclical, ritual, and mythical time do not, or not nearly as readily. Moreover, text-marked historical periods are measured within centuries, decades or individual years; prehistory is more often scaled in multiple centuries or millennia. Specifically, Bradley criticizes archaeologists accustomed to studying historical periods for mistakenly inferring continuity from Bronze Age to post-Roman times in ritual observance at Yeavering, in Northumbria. The time spans involved are not alike, and their "sequential" occurrence implies continuity far less plausibly than discontinuity; as an alternative, Bradley suggests that elites of the later, historic periods invoked what seemed timeless authority by associating themselves spatially with the ruins, and in so doing, claiming ties with primordial ancestral or mythical antecedents. The "afterlife of monuments" is not simply the physical formation of ruins, but integral to understanding landscape as social history.

In landscape studies as in other archaeological inquiries, Barrett (1988) opposes functionalist views and emphases on moments in time, attending instead to material evidence as traces of ongoing and emergent social practices. Similarly, he opposes structuralist views (together with functionalism) as diverting attention from agency and history (e.g., 2000). He takes issue with those who describe landscape "as a history of things that have been done to the land" (1999a: 26), instead espousing inquiry into *inhabitation*, the social practices and experiences that made particular monuments possible – and, as important, into those that subsequently made continued living with those monuments in that landscape either possible or problematic (1999a, 1999b). His stimuli include the writings of Giddens on structuration, Bourdieu on practice, Foucault on embodied agency, Ingold on dwelling, and multiple authors on discourse theory and hermeneutics. Barrett's views are broadly compatible with Bradley's, but more aggressively thorough in departing from processualist modes of thinking and in urging archaeology to shift from solely consumer to active producer of social theory.

Social and spatial scale

Variable scale in time has already been mentioned; multiple authors also draw attention to the importance of social and spatial scale in landscape inquiries. Regions are often the "type size" for landscape (e.g., Fish and Kowalewski 1990; Sherratt 1996), and such scale is one reason that landscape inquiry melds with region-based research agendas central to processualism (e.g., Anschuetz, Wilshusen, and Scheick 2001; Sabloff and Ashmore 2001). But in practice, many scales are recognized, and of course, even the scales of regions vary. For example, Kirch (1999:38) suggests that both social and geographic scales were key factors in why people of Mangaia and Tikopia reacted so dramatically differently to ecosystem perturbations. Each region is a whole island, but from an adaptationist vantage, Kirch proposes that the much smaller size of Tikopia and concomitant social proximity discouraged an "us/them" distinction and instead, fostered shared coping with changes in food availability, changes in quality of landscape, and quality of life. Landscape scale shapes social actions in multiple ways.

Crumley and Marquardt contend that choosing among scales is critical for understanding landscapes. Scale defines the *grain* of the inquiry, shapes the questions that can be posed, and "activates both human environmental relations and our study of those relations. Just as specific models of reality are conceived, negotiated among human groups and applied at specific scales, so are our investigations of landscapes undertaken – and the results of our studies applied – at specific spatial and temporal scales" (1990:74–75). In the Burgundy research, Crumley (1987) explores how particularities of topography influenced definition of boundaries and defense, and through them, Celtic rules of descent, inheritance, and political and economic decision-making of varied social breadth.

Bender stresses *fluidity* and nesting of landscape scale, from quite localized to global settings (Bender 2001; Bender, Hamilton, and Tilley, 1997). Her position exemplifies a wider merging, even blurring, of burgeoning literatures on "landscape" and "place," and the congruence of social theory informing those lines of inquiry across many disciplines (e.g., Feld and Basso 1996; Groth and Bressi 1997; Hirsch and O'Hanlon 1995). As noted earlier, Bender engages such fluid and shifting landscape scales and referents as means for understanding wider social fragmentation current in the post-imperial world (1993a: 9, 2001).

Matters of scale figure, also, in landscapes characterized as structuralist replications of the cosmos or of social and political structure. These scales may also be nested, but replication of form and constituent elements is more standardized than in the kind of nesting Bender and others describe. For example, taking inspiration from Colby's cultural grammars, as well as Rapport's systems linkage of ideology and adaptation, Fritz (1978) describes the constructed landscape of Chaco Canyon as a system mapping society, mapping functional roles by creation of symmetry and asymmetry, within and among buildings – and inferentially, within and among the social groups that built them. Stein and Lekson (1992) examine the same landscape, but drawing instead from Leach, Eliade, Rapoport, and others, identify the critical components as earth and stone constructions mimicking the ambient world at several scales, thereby merging understanding of what analysts view as built and natural, and situating Chacoan peoples within nested settings, from individual buildings to cosmos. The latter approach is exemplified in a wide array of other contexts, from Neolithic Orkney (Richards 1996) to dynastic Egypt (Richards 1999), Iron Age and later East Africa (Schmidt 1983, 1997), and the Classic-period Maya lowlands (Ashmore 1991; Ashmore and Sabloff 2002). At all scales in which the structure is reproduced within a particular society, meaning is inferred to be substantially the same.

Meaning and its attachment

The foregoing raises questions about ascribing meaning to landscapes, ascriptions increasingly prominent in the more humanistic approaches to landscape study – that is, in social archaeologies of landscape. The issues are the social mechanisms by which meaning is attached, as well as the range of meanings that can be encompassed.

Meaning is attached through memory, and ritual and other forms of practice are the means of creating memory. As indicated earlier, movement within and across the landscape is considered the key to creation of memory (e.g., Bradley); some look explicitly to phenomenology, bodily immersion, and inhabitation to conceptualize movement and awareness (Barrett, Tilley, Thomas). Assertions about movement and memory find frequent recourse to wide-ranging aspects of social theory from Heidegger, Merleau-Ponty, Bourdieu, Giddens, and less often, Schama. Multiple traverses strengthen memories, reinforced further by the mnemonics of buildings, sculpture, other material inscriptions, and oral tradition (Basso 1996; Taçon 1999; van de Guchte 1999). Topography and monuments shape visual experience and movement (Bradley, Thomas, Tilley); monuments and movement can channel access to spectacles of sound or light, manifestations of the sacred that Eliade calls hierophany. Frequently emphasized, as well, are the repeated visitations and movements of ritual, especially procession and pilgrimage. But distinctions of ritual from everyday actions are sometimes unclear; seasonal or more opportunistic passages are also potent, especially with oral narrative and inscribed landmarks guiding the way. Among individuals and across generations, memories are created afresh; social conflict or periods of abandonment enhance the opportunities for attaching differing meanings (Barrett 1994, 1999b; Bender 1998; Bradley 1993, 1998).

Prominent among the meanings of landscape are power and identity, variously defined and expressed in sundry forms. These two labels gloss broad and overlapping ranges of specific meanings; theoretical foundations shape selection of emphasis. Among nonsedentary societies, familiar landscape can provide identity and moral foundation, a sense of history and genealogy, as well as coherence, stability, and attachment as people move through seasonal and annual rounds. Taçon (1999) describes such phenomena for Aboriginal Australia, and how stories of the Dreamtime combine with marked and simply recognized landmarks to ground people and empower them in conflicts over land claims. Although not embedded in a capitalist world, Bradley and others infer parallel phenomena for mobile Neolithic people of Atlantic Europe. In sedentary, even state-level societies, processions, pilgrimages, and ritualized political spectacle can serve similar ends, while simultaneously buttressing state authority and the identity of rulers. Landscape marking and movements have been taken to evince sanctification of royal authority in pharaonic Egypt (Richards 1999), medieval South India (Fritz 1986), and Maya lowlands (Ashmore 1991). Choreographed hierophanies of light or sound magnify the sense of the ruler's supernaturally sanctioned authority (Brady and Ashmore 1999).

Meanings of identity and power take many other landscape forms, as well. In US historical archaeology, for example, landscapes conventionally comprise formal gardens, interpreted most often as assertions of identity and of power among capitalist landowners in colonial North America (e.g., Kealhofer 1999; Yamin and Metheny 1996). Epperson (2000) examines landscapes of slaveholders, drawing on Foucault's discussions of Bentham's panopticon to understand gardens at Monticello and elsewhere as means for slave control. Reversing the focus, however, Pulsipher considers slaves' own gardens in the Caribbean as to have constituted strategies "to construct a decent life for themselves within a hostile system" (1994: 217), wherein movement and immersion in this material landscape could yield meaning, an identity of resistance, independence, and security. Building from ideas on concepts of ideology and its manipulation expressed by Shanks, Tilley, Lukács, and Rowe, Leone (1984) isolates a garden from near the opposite end of the colonial social spectrum and picks out its landscape materialization of social identity and power. Specifically, he interprets William Paca's garden as comprising that eighteenth-century landowner's assertion of exalted and unchallengeable social standing, by having created vanishing perspectives across descending terraces to extend the apparent size of the Annapolis property, and by having planted a carefully contrived geometric "wilderness" to affirm his "natural" control of social order.

Identity and power are also expressed in landscapes linking the living with the dead. Stonehenge, for example, joined other monuments and the Great Cursus to direct movements, control perceptions of topography and hierophany, and in the process to create memories about the proper manner of articulating the living and dead. Authors cited earlier seek to understand that landscape as ongoing social history, of phenomenology, inhabitation, and the afterlife of monuments. Parker Pearson takes a more structuralist tack (2002; Parker Pearson and Ramilisonina 1998). Using a relational analogy from Madagascar at Stonehenge and other Neolithic henge monuments in Wessex, he describes the replacement of wood with stone in construction as metaphorical transformation of an arena of the living to that of the ancestors; the stone circle, itself, embodied the ancestors. Barrett and Fewster (1998) reject the analogy as universalizing and ahistorical, privileging structure over practice. Buikstra and Charles, in turn, take issue with inhabitation and with phenomenology as privileging inferred memory and recognition over documentable events of social practice. Writing of the lower Illinois valley, they identify shifts in form and topographic location of burials and cemeteries (Buikstra and Charles 1999); inferences about differences in choices made and practices engaged allow them to relate changing emphases on mortuary ritual versus ancestor cult to sometimes dramatically altered social, economic, and political milieus (Charles and Buikstra 2002).

Roles of alternative voices

Despite notably diverse views, the foregoing discussions scarcely capture the range of voices. Focusing here on scholars based in the United Kingdom and in the United States underrecognizes or omits vibrant dialogues and landscape inquiries in other parts of the world. Papers from the Third World Archaeological Congress, in 1994, highlight multiple traditions (Ucko and Layton 1999), as do portions of recent compendia on rock-art research (Chippindale and Taçon 1998; Whitley 2001). But these still cannot encompass the full range. In Spain, for example, landscapes and their markings are subjects of intensive study; Parcero Oubiña, Criado Boado, and Santos Estévez (1998) draw on Derrida and Foucault to analyze structured meaning in sacred landscapes of Iberia, from prehistoric and historic times. In Australia, Head (1993) writes of merging perspectives from physical and cultural geography in pursuit of more sophisticated understandings of prehistoric landscapes. Along with many others, she writes of the Aboriginal Dreamtime and of potentials for its understanding in archaeology, treating issues not only of the sort discussed earlier here, but also moral, ethical, and political issues only implicit in preceding pages.

In such contexts, voices of aboriginal and other indigenous peoples in colonized nation-states are heard with increasing volume. Anschuetz and his colleagues (2001: 190–191) suggest that landscape study can facilitate dialogue between indigenous or traditional residents and archaeologists working there. Writing of archaeological research in the US Southwest, Zedeño (2000: 102) describes the current "compliance-driven" milieu as "a golden field of untapped possibilities for theoretical and methodological advance," including place-oriented Native American perspectives rather than expanse-oriented Western views (see also Snead and Preucel 1999). Other writings disseminate traditional interpretations, or pair them with archaeologists' inferences. And Bender (1998, 2001) contributes to this dialogue with regard to disenfranchised people in post-imperial times, for landscapes as starkly different as Stonehenge and post-apartheid South Africa.

A growing proportion of the discourse involves claims against colonized usurpation, both of physical possession and of interpretation. Indeed, several authors have attributed much current fascination with landscape to the rapid pace and dramatic scale of encroachment on traditional landscapes (Knapp and Ashmore 1999). The emerging focus of "cultural heritage" adopts concepts related to tradition, memory, and the cultural landscape in evaluating potentially significant sites (Cleere 1995). The landscape of Uluru/Ayers Rock is a particularly prominent Australian case of contested land rights, but far from the only one (e.g., Taçon 1999).

Future Trends

Concern with the issues outlined to this point is far from exhausted; dialogue will surely continue. Within social archaeologies of landscape, in particular, the roles of alternative voices will expand, such expansion shaped by political, ethical, and theoretical stances of the participants. Debates over appropriate characterization of space–time dynamics and life histories of landscapes will also continue, at issue being consideration of landscape as palimpsest of events or more socially fluid trajectories of inhabitation. Links between landscape and gender, landscape and the body have been little treated in this review; they merit a separate review (e.g., Bender 1999a; Gillespie 2000; Schmidt 1983; and several papers in Bender 1993a, and Ucko and Layton 1999), and certainly further development in landscape applications. I see every reason to expect that the assertions by Barrett and Stoddart, quoted at the outset of this chapter, will continue to be true for some time to come.

ACKNOWLEDGMENTS

I thank Lynn Meskell and Robert Preucel for inviting me to write this chapter. Many people have helped shape my thinking on these matters in recent years, and I am grateful especially to the editors and to Chelsea Blackmore, James Brady, Jane Buikstra, Carole Crumley, Clark Erickson, Rebecca Huss-Ashmore, Angela Keller, Bernard Knapp, Jeremy Sabloff, and Tom Patterson.

REFERENCES

Anschuetz, K. F., R. H. Wilshusen, and C. L. Scheick. 2001. An archaeology of landscapes: Perspectives and directions. *Journal of Archaeological Research* 9: 157–211.

Ashmore, W. 1991. Site planning principles and concepts of directionality among the ancient Maya. *Latin American Antiquity* 2: 199–226.

——, and A. B. Knapp (eds.) 1999. *Archaeologies of Landscape: Contemporary Perspectives*. Oxford: Blackwell.

——, and J. A. Sabloff. 2002. Spatial order in Maya civic plans. *Latin American Antiquity* 13: 201–15.

Barrett, J. C. 1988. Fields of discourse: reconstituting a social archaeology. *Critique of Anthropology* 7(3): 5–16.

——1994. *Fragments from Antiquity: An Archaeology of Social Life in Britain*. Oxford: Blackwell.

——1999a. Chronologies of landscape. In P. J. Ucko and R. Layton (eds.), *The Archaeology and Anthropology of Landscape: Shaping Your Landscape*. London and New York: Routledge, pp. 20–30.

——1999b. The mythical landscapes of the British Iron Age. In W. Ashmore and A. B. Knapp (eds.), *Archaeologies of Landscape: Contemporary Perspectives*. Oxford: Blackwell, pp. 253–265.

——.2000. A thesis on agency. In M-A. Dobres and J. Robb (eds.), *Agency in Archaeology*. London and New York: Routledge, pp. 61–68.

——, and K. J. Fewster. 1998. Stonehenge: *Is* the medium the message? *Antiquity* 72: 847–852.

Basso, K. 1996. *Wisdom Sits in Places: Landscape and Language among the Western Apache*. Albuquerque: University of New Mexico Press.

Bender, B. (ed.) 1993a. *Landscape: Politics and Perspectives*. Oxford: Berg.

——1993b. Stonehenge – contested landscapes (medieval and present day). In B. Bender (ed.), *Landscape: Politics and Perspectives*. Oxford: Berg, pp. 245–79.

——1998. *Stonehenge: Making Space*. Oxford: Berg.

——1999a. Subverting the western gaze: Mapping alternative worlds. In P. J. Ucko and R. Layton (eds.), *The Archaeology and Anthropology of Landscape: Shaping Your Landscape*. London and New York: Routledge, pp. 31–45.

——1999b. Introductory comments. *Antiquity* 73: 632–634.

——2001: Landscapes on-the-move. *Journal of Social Archaeology* 1: 75–89.

——, S. Hamilton, and C. Tilley. 1997. Leskernick: Stone worlds, alternative narratives, nested landscapes. *Proceedings of the Prehistoric Society* 63: 147–178.

Billman, B. R. 1999. Settlement pattern research in the Americas: Past, present, and future. In B. R. Billman and G. M. Feinman (eds.), *Settlement Pattern Studies in the Americas: Fifty Years Since Virú*. Washington, DC: Smithsonian Institution Press, pp. 1–5.

Bradley, R. 1987. Time regained – the creation of continuity. *Journal of the British Archaeological Association* 140: 1–17.

——1993. *Altering the Earth: The Origins of Monuments in Britain and Continental Europe*. Edinburgh: Society of Antiquaries of Scotland, The Rhind Lectures 1991–92. Monograph Series no. 8.

——1997. *Rock Art and the Prehistory of Atlantic Europe: Signing the Land*. London and New York: routledge.

——1998. Ruined buildings, ruined stones: Enclosures, tombs and natural places in the Neolithic of south-west England. *World Archaeology* 30: 13–22.

——2000. *An Archaeology of Natural Places*. London: Routledge.

Brady, J. E., and W. Ashmore. 1999. Caves, mountains, water: Ancient Maya ideational landscapes. In W. Ashmore and A. B. Knapp (eds.), *Archaeologies of Landscape: Contemporary Perspectives*. Oxford: Blackwell, pp. 124–145.

Buikstra, J. E., and D. K. Charles. 1999. Centering the ancestors: Cemeteries, mounds, and sacred landscapes in the ancient North American midcontinent. In W. Ashmore and A. B. Knapp (eds.), *Archaeologies of Landscape: Contemporary Perspectives.* Oxford: Blackwell, pp. 201–28.

Charles, D. K., and J. E. Buikstra. 2002. Siting, sighting, and citing the dead. In H. Silverman and D. B. Small (eds.), *The Space and Place of Death.* Arlington, VA: American Anthropological Association, Archeological Papers of the AAA, 11, pp. 13–26.

Chippindale, C., and P. S. C. Taçon (eds.) 1998. *The Archaeology of Rock Art.* Cambridge: Cambridge University Press.

Cleere, H. 1995. Cultural landscapes as world heritage. *Conservation and Management of Archaeological Sites* 1: 63–68.

Cronon, W. (ed.) 1996. *Uncommon Ground: Rethinking the Human Place in Nature.* New York: W. W. Norton.

Crumley, C. L. 1987. Celtic settlement before the conquest: The dialectics of landscape and power. In C. L. Crumley and W. H. Marquardt (eds.), *Regional Dynamics: Burgundian Landscapes in Historical Perspective.* San Diego, CA: Academic Press, pp. 403–429.

——1994. Historical ecology: A multidimensional ecological orientation. In C. L. Crumley (ed.), *Historical Ecology: Cultural Knowledge and Changing Landscapes.* Santa Fe, NM: SAR Press, pp. 1–13.

——, and W. H. Marquardt (eds.) 1987. *Regional Dynamics: Burgundian Landscapes in Historical Perspective.* San Diego, CA: Academic Press.

——, and W. H. Marquardt. 1990. Landscape: A unifying concept in regional analysis. In K. M. S. Allen, S. W. Green, and E. B. W. Zubrow (eds.), *Interpreting Space: GIS and Archaeology.* London: Taylor & Francis, pp. 73–79.

——, with A. E. van Deventer and J. J. Fletcher (eds.) 2001. *New Directions in Anthropology and Environment.* Walnut Creek, CA: AltaMira/Rowman & Littlefield.

Epperson, T. W. 2000. Panoptic plantations: The garden sights of Thomas Jefferson and George Mason. In J. A. Delle, S. A. Mrozowski, and R. Paynter (eds.), *The Lines that Divide: Historical Archaeologies of Race Class, and Gender.* Knoxville: University of Tennessee Press, pp. 58–77.

Erickson, C. L. 1993. The social organization of Prehispanic raised field agriculture in the Lake Titicaca basin. In V. L. Scarborough and B. L. Isaac (eds.), *Economic Aspects of Water Management in the Prehispanic New World.* Greenwich, CT: JAI Press, Research in Economic Anthropology, Supplement 7, pp. 369–426.

——1999. Neo-environmental determinism and agrarian "collapse" in Andean prehistory. *Antiquity* 73: 634–642.

Feinman, G. M. 1999. Defining a contemporary landscape approach: Concluding thoughts. *Antiquity* 73: 684–685.

Feld, S., and K. H. Basso (eds.) 1996. *Senses of Place.* Santa Fe, NM: SAR Press.

Fish, S. K. 1999. Conclusions: The settlement pattern concept from an Americanist perspective. In B. R. Billman and G. M. Feinman (eds.), *Settlement Pattern Studies in the Americas: Fifty Years Since Virú.* Washington, DC: Smithsonian Institution Press, pp. 203–208.

——, and S. A. Kowalewski (eds.) 1990. *The Archaeology of Regions: A Case for Full-coverage Survey.* Washington, DC: Smithsonian Institution Press.

Fisher, C. T., and T. L. Thurston (eds.) 1999. Special Section: Dynamic landscapes and sociopolitical process: The topography of anthropogenic environments in global perspective. *Antiquity* 73: 630–688.

Flannery, K. V. (ed.) 1976: *The Early Mesoamerican Village.* New York: Academic Press.

Fritz, J. M. 1978. Paleopsychology today: Ideational systems and adaptation in prehistory. In C. L. Redman, M. J. Berman, E. V. Curtin, W. T. Langhorne, Jr., N. M. Versaggi, and J. C.

Wanser (eds.), *Social Archaeology: Beyond Subsistence and Dating*. New York: Academic Press, pp. 37–59.

——1986. Vijayanagara: Authority and meaning of a South Indian imperial capital. *American Anthropologist* 88: 44–55.

Gillespie, S. D. 2000. Maya "nested houses": The ritual construction of place. In R. A. Joyce and S. D. Gillespie (eds.), *Beyond Kinship: Social and Material Reproduction in House Societies*. Philadelphia: University of Pennsylvania Press, pp. 135–160.

Gosden, C., and L. Head. 1994. Landscape – a usefully ambiguous concept. *Archaeology in Oceania* 29: 113–116.

Groth, P., and T. W. Bressi (eds.) 1997. *Understanding Ordinary Landscapes*. New Haven, CT: Yale University Press.

Head, L. 1993. Unearthing prehistoric cultural landscapes: A view from Australia. *Transactions of the Institute of British Geographers* 18: 481–499.

Hirsch, E., and M. O'Hanlon (eds.) 1995. *The Anthropology of Landscape: Perspectives on Place and Space*. Oxford: Clarendon Press.

Hodder, I., and C. Orton. 1976. *Spatial Analysis in Archaeology*. Cambridge: Cambridge University Press.

Ingold, T. 1986. *The Appropriation of Nature: Essays on Human Ecology and Social Relations*. Iowa City: University of Iowa Press.

Johnson, M. 1999. *Archaeological Theory: An Introduction*. Oxford: Blackwell.

Kealhofer, L. 1999. Creating social identity in the landscape: Tidewater, Virginia, 1600–1750. In W. Ashmore and A. B. Knapp (eds.), *Archaeologies of Landscape: Contemporary Perspectives*. Oxford: Blackwell, pp. 58–82.

Kirch, P. V. 1999. Microcosmic histories: Island perspectives on "global change." *American Anthropologist* 99: 30–42.

——2000. *On the Road of the Winds: An Archaeological History of the Pacific Islands before European Contact*. Berkeley: University of California Press.

Knapp, A. B. 1997. *The Archaeology of Late Bronze Age Cypriot Society: The Study of Settlement, Survey and Landscape*. Glasgow: University of Glasgow, Department of Archaeology, Occasional Paper 4.

——, and W. Ashmore. 1999. Archaeological landscapes: Constructed, conceptualized, ideational. In W. Ashmore and A. B. Knapp (eds.), *Archaeologies of Landscape: Contemporary Perspectives*. Oxford: Blackwell, pp. 1–30.

Layton, R., and P. J. Ucko. 1999. Introduction: Gazing on the landscape and encountering the environment. In P. J. Ucko and R. Layton (eds.), *The Archaeology and Anthropology of Landscape: Shaping Your Landscape*. London and New York: Routledge, pp. 1–20.

Lekson, S. H. 1996: Landscape with ruins: Archaeological approaches to built and unbuilt environments. *Current Anthropology* 37: 886–892.

Leone, M. P. 1984. Interpreting ideology in historical archaeology: Using the rules of perspective in the William Paca Garden in Annapolis, Maryland. In D. Miller and C. Tilley (eds.), *Ideology, Power and Prehistory*. Cambridge: Cambridge University Press, pp. 25–35.

Muir, R. 2000. Conceptualising landscape. *Landscapes* 1: 4–21.

Parcero Oubiña, C., F. Criado Boado, and M. Santos Estévez. 1998. Rewriting landscape: Incorporating sacred landscapes into cultural traditions. *World Archaeology* 30: 159–176.

Parker Pearson, M. 2002. Placing the physical and the incorporeal dead: Stonehenge and changing concepts of ancestral space in Neolithic Britain. In H. Silverman and D. B. Small (eds.), *The Space and Place of Death*. Arlington VA: American Anthropological Association, Archeological Papers of the AAA 11, pp. 145–160.

——, and Ramilisonina. 1998. Stonehenge for the ancestors: The stones pass on the message. *Antiquity* 72: 308–326.

Pulsipher, L. M. 1994. The landscapes and ideational roles of Caribbean slave gardens. In N. F. Miller and K. L. Gleason (eds.), *The Archaeology of Garden and Field*. Philadelphia: University of Pennsylvania Press, pp. 202–221.

Richards, C. 1996. Monuments as landscape: Creating the centre of the world in late Neolithic Orkney. *World Archaeology* 28: 190–208.

Richards, J. E. 1999. Conceptual landscapes in the Egyptian Nile valley. In W. Ashmore and A. B. Knapp (eds.), *Archaeologies of Landscape: Contemporary Perspectives*. Oxford: Blackwell, pp. 83–100.

Rossignol, J. 1992. Concepts, methods, and theory building: A landscape approach. In J. Rossignol and L. Wandsnider (eds.), *Space, Time, and Archaeological Landscapes*. New York: Plenum, pp. 3–19.

——, and L. Wandsnider (eds.) 1992. *Space, Time, and Archaeological Landscapes*, New York: Plenum.

Sabloff, J. A., and W. Ashmore. 2001. An aspect of archaeology's recent past and its relevance in the new millennium. In G. M. Feinman and T. D. Price (eds.), *Archaeology at the Millennium: A Sourcebook*. New York: Kluwer/Plenum, pp. 11–32.

Sauer, C. 1925. The morphology of landscapes. *University of California Publications in Geography* 2: 19–54.

Schama, S. 1995. *Landscape and Memory*. New York: Knopf.

Schlanger, S. 1992. Recognizing persistent places in Anasazi settlement systems. In J. Rossignol and L. Wandsnider (eds.), *Space, Time, and Archaeological Landscapes*. New York: Plenum, pp. 91–112.

Schmidt, P. R. 1983. An alternative to a strictly materialist perspective: A review of historical archaeology, ethnoarchaeology, and symbolic approaches in African archaeology. *American Antiquity* 48: 62–79.

——1997. *Iron Technology in East Africa: Symbolism, Science, and Archaeology*. Bloomington: Indiana University Press.

Sherratt, A. 1996. "Settlement patterns" or "landscape studies"? Reconciling reason and romance. *Archaeological Dialogue* 3: 140–159.

Snead, J. E., and R. W. Preucel. 1999. The ideology of settlement: Ancestral Keres landscapes in the northern Rio Grande. In W. Ashmore and A. B. Knapp (eds.), *Archaeologies of Landscape: Contemporary Perspectives*. Oxford: Blackwell, pp. 169–197.

Spirn, A. W. 1996. Constructing nature: The legacy of Frederick Law Olmsted. In William Cronon (ed.), *Uncommon Ground: Rethinking the Human Place in Nature*. New York: W. W. Norton, pp. 91–113.

Stein, J. R., and S. H. Lekson. 1992. Anasazi ritual landscapes. In D. E. Doyel (ed.), *Anasazi Regional Organization and the Chaco System*. Albuquerque, NM: Maxwell Museum of Anthropology, Anthropological Papers 5, pp. 87–100.

Stoddart, S. (ed.) 2000. *Landscapes from Antiquity*. Cambridge and Oxford: Antiquity and Oxbow.

——, and E. B. W. Zubrow. 1999. Changing places. *Antiquity* 73: 686–688.

Stone, G. D. 1996. *Settlement Ecology: The Social and Spatial Organization of Kofyar Agriculture*. Tucson: University of Arizona Press.

Taçon, P. S. C. 1999. Identifying ancient sacred landscapes in Australia: From physical to social. In W. Ashmore and A. B. Knapp (eds.), *Archaeologies of Landscape: Contemporary Perspectives*. Oxford: Blackwell, pp. 33–57.

Thomas, J. 1990. Monuments from the inside: The case of the Irish megalithic tombs. *World Archaeology* 22: 168–178.

——1991. *Rethinking the Neolithic*. Cambridge: Cambridge University Press.

—— 1993a. The politics of vision and the archaeologies of landscape. In B. Bender (ed.), *Landscape: Politics and Perspectives*. Oxford: Berg, pp. 19–48.

—— 1993b. The hermeneutics of megalithic space. In C. Tilley (ed.), *Interpretative Archaeology*. Providence, RI and Oxford: Berg, pp. 73–97.

—— 2001. Archaeologies of place and landscape. In I. Hodder (ed), *Archaeological Theory Today*. Cambridge: Polity Press, pp. 165–186.

Tilley, C. 1993. Art, architecture, landscape [Neolithic Sweden]. In B. Bender (ed.), *Landscape: Politics and Perspectives*. Oxford: Berg, pp. 49–84.

—— 1994. *A Phenomenology of Landscape: Places, Paths and Monuments*. Oxford: Berg.

Ucko, P. J., and R. Layton (eds.) 1999. *The Anthropology and Archaeology of Landscapes: Shaping Your Landscape*. London: Routledge.

van de Guchte, M. 1999. The Inca cognition of landscape: Archaeology, ethnohistory, and the aesthetics of alterity, In W. Ashmore and A. B. Knapp (eds.), *Archaeologies of Landscape: Contemporary Perspectives*. Oxford: Blackwell, pp. 149–168.

Wandsnider, L. 1998. Regional scale processes and archaeological landscape units. In A. F. Ramenofsky and A. Steffen (eds.), *Unit Issues in Archaeology: Measuring Time, Space, and Material*. Salt Lake City: University of Utah Press, pp. 87–102.

Whitley, D. S. (ed.) 2001. *Handbook of Rock Art Research*. Walnut Creek, CA: AltaMira/Rowman & Littlefield.

Yamin, R., and K. B. Metheny (eds.) 1996. *Landscape Archaeology: Reading and Interpreting the American Historical Landscape*. Knoxville: University of Tennessee Press.

Zedeño, M. N. 2000. On what people make of places: A behavioral cartography. In M. B. Schiffer (ed.), *Social Theory in Archaeology*. Salt Lake City: University of Utah Press, pp. 97–111.

12

Living and Working at Home: The Social Archaeology of Household Production and Social Relations

Julia A. Hendon

This chapter discusses a topic that has been at the heart of archaeology for a long time. Although not always named as such, a concern with household production and social relations has informed archaeological research of different theoretical orientations and operating under various paradigms. The study of household production and social relations is integral to numerous questions of archaeological inquiry, including the nature of ancient economies and social organization; the relationship between ideology and power; the evolution of social complexity; structure and agency; the construction of social identity and difference; and the study of conflict. The question for this chapter becomes, then, what would a social archaeology of household production and social relations look like? I argue that it would be embodied, agent-centered, concerned with understanding social identity and difference through the analysis of the lived experience of social groups, and that it would recognize the importance of understanding meaning as well as function.

These issues can only be addressed successfully within a social archaeology framework if we avoid thinking of "the household" as an analytical unit representative of some set of behaviors (Pauketat 2001), and instead see households as the result of the interaction of structure and agency, larger social forms, and the individual (Cowgill 1993; Dobres and Robb 2000; Johnson 1989). The household has achieved the status of an ontological category in anthropology that stands in contrast to the family, even though these categories are generalizations from a specific historical and cultural context (Birdwell-Pheasant and Lawrence-Zúñiga 1999:26). If the household is not an ontological category, when is it useful to speak of the household? I would suggest that it becomes a useful category to social archaeology when we seek to connect social identity and economic production with a locale (Giddens 1985): the house, or the spatial setting in which people live and carry out their day-to-day practices. A social archaeology of household production and social relations must therefore not only come to terms with the household but also with the house, recognizing that houses and the people who live in them are in a "mutually constituting" relationship (Birdwell-Pheasant and Lawrence-Zúñiga 1999:4).

The household emerged as a named unit in archaeology with the publication of a special edition of *American Behavioral Scientist* edited by Richard Wilk and William Rathje (Wilk and Rathje 1982a). The rapid adoption of the household as a focus of archaeological inquiry and the identification of household archaeology as a kind of archaeology, particularly in North America, demonstrate that the household filled a gap in our conceptual framework (see Allison 1999; Hendon 1996; Manzanilla 1990; Robin 2003; Svensson 1998 for recent discussions of the household and household archaeology).

Household archaeology starts with a particular social institution, the household. Households entered archaeological discourse as a conceptual alternative to family or kinship, which were seen as too intangible to be defined adequately with archaeological evidence and which were becoming increasingly problematic concepts in sociocultural anthropology (Yanagisako 1979). As something that could be usefully defined on the basis of task and activities, or function, household provided a better starting point than the family for research operating within a materialist or ecological paradigm (Wilk and Rathje 1982b). The exact relationship among household members, or how they thought about their relationship, however, were seen as unimportant. What mattered was that the household could be defined as the minimal social unit that allowed certain basic personal and social needs to be filled, including economic production and the reproduction of people and institutions (Santley and Hirth 1993). Furthermore, households have a spatial referent, the house or the residential area, that archaeologists can identify and study. For American-trained archaeologists interested in the household, therefore, houses or living areas became a proxy for the social institution under study.

The social institution of the household has not become the focus of research by European-trained archaeologists to the same extent (but see Allison 1999; Svensson 1998). A comparable focus might be termed "house archaeology." British-trained archaeologists have, for example, studied houses less as a proxy for a particular kind of social group and more as a material representation of social relations and of the symbolic meaning structuring those relations. Thus, Scott (1990) argues that changes in the design of villas in Britain during the Roman occupation are related to and a reflection of changing socioeconomic relations between family and outsiders. Combining information on the design and layout of houses with material culture and visual imagery, Ian Hodder has argued that symbolic rather than functional concerns underlie and explain spatial arrangements, choice of images, and location of activities at such sites as Çatalhöyük. Hodder suggests that Neolithic societies of Europe and the Near East made a distinction between what he labels *habitus* and *domus* (Hodder 1992; see also Hodder 1990). Hodder contends that the meanings associated with these binary categories encapsulate how early farming societies made sense of their social and natural world. Thus the domus and habitus meant different things to Neolithic societies in southeastern Europe than they did to the later Bronze Age societies in the same region. Influenced by Hodder's structuralist approach, other archaeologists have argued for similar kinds of ways of thinking about space and the house in prehistoric European societies (see, e.g., Hingley 1990; Richards 1990). This focus on the contrasts created by being inside or outside of the house, on the left or right sides, in the light or dark, or in public or private space, draw our attention to the importance of meaning but nevertheless leave us with models that do not display much real concern for the texture and variability of social relations.

Such functionalist or cognitive approaches do not, by themselves, provide a way to create a social archaeology of household production and social relations. Both suffer from a lack of people as subjects, agents, and embodied beings. The interest in reconstructing women's roles in ancient societies that emerged around the same time as household archaeology, although still functionalist to some degree, nevertheless made it necessary to consider households as something more than a minimal unit of production and reproduction. Both womanist (Joyce and Claassen 1997) and gendered perspectives have helped move us toward a social archaeology of household production and social relations by requiring archaeologists to think of households as made up of people, or at least types of people. These perspectives have also required us to recast questions of household production and social relations as questions of practice, in order to address such issues as whose labor was involved, how it was controlled, how decisions were made, and what meaning was given to production by different types of people (Hendon 1996; Tringham 1991). Such questions show the influence of feminist anthropologists, who pointed to the necessity of reworking the concept of the household from a functionalist to a conflict theory-oriented perspective (see Hart 1992; Moore 1992). Interrogating the relationship between gender and production raises questions of value and meaning that go beyond energetic investment, practical use, or scarcity and satiety. In developing pottery vessels and adopting them as the primary food processing and storing containers, the prehistoric societies in the American Southwest increased women's workloads (Crown and Wills 1995). The effort of producing cloth by Aztec and Maya women in Prehispanic Mesoamerica was legitimated through ideologies creating a complementary interplay between two particular social identities of great import to the political economy of Mesoamerican complex societies: male warrior and female weaver. These particular identities were enacted through practice, inscribed through repeated training, validated through periodic ritual, and held up as ideals through permanent visual media such as figurines (Brumfiel 1991, 1996; Hendon 1999; Joyce 1993, 2000a). Crown and Fish (1996) postulate that Hohokam women's status changed over time based in part on the enclosure of patios and houses, making these day-to-day activities less visible. Under these circumstances, houses and the domestic setting become not just a neutral location for activities but also a space within which certain kinds of social relations and identities are defined, created, and emphasized through meaningful action. Socially constructed identities are constituted from multiple elements, of course, of which gender is only one aspect (Gilchrist 1999; Joyce 2000a; Meskell 1999; Moore 1994). Gender has nevertheless served as a rewarding entry point into "peopling" household production and social relations.

Just as thinking about gender has the potential to bring attention to the construction of the person, the increasing study of agency has the potential to further social archaeology's study of the meaning and consequences of people's actions, the mutually constituting connection between production, the objects produced, and the social identity of the producers, and the role of day-to-day practice in these processes. Archaeologists do not all define or use agency in the same way (see Dobres and Robb 2000; Saitta 1994), and not all of these definitions will help advance a social archaeology of household production and social relations. Methodological individualism or limiting agency to the actions of a few are not useful approaches for an embodied, actor-centered approach (see Clark 2000; Gero 2000). So-called big man or "aggrandizer" models for the development of social inequality, for example, put too much weight on the explanatory significance of the aggressive personalities and accumulative abilities of a small subset of men. Such personalities are assumed to be a cross-cultural psychological type (Hayden 1996). Regardless of the validity of this assumption, aggrandizer models are inherently unsatisfactory because of the way that they ignore the agency of those who support – or fail to support – through their labor and production, the activities of these status-seeking individuals (Clark 2000). A much more useful approach is to study the interrelation between structure and agency as part of a consideration of the actions of social collectivities as a way of defining identity, reproducing social relations, and causing change.

Underlying both of these starting points for analysis – i.e., gender and agency – is a recognition that a social archaeology must take into account practice. It is not sufficient to identify what households do or where they do it. It is not even sufficient to identify what particular household members do or where they do it (e.g., Inomata et al. 2002). The meaning of these actions, as part of a process of creating and defining social relations and identities, is crucial to any effective understanding of how activities and relations, at the scale of the household, can inform us about how societies constitute themselves and how they change.

Household, gender, and house archaeology provide the foundation upon which a social archaeology of the household may be built. That such a structure has barely begun to be constructed can be traced to two main causes. First is the assumption that households or houses are only interesting for certain kinds of analyses, and second is the marginalization of gender as being about women rather than identity (see Joyce, chapter 4, this volume). Four things are crucial to a social archaeology of the household: (1) an immersion in the materiality of the domestic (Tringham 1994); (2) a focus on the nature and meaning of day-to-day experiences and practices (Mizoguchi 1995) rather than just their function; (3) a recognition of the variability of households (Hendon 1996); and (4) an appreciation of the importance of understanding social processes at different social scales (Tringham 1991).

The Materiality of the Domestic

Household archaeology, as discussed above, has turned to the house as a proxy, to the point where archaeologists write of excavating the household when they really mean they have excavated buildings and spaces that form part of domestic life. However, a certain unease has pervaded household archaeology, precisely because of the assumption that the true focus of interest is a social institution which must be an abstraction or an idea in people's heads, not a material form. Thus, houses become a stand-in that must always be qualified as less than ideal. British-influenced "house" archaeology has used houses as a reflection of cognitive models that structure worldviews. This approach is more sensitive to questions of meaning but often treats the house as a static by-product of such models rather than an integral part of them. Although the point often goes unrecognized, or at least undiscussed, this is an issue of theory as much as of method. It is not just about operationalizing the connection between artifact and interpretation but is also, and most importantly, about how one theorizes material culture. A social archaeology of the household should start from the standpoint that "social life is lived out *through* the material world" (Thomas 1996:55). We need to study that material world not just as a reflection of past behavior or the record of past events but as a "dialectical web of material production and social reproduction" (Dobres 2000:126).

The value of studying household production and social relations lies in its ability to shed light not just on the function of the household or its contribution to adaptation but on the ways that human subjects are created and shaped, identities defined and embodied, and roles enacted and changed through practices carried out by human and material agents, including the house itself and the material culture used within the domestic setting (Birdwell-Pheasant and Lawrence-Zúñiga 1999; Dobres 2000; Meskell 2002; Tringham 1995), even when the buildings are not well preserved. Meadows (1999) demonstrates the degree to which material culture and refuse can define the spatial and social areas on the landscape that less "romanized" Britons used as the focus of household interaction. Houses, like people, have biographies, not stages of construction (Ullén 1994). Tringham's (1994, 1995) work on creating an archaeological poetics that captures both biographies, that of house and person, has done much to make clear the intimate connection between people and their dwellings. As she and others have discussed, such biographies extend through and beyond actual use to include house destruction and replacement (Bailey 1990; Boivin 2000; Martin and Russell 2000; Stevanović 1997). The design, siting, and use of residential space interact with human action and meaning to create lived space in which the house becomes integral to the construction of social identities through a process of unexamined movements, views, and spatial arrangements (Hendon 2002b; Joyce and Hendon 2000; Malan 1997). The transmission of knowledge and technique, the bodily discipline, the arrangement of productive action, and the negotiation among household members do not occur in a spatial vacuum. They take place in some kind of constructed space which is not a neutral backdrop, but rather a shaper of people's actions and a contributor to the meaning given to those actions (Kokkinidou and Nikolaidou 1997). Even such apparently static activity as storage becomes part of the biography of lived space and thus of the people living there (Hendon 2000; Wesson 1999).

The Day-To-Day

Activities, related to day-to-day living and to the celebration of special events, serve as the primary way that the interaction between structure and agency may be studied. Activities should not be used to establish a type (of economic production, of social relations, of behavior), that we can label the "the household," or "the household mode of production." They should be used as a way to study how production and social relations are constituted through actions in a particular setting (see Tringham 1996). "Artifacts 'speak,' not so much because actors created them as 'texts' but because they are marked with the gestures and habits of their production and use, they are inscribed by the social processes involved in their creation, employment, and abandonment" (McCall 1999:18). Vitelli's (1999) intriguing attempts to understand why pottery develops when and how it does in the Greek Neolithic illustrate the value of focusing on the different ways social processes are inscribed on material culture. Her detailed contextual analyses and her understanding of clay as a medium allow her to move beyond common assumptions about "behavior" and common-sense reasons for why early farmers would "invent" pottery. Her work exemplifies Dobres's (2000) argument that technology needs to be reconceptualized as a set of social processes involving materials, action, knowledge, and relationships between human and material agents.

Studies of household-level production have often really been of the exchange of objects that were produced within a domestic setting and have been oriented toward assessing the evolutionary or developmental role of economic specialization and exchange (see Costin 1991). In these models, production and exchange only become significant when they result in non-utilitarian objects or when control of the labor or the product shifts from producer to someone else. Such shifts represent important transformations in social relations, often leading to a permanent rearrangement of the social order. The effect on the households themselves – or on the groups who are not part of those in control – needs to be considered as part of our understanding of larger-scale social changes in economy and social structure (e.g., Bowen 1992; Emerson 1997; Hagstrum 2001; Junker, Mudar, and Schwaller 1994; Mehrer 1995; Scott 1990). The tendency has been to focus on the consequences of changing social relations of production without also considering the reaction to such changes. How are inequities recognized, made sense of, responded to, or resisted?

Just as technology is a set of social processes, so are production and exchange. Approached from this perspective, all kinds of production have the potential to inform us about social relations. Production situated in the domestic space of the household or the house offers one conjunction of social action and locale, the study of which contributes to our understanding of agency and social identity. However, in order to realize fully the potential of this study, we need to let go of certain assumptions, including that of household self-sufficiency (Hagstrum 2001), of agency as synonymous with modern notions of the individual (Inomata et al. 2002), of the production of prestige goods as the only important kind of production, and, more broadly, of the household as a functional unit rather than a set of social relations enacted through practice (Meskell 1999; Woolf 1997).

The production, exchange, and use of "ordinary goods" (Smith 1999) can be equally significant in the creation and maintenance of multiple group identities and affiliations. Wattenmaker (1995, 1998) notes that non-elite households at the small third millennium BC site of Kurban Höyük (Turkey) acquired large flint blades and wheel-made pottery from specialists while continuing to produce other kinds of stone tools and make some pottery vessels by hand. The types of goods produced by specialists that were found in Kurban domestic contexts suggest to Wattenmaker that people living in this small town were not only part of a diversified regional economy but also used these goods as items of social display. Wheel-made ceramics were used for serving food, which would increase their social visibility and thus their use as conveyers of social and symbolic information. The ability to manipulate such social symbols was as important to the non-elite households operating at the small scale of the domestic setting as it was to the elite. Working on a more recent society marked not only by social stratification but also by inequities based on ethnicity, Silliman (2001) has argued that nineteenth-century Californian Native Americans who had become laborers in a colonial ranching economy persisted in making and using stone tools as part of a conscious attempt to create a separate social identity. Even seemingly simple and utilitarian actions, such as food choices and refuse disposal, contribute to social identity construction (Lightfoot, Martinez, and Schiff 1998; Martin and Russell 2000; Meadows 1999), an issue studied in detail by Lightfoot, Martinez, and Schiff as part of their research on the multi-ethnic nineteenth-century settlement of Fort Ross in California. Attention to nondiscursive practices *as* nondiscursive practices moves us beyond behavioral approaches and site formation processes to a consideration of the spatiality of the material world (Boivin 2000; Martin and Russell 2000).

The identities created through productive action, material culture, and the setting contribute to the definition of relations of power within and among groups. Rather than construe power as something certain people have or as a particular capacity, a social archaeological perspective starts from the premise that "power is an effect of the operation of social relations" (Moore 1996:205). Studying power, therefore, needs to take a multi-scalar approach (O'Donovan 2002; see also Sweely 1999). The household represents one level of social relations and interaction where differences in relations of power are enacted not only through the control of such tangible factors as material resources or labor (Blanton 1995) but through the identities that are defined and inscribed through routinized quotidian and periodic action (Joyce 2000a, 2000b; Kokkinidou and Nikolaidou 1997; Robin 2002; Tringham 1994). Practice- and agency-oriented studies of the household and the domestic space of the house can shed light on how gender, age, class, and other factors intersect to shape these identities (Brumfiel 1992, 1996; Meskell 1999). Such studies can also help us understand how households were altered by their interaction with other households, communities, and larger forms of political control (Emerson 1997; Hendon 2002a, b; Henshaw 1999; Meadows 1999; Pauketat 1994; Tringham 1995; Wesson 1999).

Variability

These identities and interactions can only be understood if we refrain from reducing the household to a behavioral unit. Treating the complex of relations and actions as "the household" creates an analytic construct that impedes effective study of household dynamics and their relationship to larger theoretical questions. It is vital that a social archaeology of household production and social relations accepts the importance of studying the variability of households and their settings. Research that has done so (e.g., Gonlin 1994, 1996; Hoffman 1999; Junker, Mudar, and Schwaller 1994; Samuel 1999; Wattenmaker 1998) has been far more productive than research which has not. Archaeologists are always working with a limited body of data and the ability to define a type may seem to be a way to achieve generalizations about ancient societies. In the process, however, we often fail to appreciate the explanatory value of variation. If all households are the same because they are a type (of settlement, of relationships, of function), then there is very little of interest to say about them once one has described the architectural features and enumerated the activities associated with each type (see Praetzellis 1998). One now knows the characteristics of the type and has reaffirmed the functions associated with that type. It is only by working against this assumption of uniformity that one can begin to see how people used day-to-day action in the setting of the house to create differences of political, moral, and social significance.

Research on the seventh- to eleventh-century Maya occupation of the Copan Valley, Honduras, demonstrates the limitations of a typological approach. Intensive settlement pattern studies carried out in the 1970s and 1980s resulted in fine-grained recording of the final phase of occupation throughout the valley and the categorization of all sites into a four-level typology. Although each type is based on the physical appearance of the site, including the number of buildings, their height and construction material, and the overall size of the site, the types are also intended to reflect differences in house-hold size, wealth, and status (Hendon 1992). Although useful as a first approximation of social variation based primarily on the recording of unexcavated buildings, this site typology has proved increasingly unable to capture the different ways that Copan Valley households varied internally and from one another. Research on sites assigned to the lowest level of the typology has demonstrated not only that rural and urban households belonging to the same type differ markedly in terms of activities and measures of wealth, but also that rural households were not equivalent in the kinds of specialized production they engaged in or in their access to imported materials or objects, such as green obsidian, polychrome pottery from northern Honduras, and jade or greenstone jewelry (Gonlin 1994, 1996). Like the Kurban Höyük villagers studied by Wattenmaker, rural Copan households created and reinforced social relations and social difference through the use of special tableware and objects for personal use that were visible to others.

Scale

The household, as a set of relations, a focus of action, and a physical setting, must become an object of study in its own right. If we are indeed interested in *what* societies were like for different kinds of people (Tringham 1994) and in *how* societies change (Pauketat 2001), then we need to study economic production and social relations at several different scales. The household, the social institution most often invoked when considering these processes at a small or micro scale, is interesting precisely because of its articulation with other social institutions and its involvement in social processes that help explain how change occurs, what form it takes, and what its consequences are. The development of more formal, institutionalized kinds of governance, of more enduring social hierarchies, or of the complex features called "the state," does not make the domestic any less important. It merely changes the ways that the intimate setting of the house intersects with other settings and provides a greater set of con-trasts (Pollock, Pope, and Coursey 1996; Wattenmaker 1995). Nor is this a one-way flow of change or influence. The domestic is not just acted upon differently or subject to a greater weight of community-wide influence. It is also, simultaneously, part of the construction and negotiation of social relations.

A multi-scalar approach also leads to a more careful consideration of the role of place and the spatial dimension of domestic life in the shaping of social relations. I noted at the beginning of this chapter that a social archaeology of household produc-tion and social relations would be embodied, agent-centered, and concerned with understanding social identity and difference through the analysis of the lived experience of social groups. Embodiment, agency, and the lived experience all involve, to at least some extent, actions and interactions situated in time and space. Moreover, these situated actions and interactions are shaped by the space in which they take place as much as by the people involved (Hendon 2000; Richards 1990). In this sense, the house, or more broadly, the lived space, becomes an agent in the construction of social identity (Birdwell-Pheasant and Lawrence-Zúñiga 1999; Tringham 1994). Movement through interior and exterior spaces (Joyce and Hendon 2000), degrees of visibility (Hendon 2002b), and the design of houses and other living areas (Bachand et al. in press; Lightfoot, Martinez, and Schiff 1998; Meskell 2002; Uruñuela Ladrón de Guevara and Plunket Nagoda 1998) are all ways that domestic space becomes a meaningful locale.

Conclusions

In my own work on sixth- to eleventh-century high-status urban households of the Copan Valley, this lived space has proved to be a productive scale at which to study the construction of social identity, maintenance of social relations, and the creation of social difference as embodied in the built environment and peoples' actions within that built environment. In their residential compounds, the Copan elite engaged in specialized production of prestige goods such as textiles and shell ornaments as well as materials needed for daily life, such as obsidian tools (Hendon 1997). They made visible their claims to be considered important and wealthy through the design and construction of their houses and in the layout of buildings, creating particular ways to see into or to enter their living areas (Hendon 2002b). Variation in the location of storage areas was another way that households differentiated themselves. Residents in the most elaborate residential compounds concealed storage areas inside their houses. Other households put their storage areas on display through the construction of free-standing storehouses. These choices created differences in knowledge between the people living in a particular residential compound and their neighbors or visitors (Hendon 2000). Appropriate patterns of embodiment were made visible through large-scale stone sculpture of young men and small-scale clay figures of mature men and women (Bachand, Joyce, and Hendon 2003; Hendon 2003c). Life-cycle rituals, accompanied by feasting and music-making, as well as the daily activities of production, reinforced these images of ideal appearance and behavior as well as reaffirming household solidarity and social relations (Hendon 2003b). Burial of people, objects, and even parts of earlier buildings inside buildings or pavements further reinforced the affiliation between individual and the social group defined by shared residence and practices. These types of interment also created another area of differentially shared knowledge through selective remembering and forgetting (Hendon 2000, 2003a).

The very complexity of Copan society ensures that people were members of many different social groups, who engaged in the construction and maintenance of the social relations underlying political and economic structures through multiple forms of social interaction taking place in various locales and operating at different social scales. One cannot reduce all these aspects of social life to a single variable, whether it be class (the elite), political institution (leadership), or social organization (the household). Nor can one concentrate only on a single setting or type of physical space in order to learn everything about a particular society. Instead, one must ask what is to be learned from focusing at a particular scale or on a particular locale. The study of the places where members of the elite lived, in some cases over many generations, in organized social collectivities yields a finer-grained understanding of what practices were central to their ability to maintain the patterns of everyday life and gives us a sense of how these high-status people re-created the social relations central to their role as an elite within the larger society of the Copan Valley. None of these insights would be possible from assuming that all households were alike or even that all elite households were alike due to their shared class membership. Nor does the texture of elite life at Copan – its emphasis on control of production, rituals, knowledge, and even the very bodies of its members, both living and dead – become apparent when working at a different scale, such as that provided by a study of settlement pattern, or with different sources of information, such as that furnished by the written records of Maya royalty.

Plausible, useful, and intellectually interesting interpretations will not emerge on their own from the description of artifact types, settlement patterns, site formation processes or other archaeological data. Such exercises in "hyperscience" (Majewski 2000), no matter how detailed the archaeological record, serve merely to conceal the implicit theorizing that underlie them and, in the process, violate the nature of archaeological research. Barrett (1994:92) notes that the study of domestic architecture "is fixed at the intersection of a number of interpretive regimes." We need to consider what those regimes are. Theorizing meaning, practice, and agency is crucial to a social archaeology of household production and social relations. Central to this process of understanding is a greater attention to materiality, the day-to-day, variability, and scale.

REFERENCES

Allison, P. M. (ed.) 1999. *The Archaeology of Household Activities*. London: Routledge.

Bachand, H., R. A. Joyce, and J. A. Hendon. 2003. Bodies moving in space: Ancient Mesoamerican human sculpture and embodiment. *Cambridge Archaeological Journal* 13(2): 238–247.

Bailey, D. W. 1990. The living house: Signifying continuity. In R. Samson (ed.), *The Social Archaeology of Houses*. Edinburgh: Edinburgh University Press, pp. 19–48.

Barrett, J. C. 1994. Defining domestic space in the Bronze Age of southern Britain. In M. Parker Pearson and C. Richards (eds.), *Architecture and Order: Approaches to Social Space*. London: Routledge, pp. 87–97.

Birdwell-Pheasant, D., and D. Lawrence-Zúñiga. 1999. Introduction: Houses and families in Europe. In D. Birdwell-Pheasant and D. Lawrence-Zúñiga (eds.), *House Life: Space, Place and Family in Europe*. Oxford: Berg, pp. 1–35.

Blanton, R. E. 1995. The cultural foundations of inequality in households. In T. D. Price and G. M. Feinman (eds.), *Foundations of Social Inequality*. New York: Plenum, pp. 105–127.

Boivin, N. 2000. Life rhythms and floor sequences: Excavating time in rural Rajasthan and Neolithic Çatalhöyük. *World Archaeology* 31: 367–388.

Bowen, J. 1992. Faunal remains and urban household subsistence in New England. In A. E. Yentsch and M. C. Beaudry (eds.), *The Art and Mystery of Historical Archaeology: Essays in Honor of James Deetz*. Boca Raton, FL: CRC Press, pp. 267–281.

Brumfiel, E. M. 1991. Weaving and cooking: Women's production in Aztec Mexico. In J. M. Gero and M. W. Conkey (eds.), *Engendering Archaeology: Women and Prehistory*. Oxford: Basil Blackwell, pp. 224–251.

—— 1992. Distinguished lecture in archeology: Breaking and entering the ecosystem – gender, class, and faction steal the show. *American Anthropologist* 94: 551–567.

—— 1996. Figurines and the Aztec state: Testing the effectiveness of ideological domination. In R. P. Wright (ed.), *Gender and Archaeology*. Philadelphia: University of Pennsylvania Press, pp. 143–166.

Clark, J. E. 2000. Towards a better explanation of hereditary inequality: A critical assessment of natural and historic human agents. In M-A. Dobres and J. Robb (eds.), *Agency in Archaeology*. London: Routledge, pp. 92–112.

Costin, C. L. 1991. Craft specialization: Issues in defining, documenting, and explaining the organization of production. *Archaeological Method and Theory* 3: 1–56.

Cowgill, G. L. 1993. Distinguished lecture in archeology: Beyond criticizing New Archeology. *American Anthropologist* 95: 551–573.

Crown, P. L., and S. K. Fish. 1996. Gender and status in the Hohokam Pre-Classic to Classic tradition. *American Anthropologist* 98: 803–817.

Crown, P. L., and W. H. Wills. 1995. The origins of Southwestern ceramic containers: Women's time allocation and economic intensification. *Journal of Anthropological Research* 51: 173–186.

Dobres, M-A. 2000. *Technology and Social Agency*. Oxford: Blackwell.

——, and J. Robb 2000. Agency in archaeology: Paradigm or platitude? In M-A. Dobres and J. Robb, *Agency in Archaeology*. London: Routledge, pp. 3–17.

Emerson, T. E. 1997. *Cahokia and the Archaeology of Power*. Tuscaloosa: University of Alabama Press.

Gero, J. 2000. Troubled travels in agency and feminism. In In M-A. Dobres and J. Robb, *Agency in Archaeology*. London: Routledge, pp. 34–39.

Giddens, A. 1985. Time, space, and regionalisation. In D. Gregory and J. Urry (eds.), *Social Relations and Spatial Structures*. New York: St. Martin's Press, pp. 265–295.

Gilchrist, R. 1999. *Gender and Archaeology: Contesting the Past*. London: Routledge.

Gonlin, N. 1994. Rural household diversity in Late Classic Copan, Honduras. In G. M. Schwartz and S. E. Falconer (eds.), *Archaeological Views from the Countryside: Village Communities in Early Complex Societies*. Washington, DC: Smithsonian Institution Press, pp. 177–197.

—— 1996. Methodological analysis of the Copan testing program. In A. Guadalupe Mastache, J. R. Parsons, R. S. Santley, and M. C. Serra Puche (eds.), *Arqueología Mesoamericana: Homenaje a William T. Sanders*, Vol. 2. México, DF: Instituto Nacional de Antropología e Historia, pp. 231–252.

Hagstrum, M. 2001. Household production in Chaco Canyon society. *American Antiquity* 66: 47–55.

Hart, G. 1992. Imagined unities: Constructions of "the household" in economic theory. In S. Ortiz and S. Lees (eds.), *Understanding Economic Process*. Lanham, MD: University Press of America, Monographs in Economic Anthropology 10, pp. 111–129.

Hayden, B. 1996. Feasting in prehistoric and traditional societies. In P. Wiessner and W. Shiefenhöve (eds.), *Food and the Status Quest: An Interdisciplinary Perspective*. Providence, RI: Berghahn Books, pp. 127–147.

Hendon, J. A. 1992. The interpretation of survey data: Two case studies from the Maya area. *Latin American Antiquity* 3: 22–42.

—— 1996. Archaeological approaches to the organization of domestic labor: Household practice and domestic relations. *Annual Review of Anthropology* 25: 45–61.

—— 1997. Women's work, women's space and women's status among the Classic Period Maya elite of the Copan Valley, Honduras. In C. Claassen and R. A. Joyce, *Women in Prehistory: North America and Mesoamerica*. Philadelphia: University of Pennsylvania Press, pp. 33–46.

—— 1999. Multiple sources of prestige and the social evaluation of women in Prehispanic Mesoamerica. In J. E. Robb (ed.), *Material Symbols: Culture and Economy in Prehistory*. Carbondale: Southern Illinois University, Center for Archaeological Investigations Occasional Paper 26, pp. 257–276.

—— 2000. Having and holding: Storage, memory, knowledge, and social relations. *American Anthropologist* 102: 42–53.

—— 2002a. Household and state in Prehispanic Maya society: Gender, identity, and practice. In L. Gustafson and A. Trevelyan (eds.), *Ancient Maya Gender Identity and Relations*. Westport, CT: Greenwood, pp. 75–92.

—— 2002b. Social relations and collective identities: Household and community in ancient Mesoamerica. In M. O'Donovan (ed.), *The Dynamics of Power*. Carbondale: Southern Illinois University, Center for Archaeological Investigations Occasional Paper 30, pp. 273–300.

—— 2003a. El papel de los enterramientos en la construcción y negociación de la identidad social en los mayas prehispánicos. In A. C. Ruiz, M. H. Ruz Sosa, and M. J. Iglesia de Ponce de León (eds.), *Antropología de la eternidad: La muerte en la cultura maya*. Madrid: Sociedad Española de Estudios Mayas and Centro de Estudios Mayas, Instituto de Investigaciones Filológicas, Universidad Nacional Autónoma de México, pp. 161–174.

—— 2003b. Feasting at home: Community and house solidarity among the Maya of Southeastern Mesoamerica. In T. Bray (ed.), *The Archaeology and Politics of Food and Feasting in Early States and Empires*. New York: Kluwer/Plenum, pp. 203–233.

—— 2003c. In the house: Maya nobility and their figurine-whistles. *Expedition* 45(3): 28–33.

Henshaw, A. S. 1999. Location and appropriation in the Arctic: An integrative zooarchaeological approach to historic Inuit household economies. *Journal of Anthropological Archaeology* 18: 79–118.

Hingley, R. 1990. Domestic organisation and gender relations in Iron Age and Roman-British households. In R. Samson (ed.), *The Social Archaeology of Houses*. Edinburgh: Edinburgh University Press, pp. 125–147.

Hodder, I. 1990. *The Domestication of Europe*. Oxford: Basil Blackwell.

—— 1992. The domestication of Europe. In I. Hodder, *Archaeological Theory and Practice*. London: Routledge, pp. 241–253.

Hoffman, B. W. 1999. Agayadan Village: Household archaeology on Unimak Island, Alaska. *Journal of Field Archaeology* 26: 147–161.

Inomata, T., D. Triadan, E. Ponciano, E. Pinto, R. E. Terry, and M. Eberl. 2002. Domestic and political lives of Classic Maya elites: The excavation of rapidly abandoned structures at Aguateca, Guatemala. *Latin American Antiquity* 13: 305–330.

Johnson, M. H. 1989. Conceptions of agency in archaeological interpretation. *Journal of Anthropological Archaeology* 8: 189–211.

Joyce, R. A. 1993. Women's work: Images of production and reproduction in pre-Hispanic southern Central America. *Current Anthropology* 34: 255–274.

—— 2000a. *Gender and Power in Prehispanic Mesoamerica*. Austin: University of Texas Press.

—— 2000b. Girling the girl and boying the boy: The production of adulthood in ancient Mesoamerica. *World Archaeology* 31: 473–483.

——, and C. Claassen. 1997. Women in the ancient Americas: Archaeologists, gender, and the making of prehistory. In C. Claassen and R. A. Joyce (eds.), *Women in Prehistory: North America and Mesoamerica*. Philadelphia: University of Pennsylvania Press, pp. 1–14.

——, and J. A. Hendon. 2000. Heterarchy, history, and material reality: "Communities" in Late Classic Honduras. In M-A. Canuto and J. Yaeger, *The Archaeology of Communities: A New World Perspective*. London: Routledge, pp. 143–160.

Junker, L. L., K. Mudar, and M. Schwaller. 1994. Social stratification, household wealth, and competitive feasting in 15th/16th-century Philippine chiefdoms. *Research in Economic Anthropology* 15: 307–358.

Kokkinidou, D., and M. Nikolaidou. 1997. Body imagery in the Aegean Neolithic: Ideological implications of anthropomorphic figurines. In J. Moore and E. Scott, *Invisible People and Processes: Writing Gender and Childhood into European Archaeology*. London: Leicester University Press, pp. 88–112.

Lightfoot, K., A. Martinez, and A. M. Schiff. 1998. Daily practice and material culture in pluralistic social settings: An archaeological study of culture change and persistence from Fort Ross, California. *American Antiquity* 63: 199–222.

Majewski, T. 2000. "We are all storytellers": Comments on storytelling, science, and historical archaeology. *Historical Archaeology* 34: 17–19.

Malan, A. 1997. The material world of family and household: The Van Sitterts in eighteenth-century Cape Town 1748–1796. In L. Wadley (ed.), *Our Gendered Past: Archaeological Studies of Gender in Southern Africa*. Johannesburg: Witwatersrand University Press, pp. 273–301.

Manzanilla, L. 1990. Niveles de análisis en el estudio de unidades habitacionales. *Revista Española de Antropología Americana* 20: 9–18.

Martin, L., and N. Russell. 2000. Trashing rubbish. In I. Hodder (ed.), *Towards Reflexive Method in Archaeology: The Example of Çatalhöyük*. Cambridge: McDonald Institute for Archaeological Research, British Institute of Archaeology at Ankara Monograph 28, pp. 57–69.

McCall, J. C. 1999. Structure, agency, and the locus of the social: Why poststructural theory is good for archaeology. In J. E. Robb (ed.), *Material Symbols: Culture and Economy in Prehistory*. Carbondale: Southern Illinois University, Center for Archaeological Investigations Occasional Paper 26, pp. 16–20.

Meadows, K. 1999. The appetites of households in Early Roman Britain. In P. M. Allison (ed.), *The Archaeology of Household Activities*. London: Routledge, pp. 101–120.

Mehrer, M. W. 1995. *Cahokia's Countryside: Household Archaeology, Settlement Patterns, and Social Power*. DeKalb: Northern Illinois University Press.

Meskell, L. 1999. *Archaeologies of Social Life*. Oxford: Blackwell.

—— 2002. *Private Life in New Kingdom Egypt*. Princeton, NJ: Princeton University Press.

Mizoguchi, K. 1995. A comment upon agency, experience, and a Japanese perspective. In I. Hodder, M. Shanks, A. Alexandri, V. Buchli, J. Carman, J. Last, and G. Lucas (eds.), *Interpretive Archaeology: Finding Meaning in the Past*. London: Routledge, p. 228.

Moore, H. L. 1992. Households and gender relations: The modeling of the economy. In S. Ortiz and S. Lees (eds.), *Understanding Economic Process*. Lanham, MD: University Press of America, Monographs in Economic Anthropology 10, pp. 131–148.

—— 1994. *A Passion for Difference*. Bloomington: Indiana University Press.

—— 1996. *Space, Text, and Gender: an Anthropological Study of the Marakwet of Kenya*. New York: Guilford Press.

O'Donovan, M. 2002. Grasping power: A question of relations and scales. In M. O'Donovan (ed.), *The Dynamics of Power*. Carbondale: Southern Illinois University, Center for Archaeological Investigations Occasional Paper 30, pp. 19–34.

Pauketat, T. R. 1994. *The Ascent of Chiefs: Cahokia and Mississippian Politics in Native North America*. Tuscaloosa: University of Alabama Press.

—— 2001. Practice and history in archaeology: An emerging paradigm. *Anthropological Theory* 1: 73–98.

Pollock, S., M. Pope, and C. Coursey. 1996. Household production at the Uruk Mound, Abu Salabikh, Iraq. *American Journal of Archaeology* 100: 683–698.

Praetzellis, A. 1998. Introduction: Why every archaeologist should tell stories once in a while. *Historical Archaeology* 32: 1–3.

Richards, C. 1990. The Late Neolithic house in Orkney. In R. Samson (ed.), *The Social Archaeology of Houses*. Edinburgh: Edinburgh University Press, pp. 111–124.

Robin, C. 2002. Outside of houses: The practices of everyday life at Chan Noohol, Belize. *Journal of Social Archaeology* 2: 245–268.

—— 2003. New directions in Classic Maya household archaeology. *Journal of Archaeological Research* 11(4): 279–356.

Saitta, D. J. 1994. Agency, class, and archaeological interpretation. *Journal of Anthropological Archaeology* 13: 201–227.

Samuel, D. 1999. Bread making and social interactions at the Amarna Workmen's Village, Egypt. *World Archaeology* 31: 121–144.

Santley, R. S., and K. G. Hirth. 1993. Household studies in Western Mesoamerica. In R. S. Santley and K. G. Hirth (eds.), *Prehispanic Domestic Units in Western Mesoamerica: Studies of the Household, Compound, and Residence*. Boca Raton, FL: CRC Press, pp. 3–17.

Scott, E. 1990. Romano-British villas and the social construction of space. In R. Samson (ed.), *The Social Archaeology of Houses*. Edinburgh: Edinburgh University Press, pp. 149–172.

Silliman, S. 2001. Agency, practical politics and the archaeology of culture contact. *Journal of Social Archaeology* 1: 190–209.

Smith, M. L. 1999. The role of ordinary goods in premodern exchange. *Journal of Archaeological Method and Theory* 6: 109–135.

Stevanović, M. 1997. The age of clay: The social dynamics of house destruction. *Journal of Anthropological Archaeology* 16: 334–395.

Svensson, E. 1998. Expanding the household. *Lund Archaeological Review* 4: 85–100.

Sweely, T. L. 1999. Introduction. In T. L. Sweely (ed.), *Manifesting Power: Gender and the Interpretation of Power in Archaeology*. London: Routledge, pp. 1–14.

Thomas, J. 1996. *Time, Culture and Identity: An Interpretive Archaeology*. London: Routledge.

Tringham, R. 1991. Households with faces: The challenge of gender in prehistoric architectural remains. In J. M. Gero and M. W. Conkey (eds.), *Engendering Archaeology: Women and Prehistory*. Oxford: Basil Blackwell, pp. 93–131.

—— 1994. Engendered places in prehistory. *Gender, Place and Culture* 1: 169–203.

—— 1995. Archaeological houses, households, housework and the home. In D. N. Benjamin (ed.), *The Home: Words, Interpretations, Meanings, and Environments*. Aldershot: Avebury, pp. 79–107.

—— 1996. "But Gordon, where are the people?" Some comments on the topic of craft specialization and social evolution. In B. Wailes (ed.), *Craft Specialization and Social Evolution: In Memory of V. Gordon Childe*. Philadelphia: University Museum of Archaeology and Anthropology, University of Pennsylvania. University Museum Symposium Series 6, pp. 233–239.

Ullén, I. 1994. The power of case studies: Interpretation of a Late-Bronze-Age settlement in central Sweden. *Journal of European Archaeology* 2: 249–262.

Uruñuela Ladrón de Guevara, G., and P. P. Nagoda. 1998. Areas de actividad en unidades domésticas del Formative terminal en Tetimpa, Puebla. *Arqueología* 20: 3–19.

Vitelli, K. D. 1999. "Looking up" at early ceramics in Greece. In J. M. Skibo and G. M. Feinman (eds.), *Pottery and People: A Dynamic Interaction*. Salt Lake City: University of Utah Press, pp. 184–198.

Wattenmaker, P. 1995. Household economy in early state society: Material value, productive context and spheres of exchange. In E. M. Brumfiel (ed.), *The Economic Anthropology of the State*.

Lanham, MD: University Press of America, Monographs in Economic Anthropology 11, pp. 93–117.

—— 1998. *Household and State in Upper Mesopotamia: Specialized Economy and the Social Uses of Goods in an Early Complex Society*. Washington, DC: Smithsonian Institution Press.

Wesson, C. 1999. Chiefly power and food storage in Southeastern North America. *World Archaeology* 31: 145–164.

Wilk, R. R., and W. L. Rathje (eds.) 1982a. *Archaeology of the Household: Building a Prehistory of Domestic Life. American Behavioral Scientist* 25.

—— 1982b. Household archaeology. In R. R. Wilk and W. L. Rathje, *Archaeology of the Household: Building a Prehistory of Domestic Life, American Behavioral Scientist* 25: 617–639.

Woolf, A. 1997. At home in the long Iron-Age: A dialogue between households and individuals in cultural reproduction. In J. Moore and E. Scott, *Invisible People and Processes: Writing Gender and Childhood into European Archaeology*. London: Leicester University Press, pp. 68–74.

Yanagisako, S. J. 1979. Family and household: The analysis of domestic groups. *Annual Review of Anthropology* 8: 161–205.

13

Diaspora and Identity in Archaeology: Moving beyond the Black Atlantic

Ian Lilley

At the heart of the notion of diaspora is the image of a journey. Yet not every journey can be understood as diaspora. (Brah 1996:182)

... the post-modern, in spite of all the cant of modernization, reproduces the "pre-modern" on another scene. (Spivak 1988:169)

Diaspora theory is about creating and maintaining identity in communities dispersed amongst other peoples. It is about the local and non-local, and how through processes of hybridity and creolization some groups of people can be both at the same time. The studies considered in this chapter show that in addition to intersecting with orthodox empirical research and theorizing on colonization and colonialism, identity, migration, and nationalism, aspects of diaspora studies also overlap with more exploratory post-colonial and postmodernist perspectives, as well as globalization theory and cultural studies (all of which themselves interfinger to a considerable extent). Yet diaspora theory remains distinct owing to the peculiarities of its subject matter. Many people equate that subject matter solely with forced exile, political oppression, and ideologies of return to a homeland, on the basis of the Jewish and Black African experiences in particular. As discussed below, however, diaspora is a fluid term which has long had other connotations as well, which makes it applicable to a considerably more diverse array of related phenomena. Some diaspora scholars are concerned that continual broadening of the term may blunt its critical edge, even though their own work itself has made it more encompassing. The attitude adopted here is that the breadth of the term makes it more rather than less useful because it offers archaeologists a greater number of intellectual avenues to consider in their approaches to past population dispersals.

Exploring the application of these various perspectives on diaspora can do three things for the discipline. First, it can enhance understanding at a human scale of the communities, localities, and identities entailed in particular kinds of population move-ments in the past, adding a dimension to the explanation of archaeological migrations not normally afforded by either culture-historical or processual approaches. Second, it can enable comparison between ancient and modern population dispersals, bolstering archaeology's role in lending much-needed historical subtlety to contemporary social theory. Third, from a different but related angle, it can help archaeologists understand the sociopolitical condition and perspectives on the past of many of the contemporary descendant communities with which they work, be they communities in diaspora such as African Americans, or colonized indigenous minorities which exist in diaspora-like circumstances within settler nations such as Australia or those throughout the Americas (Clifford 1994:307–310; Smith 1992:453 fn. 25; for Australian examples see Rigsby 1995; Smith 2000; Weiner 2002).

This last theme is vitally important to archaeology's future in many parts of the world but requires separate treatment elsewhere. The present chapter is primarily concerned with the first theme, though it touches on some implications for the second. It considers the application of diaspora theory to the earliest stage of the Lapita dispersal through the western Island Pacific about 3,300 years ago. Described in more detail below, Lapita is broadly contemporaneous with the Phoenician and western Greek expansions in the Mediterranean and has some intriguing parallels with both. However, in the nature and pattern of its material manifestations, in its origins at a processual level, and in the history of its archaeological conceptualization, Lapita is much more akin to phenomena such as the *Linearbandkeramik* (Linear Pottery/LBK) and Cardial Ware dispersals in early Neolithic Europe (e.g., Bellwood 2001; Price 2000; Price et al. 2001; Sommer 2001). These potentially informative convergences warrant further thought but cannot be dealt with at length here. As a start, I refer the reader to Price (2000), especially the chapters by Barnett, Bogucki, Zilhão (2000, also 2001), and Zvelebil and Lillie (2000), as well as Price's own introduction and conclusion.

There is continuing debate about the identity of the groups involved in the historically recorded dispersions of the Phoenicians and western Greeks (e.g., Descoeudres 1990; Kaiser 2000; Muhly 1999; Rowlands 1998; Vella 1996). Nonetheless, the population movements in question have long been explicitly conceptualized as diasporas in ways that Lapita and similar prehistoric dispersals such as the LBK and Cardial expansions have not. The standing of these prehistoric examples as diasporas should be investigated if we are to comprehend the social formations they embody and grasp the implications of their existence for contemporary social-theoretical approaches to movement and identity in the modern world. One need not resurrect Childe's Danubians and their ilk to do this; even the most hesitant dip into the vast literature on social identity is sufficient to confirm that Renfrew (1988:438) is right to insist that "the notion of ethnicity cannot properly be used as the fundamental organizing principle for the prehistoric past." By the same token, even though there are significant conceptual and practical difficulties involved (e.g., Gosden 1992a:807–808; Jones 1999; Meskell 1999:44; Morris 2000:5–8; Shennan 1989), archaeologists should not shy away from prehistoric social identity to focus solely on the underlying regularities of the *longue durée*. As Ucko (1989:xiii; original emphasis) observes, "[w]hat can legitimately be inferred about the social groups which produced the material culture objects which are the primary evidence of archaeology" is "one of the most – possibly *the* most – fundamentally important questions of archaeological enquiry and interpretation."

Approaching it boldly is the only way archaeologists can get beyond "uninhabited histories and unpeopled pasts" (Meskell 1996:7).

Diaspora

The simplest meaning of diaspora is to scatter people as seed is scattered for planting, from the Greek *dia*, "across," and *speirein*, "to scatter." There are scholars who see diaspora primarily as a type of society characterized by particular attributes. Others see it more as a social condition produced by experiencing such attributes. Despite the impression created by some contemporary writing, use of the term is by no means restricted to events and processes in the late modern/postcolonial world. Hall (1992:310), for instance, describes the social condition inhering in "the new diasporas created by the postcolonial migrations" as "one of the distinctly novel types of identity produced in the era of late modernity." Diasporas are unquestionably embedded in the development of the modern world, owing to their pivotal role in what Davis (1973) calls "the rise of the Atlantic economies" from the late 1400s (also Curtin 1990). Diasporas are also inextricably implicated in the emergence of the supposedly "postcolonial" manifestation of the world system these "Atlantic" economies have shaped (e.g., Anderson 1994; Anthias 1998; Brah 1996; Cheah and Robbins 1988; Clifford 1994; R. Cohen 1997; Gilroy 1993; Gordon and Anderson 1999; Hall 1990; McClintock 1992; Shukla 2001; Yelvington 2001). As Bender (2001:83) has reflected, however, from an archaeological perspective "these contemporary movements are only a particular reworking of age-old scenarios." Thus it is, to paraphrase Spivak, that the premodern, indeed, the prehistoric, prefigures the postmodern.

While no one could reasonably argue that the late modern world has no unique features, Bender's sentiment is echoed by a variety of non-archaeological social theorists other than Spivak, including Appadurai, Clifford, and Shami.[1] Appadurai and Spivak make general comments about history, such as the epigram at the opening of this chapter, or Appadurai's (1996:2) observation that "[a]ll major social forces have precursors, precedents, analogs, and sources in the past." Clifford (1994:328) and Shami (2000), on the other hand, use explicitly archaeological metaphors to take things much further in their discussions of the "pre-history of postcolonialism" and "prehistories of globalization" (see also Buell 1998).

Clifford (1994:238) proposes that looking to (pre)history is "about recovering non-Western, or not-only-Western, models for cosmopolitan life...— resources for a fraught [postmodern/postcolonial/postnational] life." Shami extends this point. She (2000:189) argues that the archaeological concept of "prehistory" is a chronological label, but that the notion is more powerful as a metaphor that builds upon its chronological connotation to become "a historical device — more a way of thinking about the past than a fixed reality." On this basis,

> a prehistory of globalization seeks pasts characterized by mobility, cosmopolitanism, and vertical and horizontal linkages that displace the notion of the past as stagnant and bound by empire and tradition.... The use of the term does not aim to fix the characteristics of a certain age, but to enable the mobilization of alternative pasts in order to challenge the teleological certainty of the present. (Shami 2000:189)

Shami (2000:189–90) goes on to propose that if prehistory as metaphor "is to be deployed to reveal, rather than gloss, ways of seeing," it needs to be reconceptualized so as to "see through categorizations of time that produce the past as a foreign country," to undermine the "territorializing" of identity "and capture it 'in motion,'" and to deconstruct the "teleological necessity of prehistory unfolding into 'real' history." I am wary of Shami's subsequent millenarian implication that we should be preparing for, and indeed, work to hasten the imminent demise of the nation-state (cf. Buell 1998). Nonetheless, I have considerable sympathy with her general position and especially with her (and Clifford's) metaphorical use of "prehistory" to add historical nuance to contemporary social theory. However, from an archaeological vantage it is clear that their positions, and thus the broader social-theoretical value of the idea of "prehistory," would be immeasurably strengthened if archaeologists themselves brought the unique materiality of real prehistoric evidence to bear on the theoretical reconceptualization and deployment of the term in its metaphorical sense. Hence my interest in applying diaspora theory to actual prehistoric phenomena such as Lapita.

Although archaeologists have not been much involved as yet, new societies and hybrid cultural forms of the sort entailed in diaspora have long been described by scholars of Mediterranean history (e.g., Caröe 1932; Descoeudres 1990; see also Rowlands 1998), as well as by anthropologists and others researching precolonial and modern but "pre-postcolonial" patterns of culture contact and cross-cultural interaction (e.g., A. Cohen 1971; Curtin 1975, 1984). Indeed, all current conceptualizations of diaspora are ultimately based on post hoc biblical and Classical accommodations of even earlier and sometimes only hazily documented historical events and processes. Old Testament references to Jewish exile have been continually reworked by Jewish and Christian writers, while Classical Greek and Roman visions of the world have been refracted through modern European imperial and anti-imperial experience (e.g., De Angelis 1998; Hingley 2001; Jones 1999; Morris 2000; Rowlands 1998; van Dommelen 1997; Woolf 1997). Possible *prehistoric* examples of cultural creolization or hybridity such as Lapita and the LBK have so far been left out of the equation altogether, but if not approached with the foregoing in mind will be "explained" in a thoroughly confused and confusing manner which does little to enlighten us about prehistory or understand its implications for contemporary social theory. Ancient and modern diasporas should be critically compared through empirical investigation rather than have their differences (or similarities) merely asserted. Some history is in order.

Without reference to the historiographical issues just mentioned, sociologist Robin Cohen (1997:2) states that the Ancient Greeks coined the term "diaspora" to refer in a positive vein to "the colonization of Asia Minor and the Mediterranean in the Archaic period (800–600 BC)...through plunder, military conquest, colonization and migration." He (1997:26) contends that this original broad meaning was "highjacked" over the last two millennia by the notion of the Jewish "victim diaspora," which rests upon the connotations of forced exile and continuing exclusion. Thus it is, in his view, that this "more sinister and brutal" (1997:ix) perception underpins early scholarly consideration of diaspora by Weber, for example, in his discussion of "pariah peoples," and by Toynbee in his "Jewish model of civilisation" (R. Cohen 1997:101–102).

Ironically, in view of this outlook, R. Cohen's own survey builds upon the Jewish experience to consider the meaning of diaspora in contemporary social theory, as do other general treatments such as those of Safran (1991), Clifford (1994, also 1992) and Chaliand and Rageau (1995). All acknowledge that the Jewish victim model "has a strong entailment...on the language of diaspora" (Clifford 1994:306). They also point out that it helps us understand certain other cases, including the spread of sub-Saharan Africans through the New World and elsewhere, principally as a result of the post-Columbian slave trade. Critically, though, all also stress that the classical Jewish model of diaspora is too restrictive to apply to the range of phenomena now subsumed by the term, including aspects of the Jewish diaspora itself (cf. Spencer-Wood 1999). Safran (1991:83) notes in this connection that the terms "diaspora" and "diaspora community" "seem increasingly to be used as metaphoric designations for several categories of people – expatriates, expellees, political refugees, alien residents, immigrants, and ethnic and racial minorities *tout court*."

On that basis, Safran proffers a polythetic set of the critical attributes of a diaspora, including dispersal, memories or myths of a homeland, distinction from the host society, an ethic of eventual return to the homeland, a commitment to the "maintenance or restoration" of the homeland, and finally, a continuing, direct or vicarious individual and community relationship with the homeland. As a polythetic definition, this means that to be identified as a diaspora rather than some other sort of migration, a population dispersal should exhibit most of these characteristics most of the time. Clifford (1994:304–310) and R. Cohen (1997:21–29) take a similar route. They expand upon Safran's list in their own ways, common denominators being a de-emphasis of forced exile and commitment to a homeland but the retention of dispersal amongst "alien" host communities as central characteristics of the diasporic condition.

Robin Cohen furnishes a descriptive typology of diasporas linked by his own set of attributes (1997:26) and presents exemplars of each of his types. In addition to considering the classic Jewish case at length, he also includes the African and Armenian situations as "victim" diasporas. He goes on to discuss the Indian "labour" and British "imperial" diasporas, the Chinese and Lebanese "trade" diasporas and the Caribbean "cultural" diaspora. Clifford, on the other hand, looks instead to the psycho-sociological effects of diasporic experience. As Anthias describes it (1998:557, original emphasis), Clifford and other postmodernists such as Hall (1990), Gilroy (1993), and Brah (1996) see diaspora as a "*social condition* and social process." This condition is structured by movement and "the experience of being *from* one place and *of* another...where one is constructed in and through *difference*" as well as "cultural accommodation or syncretism: in some versions hybridity" (Anthias 1998:565, original emphasis).

The views of Safran, Clifford, and R. Cohen underlie my own approach to diaspora as a general phenomenon, because although they are more inclusive than the classic "victim" model, their polythetic definitions retain a set of core characteristics that prevent the term "diaspora" from losing all capacity to distinguish particular sorts of population movements from others. Of all the sorts of diaspora considered by Cohen, I find the concept of a trade diaspora of most value in thinking about the Lapita case, but in terms more like those of Clifford than R. Cohen himself. The latter relies on Curtin (1984) for background material on trade diasporas, but as Curtin acknowledges, the term "trade diaspora" was coined by the British social anthropologist Abner Cohen (1971, also 1967, 1969). With Barth (e.g., 1969), though rarely in agreement with him, A. Cohen was a founder in sociocultural anthropology of the constructivist approach to ethnicity (see Banks 1996, esp. 32–37, for extended discussion). His ideas regarding the social strategies entailed in diaspora thus prefigure those discussed by postmodernists such as Clifford and Hall. Defending his use of the word "diaspora" to describe something other than the classic Jewish condition in the light of Fallers (1967) earlier example, A. Cohen (1971:267) applied it from an explicitly instrumentalist perspective to refer to a distinctive social formation created by the dispersal of Hausa traders amongst Yoruba people in one part of colonial Nigeria. First painting the Hausa in the city of Ibadan as a stranger community (1967), he then proposed that such social formations create ethnicity while being created by it. This was because dispersed Hausa elsewhere in Nigeria did *not* create similar social formations, but rather were largely integrated with surrounding Yoruba people. Thus rather than being ethnic survivals from a migration source-area, A. Cohen argued that the distinctive groups he observed comprise "new social forms...[which] have continuously re-created their distinctiveness in different ways, not because of conservatism, but because these ethnic groups are in fact interest groupings whose members share some common economic and political interests and who, therefore, stand together in the continuous competition for power with other groups" (1969:192).

By 1971, A. Cohen (1971: 267) had determined that "diaspora" was the best word to apply to the Hausa because in his view it captured their status as "a nation of socially interdependent, but spatially dispersed, communities" of people who are "culturally distinct from both their society of origin and from the societies among which they live." Their ties create a new social formation which has a "stability of structure but allows a high degree of mobility of personnel." I think that this sort of conceptualization gets us closer to what diaspora may mean to the people involved than does R. Cohen's typological approach.

A. Cohen's ideas are certainly not unproblematic, particularly in their application to Lapita. Lovejoy (pers. comm.), an historian of West African trade and former student of Curtin, points out that the Hausa diaspora was terrestrial, while Lapita was a phenomenon of the Island Pacific and thus to a large extent maritime. He also notes that A. Cohen does not discuss Hausa relations with their homeland, or the diaspora's precolonial history, this last meaning by implication that the diaspora A. Cohen describes may be entirely a product of colonialism. That is true, but Curtin's (1975, 1984) own treatments of trading diasporas in precolonial West Africa refer to A. Cohen without any such criticism. Indeed, Curtin (1975:59–60) plainly describes A. Cohen's conception as "[a]n analytical model closer to historical reality" than popular Western depictions of cross-cultural engagement in West Africa, such as itinerant peddlers or so-called "silent trade." On the other hand, Curtin (1975:2) is clear that trade diasporas are in his view a feature of urbanized society, arguing that earlier forms of cross-cultural trade "are lost beyond any possibility of historical reconstruction." As implied earlier, however, such questions are not simply a matter for assertion. Rather, they should be the focus of empirical investigation of precisely the sort explored in this chapter.

The general concept of diaspora also has its critics. Anthias (1998:557) argues that the postmodernist and classificatory approaches equally "are problematised by their reliance on a notion of deterritorialised ethnicity which references the primordial bonds of 'homeland'...[and by an inability] to attend fully to...issues of class, gender and trans-ethnic alliances"; in sum, "the problems identified with the 'ethnicity' problematic." I return to this point at the end of the chapter. It is interesting to note here, however, that despite the explicit constructivism of ethnographers such as A. Cohen as well as the postmodernists, others propose that "the cosmopolitan migrant... obeys the logic of a bounded essentialized ethnicity that remains unchanged in exile" (Cheah 1988a:22; see also Anderson 1988).

Idealist notions of identity may be questionable on empirical as well as theoretical grounds, but constructivist perspectives have their own difficulties. They can be functionalist and teleological, and can overemphasize the importance of agency at the expense of structure and history. As Jones (1997:100; also 1999) divines, a position which allows for elements of both is heuristically the most useful. Though obviously instrumentalist in tone, A. Cohen's formulation includes a role for shared history and biocultural background amongst the groups which create an ethnic identity in diaspora. These characteristics-in-common provide the foundation upon which instrumental interests build ethnicity, much in the way Jones (1997, 1999) and others argue Bourdieu's *habitus* does. A. Cohen's position thus does not define ethnicity as a *purely* contingent or situational phenomenon. Rather, his stance acknowledges the importance of situational factors in a way that unalloyed essentialist perspectives do not. Adopting this standpoint is the key, I think, because it helps us avoid the teleologies which inhere in wholly instrumentalist views while also circumventing the essentialist traps of an entirely primordialist outlook.

The material conditions of diaspora are of signal importance to Cheah (1988a, 1988b). He goes beyond questions of essentialized identity to call very pointedly into question postmodernism's weighty Hegelian/Marxist baggage regarding the impending transcendence of modernity by hybrid postmodernity and concomitant end of the modern capitalist state. Cheah thus returns us to the question of whether social-theoretical frameworks, which at root are intended to explain and/or advance a particular political agenda regarding the modern capitalist world (including A. Cohen's understanding of the Hausa diaspora under colonial conditions), are likely to be of much help in archaeological and especially prehistoric circumstances.

Diaspora in Archaeology

Diaspora and all it entails in social theory have yet to have much impact in archaeology conceptually or geographically beyond what Gilroy (1993) famously labelled the "Black Atlantic": the world initially created by the post-Columbian African slave trade. In fact, as Orser (1998) has observed, within that already quite narrow world archaeological study has not extended much beyond New World slavery, and then has been concerned primarily with the Caribbean and American South. This last has occurred despite the efforts of local and US scholars such as Funari (e.g., 1999), Orser himself (e.g., 1994), and others in Brazil, where by far the most slaves were actually sent, "where the characteristic elements of New World tropical slave plantations were first put together... [and which,] in 1888,... was the last country in the Western Hemisphere to abolish slavery" (Curtin 1990:46). Moreover, it remains the case even though expatriate and local archaeological interest in the African end of the slave trade is increasing (e.g., Kelly 1997; also papers given at the World Archaeological Congress Intercongress on the African Diaspora, Curaçao, 2001). Orser (1998:65) suggests this situation arose owing to the effects on American archaeological research interests of the US civil rights movement and "the immaturity of historical archaeology" in and more particularly beyond the United States – the archaeology, that is, of the colonial/neocolonial post-Columbian world.

Archaeological insights into New World slavery undoubtedly have profound substantive and moral implications for our understanding of modernity as an historical phenomenon as well as of broader issues such as culture contact and cultural change. Yet the overwhelming focus on the New World has distorted archaeological understanding of the African diaspora more generally (Orser 1998:63–66). This dispersal began well over a millennium before the expansion of Europe. It also extended into Europe, the Middle East, and Asia in addition to the New World (e.g., Brandt and Walz 2001). The concentration on the Black Atlantic has also distracted archaeological attention from other modern diasporas and their implications for diaspora theory generally and for the comparative study of the African diaspora in particular. Thus while non-archaeologists continue to explore modern diaspora in all its theoretical and geohistorical permutations *including but not limited to* the post-Columbian African case, one looks almost in vain for archaeological consideration of any of the other recent diasporas canvassed by R. Cohen (1997) *except* the post-Columbian African case (e.g., Blakey 2001; Franklin 1997; Haviser 1999; Orser 1998). There are two principal exceptions. One is an emergent archaeology of the British – R. Cohen's (1997:66) exemplar of an imperial diaspora – which scholars such as Susan Lawrence (1999, 2003, in press) are developing into a specific focus within historical archaeology on the basis of Deetz's pioneering efforts in the United States and South Africa (e.g., Deetz 1977; Winer and Deetz 1990). The other is the archaeology of the overseas Chinese, best developed in Australasia and North America (Schulz and Allen 2002).

There is also only limited reflection on the archaeological application of diaspora theory to population movements in more ancient times. This is not to say that ancient population movements are not investigated by archaeologists. Despite the "retreat from migrationism" in Anglo-American archaeology that was explored some years ago by Adams, van Gervan, and Levy (1978), population movement (whether described as such or as colonization, diaspora, migration or something else) has remained a critical focus of archaeological attention around the world since the inception of the discipline (Rouse 1986) and migration in particular has in recent years made a return in Anglo-American archaeology (e.g., Anthony 1990, 1997; Burmeister 2000; Härke 1998; cf. Clark 1994). Burmeister and others interested in migration (e.g., Frankel 2000; Frankel and Webb 1998; cf. Knapp 2001) have experimented with the application of social theory in the form of Bourdieu's ideas (see also Jones 1997, 1999). However, the premodern population movements that are being (re-)examined in the recent literature are generally not called diasporas, or examined in the light of contemporary diaspora theory of either a typological or postmodern stripe. The term diaspora is sometimes used in its broadest connotation, as a synonym of migration, colonization or dispersal (e.g., Bellwood 2001; Bogucki 2000). Bellwood (2001:191) very briefly canvasses the diasporas in recent history and Bogucki (2000:212–218) considers complex self-organizing systems in ways which are relevant to diaspora theory, but neither considers whether the examples of Neolithic colonization they refer to parallel any of the types of diaspora discussed by R. Cohen, or whether such dispersals entailed a social condition such as that described by A. Cohen or postmodernists such as Clifford or Hall.

The foregoing does not mean there has been no theoretically informed consideration of diaspora by archaeologists. It is fair to say, however, that comprehensive discussion is still rare, being limited largely to Bender's (e.g., 2001) thought-provoking work on "landscapes on-the-move." She (2001:76) notes that despite increasing convergence between archaeological and anthropological social theorizing about location and identity, "[t]here is ... one domain in which archaeology has been slow to keep pace with anthropology.... [I]t seems surprising in that trying to understand great sweeps of prehistory, there has been a reluctance in recent years to think about the dynamics of people on the move" at the lived, human scale. Bender's (2001:83) published position nonetheless relies on ethnographic examples. She claims she could just as easily "have used examples drawn from ... prehistory," but it remains the case to my knowledge that neither she nor any other archaeologist has explicitly drawn upon diaspora theory to help explain a major prehistoric population movement anywhere in the world. As Bender herself notes, in Anglo-American archaeology this is undoubtedly linked in part with the aforementioned "retreat from migrationism." It is also partly owed to the almost exclusive focus of the discipline's substantive diaspora research on the Black Atlantic, especially in the Americas.

Generally speaking, the archaeology of the African Diaspora does not explicitly employ or explore diaspora theory so much as advance on the implicit understanding that the phenomenon in focus is unquestionably a diaspora. Thus while the nature of the diasporic status of the African Diaspora continues to be discussed outside archaeology (e.g., Gordon and Anderson 1999), there is little or no archaeological reflection on what this may mean for archaeological study or on the implications of archaeological results for studies of the African Diaspora or diaspora theory more broadly. This is understandable: as noted earlier, the African slave trade is one of the most well-known examples of diaspora after the Jewish *locus classicus*. Indeed, the two are often seen to be closely tied conceptually (and by some, such as Rastafarians, historically; see Clifford 1994:321–325; R. Cohen 1997:31–42; Gilroy 1993:205–212). However, the African Diaspora is emphatically *not* an unproblematical phenomenon. In calling for "*ethnographic* attention to the process of diaspora identification," for instance, Gordon and Anderson (1999:282, original emphasis) ask: "[i]n what sense are people whose ancestry is undeniably mixed – for example, Blacks in the United States, Nicaragua and Honduras – more African than anything else? Are there criteria other than continuities from Africa which can serve as the basis of diasporic identity? In sum, who are the members of the African diaspora and what makes them members?" Archaeologists interested in diaspora, African or otherwise, need to ask themselves similar sorts of questions.

Lapita

Lapita is a place in New Caledonia where, in 1952, archaeologists found a distinctively decorated handmade pottery they realized was stylistically the same as pottery reported from localities as widely separated as Fiji, the Bismarck Archipelago northeast of New Guinea, and, with less assurance, Island Southeast Asia (Gifford and Shutler 1956:7, 94) (figures 13.1 and 13.2). Named for the locality, Lapita pottery is now known from the Bismarck Archipelago to Samoa and Tonga on the western edge of Polynesia, and to have generic relationships with Southeast Asian wares. Lapita is also the earliest pottery known in the Pacific. It is presently dated in its classic form to between about 3300 and 2700 BP, though decoratively and morphologically simplified "late" Lapita may have been made for up to five centuries longer in the Bismarcks.

Lapita's elaborate decoration includes stylized human faces and was characteristically created with a dentate (toothed) stamp following systematic rules. Most excavated Lapita ceramics are of local manufacture but the decorative patterns represented are very similar between often very widely dispersed sites and vary synchronously through time across very large areas, indicating highly effective intersite communication and a high degree of social cohesion. Lapita is typically associated with a suite of other archaeological markers including distinctive ground stone adzes and shell artefacts (perhaps including valuables), the first domesticated pigs, dogs, and chickens in the Pacific, and intensive root and tree crop agriculture combined with inshore and reef fishing and mollusc gathering. In western regions, villages are generally found on small offshore islands or the beaches of larger islands, though some later ones have recently been found some distance inland in New Britain, in the vicinity of some of Island Melanesia's principal obsidian sources. Sometimes built on stilts over lagoons, the villages were in locations that allowed easy access for seagoing canoes and long-distance movement of goods, particularly obsidian, which was very widely transported, and perhaps also shell artefacts. Lapita villages in the eastern archipelagos were all on land, some a considerable distance inland.

The Bismarcks and other parts of Near Oceania[2] were first colonized around 30000–35000 BP (e.g., Allen, Gosden, and White 1989; Wickler and Spriggs 1988), and Lapita sites are found no closer to Asia than the Siassi Islands off western New Britain (Lilley 1988, 2002, in press). However, there is an unambiguous and undisputed association in the first colonists of Remote Oceania of archaeological markers of Lapita occupation and biological and linguistic markers of undoubted Island Southeast Asian origin (Green 1997). Thus despite the almost exclusively Melanesian distribution of the distinctive archaeological signature outlined above, the makers and users of Lapita are on this basis argued to have been of primarily Southeast Asian descent and to have spoken Proto-Oceanic, the precursor of all languages in the Oceanic branch of the otherwise Asian[3] Austronesian language family. Together with the archaeological evidence, these biological and linguistic attributes are conventionally taken as evidence for the existence of a bioculturally coherent Lapita Cultural Complex (Green 1991b, 1992; of a vast literature, see also for example Allen and Gosden 1991; Bedford, Sand, and Burley 2002; Bellwood 1997; Bellwood, Fox, and Tryon 1995; Best 2002; Burley, Nelson, and Shutler 1999; Clark, Anderson, and Vunidilo 2001; Davidson et al. 1996; Galipaud 1992; Galipaud and Lilley 1999; Irwin 1992; Kirch 1997; Kirch 2000; Sand 2001; Spriggs 1997; Summerhayes 2000).

Leaving aside the Asian connection for the moment, the current culture-historical consensus regarding the Lapita complex is that it resulted from a rapid but clinal dispersal from the Bismarcks to Tonga of identity-conscious fisher-farmer sailor-

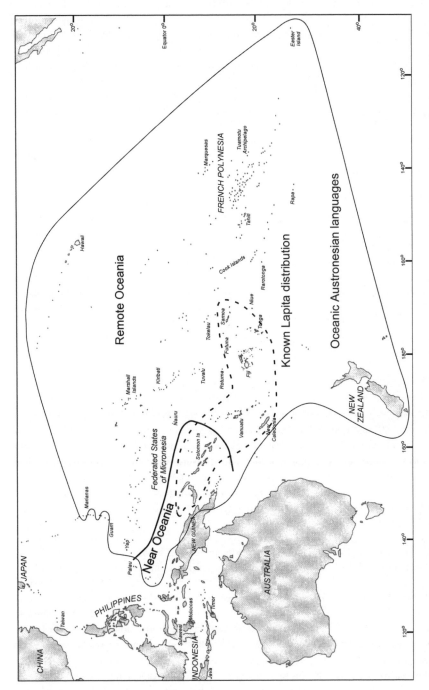

Figure 13.1 *The region of interest, showing places mentioned in the text, the boundary between Near and Remote Oceania, the known distribution of Lapita sites, and the extent of the Oceanic subgroup of the Austronesian language family (after Ross, Pawley, and Osmond 1998: xxi)*

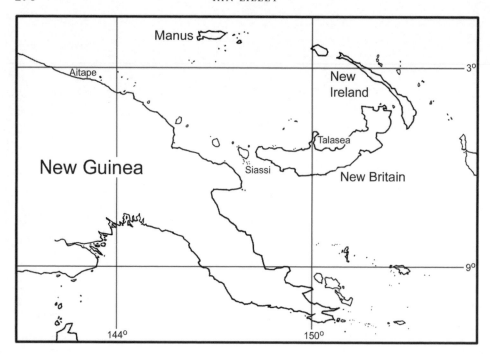

Figure 13.2   *The Bismarck Archipelago and eastern New Guinea, showing places mentioned in the text*

potters. Some became the first humans to colonize Remote Oceania. Others stayed in the Bismarcks and other island groups en route to Western Polynesia, where they contributed variably to the ancestry of modern Island Melanesians. They also contributed to the ancestry of some people on the coasts of mainland New Guinea as well, though Lapita-makers themselves appear to have avoided the island completely.[4] Lapita culture in Melanesia evolved into various regional cultural forms which to differing degrees must have melded in some manner with existing cultures. In some places, such as Vanuatu and New Caledonia (Bedford and Clark 2001; Sand 2001), Lapita ceramics developed into other styles, though none was ever nearly as widespread as Lapita. In many other parts of Melanesia, pottery manufacture ceased altogether or, in places such as the Siassi-west New Britain region in the Bismarcks, may have disappeared for periods of up to 1,000 years before re-emerging seemingly *de novo* in quite different forms of as-yet uncertain origin (Lilley 1999, 2000, 2002, in press).

The colonists who reached Western Polynesia some 2,800–2,900 years ago paused in Fiji–Samoa–Tonga for perhaps 1,000 years, during which time they evolved physically, culturally, and linguistically into the ancestors of the Polynesians. This homogenous group then colonized the islands from Samoa and Tonga in the west to Hawai'i in the north, Easter Island in the east and New Zealand in the southwest (as well as some outliers back in Melanesia). Western Polynesian ceramics became much simplified soon after initial colonization, and rapidly ceased to be made altogether, though pottery manufacture persisted in Fiji. No pottery to speak of was carried further into Polynesia. The thirty millennia separating the colonization of Near and Remote Oceania are attributed to people's inability to cross the vast water-gaps beyond the Solomons prior to the introduction of superior Lapita maritime technology. Similarly, the successful colonization of the resource-poor islands of Remote Oceania is attributed to more advanced Lapita agriculture, use of domestic animals, and seafaring technology which permitted long-distance links back to existing communities. Production of the highly distinctive pottery is also seen as critical to successful colonization, as it is held to be a symbol of shared social identity and strong, supportive intercommunal links.

Aspects of the foregoing "phylogenetic" culture-historical model have long been criticized by Terrell and like-minded colleagues, particularly in relation to what they see as its (neo)colonialist essentialism and over-dependence on historical-linguistic reconstructions of the Austronesian language family (e.g. Terrell 1981, 1986, 1988, 1989; Terrell, Hunt, and Gosden 1997; Terrell, Kelly, and Rainbird 2001). However, there appears to be general agreement that whatever else it may or may not have been, the Lapita phenomenon:

1   appeared suddenly and without precedent in about 3300 BP in widely dispersed coastal locations throughout the already inhabited Bismarck Archipelago;
2   reflects connections among Island Southeast Asian and Island Pacific populations and at least some movement of people from west to east;
3   comprised at least four major space–time provinces, being in temporal order Early (or Far Western), Western, Southern and Eastern, and;
4   at least in the Eastern and probably also the Western and Southern provinces, resulted from the dispersal from the Bismarcks–Solomons region of a single, biologically, culturally and linguistically identifiable group.

Despite this broad consensus, neither conventional nor contrarian models concerning the Lapita dispersal address the mechanisms or processes which led to the emergence of the coherent ethnolinguistic group, which all agree was involved in the initial human colonization of the Eastern and probably also the Western and Southern Lapita provinces. Until recently, conventional models saw the situation in very straightforward terms: an identity-conscious group of Island Southeast Asians once characterized as "Vikings of the sunrise" (Buck 1938) migrated into Island Melanesia and onward into the remote Pacific with little or no contact with existing populations in Melanesia, as part of a very large-scale population dispersal driven by population growth in newly Neolithic East and Southeast Asia (e.g., Bellwood 1978). As continuing debate in *Nature* demonstrates (e.g., Diamond 2000, 2001; Oppenheimer and Richards 2001), this "express train to Polynesia" (Diamond 1988) scenario still has its high-profile advocates. This is the case even though since at least the early 1990s most migrationists close to the coalface have admitted greater local input, culturally and biologically, than they once did (e.g., Spriggs 1999). Kirch (1997:335 n. 15), for instance, long a confirmed migrationist, calls the express train idea "nonsensical."

The revision results largely from the efforts of White and especially Allen (e.g., Allen 1996, 1984; Allen and White 1989; White 1999; White, Allen, and Specht 1988). In the early 1980s, they assertively advanced an indigenist alternative founded on Green's (1979:45) observation that the distinctive archaeological signature of Lapita developed in the Bismarcks, not Southeast Asia, where despite the linguistic and biological connections, ceramics and other archaeological remains exhibit only generic rather than obviously directly "ancestral" similarities with Lapita materials. Allen sought to test the indigenist position through a major international research effort beginning in the mid-1980s (Allen 1984; Allen and Gosden 1991).The results concerning Lapita (there were also groundbreaking findings concerning the Pleistocene) tended to support the migrationist position, but did reveal varying degrees of local input. On this basis and the results of continuing researches, most of the scholars involved take their lead from further work by Green (1991b, 1992) to now describe the processes underlying the emergence of the Lapita as some combination of intrusion, innovation, and integration ("Triple I").

There is criticism of Green's model (e.g., Spriggs 1996, 1999), to which he has responded with detailed refinements (Green 2000). However, neither Green nor anyone else discusses in detail how the "Triple I" processes or any alternatives may have actually worked at a human rather than abstract, processual scale, why they may have worked in one way rather than another, or what they may have meant for the people involved in terms of the processes of identity and community formation which are implicitly involved but inevitably avoided by current explanatory frameworks. These – especially the last – are the questions which intrigue me. That is why I am interested in exploring the application of diaspora theory to the Lapita case: "once identity becomes the subject of analysis itself, rather than an essential, taken-for-granted character, it becomes necessary to consider the nature of the social and cultural processes involved in the construction of ethnic identities" (Jones 1999:221).

A Lapita Diaspora?

Can we explain the Lapita dispersal as a diaspora? There is little question that the rapid west–east spread of the Lapita Cultural Complex represents a migration – a journey, in terms of Brah's epigram at the start of this chapter – but can it and should it be called a diaspora in terms such as those used by either R. Cohen or A. Cohen? I believe it can and should, at least in the Early (a.k.a. Far Western) Lapita period, before the spread of the cultural complex into Remote Oceania saw the emergence of the Western, Eastern, and Southern Lapita space–time provinces. This is because it occurred in previously inhabited regions, and entailed the creation and maintenance of a dispersed but coherent community distinct from those that surrounded it as well as those in the migration source-area. By general consensus, these are core characteristics of a diaspora of any sort, "victim," "trade" or other.

Orthodox explanations for Lapita generally rest on the motive power of Neolithic expansion from China through Island Southeast Asia (e.g., Bellwood 2001). Anderson (2001) develops this theme to show how the Lapita dispersal appears to be one of a series of large-scale and increasingly frequent pulse-like movements of expanding Neolithic populations through Southeast Asia and the Pacific, each separated by a period of relative stability. He (2001:15) suggests that this pattern reflects a deep demographic rhythm, which indicates that more specific models of Lapita origins "might eventually become integrated to a greater or lesser degree into a broad general explanation." Unlike short-distance population movements, migrations of the sort entailed by Lapita do seem dependent on population density and are thus likely to be linked ultimately to the emergence of farming (Clark 1994:335), just as Anderson, Bellwood, and others contend. I have no quarrel with this idea, but large-scale processes of the *longue durée* such as those illuminated by Anderson or Bellwood do not cause phenomena such as the Lapita florescence in anything but the most remote sense.

Building on an aside by Kirch (1988:162; see also 1997:64–65 and Spriggs 1997:73–76), I would advance involvement in obsidian trade as a more proximal cause of Austronesian expansion into Melanesia. Obsidian from a single set of sources in the Talasea–Cape Hoskins region in central northern New Britain was moved around the Bismarcks for more than 15,000 years before Lapita appeared. Torrence's (1994, 1992; Torrence and Stevenson 2000) work around Talasea suggests there was long-term intensification in resource use in the obsidian source-area prior to the appearance of Lapita (see also White 1996; White and Harris 1997). I hypothesize that long-distance distribution of obsidian was intensifying as part of this process, with far-reaching ramifications for down-the-line coastal exchange networks at a time when Goodenough (1982) and Swadling (1995) suggest there may have been growing Southeast Asian interest in products from northwest Melanesia. Although no Melanesian obsidian is known in Southeast Asian contexts predating Lapita, Talasea obsidian dating to the late Lapita period has been found in Borneo (Bellwood and Koon 1989). In addition, on the basis of a personal communication from Ambrose, White (1996) mentions that in historic times New Britain obsidian reached as far west as Biak Island, off the far western end of the New Guinea mainland. Both these facts lend support to my propositions and Kirch's original comments regarding the role of obsidian trade in Lapita origins.

Approximately three centuries prior to the appearance of Lapita, there was a volcanic eruption of staggering proportions in the eastern part of the obsidian source-area on New Britain. Spriggs (1997:76) has described it as "one of the most massive eruptions to occur anywhere on earth during the time modern humans have existed." An event of this magnitude must have had a role in the developments in question. Both Torrence's (above) and Pavlides's (1996; Pavlides and Gosden 1994) work in New Britain indicates significant shifts in the nature of activity after the eruption, when Lapita sites suddenly appear on the coast in the vicinity of the obsidian sources and elsewhere. Developing Spriggs's thoughts on the matter (1997:73–76), I propose that the eruption created various technical problems of communication and control in pre-Lapita exchange networks in which obsidian played a critical role, problems which local communities were unable to accommodate in the short term. I further hypothesize that the appearance of Lapita is intimately connected with the process of recovery.

My view is that these difficulties of communication and control created perturbations down the line from the Bismarcks along the north coast of New Guinea into the easternmost fringes of Austronesian-speaking Island Southeast Asia, from where highly mobile traders (or would-be traders) with interests that ultimately reached into the Bismarcks departed to reinvigorate obsidian-dependent trading links. In addition to any benefits (or, indeed, disadvantages) this activity may have had for existing Melanesian populations, being on site rather than at a significant geographical remove from the obsidian sources would almost certainly have provided the migrant traders with economic and sociopolitical opportunities not available in their home communities.

This notion of immediately pre-Lapita Austronesian exploration of the Bismarcks has a checkered history. Yet in the light of contemporary research on migration there can be little question that such "scouts," as Anthony (1990) calls them, investigated the Bismarcks to assess opportunities and relay information back to potential source-areas for migration prior to any larger-scale population movement. Evidence is sparse and equivocal, but that such scouting occurred in Lapita times may be indicated by Kirch and Yen's finds on Tikopia (Kirch 2000:335 n. 16) and Spriggs's "Lapita without pots" on Nissan. Spriggs (1991:309–310) dismisses the possibility that his finds might represent pre-Lapita Austronesian activity, but in the light of Anthony's work he (1995:124–125) speculates that "Lapita without pots" may represent Lapita exploration beyond the Bismarcks. I think there is every reason to believe that Lapita-makers explored ahead as part of the colonizing process, and, despite a complete lack of evidence at present, that similar exploration was undertaken by Austronesian-speakers from Southeast Asia immediately prior to the Lapita florescence as well. As Graham (1990:45) observes in relation to the Ancient Greeks, "[i]t is obvious that any serious colonization requires previous knowledge, both of the land to be settled and the people who inhabit it." Irwin's (1992) discussion of Pacific exploration and colonization by return voyaging makes the same point.

We must heed Ambrose's (1978) caveat that the evidence suggests that Lapita traders were very different from ethnographically described long-distance middleman (or "freelance") traders in Melanesia. Yet of the various choices of scouts listed by Anthony, merchants (i.e., traders) are by far the most likely in the present context even if trade with existing populations had nothing to do with subsequent Lapita expansion into uninhabited Remote Oceania. Anthony (1990:903) remarks: "initial migrants (the scouts) might have had motives and organization very different from those of the group that followed." If this were the case, we have to ask what such motives and organization may have been. What caused the putative Lapita diaspora in human terms? Why did any migrants not just integrate with existing local communities? Thinking about the way Lapita society and culture are characterized above, and especially Green's "Triple I" model, it is time to return to diaspora theory, and specifically to A. Cohen's conception of trading diasporas.

A. Cohen's work describes and explains a situation close to the one which I suspect obtained in the Bismarcks in the period from just before Lapita emerged to the time it began to spread beyond the archipelago and out into the remote Pacific. It thus allows us to flesh out the processes of intrusion, innovation, and integration. Specifically, through the instrumental (that is, self-interested) construction of an ethnically distinct trading diaspora it provides a mechanism which analytically and historically gets us from individual pre-Lapita Austronesian-speaking trader-scouts penetrating the Bismarcks by way of individual trade connections to the emergence in the same region of the fully developed Lapita cultural complex during the Early Lapita period. This is because a trade diaspora could have solved problems in obsidian-dependent down-the-line trade engendered by volcanic instability. A. Cohen argues that the

> conduct of long-distance trade requires finding solutions to a number of basic technical problems [of communication and control]. ... Under pre-industrial social conditions ... these technical problems have often been overcome when men from one ethnic

group control all or most of the trade in specific commodities. ... [E]thnic control or monopoly [of trade] can be achieved only in the course of continuous rivalry and opposition from other ethnic groups. In the process, the monopolizing group is forced to organize itself for political action in order to deal with external pressure, to co-ordinate the co-operation of its members in the common cause and establish channels of communication and mutual support with members from communities of the same ethnic group in neighbouring localities who are engaged in the trading network. In this way, a trading diaspora, consisting of dispersed, but highly interrelated communities, comes into being. ... A diaspora of this kind is distinct as a type of social grouping in its culture and structure. Its members are culturally distinct from both their society of origin and from the societies among which they live. (1971: 266)

I suggest the original, far-flung, pre-Lapita "trader-scouts" would have begun the process of diaspora formation, possibly but not necessarily consciously. Recalling A. Cohen's comments about stability and mobility, the most critical outcome of their activity in this regard would have been to build a form of society which, as Gosden (1992:25) puts it, allowed them "to stay in motion and yet maintain balance." In beginning this process, they laid the blueprint for the emergence during the Early Lapita period of a fully-fledged trading diaspora, as economic expansion created by their interactions with local people, and information about it they relayed back to their home regions, encouraged a more significant movement of population from Southeast Asia into the Bismarcks.

What sort of social formation would have characterized Early Lapita society thus conceptualized? A. Cohen (1969:201) proposes that the distinctive social features of a trading diaspora result from the way certain basic organizational problems are solved by "groups whose political corporateness is not formally institutionalized within the contemporary situation." The problems to which he (1971:271–278, also 1969:201–211) refers are those of distinctiveness, continual demographic adjustment, communication, the organization of trust and credit, and the organization of authority. An effective diaspora "must define its membership and its sphere of operation by defining its identity and exclusiveness." Maintaining distinctiveness has implications for recruitment, if dying members are to be replaced and, where a diaspora is expanding, new members admitted. Distinctiveness is also related to communication, which is crucial to the conduct of trade and the maintenance of the interdependence of the diaspora. Communication, however, while necessary, "is not sufficient for a distinct group to function politically." This requires authority, the legitimate use of power, which has to be supported by political ideology.

The Hausa in question overcome these problems through distinctive behavior, by focusing their primary relationships within their community, by enforcing endogamy, through "the speedy homogenization of diaspora culture," by using a common distinctive language, and, most importantly, by maintaining a moral community founded on a shared ideology, in their case derived from a mystical order of Islam. I am not suggesting the makers and movers of Lapita were mystics. I do contend, however, that what we know or at least postulate about Lapita, and especially about the social-communicative and perhaps ideological role(s) of elaborately decorated Lapita ceramics, indicates that similar effort went into similar means of establishing and reinforcing distinctiveness, facilitating communication, and maintaining authority among the communities scattered through the Bismarcks.

Much more detailed comparative work on the modern and ancient material manifestations of diasporas is undoubtedly required before I can be confident of my ground on this issue. Moreover, it must be remembered that Lapita reflects a maritime expansion, whereas the Hausa diaspora was entirely terrestrial, which may introduce critical differences which remain to be addressed. The same applies to the potential strictures of the colonial situation in Nigeria, which obviously have no parallel in the Lapita case, though the disruption of colonialism may well mirror that of long-distance migration to a considerable degree. Such strictures also apply to other potentially useful parallel cases, such as those of the six groups of historical German migrants studied by Waters (1995:516), some of which integrated but others of which maintained distinctive enclaves when "it was in the material interests of individuals to do so." Nonetheless, on the grounds of the foregoing exploration of the issues, I think it reasonable to propose that in the Lapita Cultural Complex we are dealing with a broadly similar class of social *formation* to the trade diaspora described by A. Cohen (see also Curtin 1975:59–66 and Waters 1995). This means, therefore, that we are likely to be dealing with the same general sort of social *condition* that Clifford, Hall, and others argue is engendered by diasporic experiences of communities dispersed amongst other peoples in the (post)-modern, postcolonial world. A feature of late modernism they may well be, but diasporas characterized by fluid identities and hybridity thus also appear to date into deep prehistory. What is more, if they are seen to be constructed in the manner A. Cohen discerns, the definition and explanation of prehistoric diasporas such as Lapita can largely avoid "the 'ethnicity' problematic" which is so familiar to archaeologists engaging with questions of social identity (Jones 1997, 1999; cf. Lamberg-Karlovsky 1997, 1998).

ACKNOWLEDGMENTS

I thank Lynn Meskell for so generously inviting me to contribute this piece and Tamsin Smith at Blackwell for her encouraging assistance with its production. As always, I thank Michael Williams for providing a work environment so conducive to scholarly productivity and a vision which has led me to think about a great many things I may otherwise have missed. Sean Ulm greatly assisted with the figures and Lynn Meskell and Robert Preucel made insightful comments which improved the text, but I remain responsible for the final product.

NOTES

1   Three of these four writers live "in diaspora," as do many other stars in the contemporary social-theoretical firmament. Thus they and the likes of Bhabha, Naipaul, Rushdie, Said, and the late Frantz Fanon embody the intimate relationship between diasporic experience and the condition of postcoloniality. Though the relationship is not nearly as strong across the entire field of study, much the same can be said of cultural studies and scholars such as Brah, Gilroy, and Hall. Similarly, Benedict Anderson, of *Imagined Communities* fame, explicitly draws attention in "Exodus," a 1994 paper about diaspora, to the fact that he is an Irish citizen living in the United States.

2   "Near Oceania" is New Guinea and the other islands east as far as the end of the Solomons, while "Remote Oceania" is the Pacific beyond the southernmost end of the main Solomons chain; see figure 13.1 and Green (1991a).

3   Within Asia, Austronesian languages are spoken by aboriginal people in Taiwan and in one location in coastal Vietnam, but are otherwise restricted to Island Southeast Asia. Astonishingly, speakers of a Southeast Asian Austronesian tongue were also the first colonists of Madagascar off southern Africa.

4   Two Lapita sherds (one broken in two) have been found on the Sepik coast of the New Guinea mainland. The broken one, from Aitape, is otherwise unprovenanced, while the second is a recent surface find on Ali Island (Terrell and Welsch 1997:558).

REFERENCES

Adams, W., D. van Gervan, and R. Levy. 1978. The retreat from migrationism. *Annual Review of Anthropology* 7: 483–532.

Allen, J. 1984. In search of the Lapita homeland. *Journal of Pacific History* 19: 186–201.

——1996. The pre-Austronesian settlement of Island Melanesia: Implications for Lapita archaeology. *Transactions of the American Philosophical Society* 86:11–27.

——, and C. Gosden. 1991. *Report of the Lapita Homeland Project*. Canberra: Department of Prehistory, Research School of Pacific Studies, Australian National University, Occasional Papers in Prehistory 20.

——, C. Gosden, and J. P. White. 1989. Human Pleistocene adaptations in the tropical island Pacific. *Antiquity* 63: 548–561.

——, and J. P. White. 1989. The Lapita homeland: some new data and an interpretation. *Journal of the Polynesian Society* 98: 129–146.

Ambrose, W. 1978. The loneliness of the long-distance trader in Melanesia. *Mankind* 11: 326–333.

Anderson, A. 2001. Mobility models of Lapita migration. In G. Clark, A. Anderson, and T. Vunidilo (eds.), *The Archaeology of Lapita Dispersal in Oceania: Papers from the Fourth Lapita Conference, June 2000, Canberra, Australia*. Canberra: Pandanus Books, Terra Australis 17, pp. 15–23.

Anderson, B. 1988. Nationalism, identity and the world-in-motion: On the logics of seriality. In P. Cheah and B. Robbins (eds.), *Cosmopolitics: Thinking and Feeling beyond the Nation*. Minneapolis: University of Minnesota Press, pp. 117–133.

——1994. Exodus. *Critical Inquiry* 20: 314–327.

Anthias, F. 1998: Evaluating "diaspora": Beyond ethnicity? *Sociology* 32: 557–580.

Anthony, D. 1990. Migration in archaeology: The baby and the bathwater. *American Anthropologist* 92: 895–914.

——1997. Prehistoric migration as social process. In J. Chapman and H. Hamerow (eds.), *Migrations and Invasions in Archaeological* Explanation. Oxford: British Archaeological Reports International Series 664, pp. 21–32.

Appadurai, A. 1996. *Modernity at Large. Cultural Dimensions of Globalization*. Public Worlds, Vol. 1. Minneapolis: University of Minnesota Press.

Banks, M. 1996. *Ethnicity: Anthropological Constructions*. London, Routledge.

Barnett, W. 2000. Cardial pottery and the agricultural transition in Mediterranean Europe. In T. D. Price (ed.), *Europe's First Farmers*. Cambridge: Cambridge University Press, pp. 93–116.

Barth, F. 1969. Introduction. In F. Barth (ed.), *Ethnic Groups and Boundaries*. London: George Allen & Unwin, pp. 9–38.

Bedford, S., and G. Clark, 2001. The rise and rise of the incised and applied relief tradition: A review and reassessment. In G. Clark, A. Anderson, and T. Vunidilo (eds.), *The Archaeology of the Lapita Dispersal in Oceania: Papers from the Fourth Lapita Conference, June 2000, Canberra, Australia*. Canberra: Pandanus Books, Terra Australis 17, pp. 61–74.

Bedford, S., C. Sand, and D. Burley. 2002. *Fifty Years in the Field: Essays in Honour and Celebration of Richard Shutler Jr's Archaeological Career*. Auckland: New Zealand Archaeological Association, Monograph 25.

Bellwood, P. 1978. *Man's Conquest of the Pacific*. London: Collins.

——1997. *Prehistory of the Indo-Malaysian Archipelago*. Rev. edn. Honolulu: University of Hawai'i Press.

——2001. Early agriculturalist population diasporas? Farming, languages, and genes. *Annual Review of Anthropology* 30: 181–207.

——, J. Fox, and D. Tryon (eds.) 1995. *The Austronesians: Historical and Comparative Perspectives*. Canberra: Department of Anthropology, Australian National University.

Bellwood, P., and P. Koon, 1989. Lapita potters leave boats unburned! The question of Lapita links with Island Southeast Asia. *Antiquity* 63: 613–622.

Bender, B. 2001. Landscapes on-the-move. *Journal of Social Archaeology* 1: 75–89.

Best, S. 2002. *Lapita: A View from the East*. Auckland: New Zealand Archaeological Association, Monograph 24.

Blakey, M. 2001. Bioarchaeology of the African Diaspora in the Americas: Its origins and scope. *Annual Review of Anthropology* 30: 387–422.

Blust, R. 1980. Early Austronesian social organization: The evidence of language. *Current Anthropology* 21: 205–226.

Bogucki, P. 2000. How agriculture came to north-central Europe. In T. D. Price (ed.), *Europe's First Farmers*. Cambridge: Cambridge University Press, pp. 197–218.

Brah, A. 1996. *Cartographies of Diaspora: Contesting Identities*. London: Routledge.

Brandt, S. and J. Walz 2001. Toward an Archaeology of the Other African Diaspora: The Slave Trade in the Indian Ocean. Paper presented in Session III, Global Processes and Local Identities, World Archaeological Congress Intercongress on the African Diaspora, April 23–29, Curaçao, Netherlands Antilles.

Buck, P. (Te Rangi Hiroa). 1938. *Vikings of the Sunrise*. New York: Frederick A. Stokes.

Buell, F. 1998. Nationalist postnationalism: Globalist discourse in contemporary American culture. *American Quarterly* 50: 548–591.

Burley, D., D. Nelson, and R. Shutler, 1999. A radiocarbon chronology for the Eastern Lapita frontier in Tonga. *Archaeology in Oceania* 34: 59–70.

Burmeister, S. 2000. Archaeology and migration: approaches to an archaeological proof of migration. *Current Anthropology* 41: 539–567.

Caröe, A. 1932. Cyprus architecture. The fusion of Byzantine, Western and Mahommedan architectural styles in Cyprus. *Journal of the Royal Institute of British Architects* 26: 45–56.

Chaliand, G., and J-P. Rageau, 1995. *The Penguin Atlas of Diasporas*. Trans. A. M. Berrett. Harmondsworth: Viking.

Cheah, P. 1988a. Introduction Part II: The cosmopolitical today. In P. Cheah and B. Robbins (eds.), *Cosmopolitics: Thinking and Feeling beyond the Nation*. Minneapolis: University of Minnesota Press.

——1988b. Given culture: Rethinking cosmopolitical freedom in transnationalism. In P. Cheah and B. Robbins (eds.), *Cosmopolitics: Thinking and Feeling beyond the Nation*. Minneapolis: University of Minnesota Press, pp. 290–328.

——, and B. Robbins (eds.) 1988. *Cosmopolitics: Thinking and Feeling beyond the Nation*. Minneapolis: University of Minnesota Press.

Clark, G. 1994. Migration as an explanatory concept in Paleolithic archaeology. *Journal of Archaeological Method and Theory* 1: 305–343.

——, A. Anderson, and T. Vunidilo (eds.) 2001. *The Archaeology of the Lapita Dispersal in Oceania: Papers from the Fourth Lapita Conference, June 2000, Canberra, Australia*. Canberra: Pandanus Books, Terra Australis 17.

Clifford, J. 1992. Traveling cultures. In L. Grossberg, C. Nelson, and P. Treichler (eds.), *Cultural Studies*. New York: Routledge, pp. 96–116.

—— 1994. Diasporas. *Cultural Anthropology* 9: 302–338.

Cohen, A. 1967. Stranger communities. The Hausa. In P. Lloyd, A. Mbogunje, and B. Awe (eds.), *The City of Ibadan*. Cambridge University Press, pp. 117–127.

—— 1969. *Custom and Politics in Urban Africa*. London: Routledge & Kegan Paul.

—— 1971. Cultural strategies in the organization of trading diasporas. In C. Meillassoux (ed.), *L'évolution du commerce Africain dupuis le XIXe siècle en Afrique du l'ouest*. Oxford: Oxford University Press, pp. 266–281.

Cohen, R. 1997. *Global Diasporas: An Introduction*. London: UCL Press.

Curtin, P. 1975. *Economic Change in Precolonial Africa*. Madison: University of Wisconsin Press.

—— 1984. *Cross-Cultural Trade in World History*. Cambridge: Cambridge University Press.

—— 1990. *The Rise and Fall of the Plantation Complex*. Cambridge: Cambridge University Press.

Davidson, J., G. Irwin, F. Leach, A. Pawley, and D. Brown (eds.) 1996. *Oceanic Culture History: Essays in Honour of Roger Green*. Dunedin: *New Zealand Journal of Archaeology* Special Publication.

Davis, R. 1973. *The Rise of the Atlantic Economies*. London: Weidenfeld & Nicolson.

De Angelis, F. 1998. Ancient past, imperial present: the British Empire in T. J. Dunbabin's *The western Greeks*. *Antiquity* 72: 539–549.

Deetz, J. 1977. *In Small Things Forgotten*. New York: Doubleday.

Descoeudres, J-P. (ed.) 1990. *Greek Colonists and Native Populations. Proceedings of the First Australian Congress of Classical Archaeology, held in Honour of Emeritus Professor A. D. Trendall, Sydney, 9–14 July 1985*. Oxford: Clarendon Press.

Diamond, J. 1988. Express train to Polynesia. *Nature* 336: 307–308.

—— 2000. Taiwan's gift to the world. *Nature* 403: 709–710.

—— 2001. Slow boat to Melanesia? Diamond replies. *Nature* 410: 167.

Fallers, L. A. (ed.) 1967. *Immigrants and Associations*. The Hague: Mouton.

Frankel, D. 2000. Migration and ethnicity in prehistoric Cyprus: Technology as habitus. *European Journal of Archaeology* 3: 167–187.

——, and J. M. Webb. 1998. Three faces of identity: Ethnicity, community and status in Bronze Age Cyprus. *Mediterranean Archaeology* 11: 1–12.

Franklin, M. 1997. "Power to the people": Sociopolitics and the archaeology of Black Americans. *Historical Archaeology* 31:36–50.

Funari, P. 1999. Maroon, race and gender: Palmares material culture and social relations in a runaway settlement. In P. Funari, M. Hall, and S. Jones (eds.), *Historical Archaeology: Back from the Edge*. London: Routledge, pp. 308–327.

Galipaud, J-C. (ed.) 1992. *Poterie Lapita et Peuplement*. Noumea: ORSTOM.

——, and I. Lilley (eds.) 1999. *Le Pacifique de 5000 à 2000 BP. Suppléments à l'histoire d'une colonisation*. Actes du colloque Vanuatu, 31 juillet–6 août 1996. Collections Colloques et séminaires. Paris: Editions de l'Institut de Recherche pour le Développement.

Gifford, E., and D. Shutler. 1956. *Archaeological Excavations in New Caledonia*. Berkeley: University of California, Anthropological Records 18:1.

Gilroy, P. 1993. *The Black Atlantic: Modernity and Double Consciousness*. London: Verso.

Goodenough, W. 1982. Ban Chiang in world perspective. In J. C. White (ed.), *Ban Chiang: Discovery of a Lost Bronze Age*. Philadelphia: University Museum, pp. 52–53.

Gordon, E., and M. Anderson. 1999. The African Diaspora. Toward an ethnography of diasporic identity. *Journal of American Folklore* 112: 282–296.

Gosden, C. 1992a. Endemic doubt: Is what we write right? *Antiquity* 66: 803–808.

——1992. Dynamic traditionalism: Lapita as a long term social structure. In J-C. Galipaud (ed.), *Poterie Lapita et Peuplement*. Noumea: ORSTOM, pp. 21–26.

Graham, A. 1990. Pre-colonial contacts: Questions and problems. In J-P. Descoeudres (ed.), *Greek Colonists and Native Populations. Proceedings of the First Australian Congress of Classical Archaeology, held in Honour of Emeritus Professor A. D. Trendall, Sydney, 9–14 July 1985*. Oxford: Clarendon Press.

Green, R. 1979. Lapita. In J. Jennings (ed.), *The Prehistory of Polynesia*. Canberra: Australian National University Press, pp. 27–60.

——1991a. Near and remote Oceania: disestablishing "Melanesia" in culture history. In A. Pawley (ed.), *Man and a Half: Essays in Pacific Anthropology and Ethnobotany in Honour of Ralph Bulmer*. Auckland: Polynesian Society, pp. 491–502.

——1991b. The Lapita cultural complex. *Bulletin of the Indo-Pacific Prehistory Association* 11: 295–305.

——1992. Definitions of the Lapita cultural complex and its non-ceramic component. In J-C. Galipaud (ed.), *Poterie Lapita et Peuplement*. Noumea: ORSTOM, pp. 7–20.

——1997. Linguistic, biological and cultural origins of the initial inhabitants of Remote Oceania. *New Zealand Journal of Archaeology* 17: 5–27.

——2000. Lapita and the cultural model for intrusion, integration and innovation. In A. Anderson and T. Murray (eds.), *Australian Archaeologist: Collected Papers in Honour of Jim Allen*. Canberra: Centre for Archaeological Research and Department of Archaeology and Natural History, Australian National University, with the Department of Archaeology, La Trobe University, pp. 372–392.

Hall, S. 1990. Cultural identity and diaspora. In J. Rutherford (ed.), *Identity*. London: Lawrence & Wishart, pp. 222–237.

——1992. The question of cultural identity. In S. Hall, D. Held, and T. McGrew (eds.), *Modernity and its Futures*. London: Polity Press in association with the Open University, pp. 273–325.

Härke, H. 1998. Archaeologists and migrations: A problem of attitude? *Current Anthropology* 39: 19–45.

Haviser, J. (ed.) 1999. *African Sites Archaeology in the Caribbean*. Princeton, NJ and Kingston: Markus Weiner and Ian Randle.

Hingley, R. (ed.) 2001. *Images of Rome: Perceptions of Ancient Rome in Europe and the United States in the Modern Age*. Journal of Roman Archaeology Supplementary Series 44.

Irwin, G. 1992. *The Prehistoric Exploration and Colonization of the Pacific*. Cambridge: Cambridge University Press.

Jones, S. 1997. *The Archaeology of Ethnicity*. London: Routledge.

——1999. Historical categories and the praxis of identity: the interpretation of ethnicity in historical archaeology. In P. Funari, M. Hall, and S. Jones (eds.), *Historical Archaeology: Back from the Edge*. London: Routledge, pp. 119–232.

Kaiser, A. 2000. Ethnic identity and urban fabric: The case of the Greeks at Empúries, Spain. *Journal of Mediterranean Archaeology* 13: 189–203.

Kelly, K. 1997. The archaeology of African–European interaction: Investigating the social roles of trade, traders, and the use of space in the seventeenth- and eighteenth-century *Hueda* Kingdom, Republic of Benin. *World Archaeology* 28: 351–69.

Kirch, P. 1988. Problems and issues in Lapita archaeology. In P. Kirch and T. Hunt (eds.), *Archaeology of the Lapita Cultural Complex*. Seattle: Burke Museum, Research Report 5, pp. 157–165.

—— 1997. *The Lapita Peoples: Ancestors of the Oceanic World*. Oxford: Blackwell.

—— 2000. *On the Road of the Winds: An Archaeological History of the Pacific Islands before European Contact*. Berkeley: University of California Press.

Knapp, B. 2001. Archaeology and ethnicity: A dangerous liaison. *Archaeologia Cypria* 4: 29–46.

Lamberg-Karlovsky, C. 1997. Politics and archaeology: Colonialism, nationalism, ethnicity and archaeology. Part 1. *Review of Archaeology* 18: 1–14.

—— 1998. Politics and archaeology: Colonialism, nationalism, ethnicity and archaeology. Part 2. *Review of Archaeology* 19: 35–47.

Lawrence, S. 1999. The Nineteenth Century British Diaspora. Paper presented in the Symposium on the Archaeology of the British, World Archaeological Congress IV, Cape Town, South Africa.

—— 2003. Archaeology and the nineteenth-century British Empire. *Historical Archaeology* 37: 20–33.

—— in press. Introduction: Comparative archaeologies of empire. In S. Lawrence (ed.), *Archaeologies of the British: Explorations of Identity in Great Britain and its Colonies 1600–1945*. London: Routledge.

Lilley, I. 1988. Prehistoric exchange across the Vitiaz Strait, Papua New Guinea. *Current Anthropology* 29: 513–516.

—— 1999. Post-Lapita scenarios for archaeology and language in north New Guinea-west New Britain. In P. Bellwood, D. Bowdery, M. Fiskesjo, I. Lilley, and B. Maloney (eds.), *The Melaka Papers, Volume 2*. Canberra: Indo-Pacific Prehistory Association, pp. 25–34.

—— 2000. Migration and ethnicity in the evolution of Lapita and post-Lapita maritime societies in northwest Melanesia. In S. O'Connor and P. Veth (eds.), *Voyaging with Wallace: Studies of Past and Present Maritime Cultures of the Indo-Pacific Region*. Rotterdam: A. A. Balkema, pp. 177–195.

—— 2002. Lapita and Type Y pottery in the KLK site, Siassi, Papua New Guinea. In S. Bedford, D. Burley, and C. Sand (eds.), *Fifty Years in the Field: Essays in Honour and Celebration of Richard Shutler Jr's Archaeological Career*. Auckland: New Zealand Archaeological Association Monograph Series 25, pp. 79–90.

—— in press. Trade and culture history across the Vitiaz Strait: The emerging mid- to late Holocene sequence. In V. Attenbrow and R. Fullagar (eds.), *Festschrift for Jim Specht* (working title). Sydney: Australian Museum, Records of the Australian Museum.

McClintock, A. 1992. The angel of progress: pitfalls of the term "postcolonialism." *Social Text* 31/32: 84–98.

Meskell, L. 1996. The somatisation of archaeology: Institutions, discourses, corporeality. *Norwegian Archaeological Review* 29: 1–16.

—— 1999. *Archaeologies of Social Life: Age, Sex, Class et cetera in Ancient Egypt*. Oxford: Blackwell.

Morris, I. 2000. *Archaeology as Cultural History*. Oxford: Blackwell.

Muhly, J. 1999. The Phoenicians in the Aegean. *Aegaeum* 20: 517–526.

Oppenheimer, S., and Richards, M. 2001. Polynesian origins: Slow boat to Melanesia? *Nature* 410: 166–167.

Orser, C. 1994. Toward a global historical archaeology: an example from Brazil. *Historical Archaeology* 28, 5–22.

—— 1998. The archaeology of the African Diaspora. *Annual Review of Anthropology* 27: 63–82.

Pavlides, C. 1996. Transformations in Stone: Characterizing the Structure and Organization of Holocene Assemblages in the Rain Forests of West New Britain. Paper presented to the Vanuatu National Museum-ANU-ORSTOM Conference on The Western Pacific, 5000 to 2000 BP: Colonisations and Transformations. Port Vila, Vanuatu.

——, and Gosden, C. 1994. 35,000-year-old sites in the rainforests of West New Britain, Papua New Guinea. *Antiquity* 68: 604–10.

Price, T. D. (ed.) 2000. *Europe's First Farmers*. Cambridge: Cambridge University Press.

——, R. A. Bentley, J. Luning, D. Gronenborn, and J. Wahl. 2001. Prehistoric human migration in the *Linearbandkeramik* of Central Europe. *Antiquity* 75: 593–603.

Renfrew, C. 1988. Archaeology and language: The puzzle of Indo-European origins. *Current Anthropology* 29: 437–468.

Rigsby, B. 1995. Tribes, diaspora people and the vitality of law and custom: Some comments. In J. Fingleton and J. Finlayson (eds.), *Anthropology in the Native Title Era*. Canberra: Australian Institute of Aboriginal and Torres Strait Islander Studies, pp. 25–27.

Ross, M., A. Pawley, and M. Osmond. 1998. *The Lexicon of Proto Oceanic. The Culture and Environment of Ancestral Oceanic Society. 1: Material Culture*. Canberra: Pacific Linguistics C-152.

Rouse, I. 1986. *Migrations in Prehistory: Inferring Movement from Cultural Remains*. New Haven, CT: Yale University Press.

Rowlands, M. 1998. The archaeology of colonialism. In K. Kristiansen and M. Rowlands (eds.), *Social Transformations in Archaeology*. London, Routledge, pp. 327–333.

Safran, W. 1991. Diasporas in modern societies: Myths of homeland and return. *Diaspora* 1: 83–99.

Sand, C. 2001. Evolutions on the Lapita Cultural Complex: A view from the Southern Lapita Province. *Archaeology in Oceania* 36: 65–76.

Schulz, P., and R. Allen. 2002. Archaeology and architecture of the Overseas Chinese: A bibliography. http://www.sha.org/ChinBibDec02fnl.pdf (accessed 29 May 2003).

Shami, S. 2000. Prehistories of globalization: Circassian identity in motion. *Public Culture* 12: 177–204.

Shennan, S. 1989. Introduction. In S. Shennan (ed.), *Archaeological Approaches to Cultural Identity*. London: Unwin Hyman, pp. 1–32.

Shukla, S. 2001. Locations for South Asian diasporas. *Annual Review of Anthropology* 30: 551–572.

Smith, A. 1992. Chosen peoples: Why ethnic groups survive. *Ethnic and Racial Studies* 15: 436–56.

Smith, B. 2000. *"Local" and "Diaspora" Connections to Country and Kin in Central Cape York Peninsula*. Land, Rights, Laws: Issues of Native Title. Vol. 2. Canberra: Australian Institute of Aboriginal and Torres Strait Islander Studies, Issues Paper 6.

Sommer, U. 2001. "Hear the instruction of thy father, and forsake not the law of thy mother": Change and persistence in the European early Neolithic. *Journal of Social Archaeology* 1: 244–70.

Spencer-Wood, S. 1999. The formation of ethnic-American identities: Jewish communities in Boston. In P. Funari, M. Hall, and S. Jones (eds.), *Historical Archaeology: Back from the Edge*. London: Routledge, pp. 284–307.

Spivak, G. 1988. *In Other Worlds: Essays in Cultural Politics*. London: Routledge.

Spriggs, M. 1991. Lapita origins, distribution, contemporaries and successors revisited. *Bulletin of the Indo-Pacific Prehistory Association* 11: 306–312.

—— 1995. The Lapita culture and Austronesian prehistory in Oceania. In P. Bellwood, J. Fox, and D. Tryon (eds.), *The Austronesians: Historical and Comparative Perspectives*. Canberra: Department of Anthropology, Australian National University, pp. 112–133.

—— 1996. What is southeast Asian about Lapita? In T. Akazawa and E. Szathmáry (eds.), *Prehistoric Mongoloid Dispersals*. Oxford: Oxford University Press, pp. 324–48.

—— 1997. *The Island Melanesians*. London: Blackwell.

—— 1999. Pacific archaeologies: Contested ground on the construction of Pacific history. *Journal of Pacific History* 34: 109–22.

Stein, G. 1999. *Rethinking World Systems: Diasporas, Colonies, and Interaction in Uruk Mesopotamia*. Tucson: University of Arizona Press.

Stein, G. 2002. Colonies without colonialism: A trade diaspora model of 4th Millennium BC Mesopotamian enclaves in Anatolia. In C. Lyons and J. Papadopoulos (eds.), *The Archaeology of Colonialism*. Los Angeles: J. Paul Getty Museum Publications, pp. 26–64.

Summerhayes, G. 2000. *Lapita Interaction*. Canberra: ANH Publications and Centre for Archaeo-logical Research, Australian National University, Terra Australis 15.

Swadling, P. 1995. *Plumes from Paradise*. Brisbane: Robert Brown & Associates.

Terrell, J. 1981. Linguistics and the peopling of the Pacific Islands. *Journal of the Polynesian Society* 90: 225–258.

——1986. *Prehistory in the Pacific Islands*. Cambridge: Cambridge University Press.

——1988. History as a family tree, history as an entangled bank: Constructing images and interpretations of prehistory in the South Pacific. *Antiquity* 62: 642–657.

——1989. What Lapita is and what Lapita isn't. *Antiquity* 63: 623–626.

——, T. Hunt, and C. Gosden. 1997. The dimensions of social life in the pacific. Human diversity and the myth of the primitive isolate. *Current Anthropology* 38: 155–195.

——, K. Kelly, and P. Rainbird. 2001. Foregone conclusions? An analysis of the concepts of "Austronesians" and "Papuans". *Current Anthropology* 42: 97–124.

——, and R. Welsch. 1997. Lapita and the temporal geography of prehistory. *Antiquity* 71: 548–572.

Torrence, R. 1992. What is Lapita about obsidian? A view from the Talasea source. In J-C. Galipaud (ed.), *Poterie Lapita et peuplement*. Noumea, ORSTOM, pp. 111–126.

——1994. Processes and events: Differential rates of change in the Talasea region of West New Britain, Papua New Guinea. Paper presented to the 15th IPPA Congress, Chang Mai, Thailand.

——, and C. Stevenson. 2000. Beyond the beach: Changing Lapita landscapes on Garua Island, Papua New Guinea. In A. Anderson and T. Murray (eds.), *Australian Archaeologist: Collected Papers in Honour of Jim Allen*. Canberra: Centre for Archaeological Research and Department of Archaeology and Natural History, Australian National University, with the Department of Archaeology, La Trobe University, pp. 324–345.

Ucko, P. 1989. Foreword. In S. Shennan (ed.), *Archaeological Approaches to Cultural Identity*. London: Unwin Hyman, pp. ix–xx.

van Dommelen, P. 1997. Colonial constructs: Colonialism and archaeology in the Mediterra-nean. *Antiquity* 28: 305–323.

Vella, N. 1996. Elusive Phoenicians. *Antiquity* 70: 245–250.

Waters, T. 1995. Towards a theory of ethnic identity and migration: The formation of ethnic enclaves by migrant Germans in Russia and North America. *International Migration Review* 29: 515–544.

Weiner, J. 2002. *Diaspora, materialism, tradition: Anthropological issues in the recent High Court appeal of the Yorta Yorta*. Land, Rights, Laws: Issues of Native Title Vol. 2. Canberra: Native Title Research Unit, Australian Institute of Aboriginal and Torres Strait Islander Studies, Issue Paper 18.

White, J. P. 1996. Rocks in the head. In J. Davidson, G. Irwin, F. Leach, A. Pawley, and D. Brown (eds.), *Oceanic Culture History: Essays in Honour of Roger Green*. Dunedin: New Zealand Archaeological Association, pp. 199–209.

——1999. Who is the potter, pray, and who the pot? *Review of Archaeology* 20: 12–14.

——, J. Allen, and J. Specht. 1988. Peopling the Pacific: The Lapita Homeland Project. *Austra-lian Natural History* 22: 410–416.

——, and M-N. Harris. 1997. Changing sources: Early Lapita period obsidian in the Bismarck Archipelago. *Archaeology in Oceania* 32: 97–107.

Wickler, S., and Spriggs, M. 1988. Pleistocene human occupation of the Solomon Islands, Melanesia. *Antiquity* 62: 703–706.

Winer, M., and Deetz, J. 1990. The transformation of British culture in the Eastern Cape, 1820–1860. *Social Dynamics* 16: 55–75.

Woolf, G. 1997. Beyond Romans and natives. *World Archaeology* 28: 339–350.

Yelvington, K. 2001. The anthropology of Afro-Latin America and the Caribbean: Diasporic dimensions. *Annual Review of Anthropology* 30: 227–260.

Zilhão, J. 2000. From the Mesolithic to the Neolithic in the Iberian peninsula. In T. D. Price (ed.), *Europe's First Farmers*. Cambridge: Cambridge University Press, pp. 144–182.

——2001. Radiocarbon evidence for maritime pioneer colonization at the origins of farming in west Mediterranean Europe. *Proceedings of the National Academy of Sciences* 98: 14180–14185.

Zvelebil, M., and M. Lillie. 2000. Transition to agriculture in eastern Europe. In T. D. Price (ed.), *Europe's First Farmers*. Cambridge: Cambridge University Press, pp. 57–92.

Part IV

Politics

Lynn Meskell and Robert W. Preucel

Never before have debates about nationalism, heritage, and politics stimulated by the destruction of archaeological sites and the looting of archaeological objects circulated as widely in the public consciousness as they have since the 1990s. During the two recent Gulf wars aimed at the destruction of the Iraqi regime, there was a sharp public outcry over the protection of archaeological heritage. The looting of the Baghdad Museum and others became a nodal point for archaeologists and the international community alike. A similar concern was raised with the Taliban's control over its multiethnic, multireligious heritage, whether in national museums or in the Bamiyan Valley of Afghanistan (Colwell-Chanthaphonh 2003; Meskell 2002b; see Bernbeck and Pollock, chapter 14, this volume). The Middle East has been characterized as a repository of precious archaeological resources constituting a universal world heritage, but a heritage that requires control and management by Western experts and their respective governments.

In February 2003, before the full-scale coalition military action in late March, a group of wealthy collectors and curators met with the US Defense and State departments to discuss the impending fate of archaeological sites, museums, and collections (Lawler 2003). Some months earlier, President George W. Bush discussed the possibility of resuming discussions with UNESCO after a 30-year silence. Meanwhile countries including Britain, Germany, Switzerland, and Japan have still failed to ratify the 1970 UNESCO convention to prevent the international trade in stolen art and antiquities (Meskell 2002b). For any archaeologists who perhaps imagined that our discipline might be kept unsullied from the political arena, these recent events underscore the intensely political nature of the archaeological enterprise. The key point to keep in mind is that these examples are exceptions only in their specifics. The discursive fields of identity and politics are deeply entwined. Identities, past and present, are multiply constructed and revolve around a set of iterative practices that are always in process, despite their material and symbolic substrata. Who we are, what we study, and the questions we ask have real-time effects. These configurations underscore the types of archaeology, the level of political engagement, and the points of connection archaeologists experience. The *politics of location* is central to our understanding of archaeological subjects and affects us as practitioners today.

Archaeology as a discipline was forged in conjunction with burgeoning national identity and state formation in Europe and elsewhere, in itself a very specific and reductionist construal of identity. During that era and for much archaeology afterward, criteria such as establishing identity or ethnic boundaries played into nationalist tropes of governance and supremacy. Ethnicity has been paramount since the nineteenth century, foregrounded by writers such as Morgan, Kossina, and Childe (Trigger 1989), and spurred on by the refashioning of national boundaries, diasporic movements, and ethnic tensions within twentieth-century Europe. From the outset, archaeological heritage was entangled with issues of identity, locality, territory, ethnicity, religion, and economic value. Historically, our present concept of archaeological heritage crystallized in Europe in synchrony with the origins of the nation-state, while the notion of the past as a resource to be managed by the present is also characteristic of the modern era. Intimately connected to the Enlightenment, the formation of national identity relied on a coherent national heritage that could be deployed to fend off the counter-claims of other groups and nations. We might look to the negative associations of early ethnic studies and their political deployment in order to explain the subsequent time lag between the first half of the twentieth century and its rather different articulation in very recent scholarship.

Heritage Places

Heritage is history with a purpose. It is history embedded in a political location. Places of heritage are intensely political spaces where links are forged across temporal, material, and symbolic landscapes. As we have seen in Europe and the Middle East, they are contested geographies where specific histories and cultural memories may be either enshrined or erased, depending on state sanctioning, collective amnesia, and, quite simply, the willingness to remember or forget. In archaeology, heritage studies once inhabited the undertheorized end of an "applied archaeology" spectrum (Meskell 2002b). As Bernbeck and Pollock argue (chapter 14), archaeology is distinct from other historical disciplines in that it engages with the lives of people by means of concrete things that take the form of material remains and their relationships to one another. This makes for volatile geographies and contested spaces where past, present, and future collide. Given the outcry over recent destruction of heritage in Afghanistan and Iraq, archaeologists might move to historicize and interrogate the apparently un-controversial construction of "heritage," particularly through the lens of interdisciplin-ary scholarship devoted to the entanglements of identity, place, politics, memory, and tourist economies (Matero 2000). In disciplines such as social geography, historic preservation, or museum studies the category of "heritage" is approaching meaning overload, evidenced by an outpouring of writing devoted to materiality, commemor-ation, and nationalism.

Heritage has been extremely politicized and deployed by various factions in recent conflicts and war zones, whether that of the Balkans (Brown 1998; Chapman 1994) or the Middle East (Meskell n.d. Naccache 1998; Pollock and Lutz 1994). Many of the most vigorous critiques have come from Western museums, collectors, and archaeolo-gists. Despite Colin Renfrew and others' call for protection for "the extraordinary global significance of the monuments, museums and archaeological sites of Iraq," many countries have yet to sign the 1954 Hague Convention, including Afghanistan, the United States, the United Kingdom, and Japan. The Convention states that "damage to cultural property belonging to any people whatsoever means damage to the cultural heritage of all mankind, since each people makes its own contribution to the culture of the world" (UNESCO 2000:1). The Cold War destabilized the United States' and United Kingdom's commitment to preserving heritage in the context of war, and specific countries were unwilling to place limitations on the means of warfare. Since the Balkan crisis there has been active prosecution of offenses against cultural property by an international tribunal in The Hague, specifically the destruction of the Mostar Bridge and Dubrovnik (Prott, de la Torre, and Levin 2001:13). Phrased in terms of war crimes, this has set a precedent for future actions, perhaps potentially even those such as the bombing of Afghanistan and Iraq. Speaking specifically about Afghanistan, Colin Renfrew has stated that "the time is ripe for an international convention to make the destruction of cultural artefacts a crime against humanity" (Bone 2001). The loss of heritage can easily be decried as a crime that affects multiple generations, erasing cultural memory and severing links with the past that are integral to forging and maintaining modern identities. Yet it is extremely dangerous to place commensurate value on people and things and to couch these acts in a language reserved for genocide, since they do not inhabit the same order of existence (Meskell 2002b: 564).

The material world, as it exists today, is a constant reminder of an ever-present past, and yet certain decisions by particular individuals and organizations render particular places valuable, important, aesthetic, and meaningful. Heritage inhabits spatial, temporal, cultural, and economic domains. However, the notion of cultural good is often synonymous with economic success. Heritage is embedded within narratives of ownership and, like other natural, non-renewable resources, is depicted as a scarce commodity or property. There are two implications that follow from that position: the first deals with notions of ownership and control, the second with an essentialized vision of the past as a "natural" resource. Amongst many Native American (Goldstein 1992; Lilley 2000a; Swidler et al. 1997; Watkins 2001) or Australian Aboriginal communities (Byrne 2003a; Meehan 1995), "the past" is not something to be bought or sold, studied or scientifically tested, displayed or objectified. In fact many other groups do not consider that the past is past at all. Relationships to heritage such as these cannot be captured in the language of patrimony or ownership, nor can they reside within the dominant perspective that valorizes a value-hierarchical, dualistic, rights-based framework (Warren 1999: 15–16), thus challenging the adequacy of our semantic categories, and our fundamental conceptual taxonomies that reflect the very hallmarks of our distinctive modernity (Meskell 2002a: 567–8).

The production and maintenance of heritage are foundational to the archaeological endeavor and certainly more complex when we are involved in crafting pasts for other communities. Foreign archaeologists, according to Bernbeck and Pollock, in contrast to native ones, generally work in an imperialist tradition that treats archaeology as a global endeavor. This is tied to the notion of a global world heritage and often erases local specificities. Thus we are seen as excavating humanity's past, leading to forms of departicularization rather than contextual understandings of local practices and histories.

Deployed Pasts: Nationalism

Since the 1980s a burgeoning literature has focused attention upon archaeology and archaeological narratives in the service of the state. This is, in part, an outgrowth of earlier studies that linked the rise of archaeology with the construction of the modern nation-state (Fowler 1987; McGuire 1992; Patterson 1994). Ensuing studies focused more closely upon European nation-building, whereas more recent work has brought this into a wider global and contemporary perspective (Kohl 1998; Kohl and Fawcett 1995; Meskell 1998b; Ucko 1995).

In the 1990s questions of theory in specific countries and the relationships between national concerns and theoretical developments also emerged as an important issue (Hodder 1991; Ucko 1995). It is also crucial to provide sociopolitical linkages between historical events and the emergence of archaeological discourse: the twentieth century was rife with political restructuring and ethnic/religious upheavals (e.g. in the Balkans, the Soviet Union, Israel, and India) that sparked relationships with particular historical trajectories, nostalgia, and memory, and the tacit materiality of archaeological remains. The chapters in this section explore how cultural heritage has been deployed in quests for specific modernities, sometimes at the expense or erasure of others, and the ways in which political agendas inhere in monumentalized space.

Numerous papers and books have dealt with the national character of archaeology in particular European countries (Demoule 1999; Dietler 1994; Fleury-Ilett 1993; Hamilakis 1996; Kasier 1995; Kotsakis 1998; Schnapp 1996; Shnirelman 1995; Wailes and Zoll 1995). More substantial studies have been undertaken for Germany, specifically its relationship to the Nazi regime (Anthony 1995; Arnold 1990; Härke 2000; Härke and Wolfram 1993) and the divisive effects of the Berlin Wall. Greece has also been at the center of attention, not least because of the ongoing battle for the Parthenon (Elgin) Marbles (Hamilakis 1999; Hamilakis and Yalouri 1996; Yalouri 2001) now housed in the British Museum. The Middle East is also receiving well-warranted attention in terms of the centrality and mobilizing force of its unique histories and historiographies (Abdi 2001; Meskell 1998b; Naccache 1998; Özdogan 1998; Pollock and Lutz 1994; Reid 2002; Scham 1998; Silberman 1995; Wood 1998). More recently, studies by Asian specialists have foregrounded the role of archaeology within national modernities (Fawcett 1995; Pai 2000; Tong 1995; Tsude 1995; Von Falkenhausen 1995).

As Koji Mizoguchi (chapter 17) documents for Japan, individual nation-states functioned, and continue to function, as boundary-markers in the constitution and reproduction of modern institutions and archaeology as a discipline. Specifically, he asks, why did the formation of modern nation-states in many cases coincide with the disciplinary foundations of archaeology? Why was archaeology mobilized particularly intensively in the constitution of national identity? Here the history of Japanese archaeology, and Japan as a modern nation-state, offer a particularly salient example, since modernization and the formation of a modern nation–state took place as a tightly combined process and archaeology was deeply imbricated. Newer areas such as South Asia have recently focused upon identity, nationalism, and the place of the past (Chakrabarti 1995, 1997, 2000; Colwell-Chanthaphonh 2003; Coningham and Lewer 2000a; Coningham and Lewer 2000b; Lahiri 2000; Paddayya 1995), especially after the volatile incidents around Ayodya mosque (Bernbeck and Pollock 1996; Mandal 1993; Rao 1994; Shaw 2000). In chapter 14 Bernbeck and Pollock argue that the Ayodhya example is a not uncommon case in which members of two religious groups claim the same place as sacred to their religion. The material residues of archaeology were invoked as concrete evidence if and when they were (or could be made to be) useful. Inevitably, no amount of debate over the physical evidence mattered: both parties assumed that they were correct. The Babri Mosque was dismantled and, since 1992; Ayodhya has remained a volatile geography where endeavors to rebuild the Ram temple have run parallel to outbreaks of violence between religious factions.

While these aforementioned themes unite many groups across the globe, it has taken time to connect scholars writing on the topic from Europe, the Caribbean, Latin America, North America, India, and Australia. An important body of writing on the politics of archaeology in Latin America provides salient insights for those working elsewhere (Funari 1995; Higueras 1995; Mamani Condori 1996; McGuire and Navarrete 1999; Patterson 1995; Politis 1995, 2001; Ramos 1994; Schmidt and Patterson 1995; Vargas Arenas 1995). In Guatemala, the Copan excavations influenced the independence movement, providing the new nation with its own ennobling history (Chinchilla Mazariegos 1998). In Mexican archaeology, ethnicity, class, and race are cross-cut by competing narratives and representations (Bernal 1980; Castañeda 1997; Hyland 1992; Jones 1997). New collaborative projects are also underway in Brazil, where public archaeology, anthropology, and new forms of media are being experimented with in relation to educational and developmental activities with local communities (Fordred Green, Green, and Neves 2003). Despite the sensational nature of archaeological discoveries and their political mobilizations, few archaeologists have explored the potentials for linking heritage, national modernity, and tourism. Archaeological monuments lie at a powerful nexus between Appadurai's (1997) *ethnoscapes* and *finanscapes*, and so on. Alternatively, ethnographers and sociologists have theorized the intersection between performing the past, potent tourist locales, and divergent interest groups (e.g., Abu el-Haj 1998, 2001; Ashworth 1995; Edensor 1998; Herbert 1995; Kirshenblatt-Gimblett 1998).

Geographically, there are clear imbalances between the scope of literature produced, and these are undoubtedly linked to the development of social archaeology and the place of sociopolitics (Meskell 2002a: 289). A growing number of studies have been produced for African countries (Andah 1995a, 1995b; Elamin 1999; Jeppson 1997; Lewis-Williams 1995; Schrire 1995; Shepherd 2002; 2003). In South Africa Martin Hall attacked the apartheid regime (1984, 1988) and its legacy in an attempt to resituate archaeology as a political endeavor, and to foreground the ethical responsibility of practitioners (Hall 1992; 1994a, 1994b, 1999; 2001). He has recently (2000) documented Cape Town's District Six, its destruction, and subsequent rise with the success of protest against the apartheid state. In Johannesburg, the Rock Art Research Institute has materialized this commitment by instigating a series of collaborative projects around the presentation of rock-art sites that involves diverse local communities and publics (Blundell 1996, 2002; Laue, Turkington, and Smith 2002).

Colonial Contexts

A social archaeology is committed to addressing larger worldwide processes that engulf us all, such as colonialism, globalism, and exploitation (Hodder 1999; 2000a; Meskell 1998a). This is appropriate since archaeology, like anthropology, grew up embedded within a colonial framework. In the last two decades of postprocessual and indigenous archaeologies, scholars have become more politicized and outspoken in this regard. Central to this development has been a recognition of the politics of location, both in respect to the effects of colonial hegemonies or transnational tensions, and in terms of our own situated scholarship. In chapter 7 of this volume Chris Gosden argues that colonialism is the dominant social fact of the last five centuries and concomitantly, colonial relations had profound intellectual, economic, and social implications for all concerned, the colonizers as well as the colonized. Epistemically, we as archaeologists work in a type of in-between space. In reaction to this phenomenon, a postcolonial archaeology takes as its object of study the types of cultural forms and identities created through colonial encounters (Gosden 1999; 2001:241). As archaeologists, then, we are not seeking to uncover pristine identities of colonizer and colonized, since these groups cannot sustain their own separate identities. Rather, in line with other postcolonial theorists, we acknowledge the creation of hybrid and creole cultures that result from sustained colonial contact and seek to engage with their material traces. So, on the one hand, archaeologists have begun revealing the impacts of colonial hegemonies on archaeology as a discipline (Byrne 1991, 2003b; Shepherd 2003; van Dommelen 1997) and its concomitant histories and, on the other, have attempted to forge a new postcolonial archaeology in practice (Byrne, Brayshaw, and Ireland 2001; Colwell-Chanthaphonh and Ferguson 2004; Hall 2001; Hodder 1999, 2000b; Lilley 2000a; Preucel 2002).

Unsurprisingly, the residual effects of colonialism, be it English, Dutch, French, Portuguese, or Spanish, have occupied distinct trajectories in different countries. There has been an outpouring of literature on Native American issues since the 1990s, specifically the problematics of archaeological intervention (Goldstein 1992; Swidler et al. 1997), reburial and repatriation (Bray 2001; Bray and Killion 1994; Fforde, Hubert, and Turnbull 2002; Fine-Dare 2002; Goldstein and Kintigh 1990; Ridington and Hastings 1997; Thomas 2000; Tweedie 2002; Watkins 2004; Wylie 2001), representation, the place of Cultural Resource Management (CRM) (Dowdall and Parish 2003; Stoffle, Zedeno, and Halmo 2001), collaborative field practices (Colwell-Chanthaphonh and Ferguson 2004), museums, and so on. As McGuire outlines in chapter 16, repatriation and reburial have become facts of life for North American archaeology, with numerous large repatriations of museum collections to native communities. He states that every major archaeological museum in the United States has an office of repatriation and is actively involved in negotiations with Native American nations. Reburial, and inclusion of Native American observers, have also become standard practice in CRM excavations and for most grant-funded research projects and even field schools. Numerous publications now attest to the ethical centrality of these issues in terms of cultural patrimony and stewardship, as well as our professional engagement with native communities (Dongoske, Aldenderfer, and Doehner 2000; Dongoske et al. 1997). Significantly, the impetus for this shift was initiated by indigenous activists, rather than being an emergent recognition by archaeologists. Comparatively speaking, North American archaeologists were slow in acknowledging the rights of indigenous peoples, especially when compared to legislation in Australia. They "seem not to have recognized an emergent pressing need to single out Native Americans for attention before such a course of action was imposed upon them by interests which are not naturally sympathetic to archaeological concerns and perhaps even middle-class concerns more generally" (Lilley 2000b:113).

Yet the recognition of Native rights in the United States, accompanied by NAGPRA (the Native American Graves Protection and Repatriation Act of 1990), has ineluctably entered the slippery terrain of identity politics (Watkins 2004; see also McGuire, chapter 16; this volume). On one side, there has been a scientific desire to definitively answer the specificities of ancient identity (Clark 2001). This has resulted in some absurd claims. As Watkins demonstrates, taxonomically Kennewick man or "the ancient one," as he is called by native peoples, has been reconfigured as a Paleoamerican not a Paleoindian, with the concomitant politics that follow on from such labeling. Spurred on by a positivist ethos in archaeology that advocates a literal concordance between artifacts, and human remains, and modern Native people, we have seen the results of manipulation and misuse (Meskell 2002a). On the other side, archaeologists of a more postpositivist theoretical persuasion have spent decades problematizing the connection between ethnicity and artifacts, thus arguing for a more fluid and ongoing constitution of identity. This perspective, ironically, has been hijacked by some high-profile anthropologists who want unrestricted access to studying ancient human remains irrespective of the needs or wishes of Native Americans, or our ethical responsibilities as archaeologists.

NAGPRA requires a literal identification and correlation. Cultural affiliation is broadly defined as "a relationship of shared group identity which can reasonably be traced historically or prehistorically between members of a present-day Indian tribe or Native Hawaiian organization and an identifiable earlier group," a "relationship of shared group identity," and is established "when the preponderance of the evidence – based on geographical, kinship, biological, archeological, linguistic, folklore, oral tradition, historical evidence, or other information or expert opinion – reasonably leads to such a conclusion." Significantly, this standard of proof is not isomorphic with scientific testing. NAGPRA's acknowledgment of Native American rights and concerns is not at issue here. What is at issue is the series of foundational claims upon which connections between contemporary communities and ancient cultural property are premised (Meskell 2002a:291). A more politically responsible and socially engaged archaeology can be forged without recourse to such reductionist science. With the recognition that other communities and groups have equally legitimate claims to stewardship, the resolution of such disagreements requires a clear understanding of the different standpoints, structures of power, and politics involved (Patterson 1999). Significantly, sacred objects and objects of cultural patrimony are kept separate in the language of NAGPRA, but they still reside within a Western scientific purview that has yet to be satisfactorily interrogated from the point of view of indigenous knowledge. Within this Western framework, it may be legally permissible to argue that emphasis should be placed on the patrimonial relationship, which acknowledges traditional or historic continuity of connection in addition to linear descent. But rather than trying to quantify past and present identities in the face of significant methodological hurdles, it may prove more ethically appropriate to argue that specific groups constitute appropriate custodians because they have legitimate cultural or spiritual responsibility for the cultural property at issue. This places rightful emphasis upon living groups and foregrounds reconciliation in the wake of colonization, rather than attributing salience entirely to the needs of archaeologists.

As a comparison, a more progressive position toward indigenous issues has been central in Australian archaeology for some time. (Attwood and Arnold 1992; Byrne 1991, 1996; Byrne, Brayshaw, and Ireland 2001; Hemming 2000; Meehan 1995; Moser 1995; Pardoe 1990). Ian Lilley has recently compared Australian legislation with that of other "settler societies," such as New Zealand, Canada, and South Africa, where indigenous claims are often prioritized over those of all other interested parties (Lilley 2000b); whereas in the United States many publics and multiple interests are acknowledged. He asserts that archaeologists and their institutional politics have been very different in the United States as compared to the aforementioned Commonwealth countries, a situation tacitly linked to nation-building. The latter are largely middle-class and postcolonialist in their perspectives (see also Pokotylo and Guppy 1999). Lilley and Williams (n.d) argue that in Australia, archaeologists and Aboriginals alike have vigorously critiqued universalist thinking (Bowdler 1992; Langford 1983) and that even non-indigenous efforts against institutionalized racism are, in themselves, forms of paternalism. As many have made clear (Moser 1995; Murray 1996, 2000), archaeologists need indigenous people much more than indigenous people need archaeologists!

Colonialism, a topic of sustained interest in anthropology and history, has also been revitalized through the influence of postcolonial theory in archaeology. Archaeologists are now pursuing notions of hybridity and creolization in the construction of material culture and social identity (Wilkie 2000, 2003; Zimmerman et al. 2003), moving between notions of blended or reworked articulations and the hard realities of repression. While such studies make claims about past life experiences, they also connect our discipline to the contemporary struggles and oppressions of living people.

Ethical Engagements

Locating and engaging ethics in archaeology remain relatively recent undertakings (Green 1984; Lynott and Wylie 2000; Vitelli 1996; Zimmerman et al. 2003). Part of this problem hinges on the false assumption that the subjects of our research are dead and buried (Meskell 2002b, n.d.) – as opposed to the dilemmas faced by ethnographers and their subjects. Archaeologists have traditionally assumed that they are not implicated in the concerns of specific living peoples and instead are contributing to the production of a universal world heritage. From this perspective, the ancestral puebloan cliff dwellings of Mesa Verde share more with the Colosseum of ancient Rome and the pyramids of Egypt than they do with the modern pueblo villages of the Rio Grande. The ethical dimension of this view is often overlooked or rendered mute by force of scientific objectivity and research agendas. For the most part, a social archaeology, influenced by the voices of indigenous people, is recognizing the role of ethics at all levels of the archaeological enterprise (Cantwell, Friedlander, and Tramm 2000; Lynott and Wylie 2000; Meskell and Pels n.d; Vitelli 1996; Wilk and Pyburn 1998).

Archaeologists have always been implicated in politics, whether in negotiations with governments and their representatives, organizations such as the World Bank or UNESCO, as well as tourist agencies, heritage brokers, local communities, and innumerable individuals. All of these groups might be seen as stakeholders with specific claims and interests upon the past. Given the new climate of social archaeology, the older vision of "pure" academic research has been challenged by political realities including the indigenization of archaeology, the Balkan crisis, wars in Iraq and Afghanistan, and so on. A move toward social responsibility has been slow and uneven and much of the controversy has been hampered by an overweening polemic over constructive cooperation and debate (Wilk and Pyburn 1998: 197). Thus it is possible to argue that the legacy of positivism has postponed a sustained disciplinary engagement with ethical discourse. Our lack of personal positioning, self-reflexivity, and ethical self-monitoring has been a crucial factor in this ontological impasse.

Ethical guidelines could be seen to cover several key components of archaeological practice: stewardship, accountability, commercialization, public education and outreach, intellectual property, preservation, and publication (see Wilk and Pyburn 1998). Ethical codes and programmatic guidelines have traditionally been conducted under the auspices of national bodies, such as the Society for American Archaeology (SAA), AAA or Archaeological Institute of America (AIA) in the United States, the AAA in Australia or the one international body, the World Archaeology Congress (WAC) (see Lilley 2000b; Lynott and Wylie 2000). A genealogy of ethics underscores the dearth of writing devoted to conducting archaeology in overseas countries, where practitioners and situational interests take on more complex layerings (but see papers in Meskell and Pels n.d.). Here we face the thorny issue of reconciling archaeological representations in situations where archaeologists are separated, but not disentangled, from the construction and effects of national and international heritage. Problems inhere, for example, with global legislation such as that of UNESCO (Meskell 2002b). Constructions of shared world heritage are easily subject to residual colonial inflections, as we have seen in Afghanistan and Iraq. Culture might best be understood as a suite of mobile metaphors rather than a *thing*, cultural variability occurs between individuals who experience different life histories, and cultural consensus emerges out of further experiences in shared social fields and common social discourse (Handwerker 1997:805).

Effective collaborative work is key in our new, more ethically inflected, practice (e.g., Colwell-Chanthaphonh and Ferguson 2004; Fordred Green, Green, and Neves 2003). We need to bring our analytical techniques to bear on questions relevant and interesting to indigenous communities, thus producing more comprehensive understandings of the past. Writing about collaborative work of mutual significance for indigenous people as well as archaeologists, Lilley and Williams (n.d.) outline a useful set of imperatives. Archaeologists should acknowledge indigenous people have other sets of legitimate interests in the archaeological record different to our own and all that entails; accept that questions and approaches of one side should not dominate or diminish the approaches of the other; determine areas of mutual interest that can enhance both archaeological and non-archaeological aims and bridge the gap between interest groups. As they note, this does not necessarily mean that archaeologists need to incorporate beliefs about the Rainbow Serpent in their own interpretations or that Aboriginal people need to replace their origin myths with arch-aeological narratives.

Working together, anywhere in the world, can no longer entail using indigenous people as if they were simply another set of volunteers or consultants. It means making a commitment to the indigenous community at a variety of levels, be they personal, professional, or places in-between. Moreover, we need to move to consider questions that are of interest to these groups. We need to

> seek out and discuss with Indigenous people what archaeology does; what they, the archaeologists, want from the study; what the study might offer Indigenous people in relation to conventional archaeological results; and, most importantly, what [indigenous] people think the archaeology might be able to do for them from a purely Indigenous, *non-archaeological* perspective at the same time as it contributes to science in the way the archaeologists claim it will ... [indigenous] people need to insist on this last matter even when it is not raised by archaeologists. Archaeologists should resist any urge to promise more than their methods and theories can deliver in such circumstances, but they should not be timid in exploring the boundaries of those methods and theories in determining just what it is they can offer. (Lilley and Williams n.d.)

The Past as Intellectual Property

A new arena that archaeologists will inexorably confront is the issue of intellectual property rights. While there is little extant publication on this arena of archaeological practice, we feel it is important to flag upcoming debates and issues within the purview of social archaeology. Wilk and Pyburn (1998:200) described intellectual property as

> contained in knowledge and documents created through the study of archaeological resources is part of the archaeological record and, therefore, [is] held in stewardship rather than as a matter of personal possession. If there is a compelling reason, and no legal restrictions, a researcher may have exclusive access to original materials and documents for a limited and reasonable time, after which these materials and documents must be made available to others. Knowledge must be made available, by publication or other-wise, within a reasonable time, and documents deposited in a suitable place for permanent safekeeping. The preservation and protection of in situ archaeological sites must be considered in the publication or distribution of information about them.

This takes one important view of intellectual property, namely the ways in which archaeologists control information about the past. But what about the dissemination of images or information for commercial uses and profits that extend beyond the discip-line of archaeology and our perceived responsibilities? While Wilk and Pyburn have a very useful discussion of *commercialization*, this in fact refers to the problems of looting, the loss of data, and the vices of the antiquities market: each of which is both crucial and well known to archaeologists. We are suggesting here that archaeologists need to go further. Since archaeologists are producers of data, we play a greater role in the circulation of our products, especially as they pertain to the representation of indigen-ous people and their respective pasts. Two case studies are compelling here with regard to the commercialization of indigenous culture – Australia and South Africa.

Issues of intellectual property are becoming hotly debated in postcolonial contexts. They are integral in every stage of the excavation process, from initial planning strategies and permit granting to the publication of results and interpretations. In the case of Australia, Janke (1998) succinctly states: "[i]ndigenous Australians are concerned that their culture is currently under threat. In an age of commercialisation, new technology and increased globalisation, Indigenous people are concerned for the ongoing mainten-ance of the culture. Indigenous people seek better recognition and protection." In Aus-tralia, awareness of these issues began in the 1990s when it became clear to Aboriginal people that their culture was being "ripped off." In legal terms heritage has a broad remit covering performance, literary, and artistic works; languages; scientific, agricultural, tech-nical, and ecological knowledge; spiritual knowledge; moveable cultural property includ-ing burials; ancestral remains; immovable cultural property including sites and burials; genetic materials; cultural environment resources; and documentation of heritage in all forms of media. Academic research, alongside art, tourism, and biotechnology, is listed as one of the areas that has commercial uses for indigenous heritage. Maori scholar Linda Tuhiwai Smith (1999) imputes that the word "research" is one of the dirtiest words for indigenous people globally. Aboriginal people are now claiming compensation for the use of indigenous culture and, alternatively, assert that they must be able to stop com-modification of certain aspects of their culture: certain objects and information are not saleable. Cultural heritage laws are not sufficient to cover this terrain, nor are the Patents Act, Designs Act, Trade Marks Act, and so on. New legislation is intended to empower indigenous communities, to grant them control and ownership over cultural heritage and for that property to be vested within the local community.

Since the 1990s, indigenous cultural and intellectual property rights have become central to a distinctive Australian national identity and its subsequent marketing abroad. Much of this material falls within the purview of archaeology and the visual arts. The interest in Aboriginal and Torres Strait Islander cultures has been cited as a major reason for the growth of Australia's international tourism industry. The indigenous arts and crafts market is worth around $200 million per year in Australia and some 50 percent of sales relate to the tourism market. Some hold that such practices engage living, evolving cultural traditions, and fossilize them, rendering apparently immutable and fixed that which is evolving. Objects of traditional study – whether bark paintings or songs – are not simply productions transformed into "works of art" (Morris 1997). For example, the antiquity of images, passed down through millennia, is what gives the cultural product its aesthetic potency, not the newness of its creation by one particular person. Moreover, archaeologists and heritage practitioners are implicated in various collecting agencies including museums, galleries, universities, and research institutions. Throughout Austra-lia and globally, collections of indigenous cultural materials, ancestral human remains, and other items important to indigenous cultural identity are archived and displayed. Indigenous peoples are seeking recognition of their rights over these materials, including ownership rights, and for these materials to be returned to their communities. The recognition of native title and land rights has done much to enlighten Australians about the depth of meaning of cultural productions. And this entails maintaining and preserv-ing the oldest continuous culture in the world: "All Australians should embrace this as part of their responsibility to world heritage, rather than *terra nullius* it out of their lives" (Morris 1997).

In the case of South Africa, less has been produced in the way of reports on intellectual property and ensuing legislation, but certainly there is plenty of concern about the incursions of the pharmaceutical companies and the tourism and craft industries in terms of exploiting the resources, knowledge, and artistic traditions of indigenous people. The rich and evocative histories of communities such as the San (often referred to as "bushman") are probably most at issue and most vulnerable. Medical and herbal knowledge are being gleaned and patented by international companies with little concern for the adequate remuneration, much less the well-being, of the native communities involved. Perhaps more archaeological are the countless reproductions of San rock art that adorn innumerable objects for the tourist market and are found in tourist contexts such as hotels. Many of these items, from candles and tea towels to full-scale replica rock art, are for sale within South Africa and are exported globally. In the absence of a fully operational heritage agency at the time of writing, indigenous groups in South Africa may do well to lobby for something akin to the Australian model of protection and compensation (see Byrne, Brayshaw, and Ireland 2001; Janke 1998). In 2001 steps were taken by the delegates of the National Khoisan Consultative Conference on Khoisan diversity in National Unity that would ultimately be submitted to the South African Heritage Resources Agency (SAHRA) and the University of the Western Cape (UWC) Institute for Historical Research. They argued that although the National Khoisan Legacy Project contributes to the unified ideal of nation-building, the direct involvement and consultation of Khoisan communities had to be ensured, and the renaming of natural and cultural resources should enjoy preference (Le Fleur 2001). They addressed the issue of repatriation, specifically that of Sarah Baartman as well as other Khoisan human remains: the former occurred in July of 2002 followed by a reburial ceremony. Additionally, they asked for the closure of the San diorama (casts taken from living people) at the South African Museum (see Skotnes 1996), and the establishment of a consultative process with the affected Khoisan groups: both were subsequently achieved. Other issues raised involved the establishment of ten Khoisan regions to remedy the matter of land restitution and access to ancestral areas, and the registering of a Trust with the high court to mobilize resources for self-development.

Conclusions

While slow to take root due to the intransigence of positivistic thinking, a politicized social archaeology represents one of the most significant growth areas in our discipline. It represents our contemporary engagement with other fields and audiences, and fulfils part of our ethical responsibility as public figures charged with the stewardship or trusteeship (Bender 1998; Scham 1998) of the past. One important development has been the deconstruction of field practices, including recognizing the place of local workers, and an investigation of remnant colonial hegemonies. Fieldwork practices and the subsequent production of heritage sites, their interventions and ramifications, forms a critical arena of analysis for archaeologists today (Fotiadis 1993; Hodder 1998; Meskell 2001; Politis 2001). Archaeologists need to interrogate the discipline's public face, specifically our growing set of responsibilities to many different constituencies. Our roles as stewards or trustees of the past are mobilized in a variety of contexts, but are more critically inflected when we speak for others, either with indigenous communities at home or within the locus of foreign countries. Mathew Spriggs (1991), writing on fieldwork in the Pacific, has called for six practical levels of engagement: recognition of prior indigenous landownership; consultation with indigenous groups; useful presentation of archaeological fieldwork to local communities; employment and training within the indigenous community; protection of sites and burials; and allowing for variant interpretations between archaeologists and indigenous people. Written over a decade ago, this is an excellent starting point for all archaeological engagements at home and abroad. Given the complexities of archaeology on the ground, one cannot simply prepare a universal mandate for the practice of archaeology in the global milieu. However, there is one constant that pervades the constitution of a social archaeology, namely that all archaeological engagements must be examined in context.

REFERENCES

Abdi, K. 2001. Nationalism, politics, and the development of archaeology in Iran. *American Journal of Archaeology* 105: 51–76.

Abu el-Haj, N. 1998. Translating truths: Nationalism, the practice of archaeology, and the remaking of past and present in contemporary Jerusalem. *American Ethnologist* 25: 166–188.

——2001. *Facts on the Ground: Archaeological Practice and Territorial Self Fashioning in Israeli Society.* Chicago: University of Chicago Press.

Almond, B. 1991. Rights. In P. Singer (ed.), *A Companion to Ethics.* Oxford: Blackwell, pp. 259–269.

Andah, B. W. 1995a. European encumbrances to the development of relevant theory in African archaeology. In P. J. Ucko (ed.), *Theory in Archaeology: A World Perspective.* London: Routledge, pp. 96–109.

——1995b. Studying African societies in cultural context. In P. R. Schmidt and T. C. Patterson (eds.), *Making Alternative Histories: The Practice of Archaeology and History in Non-Western Settings.* Santa Fe: School of American Research Press, pp. 149–181.

Anthony, D. 1995. Nazi and eco-feminist prehistories: Counter points in Indo-European archaeology. In P. Kohl and C. Fawcett (eds.), *Nationalism, Politics and the Practice of Archaeology.* Cambridge: Cambridge University Press, pp. 82–96.

Appadurai, A. 1997. *Modernity at Large: Cultural Dimensions of Globalization.* Minneapolis: University of Minnesota Press.

Arnold, B. 1990. The past as propaganda: Totalitarian archaeology in Nazi Germany. *Antiquity* 64: 464–478.

Ashworth, G. 1995. Heritage, tourism and Europe: A European future for a European past? In D. Herbert (ed.), *Heritage, Tourism and Society.* New York: Mansell, pp. 69–84.

Attwood, B., and J. Arnold (eds.) 1992. *Power, Knowledge and Aborigines.* Bundoora: La Trobe University Press.

Bender, B. 1998. *Stonehenge: Making Space.* Oxford: Berg.

Bernal, I. 1980. *A History of Mexican Archaeology.* London: Thames & Hudson.

Bernbeck, R., and S. Pollock. 1996. Ayodhya, archaeology, and identity. *Current Anthropology* 37: 138–142.

Blundell, G. 1996. Presenting South Africa's rock art sites. In J. Deacon (ed.), *Monuments and Sites: South Africa*, pp. 71–80. Sri Lanka: International Council on Monuments and Sites.

——2002. *The Unseen Landscape: A Journey to Game Pass Shelter (Guide Booklet).* Johannesburg: Rock Art Research Institute.

Bone, J. 2001. Afghan warlord calls for statues to be rebuilt. *The Times*, London, December 10.

Bowdler, S. 1992. Unquiet slumbers: The return of the Kow Swamp burials. *Antiquity* 66: 103–106.

Bray, T. (ed.) 2001. *The Future of the Past: Archaeologists, Native Americans and Repatriation*. New York: Garland.

——, and T. W. Killion (eds.) 1994. *Reckoning with the Dead: The Larsen Bay Repatriation and the Smithsonian Institution*. Washington, DC: Smithsonian Institution Press.

Brown, K. S. 1998. Contests of heritage and the politics of preservation in the Former Yugoslav Republic of Macedonia. In L. M. Meskell (ed.), *Archaeology Under Fire: Nationalism, Politics and Heritage in the Eastern Mediterranean and Middle East*. London: Routledge, pp. 68–86.

Byrne, D. 1991. Western hegemony in archaeological heritage management. *History and Anthropology* 5: 269–276.

——1996. Deep nation: Australia's acquisition of an indigenous past. *Aboriginal History* 20: 82–107.

——2003a. Messages to Manila. *Aboriginal History*: forthcoming.

——2003b. Nervous landscapes: Race and space in Australia. *Journal of Social Archaeology* 3: 169–193.

——, H. Brayshaw, and T. Ireland. 2001. *Social Significance: A Discussion Paper*. Sydney: New South Wales National Parks and Wildlife Service.

Cantwell, A-M., E. Friedlander, and M. L. Tramm (eds.) 2000. *Ethics and Anthropology: Facing Future Issues in Human Biology, Globalism and Cultural Property*. New York: New York Academy of Sciences, Annals of the New York Academy of Sciences.

Castañeda, Q. E. 1997. *In the Museum of Maya Culture: Touring Chichén Itzá*, Minneapolis: University of Minnesota Press.

Chakrabarti, D. K. 1995. Buddhist sites across South Asia as influenced by political and economic forces. *World Archaeology* 27: 185–202.

——1997. *Colonial Indology: Sociopolitics of the Ancient Indian Past*. New Delhi: Munshiram Manoharlal.

——2000. Colonial indology and identity. *Antiquity* 74: 667–671.

Chapman, J. 1994. Destruction of a common heritage: The archaeology of war in Croatia, Bosnia and Hercegovina. *Antiquity* 68: 120–126.

Chinchilla Mazariegos, O. 1998. Archaeology and nationalism in Guatemala at the time of independence. *Antiquity* 72: 376–386.

Clark, G. A. 2001. Letter to the editor. *Society for American Archaeology: Archaeological Record*, March: 3.

Colwell-Chanthaphonh, C. 2003. Dismembering/disremembering the Buddhas: Renderings on the Internet during the Afghan purge of the past. *Journal of Social Archaeology* 3(1): 75–98.

——, and T. J. Ferguson. 2004. Virtue ethics and the practice of history: Native Americans and archaeologists along the San Pedro Valley of Arizona. *Journal of Social Archaeology* 4: 5–27.

Coningham, R., and N. Lewer. 2000a. Archaeology and identity in south Asia – interpretations and consequences. *Antiquity* 74: 664–667.

——2000b. The Vijayan colonization and the archaeology of identity in Sri Lanka. *Antiquity* 74: 707–712.

Demoule, J. 1999. Ethnicity, culture and identity: French archaeologists and historians. *Antiquity* 73: 190–198.

Dietler, M. 1994. "Our ancestors the Gauls": Archaeology, ethnic nationalism, and the manipulation of Celtic identity in modern Europe. *American Anthropologist* 96: 584–605.

Dongoske, K. E., M. Aldenderfer, and K. Doehner (eds.) 2000. *Working Together: Native American and Archaeologists*. Washington, DC: Society for American Archaeology.

Dongoske, K. E., M. Yeatts, R. Anyon, and T. J. Ferguson. 1997. Archaeological cultures and cultural affiliation: Hopi and Zuni perspectives in the American southwest. *American Antiquity* 62: 600–608.

Dowdall, K., and O. Parish. 2003. A meaningful disturbance of the earth. *Journal of Social Archaeology* 3: 99–133.

Edensor, T. 1998. *Tourists at the Taj: Performance and Meaning at a Symbolic Site.* New York: Routledge.

Elamin, Y. M. 1999. Archaeology and modern Sudanese cultural identity. *African Archaeological Review* 16: 1–3.

Fawcett, C. 1995. Nationalism and postwar Japanese archaeology. In P. L. Kohl and C. Fawcett (eds.), *Nationalism, Politics, and the Practice of Archaeology.* Cambridge: Cambridge University Press, pp. 232–246.

Fforde, C., J. Hubert, and P. Turnbull (eds.) 2002. *The Dead and their Possessions: Repatriation in Principle, Policy and Practice.* London: Routledge.

Fine-Dare, K. 2002. *Grave Injustice: The American Indian Repatriation Movement and NAGPRA.* Norman: University of Oklahoma Press.

Fleury-Ilett, B. 1993. Identity of France: the archaeological interaction. *Journal of European Archaeology* 1: 169–180.

Fordred Green, L., D. R. Green, and E. G. Neves. 2003. Indigenous knowledge and archeological science: The challenges of public archeology in the Reserva Uaçá. *Journal of Social Archaeology* 3: 366–398.

Fotiadis, M. 1993. Regions of the imagination: archaeologists, local people, and the archaeological record in fieldwork, Greece. *Journal of European Archaeology* 1: 151–170.

Fowler, D. D. 1987. Uses of the past: Archaeology in the service of the state. *American Antiquity* 52: 229–248.

Funari, P. P. A. 1995. Mixed features of archaeological theory in Brazil. In P. J. Ucko (ed.), *Theory in Archaeology: A World Perspective.* London: Routledge, pp. 236–250.

Goldstein, L. (1992). The potential for future relationships between archaeologists and Native Americans. In L. Wandsnider (ed.), *Quandaries and Quests: Visions of Archaeology's Future.* Carbondale: Southern Illinois University Press, pp. 59–71.

——, and K. Kintigh. 1990. Ethics and the reburial controversy. *American Antiquity* 55: 585–591.

Gosden, C. 1999. *Anthropology and Archaeology: A Changing Relationship.* London: Routledge.

—— 2001. In I. Hodder (ed.), *Archaeological Theory Today.* Cambridge: Polity Press. pp. 241–261.

Green, E. L. (ed.) 1984. *Ethics and Values in Archaeology.* New York: The Free Press.

Hall, M. 1984. The burden of tribalism: The social context of southern African Iron Age Studies. *American Antiquity* 49: 455–467.

—— 1988. Archaeology under apartheid. *Archaeology* 41: 62–64.

—— 1992. Small things and the mobile, conflictual fusion of power, fear, and desire. In A. Yentsch and M. Beaudry (eds.), *The Art and Mystery of Historical Archaeology.* Boca Raton: CRC Press, pp. 373–399.

—— 1994a. Lifting the veil of popular history: Archaeology and politics in urban Cape Town. In G. C. Bond and A. Gilliam (eds.), *Social Construction of the Past.* London and New York: Routledge, pp. 176–184.

—— 1994b. The secret lives of houses: Women and gables in the eighteenth-century Cape. *Social Dynamics* 20: 1–48.

—— 1999. Virtual colonization. *Material Culture* 4: 39–55.

—— 2000. *Archaeology and the Modern World: Colonial Transcripts in South Africa and the Chesapeake.* London: Routledge.

—— 2001. Social archaeology and the theaters of memory. *Journal of Social Archaeology* 1: 50–61.

Hamilakis, Y. 1996. Through the looking glass: Nationalism, archaeology and the politics of identity. *Antiquity* 70: 975–978.

——1999. Stories from exile: Fragments from the cultural biography of the Parthenon (or "Elgin") marbles. *World Archaeology: The Cultural Biography of Objects* 31: 303–320.

——, and E. Yalouri. 1996. Antiquities as symbolic capital in modern Greek society. *Antiquity* 70: 117–129.

Handwerker, W. P. 1997. Universal human rights and the problem of unbounded cultural meanings. *American Anthropologist* 99: 799–809.

Härke, H. (ed.) 2000. *Archaeology, Ideology and Society: The German Experience. Gesellschaften und Staaten im Epochanwandel* 7. Frankfurt: Peter Lang.

——, and S. Wolfram. 1993. The power of the past. *Current Anthropology* 34: 182–184.

Hemming, S. 2000. Ngarrendjeri burials as cultural sites: Indigenous heritage issues in Australia. *World Archaeology Bulletin* 11: 58–66.

Herbert, D. (ed.) 1995. *Heritage, Tourism, and Society.* London: Mansell.

Higueras, A. 1995. Archaeological research in Peru: Its contribution to national identity and to the Peruvian public. *Journal of the Steward Anthropological Society* 23: 391–407.

Hodder, I. (ed.) 1991. *Archaeological Theory in Europe: The Last Three Decades.* London: Routledge.

——1998. The past and passion and play: Çatalhöyük as a site of conflict in the construction of multiple pasts. In L. M. Meskell (ed.), *Archaeology Under Fire: Nationalism, Politics and Heritage in the Eastern Mediterranean and Middle East.* London: Routledge, pp. 124–139.

——1999. *The Archaeological Process: An Introduction.* Oxford: Blackwell.

——2000a. Archaeology and globalism. David Skomp Distinguished Lectures in Anthropology, 1999–2000, Indiana University, February 18.

——(ed.) 2000b. *Towards Reflexive Method in Archaeology: The Example at Çatalhöyük.* Cambridge: McDonald Institute for Archaeological Research.

Hyland, J. 1992. Archaeological meditations of the Conquest and constructions of Mexican national identity. *Kroeber Anthropological Society Papers* 73–4: 92–114.

Janke, T. 1998. *Our Culture: Our Future. Report on Australian Indigenous Cultural and Intellectual Property Rights.* Surrey Hills: Australian Institute of Aboriginal and Torres Strait Islander Studies and Aboriginal and Torres Strait Islander Commission.

Jeppson, P. L. 1997. "Leveling the playing field" in the contested territory of the South African past: A "public" versus a "people's" form of historical archaeology outreach. *Historical Archaeology* 31: 65–83.

Jones, L. 1997. Conquests of the imagination: Maya–Mexican polarity and the story of Chichén Itzá. *American Anthropologist* 99: 275–290.

Kasier, T. 1995. Archaeology and ideology in southeastern Europe. In P. L. Kohl and C. Fawcett (eds.), *Nationalism, Politics and the Practice of Archaeology,* Cambridge: Cambridge University Press, pp. 99–119.

Kirshenblatt-Gimblett, B. 1998. *Destination Culture: Tourism, Museums, and Heritage.* Berkeley: University of California Press.

Kohl, P. L. 1998. Nationalism and archaeology: On the constructions of nations and the reconstructions of the remote past. *Annual Review of Anthropology* 27: 223–246.

——, and C. Fawcett (eds.) 1995. *Nationalism, Politics and the Practice of Archaeology.* Cambridge: Cambridge University Press.

Kotsakis, K. 1998. The past is ours: Images of Greek Macedonia. In L. M. Meskell (ed.), *Archaeology Under Fire: Nationalism, Politics and Heritage in the Eastern Mediterranean and Middle East.* London: Routledge, pp. 44–67.

Lahiri, N. 2000. Archaeology and identity in colonial India. *Antiquity* 74: 687–692.

Langford, M. 1983. Our heritage – your playground. *Australian Archaeology* 16: 1–6.

Laue, G., T. Turkington, and B. Smith. 2002. Presenting South African rock art to the world: Two major new public rock art site developments for 2002. *The Digging Stick* 18: 5–7.

Lawler, A. 2003. Impending war stokes battle over fate of Iraqi antiquities. *Science* 299: 643.

Le Fleur, C. A. 2001. Resolutions as agreed by Official and Associate Delegates to the National Khoisan Consultative Conference on Khoisan diversity in National Unity, Anthropology edition, vol. http://www.und.ac.za/und/ccms/anthropology (last accessed April 2003).

Lewis-Williams, J. D. 1995. Some aspects of rock art research in the politics of present-day South Africa. In K. Helskog and B. Olsen (eds.), *Perceiving Rock Art: Social and Political Perspectives*. Oslo: Institute for Comparative Research in Human Culture, pp. 317–337.

Lilley, I. (ed.) 2000a. *Native Title and the Transformation of Archaeology in the Postcolonial World*. Sydney: University of Sydney, Oceania Monographs 50.

—— 2000b. Professional attitudes to indigenous interests in the native title era: Settler societies compared. In I. Lilley (ed.), *Native Title and the Transformation of Archaeology in the Postcolonial World*. Sydney: Oceania Publications, Monograph 50, pp. 99–119.

——, and M. Williams, n.d. Archaeological and indigenous significance: A view from Australia. In C. Mathers, T. Darvill, and B. Little (eds.), *Heritage of Value, Archaeology of Renown: Reshaping Archaeological Assessment and Significance*. Gainesville: University of Florida Press.

Lynott, M. J., and A. Wylie (eds.) 2000. *Ethics in American Archaeology*. Washington, DC: Society for American Archaeology.

Mamani Condori, C. 1996. History and prehistory in Bolivia: What about the Indians? In R. W. Preucel and I. Hodder (eds.), *Contemporary Archaeology in Theory: A Reader*. Oxford: Blackwell, pp. 632–645.

Mandal, D. 1993. *Ayodhya: Archaeology After Demolition*. New Delhi: Orient Longman.

Matero, F. 2000. Ethics and policy in conservation. *Conservation: The GCI Newsletter* 15: 5–9.

McGuire, R. H. 1992. Archaeology and the first Americans. *American Anthropologist* 94: 816–836.

——, and R. Navarrete. 1999. Entre motocicletas y fusiles: Las arqueologías radicales anglosajona y latinoamericana. *Boletín de Antropología Americana* 34: 89–110.

Meehan, B. 1995. Aboriginal views on the management of rock art sites in Australia. In K. Helskog and B. Olsen (eds.), *Perceiving Rock Art: Social and Political Perspectives*. Oslo: Institute for Comparative Research in Human Culture, pp. 295–316.

Meskell, L. M. 1998a. Archaeology matters. In L. M. Meskell (ed.), *Archaeology Under Fire: Nationalism, Politics and Heritage in the Eastern Mediterranean and Middle East*. London: Routledge, pp. 1–12.

—— (ed.) 1998b. *Archaeology Under Fire: Nationalism, Politics and Heritage in the Eastern Mediterranean and Middle East*. London: Routledge.

—— 2001. The practice and politics of archaeology in Egypt. In A.-M. Cantwell, E. Friedlander, and M. L. Tram (eds.), *Ethics and Anthropology: Facing Future Issues in Human Biology, Globalism, and Cultural Property*. New York: Annals of the New York Academy of Sciences, pp. 146–169.

—— 2002a. The intersection of identity and politics in archaeology. *Annual Review of Anthropology* 31: 279–301.

—— 2002b. Negative heritage and past mastering in archaeology. *Anthropological Quarterly* 75: 557–574.

—— n.d. Sites of violence: Terrorism, tourism and heritage in the archaeological present. In L. M. Meskell and P. Pels (eds.), *Embedding Ethics*. Oxford: Berg, forthcoming.

——, and P. Pels (eds.) n.d. *Embedding Ethics*. Oxford: Berg, forthcoming.

Morris, C. 1997. Indigenous intellectual property rights: The responsibilities of maintaining the oldest continuous culture in the world. *Indigenous Law Bulletin 19*: http://www.austlii.edu.au/au/journals/ ILB/1997/19.html (last consulted April 2003).

Moser, S. 1995. Archaeology and its Disciplinary Culture: The Professionalisation of Australian Prehistoric Archaeology. Ph.D. dissertation, University of Sydney.

Murray, T. 1996. Coming to terms with the living: Some aspects of repatriation for the archae-ologist. *Antiquity* 70: 217–220.

—— 2000. Conjectural histories: Some archaeological and historical consequences of indigenous dispossession in Australia. In I. Lilley (ed.), *Native Title and the Transformation of Archaeology in the Postcolonial World*, pp. 64–77. Sydney: University of Sydney, Oceania Monographs 50.

Naccache, A. F. H. 1998. Beirut's memoryside: Hear no evil, see no evil. In L. M. Meskell (ed.), *Archaeology Under Fire: Nationalism, Politics and Heritage in the Eastern Mediterranean and Middle East*. London: Routledge, pp. 140–158.

Özdogan, M. 1998. Ideology and archaeology in Turkey. In L. M. Meskell (ed.), *Archaeology Under Fire: Nationalism, Politics and Heritage in the Eastern Mediterranean and Middle East*. London: Routledge, pp. 111–123.

Paddayya, K. 1995. Theoretical perspectives in Indian archaeology. In P. J. Ucko (ed.), *Theory in Archaeology: A World Perspective*. London: Routledge, pp. 110–149.

Pai, H. 2000. *Constructing "Korean" Origins: A Critical Review of Archaeology, Historiography, and Racial Myth in Korean State-Formation Theories*. Cambridge, MA: Harvard University Asia Center/Harvard University Press.

Pardoe, C. 1990. Sharing the past: Aboriginal influence on archaeological practice, a case study from New South Wales. *Aboriginal History* 14: 208–223.

Patterson, T. C. 1994. *Toward a Social History of Archaeology in the United States*, New York: Harcourt Brace.

—— 1995. Archaeology, history, *Indigenismo*, and the state in Peru and Mexico. In P. R. Schmidt and T. C. Patterson (eds.), *Making Alternative Histories: The Practice of Archaeology and History in Non-Western Settings*. Santa Fe, NM: School of American Research Press, pp. 69–85.

—— 1999. The political economy of archaeology in the United States. *Annual Review of Anthropology* 28: 155–174.

Pokotylo, D., and N. Guppy. 1999. Public opinion and archaeological heritage: Views from outside the profession. *American Antiquity* 64: 400–416.

Politis, G. 1995. The socio-politics of the development of archaeology in Hispanic South America. In P. J. Ucko (ed.), *Theory in Archaeology: A World Perspective*. London: Routledge, pp. 197–235.

—— 2001. On archaeological praxis, gender bias and indigenous peoples in South America. *Journal of Social Archaeology* 1: 90–107.

Pollock, S., and C. Lutz. 1994. Archaeology deployed for the Gulf War. *Critique of Anthropology* 14: 263–284.

Preucel, R. W. (ed.) 2002. *Archaeologies of the Pueblo Revolt: Identity, Meaning and Renewal in the Pueblo World*. Albuquerque: University of New Mexico Press.

Prott, L., M. de la Torre, and D. Levin. 2001. A conversation with Lyndel Prott. *Getty Conservation Institute Newsletter* 16: 12–15.

Ramos, A. 1994. From Eden to limbo: The construction of indigenism in Brazi. In G. C. Bond and A. Gilliam (eds.), *Social Construction of the Past: Representation as Power*. London: Routledge, pp. 74–88.

Rao, N. 1994. Interpreting silences: Symbol and history in the case of Ram Janmabhoomi/Babri Masjid. In G. C. Bond and A. Gilliam (eds.), *Social Construction of the Past: Representation as Power*. London: Routledge, pp. 154–164.

Reid, D. M. 2002. *Whose Pharaohs? Archaeology, Museums, And Egyptian National Identity From Napoleon to World War I*. Berkeley: University of California Press.

Ridington, R., and D. Hastings. 1997. *Blessing for a Long Time: The Sacred Pole of the Omaha Tribe*. Lincoln: University of Nebraska Press.

Scham, S. A. 1998. Mediating nationalism and archaeology: A matter of trust? *American Anthropologist* 100: 301–308.

Schmidt, P. R., and T. C. Patterson (eds.) 1995. *Making Alternative Histories: The Practice of Archaeology and History in Non-Western Settings*. Santa Fe, NM: School of American Research Press.

Schnapp, A. 1996. French archaeology: Between national identity and cultural identity. In M. Díaz-Andreu and T. Champion (eds.), *Nationalism and Archaeology in Europe*. London: University College London Press, pp. 48–67.

Schrire, C. 1995. *Digging Through Darkness: Chronicles of an Archaeologist*. Charlottesville: University Press of Virginia.

Shaw, J. 2000. Ayodhya's sacred landscape: Ritual memory, politics and archaeological "fact." *Antiquity* 74: 693–700.

Shepherd, N. 2002. The politics of archaeology in Africa. *Annual Review of Anthropology* 31: 189–209.

—— 2003. "When the hand that holds the trowel is black ...""; disciplinary practices of self-representation and the issue of "native" labour in archaeology. *Journal of Social Archaeology* 3: 334–352.

Shnirelman, V. A. 1995. Alternative prehistory. *Journal of European Archaeology* 3: 1–20.

Silberman, N. A. 1995. Promised lands and chosen peoples: The politics and poetics of archaeological narrative. In P. L. Kohl and C. Fawcett (eds.), *Nationalism, Politics and the Practice of Archaeology*. Cambridge: Cambridge University Press, pp. 249–262.

Skotnes, P. (ed.) 1996. *Miscast: Negotiating the Presence of the Bushmen*. Cape Town: University of Cape Town Press.

Smith, L. T. 1999. *Decolonizing Methodologies*. London: Zed Books.

Spriggs, M. 1991. Facing the nation: Hawaiians and archaeologists in an era of sovereignty. *The Contemporary Pacific* 3: 379–392.

Stoffle, R. W., M. N. Zedeno, and D. B. Halmo (eds.) 2001. *American Indians and the Nevada Test Site: A Model of Research and Consultation*. Washington, DC: US Government Printing Office.

Swidler, N., K. E. Dongoske, R. Anyon, and A. S. Downer (eds.) 1997. *Native Americans and Archaeologists: Stepping Stones to Common Ground*. Walnut Creek, CA: AltaMira Press.

Thomas, D. H. 2000. *Skull Wars: Kennewick Man, Archaeology, and the Battle for Native American Identity*. New York: Basic Books.

Tong, E. 1995. Thirty years of Chinese archaeology (1949–1979). In P. L. Kohl and C. Fawcett (eds.), *Nationalism, Politics, and the Practice of Archaeology*. Cambridge: Cambridge University Press, pp. 177–197.

Trigger, B. G. 1989. *A History of Archaeological Thought*. Cambridge: Cambridge University Press.

Tsude, H. 1995. Archaeological theory in Japan. In P. J. Ucko (ed.), *Theory in Archaeology: A World Perspective*. London: Routledge, pp. 298–311.

Tweedie, A. M. 2002. *Drawing Back Culture: The Makah Struggle for Repatriation*. Seattle: University of Washington Press.

Ucko, P. J. (ed.) 1995. *Theory in Archaeology: A World Perspective*. London: Routledge.

UNESCO. 2000. Convention concerning the protection of the world cultural and natural heritage (Paris 16 November 1972). *US/ICOMOS Scientific Journal – International Cultural Heritage Conventions* 2: 19–36.

van Dommelen, P. 1997. Colonial constructs: colonialism and archaeology in the Mediterranean. *World Archaeology* 28: 305–323.

Vargas Arenas, I. 1995. The perception of history and archaeology in Latin America: A theoretical approach. In P. R. Schmidt and T. C. Patterson (eds.), *Making Alternative Histories: The*

Practice of Archaeology and History in Non-Western Settings. Santa Fe, NM: School of American Research Press, pp. 47–67.

Vitelli, K. D. (ed.) 1996. *Archaeological Ethics*. Walnut Creek, CA: AltaMira Press.

Von Falkenhausen, L. 1995. The regionalist paradigm in Chinese archaeology. In P. L. Kohl and C. Fawcett (eds.), *Nationalism, Politics, and the Practice of Archaeology*. Cambridge: Cambridge University Press, pp. 198–217.

Wailes, B., and A. L. Zoll. 1995. Civilization, barbarism and nationalism in European archaeology. In P. L. Kohl and C. Fawcett (eds.), *Nationalism, Politics and the Practice of Archaeology*. Cambridge: Cambridge University Press, pp. 21–38.

Warren, K. J. 1999. A philosophical perspective on the ethics and resolution of cultural property issues. In P. M. Messenger (ed.), *The Ethics of Collecting Cultural Property*. Albuquerque: University of New Mexico Press, pp. 1–25.

Watkins, J. 2001. *Indigenous Archaeology*. Walnut Creek, CA: AltaMira Press.

——2004. Becoming American or becoming Indian? NAGPRA, Kennewick, and cultural affiliation. *Journal of Social Archaeology* 4: 60–80.

Wilk, R., and K. A. Pyburn. 1998. Archaeological ethics. *Encyclopedia of Applied Ethics* 1: 197–207.

Wilkie, L. A. 2000. Culture bought: Evidence of creolization in the consumer goods of an enslaved Bahamian family. *Historical Archaeology* 34: 10–26.

——2003. *An Archaeology of Mothering*. London: Routledge.

Wood, M. 1998. The use of the Pharaonic past in modern Egyptian nationalism. *Journal of the American Research Center in Egypt* 35: 179–196.

Wylie, A. 2001. Ethical dilemmas in archaeological practice: Looting, repatriation, stewardship, and the (trans)formation of disciplinary identity. In M. Lynott and A. Wylie (eds.), *Ethics in American Archaeology*. Washington, DC: Society for American Archaeology, pp. 138–68.

Yalouri, E. 2001. *The Parthenon: Global Fame, Local Claim*. Oxford: Berg.

Zimmerman, L. J., K. D. Vitelli, J. Hollowell-Zimmer, and R. D. Maurer (eds.) 2003. *Ethical Issues in Archaeology*. Walnut Creek, CA: AltaMira Press.

14

The Political Economy of Archaeological Practice and the Production of Heritage in the Middle East

Reinhard Bernbeck and Susan Pollock

"Who controls the past," ran the Party slogan, "controls the future: who controls the present controls the past." (Orwell 1961 [1949]: 32)

Introduction

Archaeology embodies a temporal paradox: while its object of study is the human past, the practice of archaeology is firmly situated in the present.[1] Archaeology is not alone in this paradox; any historical discipline faces a similar dilemma. But archaeology is distinct in that it engages with the lives of people in the past by means of concrete things that take the form of material remains and their relationships to one another. Oddly, it is the concreteness of its evidence that lends archaeology much of its ambiguity. As every student of the subject learns, archaeologists are faced continually with the problems of how to interpret the mute material remains they uncover, especially in prehistoric contexts where there are no written records to offer keys to the meanings of the objects. The potential multivocality of material remains means that few interpretations of archaeological evidence are fixed; ever subject to challenge and reinterpretation, they lend themselves to a wide variety of uses and abuses for purposes in the present.

In this chapter, we examine the contemporary practice of archaeology in the Middle East, in addition drawing for comparative purposes on some examples from South Asia. Geographically, this is an area that runs from Jerusalem and Turkey in the west to Delhi and Afghanistan in the east. We consider such questions as who conducts archaeology in these parts of the world, the intellectual underpinnings that shape their work, and how that work is funded. We explore some of the ways in which the interests and practices of non-archaeologists and archaeologists alike shape their engagements with the archaeological record, contributing to a definition of which pasts matter – that is, which are considered to have relevance for the present – and which do not. Although each of these themes will be treated separately, they are, as we hope our exposition will reveal, closely intertwined. Furthermore, in addressing each of these questions, it will be important to consider not just positive answers; in each case, what and who are left out of present-day archaeological practice are at least as crucial for understanding those practices (Glock 1999a).

While the issues that we raise in this chapter are by no means unique to the archaeology of the Middle East or South Asia, the connections between archaeology and politics there have resulted in especially bloody encounters in the late twentieth and early twenty-first centuries. We contend that the Middle Eastern origins of three major world religions and contemporary conflicts among their adherents play a significant role in exacerbating tensions surrounding the use and practice of archaeology in the region in ways that differ from those in many other world areas. We also suggest that rather than focusing principally on archaeology's connection to nationalism in the contemporary world (Díaz-Andreu and Champion 1996; Kohl and Fawcett 1995), it is also important to consider archaeology's relationship to current trends, ranging from globalization to the breakdown of nation-states into ethnically defined units.

An underlying theme throughout this chapter is that archaeology never takes place outside hegemonic structures. By hegemonic structures we mean those structures, both economic and other, that help to achieve the consent of subordinate groups to a dominant ideology and which do so in such a way as to define the "field of common sense" (Grossberg 1996: 162), the "ruling definitions of the 'natural'" (Comaroff 1985: 6). Hegemony is "a whole body of practices and expectations...a lived system of meanings and values. ...It thus constitutes a sense of reality for most people in the society, a sense of absolute because experienced reality beyond which it is very difficult for most members of the society to move, in most areas of their lives" (Williams 1977: 110). The connection of archaeology with hegemonic structures means that as archaeologists we must constantly question who controls the definition of current hegemonies and ask ourselves how, through our work, we are implicated in them.

The Practice of Archaeology: Who Are Archaeologists, and How Do They Do Their Work?

A consideration of the practice of archaeology is broad indeed and far exceeds the scope of this chapter. We concentrate principally on what we regard as the largely unquestioned aspects of archaeological practice in the Middle East: the engagement of Western archaeologists who work in that region today (Hamilakis 1999). In doing so we devote only passing attention to the earlier history of archaeology in the region, which has been the subject of a number of other recent studies (e.g., Kuklick 1996; Larsen 1996; Özdoğan 1998; Silberman 1982), as well as to the contemporary practice of archaeologists native to the region (e.g., Abu el-Haj 1998). Our relative neglect of these topics is in no way a commentary on their importance, but rather a choice we have made in delimiting the scope of this chapter.

Who are the archaeologists working in the Middle East?

A simple answer to the question of who conducts archaeology in the Middle East today is: both archaeologists who are native to the region and foreigners. Those foreigners, however, are by no means drawn equally from other countries. Most are Westerners, coming from the United States, Europe, and Australia. Few South American, African or East Asian archaeologists (apart from Japanese) are engaged in Middle Eastern archaeology. One might reasonably ask why archaeologists from these areas of the world are not actively involved in fieldwork in the Middle East, especially since archaeology as a discipline is well represented there.

We suggest that the answer stems at least in part from the relationship between archaeologists and the particular, regionally determined object of their study. Following Trigger (1984), one can argue that "native" archaeologists – whether Argentinians working in Argentina, Austrians in Austria, or whatever – tend to work within a nationalist tradition. In this tradition the questions posed and the work conducted involve attempts to glorify, whether explicitly or implicitly – and in many cases to create – a national past. In her discussion of the "archaeology of the disenfranchised," Scham (2001a) has drawn attention to important distinctions among the archaeologies practiced by various disenfranchised groups.[2] She points out that only some of these may actually become nationalist archaeologies, in the sense that they seek to create or support a national identity (Scham 2001a: 190). Yet they share with Trigger's notion the salience of a past that provides roots of and justification for a group in the present that is struggling – or recently has struggled – for recognition, if not existence. Foreign archaeologists, in contrast to native ones, are generally working in an imperialist tradition which treats archaeology as a global endeavor ("we excavate *humanity's* past"), a kind of "departicularization," in Alonso's terms (1988: 44–45). This latter point is nicely illustrated by a recent case that received international attention: the destruction of the Bamiyan Buddhas by the former Taliban government of Afghanistan. In response, the Exccutive Board of UNESCO adopted a draft resolution "condemning the acts of destruction committed against cultural monuments in Afghanistan as crimes against *the common heritage of humanity*" (Manhart 2001: 388; our emphasis).

Western archaeologists are in many, if not most, cases educated in a Judeo-Christian tradition that views the Middle East as the birthplace of their religious heritage (Kuklick 1996; Silberman 1982) and, by extension, the cradle of *Western* civilization (Bahrani 1998; Pollock and Lutz 1994). Armed with these (often implicit) underlying assumptions, research on the Middle Eastern past can easily be understood as a part of an investigation of the roots of one's own heritage, albeit with a quite different twist than in the case of native archaeologists. Whereas in the nineteenth century the interests of foreign, almost exclusively Christian researchers were clearly in what they perceived as *their* past (simply transposed in space), in the twentieth century there was a tendency to broaden this to the notion of humanity's past, thereby attempting to make it acceptable to postcolonial sensibilities. For those archaeologists in other parts of the world who come from different religious/intellectual traditions, the "relevance" of the Middle Eastern past for their own interests may be correspondingly lower. Availability of funding permitting archaeologists to journey substantial distances to conduct their research also plays an important role, a topic we take up below.

Intellectual underpinnings of foreign archaeologists working in the Middle East

If we look more closely at foreign (i.e., Western) archaeologists working in the Middle East, we can see clear lines of distinction among them. Some work in a tradition that is historical and particularist in orientation, whereas others follow a more generalizing, anthropological tradition. To understand why these distinctions exist and what their implications are, it is useful to consider the intellectual underpinnings and training of archaeologists who follow these two traditions. In contrasting two traditions, we wish to make clear at the outset that we are painting a picture with broad brushstrokes; it should be obvious that much detail and differences among individual practitioners or "sub-traditions" is glossed over in this way.[3]

The first tradition we consider is one that is most closely allied in its approach and interests to history. In this tradition, an intellectual focus on a particular area is seen as important and relevant in and of itself; there need be no broader goal than investigating the history of a region. This approach is connected to the idea of *Bildung* which was promoted in the nineteenth century by Wilhelm von Humboldt, among others. *Bildung* refers to several things, including the importance of lifelong learning for its own sake (Menze 1975: 266–267; Nipperdey 1990: 590). This tradition is most commonly, though not exclusively, found in Europe, and we will call it, for the sake of simplicity, the Europeanist tradition.

An emphasis on studying the history of a particular area often results in a long-term commitment to a specific (small) region and/or country, an engagement that encourages a considerable depth of knowledge not only about its archaeology and history but also about contemporary conditions and local language(s). Practitioners of this approach may devote a substantial portion of their career to the investigation of a single site (e.g., Matthiae at Ebla; Oateses at Brak; Korfmann at Troy). Even incremental gains in knowledge or understanding of an ancient settlement are seen as important, regardless of whether long-term work produces any major new insights. Sites chosen tend to be large, in part because of the intention to spend many years investigating them but also because of the types of finds desired, a point to which we return in a moment.

The emphasis on archaeology's alliance with (a certain kind of) history has tended to mean that archaeologists working in a Europeanist tradition share a common prejudice of historians that archaeological remains are less informative than written sources. In other words, archaeology is essentially a handmaiden to history, helping to uncover texts and inscribed objects as well as other items (architecture, artifacts) that aid in illustrating the historical understanding won from written sources. As a result, archaeologists working in this tradition are inclined to focus on textually documented periods and on sites – principally large ones – that are judged likely to produce cuneiform tablets and, preferably, major architecture.

In principle, a Europeanist approach to archaeology has as its ultimate goal the writing of histories. But Europeanist archaeologists working in the Middle East have, as yet, seldom done so (however, see Nissen 1988, 1998; Postgate 1992). One might suspect that history-writing within this archaeological tradition would likely be of a kind that concentrates on documenting the accomplishments of elite sectors of society, although this has not been strictly the case for those that have appeared.

The ideology of *Bildung* in the Europeanist tradition produces, on the one hand, a salutary acceptance of knowledge acquisition as valuable in and of itself, without the need for additional rationale. At the same time, it is an ideology that obscures an underlying class structure. Knowledge serves as a means to preserve power; in its self-referential, "valueless" form, it is no longer the *content* of knowledge that is related to power, but one's ability to refer to such esoteric wisdom. Even today, being able to talk about Greek mythology serves as a means to distinguish oneself from the working classes (Bourdieu 1984). An archaeological tradition underpinned by an ideology of *Bildung* is one that implicitly understands Western archaeologists' attention to the Middle Eastern past as a demonstration of the superior claims of Westerners (as opposed to natives) to (supposedly) disinterested knowledge.

The second tradition of foreign archaeological practice in the Middle East is one that is most closely connected to the social sciences and especially anthropology. In this tradition, primary attention is devoted to comparative work and generalizations that can result from it. Research is typically framed in terms of certain problems or questions to be addressed by means of specific fieldwork and analyses. The focus of these problems tends to be on questions of why or how (processes, structures, and other abstractions), rather than on the specifics of what happened in the past, except as these are a means to the end of answering the why and how questions. This tradition is most commonly, although not exclusively, associated with North American archaeologists, and we refer to it as the Americanist tradition.

Archaeological work in the Americanist tradition usually puts an emphasis on short-term projects that are designed to answer a particular question with a relatively small amount of fieldwork (e.g., Hole, Flannery, and Neely 1969; Pollock et al. 2001; Wright 1981). This is typically followed by a project at another site, region, or perhaps country where comparative work is carried out. In contrast to the Europeanist tradition, an Americanist one views relevant knowledge as primarily that which helps to address a specific question; the acquisition of information that contributes to an overall accumulation of data is considered insufficient by itself. Field research is planned with the goal of finding an efficient means to address one's research question. In other words, research is governed by an instrumental rationality that requires that it justify itself in terms of the expected outcome. This is often thought to be best achieved by the selection of smaller sites – including those sites disproportionately endangered by construction projects and frequently neglected in a Europeanist tradition – which may require a small overall input of time to acquire a "representative" sample. At the same time, the dissociation of archaeology and history means that Americanist archaeologists are much less driven by the desire to recover texts than their Europeanist counterparts; indeed, Americanist archaeologists are more likely to work on prehistoric periods. The overall focus on short-term projects means that researchers working in this tradition may lack the in-depth knowledge of a particular area that their Europeanist colleagues tend to have, especially the understanding of a contemporary context that comes from long association with local people and fluency in their language.

The Americanist tradition aims to produce broad, generalizable statements about the past rather than particular histories. These aims have often led to a neglect of historical detail, in a rush to come up with general statements of greater scope. The alliance with cultural anthropology and tendency toward disinterest in history have meant that relatively few archaeologists educated in this tradition have substantial training in ancient languages. Appropriate models and analogies for understanding the prehistoric past are seen as coming principally from ethnographic work in other parts of the world rather than from the later historical tradition of the Middle East.

A result of the emphasis on short-term projects and comparative goals is that, at least in principle, the Americanist archaeological presence can and should be everywhere. The whole world is, in a sense, the anthropological archaeologist's laboratory. The desirability of the comparative enterprise is fostered by the make-up of many anthropology departments in which most, if not all, of the Middle Eastern archaeologist's colleagues are likely to work in entirely different parts of the world and have little common knowledge of particular regions. Knowledge sharing becomes by necessity a matter of common theoretical or methodological interests rather than occurring at the level of data or detailed historical understandings.

These distinctive intellectual traditions help explain why there are also some marked differences in Europe and the United States in supporting institutions and modes of publication. Institutions such as the Deutsches Archäologisches Institut (DAI) in Germany and the Centre National de la Recherche Scientifique (CNRS) in France have no counterpart in the United States. They are dedicated to long-term, slow accumulations of detailed knowledge about an area or subject. Researchers connected to them are not typically required to demonstrate rapid turnarounds or to meet set output or productivity goals. In the United States in contrast, a much more capitalist equation governs research: one is expected to calculate how much money and other resources, especially time, one needs to expend in order to reach a specific, desired outcome. The ability to achieve that outcome with the lowest expenditure of resources is a mark of a successful researcher.

The Europeanist archaeological tradition supports the publication of small-run, expensively produced (and priced) site reports and catalogs that are of interest to only a small group of specialist scholars. Once again, knowledge for its own sake is seen as valuable, and the publication of such volumes is accorded high esteem within the scholarly community. In contrast, American publishers are increasingly restricting their output to books that sell to a sizable audience, resulting in an emphasis on those scholarly publications that can be marketed as textbooks. The publication of site reports suffers in this atmosphere, exacerbating a situation to which funding priorities also contribute, a point to which we return below. At the same time, the Americanist focus on general questions that have applications beyond one's own particular area of study allows insights into general processes beyond the particular case researched.

"Native" traditions in Middle Eastern archaeology are typically more similar to Europeanist ones in their intellectual orientation than to the Americanist approach (Glock 1999b). This is due in part to the tendency for many Middle Eastern archaeologists to receive their advanced training in Europe rather than the United States.[4] In addition, however, an historically oriented approach matches more closely the interests of nationalist or disenfranchised archaeologies that are generally favored by practitioners in Middle Eastern countries.

Paying for archaeology

Along with the training of archaeologists, sources of funding for archaeological research have a significant impact on the kinds of fieldwork conducted and the ways in which it is done (cf. Gero 1985; Kramer and Stark 1994; Yellen 1991). To a large extent, funding sources reproduce the existing structures of archaeological practice set out by educational institutions.

One of the premier funding agencies for archaeologists based at US institutions is the National Science Foundation (NSF), which supports projects that have explicitly anthropological significance, i.e., broad, problem-oriented goals.[5] Far less likely to be funded are projects that seek to acquire detailed, culture-historical-type understandings of a specific place or time without an additional justification for how or why such basic data will be used in the service of anthropological goals. Due in part to a chronic shortage of funds, the NSF archaeology program is reluctant to commit to long-term support of a single project. The maximum duration of a grant is five years, but in 2000, the most recent year for which data are available, 55 percent of awards were for two years or less and only 5 percent for more than three years (http://www.nsf.gov/sbe/bcs/arch/senior.htm). A renewal requires a completely new application with a rationale that justifies why continued work will produce substantially new insights. In contrast, the excavations by the Deutsches Archäologisches Institut at Boğazköy (Turkey) have been undertaken continuously since 1931, with the sole exception of an interruption during World War II. This project of more than 70 years' duration has long-term funding and therefore the possibility to systematically and extensively uncover the Hittite capital, focusing successively on different areas of the city (Neve 1996: 11–15, 99–104).

US-based archaeologists working in the Middle East face high costs of transportation to their field sites. That, together with a need to show "output on investment" in order to justify their research and especially to be funded in the next round of grant applications, dictates certain approaches to fieldwork. Only in exceptional cases, such as at Çatalhöyük, can very time-consuming, highly detailed work be sustained by full-scale projects (Hodder 1996, 2000a). An economic emphasis on working quickly and efficiently is coupled with a longstanding tradition of employing local villagers as workmen to assist with the physical labor, or in some cases to do most of it, with archaeologists' roles being confined principally to note-taking, drawing, and other forms of recording as well as directing the workmen. In the context of long-term projects such as those more typical of the Europeanist tradition, there is the – often unrealized – potential to train local workmen to become highly skilled excavators, one of the most famous examples being the Sherqatis in Iraq (Lloyd 1963: 24). In the more common situation in which projects remain at one site for only a few years, it is frequently the case that archaeologists must start afresh each time with an inexperienced workforce. Relative lack of experience, combined with a Western work ethic that believes in keeping a paid workforce busy at all times, affects both the pace and quality of work conducted as well as archaeologists' relationships to workers.

An additional constraint on fieldwork comes from the archaeological services in many Middle Eastern countries which expect project directors to demonstrate continuing interest in "their" site through regular, i.e., annual, presence and fieldwork.[6] As a result, time for analysis and publication is minimized, as summer months are spent in the field, and available time during teaching semesters is largely absorbed in writing grant proposals, permit applications, and obligatory reports for government and funding agencies. This situation is further exacerbated by the reluctance of many American granting agencies to fund the less glamorous and more time-consuming aspects of fieldwork, namely analysis and publication, thereby contributing to the small number of completed site reports.

The European situation is different in a number of respects.[7] Funding agencies, for example, the Deutsche Forschungsgemeinschaft in Germany, the CNRS in France, or the British Schools of Archaeology in Great Britain, show a greater willingness to support individual projects over the long term. In line with the general intellectual orientation of Europeanist archaeology, it is understood that the gradual accumulation of data is an important end in itself and may lead to unspecified(able) benefits in the future. There is less pressure to strive to answer a particular question posed prior to beginning the research. Along with the importance placed on basic data acquisition is an acceptance of the costs incurred in working up such material for publication and a greater readiness to fund those later stages of the research process.

The commitment to years of work at a single site results in a trained local workforce that might, in principle, permit a slower and more detail-oriented approach to excavation. However, the Europeanist emphasis on recovering substantial architecture and elite remains usually precludes an interest in such field methods. Instead, large clearances that expose full architectural plans are common, an approach that often dovetails closely with the interests of local officials who wish to use archaeology to promote tourism.

On the other hand, European funding agencies' readiness to commit to large, long-term projects often works to the detriment of newer or smaller projects that have a hard time "getting a foot in the (funding) door." The Americanist tendency to spread the money around, albeit thinly, thereby encouraging younger researchers who may bring different approaches to their work, is more likely to be stifled in the European context.

Archaeological Evidence and the Practices of Non-Archaeologists

Archaeological sites, artifacts, and monuments are, of course, not the sole property of archaeologists, nor are archaeologists able to maintain a monopoly on the interpretations of archaeological evidence, however much they may at times desire to do so. We turn now to issues surrounding the use of archaeology by those who are not professionals in the field.

The production of cultural heritage

The issue of "public"[8] interest in and use of archaeology can be understood as a series of challenges to an expert discourse (conducted by professional archaeologists) that seeks to maintain a hegemonic control over interpretations of the archaeological record. We consider this matter in terms of the production of heritage, which involves the preservation, neglect, and destruction of archaeological sites and remains.

The production of cultural heritage includes the selection of certain (kinds and parts of) sites for preservation and/or reconstruction in order to make them potential tourist attractions. These are places that a government or particular group wishes to exhibit – whether to their own constituents or to others – as important in or characteristic of their past (cf. Abu el-Haj 1998: 171; Dietler 1994; Glock 1999a). Sites such as Babylon, Boğazköy, Petra, and Persepolis are among the best known examples of places that have come, at various times, to *stand for* the past of the modern countries in which they are located. While it is certainly the case that some types of archaeological sites lend themselves more easily to presentation for tourist consumption, the choice of sites for preservation and/or reconstruction is guided to a significant extent by other consider-ations rather than by intrinsic features of archaeological remains (cf. Scham 2001a: 204). The specific reasons for particular choices must be examined in historical con-text; only that way can one begin to understand the odd choice of Masada, where the Jews suffered defeat at the hands of the Romans, as a key symbol of modern Israel (Ben-Yehuda 1995; Scham 2001a: 202–203).

In contrast to the effort and money invested to preserve and even reconstruct some sites, others may be deliberately destroyed. A notable recent example is the demolition of the Bamiyan Buddhas by the Taliban, but the destruction of the site of Zeugma/Belkis in Turkey, a substantial portion of which was submerged by the lake formed behind the Birecik dam despite international outcry, is a related case (Başgelen and Ergeç 2000). In the one case (Zeugma), we tend to "understand" the economic ration-ale for building dams; in the other (Bamiyan), the religious "logic" appears indefensible to us. Still other sites are left to decay or fall prey to petty vandalism (e.g., the Armenian site of Akdamar on an island in Lake Van), itself a deliberate choice *not* to preserve certain remains.

In the examples just cited, it is important to note that both the Taliban and the Turkish government engaged in the destruction of sites – whether deliberate or by leaving them to decay or be submerged – and at the same time both worked to preserve other archaeological remains. The many well-known archaeological sites in Turkey that draw tourists, both Turkish and foreign, need little mention. Despite the large-scale and seemingly wanton destruction perpetrated by the Taliban during the years in which they governed Afghanistan, observations by one of us indicated that they took the utmost care to restore and preserve all mosques that had suffered from attacks. This is in line with the reopening of the Kabul Museum as a National Museum of Islamic Art, following the destruction of pre-Islamic statues and other artifacts. In this way, the Taliban not only negatively, but also positively worked on *their* preferred version of Afghanistan's past.[9] As much as one may condemn the Taliban's actions, one must nonetheless call into question a statement that appeared in a prominent newspaper describing the Taliban as "taking with them into the dark practically every-thing that linked the country to its past" (*Independent* [London], November 29, 2001). The issue, rather, is *which* past? It is perhaps also worth noting here that the outrage felt by many Western observers at the destruction of irreplaceable antiquities by the Taliban may be one (of many) instances in which cultural misunderstandings play a significant role. More than one Middle Eastern religion has a long history of mistrust of images and tendency toward iconoclasm that sits ill with those of us who live today in societies saturated with visual imagery.

The tyranny of stratigraphy

The production of cultural heritage involves the selective use of aspects of a group's or nation's past to highlight those times, events, or conditions it sees as most favorable to its present agenda. In attempting to choose certain monuments or locations to represent its preferred past, a group may be confronted with a variety of dilemmas. Here we highlight one of those which we refer to as the tyranny of space. Archaeological sites – unlike the artifacts they contain – are intimately bound to particular spaces. The very location of a site has a meaning, a "social character" as an identifier with the past. When two (or more) sites that are claimed by different groups are superimposed, thereby occupying the same spot, a conflict may ensue that has no apparent resolution, because neither destruction nor preservation is easily possible. Put differently, superposition, which involves the vertical dimension of space, has a different meaning than horizontal proximity, even if the physical distance between two sites or buildings is the same. Horizontal distance implies a sense of equality or at least lack of inherent distinction, whereas vertical distance confers a sense that what is above is also superior. Meanings attached to superimposed monuments can be used strategically in two different ways. What is underneath is older, and because of this temporal precedence becomes a powerful symbol of the "original," the primordial. On the other hand, the upper layers of buildings are more recent and therefore may be argued to be more "developed" and "civilized"; and often, they are also simply what is *there*. We illustrate these points with two examples, Ayodhya and Jerusalem.

Ayodhya   In December 1992 a crowd of Hindu militants attacked and destroyed the sixteenth-century Babri Mosque at Ayodhya in Uttar Pradesh (India), believed by some to have been built over the site of a Hindu temple marking the birthplace of the mythical king Ram (Bernbeck and Pollock 1996; Brandtner 1994; Teuscher 1994). According to the view espoused by the Hindu militants, the construction of the mosque by the Mughal emperor Babur was responsible for the razing of the temple. Tensions had existed well before December, but they escalated dramatically with the mosque's destruction, which led to riots in India and Bangladesh that left hundreds dead (Nasrin 1994).

Archaeological excavations took place at the site on several occasions. The most extensive work was carried out by the archaeologist B. B. Lal in the mid-1970s (Lal 1980, 1983). At the time he reported that there was little of interest in the medieval levels, but a decade later he published an article in which he claimed that he had found the remains of a columned temple beneath the mosque (Lal 1990: 15). The clear implication was that this columned building was the remains of the Ram temple said to have been destroyed by Babur. In addition, numerous objects were alleged to have been found immediately following the destruction of the mosque that were said to have come from the earlier temple (Gupta 1994). However, examination of the various pieces of evidence indicates that the archaeological picture is far from clear in its support of the existence of a temple that was destroyed by the construction of the mosque (Engineer 1992; Mandal 1993; Rao 1994; Teuscher 1994).

The Ayodhya example is a (not uncommon) case in which members of two religious groups claim the same place as sacred to their religion; archaeological remains were summoned as pieces of evidence if and when they were (or could be made to be) useful (cf. Brandtner 1994: 227). No amount of debate over the physical evidence mattered in the long run – both parties *knew* that they were right, and the question became one of whether or not the standing religious building – the mosque – would or would not be preserved. In the end it was not.

The destruction of a monument is intended to eradicate memories. However, the act of destruction often has the reverse effect of perpetuating memory. In 2002, violence related to Ayodhya once again erupted. In February, a trainload of Hindus, members of the ultranationalist World Hindu Council, was attacked – seemingly after a drunken provocation – by angry Muslims who set fire to the train, killing 58. The Hindus aboard the train were returning to their homes in Gujarat from Ayodhya, where they had been making preparations for the erection of a new temple to Ram on the spot where the Babri Mosque had stood. The attack on the train was followed by days of violence, killing hundreds, mostly Muslims (*New York Times*, February 28, 2002, late edition; *Independent* [London], March 20, 2002).

Plans to build a temple on the same spot as the demolished mosque have been underway in some Hindu circles since 1992. The World Hindu Council announced plans to begin erecting the temple on March 15. Although originally favored by the Bharatiya Janata Party government, the Prime Minister, Mr. Vajpayee, withdrew his support following the February violence and a ruling by the Indian Supreme Court against building the temple. Interestingly, the Vajpayee government proposed instead that a temple be built *close* to the razed mosque; Muslim leaders, however, expressed their fears that if the work began, the temple would end up being erected on the *same spot* as the mosque (*Guardian* [London], March 15, 2002).

Jerusalem In Jerusalem, a city claimed by three major religions, the problem is magnified. The place known to Jews as the Temple Mount and to Muslims as the Haram al-Sharif is another example of the superimposition of sites. For Muslims, this is the place from which Mohammed ascended to heaven, and it is therefore one of the holiest places in Islam. For Jews, the Temple Mount is the place where the Jewish temple stood in the days of Herod; it is one of the holiest places in Judaism. Today the Dome of the Rock and the Al-Aqsa Mosque stand at this spot, buildings that date to the seventh century AD. Israel maintains secular control of the area, whereas a Muslim religious trust, the Waqf, is in charge of managing the religious buildings (Scham 2001b).

In this case, once again, the *very place* is sacred to two major religions. The construction of a new stairway and exit, authorized by the Waqf, provoked a storm of protest by a number of Israeli archaeologists and politicians, who charged that inadequate archaeological methods were used in removing material in preparation for the building activity. The Waqf claimed that it used appropriate procedures and found that the deposits were all thoroughly mixed (Scham 2001b). As a result of this conflict, Israeli archaeologists and other prominent intellectuals formed a "Committee to Prevent the Destruction of Antiquities on the Temple Mount" with the aim of monitoring the Waqf's archaeological activities. Despite accusations that the Waqf undertook large-scale excavations, committee members were unable to present hard evidence for this (*Jerusalem Post*, February 2, 2001).

Politicians attempted to propose a solution to this dilemma of how to deal with one spot claimed by two conflicting groups. A proposal was forwarded by the United

States and Israel to divide the hill *horizontally*, turning the standing buildings over to Palestinian control and the Western wall to the Israelis. This proposal is said to have been the most significant factor in the breakdown of the Camp David II meetings in 2000, with the Palestinian delegation unwilling to consider any division of the spot and the Israelis equally unwilling to cede sovereignty of it to the Palestinians (Scham 2001b).

A related case concerns a tunnel running along the outer wall of the Haram al-Sharif/Temple Mount. The tunnel was dug in ancient times, and it includes remains from Roman, Byzantine, medieval Islamic, and Crusader periods. Until 1996 the tunnel was accessible through a single entrance at its southern end. In September of that year, just after conservative politician Binyamin Netanyahu had won the elections, the Israeli government opened the (blocked) entrance at the northern end which is located in the Muslim Quarter of Jerusalem. Violent protests by Palestinians ensued, claiming the lives of over sixty Palestinians and Israelis, and endangering the already weakened peace process. In the following months, Palestinian protesters charged that the tunnel endangered the integrity of buildings above it (*Jerusalem Post*, January 29, 1997).

Where superimposed archaeological remains – occupying the same location – are of interest to two or more groups, the production of heritage is likely to be challenged in politically contested situations, especially where one group is dominant over the other but not to the extent that subordinate one(s) can be totally ignored. Put differently, such challenges are probable in the rather common situations in which there is no clearly established hegemony, but rather various groups struggling for it (Brow 1990: 3). The archaeological/ heritage examples around which disputes revolve are those that are used to stake claims to broader spaces: in the case of Ayodhya, to India as a solely Hindu versus a Hindu *and* Muslim society; for the Haram al-Sharif/Temple Mount, the question of sovereignty over Jerusalem.

Interestingly, these examples suggest that in a world dominated by (manipulated) images that are often more "real" than what they purport to represent, the tangibility and uniqueness – or aura (Benjamin 1968 [1936]) – of particular places remain inviolable. If indeed the aura of "real" monuments remains key, it would imply re-presentations of an archaeological monument – whether in the form of a reconstruction (e.g., the Buddhas in Bamiyan), simulacrum constructed elsewhere (e.g., the Parthenon in Nashville, Tennessee), or in images – *enhance* rather than weaken the power of the "original" (contra Baudrillard 1994 [1981]).

A Larger Framework

A consideration of who does archaeology, the intellectual traditions within which it is conducted, how it is paid for, and public interests in archaeology brings us to the question of which pasts matter, and, by implication, which do not? A closely related question must also be posed: *to whom* do certain pasts matter? Addressing these questions requires us to consider the contradictions within and between the practices of archaeologists and the practices of others with interests in archaeological evidence.

The production of heritage – pasts that matter – involves a dialectical relationship between the preservation of the archaeological record and a neglect or downright destruction of (portions of) it. What gets preserved depends to a significant degree on who has the power to define the past that matters and, by implication, which pasts do not. When we as archaeologists condemn the ravaging of sites or monuments, we might also remember that, as we tell our introductory classes, excavation is itself destruction. The production of heritage comes as much from the neglect and destruction of remains of the past as it does from the preservation and reconstruction of other parts (Naccache 1998) – as Trouillot (1995) points out, history is produced through silences.

We have also problematized the use of the past by non-archaeologists. Much of the anthropological literature since the late 1980s claims that archaeology figures prominently in attempts at nation-building (Blakey 1995; Díaz-Andreu and Champion 1996; Kohl and Fawcett 1995; Meskell 1998; Trigger 1984). However, in the post-Cold War world, four trends contribute to a repositioning of archaeology. First, there are processes that work toward the creation of supranational identities. These may originate in the conscious efforts of an emerging political supranational entity, such as Europe. In that case, the construction of a past that coincides geographically with the new political boundaries is actively pursued using financial incentives, as, for example, in the case of "Celtic Europe," which was touted in a number of highly advertised exhibits (e.g., Rieckhoff and Biel 2001; Weber and Hollein 2002). The use of an African past in the search for pan-African identity (Andah 1995; cf. Holl 1995: 197–204) works on a similarly supranational scale but is not spearheaded by an entity that has substantial political-economic powers. The lack of a politically driven funding body turns the generation of pan-African identity into an intellectual endeavor that has far less impact on concerned populations than in the European case. Second, the breakdown of nations and whole imperia (Yugoslavia, the Soviet Union) into smaller, often "ethnically clean" units that can barely be called "nations" is accompanied by a quest for a parochial past. Strictly delimited in its spatial extent, it serves not only to aggrandize a new nation's *ethnic* identity but to antagonize its neighbors (Kaiser 1995).

A third trend consists of globalization of pasts that had traditionally been sources for local or regional identity. Local pasts are increasingly turned into a playground for rich tourists (MacCannell 1999), as well as a reservoir for diasporic groups (Lavie and Swedenburg 1996). Archaeological tourism and its capitalist appendages such as tour organizations, hotels, restaurants, etc., impinge substantially on local populations; economic benefits often accrue principally to outside organizations or those segments of local populations that are already better off (cf. Hodder 1999: 202–204). Globalization of the past also includes its virtualization, the tourist who stays at home and "experiences" pasts through media such as television and the internet. For global consumers, whether real or virtual, it is principally globalized pasts that are emphasized, the features of "our common humanity." These are served up in a way that will be inoffensive to major transnational economic interests. Finally, globalization's encroachment on lower-class populations and "indigenous cultures" is at best ambiguous. Some archaeologists still want to see the positive aspects of this intrusion by focusing on indigenous activists who connect with the nodes of the global net to propagate their past (Smith and Ward 2000). But what about the millions of people who not only lack the economic means to access the internet but also the basic skills to do so, most importantly, literacy? An emphasis solely on an educated, activist community leaves the large interstices – the gaping holes – of the global net out of sight, where traditional social structures are being erased in order to exploit uprooted local populations economically (Kurz 1999: 871–879).

As elsewhere in the world, such intertwined processes of nationalism, "indigenism," and globalization are at work in the Middle East. However, the situation is complicated by two additional components of generating pasts. In most Middle Eastern countries, no real unified national past has taken hold, even when officially propagated by a government. Instead, adherents of different religions (Islam, Judaism, Christianism, Hinduism, Buddhism) promote their own history as *the* true past. This often leads to violent conflicts within nation-states between different religious pasts, of which those over Ayodhya and the Al-Aqsa Mosque are only particularly salient cases.

Furthermore, many states – including Iraq, Turkey, Jordan, pre-revolutionary Iran, Syria, and Egypt – have secular foundations. This secularism as well as state borders are the outcomes of the colonial order. Leaders of such states continue attempting to ensure national unity through a tradition that skips over the religiously contentious periods. As a result, it is very often the chronologically remote periods (in Turkey the Hittites [Özgüç 2002: 15], in pre-revolutionary Iran the Achaemenids, in Iraq the Neo-Babylonians) extending back to prehistory that serve as building blocks for the "invention of tradition," rather than (more recent) pasts that people can easily connect with. For example, the Iranian pre-revolutionary calendar, introduced in the 1970s, began with Cyrus the Great's accession year and reminded people on a daily basis of the artificiality of a time system that disavowed the Islamic calendar. To name but one other example, a small find – a bronze standard from a burial – from the third-millennium site of Alaca Höyük in Turkey has been turned into a huge monument in one of the busiest traffic circles in the capital, Ankara. Such an enforced presence of alienated pasts has led to clashes between the local, mainly religiously oriented population and those who most clearly represent the interests of the secular and global order: tourists (*Guardian* [London], November 18, 1997; Hodder 2000b: 8).

The combination of conflicts over religious pasts and the clash between religious and secular orders gives the politics of archaeology in the Middle East a particular complexity and acuteness, especially because most foreign archaeologists working in the region share ties to one or another of the major Middle Eastern religions. The claim to absolute truth, including historical truth, is a mainstay of many of these religions and contributes to the ardent and intolerant character of many conflicts over archaeological sites. What is more, many secular governments, for fear of losing their legitimization, try to undermine or prohibit religiously based political parties. By doing so, the secular world and the promotion of a secular past become part and parcel of an anti-democratic, repressive state apparatus. Near Eastern archaeology is openly exploited by the "players" in this political game for various global, national, and religious endeavors.

We have considered here the position of foreign archaeologists and have claimed that their work in the Near East is fraught with dilemmas that are at present insoluble because we are all caught in the web of global economic and ideological structures as well as local religious practices. Most foreign archaeologists work on pre-Islamic periods, presumably in part because they wish to avoid becoming involved in heated conflicts over religious pasts. Whatever the reasons, the emphasis on pre-Islamic pasts unwillingly contributes to conflict by furthering a refined knowledge of a secular, "national" past that is one of the hallmarks of cultural alienation between many Near Eastern governments and populations. However, the alternative – to work on later, usually Islamic periods – would involve archaeologists in the kinds of interreligious conflicts alluded to earlier. For these reasons, we contend that archaeological practice in the Near East at present not only forfeits any claim to a politically neutral position, but in many cases plays a politically harmful role. It is our responsibility to recognize the situation and to work toward ways to ameliorate it, which by necessity involves working both from within *and* from outside archaeology.

NOTES

1   There are, of course, some who argue that archaeology studies material culture, whether past or present. However, by far the majority of archaeologists understand their work as involving the study of the past.

2   By disenfranchised, Scham refers principally to cultural and historical disenfranchisement, meaning "groups who have been deprived of control over the presentation of their pasts" (2001a: 187).

3   A few words about our own backgrounds are in order here. One of us (RB) was trained in the scholarly tradition we call Europeanist, the other (SP) in the Americanist one. Both of us have spent considerable time working in the other context, through fellowship opportunities, jobs, and/or field projects. We would like to emphasize that reflections on these experiences have led both of us to appreciate certain features of both traditions and to view other aspects of them critically, a sense of which we try to convey in this chapter.

4   Turkey, Israel, and Jordan (as well as India) all have their own quite well-developed university systems of training archaeologists, but even in these cases it is not unusual – with the exception of Israel – for students to do their graduate study abroad. Other Middle Eastern countries have notably fewer opportunities for university degrees in archaeology.

5   According to its website, the "Archaeology Program provides support for anthropologically relevant archaeological research" (http://www.nsf.gov/sbe/bcs/arch/start.htm, last accessed Jan. 9, 2002).

6   With few exceptions, permits to excavate are given to individual projects that then are understood to have exclusive "rights" to work at that particular site as long as they adhere to written and unwritten rules of conduct.

7   There are, of course, substantial differences in amounts and sources of funding in different European countries. Nonetheless, we think there is a legitimate distinction to be drawn between European and American approaches to funding archaeological fieldwork.

8   There are, of course, numerous publics, whose composition may shift depending upon the issues at stake.

9   We wish to be clear here that we in no way condone the destruction of antiquities by the Taliban. However, we believe that it is crucial to view their actions in the context of those of other governments and interest groups. In that way, it is evident that the destruction perpetrated at the hands of the Taliban is a more extreme form of a common, worldwide phenomenon. One need only consider the efforts made to destroy statues of Lenin, Stalin, Marx, and others throughout post-1989 eastern Europe (Verdery 1999).

REFERENCES

Abu el-Haj, N. 1998. Translating truths: Nationalism, the practice of archaeology, and the remaking of past and present in contemporary Jerusalem. *American Ethnologist* 25: 166–188.

Alonso, A. M. 1988. The effects of truth: Re-presentations of the past and the imagining of community. *Journal of Historical Sociology* 1: 33–57.

Andah, B. 1995 Studying African societies in cultural context. In P. R. Schmidt and T. C. Patterson (eds.), *Making Alternative Histories*. Santa Fe, NM: School of American Research Press, pp. 149–182.

Bahrani, Z. 1998. Conjuring Mesopotamia: Imaginative geography and a world past. In L. Meskell (ed.), *Archaeology under Fire: Nationalism, Politics and Heritage in the Eastern Mediterranean and the Middle East*. London: Routledge, pp. 159–174.

Başgelen, N., and R. Ergeç. 2000. *Belkis/Zeugma – Halfeti – Rumkale. A Last Look at History*. Istanbul: Archaeology and Art Publications.

Baudrillard, J. 1994 [1981]. *Simulacra and Simulation*. Trans. S. F. Glaser. Ann Arbor: University of Michigan Press.

Benjamin, W. 1968 [1936]. The work of art in the age of mechanical reproduction. In H. Arendt (ed.), *Illuminations*. Trans. Harry Zohn. New York: Schocken Books, pp. 217–251.

Ben-Yehuda, N. 1995. *The Masada Myth: Collective Memory and Mythmaking in Israel*. Madison: University of Wisconsin Press.

Bernbeck, R., and S. Pollock. 1996. Ayodha, archaeology, and identity. *Current Anthropology* 37 (Suppl.): 138–142.

Blakey, M. L. 1995. Race, nationalism and the Afrocentric past. In P. R. Schmidt and T. Patterson (eds.), *Making Alternative Histories*. Santa Fe, NM: School of American Research Press, pp. 213–228.

Bourdieu, P. 1984. *Distinction: A Social Critique of the Judgement of Taste*. Trans. R. Nice. Cambridge, MA: Harvard University Press.

Brandtner, M. 1994. Die indischen Epen als Gegenstand archäologischer Forschung: Graben im Dienst des "Hindutums" oder: "Digging for God and Country." *Internationales Asienforum* 25: 213–238.

Brow, J. 1990. Notes on community, hegemony, and the uses of the past. *Anthropological Quarterly* 63: 1–6.

Comaroff, J. 1985. *Body of Power, Spirit of Resistance: The Culture and History of a South African People*. Chicago: University of Chicago Press.

Díaz-Andreu, M., and T. Champion (eds.) 1996. *Nationalism and Archaeology in Europe*. London: University College London Press.

Dietler, M. 1994. "Our ancestors the Gauls": Archaeology, ethnic nationalism, and the manipulation of Celtic identity in modern Europe. *American Anthropologist* 96: 584–605.

Engineer, A. A. (ed.) 1992. *Politics of Confrontation: The Babri–Masjid Ramjanmabhoomi Controversy Runs Riot*. New Delhi: Ajanta Press.

Gero, J. 1985. Socio-politics and the woman-at-home ideology. *American Antiquity* 50: 342–350.

Glock, A. 1999a. Cultural bias in archaeology. In T. Kapitan (ed.), *Archaeology, History and Culture in Palestine and the Near East: Essays in Memory of Albert E. Glock*. Atlanta, GA: Scholars Press, pp. 324–342.

——1999b. Archaeology as cultural survival: The future of the Palestinian past. In T. Kapitan (ed.), *Archaeology, History and Culture in Palestine and the Near East: Essays in Memory of Albert E. Glock*. Atlanta, GA: Scholars Press, pp. 302–323.

Grossberg, L. 1996. History, politics and postmodernism: Stuart Hall and Cultural studies. In D. Morley and K-H. Chen (eds.), *Stuart Hall: Critical Dialogues in Cultural Studies*. London: Routledge, pp. 151–173.

Gupta, S. P. 1994. Government sitting tight over clinching archaeological evidence? *Organiser* 46(18): 3.

Hamilakis, Y. 1999. La trahison des archéologues? Archaeological practice as intellectual activity in postmodernity. *Journal of Mediterranean Archaeology* 12(1): 60–79.

Hodder, I. (ed.) 1996. *On the Surface: Çatalhöyük 1993–95*. Cambridge: McDonald Institute for Archaeological Research.

—— 1999. *The Archaeological Process. An Introduction*. Oxford: Blackwell.

—— (ed.) 2000a. *Towards Reflexive Method in Archaeology: The Example at Çatalhöyük*. Cambridge: McDonald Institute for Archaeological Research.

—— 2000b. Archaeology and globalism. David Skomp Distinguished Lectures in Anthropology 1999–2000, Indiana University, February 18.

Hole, F., K. Flannery, and J. Neely, J. 1969. *Prehistory and Human Ecology of the Deh Luran Plain*. Ann Arbor: University of Michigan Museum of Anthropology, Memoirs 1.

Holl, A. F. C. 1995. African history: Past, present, and future. The unending quest for alternatives. In P. R. Schmidt and T. C. Patterson (eds.), *Making Alternative Histories*, Santa Fe, NM: School of American Research Press, pp. 183–212.

Kaiser, T. 1995. Archaeology and ideology in southeast Europe. In P. L. Kohl and C. Fawcett (eds.), *Nationalism, Politics, and the Practice of Archaeology*. Cambridge: Cambridge University Press, pp. 99–119.

Kohl, P., and C. Fawcett (eds.) 1995. *Nationalism, Politics, and the Practice of Archaeology*. Cambridge: Cambridge University Press.

Kramer, C., and M. Stark. 1994. The status of women in archeology. In M. Nelson, S. Nelson, and A. Wylie (eds.), *Equity Issues for Women in* Archeology. Washington, DC: Archeological Papers of the American Anthropological Association 5, pp. 17–22.

Kuklick, B. 1996. *Puritans in Babylon: The Ancient Near East and American Intellectual Life, 1880–1930*. Princeton, NJ: Princeton University Press.

Kurz, R. 1999. *Schwarzbuch des Kapitalismus*. Frankfurt/Main: Ullstein.

Lal, B. B. 1980. Excavations at Ayodhya, District Faizabad. *Indian Archaeology, 1976–77: A Review*, pp. 52–53.

—— 1983. Excavations at Ayodhya, District Faizabad. *Indian Archaeology, 1979–80: A Review*, pp. 76–77.

—— 1990. Archaeology of the Ramayana Sites Project. *Manthan*, October: 9–21.

Larsen, M. T. 1996. *The Conquest of Assyria: Excavations in an Antique Land 1840–1860*, London: Routledge.

Lavie, S., and T. Swedenburg (eds.) 1996. *Displacement, Diaspora, and Geographies of Identity*. Durham, NC: Duke University Press.

Lloyd, S. 1963. *Mounds of the Near East*. Edinburgh: Edinburgh University Press.

MacCannell, D. 1999. *The Tourist. A New Theory of the Leisure Class*, 2nd edn. Berkeley: University of California Press.

Mandal, D. 1993. *Ayodhya: Archaeology after Demolition*. New Delhi: Orient Longman.

Manhart, C. 2001. The Afghan cultural heritage crisis: UNESCO's response to the destruction of statues in Afghanistan. *American Journal of Archaeology* 105: 387–388.

Menze, C. 1975. *Die Bildungsreform Wilhelm von Humboldts*. Hanover: Schroedel.

Meskell, L. (ed.) 1998. *Archaeology Under Fire: Nationalism, Politics and Heritage in the Eastern Mediterranean and Middle East*. London: Routledge.

Naccache, A. H. F. 1998. Beirut's memorycide: Hear no evil, see no evil. In L. Meskell (ed.), *Archaeology under Fire: Nationalism, Politics and Heritage in the Eastern Mediterranean and the Middle East*. London: Routledge, pp. 140–158.

Nasrin, T. 1994. *Lajja (Shame)*. Trans. T. Gupta. New Delhi: Penguin.

Neve, P. 1996. *Hattusa. Stadt der Götter und Tempel*, 2nd edn. Mainz: Philipp von Zabern.

Nipperdey, T. 1990. *Deutsche Geschichte I, 1866–1918. Arbeitswelt und Bürgergeist*, Munich: C. H. Beck.

Nissen, H. 1988. *The Early History of the Ancient Near East, 9000–2000* B.C. Chicago: University of Chicago Press.

——1998. *Geschichte Alt-Vorderasiens*. Munich: Oldenbourg.

Orwell, G. 1961 [1949]. *1984*. New York: New American Library.

Özdoğan, M. 1998. Ideology and archaeology in Turkey. In L. Meskell (ed.), *Archaeology under Fire: Nationalism, Politics and Heritage in the Eastern Mediterranean and the Middle East*. London: Routledge, pp. 111–123.

Özgüç, T. 2002. Die Stellung der Hethiter im kulturellen Erbe der Türkei. In *Die Hethiter und ihr Reich*. Stuttgart: Theiss, Exhibition Catalogue, pp. 14–15.

Pollock, S., and C. Lutz. 1994. Archaeology deployed for the Gulf War. *Critique of Anthropology* 14: 263–284.

Pollock, S., R. Bernbeck, S. Allen, et al. 2001. Excavations at Fistikli Höyük, 1999. In N. Tuna, J. Öztürk, and J. Velibeyoğlu (eds.), *Salvage Project of the Archaeological Heritage of the Ilisu and Carchemish Dam Reservoirs. Activities in 1999*. Ankara: Middle East Technical University, pp. 1–63.

Postgate, J. N. 1992. *Early Mesopotamia: Society and Economy at the Dawn of History*. London: Routledge.

Rao, N. 1994. Interpreting silences: Symbol and history in the case of Ram Janmabhoomi/Babri Masjid. In G. C. Bond and A. Gilliam (eds.), *Social Construction of the Past: Representation of Power*. London: Routledge, pp. 154–164.

Rieckhoff, S., and J. Biel (eds.) 2001. *Die Kelten in Deutschland*. Stuttgart: Theiss.

Scham, S. 2001a. The archaeology of the disenfranchised. *Journal of Archaeological Method and Theory* 8: 183–213.

——2001b. A fight over sacred turf: Who controls Jerusalem's holiest shrine? *Archaeology* 54(6): 62–74.

Silberman, N. A. 1982. *Digging for God and Country*. New York: Knopf.

Smith, C., and G. K. Ward (eds.) 2000. *Indigenous Cultures in an Interconnected World*. St. Leonards: Allen & Unwin.

Teuscher, U. 1994. Ayodhya – Die archäologischen Befunde und die Kontroverse um ihre Deutung. *Internationales Asienforum* 25: 239–253.

Trigger, B. 1984. Alternative archaeologies: Nationalist, colonialist, imperialist. *Man* n.s. 19: 355–370.

Trouillot, M-R. 1995. *Silencing the Past: Power and the Production of History*. Boston: Beacon.

Verdery, K. 1999. *The Political Lives of Dead Bodies: Reburial and Postsocialist Change*. New York: Columbia University Press.

Weber, K., and M. Hollein (eds.) 2002. *Das Rätsel der Kelten vom Glauberg*. Stuttgart: Theiss.

Williams, R. 1977. *Marxism and Literature*. Oxford: Oxford University Press.

Wright, H. T. (ed.) 1981. *An Early Town on the Deh Luran Plain: Excavations at Tepe Farukhabad*. Ann Arbor: University of Michigan Museum of Anthropology, Memoirs 13.

Yellen, J. 1991. Women, archeology, and the National Science Foundation: An analysis of fiscal year 1989 data. In D. Walde and N. Willows (eds.), *The Archaeology of Gender*. Calgary: University of Calgary Archaeological Association, pp. 201–210.

15

Latin American Archaeology: From Colonialism to Globalization

Gustavo G. Politis and José Antonio Pérez Gollán

Introduction

Social archaeology, or "the social" in archaeology, is a concept with a variety of meanings that depend on historical context and theoretical perspective (Meskell et al. 2001). Of the many ways in which these issues are approached in Latin American archaeology, we focus on the explicit social commitment of archaeological praxis in the continent. We further explore how the colonial past of the region and the current process of globalization have affected the practice of archaeology and both its conceptual and theoretical development; however, not all archaeologists recognize the social implications or political dimensions of their work. This is especially true in a continent with a high percentage of Native Americans, *mestizos*, and Afro-Americans, for whom, apart from their own traditional knowledge (now extinct in many cases), archaeology is the only way they can learn about their past, and a continent where most (if not all) of the research is undertaken by non-indigenous or foreign scholars.

Over the twentieth century Latin American archaeologists have adopted various ideological and political stances about the social conditions of the ethnic groups and classes – urban and rural alike – within their continent's different countries. In this chapter we review this complex interaction and the present situation; we also discuss the social aspects of archaeological praxis within the Latin American context, even though the region is heterogeneous in terms of geography and culture, and has an intricate internal diversity resulting from different historical processes.

Up to now there has been little critical reflection about the social aspects of Latin American archaeology and the sociopolitical context in which it developed. Most studies have summarized the archaeological research in particular countries (Cabrera Pérez 1988; Fernández 1982; Mendonça de Souza 1991; Orellana Rodríguez 1996), and few have taken sociopolitical aspects specifically as an axis of their analysis (Barreto 1999; Echevarría Almeida 1996; Fernández Leiva 1992; Funari 1995; Gnecco 1995; Lorenzo 1981; Madrazo 1985; Politis 1992; Vargas Arenas 1999). Less frequently, investigations have highlighted the political dimensions of certain trends in archaeological theory, such as those of the Austro-German *Kulturkreise* school in

Argentina (Boschín and Llamazares 1984; Kohl and Perez Gollán 2002; Núñez Regueiro 1972), American cultural ecology in Brazil (Barreto 1999; Funari 1991), or even the influence of Gordon Childe's works (Pérez Gollán 1981). Few authors have carried out historiographic studies concerning the development of archaeology in particular countries (e.g., Chaves Chamorro 1986 for Colombia, Vázquez León 1996 for Mexico), or have written from a biographical perspective (e.g., Alonso and Baranda 1984; González 1985, Mirambell and Pérez Gollán 2000; Rojas 1987). Attempts to carry out broader, continent-wide studies encompassing the historical processes of archaeology in the Americas are scarce (Oyuela-Caycedo 1994; Politis 1995). We will begin with an analysis of the sociopolitical framework of production to try and understand the causes and characteristics of an explicitly social archaeological practice, taking as examples models of research carried out in other regions (Kohl and Fawcett 1995; Lamberg-Karlovsky 1990; Trigger 1989; Ucko 1995).

Social Issues in Latin American Archaeology: An Historical Perspective

Archaeology in Latin America was deeply affected from the start by the cataclysmic European colonial invasion. This powerful and contradictory event is constructed and reconstructed on the basis of the representations of past indigenous and *mestizo* societies. Given Latin America's notable historical diversity, such representations encompass the broad spectrum of social complexity achieved by local pre-Columbian societies.

In Europe historical continuity is taken for granted, and so a strong bond has developed between prehistory (archaeology), protohistory, and history. In contrast, in the colonial world discontinuity is clearly reflected in the classic structure where indigenous cultures are exhibited in anthropological museums and European cultures in history museums. Efforts should be made to break with the schematization of a past that lacks contemporary relevance (archaeology), an ethnographic present of Indians and *mestizos* frozen in their "otherness" (anthropology), and a dominant European society (history).

Two historical examples shed some light on this colonial fissure. The first is the book *Comentarios Reales* by the *mestizo* Inca Garcilaso de la Vega (1995 [1609]), which develops an elaborate theory on the character of Inca religion. According to Duviols (1964:43), the best apologist argument of the *Comentarios* is the providential sacralization of the Inca nobility: "But the masterpiece of this defense is the religion attributed to the Incas. ... Their conquests were primarily spiritual conquests to spread the religion of the Sun and the deism of Pachacámac, indispensable stages in God's road." Garcilaso quotes from the Lascasian, Augustinian, and Stoic traditions to bolster his attempt to refute Viceroy Toledo, and to prove that the Inca dynasty (his relatives) were not heathen barbarians (Duviols 1976:157). Garcilaso contended that, on the contrary, they had achieved the highest possible development as far as religion was concerned that could be expected of those who, being pagans, were not familiar with the Christian faith (ibid.). At the time that Garcilaso de la Vega wrote his *Comentarios*, an atmosphere of eschatological anxiety prevailed. Beyond redeeming the souls of the Indians, their past – their cultural heritage – was to be saved in order to simultaneously undertake a re-evaluation of all that was indigenous. The appropriation of the past represented the possibility of taking possession of the future, and such a course necessarily implied becoming the equals of classical antiquity (Lafaye 1984:62, 134). Garcilaso's work became a source of legitimacy for the Andean insurrectionary movements, from Túpac Amaru to the nineteenth-century wars of independence.

The second example is the discovery in 1790 of the stone sculpture of the goddess Coatlicue, "the one with the skirt of snakes," in the Plaza Mayor in Mexico City. As Octavio Paz wrote (1995), there is nothing that better illustrates the different ideas that the Western world has about pre-Columbian art – and of indigenous society as a whole – than the history of this disturbing American deity. Viceroy Revillagigedo decided that the Coatlicue sculpture should be exhibited at the Royal and Pontifical University of Mexico as "a monument of American antiquity." Shortly afterwards it was reburied, because of fears that the old "demonic" beliefs would be revived, as some Indians still worshiped the goddess. In 1804 Alexander von Humboldt succeeded in having the statue unearthed so that he could study it. Today Coatlicue occupies a privileged place in the grand Aztec Hall in the National Museum of Anthropology, Mexico City.

According to Octavio Paz:

> Coatlicue's trajectory – from goddess to demon, from demon to monster and from monster to masterpiece – illustrates the changes in sensitivity we [Westerners] have experienced over the past four hundred years. ... Since the late eighteenth century Coatlicue has abandoned the magnetic territory of the supernatural to penetrate the corridors of aesthetical and anthropological speculation; she is no longer the crystallization of the underworld's powers and has become an episode in the history of the beliefs of man. By leaving the temple for the museum, she changes in nature though not in appearance. (1995:76)

Modern Western aesthetics, which has re-evaluated African masks and Polynesian carvings, has taught us that the *otherness* imposed upon the aboriginal past is resolved whenever its artistic creations, apparently so distant from ours, turn wonderfully real in our present.

In the early nineteenth century the liberal, anti-colonial, and republican Latin American political discourse regarded the pre-Columbian past equivalent to the cultural origins of European civilization as an argument for ideological legitimacy. In some cases, it appealed to the alleged arrival of colonizing groups from Atlantis, Egypt or Greece; in others, the existence of monumental ruins could only be the result of societies with a sophisticated artistic and intellectual development, and the product of religious beliefs parallel to the paganism of the Classical world. Those who were interested in the Indian past had, on the one hand, to turn archaeological remains into the heritage of the new republics and build a common identity and an autonomous politico-cultural project (see Amigo 2001). On the other, they had to link the contemporary indigenous populations – impoverished and marginalized after centuries of colonial domination – with a splendrous history made evident through monumental material remains.

In the second half of the nineteenth century, positivism (particularly in its "Scientism"[1] variant) and Darwinism grew in strength as scientific tools to interpret reality, and fostered the belief that the proclaimed disappearance of "primitives" in the face of progress was a consequence of the survival of the fittest in the struggle for existence. This notion emphasized the seemingly negative components of indigenous populations, which explained the late arrival of modernity in Latin America. Archaeology showed the artistic and technological achievements of bygone populations who, because of their prehistoric remoteness, also were testimony to the unchallengeable extinction of the "backward peoples" by the overwhelming expansion of "universal history."

By the end of the nineteenth century dating the past was a crucial issue in prehistoric research, and it was the German scholar Max Uhle who established the first archaeological chronology in the Andes (Rowe 1998). In 1893, he traveled to South America for the Ethnographic Museum of Berlin to acquire archaeological collections in Bolivia and northwest Argentina, and remained in the region for over forty years, devoting himself to archaeological research, with the exception of a few short trips to the United States.[2] His idea of chronology was innovative: "In Americanist studies, the first thing that had to be done was to introduce the idea of time, to get people to admit that the types could change" (cited in Willey and Sabloff 1980:73). Uhle proposed a relative chronology of almost pan-Andean scope following on from the local sequences – which he named "chronological horizons" – that he linked by means of the presence of two widely extended styles: Tiwanaku and Inca (Rowe 1998). His methodological criterion lay in the appropriate mastery of both stratigraphy and gravelot seriation, this latter technique developed by Flinders Petrie (Willey and Sabloff 1980). Uhle was greatly helped by being unhampered by the parochial view of most local archaeologists, and could acknowledge the existence of a history of prehistoric Peru that was not limited to the providential Inca prelude preceded by a generalized savagery and mysterious megalithic empires. According to Uhle, in spite of some undeniable differences, their common pre-Columbian roots closely linked Ecuador, Peru, Bolivia, Chile, and Argentina (Kaulicke 1998:29–30).

In the same period, the Argentinean Juan Bautista Ambrosetti, strongly influenced by the paleontologist and paleoanthropologist Florentino Ameghino's notion of time, established a relative chronology in the archeological site of Pampa Grande, Salta (Ambrosetti 1906), applying the grave-lot seriation method that Flinders Petrie had used in Egypt; shortly afterwards, the National University at La Plata published the Spanish translation of two of Petrie's methodological articles (Petrie 1907a, 1907b).

Leaving aside Uhle's hypothesis that the origin of the coastal Andean civilization was a diffusion from the Mayan area, Julio C. Tello (1921) interpreted Peruvian archaeology from an *indigenista* and autochthonous perspective. After years of research in the Sierra Central, he proposed Chavín as the mother culture of the Andean civilization, whose emergence was to be sought in the tropical rainforests east of the Andes (Lumbreras 1989). The idea of continuity of the historical process meant that the archaeological record was interpreted as a function of the notion of Nation, inasmuch as, according to Tello himself:

European civilization makes efforts to construct the Nation on the Spanish or Latin traditions, leaving aside the foundations left by aboriginal civilizations. ... [and] not properly employing the knowledge and methods of Science, which would allow us to get acquainted with our land and our history, to subjugate the selfishness of man, to establish

the economical balance of the social classes and, thus, to strengthen our nationality. ...
Our present Hispano-Peruvian civilization can only be erected on the indigenous pedestal.
(1921:48)

In Mexico, Manuel Gamio has been considered one of the first *indigenista* scientists
because of his active position as an anthropologist in favor of the Indian population.
During the first decades of the Mexican Revolution he organized the governmental
institutions devoted to archaeology and anthropology (Marzal 1986:404–410). Gamio,
who met Franz Boas at the International School of American Archaeology and Ethnology in Mexico City, carried out the first stratigraphic excavation at Azcapotzalco that
enabled him to postulate a cultural sequence and a relative chronology for the Valley
of Mexico. In 1922 he published the results of his investigations in the valley of
Teotihuacan, an integrated research project that ranged from the first pre-Columbian
settlers to the present inhabitants (Gamio 1922). He thought that archaeology was
important inasmuch as culture – thought of as a complex of traits – was the foundation of Indian identity. Consequently, knowledge of pre-Columbian civilizations would
explain the characteristics of today's ethnic population: "the knowledge of which undoubtedly represents the true gospel of good government" (Gamio 1916:59).

With the financial support of the Carnegie Institute, in 1924 Silvanus Morley began
his excavations at Chichén Itzá (Yucatan), and for the first time undertook the reconstruction of the main buildings. His project was designed to increase the confidence of
the Mexican people and government in foreign scientific institutions, while simultaneously bearing witness to the artistic advances of the pre-Columbian Maya (Bernal
1979:169). The ideological manipulation of the monumental reconstructions – which
had more than just a few followers – began an extended and heated controversy.

As in Chavín in the central Andes, the discovery of the Olmec culture (Stirling 1939)
posed the problem of diffusion vis-à-vis autonomous development with regard to the
origins of Mesoamerican civilization. The Olmec evidence questioned both the chronology and the origins of the Maya calendar, and revealed the existence of a monumental architecture and wide-ranging and sophisticated art. The archaeologist Alfonso Caso
and the artist and museologist Miguel Covarrubias played crucial roles in the acceptance of the Olmec culture as the foundation of Mesoamerican civilization; an issue that
within the political context of the time represented the recognition of an *indigenista* and
autochthonous point of view.

After the victory of the Mexican Revolution, the new nationalistic values in science
and art were made evident in the mural paintings of Orozco and Rivera, Carlos
Chávez's music, and Manuel Gamio's anthropology (Matos Moctezuma 1972:8). In
Latin America at the beginning of the twentieth century, socialism and nationalism
were the expressions of an incipient working class and of the new middle classes.
Utopias of miscegenation began to appear, such as *Eurindia* by Ricardo Rojas (1953,
1971 [1909], 1980[1924]), and *La raza cósmica* by José Vasconcelos (1948 [1925]). José
Carlos Mariátegui (1979 [1928]) imagined a future society based on a type of pre-
Columbian socialism, and Luis Valcárcel (1972 [1927]) – archaeologist, ethnohistorian,
and politician – believed that the city of Cuzco would redeem the Indian. Art and
architecture in the versions of the Prehispanic world constructed by archaeologists
became sources of inspiration (Gutiérrez and Gutiérrez Viñuales 2000), such as

Andean textiles for the Uruguayan painter Joaquín Torres García, Chac Mool for Henry Moore, Martín Chambi's *indigenista* photography (Hopkinson 2001), Maya architecture for Frank Lloyd Wright (Braun 1993), and the *Ollantay* tragedy by Ricardo Rojas (1939).[3] In several countries archaeology's commitment to the social struggle had become part of the project of a new nation, while in others it encouraged the dream of political utopias.

In the 1940s, Mexican nationalism drifted away from the social justice promised by the Revolution and accelerated the advancement of capitalism (Halperín Donghi 1998), while official archaeology opted for monumental reconstructions pandering to the tourist. In those years Pedro Armillas, guided by the ideas of V. Gordon Childe, raised the issue of the economic and social foundations of Mesoamerican civilizations; and by turning to archaeological records and historic documents, he reconstructed archaeological landscapes, ancient agrarian technologies, and hydraulic systems. In his own words:

> the effort of most research was focused exclusively on the ceremonial aspects of the Mesoamerican civilizations and their artistic expressions … . In the future, we should try harder to study the basic techniques and the economic factors involved in the formation of any culture and in the evolutionary changes that took place within them … and to stimulate interest in many important issues, such as the spatial and temporal distribution of the different kinds of crops, their comparative significance in economic life, the importance of change in tools and the implications of social and settlement patterns. (1991 [1948]: 143)

No doubt the issues addressed by Armillas originated in his ideological and political experience during the Spanish Civil War, together with a fresh reading of Childe (see Alonso and Baranda 1984; Durand 1987; Rojas 1987); his investigations were a landmark in the archaeology of the Americas (see Litvak and Mirambell 2000 and Rojas Rabiela 1991).

Between 1940 and 1970 two versions of the culture-history archaeology expanded and consolidated in Latin America. The American variant was accepted more widely, while the Austro-German was restricted to the Southern Cone (Politis 1995). The American culture-history production is best represented in several books edited or written by North American scholars: *The Handbook of South American Indians* edited by Julian Steward (1946–50); Sol Tax's collection of articles (1962 [1951]), Alfonso Caso, Irving Rouse, and Gordon Willey; Gordon Willey's *An Introduction to American Archaeology* (1996); and *Aboriginal Development in Latin America: An Interpretative Review*, edited by Betty Meggers and Clifford Evans (1963), which includes many papers written by Latin American archaeologists. A particularly paradigmatic piece of culture-history research was that carried out by Bennett, Bleiler, and Sommer (1948) in northwestern Argentina, where the notion of the "co-tradition area" was applied:

> The term "co-tradition area" has been used for this overall history of an area in which the component cultures have been interrelated over a period of time. The co-tradition area approach assumes cultural continuity within the region and mutual influence of the component cultures, both in space and time. … So far, only two co-tradition areas have

been described for South America, namely, for the Central Andes and for northwestern Argentina. (Bennett 1962 [1951])

Taking the ideas of Bennett and his co-workers in the area as a starting point, Alberto Rex González was able to widen and systematize the cultural sequence, and obtain an absolute chronology that perhaps constitutes the best example of American culture-historical archaeology in Latin America (González 1955, 1960, 1963a, 1963b, 1965, 1979, 1980, 1999). In other countries, North American culture history was a primary tool for systematizing and organizing extant knowledge (see, e.g., Cruxent and Rouse 1958–9 and Wagner 1967 for Venezuela).

After World War II the United States consolidated its economic and cultural hegemony in Latin America, which increased the presence of North American archaeologists, particularly in the Andes and Mesoamerica. Their investigations provided more systematic and reliable data, but they also imposed upon local scholars an exclusively culture-historical theoretical and methodological approach. While analyzing this process it seems advisable to avoid ideological stereotypes and simplistic political generalizations, as well as to take into consideration the different theoretical branches of North American archaeology and the personal attitudes of the researchers involved.

Even though American culturalism prevailed almost exclusively in Latin American archaeology, by the late 1940s the Austrian school of *Kulturkreise* became strong in Argentina (and from there influenced the Southern Cone), and dominated archaeological research in the Pampas, the River Plate Basin, and Patagonia for many decades (Bórmida 1960, 1969; Menghin 1956; Menghin and Bórmida 1950). This was a direct consequence of the arrival of Oswald Menghin in Argentina after World War II.[4] Subsequently, alternative local perspectives evolved (i.e., Madrazo 1973), together with the local development of typological methodology (Aschero 1975).

Between Processualism and Marxism

During the late 1970s, some of the pioneering ideas of processual archaeology spread to Latin America, including the work of Binford (1962, 1977, 1978), Clarke (1968), Schiffer (1976), and Flannery (1976). However, both the American and Austrian culture-history approaches were still predominantly popular (Bonnin and Laguens 1984–5). Latin American archaeologists under the influence of processualism redefined their objectives and continued to relinquish specific social realities. In this new setting Latin America provided data that were used for one of the main objectives of early processual archaeology: the construction of cross-cultural and ahistorical regularities, or law-like propositions. Immersed in the enthusiasm and optimism of early processualism, many embraced the hypothetico-deductive-nomological chimera, but only a limited number made any serious attempt to apply this theory and methodology in a rigorous and consistent manner.

It is important to point out that processual archaeology has been criticized within Latin America, although in some cases it has been defended by the opinions of well-known foreign scholars, such as the case of the translation of Bayard's text (1983). More original and accurate analyses of the failures and limitations of the processual program have been exposed by the "Latin American social archaeologists"[5] (notably Gándara 1980, 1981), while other isolated criticisms were also published before the expansion of postprocessualism in Latin America (i.e., Crivelli Montero 1990; Lorenzo 1976a,b).

An interesting and atypical case is that of Brazil, where American culture history took root thanks to the endeavors of Betty Meggers and Clifford Evans, who founded and supported for many years the PRONAPA (Programa Nacional de Pesquisas Arqueológicas) and PRONAPABA (Programa Nacional de Pesquisas Arqueológicas na Bacía Amazónica) programs for regional research (Meggers 1992). Within the framework of these projects, the first generation of Brazilian professional archaeologists and academicians was formed and produced, between 1960 and 1980, a significant amount of original and systematic data which laid the foundations for subsequent research. Some of the new generation of Brazilian archaeologists have been fairly critical of PRONAPA (Barreto 1999; Funari 1992, 1995; Neves 1999), mostly for what they consider to be a lack of external evaluation of their production (see Meggers 1992, 2001 for a different point of view). However, whether or not this criticism were true, Brazilian archaeology remained on the track of American culture history, with a strong cultural ecology component. Meanwhile, in the 1970s a heated debate on processual archaeology was taking place in Anglo-Saxon countries, which slowly influenced archaeology in several areas in Latin America; and in Peru, Venezuela, the Dominican Republic, and Mexico a regional school of thought – "Latin American social archaeology" – was evolving. It was only with the second generation of professional archaeologists, and mainly in the early 1990s, that the processual debate began to take place in Brazil, shortly followed by postprocessual archaeology, which is still in its early stages (Funari 1995).

Undoubtedly, the repercussions of processual influence were not identical in all countries. In Peru, Mexico, and Venezuela, for instance, the impact of processual archaeology was muted, among other reasons, by the development of this "Latin American social archaeology"; a trend based on V. Gordon Childe's Marxism (Bate 1978; Lorenzo, Pérez Elias, and García Bárcena 1976; Lumbreras 1974; Sanoja and Vargas Arenas 1974), the significance and relevance of which have been the subject of recent debate (see Benavides 2001; McGuire and Navarrete 1999; Oyuela-Caycedo et al. 1997; Patterson 1992, 1997; Politis 2003). Within Latin America, "Latin American social archaeology" is of special interest because of its criticism of the theoretical subordination of archaeology in the continent, the questioning of the culture-history epistemology and the revindication of a radical political posture vis-à-vis social problems. In terms of characterization, McGuire and Navarrete (1999) have painted an exaggeratedly optimistic picture by using the image of Che Guevara – revolutionary, socially engaged, realistic – as its metaphor. In contrast, they represent Anglo-Saxon radical archaeology with the image of James Dean – nihilistic, individualistic, and socially negligible.

"Latin American social archaeology" has systematically incorporated Marxist thinking into contemporary Latin American archaeology, mainly through Childe's work. It is important to highlight both its sharp and reflexive criticism, and its originality and independence of thought, particularly in the pioneering works by Lumbreras (1974) and Lorenzo (Lorenzo, Pérez Elias, and García Bárcena 1976). However, the everyday practice of most Latin American social archaeologists is limited to the academic milieu, far from the arena of social conflict. In this sense, it is a valid argument that "there are few social archaeologists who in practice assume this commitment [of knowing, explaining and helping social change], as they tend to focus on the scientific explanation of reality independently of the progressive or reactionary use that the knowledge they generate is put to" (Fournier 1999:20). Moreover, while classifying and interpreting the data, it is common for social archaeologists to turn to conceptual and analytical categories of American culturalism (Cuban archaeology is an illuminating example; see Guarch 1987).

"Latin American social archaeology" has had little influence on the development of the radical, critical, and Anglo-Saxon Marxist archaeologies, which are based on the classic works by Marx and Engels and the French Marxists. As Fournier (1999) has stated, the lack of consideration of Hispano-American contributions in the many studies that have analyzed the use of concepts and principles derived from Marxism in world archaeology is astonishing. Among the few exceptions are the works by Patterson (1994, 1997) and McGuire (1992), who have acknowledged and widely discussed the contributions of their Latin American Marxist colleagues.

As one of us has argued elsewhere (Politis 1995), the variable influence of processual archaeology in Latin America has always been related to the overall political situation. Under military dictatorships – the situation in many Latin American countries during the 1970s and the 1980s – processual archaeology helped to break with the prevailing culture-historical orientation (but see the discussion above), inasmuch as processualism, from the standpoint of the search for objectivity and asepsis grounded in the "scientific method," was not considered to be as dangerous as "Latin American social archaeology" by the military governments.

Mexico and Peru hosted several generations of North American archaeologists committed to processual archaeology, but who maintained rather distant contact with the community and an asymmetrical relationship with local scholars. The administration of funds and resources, in addition to the participation of local archaeologists as trainees,[6] generated situations of dependence and inequality, even though the inclusion of local researchers was a necessary condition for securing permits. However, as we know, in bureaucratic decisions the quality of projects or the backgrounds of the directors do not always prevail (see Manzanilla 1992:13). This process of complex asymmetrical relationships has undergone a number of changes and has been analyzed from different perspectives (see Burger 1989; Lorenzo 1976a,b, 1981). Nevertheless, one should not consider Latin American archaeology as merely a passive and mechanical reflection of what happens in central countries: an example is the original and broad perspective of the research carried out by the Mexican archaeologist Linda Manzanilla on the emergence of early urban societies (Manzanilla 1997). Nor do we share Bate's simplistic views, when he states: "In practice, real and everyday archaeology [presumably in Latin America] is still over ninety percent particularist-historical, and, at the most, vulgarly evolutionist. In short, antiquated traditional" (2001:xix).

Postprocessual Approaches, Critical Reflection And The Re-Emergence of Social Archaeology in the 1990s

The heterodoxy of so-called "postprocessual" archaeology questions the epistemological foundations of processualism – its dependence on ecological models and its positivist foundations – and encourages critical reflection in archaeology. It argues for the replacement of the standard notion of objectivity with a perspective in which the production of knowledge is constrained by local contexts and conditions (Preucel and Hodder 1999:526). Postprocessualism is still at an early stage and is not central in Latin American contemporary debate (for exceptions, see Gnecco 1999a, 1999b; Haber 1997). However, among the research problems posed by postprocessual archaeology, there are subjects that seem relevant for Latin American social archaeology, and which have caught the attention of local and foreign archaeologists. Thus, issues of gender, multivocality, ethnicity, and human agency have begun to be considered, and even though such studies are still in their infancy[7] (i.e., Gero 1991; Hastorf 1991; Wüst 1999; Zarankin and Acuto 1999), they contain a reflective potential for ethics and the implications of professional practice.

In Brazil, the explicit social components of archaeological praxis only began to emerge more clearly in the 1990s through the lens of postprocessualism. Funari and Orser initiated a study of the maroon settlements in the region of Palmares, with the purpose of clarifying aspects of their social and cultural life (Allen 1995; Funari 1999; Orser 1992; Orser and Funari 1992). This project aimed to give visibility and historical legitimacy to the Afro-American population of Brazil, who fought the Europeans from the beginning for their freedom and independence, and maintained connections with Indian groups.

Forensic archaeology provides an interesting example of the social impact of archaeology, and, even though not postprocessual theoretical development, is directly related to social commitment. In the 1970s, Argentina, Bolivia, Brazil, Chile, Uruguay, and most of the Central American republics underwent periods of intense violence and repression. During the 1980s and 1990s, some of these countries successively initiated processes of democratization that promoted investigations into the human rights' violations of the recent past. In 1983, the newly elected democratic government of Argentina created the National Commission on Disappeared Persons (CONADEP) which, with the help of a delegation of the American Association for the Advancement of Science (AAAS) led by Clyde Snow, helped to establish the Argentine Forensic Anthropology Team (EAAF). This group was created to meet the historical need to exhume and attempt to identify the thousands of *desaparecidos* in Argentina. The presence of archaeologists in the EAAF was crucial to the task, as they had unique expertise in the recovery of human remains and associated evidence in a detailed and systematic manner, employing appropriate recording techniques in order to use the findings in a court of law. Suddenly, these archaeologists, trained in rigidly controlled universities under a military government, with the assistance of an American scientist, became a vital tool for providing conclusive and legally valid evidence that enabled the military juntas and other, higher-ranking military officers to be tried and sentenced. In 1987 the EAAF expanded its activities beyond Argentina and participated in investigations in many Latin American countries, as well as other parts of the world (Cohen Salama 1991). Notably, the activities of the EAAF in the post-dictatorship era have consolidated a new field in the application of archaeology in the continent, and generated new types of social demands on archaeologists. In fact, the investigations carried out by forensic archaeologists did not only help the victims' families with their right to recover the remains and histories of their loved ones, enabling them to hold the customary funeral and mourn their dead. They also contributed significantly to the recovery of the recent past, which had been distorted and veiled by the political parties or governments that were, in turn, implicated in the criminal acts under investigation (da Silva Catela 2001).

The most remarkable contributions of the postprocessual perspective have undoubtedly been the development of reflexive attitudes regarding the connotations and uses of archaeology, together with a delegitimization of hegemonic discourses of the past. Both have helped sensitize archaeologists to social problems and have given them a more open attitude toward other groups and marginalized segments of society. However, as far as the production of information and the generation of patterns or concepts are concerned, whether through interrogating the archaeological record or for data analysis and interpretation, postprocessual archaeology in Latin America has so far made no significant contribution.

Final Comments

Archaeology is a part of the scientific development of Western culture, and one of the most elaborate expressions of temporal thinking (Gnecco 1999b). As such, it has been a tool for social subordination that bestows legitimacy on science alone. Indigenous myths and visions of the cosmos are considered exoticisms or objects of scientific inquiry, rather than a different and legitimate way of perceiving the world. In historical terms, archaeology in Latin America was born into the colonial remit of the search for the exotic, explaining difference and appropriating the past and the material culture of the dominated "other" (Florescano 1993; Trigger 1980, 1989). This legacy still clouds a portion of the theory and practice of archaeology, both local and from overseas.

Even though there have been different ways of practicing archaeology in Latin America, its relevance so far has been quite limited and, with few exceptions, it has lacked the development of theoretical subjects (see the discussion in Politis 2003). To some, this is explained by the absence of a "critical mass" of researchers; they argue that it is necessary to count on a minimum total number of archaeologists, in the assumption that a percentage of them may start to produce theory. This is erroneous, as there are more archaeologists in the countries of the Southern Cone than in the universities of the United Kingdom, yet the latter have a much higher density of theoretical production. Our idea is that the lack of a "theoretical intention" among Latin American archaeologists is the consequence of their intellectual subordination, which is, in turn, the social reflection of the politico-economic dependency of the countries in the region. Latin American archaeologists produce information and, exceptionally, a more elaborate pattern or conceptual tool. Similarly, Latin American countries produce raw materials, and occasionally provide cheap labor for less complex industrial manufacturing processes. In most Latin American countries, archaeology is dependent on the state for its funding, subordinating it to political power. Any scientific field that lacks autonomy will not develop a tradition, which has long been understood as a long-established practice of original and innovative thinking (Bourdieu 1997).

Given the characteristics of education and the state of indigenous communities, there is nothing that can be labeled as an "indigenous archaeology." It is the Western discipline of archaeology that has ignored other ways of investigating the past and failed to provide a meaning for the material culture of many indigenous societies. Up to now, alternative ways of exhibiting and spreading archaeological knowledge have been scarce (see Núñez Atencio 2001; Podgorny 1999). An example is the experience of the community of Santa Ana del Valle (Oaxaca, Mexico), whose members designed and built their own local museum with the technical assistance of the National School of Anthropology and History (ENAH) and the National Institute of Anthropology and History (INAH). Another example, in Argentina, was the excavation of graves in Añelo (Neuquén), where archaeologists and the Mapuche Indians worked together for the conservation of cultural remains. The local indigenous community was left in charge of the administration of the site museum (Bisset 1989; Cúneo and Rodriguez de Tocigliani 1993). A landmark in the process of the recognition of indigenous people's rights to their cultural heritage in Argentina was the decision adopted by the National Park Service (APN) in 2000 to give the Ñorquinco Mapuche community custody of their sacred site, situated in the Lanín National Park, Neuquén. This decision marked a substantial change in the APN's attitude toward the indigenous people; for the Mapuche communities it meant the recovery of a ceremonial site – a *rehue* (from *re*, genuine, exclusive; and *hue*, place) – where they had performed *camarucos* (ritual gatherings) before they were forced to abandon it when the park was created more than sixty years before. Nevertheless, the Santa Ana del Valle Museum, the Añelo Museum, and the Lanín National Park are exceptional cases in Latin America, where archaeology is generally characterized by ignorance of, and disregard for, indigenous peoples' concern about their archaeological heritage (see the discussion in Endere 2002).

The most significant postprocessual contribution to Latin American archaeology is not the production of abundant and original knowledge different to that of the culture-historical or processual approaches. Rather, it is the delegitimization of hegemonic archaeological discourse, the criticism of the existence of only one way of seeing the past, and the rejection of a positivism that considers the generation of knowledge as devoid of political intentionality. Critical reflection of professional practice and the political implications – intentional or otherwise – of the results of research have at least begun to be discussed (for instance, at the First and Second International Meeting of South American Archaeological Theory). In turn, a few archaeological museums have begun to reflect the plural interpretations of the past and to give a voice to other cultural actors (a typical case is an exhibition at the Ethnographic Museum, University of Buenos Aires). Some of these institutions have ceased to be the repositories of the "spoils of war" of European colonization of indigenous societies, and have become places of reflection and revalorization of a plural, non-hegemonic history. James Volkert (1997), from the National Museum of the American Indian (the Smithsonian Institution, Washington, DC), has stated that museums should give the right to speak to those centrally involved – Native Americans, in the case of his institution – so that they can collaborate at the same level as technicians and researchers.

In general, contemporary Latin American archaeology constructs the regional archaeological past on the basis of foreign research agendas, which rarely pose the need to link the research with the historical and social problems of the region. But one must simultaneously warn against an aggressive and militant indigenist fundamentalism that has emerged in many countries, based on a biased interpretation of archaeological data, and which has little to do with pluralism and respect for "otherness."

The scientific contributions of Latin American archaeologists are undeniable, as they encompass the study of hunter-gatherers from the Late Pleistocene to the analysis of state societies, not to mention the contributions of symbolic archaeology, ethnoarchaeology, taphonomy, and forensic studies. However, these accomplishments are introduced in academic discussions as mere data or scattered hypotheses – rarely as compact theoretical models – which are then reelaborated in the central countries, mainly the United States. The potential of this knowledge as a tool for social change is lost within the labyrinths of "universal science." The few exceptions occur in the field of practice, and represent isolated and individual efforts from those who are committed to their work and seek modes of social transference. Such is the case, for instance, of forensic archaeology, or the efforts of some archaeologists to ensure that the knowledge they generate helps to improve the living standards of the communities with whom they work (i.e., Alvarez 1985; Erickson 1988, 1992; Olivera and Tchilinguirian 2000). Other, isolated attempts include the promotion of plans for sustainable development in archaeological areas, such as the Serra do Capibara National Park, Brazil.

Latin American archaeology seeks to "globalize" itself theoretically and methodologically in order to be included in the world discussion; but it simultaneously strengthens its dependency on the hegemonic countries by following the direction of the Anglo-American agenda – a subordination that usually leaves little room for originality and which reinforces the role of Latin American archaeologists as data-generators, but not as knowledge producers or agents of social change. Archaeology in the region remains in a condition similar to that described by Langebaeck (1996:12) for Colombian archaeology, when he defined it as a "two-fold marginality" in relation to both the international academy and the social issues of the region (see also Politis 2001).

We believe in the legitimacy of archaeology as a producer of knowledge of the past, and in the elaboration of a coherent and ethical discourse on how to transmit such knowledge. But what we do question is the hegemony of that discourse, the dissociation from local interests, and the political naiveté of the culture-historical and processual approaches. The political implications of archaeological knowledge were clearly understood by the founders of Latin American museums in the late nineteenth century, and continued to be, although in a different way, by the indigenist movements during the first decades of the twentieth century. However, this knowledge has slowly faded away almost to the point of extinction as a result of the dominance of processual archaeology in the 1980s and 1990s.

The question is whether Latin American archaeology is in a position to drop its dependency and build a project of its own, more deeply connected to local and regional interests rather than the concerns of Anglo-Saxon and Western European societies and academia. At present, the answer is far from clear, but everything seems to indicate that the Latin American scientific community will find it difficult to free itself from its subjugation, chiefly because the political and economic world is becoming increasingly "globalized," and this, in Latin America, can only lead to greater dependency.

ACKNOWLEDGMENTS

I would like to thank Ben Alberti and Xavier Martini for their comments, and for help with the translation.

NOTES

1 Scientism is the idea that the scientific spirit and methods are to be extended, without exception, to all realms of intellectual and moral life (Soler 1968:19–29).
2 In 1907 he published the results of his pioneering excavation using the stratigraphic method at Emeryville shell mound in San Francisco Bay, California (Willey and Sabloff 1980:55).
3 "According to my own aesthetic doctrine of *Eurindia*, I had to combine the most authentic indigenous substance with the most relevant theatrical piece created by the Greeks" (Rojas 1939:12).
4 For a review of Menghin's political activity before his arrival in Argentina, and how this was strongly related to his research objectives, see Arnold 1990 and Kohl and Pérez Gollán 2002.
5 This regional theoretical trend in archaeological thinking is placed between quotation marks to differentiate it from the wider notion of Latin American social archaeology as discussed in this chapter.
6 Even though, according to Lorenzo (1976a,b), little can be learned from any of them.
7 Probably with the exception of the gender studies in Mesoamerica, which are more than a decade old.

REFERENCES

Allen, S. 1995. Africanism, Mosaics and Creativity: The Historical Archaeology of Palmares. Unpublished MA thesis, Brown University, Providence, RI.

Alonso, M. S., and M. Baranda. 1984. *Palabras del exilio, 3. Contribución a la historia de los refugiados españoles en México. Seis antropólogos mexicanos.* México, DF: Departamento de Estudios Contemporáneos del INAH.

Alvarez, S. 1985. *Tecnología Prehispánica, Naturaleza y Organización Cooperativa en la Cuenca del Guayaí.* Guayaquil: CEAA-EPSOL, Colección Peñón del Río.

Ambrosetti, J. B. 1906. *Exploraciones arqueológicas en la Pampa Grande.* Buenos Aires: Facultad de Filosofía y Letras, Universidad de Buenos Aires, Publicaciones de la Sección Antropológica 1.

—— 1907. *Exploraciones arqueológicas en la ciudad prehistórica de La Paya.* Buenos Aires: Facultad de Filosofía y Letras, Universidad de Buenos Aires, Publicaciones de la Sección Antropológica 3.

Amigo, R. 2001. *Tras un inca. Los funerales de Atahualpa de Luis Montero en Buenos Aires.* Buenos Aires: Telefónica y Fundación para la Investigación del Arte Argentino (FIAAR).

Armillas, P. 1991 [1948]. Una secuencia del desarrollo cultural en Mesoamérica. In T. Rojas Rabiela (ed.), *Pedro Armillas: Vida y obra.* México, DF: CIESAS–INAH, pp. 143–158.

Arnold, B. 1990. The past as propaganda: Totalitarian archaeology in Nazi Germany. *Antiquity* 64: 464–478.

Aschero, C. 1975. *Ensayo para una clasificación morfológica de artefactos líticos aplicada a estudios tipológicos comparativos.* Buenos Aires: manuscript report to CONICET.

Barreto, C. 1999. Arqueología brasileira: Uma perspectiva histórica e comparada. In M. I. D'Agostino Fleming, *Revista do Museu de Arqueologia e Etnologia. Anais da I Reunião Internacional de Teoria Arqueológica na América do Sul.* São Paulo: MAE, pp. 201–212.

Bate, F. 1977. *Arqueología y Materialismo Histórico.* México, DF: Ediciones de Cultura Popular.

——1978. *Sociedad, Formación Económico-Social y Cultura.*, México, DF: Ediciones de Cultura Popular.

——2001. Teorías y métodos en Arqueología. ¿Criticar o proponer? In *Actas del XIII Congreso Nacional de Arqueología Argentina*, Vol. 1. Córdoba, Argentina, pp. XVII–XXIV.

Bayard, D. 1983. La "nueva arqueología." Una historia crítica. *Scripta Ethnologica. Supplementa* 2: 9–27.

Benavides, H. O. 2001. Returning to the source: Social archaeology as Latin American philosophy. *Latin American Antiquity* 12: 355–370.

Bennett, W. C. 1962 [1951]. New World culture history: South America. In S. Tax (ed.), *Anthropology Today: Selections.* Chicago: University of Chicago Press, pp. 195–209.

——, E. Bleiler, and F. H. Sommer. 1948. *North West Argentine Archaeology.* New Haven, CT: Yale University Publications in Anthropology.

Bernal, I. 1979. *Historia de la arqueología en México.* México, DF: Editorial Porrúa.

Binford, L. 1962. Archaeology as anthropology. *American Antiquity* 28: 217–225.

——(ed.) 1977. *For Theory Building in Archaeology: Essays in Archaeology.* New York: Academic Press.

——1978. *Nunamiut Ethnoarchaeology.* New York: Academic Press.

Bisset, A. M. 1989. El Museo de Añelo. Paper presented at the Jornadas sobre el Uso del Pasado, Faculated de Ciencias Naturales y Museo, UNLP, La Plata, Argentina.

Bonnin, M., and A. Laguens, 1984–5. Acerca de la arqueología Argentina de los últimos 20 años a través de las citas bibliográficas en las revistas Relaciones y Anales de Arqueología y Etnología. *Relaciones de la Sociedad Argentina de Antropología* XVI (nueva serie): 7–25. Buenos Aires.

Bórmida, M. 1960. *Prolegómeros para una arqueología de la Pampa Bonaerense.* Boletín de la dirección de Museos de la Provincia de Buenos Aires, La Plata.

——1969. El Puntarrubiense. *Trabajos de Prehistoria* 26: 1–116.

Boschín, M. T., and A. M. Llamazares, 1984. La escuela histórico-cultural como factor retardatario del desarrollo cientifico de la arqueología Argentina. *Etnía* 32: 101–156. Olavarría.

Bourdieu, P. 1997. *Les Usages Sociaux de la Science. Pour une Sociologie Clinique du Champ Scientifique.* Paris: Institut National de la Recherche Agronomique (INRA).

Braun, B. 1993. *Pre-Columbian Art and the Post-Columbian World. Ancient American Sources of Modern Art.* New York: H. N. Abrams.

Burger, R. L. 1989. An overview of Peruvian archaeology (1976–1986). *Annual Review of Anthropology* 18: 37–69.

Cabrera Pérez, L. 1988. Arqueología de Rescate en el Este Uruguayo. Departamento de Rocha. Unpublished paper delivered to the Universidad Nacional de La Plata.

Caso, A. 1962 [1951]. New World culture history: Middle America. In S. Tax (ed.), *Anthropology Today: Selections.* Chicago: University of Chicago Press, pp. 210–221.

Chaves Chamorro, M. 1986. *Trayectoria de la Antropología Colombiana.* Bogotá: Guadalupe.

Clarke, D. L. 1968. *Analytical Archaeology.* London: Methuen.

Cohen Salama, M. 1991. *Tumbas Anónimas.* Buenos Aires: Catálogos.

Crivelli Montero, E. 1990. Un campo de huesos secos: La arqueología Argentina en el último decenio. In C. E. Berbeglia (ed.), *Propuestas para una Antropología Argentina.* Buenos Aires: Editorial Biblos, pp. 111–131.

Cruxent, J. M., and I. Rouse, 1958–9. An archeological chronology of Venezuela. *Social Science Monographs* 1: 2–39.

Cúneo, E., and M. Rodríguez de Torcigliani. 1993. Evidencias prehistóricas: Antiguo poblamiento y coexistencia cultural. In S. Bandieri and O. Favaro (eds.), *Historia del Neuquén.* Buenos Aires: Plus Ultra, pp. 11–63.

da Silva Catela, L. 2001. *No habrá flores en la tumba del pasado. La experiencia de reconstrucción del mundo de los familiares de desaparecidos.* La Plata: Ediciones Al Margen.

Durand, J. 1987. Por una antropología pedestre (entrevista a Pedro Armillas). In J. L. Rojas (ed.), *La Aventura Intelectual de Pedro Armillas. Visión Antropológica de la Historia de América.* Guadalajara: Colegio de Michoacán, pp. 109–152.

Duviols, P. 1964. El Inca Garcilaso de la Vega intérprete humanista de la religión incaica. *Diógenes* 47: 31–43. Buenos Aires.

—— 1976. Punchao, idolo mayor del Coricancha: Historia y tipología. *Antropología Andina* 1–2: 156–183. Cuzco: Centro de Estudios Andinos.

Echeverría Almeida, J. 1996. *Betty J. Meggers. Personalidades y dilemas en la arqueología ecuatoriana.* Quito: Ediciones Abya-Yala.

Endere, M. L. 2000. *Arqueología y legislación en Argentina. Cómo proteger el patrimonio arqueológico.* Olavarría: INCUAPA, Universidad Nacional del Centro de la Provincia de Buenos Aires.

—— 2002. Management of Archaeological Sites and the Public in Argentina. Unpublished Ph.D. dissertation, University College London.

Erickson, C. 1986. Waru-Waru: Una tecnología agrícola del Altiplano pre-hispánico. In C. De la Torre and M. Bruga (eds.), *Andenes y Camellones en el Perú Andino. Historia Presente y Futuro.* Lima: Consejo Nacional de Ciencia y Tecnología, pp. 59–84.

—— 1988. Raised field agriculture in the lake Titicaca basin. Putting ancient agriculture back to work. *Expedition* 30(3): 8–16.

—— 1992. Applied archaeology and rural development: Archaeology's potential contribution to the future. *Journal of the Steward Anthropological Society* 20 (1–2): 1–16.

Fernández, J. 1982. Historia de la arqueología Argentina. *Anales de Arqueología y Etnología* XXXIV–XXXV (1979–80). Mendoza: Universidad Nacional de Cuyo.

Fernández Leiva, O. 1992. Arqueología de Cuba. In G. Politis (ed.), *Arqueología en America Latina Hoy.* Bogotá: Fondo de Promoción de la Cultura del Banco Popular, pp. 32–44.

Flannery, K. (ed.) 1976. *The Early Mesoamerican Village.* New York: Academic Press.

Florescano, E. (ed.) 1993. *El patrimonio cultural de México.* México, DF: Consejo Nacional para la Cultura y las Artes y Fondo de Cultura Económica.

Fournier, P. 1999. La arqueología social latinoamericana: Caracterización de una posición teórica marxista. In A. Zarankin and F. Acuto (eds.), *Sed Non Saciata. Teoría Social en la Arqueología Latinoamericana Contemporánea.* Buenos Aires: Tridente, pp. 17–32.

Funari, P. 1991. Archaeology in Brazil: Politics and archaeology in a cross-road. *World Archaeological Bulletin* 5: 122–132.

—— 1995. Mixed features of archaeological theory in Brazil. In P. Ucko (ed.), *Theory in Archaeology. A World Perspective.* London and New York: Routledge, pp. 236–250.

—— 1999. Brazilian archaeology. A reappraisal. In G. Politis and B. Alberti (eds.), *Archaeology in Latin America.* London and New York: Routledge, pp. 17–34.

Funari, P. P. A. 1992. La arqueología en Brasil: Política y academia en una encrucijada. In G. Politis (ed.), *Arqueología en América Latina Hoy.* Bogotá: Fondo de Promoción de la Cultura del Banco Popular, pp. 57–69.

Gamio, M. 1916. *Forjando Patria. Pro-nacionalismo.* México, DF: Porrúa Hermanos.

—— 1922. *La población del valle de Teotihuacán.* México, DF: Dirección de Talleres Gráficos de la Secretaría de Educación Pública.

——1972. *Arqueología e indigenismo*. Intro. and sel. Eduardo Matos Moctezuma. México, DF: Sepsetentas, Secretaría de Educación Pública.

Gándara, M. 1980. La vieja Nueva Arqueología (primera parte). *Boletín de Antropología Americana* 2: 7–45. México, DF: Instituto Panamericano de Geografía y Historia.

——1981. La vieja Nueva Arqueología (segunda parte). *Boletín de Antropología Americana* 3: 7–70. México, DF: Instituto Panamericano de Geografía y Historia.

——1998. La interpretación temática y la conservación de patrimonio cultural. In E. Cárdenas (ed.), *Memoria 60 Años de la ENAH*. México, DF: Escuela Nacional de Antropología e Historia, pp. 453–477.

Garcilaso de la Vega, I. 1995 [1609]). *Comentarios reales de los incas*. Ed. C. Araníbar. México, DF: Fondo de Cultura Económica.

Gero, J. 1991. Gender lithics: Women's roles in stone tool production. In J. Gero and M. Conkey (eds.), *Engendering Archaeology. Women in Prehistory*. Oxford: Blackwell, pp. 163–193.

——1992. Feast and females: Gender ideology and political meals in the Andes. *Norwegian Archaeological Review* 25(1): 15–30.

Gnecco, C. 1995. Praxis científica en la periferia. Notas para una historia social de la arqueología colombiana. *Revista Española de Antropología Americana* 25: 9–22.

——1999a. Archaeology and historical multivocality: A reflection from the Colombian multicultural context. In G. G. Politis and B. Alberti (eds.), *Archaeology in Latin America*. London and New York: Routledge, pp. 258–270.

——1999b. *Multivocalidad Histórica. Hacia una Cartografía Postcolonial de la Arqueología*. Bogotá: Universidad de Los Andes.

González, A. R. 1955. Contextos culturales y cronología relativa del área central del N. O. Argentino. (Nota preliminar). *Anales de Arqueología y Etnología* XI: 7–32. Año 1950. Mendoza: Universidad Nacional de Cuyo.

——1960. La estratigrafía de la gruta de Intihuasi (Prov. de San Luis, R. A.) y sus relaciones con otros sitios precerámicos de Sudamérica. *Revista del Instituto de Antropología* I: 6–290. Córdoba, Argentina: Faculated de Filosofía y Letras, Universidad Nacional de Córdoba.

——1963a. Cultural development in northwestern Argentina. In B. J. Meggers and C. Evans (eds.), *Aboriginal Development in Latin America: An Interpretative Review*. Washington, DC: Smithsonian Institution, Smithsonian Miscellaneous Collections 146(1), pp. 103–117.

——1963b. Las tradiciones alfareras del Período Temprano del N. O. Argentino y sus relaciones con las áreas aledañas. *Congreso Internacional de Arqueología de San Pedro de Atacama*. Antofagasta: Anales de la Universidad del Norte 2, pp. 49–65.

——1965. La cultura de La Aguada del N. O. Argentino. *Revista del Instituto de Antropología* II–III: 205–253. 1961–4. Córdoba, Argentina: Facultad de Filosofía y Humanidades, Universidad Nacional de Córdoba.

——1979. Dinámica cultural del N.O. Argentino. Evolución e historia en las culturas del N. O. Argentino. *Antiquitas* 28–29: 1–15. Boletín de la Asociación Amigos del Instituto de Arqueología. Buenos Aires: Faculated de Historia y Letras, Universidad del Salvador.

——1980. Patrones de asentamiento incaicos en una provincia marginal del imperio. Implicancias socio-culturales. *Prehistoric Settlement Pattern Studies: Retrospect and Prospect*. New York: Wenner-Gren Foundation for Anthropological Research, Burg Wartenstein Symposium 86, pp. 1–32.

——1985. Cincuenta años de arqueología del noroeste Argentino (1930–1980): Apuntes de un casi testigo y algo de protagonista. *American Antiquity* 50: 505–517.

——1999. *Cultura de La Aguada. Arqueología y Diseños*. Buenos Aires: Filmediciones Valero.

Guarch, J. M. 1987. *Arqueología de Cuba. Métodos y Sistemas*. La Habana: Editorial de Ciencias Sociales.

Gutiérrez, R., and R. Gutiérrez Viñuales. 2000. Fuentes prehispánicas para la conformación de un arte nuevo en América. *Temas de la Academia Nacional de Bellas Artes*, año 2, número 2. Arte prehispánico: creación, desarrollo y persistencia. Buenos Aires: Academia Nacional de Bellas Artes, pp. 21–32.

Haber, A. 1997. La casa, el sendero y el mundo. Significados culturales de la arqueología, la cultura material y el paisaje en la Puna de Atacama. *Estudios Atacameños* 14: 373–398.

Halperín Donghi, T. 1998. *Historia contemporánea de América Latina*. Madrid: Alianza.

Hastorf, C. 1991. Gender, space and food in prehistory. In J. Gero and M. Conkey (eds.), *Engendering Archaeology. Women in Prehistory*. Oxford: Blackwell Scientific, pp. 132–159.

Hodder, I. 1988. *Interpretaciones en Arqueología. Corrientes Actuales*. Barcelona: Editorial Crítica.

Hopkinson, A. 2001. *Martín Chambi*. Hong Kong: Phaidon.

Kaulicke, P. (ed.). 1998. *Max Uhle y el Antiguo Perú*. Lima: Pontificia Universidad Católica del Perú.

Kohl, P. and C. Fawcett (eds.) 1995. *Nationalism, Politics, and the Practice of Archaeology*. Cambridge: Cambridge University Press.

——, and J. A. Pérez Gollán. 2002. Religion, politics, and prehistory: The life and writings of O. Menghin and their lingering legacy for culture-historical archaeology. *Current Anthropology* 43: 561–586.

Lafaye, J. 1984. *Mesías, cruzadas, utopías. El judeo-cristianismo en las sociedades ibéricas*. México, DF: Fondo de Cultura Económica.

Lamberg-Karlovsky, C. C. (ed.) 1990. *Archaeological Thought in America*. Cambridge: Cambridge University Press.

Langebaeck, C. 1996. La arqueología después de la arqueología en Colombia. En P. Lamus (ed.), *Dos Lecturas Críticas. Arqueología en Colombia*. Bogotá: Fondo de Promoción de la Cultura.

Litvak, J., and L. Mirambell (eds.) 2000. Arqueología, historia y antropología. In *Memoriam José Luis Lorenzo Bautista*. México, DF: Colección Científica. Instituto Nacional de Antropología e Historia.

Lorenzo, J. L. 1976. La arqueología mexicana y los arqueólogos norteamericanos. *Cuadernos de Trabajo. Apuntes para la Arqueología* 14. México, DF: Departamento de Prehistoria, INAH.

——1981. Archaeology south of the Rio Grande. *World Archaeology* 13: 190–208.

Lorenzo, J. L. (ed.). 1976. *Hacia una Arqueología Social. Reunión de Teotihuacan (octubre de 1975)*. México, DF: Instituto Nacional de Antropología e Historia.

——, A. Pérez Elías, and J. García Bárcena. 1976. *Hacia una Arqueología Social: Reunión de Teotihuacan*. México, DF: Instituto Nacional de Antropología e Historia.

Lumbreras, L. 1974. *La Arqueología como Ciencia Social*. Lima: Ediciones Histar.

——1989. *Chavín de Huantar en el Nacimiento de la Civilización Andina*. Lima: Instituto Andino de Estudios Arqueológicos.

Madrazo, G. 1973. Síntesis de la Arqueología Pampeana. *Etnía* 17: 13–25.

——1985. Determinantes y orientaciones en la antropología Argentina. *Boletín de del Instituto Interdisciplinario de Tilcara*. Tilcara: Facultad de Filosofía y Letras de la UBA, Instituto Interdisciplinario de Tilcara, pp. 13–56.

Manzanilla, L. 1992. *Akapana una Pirámide en el Centro del Mundo*. México, DF: Instituto de Investigaciones Antropológicas, Universidad Nacional Autónoma de México.

——(ed.). 1997. *Emergence and Change in Early Urban Society*. New York: Plenum.

Maríategui, J. C.. 1979 [1928]. *Siete ensayos de interpretación de la realidad peruana*. México, DF: Serie Popular Era.

Marzal, M. 1986. *Historia del antropología indigenista: México y Perú*. 2nd edn. Lima: Pontificia Universidad Católica del Perú.

Matos Moctezuma, E. 1972. *Introducción*. In M. Gamio (ed.), *Arqueología e indigenismo*. México, DF: Sepsetentas, Secretaría de Educación Pública, pp. 7–23.

McGuire, R. 1992. *A Marxist Archaeology*. San Diego, CA: Academic Press.

——, and R. Navarrete. 1999. Entre motocicletas y fusiles: Las arqueologías radicales anglosajonas e hispana. *Revista do Museu de Arqueología e Etnología* 3: 181–199. São Paulo.

Meggers, B. 1992. Cuarenta años de colaboración. In B. Meggers (ed.), *Prehistoria Sudamericana: Nuevas Perspectivas*. Santiago de Chile: Taraxacum, pp. 13–26.

——2001. The continuing quest for El Dorado: Round two. *Latin American Antiquity* 13(3): 304–325.

Meggers, B. J., and C. Evans (eds.) 1963. *Aboriginal Development in Latin America: An Interpretative Review*. Washington, DC: Smithsonian Institution, Smithsonian Miscellaneous Collections 146 (1).

Mendonça de Souza, A. 1991. *História da Arqueología Brasileira*. Pesquisas: Série Antropología 46.

Menghin, O. 1956. El Poblamiento prehistórico de Misiones. *Anales de Arqueología y Etnología* XII: 19–40. Mendoza.

——, and M. Bórmida. 1950. Investigaciones prehistóricas en cuevas de Tandilia (Provincia de Buenos Aires). *Runa* 3: 5–35.

Meskell, L., C. Gosden, I. Hodder, R. Joyce, and R. Preucel. 2001. Editorial statement. *Journal of Social Archaeology* 1(1): 5–12.

Mirambell, L., and J. A. Pérez Gollán. 2000. Semblanza de José Luis Lorenzo. In J. Litvak and L. Mirambell (eds.), *Arqueología, Historia y Antropología In Memoriam José Luis Lorenzo Bautista*. Colección Científica. México, DF: Instituto Nacional de Antropología e Historia, pp. 15–43.

Netto, L. 1885. Investigacão sobre a archeologia brasileira. *Anais do Museu Nacional*, 257–553.

Neves, E. G. 1999. Changing perspectives in Amazonian Archaeology. In G. Politis and B. Alberti (eds.), *Archaeology in Latin America*. London and New York: Routledge, pp. 216–243.

Núñez Atencio, L. 2001. *Aprendamos Arqueología en Nuestra Tierra*. Antofagasta: Universidad Católica del Norte y Explora-CONICYT.

Núñez Regueiro, V. 1972. Conceptos teóricos que han obstaculizado el desarrollo de la arqueología en Sud-América. *Estudios de Arqueología* 1. Cachi: Museo Arqueológico de Cachi, pp. 11–35.

Olivera, D., and P. Tchilinguirian. 2000. De aguas y tierras: Aportes para la reactivación de campos agrícolas arqueológicos en la Puna Argentina. *Relaciones de la Sociedad Argentina de Antropología* XXV: 99–118.

Orellana Rodríguez, M. 1996. *Historia de la Arqueología en Chile*. Colección Ciencias Sociales, Universidad de Chile. Santiago: Bravo y Allende.

Orser, C. E., and P. P. Funari. 1992. Pesquisa arqueológica inicial em Palmares. *Estudos Ibero-Americanos* 18: 53–69.

Orser, C. H. 1992. *In Search of Zumbi*. Normal: Illinois State University Press.

Oyuela-Caycedo, A. 1994. *History of Latin American Archaeology*. Aldershot and Brookfield: Avebury.

——, A. Anaya, C. G. Elera, and L. Valdez. 1997. Social archaeology in Latin America? Comments to T. C. Patterson. *American Antiquity* 62: 365–374.

Patterson, T. 1992. Social archaeology in Latin America: An appreciation. *American Antiquity* 59: 531–537.

——1994. Social archaeology in Latin America: An appreciation. *American Antiquity* 59: 531–537.

——1997. A reply to A. Oyuela-Caycedo, A. Anaya, C. G. Elera and L. M. Valdez. *American Antiquity* 62(2): 365–374.

Paz, O. 1995. *El arte de México: Materia y sentido Obras completas. Los privilegios de la vista II. Arte de México*. México, DF: Círculo de Lectores y Fondo de Cultura Económica.

Pérez Gollán, J. A. 1981. *Presencia de Vere Gordon Childe*. México, DF: Instituto Nacional de Antropología e Historia.

——1988. La vida termina mejor cuando uno está alegre y fuerte. *Coloquio V. Gordon Childe*. México, DF: Universidad Nacional Autónoma de México, pp. 403–408.

Petrie, W. M. F. 1907a. *Las sucesiones de los restos prehistóricos*. Trans. S. A. Lafones Quevedo. La Plata: Universidad Nacional de La Plata, Biblioteca de Difusión Científica del Museo de La Plata, Vol. 1, pp. 221–237.

——1907b. *Métodos y propósitos en arqueología*. Trans. S. A. Lafones Quevedo. La Plata: Universidad Nacional de La Plata, Biblioteca de Difusión Científica del Museo de La Plata, Vol. 1, pp. 9–220.

Podgorny, I. 1999. *Arqueología de la educación: Textos, indicios, monumentos. La imagen del indio en el mundo escolar*. Buenos Aires: Sociedad Argentina de Antropología, Serie Tesis Doctorales.

Politis, G. 1992. Política nacional, arqueología y universidad en Argentina. In G. Politis (ed.), *Arqueología en América Latina Hoy*. Bogotá: Fondo de Promoción de la Cultura del Banco Popular, pp. 70–87.

——1995. The socio-politics of archaeology in Hispanic South America. In P. Ucko (ed.), *Theory in Archaeology. A World Perspective*. London: Routledge, pp. 197–235.

——2001. On archaeological praxis, gender bias and indigenous peoples in South America. *Journal of Social Archaeology* 1(1): 90–107.

——2003. The theoretical landscape and the methodological development of archaeology in Latin America. *American Antiquity* 2(62): 245–272.

Preucel, R., and I. Hodder. 1999. Representations and antirepresentations. In R. Preucel and I. Hodder (eds.), *Contemporary Archaeology in Theory. A Reader*. Oxford: Blackwell Science, pp. 519–530.

Rojas, J. (ed.) 1987. *La aventura intelectual de Pedro Armillas. Visión antropológica de la Historia de América*. Guadalajara: Colegio de Michoacán.

Rojas, R. 1971 [1909]. *La restauración nacionalista. Crítica de la educación argentina y bases para una reforma en el estudios de las humanidades modernas*. Prólogo de Fermín Chavez. Buenos Aires: A. Peña Lillo.

——1980 [1924]. *Eurindia. Ensayo de estética sobre las culturas americanas* (2 vols.). Buenos Aires: Centro Editor de América Latina, Biblioteca Argentina Fundamental.

——1939. *Ollantay, tragedia de los Andes*. Buenos Aires: Losada.

——1953. *Silabario de la decoración americana*. Buenos Aires: Losada.

Rojas Rabiela, T. (ed.) 1991. *Pedro Armillas: Vida y obra*. Vols. I and II. México, DF: CIESAS–INAH.

Rouse, I. 1962 [1951]. The strategy of culture history. In S. Tax (ed.), *Anthropology Today: Selections*. Chicago: University of Chicago Press, pp. 84–103.

Rowe, J. H. 1998. Max Uhle y la idea del tiempo en la arqueología americana. In P. Kaulicke (ed.), *Max Uhle y el Antiguo Perú*. Lima: Pontificia Universidad Católica del Perú, pp. 5–21.

Sanoja, M. and I. Vargas Arenas. 1974. *Antiguas Formaciones y Modos de Producción Venezolanos*. Caracas: Monte Avila Editores.

Schiffer, M. B. 1976. *Behavioral Archaeology*. New York: Academic Press.

Soler, R. 1968. *El Positivismo Argentino*. Buenos Aires: Paidos.

Steward, J. H. (ed.) 1946–50. *The Handbook of South American Indians* (6 vols.). Bureau of American Ethnology, Washington DC, Bulletin 143.

Stirling, M. 1939. Discovering the New World's oldest dated work of man. *National Geographic Magazine* LXXVI: 34–46.

Tax, S. (ed.). 1962 [1951]. *Anthropology Today: Selections*. Chicago: University of Chicago Press.

Tello, J. C. 1921. *Introducción a la historia antigua del Perú*. Lima: Editorial Euforión.

Trigger, B. G. 1980. Arqueología y etnohistoria. *Cuicuilco. Escuela Nacional de Antropología e Historia* 2: 9–15.

——1989. *A History of Archaeological Thought*. Cambridge: Cambridge University Press.

Ucko, P. (ed.) 1995. *Theory in Archaeology. A World Perspective*. London: Routledge.

Valcárcel, L. E. 1972 [1927]. *Tempestad sobre los Andes*. Lima: Editorial Universo.

Vargas Arenas. I. 1999. *La historia como futuro*. Caracas: Fondo Editorial Tropykos.

——and M. Sanoja Obediente. 1999. Archaeology as a social science. In G. Politis and B. Alberti (eds.), *Archaeology in Latin America*, pp. 59–75. London: Routledge.

Vasconcelos, J. 1948 [1925]. *La raza cósmica. Misión de la raza americana. Argentina y Brasil*. Buenos Aires: Colección Austral de Espasa-Calpe Argentina.

Vázquez León, L. 1996. *El Leviatan Arqueológico. Antropología de una Tradición Científica en México*. Leiden: Research School, CNWS 44.

Volkert, J. 1997. Los museos en los albores del siglo XXI. *Ciencia Hoy* 7:39. Buenos Aires, pp. 10–15.

Wagner, E. 1967. The prehistory and ethnohistory of the Carache Area in Western Venezuela. *Yale Publications in Anthropology* 71: 11–15.

Willey, G., and J. Sabloff. 1980. *A History of American Archaeology*. San Francisco: W. H. Freeman.

Willey, G. R. 1962 [1951]. Archaeological theories and interpretation: The New World. In S. Tax (ed.), *Anthropology Today: Selections*. Chicago: University of Chicago Press, pp. 170–193.

——1996. *An Introduction to American Archaeology* (2 vols.). Englewood Cliffs, NJ: Prentice-Hall.

Wüst, I. 1999. Etnicidade e tradições ceramistas: Algunas reflexões a partir de antigas aldeias Bororo do Mato Grosso. In M. I. D'Agostino Fleming (ed.), *Anais da I Reuinião Internacional de Teoria Arqueológica na America do Sul*. São Paulo: Universidade de São Paulo, pp. 303–318.

Zarankin, A., and F. Acuto. 1999. *Sed Non Satiata. Teoría Social en la Arqueología Latinoamericana Contemporánea*. Buenos Aires: Tridente.

16

Contested Pasts: Archaeology and Native Americans

Randall H. McGuire

For over two centuries competing histories have existed for Native America (Thomas 2000: xxv). Euro-American scholars have researched and written a national, public history that is published in books, taught in schools, and enshrined in parks and monuments. Native Americans have sustained their own histories in opposition to this dominant narrative. Native elders have taught these covert histories to the children in the home. Archaeologists tended to see their investigations as the study of things, bones, and artifacts, not as the study of a living people with a past, present, and future. They seemed to assume that real Native Americans only lived in the past, that their culture had vanished, and that their descendants had lost their heritage (McGuire 1997). The White scholars saw themselves both as the preservers of fading cultures and as liberal crusaders for the Indian's rightful place in a US national heritage. They did not realize that the archaeology of Native America is fundamentally a colonialist enterprise (Trigger 1984).

In the early 1970s Indian people made public their longstanding objections to the excavation of their ancestors' burials (McGuire 1992). They informed archaeologists that the pasts that we study are the heritages of living peoples (Deloria 1973). Most anthropologists were honestly shocked and confused when Native Americans ob-structed excavations and demanded the return of their ancestors' remains. The archae-ologists saw their actions in terms of their own intentions, in terms of debates over national heritage, in terms of a scientific search for knowledge, and in terms of the history of archaeology. Native Americans, on the other hand, saw archaeology in the larger historical context of White–Indian relations. In this larger history and set of relations the archaeological control of Indian pasts was simply one other facet that had been stripped from their control. I will examine this history in order to understand contemporary conflicts between Native Americans and archaeologists.

The struggle over who would control Indian pasts culminated in the early 1990s with various laws that now regulate the archaeology of Native America. This legislation has restructured the debates around issues of identity, science, and intellectual property rights. This debate continues within a larger backlash against tribal sovereignty. These laws also gave Native Americans more control over the archaeological study of indigenous pasts and this newfound empowerment raises the possibility of an indigenous archaeology (Watkins 2000). At the dawn of the twenty-first century Native Americans and archaeologists interact on a very complex field of relations. Questions of knowledge and power remain at the core of this field, but the more complex nature of relations opens up creative new spaces for a radically different archaeology.

Indians, Heritage, and Archaeology

Indians have an ambiguous and often contradictory position in the American cultural imagination (Deloria 1998; Huhndorf 2001). Europeans did not encounter a wilderness in North America but instead a land thickly populated with people who had to be subjected, killed, and removed to make way for European civilization (Axtell 2001). Three centuries after the first encounter the new American culture inherited the contradictory notions that Native Americans were bloodthirsty savages or that they were noble savages. Indians as bloodthirsty savages populated popular culture, literature, theater, and movies throughout the nineteenth and twentieth centuries (Kilpatrick 1999: 1–15). Yet, even as the battles of conquest raged, Euro-Americans took possession of Native American pasts and wrote a mythic history that incorporated the Noble Savage as part of the natural environment that gave rise to an American identity and heritage (McGuire 1992). This myth of the First Americans drove the development of an American four-field anthropology. The disciplines originated to record and preserve these vanishing cultures. But Native Americans refused to vanish, and the continuation of their own history was a key aspect of their refusal.

Beginning with Columbus

When Columbus landed in the Bahamas in 1492, no Indians lived in North America. Many peoples, including the Diné (Navajo), O'odham (Pima), Lakota (Sioux), Inuit (Eskimo), Ashiwi (Zuni), Wah-zah-zhe (Osage), Haida Gwaii (Haida), Numakiki (Mandan), Inuna-Ina (Arapaho), Haudenosaunee (Iroquois), Karuk, and Lenape (Delaware), peopled the land. Each of these nations had its own language, culture, and history. They only became Indians in the crucible of the European conquest of North America. Europeans used existing Renaissance concepts of human variation, mythic landscapes, morality, and wickedness to invent the Indian (Moffitt and Sebastián 1996). Embedded in this invention were categories and concepts that persist to this day in the Euro-American imagination of Indians.

Key to these concepts is both an opposition and an underlying theme that resolve the contradiction that they entail. Columbus reported two groups of indigenous peoples in the Caribbean (Moffitt and Sebastián 1996): peaceful, naive Arawaks who lived in a state of nature, and savages who ate human flesh. Both of these groups could not resist the Spanish force of arms and died in droves from diseases that did not affect the Spanish. The European invention of the Indian consistently depended upon this opposition between the peaceful child of the forest and the savage cannibals and the belief that Indians would vanish with civilization (Berkhofer 1978: 4–12).

The Enlightenment, the New Republic, and the First Americans

During the Enlightenment the image that the Spanish had drawn thrived and French philosophers recast the debate as an opposition between the Savage and the Noble Savage (Berkhofer 1978: 74–78). The Savage lurked in the forests of North America while the Noble Savage populated critiques of French society. Reformers ennobled Native Americans to critique European society and to advocate change. Their conservative critics exposed the brutish reality of Native American life and branded the reformers as romantics.

The Enlightenment also saw the development of a new legitimating ideology for state political power and sovereignty, the nation-state (Anderson 1983; Poole 1999). A state derives its legitimacy from being the government of a people who share a common identity as a nation. Poole (1999: 13–18) argues that a national identity is a cultural object that is created, maintained, and negotiated through a sense of place (a shared homeland) and a sense of history (a shared heritage). The nation-state purports to be a community of equals, who are the citizens of the state. The United States was one of the first such nation-states in the world.

The Noble Savage appeared in the discourse of North America during the Revolutionary period but would not be fully formed in that discourse until the early 1800s. The discussion was fundamental to the process of creating an American Culture and Nation. This process was ripe with contradictions, such as slaveholders proclaiming that "All men are created equal." Equally problematic was the fact that the Nation consisted of an ethnically diverse mass of Europeans who had conquered and colonized someone else's homeland (Axtell 2001). To create the Nation a shared sense of place and heritage had to be produced, and to resolve the contradiction the usurpation of Native Americans from the land had to be justified. Throughout the nineteenth century debates raged between those who saw Indians as Noble Savages, the First Americans, and those who saw them as bloodthirsty savages who must be swept aside to achieve manifest destiny. Both of these perspectives equated Indians with nature – they were savages – and both assumed that Native peoples would vanish as civilization subdued and reclaimed the wilderness. This debate gave birth to American anthropology.

American revolutionaries faced a crisis of identity: "what did it mean to be non-British, what did it mean to be an American" (Thomas 2000: 12)? Before the Revolution, on both sides of the Atlantic, Europeans had equated Americans with Indians (Moffitt and Sebastián 1996; Thomas 2000: 12). The Colonists were English, Germans, Spaniards, French, and Dutch, not Americans. The revolutionaries resolved this crisis by adopting the guise of Native Americans to practice European customs of protest (Deloria 1998: 14). Whereas people in Europe would have blackened their faces or worn sack masks to confront the authorities, the revolutionaries dressed up like Indians. The most famous such incident was the Boston Tea Party, but groups confronting authority and crises of identity in the United States have continued to play Indian from the Whiskey Rebellion of the 1790s to the modern New Age movement (Deloria 1998; Huhndorf 2001).

Thomas Jefferson and many other enlightened gentlemen pronounced Native Americans to be a vibrant and noble race (Wallace 1999). They carved out a place in the US national heritage for Native Americans as the First Americans (McGuire 1992). They did so, in part, to answer French critics who used an Enlightenment theory of environmental determinism and progress to argue that the savage nature of the Indian indicated the inability of the North American environment to support a civilized nation (Berkhofer 1978: 42–43, Wallace 1999: 76–77). They also did so to establish a sense of place for the new nation in the natural environment and link that nation to an Indian heritage that stretched back to time immemorial. In 1826 James Fenimore Cooper developed the defining saga of the First American ideology in his book *The Last of the Mohicans* (Slotkin 1986).

American anthropology and archaeology originated in the construction of the First Americans ideology. The American Philosophical Society, established in 1743, integrated Native Americans in its study of natural history. Jefferson accumulated Indian artifacts in his cabinet of curios, collected data on Native American languages, and directed Lewis and Clark to gather ethnographic and archaeological data (Kennedy 1994; Wallace 1999). He carried out what most scholars consider to be the first archaeological excavation in the United States as part of his rebuttal to the French critics (McGuire 1992). In 1794 Charles Wilson Peale established the first US museum of natural history in Philadelphia and he institutionalized Native Americans as objects of natural history (Sellers 1980). These scholars predicted a tragic fate for the First Americans, asserting that the Indians must either retreat westward or assimilate into White society, leaving behind their ancestors, graves, their ancient monuments, and their vacant lands for the civilized Euro-Americans (Wallace 1999: 334).

Mound builders and manifest destiny

The First Americans ideology thrived in the urbane atmosphere of the east coast. Americans on the cutting edge of conquest found little reality in the Noble Savage (Kennedy 1994; Wallace 1999). Directly involved in the messy reality of ethnic cleansing, they dismissed the views of Jefferson, Cooper, and their ilk as romantic. Enlightenment ideals also faded, to be replaced by religious fundamentalism (McLoughlin 1986: xvi). They claimed that Americans were God's chosen race with a manifest destiny to conquer the continent. They resolved the ideological contradiction of a European nation founded on Native American territory by denying that these lands were truly an Indian homeland. Andrew Jackson's administration (1828–36) implemented a policy of ethnic cleansing with a vengeance and the Cherokee Trail of Tears exemplifies the horrors and atrocities of this (McLoughlin 1986).

West of the Appalachian Mountains, Euro-American settlers encountered massive mounds and earthen monuments unlike any ancient remains that they had seen on the east coast (Kennedy 1994). These ancient works puzzled Enlightenment scholars like Jefferson, but they tended to accept them as evidence of Indian achievement (Wallace 1999). Liberal scholars such as Albert Gallatin, Samuel F. Haven (1856), and Henry Roe Schoolcraft (1856: 135–136) championed the Native American origin of these constructions. Schoolcraft excavated in the Grave Creek Mound in Ohio to demonstrate that Indians had built the mounds (Silverberg 1968: 107–108).

Frontiersmen, however, proposed that a civilized race of mound builders had built the great mounds of the Midwest only to be overrun by red savages from the north

(Silverberg 1968; Kennedy 1994). These men had fought Indians and built their for-
tunes from the lands that they had conquered. They included individuals such as
Presidents Andrew Jackson and William Henry Harrison, Secretary of War Lewis Cass,
and Ohio professionals Caleb Atwater, E. H. Davis, and E. G. Squire (Kennedy 1994;
Silverberg 1968). Many of these men engaged in archaeology to prove this myth of the
mound builders. In 1846 the Smithsonian Institution was founded, and its first publication was Squier and Davis's *Ancient Monuments of the Mississippi Valley* (1848).

During the war with Mexico US army columns crossed the Southwest. Army officers described the stone ruins of this region in their journals and compiled a Southwestern version of the mound-builder myth. They gave the ruins names like Aztec and
Montezuma's Castle because they believed that the Aztec or their ancestors had constructed the monuments (Fowler 2000). This myth portrayed the Pueblo Indians'
substantial homes and agricultural fields as recent borrowings from the Spanish and
not as aboriginal developments. Just as the mound-builder myth legitimated the re-
moval of Indian people from the East, the Aztec myth legitimated the taking of Pueblo
land (Lekson 1988; McGuire 1992: 231).

Debates about who built the mounds dominated American archaeology in the nineteenth century. They occurred in the larger context of disputes about the Indian's place
in the national heritage and what it meant to be an American. Artists such as George
Catlin, Karl Bodmer, and Albert Bierstadt filled their canvases with Noble Savages,
while Carl Wilmar, Caleb Bingham, and Frederic Remington portrayed bloodthirsty
savages attacking soldiers and settlers (Goetzmann and Goetzmann 1986). Mark Twain
used his own brief exposure to the brutish reality of Indian life in Nevada to sarcastic-
ally critique Cooper. Writing at mid-century, the historians George Bancroft and Francis Parkman emphasized the cruel horrors of Indian warfare to justify the ongoing
conquest of the West (Berkhofer 1978: 95–96). The scholars did not ask Native
Americans their opinion on these matters, and remained secure in their conviction that
Indians were a vanishing race.

While Euro-Americans debated the place of Native Americans in the American
consciousness, real Indians were engaged in life and death struggles. A few incidents,
such as Indian people in the 1840s asking William Pidgeon to stop digging in Minnesota burial mounds (Silverberg 1968: 139), suggest that Native Americans objected to
the Euro-Americans' research. But these concerns were secondary to resisting the
horrific process of ethnic cleansing that sought to eliminate Indian people from the
continent.

Almost gone: Assimilation, science, and evolution

In 1890 the Seventh Calvary massacred hundreds of Lakota men, women, and children
at Wounded Knee, South Dakota and the "Indian Wars" ended. In 1900 the US census
reported the nadir of the Indian population. At this same time US Indian policy moved
to assimilation, guided in part by a newly institutionalized four-field anthropology, and
the First American ideology triumphed in the official US consciousness.

In the West, as had been the case in the East, conquest and Euro-American debates
about the nature of Indian people went hand in hand. In 1865 the US Surgeon General
directed military officers to collect Indian skulls (Thomas 2000: 57). Scientists wanted

these skulls to answer questions about the racial relationship of humans; did humans have a single origin or did each race have its own Adam (Gould 1981)? Samuel George Morton of the Academy of Natural Sciences in Philadelphia initiated this research in the early nineteenth century. Morton believed that detailed measurements of skulls could both resolve the question of racial origins and reveal the relative intelligence and temperament of races. Advocates of this scientific racism amassed large collections of skulls for these measurements (Gould 1981). Army officers beheaded Indian corpses on battlefields and dug up recent graves. They made their collections in secret, over the protests of Native people, or at gunpoint. Early twentieth-century anthropologists such as Franz Boas and Alex Hrdlicka collected even more skulls to refute the racist assumptions of this research. In 1902 Hrdlicka collected Yaqui skulls from a battlefield in Mexico (McGuire 1994: 180), and at Larsen Bay, Alaska, in the 1930s he dug up Native victims of the 1918 flu pandemic (Pullar 1994: 21).

The American four-field discipline of anthropology came together in the last decades of the nineteenth century, institutionalized in the major museums of natural history and guided by a theory of cultural evolution (McGuire 1992; Patterson 1995; Thomas 2000). The major museums of natural history hired men, and a few women, trained in entomology, ichthyology, and other biological specialties as the first professional anthropologists to salvage the "vanishing" Indian cultures. These anthropologists studied Native Americans as an aspect of nature and the museums displayed their artifacts alongside stuffed birds and mammals (as they still do). They competed with each other to make massive collections of artifacts and bones (Cole 1985). These first professionals often collaborated with "assimilated" Indians such as Ely Parker (Seneca) and Francis La Flesche (Omaha) (Michaelsen 1994). In 1879 the Federal Government established the Bureau of American Ethnography (BAE) in the Smithsonian Institution. The government charged the new Bureau to provide advice and expertise for US Indian policy. The first director, John Wesley Powell, adopted the cultural evolutionary theory of Lewis Henry Morgan as the intellectual guide for the bureau. These scholars saw value in the study of the First Americans but they were also certain that Indians had failed to change or significantly progress on the evolutionary ladder (Trigger 1986: 192–194). This failure to progress made the extinction of primitive Indian cultures inevitable and Native peoples could only survive as individuals by assimilating into civilized White society.

In the 1880s several groups advocated for the reform of US Indian policy. The reformers, like the friends of the Noble Savage before them, thought that Indians could only maintain their nobility in a state of nature (Dippie 1982). Thus, they held little hope for the survival of Indian cultures; the only hope for Native people was to be assimilated into European culture. Their assimilation program included two major parts: (1) education in boarding schools that forbade Native language, dress, and culture, and (2) the General Allotment Act of 1887 that broke up tribal territories into privately owned individual allotments. The archaeologist and BAE anthropologist Alice Cunningham Fletcher was prominent in this movement and one of the principal authors of the allotment program (Thomas 2000: 64–70). The policy of allotment devastated Indian people (Parman 1994). When Congress repealed the Allotment Act in 1934 Native American tribes had lost two-thirds of the lands that they held in 1887.

The BAE became the principal advocate of the First American ideology. In 1881 the US Congress allotted $5,000 for the BAE to carry out archaeological research on the mound builders. Cyrus Thomas directed the project and a decade later he reported that the ancestors of modern Native Americans had built the mounds (Thomas 1894). In the Southwest, Aldolph Bandelier and BAE anthropologists including Jessie Fewkes, the Mindeleff brothers, and Frank Cushing disproved the Aztec myth (Fowler 2000). The mound builders faded into folklore, although Mormons and a few others in modern US society continue to embrace the mound-builder legend. The ideology of the First Americans triumphed and became institutionalized in the dominant nationalist narrative of the United States. The key debate in US archaeology would now turn from lost tribes to the antiquity of Indians on the continent.

Archaeologists led by Edgar Lee Hewett lobbied for the passage of the Antiquities Act of 1906. This act culminates the trends of the nineteenth century and fixes the relationship between archaeology and Indians for the twentieth century. The act identifies Native American heritages as part of the natural history of the continent and their artifacts and monuments as objects to be preserved with the natural wonders of the nation. The act codifies the First American ideology of US heritage and legislates that professional archaeologists will control the physical remains of Indian pasts. The liberal ideology embodied in the act asserts the humanity of Indian people and their place in a national heritage, but it defines Indians and their heritages only in terms of Euro-American interests, debates, and agendas. With this relationship twentieth-century archaeologists begin to dismiss the Indian histories as myths and their research becomes progressively alienated from living Indian people. Archaeologists come to think of themselves as the crucial protectors and true owners of Native pasts (Deloria 1973; McGuire 1997).

A new deal for the Indians

At the beginning of the twentieth century painters, writers, and social reformers began to gather in Taos and Santa Fe. They came seeking a place frozen in time, where life seemed as unsullied and as simple as it had been a thousand years before (Goetzmann and Goetzmann 1986: 354). The artists painted the Pueblo Indians as romanticized noble savages and the reformers found in the Pueblos a sense of community that they wished to restore to urban America. They also entered into political battles to help the Pueblos protect their land base and in this they enlisted the help of anthropologists and archaeologists (Goetzmann and Goetzmann 1986: 353–376; Lekson 1988). In 1924 the reformers won their battle to save Pueblo land and began mounting a national campaign to reverse assimilation and preserve Indian cultures.

Despite the prominent role of established anthropologists and archaeologists in the battle to save Pueblo land, the new generation of scholars who came of age in the first decades of the twentieth century objected to a politically involved anthropology (Thomas 2000: 91–102). At the end of the nineteenth century Franz Boas established American four-field anthropology as an academic discipline of study. In doing so he also stressed that anthropologists must adopt a professional, objective, and scientific approach. Boas disdained any political involvement and pointed to Fletcher's involvement with allotment as evidence of the peril in political action (Thomas 2000: 70). His approach privileged the professionally trained outside observer. It led anthropologists to turn away from collaboration with Indian individuals (because they were subjective insiders) to treating Native peoples as research subjects and to the dismissal of Native American oral tradition (Thomas 2000: 91–102).

In archaeology this meant an almost complete alienation of scholars from Native peoples (Trigger 1986: 199). Whereas turn-of-the-century archaeologists had avidly collected Native oral histories and applied them to the interpretations of the archaeological record, the new generation rejected these histories as myths. Archaeologists increasingly had less and less contact with Indian peoples. Even in the Southwest, where large tracts of land remained in Native hands, where Indians still practiced traditional ways, and where Native Americans labored on archaeological excavations, most archaeologists worked on Native pasts with little regard for the interests and opinions of living Indians. In the 1930s Ann Axtell Morris (1933: 74), the wife of archaeologist Early Morris, described the Pueblo people as "archaeology still alive."

Archaeology had proven that Indians were the First Americans, but the hard-nosed scientists at the beginning of the century granted them little time on the continent. Ales Hrdlicka and William Henry Holmes mobilized the Smithsonian Institution to debunk any claims that Native Americans had occupied the continent for more than a few thousand years (Meltzer 1993). They held this ground for a generation until 1927 and the finding of Folsum projectile points amongst the bones of Pleistocene bison in New Mexico. The new orthodoxy that followed this discovery was that Clovis hunters had entered North America from Asia about 11,000 years before. This position offends(ed) many Native Americans. Each Indian Nation has its own origin history and almost all of them tell of the people being created in their sacred lands in the same process as the creation of this world (Deloria 1995, 2002).

Even though the official version of the US national heritage embraced the First Americans, this was not unambiguously the case in the popular imagination. Movies became one of the most powerful expressions of popular consciousness in the twentieth-century United States. With a handful of significant exceptions, Native Americans appeared as bloodthirsty savages in the theater (Kilpatrick 1999: 16–35). But the Noble Redman also survived in that imagination and became a tourist attraction. The railroad and motorcar transformed the West into an exotic tourist destination (Howard and Pardue 1996). The Great Northern Railroad and the Fred Harvey Company marketed the West as romantic escapism and Indian peoples and their crafts as commodities (Dilworth 1996; Weigle and Babcock 1996). Also, more and more Euro-Americans, especially children, played Indian in summer camps, fraternal organizations, the Boy Scouts, hobbyist groups, and the Camp Fire Girls (Deloria 1998; Huhndorf 2001).

In 1934 Congress passed the Indian Reorganization Act (IRA), repealing the General Allotment Act and setting up tribal governments within the US federal system. The legislation was a mixed blessing for Indian people. It established a system of tribal governments that survive to this day and that have provided a mechanism within the US federal system to preserve Indian Nations. The constitutions designed for the tribes, however, ignored or abolished existing traditional governments. Also, these governments had little power because the Bureau of Indian Affairs continued to control and administer government funds and programs on the reservations. During the 1930s some archaeologists came to work with these governments when the Indian divisions of the Works Projects Administration and the Civilian Conservation Corps sponsored archaeological projects.

Termination

Following World War II conservative forces attempted to roll back the IRA (Dippie 1982: 336–344). They instituted a policy of termination to end tribal governments and a policy of relocation to move Indian people to the cities. Native Americans fought these moves and the IRA tribal governments joined together in the National Congress of American Indians to lead this fight. Bloodthirsty savages still dominated in the popular imagination but the Noble Savage was gaining ground. Archaeology continued in the path set at the beginning of the century, largely unaware of Native Americans and their struggles.

Termination required that the Federal Government resolve any legal issues regarding ownership of Indian land. In 1946 Congress established the Indians Claims Commission to settle any outstanding indigenous land claims against the US government in order to clear the way for terminating Indian Nations. For over thirty years archaeologists did research for Indian land claims and testified before the Commission. Many archaeologists point to these cases as evidence of how archaeology has helped Native people (Ford 1973). But the attitudes of Indian people about this process and the White experts who participated in it are far more ambiguous (Deloria and Lytle 1984: 191). They recognize that the commission was part of a larger strategy to destroy their cultures, and they have trouble disassociating the experts from this intent. They were also dismayed that the commission gave authority to these experts and ignored or discredited traditional Native American leaders and knowledge.

After World War II the Federal Government embarked on a massive reservoir-building campaign. In 1944 lobbying by the Society for American Archaeology led to the establishment of the River Basin Survey Program. Across the nation from North Dakota, to New York, and to Arizona the government found it cheaper, easier, and less politically dangerous to take Indian land for reservoir construction (Cahn 1969: 69; Lawson 1994). These reservoirs terminated indigenous nations by flooding them out of their homelands. Many Indians knew the story of the military conquests of the nineteenth century and they noted that this time the scientists came for the bones to prepare the ground for taking instead of to clean up after the battle.

The Historic Sites Act of 1935 had provided the authorization for the River Basin Survey Program, and during the 1960s and 1970s Congress passed a series of acts that laid the legal basis for modern cultural resource management. This legislation continued and elaborated the Antiquities Act's definition of the Indians as the First Americans. These laws legislated that Indian remains are cultural resources to be cared for by professional archaeologists. Several key laws, including the National Environmental Policy Act of 1969, reaffirmed that Indian remains were part of the natural environment of the nation and their past's part of natural history.

After the war bloodthirsty and noble savages continued to battle in the popular consciousness. In the movie theatres the Western reined supreme and the violent savage stereotype dominated through the 1960s (Kilpatrick 1999). In general, opportunities to play Indian increased (Deloria 1998: 128–153). Expanding prosperity meant more children could go to summer camp and participate in organized youth groups like the Boy Scouts and the Y-Indian Guides. More people had the time and money to be Indian hobbyists. More money also meant more opportunities to consume the commodified Indian either as object or as a backdrop for automobile vacations in the West.

The processual theory that dominated US archaeology during this time rejected the existing Normative Archaeology with its roots in Boas. But it embraced the concept of archaeologists as scientists seeking to arrive at objective understandings of the past free of political bias. Trigger (1986: 201–206) has argued that processual theory granted that Native Americans could change and be creative but that it continued to treat the study of Indian heritages as a way to address Euro-American interests. He further argues that the processualists' emphasis on developing universal laws of cultural evolution alienated them from Native Americans who were concerned with their particular heritages, histories, and struggles.

Red power and self-determination

The end of the twentieth century witnessed a dramatic increase in the power of Indian Nations. The resistance by tribal governments and various national Indian organizations to termination led to a new federal Indian policy of self-determination. In the late 1960s and early 1970s Indian radicalism erupted in the Red Power movement. Growing Indian nationalisms that gave issues of heritage greater political prominence and visibility fueled these trends. The popular imagination embraced the Noble Savage, although the Bloodthirsty Savage had not disappeared. These changes swept up archaeology and transformed it.

In the early 1970s the policy of the federal government shifted to self-determination. Under this policy, tribal governments gained real autonomy, power, and authority. New legislation gave Indian governments greater control of federal programs, education, the adoption of Indian children, sacred places, and the archaeological record. In the 1980s, Indian Nations started to exploit the special legal status of reservation trust land to sell tax-free gasoline and cigarettes and to open gambling casinos. They also began to exert authority over non-Indian residents and landowners on reservations. The Native American Graves Protection and Repatriation Act of 1990 (NAGPRA) was one of the last legislative products of this trend.

The Red Power movement made public the covert histories and grievances of Native America to confront archaeology's control of Indian pasts and remains. In his seminal book *Custer Died for Your Sins*, Vine Deloria (1969) critiqued the relationship of cultural anthropologists to Indian people, and in *God is Red* and later works he took on the archaeologists (Deloria 1973, 1995, 2002). Native Americans objected most strongly to the excavation, curation, and display of their ancestors' bones. They wanted the bones and other sacred objects repatriated to them for reburial (Hill 1977; Talbot 1984). The American Indian Movement disrupted an excavation at Welch, Minnesota in 1971, occupied the Southwest Museum in Los Angeles in the same year, and in 1972 confiscated human bones from an anthropology laboratory at Colorado State University in Fort Collins (Watkins 2000). Archaeologists did not see themselves as grave robbers. They had an honest and deep belief in the First American ideology and they saw their work as supporting the validity of a Native American heritage in the US nation. They were surprised to find out that many Indian people did not want a place in the US heritage, but rather wanted to assert their particular histories as part of their efforts to legitimate themselves as nations with their own cultures, homelands, and heritages.

The war over repatriation raged through the 1980s. Indian activists shifted their tactics from confrontation to legislation. Native Americans including Jan Hammil, Maria Pearson, and Cecil Antone met head to head with archaeologists at professional meetings (Zimmerman 1989, 1997). The Native American Rights Fund took up the fight and lobbied for federal legislation to protect Native American graves and to give Indian peoples a voice in archaeological research. Many scientists fought back, mounting a defense for the values of an objective, nonpolitical science (Buikstra 1981; Meighan 1985; Quick 1985). A handful of archaeologists supported the Native American position (Sprague 1974; Trigger 1980; Zimmerman 1989).

This war was part of an international effort to define and defend indigenous rights. In Australia and New Zealand indigenous populations asserted their right to control their own heritage, ancient remains, and ancestors (Hubert 1989a; Matunga 1991). Developments in Canada paralleled those in the United States, but differences in the conflict and in resolutions reflect differences in the national contexts (Nicholas and Andrews 1997). In countries as diverse as Finland and Bolivia indigenous peoples found common cause in their struggle to regain control of their heritages (Aikio and Aikio 1989; Condori 1989). The World Archaeological Congress organized a meeting of archaeologists and indigenous peoples in 1989 which produced "The Vermillion Accord," an international policy statement on reburial (Hubert 1989b).

The Noble Savage image became dominant in the popular imagination by the 1980s and Native Americans engendered much public sympathy for repatriation (Zimmerman 2000). The Noble Savage was revived in the guise of the ecological Indian embodied by the crying Indian anti-littering commercials (Krech 1999). The counter-culture movement of the 1960s played Indian to challenge "the system" and the New Age movement at the end of the century played Indian to find a spirituality that it could not find in modern America (Deloria 1998; Huhndorf 2001). Movies such as *Soldier Blue* (1970) pitted noble Indians against savage US troops in thinly veiled critiques of the Vietnam War. This noblization of Native Americans in film culminated in *Dances With Wolves* (1990) and *Last of the Mohicans* (1993) (Kilpatrick 1999).

Even as the battle over repatriation raged archaeology also experienced a theoretical struggle. The alternative archaeologies of the 1980s, postprocessualist, Marxist, and feminist, questioned the validity of an objective political free science of archaeology. They argued that archaeologists needed to critically examine the social, cultural, and political contexts of their research. One consequence of this theoretical shift was a series of self-critical histories of American archaeology (Kehoe 1998; Patterson 1995; Trigger 1989). In general these trends raised awareness as to the political nature of archaeology and created a theoretical space in the discipline that accommodated the Native American critique of archaeology.

Two pieces of federal legislation brought an uneasy compromise on repatriation. In 1989 Congress passed the National Museum of the American Indian Act that set up a new Smithsonian Museum of Native America that would be directed and controlled by

Native Americans. The act and a 1996 amendment also implemented a plan for reburial and repatriation for the National Museum of Natural History. In 1990 Congress passed a second act that implemented reburial and repatriation at all federally funded museums and all archaeological projects that involved federal lands, monies, or permits. The Native American Graves Protection and Repatriation Act of 1990 transformed archaeology and the relationship of archaeology to Native America.

Repatriation and reburial has become a fact of life for archaeology (Bray 1996; Mihesuah 2000). Numerous large repatriations of museum collections, such as the Larsen Bay repatriation at the Smithsonian (Bray and Killion 1994) and the Pecos Pueblo repatriation at Harvard (Tarpy 2000), have occurred. Every major archaeological museum in the United States has an office of repatriation and is actively involved in negotiations with Native American nations. Reburial, and inclusion of Native American observers, here become standard practice in cultural resource management excavations and for most grant-funded research projects and even field schools.

Self-determination has also meant more direct Native control of archaeology and heritage. One of the federal programs that many Indian Nations took over under self-determination has been archaeology. The first Native American archaeology programs appeared in the 1970s at Zuni, Hopi, and Navajo Nations in the Southwest. As of the mid-1990s over seventy-five Indian Nations employed archaeologists and 18 nations had their own State Historic Preservation Officers (SHPOs) (Ferguson 1996: 36). Many Native American Nations have built their own museums to house archaeological collections and to interpret their own heritages. The National Museum of the American Indian is under construction on the mall in Washington, DC and this new prime national facility is managed and directed by Indian people.

One of the great Indian success stories of the 1990s was the Mashantucket Pequot of Connecticut (Benedict 2001; Eisler 2001). This group of people used archaeology, history, and genealogy to gain federal recognition as an Indian Nation in 1983 and have employed archaeologists since 1983. In the 1990s the Nation developed the most successful Native American casino in the United States. In 1998 they used some of the revenue from the casino to open a museum and research center to present their own heritage to the public. They have also been one of the largest contributors to the National Museum of the American Indian. This massive investment in heritage was initially to gain federal recognition and since then to counter critics who question the authenticity of the Nation (Benedict 2001).

Cooperation and collaboration between archaeologists and Native Americans has become much more common (Watkins 2003). One clear point of common ground has been a shared desire to preserve Indian sites, but many studies have gone beyond this. Two pioneering examples were Janet Spector's (1993) feminist-inspired collaboration with Wahpeton Dakota people in Minnesota and Larry Zimmerman's work with Cheyenne people at Fort Robinson, Nebraska (McDonald et al. 1991). In 1993 the Society for American Archaeology (SAA) began a column in its newsletter entitled "Working Together" to encourage cooperation between archaeologists and Native Americans. The column has since reported on dozens of cases of cooperation and collaboration between archaeologists and Native Americans (Dongoske, Aldenderfer, and Doehner 2000). Such cooperation led Pawnee historian Rodger Echo-Hawk (2000a: 7) to comment: "American archaeology has changed greatly in only a few short years, primarily because most archaeologists simply have never seen themselves as anti-Indian, and most Indians really are curious about archaeology." Despite such optimism at the beginning of a new century serious ambiguities, contradictions, and conflicts remain in the relationship between Native Americans and archaeology.

Backlash, or an Indigenous Archaeology

The turn of the twenty-first century has witnessed a popular and political backlash against Native American autonomy and sovereignty. Several factors have fueled this backlash. The success of a few small Indian Nations located near cities to gain wealth from casinos has bred popular resentment and cynicism about Native American identity and authenticity (Benedict 2001; Eisler 2001). Newfound Native American authority over Euro-Americans living within Indian Nations, over the adoption of Native children, and over Native graves and religious artifacts has produced conflicts with various groups in US society that now seek to limit or abolish such authority (Bordewich 1997). All of this came about in a general context of attacks on multiculturalism, and a movement to "free" people from government restrictions. Several bills have been introduced to the US Congress that would limit, roll back, or abolish Native American sovereignty and self-determination. The First American ideology remains part of the official heritage of the United States, but it is under attack from varied perspectives and the uneasy compromise in the repatriation war is strained.

The ideological battle of this backlash is a recurring one. It begins with an attack on romantic and sentimental ideas about Native Americans and calls for an objective, true understanding of their condition that emphasizes the brutish and unjust aspects of Native life. Bordewich's (1997) journalistic book *Killing the White Man's Indian* recounts case after case of the suppression of individual rights by tribal governments, waste, fraud, and corruption to show why Native Americans should be freed from these governments. Within anthropology a number of scholars have continued to fight a spirited rearguard action against repatriation and reburial (Clark 1998, 1999; Meighan 1994).

Many scholarly works that question the extreme romanticization of Native Americans have intentionally or inadvertently played into the backlash. This is especially the case when scholars have engaged in, encouraged, or allowed sensationalized popularizations of their results and conclusions. Krech's (1999) *The Ecological Indian: Myth and History* provides a nuanced consideration of why Native beliefs about the environment are not congruent with Western notions of ecology, conservation, or preservation. Critiques of Native sovereignty have caricatured his position to argue that Native Americans were in fact despoilers of the environment. Steven Le Blanc (1999) and Christy Turner (Turner and Turner 1999) have argued that the ancient Southwest was a land of warfare and cannibalism to challenge the simplistic myth of peaceful Pueblo people. Unfortunately, both the extremity of their views and the popular sensationalization of them tend to simply replace the Noble Savage stereotype with the familiar Bloodthirsty Savage (McGuire 2002). In the current ideological context it is important for archaeologists to reject oppositional thinking and to challenge all stereotypes by educating the public to the complexities of ancient Native America.

In archaeology this backlash has congealed around the case of the Kennewick Man (Chatters 2001; Downey 2000; Thomas 2000; Watkins 2000: 135–154, 2003: 274–275). In July of 1996 two young men walking on federal land discovered a skeleton eroding out of the banks of the Columbia River near Kennewick, Washington. Forensic anthropologist James Chatters initially thought the skeleton was a historic Euro-American but a Paleo-Indian projectile point in the pelvis indicated a much older date. Subsequent radiocarbon dating placed the skeleton at 9,200 to 9,600 years old, making it one of the oldest skeletons in North America. Five tribal groups filed a joint claim for the remains under the provisions of NAGPRA. A group of eight scholars filed a federal court lawsuit to stop repatriation of the Kennewick Man, as the find became known. The basis for their case was that the ancient skeleton could not be linked to a living Native American group and therefore was not covered under NAGPRA. In August of 2002 the US District Court for the District of Oregon ruled that the Department of Interior's determination that the Kennewick remains were Native American was in error. Further appeals of the case are now in progress.

The backlash extends into the international arena. The United Nations has declared 1995 to 2004 as the "International Decade of the World's Indigenous People." One goal of the decade is to promote and to protect the human rights of indigenous peoples, including the repatriation of human remains and sacred objects. Governments of numerous countries such as Australia, New Zealand, and Canada have passed laws similar to NAGPRA. Like the Kennewick controversy, the backlash to these laws has questioned the authenticity of Native claims and the ancestral linkage between modern groups and the remains. These issues are clearly stated in the Australian controversy over the Hindmarsh Island burials (Hemmings 2000).

The arguments surrounding the Kennewick case renew debates about the First American ideology. Chatters (2001) argues that Kennewick Man should be seen as an ancestor to us all. He (and others) claim that North America was settled by different waves of peoples, many of whom are not ancestral to living Native Americans. Dennis Stanford and Bruce Bradley (2000) have suggested that one such wave of immigration began with Solutrean peoples in southern Europe and ended with the Clovis culture of North America. Archaeological data do not support this attempt to Europeanize the First Americans (Strauss 2000). Like the mound-builder theories of a century before, the "ancestors to us all" position attempts to deny the primacy of Indian people in North America. Unlike the mound-builder myth, this attitude does not remove Indians from the heritage of the nation but argues that a Euro-American or universal human claim to an ancient heritage in North America has as much validity as that of the Native Americans. If true, this would eliminate the privilege that NAGPRA gives indigenous people in the official heritage of the United States (Watkins 2003: 274).

Many Native Americans have always rejected the First American ideology because they do not see their heritage as part of a US nation but instead as the property of their own nation. This view is creating an indigenous archaeology. The developing indigenous archaeology has its home both in the archaeological programs sponsored by Native American nations (Ferguson et al. 1995) and among the handful of Native American archaeologists in the profession (Watkins 2000, 2003). In tribal archaeology programs the Native American Nation sets the agenda for investigation and it determines what guidelines and rules research must follow. Nations usually started such programs to provide cultural resource management services to the Nation to comply with federal historic preservation laws. They have also used such programs to gather data in support of land-claim cases. More fundamentally they have raised the possibility of an archaeology that is guided by indigenous concepts of heritage, time, and the past (Ferguson 1996; Lomaomvaya and Ferguson 1999). The vast majority of archaeologists who work for tribal archaeology programs are Euro-Americans and only a handful of Native Americans are practicing archaeologists with advanced degrees. Like other Native American professionals, these individuals often find themselves in an ambiguous and contradictory position. The struggle of these individuals with these contradictions leads them to a unique perspective on archaeology and on what we study. It gives them a heightened awareness that archaeology is not just about stones and potsherds but is the study of the past of living peoples, a study that is not objective but emotional and political (Watkins 2000: 180–181). These efforts show archaeology to be a craft that can be applied to Native American interests as well as to those of the dominant Euro-American society (Shanks and McGuire 1996).

The Complexity Of Knowledge

The ultimate question that faces Native Americans and archaeologists is about knowledge. Who will control, create, and distribute knowledge about Native American culture history: archaeologists and anthropologists, or Native peoples (Bailey, 1998)? The issue of knowledge has been crystallized, objectified, and fetishized in the skeletons and objects that we fight over. They are important to all parties not just because of what they physically are (or were) but also because they are the embodiment of knowledge.

At the basis of the conflict between archaeology and indigenous peoples is a disagreement about what knowledge is and how it is acquired (Mason 2000). These differing worldviews are usually opposed as spiritual and scientific ways to knowledge.

For many or most indigenous people knowledge is a spiritual matter. It is passed on through elders and through religious practices. "[T]he story is passed on from generation to generation and it is told in the heart because, in the spirit, this is the true story, that cannot be misinterpreted and it goes on forever" (Turner 1989: 193).

Indigenous oral histories and origin narratives create sacred landscapes that define the proper spiritual relationship of indigenous people to nature, to other peoples, and to each other (Basso 1997). In this way the past does not have to be discovered but rather exists and is knowable in the present because it is embodied in landscapes, beliefs, and the relationships between people. The remains of ancestors, artifacts, places, and archaeological sites are not the sources of this knowledge but rather the material and sacred manifestations of it. They do not require study because knowledge is imminent and all around us. People obtain knowledge through their emotive experience of the world. Spiritual knowledge is a guide for living.

Archaeologists by and large seek knowledge through science. Although considerable debate exists within the profession about exactly what science is, most archaeologists would agree that knowledge is something that we have to unearth. Archaeologists obtain knowledge by confronting, fitting, testing or in some other ways comparing their ideas with observations about the world. Thus, knowledge must be discovered or grounded in our experience of the material world. For archaeology the remains of ancestors, artifacts, places, and archaeological sites are the sources of knowledge because they are the stuff that scientists must observe to obtain knowledge. Knowledge involves temporality or a process. Scientific knowledge is practical.

If we view these two types of knowledge in terms of a simple opposition, then they must be antithetical and irreconcilable. We see this simple opposition in many of the debates between indigenous peoples and archaeology (Mason 2000). Some indigenous peoples claim that they know their histories and that archaeology offers nothing of interest to them (Turner 1989; Minthorn 1996). Some archaeologists dismiss spiritual views of humans and their relationship to nature as absurd and argue that the only valid way to know the world is through science (Clark 1998). Both types of knowledge are, however, human products and thus must have a common basis in the human condition. Indigenous peoples need practical knowledge and this is also embedded in spiritual understandings (Lomaomvaya and Ferguson 1999). Points of congruence can and do exist between indigenous spiritual knowledge and archaeological scientific knowledge (Ferguson et al. 1995; Echo-Hawk 2000b). By the same token, scientific knowledge is produced by humans who do so in a context of social and ideological relationships. Scientific knowledge has meaning or significance within these sets of relationships and because it is a human product it also has an emotive content (Shanks 1997). If science were not emotive then no scientists would become angry when their theories or interpretations were questioned.

The opposition between spiritual and scientific knowledge is not uncomplicated. Both science and spirituality necessarily entail the existence of practical knowledge and emotion. The tensions between these different ways of knowing exist both within each type of knowledge and between each type of knowledge. As a result these two forms of knowledge are not simply irreconcilable, nor are they broadly compatible.

As Garrick Bailey (1998: 24) has pointed out, the issue between archaeology and native peoples "is not religion but politics, not beliefs but control." It is ultimately a debate over intellectual property. Who will control American Indian cultural history, scholars or native peoples? The Australian sociologist J. A. Barnes (1990) contends that in these debates knowledge, either scientific knowledge or spiritual knowledge, has three overlapping properties:

1 Knowledge as a source of enlightenment (either intellectual or spiritual) enhances our understanding of the world. The more people who possess it the better; there is no zero-sum game.
2 Knowledge as power helps us alter, control, and/or manage the world, either practically or emotionally in either the material or the spiritual realm. Here there is a zero-sum game. People gain or lose depending upon their control of knowledge
3 Knowledge is a kind of property that can be possessed by individuals or groups. Knowledge as property can be concealed, bought, sold, stolen, shared, and given.

Any attempt to frame intellectual property issues or claims in terms of only one of these properties ignores the fact that all worthwhile knowledge embodies all three of these characteristics.

Archaeologists have traditionally rejected knowledge as property or power and embraced instead the notion of knowledge as enlightenment and stressed that the contribution of archaeology is expanding that enlightenment (Clark 1998; Lynott and Wylie 1995; Meighan 1994). Archaeologists usually reject the idea that knowledge of the past should be privately owned. We argue that knowledge of the past should be the property of all people so that all can share in the enlightenment that such knowledge offers. Archaeologists become the stewards of this knowledge because they possess the special training, certification, methods, and background learning to unearth it, interpret it, preserve it, and communicate or teach it to the general public. As Native Americans point out, this knowledge is also power. Archaeologists gain employment, prestige, and professional advancement with this knowledge (Bailey 1998; Deloria 1969). They also point out that this knowledge enables archaeologists to gain power over Native peoples. White scholars (including archaeologists) determine what the general public will be taught about Native peoples in schools, universities, and museums, and the courts and legislatures call on Euro-American Scholars for expert testimony when determining Native American land claims and legitimating Native identities (Campsi 1991; Field 1999). Archaeologists have this power because this stewardship is in reality a claim of ownership. This is most obvious when knowledge is embodied in human remains and artifacts that archaeologists and museums control. It is also the case, however, with knowledge in the abstract sense. Archaeologists may make knowledge publicly available but they retain ownership of the production and distribution of that knowledge.

Indigenous peoples tend to view their knowledge as a form of property: property that has been stolen from them along with their more tangible assets of land and resources (Churchill, 1994; Deloria 1973). They recognize knowledge as enlightenment but emphasize this is a spiritual enlightenment that is based in specific cultural identities and not necessarily available to non-members of specific cultural groups. In this way they lump together the activities of archaeologists, looters, anthropologists, and New Age advocates, all of whom come from the dominant culture and seek to take human remains, artifacts, and knowledge from them. Knowledge and the human remains and objects that embody it have power. In a spiritual sense it has power to maintain the harmony of the world or alternatively harm and/or destroy that harmony. A common theme in indigenous objections to the curation of human remains or sacred artifacts is that removing human remains and artifacts from their proper place has caused physical, psychological, and emotional harm to native people (Hammil and Cruz 1989; Pullar 1994). It also has power in the political realm, and indigenous critics of archaeology point out how the robbing of their graves accompanied the subjugation of native cultures.

Once we realize that worthwhile knowledge always entails aspects of enlightenment, power, and property and that these three aspects cross-cut the distinctions between scientific and spiritual ways of knowing, we are left with a very complex sense of the character of knowledge. We should be encouraged by the fact that this complexity creates numerous spaces of compatibility between archaeology and indigenous peoples. In these spaces lies the potential for a radically transformed American archaeology that serves many interests in different ways.

BIBLIOGRAPHIC NOTE

Native American commentaries on archaeology are more often presented verbally than written, and to understand Native American perspectives an archaeologist needs to talk with Indian people. Any consideration of the relationship between archaeology and Native Americans must begin with the work of Vine Deloria (1969, 1973, 1995, 2002). He has been one of archaeology's most vocal and eloquent indigenous critics. Bilosi and Zimmerman (1997) edited a reflexive volume on Deloria's impact on anthropology. In order to understand the relationship between archaeology and Native America it is necessary to understand the history of Native America and Euro-American concepts of Indians (Axtell 2001; McGuire 1992). Several key critical histories of American archaeology also discuss the development of the relationship between Indians and archaeologists (Kehoe 1998; Patterson 1995; Trigger 1989). Berkhofer's seminal work (1978) has been followed by more recent and excellent studies (Deloria 1998; Dippie 1982; Hundorf 2001; Kilpatrick, 1999). Bordewich (1997) is the key backlash work. Mihesuah (2000) contains several key works and is an excellent place to start reading the immense literature on reburial and repatriation. Bray and Killion's (1994) edited volume on the Larsen Bay repatriation at the Smithsonian is a useful case study. The body of literature on cooperation between Native Americans and archaeologists is also growing. Spector (1993) remains one of the most self-reflexive and insightful considerations of this cooperation. Dongoske, Aldenderfer, and Doehner (2000) provide a collection of key articles from the Society for American Archaeology's "Working Together" column. Nicholas and Andrews (1997) offer a useful set of cases from Canada. The literature on the Kennewick controversy is nearly as immense now as the literature on reburial and repatriation (Chatters, 2001; Downey 2000; Thomas 2000). Finally, Watkins (2000) is a thoughtful consideration of a fully transformed archaeology.

REFERENCES

Aikio, M., and P. Aikio. 1989. A chapter in the history of the colonization of Sámi lands: The force migration of Norwegian Reindeer Sámi to Finland in the 1800s. In R. Layton (ed.), *Conflicts in the Archaeology of Living Traditions*. London: Unwin Hyman, pp. 116–130.

Anderson, B. 1983. *Imagined Communities: Reflections on the Origin and Spread of Nationalism*. London: Verso.

Axtell, J. 2001. *Natives and Newcomers: The Cultural Origins of North America*. Oxford: Oxford University Press.

Bailey, G. 1998. NGPRA, politics and control. *Anthropology Newsletter* 39(4): 24–28.

Barnes, J. A. 1990. *Models and Interpretations*. Cambridge, Cambridge University Press.

Basso, K. 1997. *Wisdom Sits in Places: Landscape and Language Among the Western Apache*. Albuquerque: University of New Mexico Press.

Benedict, J. 2001. *Without Reservation: How a Controversial Indian Tribe Rose to Power and Built the World's Largest Casino*. New York: Harper Perennial.

Berkhofer, R. F., Jr. 1978. *The White Man's Indian*. New York: Knopf.

Bilosi, T., and L. J. Zimmerman (eds.) 1997. *Indians and Anthropologists: Vine Deloria Jr. and the Critique of Anthropology*. Tucson: University of Arizona Press.

Bordewich, F. M. 1997. *Killing the White Man's Indian.* New York: Anchor Books.

Bray, T. L. 1996. Repatriation, power relations, and the politics of the past. *Antiquity* 70: 440–444.

——, and T. W. Killion (eds.) 1994. *Reckoning With the Dead: The Larsen Bay Repatriation and the Smithsonian Institution.* Washington, DC: Smithsonian Institution Press.

Buikstra, J. 1981. A specialist in ancient cemetery studies looks at the reburial issue. *Early Man* 3(3): 26–27.

Cahn, E. S. (ed.). 1969. *Our Brother's Keeper: The Indian in White America.* New York: New Community Press.

Campsi, J. 1991. *The Mashpee Indians: Tribe on Trial.* Syracuse, NY: Syracuse University Press.

Chatters, J. C. 2001. *Ancient Encounters: Kennewick Man and the First Americans.* New York: Simon & Schuster.

Churchill, W. 1994. *Indians Are Us?: Culture and Genocide in Native North America.* Monroe, WI: Common Courage Press.

Clark, G. A. 1998. NAGPRA, religion and science. *Anthropology Newsletter* 39(4): 24–25.

——1999. NAGPRA, science and the demon-haunted world. *Skeptical Inquirer* May/June: 38–45.

Cole, D. 1985. *Captured Heritage: The Scramble for Northwest Coast Artifacts.* Toronto: Douglas & McIntyre.

Condori, C. M. 1989. History and prehistory in Bolivia: What about the Indians? In R. Layton (ed.), *Conflicts in the Archaeology of Living Traditions.* London: Unwin Hyman, pp. 46–59.

Deloria, P. J. 1998. *Playing Indian.* New Haven, CT: Yale University Press.

Deloria, V., Jr. 1969. *Custer Died for Your Sins: An Indian Manifesto.* New York: Macmillan.

——1973. *God is Red.* New York: Delta Books.

——1995. *Red Earth, White Lies: Native Americans and the Myth of Scientific Fact.* New York: Scribner.

——2002. *Evolution, Creationism, and Other Modern Myths.* Golden, CO: Fulcrum.

——, and C. Lytle. 1984. *The Nations Within: The Past and Future of American Indian Sovereignty.* New York: Pantheon.

Dilworth, L. 1996. *Imagining Indians in the Southwest.* Washington, DC: Smithsonian Institution Press.

Dippie, B. W. 1982. *The Vanishing American.* Middletown, CT: Wesleyan University Press.

Dongoske, K. E., M. Aldenderfer, and K. Doehner. 2000. *Working Together: Native Americans and Archaeologists.* Washington, DC: Society for American Archaeology.

Downey, R. 2000. *The Riddle of the Bones: Politics, Science, Race and the Story of Kennewick Man.* New York: Copernicus Books.

Echo-Hawk, R. 2000a. Exploring ancient worlds. In K. E. Dongoske, M. Aldenderfer, and K. Doehner (eds.), *Working Together: Native Americans and Archaeologists.* Washington, DC: Society for American Archaeology, pp. 3–8.

——2000b. Ancient history in the New World: Integrating oral traditions and the archaeological record in deep time. *American Antiquity* 65(2): 267–290.

Eisler, K. I. 2001. *Revenge of the Pequots: How a Small Native American Tribe Created the World's Most Profitable Casino.* New York: Simon & Schuster.

Ferguson, T. J. 1996. Native Americans and the practice of archaeology. *Annual Review of Anthropology* 25: 63–79.

——, K. Dongoske, M. Yeatts, and L. Jenkins. 1995. Working together Hopi oral history and archaeology: Part I: The role of archaeology. *SAA Bulletin* 13(3): 10–13.

Field, L. W. 1999. Complicities and collaborations: Anthropologists and the "unacknowledged tribes" of California. *Current Anthropology* 40(2): 193–209.

Ford, R. I. 1973. Archaeology serving humanity. In C. Redman (ed.), *Research and Theory in Current Archaeology*. New York: John Wiley, pp. 83–93.

Fowler, D. 2000. *A Laboratory for Anthropology: Science and Romanticism in the American Southwest, 1846–1930*. Albuquerque: University of New Mexico Press.

Goetzmann, W. H., and W. N. Goetzmann. 1986. *The West of the Imagination*. New York: W. W. Norton.

Gould, R. 1981. *The Mismeasure of Man*. New York: W. W. Norton.

Hammil, J., and R. Cruz. 1989. Statement of American Indians against desecration before the World Archaeological Congress. In R. Layton (ed.), *Conflicts in the Archaeology of Living Traditions*. London: Unwin Hyman, pp. 46–59.

Haven, S. F. 1856. *Archaeology of the United States*. Washington, DC: Smithsonian Institution, Smithsonian Contributions to Knowledge, Vol. 8.

Hemmings, S. 2000. Ngarrindjeri burials as cultural sites: Indigenous heritage issues in Australia. *World Archaeological Bulletin* 11: 58–66.

Hill, R. 1977. Reclaiming cultural artifacts. *Museum News* May/June: 43–46.

Howard, K. L., and D. F. Pardue. 1996. *Inventing the Southwest: The Fred Harvey Company and Native American Art*. Flagstaff, AZ: Northland Publishing.

Hubert, J. 1989a. A proper place for the dead: A critical review of reburial. In R. Layton (ed.), *Conflicts in the Archaeology of Living Traditions*. London: Unwin Hyman, pp. 131–166.

——1989b. First World Archaeological Inter-Congress, Vermillion, South Dakota, USA. *World Archaeological Bulletin* 4: 14–19.

Hundorf, S. M. 2001. *Going Native: Indians in the American Cultural Imagination*. Ithaca, NY: Cornell University Press.

Kehoe, A. B. 1998. *The Land of Prehistory: A Critical History of American Archaeology*. London: Routledge.

Kennedy, R. G. 1994. *Hidden Cities: The Discovery and Loss of Ancient North American Civilization*. New York: Penguin.

Kilpatrick, J. 1999. *Celluloid Indians*. Lincoln: University of Nebraska Press.

Krech, S., III. 1999. *The Ecological Indian: Myth and History*. New York: W. W Norton.

Lawson, M. L. 1994. *Those Dammed Indians: The Pick-Sloan Plan and the Missouri River Sioux, 1944–1980*. Norman: University of Oklahoma Press.

LeBlanc, S. A. 1999. *Prehistoric Warfare in the American Southwest*. Salt Lake City: University of Utah Press.

Lekson, S. H. 1988. The idea of the kiva in Anasazi archaeology. *Kiva* 53(3): 213–234.

Lomaomvaya, M., and T. J. Ferguson. 1999. Hisatqatsit Aw Maamatslalwa – Comprehending Our Past Lifeways: Thoughts about a Hopi Archaeology. Paper presented at the Chacmool Conference, Calgary.

Lynott, M. J., and A. Wylie (eds.) 1995. *Ethics and Archaeology: Challenges for the 1990s*. Washington, DC: Society for American Archaeology.

Mason, R. 2000. Archaeology and Native North American oral traditions. *American Antiquity* 65(2): 239–266.

Matunga, H. 1991. The Maori delegation to WAC 2: Presentation and reports. *World Archaeological Bulletin* 5: 43–54.

McDonald, J. D., L. J. Zimmerman, A. L. McDonald, William Tall Bull, and Ted Rising Sun. 1991. The Northern Cheyenne outbreak of 1879: Using oral history and archaeology as tools of resistance. In R. H. McGuire and R. Paynter (eds.), *The Archaeology of Inequality*. Oxford: Blackwell, pp. 125–150.

McGuire, R. H. 1992. Archaeology and the First Americans. *American Anthropologist* 94(4): 816–836.

——1994. Do the right thing. In T. L. Bray and T. W. Killion (eds.), *Reckoning With the Dead: The Larsen Bay Repatriation and the Smithsonian Institution*. Washington, DC: Smithsonian Institution Press, pp. 180–183.

——1997. Why have archaeologists thought the real Indians were dead and what can we do about it? In T. Biolsi and L. J. Zimmerman (eds.), *Indians and Anthropologists: Vine Deloria Jr. and the Critique of Anthropology*. Tucson: University of Arizona Press, pp. 63–91.

——2002. Stories of power, powerful tales: A commentary on ancient Pueblo violence. In M. O'Donovan (ed.), *The Dynamics of Power*. Carbondale: Southern Illinois University Press, pp. 126–147.

McLoughlin, W. G. 1986. *Cherokee Renascence in the New Republic*. Princeton, NJ: Princeton University Press.

Meighan, C. 1985. Archaeology and anthropological ethics. *Anthropology Newsletter* 26(9): 20.

——1994. Burying American archaeology. *Archaeology* 93(3): 739.

Meltzer, D. 1993. *The Search for the First Americans*. Washington, DC: Smithsonian Institution Press.

Michaelsen, S. 1994. *The Limits of Multiculturalism: Interrogating the Origins of American Anthropology*. Minneapolis: University of Minnesota Press.

Mihesuah, D. A. 2000. *Repatriation Reader: Who Owns American Indian Remains?* Lincoln: University of Nebraska Press.

Minthorn, A. 1996. Human remains should be reburied. Umatilla, OR: Confederated Tribes of the Umatilla Indian Reservation.

Moffitt, J. F., and S. Sebastián. 1996. *O Brave New People: The European Invention of the American Indian*. Albuquerque: University of New Mexico Press.

Morris, A. A. 1933. *Digging in the Southwest*. Garden City, NY: Doubleday.

Nicholas, G. P., and T. D. Andrews (eds.). 1997. *At a Crossroads: Archaeology and First Peoples of Canada*. Burnaby, BC: Archaeology Press.

Parman, D. L. 1994. *Indians and the American West in the Twentieth Century*. Bloomington: Indiana University Press.

Patterson, T. C. 1995. *Toward a Social History of Archaeology in the United States*. Fort Worth, TX: Harcourt Brace.

Poole, R. 1999. *Nation and Identity*. London, Routledge.

Pullar, G. L. 1994. The Qikertarmiut and the scientist: Fifty years of clashing world views. In T. L. Bray and T. W. Killion (eds.), *Reckoning With the Dead: The Larsen Bay Repatriation and the Smithsonian Institution*. Washington, DC: Smithsonian Institution Press, pp. 15–25.

Quick, P. 1985. *Proceedings Conference on Reburial Issues*. Washington, DC: Society for American Archaeology.

Schoolcraft, H. R. 1856. *Historical and Statistical Information Respecting the History, Condition, and Prospects of the Indian Tribes of the United States*, Vol. 4. New York: Lippincott & Grambo.

Sellers, C. C. 1980. *Mr. Peale's Museum*. New York: W. W. Norton.

Shanks, M. 1997. *Experiencing the Past*. London: Routledge.

——, and R. H. McGuire. 1968. The craft of archaeology. *American Antiquity* 61: 75–88.

Silverberg, R. 1968. *Mound Builders of Ancient America: The Archaeology of a Myth*. New York: Graphic Society.

Slotkin, R. 1986. Introduction to the 1831 edition. In J. F. Cooper, *The Last of the Mohicans*. New York: Penguin, pp. ix–xxviii.

Spector, J. 1993. *What This Awl Means: Feminist Archaeology at a Wahpeton Dakota Village*. St. Paul: Minnesota Historical Society Press.

Sprague, R. 1974. American Indians and American archaeology. *American Antiquity* 39(1): 1–2.

Squier, E. G., and E. H. Davis. 1848. *Ancient Monuments of the Mississippi Valley*. Washington, DC: Smithsonian Institution, Smithsonian Contributions to Knowledge I.

Stanford, D., and B. Bradley. 2000. The Solutrean solution – Did some ancient Americans come from Europe? *Discovering Archaeology* 2(1): 54–55.

Strauss, L. G. 2000. Solutrean settlement of North America? A review of reality. *American Antiquity* 65(2): 219–226.

Talbot, S. 1984. Desecration and American Indian religious freedom. *Akwesasne Notes* 16(4): 20–21.

Tarpy, C. 2000. Pueblo ancestors return home. *National Geographic* November: 118–125.

Thomas, C. 1894. Report on the mound explorations of the Bureau of Ethnology. *Twelfth Annual Report of the Bureau of American Ethnology 1890–1891*. Washington, DC: Smithsonian Institution.

Thomas, D. H. 2000. *Skull Wars: Kennewick Man, Archaeology, and the Battle for Native American Identity*. New York: Basic Books.

Trigger, B. 1980. Archaeology and the image of the American Indian. *American Antiquity* 45(4): 662–76.

—— 1984. Alternative archaeologies: Nationalist, colonialist, and imperialist. *Man* 19: 355–370.

—— 1986. Prehistoric archaeology and American society. In D. J. Meltzer, D. D. Fowler, and J. A. Sabloff (eds.), *American Archaeology Past and Future*. Washington, DC: Smithsonian Institution Press, pp. 187–216.

—— 1989. *A History of Archaeological Thought*. Cambridge: Cambridge University Press.

Turner, C. G., II, and J. A. Turner. 1999. *Man Corn: Cannibalism and Violence in the Prehistoric American Southwest*. Salt Lake City: University of Utah Press.

Turner, E. 1989. The souls of my dead brothers. In R. Layton (ed.), *Conflict in the Archaeology of Living Traditions*. London: Unwin Hyman, pp. 189–194.

Wallace, A. F. C. 1999. *Jefferson and the Indians: The Tragic Fate of the First Americans*. Cambridge, MA: Belknap Press.

Watkins, J. 2000. *Indigenous Archaeology: American Indian Values and Scientific Practice*. Walnut Creek, CA: AltaMira Press.

—— 2003. Beyond the margin: American Indians, First Nations, and archaeology in North America. *American Antiquity* 68(2): 273–285.

Weigle, M., and B. A. Babcock. 1996. *The Great Southwest of the Fred Harvey Company and the Santa Fe Railway*. Phoenix, AZ: Heard Museum.

Zimmerman, L. J. 1989. Made radical by my own. In R. Layton (ed.), *Conflicts in the Archaeology of Living Traditions*. London: Unwin Hyman, pp. 60–67.

——. 1997. Anthropology and responses to the reburial issue. In T. Bilosi and L. J. Zimmerman (eds.), *Indians and Anthropologists: Vine Deloria Jr. and the Critique of Anthropology*. Tucson: University of Arizona Press, pp. 92–112.

—— 2000. A new and different archaeology. In D. A. Mihesuah (ed.), *Repatriation Reader: Who Owns American Indian Remains?* Lincoln, University of Nebraska Press, pp. 294–306.

17

Identity, Modernity, and Archaeology: The Case of Japan

Koji Mizoguchi

Modernity, the Nation-State, and Archaeology

The connection between modernity and archaeology has by now been well explored (e.g., Champion and Díaz-Andreu 1996; Hodder 1991; Kohl and Fawcett 1995). It has also been pointed out that the nation-state functions as the boundary-marker for contexts in which specific connections between modern institutions and archaeology were, and are, constituted and reproduced. However, the mechanisms at work behind the seemingly organic interdependence between modernity, the nation-state, and archaeology does not appear to have yet been fully investigated. Why did the formation of modern nation-states in many cases coincide with the disciplinization of archaeology? Why was archaeology intensively mobilized in the constitution of national identity? These questions have often been answered by referring to the artificiality, or constructed-ness of the nation-state and the necessary masking or naturalization of its coercive power, and it has been claimed that archaeology and archaeological narratives have been mobilized in this process. However, the question still remains: why archaeology? Why has archaeology been mobilized to fulfill that function? In order to answer this question, we need to specify the characteristics of archaeology and archaeological materials that make them particularly appropriate to the constitution and reproduction of the entity country by country.

The history of Japanese archaeology and Japan as a modern nation-state offers a particularly good example with which to consider the issue, because modernization and the formation of a modern nation-state took place as a tightly combined process in the country, and archaeology played an important role in this (Oguma 1995: 73–86; Teshigawara 1995: 33–120). The process was accelerated by pressure from the outside, mainly from the Western colonial powers, and consequently, Japan became the only country in East Asia to colonize neighboring countries, namely Korea and Taiwan, and to practice colonial rule. Those factors influenced the way in which national identity and the identity of the Japanese were constituted (Komori 2001). As illustrated below, these identities were constituted in two semi-autonomous but mutually influencing spheres: both through colonial expansion to neighboring countries, and through negotiating the position of Japan as a newly founded nation-state with the West (Kan 2001; Komori 2001; Oguma 1995). The coexistence of those two spheres in the discursive formation of the national identity and the identity of the Japanese had a significant effect upon the way Japanese archaeology operated before World War II. After Japan's catastrophic defeat in the war in 1945, the former sphere disappeared, and the reproduction of the national identity became largely confined to that of negotiation, mainly with the West. In this, the United States played the crucial role, not only as the most influential politico-economic force in the Western bloc, but also as the symbol of the West (e.g., Osawa 1998). This landscape of self-identification basically continued to exist until the end of the Cold War, when the relatively stable structure of the post-World-War-II landscape collapsed. Since then, not only national self-identification, but also the self-identification of individual citizens, has been facing increasing difficulty. This last change is also related to intensification variously described as the high modernism, late modernity or postmodernity (Osawa 1998).

In what follows, I will briefly trace the history of Japanese archaeology from the foundation of the Japanese modern nation-state (the Meiji restoration in 1867) to the present day by focusing on the co-transformation of the basic structure of archaeological discourse and the way national identity and the identity of the Japanese are constituted. This analysis will elucidate the positionality of archaeology. Part of the investigation will examine the way in which Western theoretical arguments have been accepted or rejected. The chapter will conclude with an argument about the future direction of social archaeology, from a Japanese perspective.

The Development of Modernity and Archaeology in Japan

Edward Sylvester Morse, an American zoologist who taught biology in the Faculty of Science at the University of Tokyo between 1877 and 1879, is widely regarded as the founding father of modern Japanese archaeology. His excavation of the Omori shell-middens on the outskirts of Tokyo and the resulting publication *Shell Mounds of Omori* (Memoirs of the Science Department, Vol. I, Part I) in 1879 are highly praised today as the work of a modern Darwinian-influenced scientific mind (Kondo and Sahara 1983: 185–188; Teshigawara 1995: 33–35). However, some have pointed out that his academic legacy was limited (Kondo and Sahara 1983: 211–214). Japanese scholars have seemingly distanced themselves from his contributions. For instance, Shogoro Tsuboi, the first professor of the Department of Anthropology in the faculty of Science at the University of Tokyo (founded in 1893), and a founding father of modern Japanese archaeology, is recorded to have actively denied not only influence from, but also contact with, Morse on numerous occasions, despite the fact that Tsuboi himself recorded that he contacted Morse for the identification of potsherds (Teshigawara 1995: 39–40). It has been speculated that ill feeling toward foreign influence, in this case that from a colonial power, was the cause (Oguma 1995: 30). However, a particular part of his legacy was inherited, namely his interest in the first inhabitants of the archipelago (Kondo and Sahara 1983: 136–153): the issue of the origin(s) of the

Japanese was the subject of the heated debate during the early history of Japanese archaeology.

The modern Japanese nation-state and the concept of the national body

The issue of the origin of a nation or a race surfaces and comes to be pursued as the issue of self-identification almost whenever the condition surrounding a nation-state is problematized. The history of Japan from the Meiji restoration up to the end of World War II can be written as the continuous reproblematization of national and popular identity and the identity of the Japanese people. The above-mentioned two spheres of self-identification – through colonial expansion and through negotiations with the West, coexisted as they continuously changed their significance in relation to one another, and both spheres were integrated through the mediation of a conceptual construct, the concept of *Koku* (nation/state)-*tai* (body), the "national body."

The formation of the nation was an important prerequisite for nation-states to establish their institutions, which inevitably disembedded people from the traditional, localized bases of their existence/self-identification and transformed them into citizens. Disembedding entails the uprooting of the behavioral norm and the set of expectations for everyday life that are formerly embedded in local knowledge formed and reproduced through the direct, recurrent sharing of experiences. In order to make those who are uprooted function in a system called a nation-state, the spatio-temporal extension of which far exceeds the domain of day-to-day experience, an imaginary communal unit such as a nation, has to be created in order to re-embed them in an imaginary sphere of shared everyday experiences, to enable them to imagine and believe that they are organically connected to one another despite the distance lying between them, and to make them feel secure again.

Citizenship, a prerequisite for the establishment of a nation-state, had to be established very quickly in Japan as the new nation-state countered pressures from the Western colonial powers (Komori 2001: Chapter I). However, this was very difficult. In the case of European nation-states, the establishment of citizenship was a long process which began during the era of absolute monarchy. Predecessors of the modern institutions such as a standing army and taxation gradually disembedded people from the conceptual landscape formed through their local, everyday experiences (Foucault 1977; Giddens 1990: 21–29). The working of these institutions also prepared people for their re-embedding in the artificial conceptual landscape of the nation-state. In the case of Japan, however, the feudal system had to be transformed into a nation-state in a very short period of time. The people were unprepared to become citizens, since the mechanisms which train people to become citizens did not fully exist. The concept of the national body was invented to overcome this difficulty.

Let us examine the distinct characteristics of the national body from other variants of the nation. As a conceptual unit, the national body was embodied by the emperor. The status of the emperor, in the newly founded constitution (the so-called Meiji constitution), was designated as the constitutionally bounded absolute sovereign who had the right and obligation to make the final decision in every matter concerning the running of the country. The executive, the parliament, the judiciary, and the military were entrusted not by the people but by the emperor to fulfill their duty, and the people were assured by the emperor of the proper running of the country and had to be ever thankful for that in order to respect and obey the emperor. Those who were incorporated in the national body were encouraged to conceive of themselves as being directly connected to the emperor (Uchida 2002: 114). The relationship was often portrayed as that of a father and child. The disembedding of the people was achieved by the creation of this imaginary personal relationship with the emperor in the form of fictive kinship. The people became independent individuals and voluntarily fulfilled their responsibility to the country by becoming individual "children" of the emperor, rather than by becoming autonomous citizens. Meanwhile, individuals had to be re-embedded in this imagined community in which they were organically united as the children of the same father. This was a sophisticated conceptual strategy which disembedded people from the mental landscape of small, local agrarian communities, and re-embedded them in that of a state and integrating them as a nation without going through the process of making them citizens.

The national body was an entity with a certain spatio-temporal extension. The image and positionality of the emperor and imperial family, and the spatio-temporal boundaries of the national body became the two basic conceptual constructs which functioned as the main constitutive elements of the national body, as the perfectly preserved, pure ethnic community continuing from the beginning of time.

The concept of the nation, intrinsically, has elements of artificiality. However, as Anthony Smith (1986) suggests, nations were constructed through the mobilization of pre-existing, tangible similarities and differences and through articulating them into ethnies (ethnic communities) or traditions. In contrast, the discourse of the national body could not rely on uniquely Japanese traditions, because Westernization was the policy of the government, and, accordingly, the introduction of the items of Western civilization was as important as the articulation of uniquely Japanese traditions (Komori 2001). This contradiction had to be resolved, and the concept of the national body functioned as the framework for self-identification by accommodating those contradictory necessities, Westernization and the articulation of indigenous traditions, at the same time. In that sense, the concept needed to be founded solely in discursive formation, and, naturally, academic discourses were strictly regulated.

The national body, the emperor, and the origin of the Japanese

Archaeology was mobilized to support the above-mentioned two main constitutive elements of the national body, that is the image and positionality of the emperor and the imperial family, and the spatio-temporal boundaries of nation. The image and positionality of the emperor were the most important and at the same time the most vulnerable of these. The imperial household was kept in obscurity throughout the Edo period: it had no political power but was utilized, in a fairly low-key manner, by the Edo feudal regime for the legitimization of their authority throughout the period, and its image and positionality had to be hastily (re-)constructed over the period around the Meiji restoration and the consolidation period of the nation-state (Taki 1988). The imperial mythology featured in such chronicles as Kojiki and Nihon-shoki (Aston 1972), compiled in the late seventh and early eighth centuries in order to legitimize the then newly established ancient state of Japan and the imperial household (e.g., Isomae 1998), was used to support this effort. The mythology told that the ancestors of the imperial family descended from heaven, created the land and conquered and assimilated aboriginal populations. This provided sources for political manipulation, one of which was the premise that the migration of the ancestors of the imperial family could be traced and the origin of the Japanese would be identifiable in archaeo-logical evidence (Teshigawara 1995: 95–99). Interestingly, foreign scholars, including Edward Morse, initially argued that the heaven mentioned in the chronicles was somewhere outside the archipelago, and the ancestors of the imperial family were a migrant population (Oguma 1995: 19–24), and this view was inherited by Japanese scholars. This further implied that archaeological evidence of the period before the migration of the ancestors of the imperial family was evidence for the life of aboriginal populations, and in that sense constituted the prehistory of Japan. The official history of the Japanese, from that point of view, began when the ancestors of the imperial family arrived on the archipelago. This also meant that the study of the true history of the imperial family and the Japanese, the archaeology of the periods after the supposed migration, had to be tightly regulated, because the study of the material evidence could potentially throw doubt onto the validity of royal mythology.

The Jomon culture of hunter-gatherers, according to the officially accepted view, was the culture of aboriginal populations which were conquered and assimilated by the ancestors of the imperial family called Ten(heaven)-son(descendant)-zoku(clan/group), meaning the group descended from heaven (Teshigawara 1995: 46–47). So, the study of the Jomon culture (its position in the chronology of Japanese prehistory, particularly its transition to the Yayoi period, was not fully established until the 1920s and 1930s) was a "safe" domain for archaeologists, because it had nothing to do with the imperial history, the history of the Ten-son-zoku group. However, the cultures or periods after that (the Kofun (mounded tomb) period) were, as we can see from the above-illustrated mythological framework, the evidence for the history of the imperial family and the national body which it encapsulated. So the study of those cultures and periods was regarded as dangerous, potentially casting doubts on the authenticity of the narrative of the national body (Teshigawara 1995: 67–72). This division of archaeology into two domains, one safe and the other dangerous, constituted a key structuring principle of the archaeological discourse of pre-World-War-II Japan.

Now let us examine at length how archaeology was mobilized in the definition of the spatio-temporal boundaries of the national body. This vividly shows how the notion of the national body played a constitutive role in how the archaeological dis-course of the period was structured.

Who were the first inhabitants of the Japanese territory, and how the ethnic make-up changed after colonization were issues vigorously debated, not only by anthropologists and archaeologists but also by scholars of various other disciplines, politicians, and social activists (Oguma 1995, 1998). In part, this was because the study fell into the category of safe archaeology. This also exemplifies the significant role commonly played by intellectuals in the invention of a tradition underpinning a new nation-state (Kan 2001: Chapter II). Yet, there appears to have been another, overtly political reason.

We can identify two standpoints: (1) Japanese culture is racially singular, and its content has not changed dramatically since the colonization of Japan; and (2) Japanese culture is racially mixed and plural, and its content has changed as newcomers have invaded or joined through time. The latter standpoint is further subdivided by differences in such questions as who were the first inhabitants of Japan and how many migrant populations came to the archipelago and conquered and assimilated the aboriginal population. These occupy the poles along a continuum, and innumerable variants exist in between, but each of these nodal opinions was connected to a specific political issue and agenda (Kan 2001).

The first standpoint was associated with the creation and consolidation of the concept of the internally homogeneous national body, and was vigorously debated from the Meiji restoration until the end of the nineteenth century. It gradually ceased to be the subject of a public discourse as Japan completed the initial phase of her nation-building through Westernization and began to colonize neighboring countries. The second standpoint was linked to the colonization of neighboring countries and related to the necessity of legitimizing the territorial expansion. The discourse of the origins, not the singular origin, of the Japanese became the main locus of discursive formation supporting this move. The claim that Japan had a history of incorporating and assimilating diverse racial groups was actively mobilized for the legitimation of colonization and the policy of assimilation, seen in a particularly drastic manner in the case of the colonization of Korea (Teshigawara 1995: 95–99).

Let us examine the debate about the first inhabitants of the archipelago, because this nicely shows how the boundaries of the national body were drawn and redrawn as the situation surrounding Japan changed, and how archaeology was involved in this process.

The point of dispute was whether the Ainu were the first inhabitants or not. The Ainu (issues concerning their ethnogenesis are far too diverse to be covered here) inhabited Hokkaido and smaller islands in the vicinity, and their population was so small that they were not regarded as a threat to the security of the feudal regime (cf. Oguma 1998: Chapter 3). However, toward the end of the Edo period Russia became interested in the islands and began to make territorial claims. At this point the Ainu were put under the direct rule of the feudal domain entrusted to control Hokkaido Island, called the Matsumae feudal domain. Once the Meiji government recognized Hokkaido Island as a subject of "internal colonization" and started sending a large number of people there, the importance of controlling the Ainu and claiming them as Japanese in order to make a territorial claim against Russia ceased. As the living conditions of the Ainu rapidly degenerated as the result of the colonization, and Christian missionaries initiated various aid and educational activities, the national government was forced to take notice of the Ainu once more. The Ainu issue from the national government's point of view, has now become that of an aboriginal minority. The intellectuals' reaction to this shift varied, but Tsuboi Shogoro, the above-mentioned founder of anthropology in Japan, actively intervened in the debate about governmental policy concerning the Ainu by comparing them with the Native American population (Oguma 1995: 81), and by quoting an example of the attempt to assimilate them.

Regardless of whether the Ainu were seen as the first inhabitants or not, the early inhabitants of Japan were, without exception, argued to have been conquered by a group coming from mainland Asia, to which the genealogy of the imperial family and the Japanese nation were linked. The redifferentiation and rearticulation of the Ainu as an aboriginal minority and their assimilation was conceived as comparable to the fictive historical narrative of the formation of the national body: the ancestors of the imperial family conquered and assimilated aboriginal populations in a similar fashion to the Ainu. This imaginary equivalence was mobilized to support the concept of the national body by providing it with a fictive direct historical parallel. And, because the historical narrative of the formation of the national body was the narrative of the arrival of new groups and their assimilation of the aboriginal populations, the methods necessary were those with which to trace the diffusions and find the traces of the habitation of the old aboriginal groups. Only the methodological tools and theoretical premises to trace the migration of peoples and their assimilation by pre-existing populations were necessary, and other archaeological concepts and methods which would systematize archaeological inference were not only unnecessary, but also dangerous.

The state power and archaeological practice

Archaeology was not taught as an academic discipline until the establishment of the first Department of Archaeology in the Faculty of Literature at Kyoto University in 1916. The most basic methodological tools of archaeology, such as stratigraphic excavations and typo-chronology, were not systematically introduced and adopted until the first quarter of the twentieth century (Teshigawara 1995: 108–115). Until that time the field of archaeological knowledge production had few means with which to differentiate itself (Teshigawara 1995: 109–110), and that made the field a most suitable one in which the discourse of the national body was reproduced not by scientific exclusion but by involving a wider community of the intellectuals who consciously and unconsciously played a role in supporting the maintenance of the national body.

From the first quarter of the twentieth century, the systematization of archaeological studies progressed. Such speculative accounts as that of the Jomon culture gradually vanished in favor of the expanding horizons of new, higher cultures of the Yayoi and the Kofun (Teshigawara 1995: 139–143). Those cultures were gradually reorganized into intraregional and interregional chronological stages. The progression of the construction of a nationwide chronological network effectively threw doubts on the validity of the mythology-based diffusionist narratives such as those outlined above. However, those doubts were carefully concealed by archaeologists themselves or modified so as not to contradict the doctrine of the national body. And interestingly, the Kofun period, characterized by gigantic keyhole-shaped tumuli, the largest examples of which were designated by the imperial house as the mausolea of ancient emperors, was the period about which the construction of a chronological system was slowest (Teshigawara 1995: 69–72). The systematization of Kofun archaeology would have almost certainly contradicted the early, mythology-based imperial history, and the investigation of the period from the viewpoint of the emergence and development of social stratification was intentionally avoided. In contrast, the construction of a nationwide chronological system progressed most rapidly in the study of Jomon culture and the prehistory of the imperial family.

The practice of organizing archaeological evidence into nationwide chronological systems, aided by the notion of stratigraphic excavation and typology was introduced by Seiryo Hamada (who studied under Flinders Petrie in London and was appointed the first professor in the department of Archaeology at Kyoto University, the first archaeology department founded in Japan [Hamada 1996 [1922]]). Ironically, this department came to function as a refuge for archaeologists who were forced to conceal their political conscience and scientific observations and just immersed themselves in the mechanistic, descriptive practice (e.g., Tozawa 1978: 56–57).

Japanese archaeology, on the one hand, had to organize its discourse to be congruent with the dominant discursive formation of state power and, on the other, to accomodate elements of Western archaeological discourse concerning the past. The concept of the national body occupied such a dominant position that individual communication fields were, regardless of whether they were for or against the concept, structured in relation to the concept.

Japanese Post-World-War-II Discursive Formation and Archaeology

Post-World-War-II archaeology refers to the period between 1945 and the late 1970s, a period characterized by the continuing existence of the basic structure of pre-war discursive space and its critique. As I will show later, this was necessitated by the rapidly crystallizing Cold War equilibrium, which also stabilized the general discursive formation of the time highly stable. Let us begin by examining the cause and effect of the continuation of the basic structure of the pre-war discourse into the post-war period. The concept of the national body again played a tacit, but pivotal role.

Japan's catastrophic defeat in World War II seemingly changed the situation completely. The old systems, embodied by the Meiji constitution, were abolished and the national body ceased to be mentioned in public. However, the structuring principles of general discursive formation remained unchanged (Kan 2001: Chapter 5), and so did the structuring principles of archaeological discourse. This was partly because of the new structure of politico-economic power which was later to become the foundation of the Cold War equilibrium; Japan, in that structure, was designated to function as a front-line nation of the United States and its allies against the Soviet Union (Kan 2001). For that to be achieved, the conceptual machinery proven to be most effective in integrating the Japanese was the national body and its pillar, the emperor and his historical positionality.

The symbolic emperor system

The emperor, previously the absolute sovereign of the nation, became the symbol of the integration of the nation. He became constitutionally detached from the running of the country, but he remained officially the embodiment of the voluntary unity of the individuals constituting the nation (the symbolic emperor system). This meant that the national body as a multifunctional conceptual entity remained intact, although it was rarely mentioned. As long as what embodied this entity, the emperor and the imperial household, remained intact, the entity itself was perceived as intact (cf. Kan 2001: 88–94, 99–114). The very nature of the entity as a conceptual, artificial construct (hence extremely flexible), worked as its strength. Japan had lost its colonies and the territories it had gained during the war, but that was conceived by the intellectual class who had formerly produced narratives supporting and legitimizing the expanding spatial extension of the national body as the purification of the content of the national body (Oguma 1995: Chapter 17). They claimed that the national body now became constituted by a single ethnic community or race. They claimed that this was the original form of the national body and the authentic nature of the Japanese had become polluted through the irresponsible misadventures conducted by hyperambitious individuals in the military and the executive. Narratives about the multiple origins of the Japanese, which were mobilized for the legitimation of the colonization and occupation, were conveniently forgotten or abandoned, and the loss of the colonies and occupied areas was tacitly portrayed as a return to the genuine, authentic state of the Japanese as a single-race, hence a "pure," nation (Oguma 1995: Chapter 17).

Ironically, the rise of the single-origin theory was also convenient for those who were trying to form a counter-discourse, particularly the advocates of Marxist history and archaeology. They were under a varying degree of influence from Russian-led communism/Marxism, and a unifying element of their discourse was the doctrine of racial self-determination as a slogan against United States-led imperialism, i.e., the forceful expansion of capitalist economy and of the Western bloc (Oguma 2002: Chapter 8). The slogan increasingly gained popularity by the fact that it gradually became apparent that the United States was utilizing the emperor and the continuation of the concept of the national body to reconstruct Japan as a successful capitalist state by preserving the old institutions, both economic and political, which were regarded by many as the problem of pre-war Japan (Oguma 2002: Chapter 3). For the Marxist historians and archaeologists, the critical investigation of the origin of the imperial household as a source of the ills for pre-war Japan had to be conducted hand in hand with the historical investigation of the singular origin of the Japanese race (cf. Toma 1951). The study of the origin of the Japanese nation had to locate not only the origin of the ills of Japan but also the source of pride for those Japanese who had constructed the nation under the shadow of the successive Chinese dynasties. It can easily be inferred that China was metaphorically compared to the United States, and the struggle against US-led imperialism which was preventing the total reform and democratization of Japan was compared to the Japanese ancient state formation as a process of struggle against Chinese influence (Oguma 2002 Chapter 3). We can see a core-periphery perspective here, although it was not systematically compared to Wallerstein's version (1974) or those archaeological works influenced by it.

Those factors constituted the backbone of the post-World-War-II archaeological discourse until the 1970s. The national body continued to play a pivotal role in discursive formation, and one's position in the discursive space continued to be determined, even if unconsciously, by his/her attitude to the notion. Although the notion itself gradually became unrecognizable, it continued to legitimize the continuation of reactionary discourses and institutions from the pre-war period. That effectively preserved the pre-war division of archaeology into the safe/apolitical and the dangerous/political/anti-imperial system. The former, I would argue, was embodied by Jomon archaeology and the latter by the Yayoi-Kofun/Marxist archaeology.

Marxist archaeology: the Japanese version

Marxist archaeology dates back to the 1920s and 1930s (Yokoyama 1955: 87–88). Deepening economic difficulties and influences from communist Russia encouraged a group of historians to initiate a project to analytically reveal the historical trajectory leading to the formation of a Japanese version of an imperialist capitalist state (Hara 1972). Taking a Marxist perspective, they regarded the investigation of the origin of social inequality an absolutely vital component of the project. To understand this historical event by situating it in the universal theory of the developmental stages (which claimed that every human society evolved from the stage of primitive communism through that of ancient slavery and that of feudalism to the stage of capitalism) was of particular importance for deciding what strategy should be taken to lead a socialist revolution in Japan. According to the communist doctrine of the time, the strategy of the socialist revolution of a given country had to be decided following the historical trajectory the country had taken.

The large tumuli of the Kofun period, including the designated imperial mausolea, were thought to indicate the establishment of the despotic rulers and the coercive power which enabled them to mobilize a large number of people like slaves. Their study and the study of the preceding historical process were conducted to scientifically (from the Marxist's point of view) reveal not only the origin of social inequality as the root of the problem of capitalism but also the ills of the Japanese nation-state, namely the emperor and the imperial household, constitutive elements of the national body, and the machineries of imperialistic capitalism ideologically dependent upon the former. As mentioned in the previous section, basic archaeological tools, concepts, and systems were underdeveloped at the time, and the involvement of archaeologists in the project was minimal. Many of the practitioners were politically active historians. The outcome of the study included many shortcomings (Wajima 1955: 33). However, this pre-war development constituted the basis of the Japanese Marxist approach, which was equipped with a strong political self-awareness.

Any Marxist approach, as a holistic interpretative framework, sorts a concerned body of evidence into interconnected units and investigates where the contradiction resides. Contradictions, for the Marxist, are *the* source of social change, and change is the intrinsic nature of society. In the case of Japanese Marxist archaeology, the contradictions leading to the formation and establishment of a class based stratification, the differentiation based upon control of the means of production, were the ultimate subject of study, and the Yayoi period (between around the fifth century BC and the late third century AD) (Wajima 1966) and the Kofun period (Kondo 1966) was seen as the decisive phase in the process. Widening contradictions between tribal social organization, based upon communal labor and the communal storage of products, and smaller semi-autonomous units functioning as actual units of everyday labor and accumulating non-communal wealth, the process ignited by the introduction of rice paddy-field agriculture at the beginning of the Yayoi period, was interpreted to have reached the point when developing social stratification in individual regions resulted in the formation of an alliance of local chieftains in which the chieftains of the present-day Kinai region of central Japan were most powerful (Kondo 1983). Chieftains of the Kinai region were the ancestors of the imperial household, around which the Japanese ancient state was to be established in the seventh century A D. In order to investigate this long-term process from a Marxist perspective, archaeological evidence was classified into various elements of infrastructure and ideology, units of social integration of various scales, and so on, and their interrelations and co-transformations were studied as indicating the deepening contradiction (Wajima 1966). The study of the process of social stratification and the emergence of the ancient state resulted in the methodological systematization of the practice of Japanese archaeology, which had formerly been somewhat undisciplined, and led to the formation of a unique tradition of social archaeological theorization.

However, I should note here that what was behind the formation of this social archaeological theorization and the systematization of archaeology was the shadow of the national body. Since the 1950s, the revival of the symbols of pre-war Japan, such as the redesignation of the anniversary of the foundation of the nation as a national holiday, a date taken from the imperial mythology, was gathering pace, and the danger of once more going down the same road toward a catastrophe like World War II was acutely felt. This theorization and systematization was firmly based upon the sense of reality, the reality of doing something good for society, and this feeling gave the practitioners a stable self-identity. They felt they knew who they were in terms of the effect of what they were doing to benefit the society (Mizoguchi 1997: 153–154). Both the systematizing tendency of the Marxist theorization and the sense of connectedness to social reality provided by the historical background and the political objective of the Marxist discourse functioned as the source for stability of the archaeological discursive formation of the period.

Jomon archaeology and the culture historical tradition

Jomon archaeology shows a stark contrast. The study of Jomon culture, before World War II, constituted a safe domain, one which was considered harmless to the legitimacy of the position of the emperor and the imperial household. Jomon culture, as illustrated above, was regarded as the culture of aboriginal populations conquered and assimilated by the ancestor of the imperial family and the Japanese people. This is why attempts to reconstruct some elements of the social organization of Jomon culture (Teshigawara 1995: 129–130) could be left unchecked by the state during the pre-World-War-II period. This positionality of the study of Jomon culture, despite its recognition as a period after the establishment of the nationwide chronological system around the 1920s and 1930s, remained intact after World War II. Setting aside innumerable attempts to refine the intraregional and interregional chronological systems, the period was predominantly the subject of culture-historical reconstructions. The functional reconstruction of individual material items was a major topic of the study, and the investigation of individual settlements and their interactions was conducted for the reconstruction of the social organization of the phase to which relevant settlements belonged. The study of the Jomon period remained the reconstruction of the contents of a synchronic slice extracted from the trajectory of the reproduction and transformation of the society. This synchronism constituted a distinct characteristic of the discourse of Jomon studies and reinforced its tacitly perceived character as a pre-history, namely the changeless, hence history-less, period of Japanese prehistory.

The coexistence of two discourses and its consequences

The coexistence of those two discourses in the discursive space of the period had some significant implications. The contrast between Yayoi-Kofun archaeology and Jomon archaeology in terms of their structural principles influenced the ways in which Western archaeological theories and methodologies were introduced to Japan. The Yayoi-Kofun discourse was Marxist and political, and produced some remarkable case studies conducted with a strong critical awareness of their political implications in both micro/local and macro/national scales. A good example is the excavation of the Tsukinowa tumulus in Okayama Prefecture. The residents of a small mining town in the Chugoku mountains became interested in local history through the encouragement of a group of archaeologists. They learnt how to connect their living conditions to the past by understanding history as a sequence of episodes forming the trajectory leading to the present, that had many problems yet to be overcome (Tsukinowa kofun kanko kai 1960; Teshigawara 1995: 214–218).

The Marxist thesis of developmental stages, and the notion of contradictions between the infrastructure and superstructure of the social whole that moved society upward in those stages, helped the people connect their living conditions, and the contradictions they faced, to that of a stage in the historic trajectory and made sense of the causal connections between them. This discursive characteristic of Marxist theory, explaining the present in terms of the past, made those who advocated it feel that the ills of the present had their roots in certain points in time. This characteristic conjoined two aims of the post-World-War-II critical archaeology: first the critique of the concept of the national body, and second the continuing ills of the present. The critique of the past became the critique of the present in the discursive space of Japanese Marxist archaeology. This is a significant precursor of the critical social archaeology that emerged in the West in the 1980s as part of postprocessualism.

However neither the processual nor postprocessual developments in the West were enthusiastically accepted. On one hand the processual method and theory package looked anti-historical to the practitioners, and hence, apolitical and reactionary. On the other hand, the significant characteristic of the postprocessual approaches, i.e., its critical political self-awareness, looked all too familiar. At this point, it has to be noted that the effort of synthesizing the ways to bridge the gap between Marxist theory and archaeological reality in the past, and in the present, was rarely made. Although in actuality it was tacitly made in each individual case study in a rather undisciplined manner by classifying the evidence into analytical units and by explaining the reason why particular units were given deeper treatments than others. This anti-theorization tendency was deep-rooted and its cause was complicated. However, in the case of Japanese Marxist archaeology, the above-illustrated factors significantly constituted indifference to theoretical developments abroad.

At the same time, the discourse of Jomon archaeology, was dominated by the reconstruction of the static, synchronic slice of social reproduction and transformation, and some constitutive elements of processual archaeology such as the application of the middle-range research strategy and systemic thinking, fit nicely into the range of the analytical requirements. This formed the background against which both the autonomous development and the introduction of the processual methods and perspectives took place relatively easily. Site-catchment analysis (e.g., Akazawa et al. 1986) is a notable example.

In addition to the above, this discursive division was also supported by the differential distribution of the Jomon and the Yayoi-Kofun sites between eastern and western Japan. The distribution of the former is denser in the east than in the west, and that of the latter, vice versa. This naturally resulted in different daily archaeological experiences, such as what one saw in museums, what one dug up at sites, and what one talked about, and added a spatial dimension to the discursive division (Mizoguchi 2002: 29–42).

Fortunate stability

In all, what characterized the discursive space of the post-World-War-II period in the history of Japanese archaeology was its stability. The two discourses, the Jomon and the Yayoi-Kofun, that coexisted in the discursive space of post-World-War-II archaeology, were constituted in their positionality by pre-war archaeology. As something that had to be referred to when one identified one's position in the discursive space, regardless of being for or against it, the shadow of the national body remained the dominant referent and functioned as the pivotal axis in the structuration of the archaeological discourse of the post-war period. The Jomon discourse remained about synchronic cultural reconstruction and rarely attempted to investigate the historical process of social transformations (toward social stratification). The Yayoi-Kofun discourse, in contrast, was about the investigation of social inequality, which resulted in the emergence of the ancestor of the imperial household, one of the ills of the pre-war, imperialistic capitalist Japan.

The existence of the dominant axis of structuration for archaeological discourse, continuing from the pre-war period, made the framework of choices archaeologists had to make in their practice relatively simple. These were the existence of the stable discursive structure formed by the coexistence of the Jomon/apolitical and the Yayoi-Kofun/radical political discourses, and the principle of classifying archaeological information into a stable set of analytical categories that were automatically determined by which discourses one participated in. This minimized the difficulty of archaeologists in choosing what to see, what to say, how to talk, and so on, in their archaeological practice.

This fortunate stability came to an end when the Cold-War equilibrium collapsed and a new condition, often described as late modernity, high modernity or postmodernity, set in.

Postmodern Difficulties

This phase, which began sometime in the 1970s and still continues, can be characterized by the fragmentation of the discursive space. Fragmentation, in this case, means the coexistence of an increasing number of distinct sets of expectations upon which archaeologists reproduce their discourses. In other words, it is a fragmentation in the aim of archaeological practice. A serious consequence of this fragmentation is the discourse and the parallel rise of the narrative of the extremes. As illustrated below, the fragmentation and related phenomena can be understood as systemic reactions to deepening "function differentiation" in social formation (cf. Luhmann 1995: 460–466).

The initial phase of the fragmentation took the form of the demise of the Marxist program. This was a typical example of the end of a grand narrative-type discourse caused by the transformation of its environment. A discourse is reproduced through the reproduction of its boundary, by which the constitutive elements of the discourse are differentiated from those that are not. The differentiation goes on in a self-reflexive manner. By self-reflexive manner I mean that the differentiation is conducted by drawing upon the memory of previous differentiations. The memory constitutes a set of expectations of what reaction an act would evoke in a certain person, and how they would respond.

From "heavy" to "light" capitalism

Bearing the foregoing in mind, let us examine the change which took place in the environment of the Marxist discourse.[1] As a persuasive political program, Marxist-led socialism had lost its appeal in Japan by the mid to late 1970s, as evidenced by the decline of labor and union movements. The transformation of the workplace, from collective to more segregated conditions in the factories, gradually destroyed the locales in which workers had maintained their day-to-day contact and shared experiences which generated coherent and collective working class spirit and working class habitus.

Concurrently, the annual income of ordinary citizens rose sharply, and the feeling of "belonging to the middle class" became widespread. This feeling was partly supported by the fact that workers were now able to buy such commodities as color televisions, refrigerators, washing machines, and so on (Tomoeda 1991). Factory workers could not buy such things easily in the early 1960s, but by the end of the 1970s more than ninety percent of households owned such commodities, and purchased them not for their functional necessity but for reasons of style (Tomoeda 1991: 142). A crucial incentive of labor and union movements, the desire to improve working and living conditions by making changes in employer–employee relations, was replaced with demands for pay rises, as was the case in other industrialized countries (Bauman 1988: 71–88). The self-identity of factory workers, that had been acquired by sharing homogeneous workplace conditions and by fighting for a cause, was now realized by purchasing commodities with certain styles, appealing to certain tastes. The detachment of the mass from face-to-face encounters situated in particular time–space settings and the disappearance of experiential constraints upon the living condition of the mass went hand in hand. Zygmunt Bauman (2000: 54–59) describes this as the transformation from "heavy" to "light" capitalism.

From a pragmatic political point of view, in such social circumstances it would have seemed pointless to carry on talking about issues such as the emergence of class-based inequality and social contradictions in the past in order to make changes in the present. Enthusiasm behind the investigation of those issues, as illustrated in the previous section, had been supported by the feeling that those things had causal connections to the social contradictions of the present. The feeling described as that of *causal-connectedness* to the past, was gone, as were the collective feelings of common injustice and striving toward a common goal, i.e., the realization of socialist democracy. A foundation of the *reality* of the Marxist discourse resided in the belief that archaeological practice could have a pragmatic impact upon Japanese politics. By revealing how Japanese prehistoric societies evolved from a Marxist point of view, it was believed that the archaeologist could both verify the party policy of the communists and enrich the party's program for the future (cf. Hara 1972: 389–395). This foundational sense of reality in archaeological practice was also lost.

Fragmentation and the rise of the transcendental

What we should emphasize here is that the changes illustrated above stemmed from the increasing complexity in capitalist social formation, in which the increasing segmentation and differentiation of new domains of social interaction and expertise became the norm of social reproduction and the time–space organization of social life. In addition, the way self-identity was constituted, i.e., the technology of the self, underwent a drastic transformation as a systemic reaction to it. The institutionalization of cultural resource management (CRM) was to become a principal domain of Japanese archaeological practice, and can be understood as a reflection of such a process.

Owing to the drastic increase in large-scale developments, cultural resource management units which were usually attached to local education boards, emerged and archaeology became a stable job or an area of expert knowledge. This resulted in the rise of professionalism, in which pragmatic concerns, such as how to retrieve as much information as possible in rescue contexts took precedence over theoretical concerns such as how to consider the importance of a site.

The increasing complexity and fragmentation in capitalist social formation caused this systemic reaction in archaeology, and led to the fragmentation of the identity of the archaeologist. The segmentation and differentiation of each excavation site as a field of the life-world experience made the spatio-temporal extension of the domain, together with its set of expectations, which is drawn upon in the reproduction of an identity, very narrow indeed.

It is natural for the fragmented self to seek transcendental entities to try and regain its sense of unity. Also, the promotion of the narratives of extremes, such as the oldest and the largest in the archaeological discourse since the 1980s, can be understood as such. By referring to something transcendental, a social imaginary, we assure ourselves that we can communicate with and understand one another in that group. The articulation of such a group is influenced by various socioeconomic and cultural factors, and the relationship between the creators and the receivers of the narrative of the transcendental being is one of systemic interdependence. When yet another extreme narrative, such as that of an urban site in the Jomon hunter-gatherer period (the San'nai-Maruyama site of Aomori prefecture; Organizing Committee of the Jomon World '96 Exhibition), was generated, groups were articulated which are differentiated by sharing same sets of interests and problems. In the case of the San'nai-Maruyama site of Aomori prefecture, the narrative of the Jomon urban settlement is associated with the articulation of a group, the people of the Tohoku (meaning north-east) region of Japan. This region was disadvantaged through being heavily reliant on agriculture throughout the industrialization-led economic boom of the post-war period.

Meanwhile, the negative reflection upon the excesses of various sorts of the post-war boom era, leading up to the so-called "bubble economic boom" of the 1980s, has led to the popularization of the Jomon period as the cradle of Japanese-ness, while the Yayoi period, formerly regarded as the formative period of Japanese-ness as a rice-growing nation (and as the nation of the deep imperial genealogy), is in steep decline. The rise of the Jomon discourse to a conspicuous position is associated with the articulation of collective feeling against the industrialization-driven economic success of Japan and the fragmentation this caused. However, this Jomon discourse is a local discourse, and can easily be relativized. In other words, it is too specific to be genuinely transcendental. Hence, many competing, would-be transcendental discourses continue to emerge, and further accelerate the fragmentation. It goes without saying that this leads to the endless relativization of one's standpoint and nihilism.

Seeking a way out

Various attempts are being made to overcome what can be described as postmodern difficulties. Notably, many of them share one element, which is to emphasize the necessity of opening up a sort of a public discursive domain. The proposals attempt to open up a domain for debate by introducing new theoretical packages from the West and comparing them with Japanese equivalents (e.g., Anzai 1990). What these packages aim to do is to systematize the archaeological discursive formation, and there is a shared assessment that the *habitual* avoidance of and hostility to theorization are a significant source of the difficulties Japanese archaeology must face. The lack of inclination to articulate one's archaeological discourse by being critically aware of its position in terms of its sociopolitical implications and its relations to pre-existing theories, makes archaeology not only vulnerable to political manipulation, both vulgar and subtle, but also makes it limited in its creative imagination and critical self-consciousness (Mizoguchi 1997). Only the explicit differentiation of problematics and the articulation of self-critical discourse, secure the productive and creative continuation of archaeological communication and enable us by avoiding the danger of post-modernistic nihilism and endless relativization (Mizoguchi 1997). Many of the attempts are ongoing, and what problematization they lead to and how it will be perceived and acted upon remain to be seen.

Conclusion

The historical trajectory of Japanese archaeology has been firmly embedded in the transformative process of Japanese modern social formation. The modernizing project of Japan was embodied by the creation and reproduction of the notion of the national body, the conceptual machinery created to integrate the people who voluntarily fulfilled their duty to the nation in return for being assured of their basic rights. The notion of the national body integrated the people as the children of the emperor. This resulted from the rapid formation of a modern nation-state in Japan under pressure from the Western colonial powers. The necessity of creating a fictional device for re-embedding the displaced people also arose in other countries during the formation of modern nation-states, but the necessity of portraying the ties that bound people as organic, not voluntary ones, was felt particularly acutely in the case of Japan. Virtually every discourse was structured by referring to the nation, either for or against it, and the situation continued throughout the period from the Meiji restoration up to as late as the 1970s, although the defeat in World War II resulted in a drastic change of the idiom of the discourses in the form of the rise of the Marxism program.

The survival of the nation was associated with heavy capitalism in Zygmunt Bauman's terminology (2000: 54–59), and the Cold War equilibrium in which both the organization of the workplace and the politico-economic formation at various levels, amongst other factors, kept the structure simple. By simple here I mean that the structuring principle of the discourses was almost without exception based upon the dichotomy between the values, meanings, and their signifiers for and against capitalist social formation. Japanese Marxist archaeology and its discourse were situated in the "against" camp, and those who did not take part in it also located their positions by measuring the distance between them and the Marxist discourse. The situation can be characterized by the existence of a dominant narrative line and the production of individual narratives in both positive and negative ways. The structure of the discursive space was naturally simple, since almost every constitutive element was situated in the dichotomy.

The decline of heavy capitalism and the collapse of the Cold War equilibrium resulted in the fragmentation of the formerly simple structuring principle, in which an ever-increasing number of discursive formations were coming into being. What remains for those who produce archaeological narratives is a database whose contents are ever-changing. One has to decide which elements to choose from the database and how to combine them into a coherent narrative. There is no unified narrative line, nor anything about how many can share one opinion. The stress and anxiety of having to make choices all the time becomes increasingly hard, and the temptation to rely upon unifying narrative lines of a dangerous kind, such as those of the extreme, namely the narrative of the first, the oldest, and the largest, is always present.

The foregoing has been a social archaeological observation of the history of modern Japanese archaeology. Now we Japanese archaeologists are in a situation in which each choice and decision in our everyday archaeological practice has to be taken with a certain awareness of their political implications. The importance of the theorization of the everyday has never been more important than now, as is the importance of a critical social archaeology.

NOTE

The author wishes to thank Lynn Meskell and Robert Preucel for their useful comments on earlier drafts of this chapter. Responsibility for any errors and shortcomings lie with the author.
1   The argument in the following two sections is taken from Mizoguchi (1997).

REFERENCES

Akazawa, T., et al. (eds.) 1986. Prehistoric hunter-gatherers in Japan: New research methods. *Bulletin Tokyo daigaku sogo kenkyu shiryokan (Bulletin of the Tokyo University Museum)* 27. Tokyo: University of Tokyo Press.

Anzai, M. 1990. *Mumoji-shakai no kokogaku (The archaeology of nonliterate societies)* (in Japanese). Tokyo: Rokko shuppan.

Aston, W. G. (trans.) 1972. *Nihongi: Chronicles of Japan from the Earliest Times to A.D. 697*. Tokyo: Charles E. Tuttle.

Bauman, Z. 1988. *Freedom*. Milton Keynes: Open University Press.

—— 2000. *Liquid Modernity*. Cambridge: Polity Press.

Champion, T., and M. Díaz-Andreu (eds.) 1996. *Nationalism and Archaeology in Europe*. London: UCL Press.

Foucault, M. 1977. *Discipline and Punish: The Birth of the Prison*. London: Penguin.

Giddens, A. 1990. *The Consequences of Modernity*. Cambridge: Polity Press.

Hamada, K. 1996 [1922]. *Tsuron kokogaku (The outline of archaeology)* (reprint) (in Japanese). Tokyo: Yusankaku.

Hara, H. 1972. Nihon ni okeru kagakuteki gennshi-kodai-shi kenkyu no seiritsu to tenkai (The establishment and the development of the social-scientific study of Japanese pre and proto-history) (in Japanese). In H. Hara (ed.), *Nihon genshi kyousan sei shakai to kokka no keisei (Primitive communism and the formation of state in Japan*. Tokyo: Asakura shoten, pp. 343–409.

Hodder, I. (ed.) 1991. *Archaeological Theory in Europe: The Last 3 Decades*. London: Routledge.

Isomae, J. 1998. *Kiki shinwa no metahisutori (The meta-history of the myths features in the Japanese imperial chronicles "Kojiki" and "Nihonshoki")* (in Japanese). Tokyo: Yoshikawakobunkan.

Kan, S. 2001. *Nashonarizumu (Nationalism)* (in Japanese). Tokyo: Iwanami.

Kohl, P., and C. Fawcett (eds.) 1995. *Nationalism, Politics and the Practice of Archaeology*. Cambridge: Cambridge University Press.

Komori, Y. 2001. *Posutokoroniaru (Postcolonialism)* (in Japanese). Tokyo: Iwanami.

Kondo, Y. 1966. Kofun toha nanika (What is the Kofun mounded tomb?) (in Japanese). In Y. Kondo and C. Fujisawa (eds.), *Nihon no kokogaku (Japanese archaeology), Vol. 4: Kofun jidai (The Kofun period)*. Tokyo: Kawade shobo shinsya, pp. 2–25.

—— 1983. *Zenpo-koen-fun no jidai (The age of the keyhole-shaped tumuli)* (in Japanese). Tokyo: Iwanami.

——, and M. Sahara. 1983. Kaisetsu (Commentary) (in Japanese). In: E. S. Morse, *Omori kaizuka (Shell mounds of Omori)* (orig. 1879, trans. and commentary Y. Kondo and M. Sahara). Tokyo: Iwanami, pp. 185–219.

Luhmann, N. 1995. *Social Systems*. Stanford, CA: Stanford University Press.

Mizoguchi, K. 1997. The reproduction of archaeological discourse: The case of Japan. *Journal of European Archaeology* 5(2): 149–165.

—— 2002. *An Archaeological History of Japan, 30,000 B.C. to A.D. 700*. Philadelphia: University of Pennsylvania Press.

Oguma, E. 1995. *Tanitsu-minzoku shinwa no kigen (The myth of the homogeneous nation)* (in Japanese). Tokyo: Shin'yosha.

—— 1998. *Nihonjin no kyokai (The boundaries of the Japanese)* (in Japanese). Tokyo: Shin'yosha.

—— 2002. *Minshu to Aikoku ("Minsyu" and "Aikoku")* (in Japanese). Tokyo: Shin'yosha.

Organizing Committee of the Jomon World '96 Exhibition (ed.) 1996. *Jomon no tobira (The Jomon world '96)*. Tokyo: Organizing Committee of the Jomon World '96 Exhibition.

Osawa, M. 1998. *Sengo no shiso kukan (The discursive space of post-World-War-II Japan)* (in Japanese). Tokyo: Chikuma shobo.

Smith, A. 1986. *The Ethnic Origins of Nations*. Oxford: Blackwell.

Taki, K. 1988. *Ten 'no no shozo (The portraits of Emperor Meiji)* (in Japanese). Tokyo: Iwanami.

Teshigawara, A. 1995. *Nihon kokogaku no ayumi (A history of Japanese archaeology)* (in Japanese). Tokyo: Meicho Shuppan.

Toma, S. 1951. *Nihon mizoku no keisei (The formation of the Japanese people)*. Tokyo: Iwanami.

Tomoeda, T. 1991. Kozo to hendo (Structures and their changes) (in Japanese). In T. Imada and T. Tomoeda (eds.), *Shakai gaku no kiso (An introduction to sociology)*. Tokyo: Yuhikaku, pp. 121–149.

Tozawa, M. 1978. Nihon kokogaku-shi to sono haikei (The history of Japanese archaeology and its backgrounds) (in Japanese). In H. Otsuka et al. (eds.), *Nihon kokogaku wo manabu (An introduction to Japanese archaeology), Vol. 1: Nihon kokogaku no kiso (Fundamentals in Japanese archaeology)*. Tokyo: Yuhikaku), pp. 50–62.

Tsukinowa kofun kanko kai. 1960. *Tuskinowa kofun (The Tuskinowa tumulus)* (in Japanese). Yanahara: Tsukinowa kofun kanko kai.

Uchida, R. 2002. *Kokudo-ron (The land of Japan)* (in Japanese). Tokyo: Chikuma shobo.

Wajima, S. 1955. Hattatsu no shodankai (Stages in the development of Japanese archaeology). In T. Mikami (ed.), *Nihon kokogaku koza (Seminar in Japanese archaeology), Vol. 2: Kokogaku kenkyu no rekishi to genjo (The history and current condition of Japanese archaeology)*. Tokyo: Kawade shobo, pp. 22–36.

—— 1966. Yayoi jidai syakai no kozo (The structure of the society of the Yayoi period) (in Japanese). In S. Wajima (ed.), *Nihon no kokogaku (Japanese archaeology), Vol. 3: Yayoi jidai (The Yayoi period)*. Tokyo: Kawade shobo shinsya, pp. 2–30.

Wallerstein, I. 1974. *The Modern World-System*. New York: Academic Press.

Yokoyama, K. 1955. Kofun jidai (The Kofun period) (in Japanese). In T. Mikami (ed.), *Nihon kokogaku koza (Seminar in Japanese archaeology), Vol. 2: Kokogaku kenkyu no rekishi to genjo (The history and current condition of Japanese archaeology)*. Tokyo: Kawade shobo, pp. 77–92.

Index

Note: page numbers in italics denote illustrations or figures